Student Edition

enVision® Geometry
Common Core

SAVVAS
LEARNING COMPANY

ISBN-13: 978-1-418-40184-9
ISBN-10:   1-418-40184-6
4 2024

Contents in Brief

enVision® Geometry Common Core

Reviewers and Consultants

Mathematicians

David Bressoud, Ph.D.
Professor Emeritus of Mathematics
Macalester College
St. Paul, MN

Karen Edwards, Ph.D.
Mathematics Lecturer
Harvard University
Cambridge, MA

Teacher Reviewers

Jennifer Barkey
K-12 Math Supervisor
Gateway School District
Monroeville, PA

Miesha Beck
Math Teacher/ Department Chair
Blackfoot School District
Blackfoot, ID

Joseph Brandell, Ph.D.
West Bloomfield High School
West Bloomfield Public Schools
West Bloomfield, MI

Andrea Coles
Mathematics Teacher
Mountain View Middle School
Blackfoot, ID

Julie Johnson
Mathematics/CS teacher (9–12)
Williamsville Central Schools
Williamsville, NY

Tamar McPherson
Plum Sr HS/Math Teacher
Plum School District
Pittsburgh, PA

Melisa Rice
Math Department Chairperson
Shawnee Public Schools
Shawnee, OK

Erin Zitka
6-12 Math Coordinator
Forsyth County
Cumming, GA

Jeff Ziegler
Teacher
Pittsburgh City Schools
Pittsburgh, PA

Authors

Dan Kennedy, Ph.D

- Retired teacher and Lupton Distinguished Professor of Mathematics at the Baylor School, Chattanooga, TN
- Co-author of textbooks Precalculus: Graphical, Numerical, Algebraic and Calculus: Graphical, Numerical, Algebraic, AP Edition
- Past chair of the College Board's AP Calculus Development Committee
- Previous Tandy Technology Scholar and Presidential Award winner

Eric Milou, Ed.D

- Professor of Mathematics, Rowan University, Glassboro, NJ
- Past President, Association of Mathematics Teachers of New Jersey
- Co-author of *Invigorating High School Math*
- Co-author of NCTM's Catalyzing Change in the Middle School
- Member of the author team for Savvas' **enVision** 6-8
- Past recipient of the Max Sobel Outstanding Mathematics Educator Award

Christine D. Thomas, Ph.D

- Professor of Mathematics Education at Georgia State University, Atlanta, GA
- Past–President of the Association of Mathematics Teacher Educators (AMTE)
- Past NCTM Board of Directors Member
- Past member of the editorial panel of the NCTM journal Mathematics Teacher
- Past co-chair of the steering committee of the North American chapter of the International Group of the Psychology of Mathematics Education

Rose Mary Zbiek, Ph.D

- Professor of Mathematics Education, Pennsylvania State University, College Park, PA
- Series editor for the NCTM *Essential Understanding* project

Contributing Author

Al Cuoco, Ph.D

- Lead author of CME Project, a NSF funded high school curriculum
- Team member to revise the Conference Board of the Mathematical Sciences (CBMS) recommendations for teacher preparation and professional development
- Co-author of several books published by the Mathematical Association of America and the American Mathematical Society
- Consultant to the writers of the Common Core State Standards for Mathematics and the PARCC Content Frameworks for high school
- Recipient of Mary P. Dolciani Award for contributions to the mathematical education of K-16 students

About :enVision® Geometry

enVision® Geometry offers a carefully constructed lesson design to help you succeed in math.

Step 1 At the start of each lesson, you and your classmates will work together to come up with a solution strategy for the problem or task posed. After a class discussion, you'll be asked to reflect back on the processes and strategies you used in solving the problem.

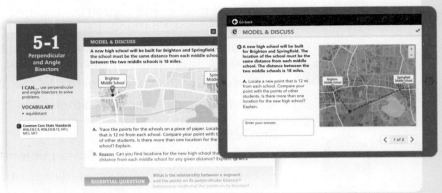

Step 2 Next, your teacher will guide you through new concepts and skills for the lesson.

After each example **a**, you work out a problem called the **Try It!** **b** to solidify your understanding of these concepts.

Side notes **c** help you with study tips, suggestions for avoiding common errors, and questions that support learning together and having a growth mindset.

In addition, you will periodically answer **Habits of Mind** **d** questions to refine your thinking and problem-solving skills.

Step 2 cont.

This part of the lesson concludes with a Lesson Check that helps you to know how well you are understanding the new content presented in the lesson. With the exercises in the **Do You Understand?** and **Do You Know How?**, you can gauge your understanding of the lesson concepts.

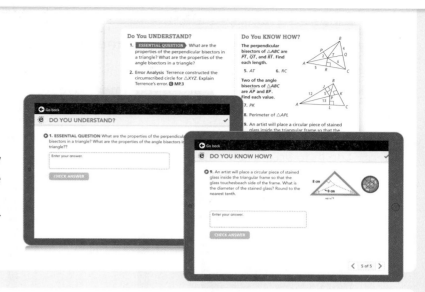

Step 3

In Step 3, you will find a balanced exercise set with **Understand** exercises that focus on conceptual understanding, **Practice** exercises that target procedural fluency, and **Apply** exercises for which you apply concept and skills to real-world situations **e**.

The **Assessment and Practice f** exercises offer practice for high stakes assessments. Your teacher may have you complete the assignment in your Student Edition, Student Companion, or online at SavvasRealize.com.

Step 4

Your teacher may have you take the Lesson Quiz after each lesson. You can take the quiz online or in print. To do your best on the quiz, review the lesson problems in that lesson.

Digital Resources

Everything you need for math, anytime, anywhere.

SavvasRealize.com is your gateway to all of the digital resources for **enVision® Geometry**. Log in to access your interactive student edition, called Realize Reader.

 INTERACTIVE STUDENT EDITION
Log in to access your interactive student edition, called Realize Reader.

 FAMILY ENGAGEMENT
Involve family in your learning.

 ACTIVITIES Complete *Explore & Reason, Model & Discuss, Critique & Explain* activities. Interact with *Examples* and *Try Its.*

 ANIMATIONS View and interact with real-world applications.

 PRACTICE
Practice what you've learned.

 VIDEOS Watch clips to support Mathematical Modeling in 3 Acts Lessons and **enVision®** STEM Projects.

ADAPTIVE PRACTICE
Practice that is *just right* and *just for you.*

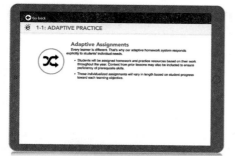

GLOSSARY Read and listen to English and Spanish definitions.

CONCEPT SUMMARY Review key lesson content through multiple representations.

ASSESSMENT
Show what you've learned.

TUTORALS Get help from Virtual Nerd, right when you need it.

MATH TOOLS Explore math with digital tools and manipulatives.

CONCEPT SUMMARY

DESMOS Use Anytime and as embedded Interactives in Lesson content.

QR CODES Scan with your mobile device for *Virtual Nerd Video Tutorials* and *Math Modeling Lessons.*

ⓒ Standards for Mathematical Practice

Making Sense of and Solving Problems

Make sense of problems and persevere in solving them.

Proficient math thinkers read through a problem situation and can put together a workable solution path to solve the problem posed. They analyze the information provided and identify constraints and dependencies. They identify multiple entries to a problem solution and choose an efficient and effective entry point.

Consider these questions to help you make sense of problems.

- What am I asked to find?
- What are the quantities and variables? What are the dependencies and the constraints? How do they relate?
- What are some possible strategies to solve the problem?

Attend to precision.

Proficient math thinkers communicate clearly and precisely the approach they are using. They identify the meaning of symbols that they use and always remember to specify units of measure and to label graphical models accurately. They use mathematical terms precisely and express their answers with the appropriate degree of accuracy.

Consider these questions to help you attend to precision.

- Have I stated the meaning of the variables and symbols I am using?
- Have I specified the units of measure I am using?
- Have I calculated accurately?

Reasoning and Communicating

Reason abstractly and quantitatively.

Proficient math thinkers make sense of quantities in problem situations. They represent a problem situation using symbols or equations and explain what the symbols or equation represent in relationship to a problem situation. As they model a situation symbolically or mathematically, they explain the meaning of the quantities.

Consider these questions to help you reason abstractly and quantitatively.

- How can I represent this problem situation using equations or formulas?
- What do the numbers, variables, and symbols in the equation or formula represent?

Construct viable arguments and critique the reasoning of others.

Proficient math thinkers and problem solvers communicate their problem solutions clearly and convincingly. They construct sound mathematical arguments and develop and defend conjectures to explain mathematical situations. They make use of examples and counterexamples to support their arguments and justify their conclusions. When asked, they respond clearly and logically to the positions and conclusions of others, and compare two arguments, identifying any flaws in logic or reasoning that the arguments may contain. They ask questions to clarify or improve the position of a classmate.

Consider these questions to help you construct mathematical arguments.

- What assumptions can I make when constructing an argument?
- What conjectures can I make about the solution to the problem?
- What arguments can I present to defend my conjectures?

Representing and Connecting

Model with mathematics.

Proficient math thinkers use mathematics to represent a problem situation and make connections between a real-world problem situation and mathematics. They see the applicability of mathematics to solve everyday problems and explain how geometry can be used to solve a carpentry problem or algebra to solve a proportional relationship problem. They define and map relationships among quantities in a problem, using appropriate tools. They analyze the relationships and draw conclusions about the solutions.

Consider these questions to help you model with mathematics.

- What representations can I use to show the relationship among quantities or variables?
- What assumptions can I make about the problem situation to simplify the problem?

Use appropriate tools strategically.

Proficient math thinkers strategize about which tools are more helpful to solve a problem situation. They consider all tools, from paper and pencil to protractors and rulers, to calculators and software applications. They articulate the appropriateness of different tools and recognize those that would best serve the needs for a given problem. They are especially insightful about technological tools and use them in ways that deepen or extend their understanding of concepts. They also make use of mental tools, such as estimation, to determine the appropriateness of a solution.

Consider these questions to help you use appropriate tools.

- What tools can I use to help me solve the problem?
- How can technology help me solve the problem?

Seeing Structure and Generalizing

Look for and make use of structure.

Proficient math thinkers see the structure of mathematics in the problems they are solving and generalize mathematics principles from this structure. They see complicated expressions or equations as single objects composed of many parts.

Consider these questions to help you see structure.

- Can I see a pattern or structure in the problem or solution strategy?
- How can I use the pattern or structure I see to help me solve the problem?

Look for and express regularity in repeated reasoning.

Proficient math thinkers notice when calculations are repeated and can uncover both general methods and shortcuts for solving similar problems.

Consider these questions to help you look for regularity in repeated reasoning.

- Do I notice any repeated calculations or steps?
- Are there general methods that I can use to solve the problem?
- What can I generalize from one problem to another?
- How reasonable are the results that I am getting?

Geometry

Congruence

Experiment with transformations in the plane.

HSG.CO.A.1   Know precise definitions of angle, circle, perpendicular line, parallel line, and line segment, based on the undefined notions of point, line, distance along a line, and distance around a circular arc.

HSG.CO.A.2   Represent transformations in the plane using, e.g., transparencies and geometry software; describe transformations as functions that take points in the plane as inputs and give other points as outputs. Compare transformations that preserve distance and angle to those that do not (e.g., translation versus horizontal stretch).

HSG.CO.A.3   Given a rectangle, parallelogram, trapezoid, or regular polygon, describe the rotations and reflections that carry it onto itself.

HSG.CO.A.4   Develop definitions of rotations, reflections, and translations in terms of angles, circles, perpendicular lines, parallel lines, and line segments.

HSG.CO.A.5   Given a geometric figure and a rotation, reflection, or translation, draw the transformed figure using, e.g., graph paper, tracing paper, or geometry software. Specify a sequence of transformations that will carry a given figure onto another.

Understand congruence in terms of rigid motions.

HSG.CO.B.6   Use geometric descriptions of rigid motions to transform figures and to predict the effect of a given rigid motion on a given figure; given two figures, use the definition of congruence in terms of rigid motions to decide if they are congruent.

HSG.CO.B.7   Use the definition of congruence in terms of rigid motions to show that two triangles are congruent if and only if corresponding pairs of sides and corresponding pairs of angles are congruent.

HSG.CO.B.8   Explain how the criteria for triangle congruence (ASA, SAS, and SSS) follow from the definition of congruence in terms of rigid motions.

Prove geometric theorems.

HSG.CO.C.9   Prove theorems about lines and angles. *Theorems include: vertical angles are congruent; when a transversal crosses parallel lines, alternate interior angles are congruent and corresponding angles are congruent; points on a perpendicular bisector of a line segment are exactly those equidistant from the segment's endpoints.*

HSG.CO.C.10   Prove theorems about triangles. *Theorems include: measures of interior angles of a triangle sum to 180°; base angles of isosceles triangles are congruent; the segment joining midpoints of two sides of a triangle is parallel to the third side and half the length; the medians of a triangle meet at a point.*

HSG.CO.C.11   Prove theorems about parallelograms. *Theorems include: opposite sides are congruent, opposite angles are congruent, the diagonals of a parallelogram bisect each other and conversely, rectangles are parallelograms with congruent diagonals.*

Make geometric constructions.

HSG.CO.D.12   Make formal geometric constructions with a variety of tools and methods (compass and straightedge, string, reflective devices, paper folding, dynamic geometric software, etc.). *Copying a segment; copying an angle; bisecting a segment; bisecting an angle; constructing perpendicular lines, including the perpendicular bisector of a line segment; and constructing a line parallel to a given line through a point not on the line.*

HSG.CO.D.13   Construct an equilateral triangle, a square, and a regular hexagon inscribed in a circle.

Similarity, Right Triangles, and Trigonometry

Understand similarity in terms of similarity transformations.

HSG.SRT.A.1 Verify experimentally the properties of dilations given by a center and a scale factor:

HSG.SRT.A.1.A A dilation takes a line not passing through the center of the dilation to a parallel line, and leaves a line passing through the center unchanged.

HSG.SRT.A.1.B The dilation of a line segment is longer or shorter in the ratio given by the scale factor.

HSG.SRT.A.2 Given two figures, use the definition of similarity in terms of similarity transformations to decide if they are similar; explain using similarity transformations the meaning of similarity for triangles as the equality of all corresponding pairs of angles and the proportionality of all corresponding pairs of sides.

HSG.SRT.A.3 Use the properties of similarity transformations to establish the AA criterion for two triangles to be similar.

Prove theorems involving similarity.

HSG.SRT.B.4 Prove theorems about triangles. *Theorems include a line parallel to one side of a triangle divides the other two proportionally and conversely; the Pythagorean Theorem proved using triangle similarity.*

HSG.SRT.B.5 Use congruence and similarity criteria for triangles to solve problems and to prove relationships in geometric figures.

Define trigonometric ratios and solve problems involving right triangles.

HSG.SRT.C.6 Understand that by similarity, side ratios in right triangles are properties of the angles in the triangle, leading to definitions of trigonometric ratios for acute angles.

HSG.SRT.C.7 Explain and use the relationship between the sine and cosine of complementary angles.

HSG.SRT.C.8 Use trigonometric ratios and the Pythagorean Theorem to solve right triangles in applied problems.★

Apply trigonometry to general triangles.

HSG.SRT.D.9 (+) Derive the formula $A = \frac{1}{2}ab \sin(C)$ for the area of a triangle by drawing an auxiliary line from a vertex perpendicular to the opposite side.

HSG.SRT.D.10 (+) Prove the Law of Sines and Cosines and use them to solve problems.

HSG.SRT.D.11 (+) Understand and apply the Law of Sines and the Law of Cosines to find unknown measurements in right and non-right triangles (e.g., surveying problems, resultant forces).

COMMON CORE STATE STANDARDS

* indicates a modeling standard

Standards for Mathematical Content in Geometry

Circles

Understand and apply theorems about circles.

HSG.C.A.1   Prove that all circles are similar.

HSG.C.A.2   Identify and describe relationships among inscribed angles, radii, and chords. *Include the relationship between central, inscribed, and circumscribed angles; inscribed angles on a diameter are right angles; the radius of a circle is perpendicular to the tangent where the radius intersects the circle.*

HSG.C.A.3   Construct the inscribed and circumscribed circles of a triangle, and prove properties of angles for a quadrilateral inscribed in a circle.

HSG.C.A.4 (+)   Construct a tangent line from a point outside a given circle to the circle.

Find arc lengths and areas of sectors of circles.

HSG.C.B.5   Derive using similarity the fact that the length of the arc intercepted by an angle is proportional to the radius, and define the radian measure of the angle as the constant of proportionality; derive the formula for the area of a sector.

Expressing Geometric Properties with Equations

Translate between the geometric description and the equation for a conic section.

HSG.GPE.A.1   Derive the equation of a circle of given center and radius using the Pythagorean Theorem; complete the square to find the center and radius of a circle given by an equation.

HSG.GPE.A.2   Derive the equation of a parabola given a focus and directrix.

Use coordinates to prove simple geometric theorems algebraically.

HSG.GPE.B.4   Use coordinates to prove simple geometric theorems algebraically.

HSG.GPE.B.5   Prove the slope criteria for parallel and perpendicular lines and use them to solve geometric problems (e.g., find the equation of a line parallel or perpendicular to a given line that passes through a given point).

HSG.GPE.B.6   Find the point on a directed line segment between two given points that partitions the segment in a given ratio.

HSG.GPE.B.7   Use coordinates to compute perimeters of polygons and areas of triangles and rectangles, e.g., using the distance formula. ★

Geometric Measurement and Dimension

Explain volume formulas and use them to solve problems.

HSG.GMD.A.1   Give an informal argument for the formulas for the circumference of a circle, area of a circle, volume of a cylinder, pyramid, and cone. *Use dissection arguments, Cavalieri's principle, and informal limit arguments.*

HSG.GMD.A.2 (+)   Give an informal argument using Cavalieri's principle for the formulas for the volume of a sphere and other solid figures.

HSG.GMD.A.3   Use volume formulas for cylinders, pyramids, cones, and spheres to solve problems. ★

Visualize relationships between two-dimensional and three-dimensional objects.

HSG.GMD.B.4   Identify the shapes of two-dimensional cross-sections of three-dimensional objects, and identify three-dimensional objects generated by rotations of two-dimensional objects.

Modeling with Geometry

Apply geometric concepts in modeling situations.

HSG.MG.A.1   Use geometric shapes, their measures, and their properties to describe objects (e.g., modeling a tree trunk or a human torso as a cylinder). ★

HSG.MG.A.2   Apply concepts of density based on area and volume in modeling situations (e.g., persons per square mile, BTUs per cubic foot). ★

HSG.MG.A.3   Apply geometric methods to solve design problems (e.g., designing an object or structure to satisfy physical constraints or minimize cost; working with typographic grid systems based on ratios). ★

* indicates a modeling standard

Statistics and Probability

Conditional Probability and the Rules of Probability

Understand independence and conditional probability and use them to interpret data.

HSS.CP.A.1 Describe events as subsets of a sample space (the set of outcomes) using characteristics (or categories) of the outcomes, or as unions, intersections, or complements of other events ("or," "and," "not").

HSS.CP.A.2 Understand that two events A and B are independent if the probability of A and B occurring together is the product of their probabilities, and use this characterization to determine if they are independent.

HSS.CP.A.3 Understand the conditional probability of A given B as $\frac{P(A \text{ and } B)}{P(B)}$ and interpret independence of A and B as saying that the conditional probability of A given B is the same as the probability of A, and the conditional probability of B given A is the same as the probability of B.

HSS.CP.A.4 Construct and interpret two-way frequency tables of data when two categories are associated with each object being classified. Use the two-way table as a sample space to decide if events are independent and to approximate conditional probabilities.

HSS.CP.A.5 Recognize and explain the concepts of conditional probability and independence in everyday language and everyday situations.

Use the rules of probability to compute probabilities of compound events in a uniform probability model.

HSS.CP.B.6 Find the conditional probability of A given B as the fraction of B's outcomes that also belong to A, and interpret the answer in terms of the model.

HSS.CP.B.7 Apply the Addition Rule, $P(A \text{ or } B) = P(A) + P(B) - P(A \text{ and } B)$, and interpret the answer in terms of the model.

HSS.CP.B.8 (+) Apply the general Multiplication Rule in a uniform probability model, $P(A \text{ and } B) = P(A)P(B|A) = P(B)P(A|B)$, and interpret the answer in terms of the model.

HSS.CP.B.9 (+) Use permutations and combinations to compute probabilities of compound events and solve problems.

Using Probability to Make Decisions

Calculate expected values and use them to solve problems.

HSS.MD.A.1 (+) Define a random variable for a quantity of interest by assigning a numerical value to each event in a sample space; graph the corresponding probability distribution using the same graphical displays as for data distributions.

HSS.MD.A.2 (+) Calculate the expected value of a random variable; interpret it as a means of the probability distribution.

HSS.MD.A.3 (+) Develop a probability distribution for a random variable defined for a sample space in which theoretical probabilities can be calculated; find the expected value.

HSS.MD.A.4 (+) Develop a probability distribution for a random variable defined for a sample space in which probabilities are assigned empirically; find the expected value.

Use probability to evaluate outcomes of decisions.

HSS.MD.B.5 (+) Weigh the possible outcomes of a decision by assigning probabilities to payoff values and finding expected values.

HSS.MD.B.5.A (+) Find the expected payoff for a game of chance.

HSS.MD.B.5.B (+) Evaluate and compare strategies on the basis of expected values.

HSS.MD.B.6 (+) Use probabilities to make fair decisions (e.g., drawing by lots, using a random number generator).

HSS.MD.B.7 (+) Analyze decisions and strategies using probability concepts (e.g., product testing, medical testing, pulling a hockey goalie at the end of a game).

Foundations of Geometry

Geometry

Congruence

- Prove geometric theorems
- Make geometric constructions

Expressing Geometric Properties with Equations

- Use coordinates to prove simple geometric theorems algebraically

Geometry

Expressing Geometric Properties with Equations

- Use coordinates to prove simple geometric theorems algebraically

Modeling with Geometry

- Apply geometric concepts in modeling situations

Transformations

Geometry

Congruence

- Experiment with transformations in the plane
- Understand congruence in terms of rigid motions

TOPIC 4

Triangle Congruence

Geometry

Congruence

- Experiment with
  transformations in the plane
- Understand congruence in
  terms of rigid motions
- Prove geometric theorems

Geometry

Congruence
- Prove geometric theorems

Geometry

Congruence
• Prove geometric theorems

TOPIC 7

Similarity

Geometry

Similarity, Right Triangles, & Trigonometry

- Understand similarity in terms of similarity transformations
- Prove theorems involving similarity

Expression Geometric Properties with Equations

- Use coordinates to prove simple geometric theorems algebraically

Right Triangles and Trigonometry

Geometry

Similarity, Right Triangles, & Trigonometry

- Define trigonometric ratios and solve problems involving right triangles
- Apply trigonometry to general triangles

TOPIC 9

Coordinate Geometry

Geometry

Congruence

- Experiment with transformations in the plane
- Prove geometric theorems

Expressing Geometric Properties with Equations

- Use coordinates to prove simple geometric theorems algebraically

Circles

Geometry

Congruence

- Experiment with transformations in the plane

Circles

- Understand and apply theorems about circles
- Find arc lengths and areas of sectors of circles

Two- and Three-Dimensional Models

Geometry

Geometric Measurement & Dimension

- Explain volume formulas and use them to solve problems
- Visualize relationships between two-dimensional and three-dimensional objects

Modeling with Geometry

- Apply geometric concepts in modeling situations

Statistics & Probability

Conditional Probability & the Rules of Probability

- Understand independence and conditional probability and use them to interpret data
- Use the rules of probability to compute probabilities of compound events.

Using Probability to Make Decisions

- Calculate expected values and use them to solve problems
- Use probability to evaluate outcomes of decisions

Foundations of Geometry

What are some of the fundamentals of geometry?

Topic Overview

enVision® STEM Project:
Design a Tablet

1-1 Measuring Segments and Angles

1-2 Basic Constructions

1-3 Midpoint and Distance

1-4 Inductive Reasoning

Mathematical Modeling in 3 Acts:
The Mystery Spokes

1-5 Conditional Statements

1-6 Deductive Reasoning

1-7 Writing Proofs

1-8 Indirect Proof

Topic Vocabulary

- angle bisector
- biconditional
- conditional
- conjecture
- construction
- contrapositive
- converse
- counterexample
- deductive reasoning
- inductive reasoning
- inverse
- Law of Detachment
- Law of Syllogism
- negation
- proof
- postulate
- theorem
- truth table
- truth value

Digital Experience

INTERACTIVE STUDENT EDITION Access online or offline.

ACTIVITIES Complete *Explore & Reason, Model & Discuss*, and *Critique & Explain* activities. Interact with *Examples* and *Try Its.*

CONCEPT SUMMARY Review key lesson content through multiple representations.

ASSESSMENT Show what you've learned.

Go online | **SavvasRealize.com**

The Mystery Spokes

Some photos are taken in such a way that it is difficult to determine exactly what the picture shows. Sometimes this is because the photo is a close up of an object, and you do not see the entire object. Other times, it might be because the photographer used special effects when taking the photo.

You can often use clues from the photo to determine what is in the photo and also what the rest of the object might look like. What clues would you look for? Think about this during the Mathematical Modeling in 3 Acts lesson.

VIDEOS Watch clips to support *Mathematical Modeling in 3 Acts Lessons* and **enVision**® *STEM Projects.*

TUTORIALS Get help from *Virtual Nerd*, right when you need it.

PRACTICE Practice what you've learned.

ADAPTIVE PRACTICE Practice that is *just right* and *just for you.*

FAMILY ENGAGEMENT Involve family in your learning.

GLOSSARY Read and listen to English and Spanish definitions.

MATH TOOLS Explore math with digital tools and manipulatives.

DESMOS Use Anytime and as embedded Interactives in Lesson content.

Did You Know?

The **golden ratio**, $(1 + \sqrt{5}) : 2$, has been explored in mathematics for over 2400 years. A golden rectangle has side lengths in the golden ratio.

$$(1 + \sqrt{5}) : 2$$

Golden rectangles are used in webpage design to allocate space for content areas.

The main door of the Taj Mahal, in Agra, India, is in the shape of a **golden rectangle**.

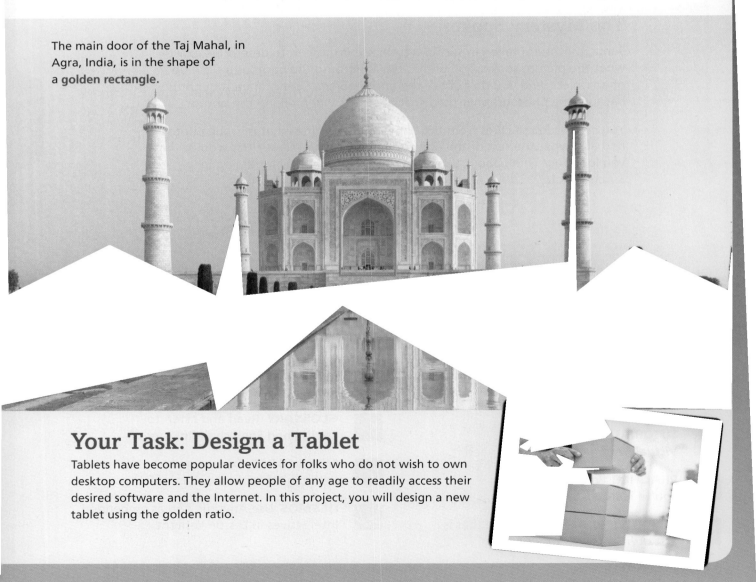

Your Task: Design a Tablet

Tablets have become popular devices for folks who do not wish to own desktop computers. They allow people of any age to readily access their desired software and the Internet. In this project, you will design a new tablet using the golden ratio.

1-1
Measuring Segments and Angles

I CAN... use properties of segments and angles to find their measures.

VOCABULARY
- collinear points
- line
- plane
- point
- postulate

Common Core State Standards
HSG.CO.A.1, MP.1, MP.2, MP.7

EXPLORE & REASON

A teacher labels two points on the number line.

A. What are some methods for finding the distance between points *A* and *B*?

B. **Construct Arguments** Which method of finding the distance is the best? Explain. **© MP.3**

ESSENTIAL QUESTION How are the properties of segments and angles used to determine their measures?

CONCEPT Undefined Terms

Undefined terms are terms whose meanings are accepted without formal definition. The undefined terms point, line, and plane are the basic building blocks of geometry.

Description	Diagram	Notation
A **point** is a location and has no size.	•*P*	a single capital letter *P*
A **line** consists of infinitely many points on a straight path that extends in two opposite directions with no end and no thickness.	A ——— B ℓ	a single letter or any two points on the line line ℓ $\overleftrightarrow{AB}$
A **plane** consists of infinitely many points and lines on a flat surface that extends without end and has no thickness.	•*X* •*Y* •*Z* *M*	a single capital letter or three points in the plane that do not lie on the same line plane *M* plane *XYZ*

CONCEPT Defined Terms

In geometry, new terms are defined using previously defined or known terms.

Description	Diagram	Notation
A segment is the part of a line that consists of two *endpoints* and all points between them.	A •——————————• B	A line segment is named by its two endpoints. $\overline{AB}$
A ray is the part of a line that consists of one *endpoint* and all the points of the line on one side of the endpoint.	M •——————————→ N	A ray is named using its endpoint first and any other point on the ray. $\overrightarrow{MN}$
Opposite rays are rays with the same endpoint that lie on the same line.	←——•——•——•——→ S T U	$\overrightarrow{TS}$ and $\overrightarrow{TU}$
An angle is formed by two rays with the same endpoint. Each ray is a side of the angle and the common endpoint is the vertex of the angle.	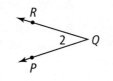	An angle can be named by its vertex, three points, or a number. $\angle Q$ $\angle PQR$ $\angle 2$

EXAMPLE 1 · Find Segment Lengths

How can you find the length of $\overline{CD}$?

The length of a segment is a positive real number. You can use the number line to find the length of $\overline{CD}$.

The notation CD represents the length of $\overline{CD}$.

To find the length of a segment, count the units of length between the endpoints. The length of $\overline{CD}$ is 3.

COMMUNICATE PRECISELY
Think about how notation and symbols are used. How does the name of a segment differ from the notation for the length of a segment? Ⓒ **MP.6**

Try It! **1.** Refer to the figure in Example 1. How can you find the length of $\overline{AC}$?

POSTULATE 1-1 Ruler Postulate

Every point on a line can be paired with a unique real number. This number is called the *coordinate* of the point.

The coordinate of *X* is 3.
The coordinate of *Y* is 7.

CONCEPT Distance on a Line

The distance between any two points *X* and *Y* is the absolute value of the difference of their coordinates.

$$XY = |7 - 3| = 4$$
$$XY = |3 - 7| = 4$$

CONCEPTUAL UNDERSTANDING

EXAMPLE 2 ▶ Find the Length of a Segment

What are *KM*, *LM*, and *KL*?

A **postulate** is a statement that is assumed to be true.

Use the Ruler Postulate to find the coordinates of *K*, *L*, and *M*. Then, find the distances between *K* and *M*, *L* and *M*, and *K* and *L*.

STUDY TIP
Remember that distance is always positive. When finding the distance between two points, use the absolute value of the difference.

$KM = |27 - 12| = 15$ or $KM = |12 - 27| = 15$
$LM = |27 - 16| = 11$ or $LM = |16 - 27| = 11$
$KL = |16 - 12| = 4$ or $KL = |12 - 16| = 4$
The length of $\overline{KM}$ is 15.
The length of $\overline{LM}$ is 11.
The length of $\overline{KL}$ is 4.

Try It! 2. Refer to the figure in Example 2.

a. What is *JK*?   **b.** What is *JM*?

POSTULATE 1-2 Segment Addition Postulate

Powered By desmos

If points *A*, *B*, and *C* are on the same line with *B* between *A* and *C*, then $AB + BC = AC$.

If...

Then... $AB + BC = AC$

EXAMPLE 3 ▸ Use the Segment Addition Postulate

Points *F*, *G*, and *H* are collinear. — Collinear points lie on the same line.
If *GH* = 16, what is *FH*?

| F | G | H |

$3x - 1$ $2x + 2$

COMMON ERROR
Be sure to answer the question that is posed. You may think the value of *x* is the answer, but you actually need to use *x* to find *FH*.

Step 1 Use the expression for *GH* to find *x*.

$$GH = 16$$
$$2x + 2 = 16$$
$$2x = 14$$
$$x = 7$$

Step 2 Find *FH*.

$$FH = FG + GH$$
$$= 5x + 1$$
$$= 5(7) + 1$$
$$= 36$$

Apply the Segment Addition Postulate.

Try It! **3. Points *J*, *K*, and *L* are collinear.**

| J | K | L |

$3n$ $5n - 7$

a. If *JL* = 25, what is *n*?   **b.** What is *JK*? *KL*?

POSTULATE 1-3 Protractor Postulate

Given $\overrightarrow{BA}$ and a point *C* not on $\overrightarrow{BA}$, a unique real number from 0 to 180 can be assigned to $\overrightarrow{BC}$.

0 is assigned to $\overrightarrow{BA}$.
180 is assigned to $\overrightarrow{BD}$.

EXAMPLE 4 ▸ Use the Protractor Postulate to Measure an Angle

STUDY TIP
Remember, the measure of ∠*BEC* is denoted as *m*∠*BEC*.

What is *m*∠*BEC*?

Since $\overrightarrow{EA}$ lines up with 0 on the top scale, use the top scale for all of the other rays in the figure.

By the Protractor Postulate, real numbers are assigned to $\overrightarrow{EB}$ and $\overrightarrow{EC}$.

47 is assigned to $\overrightarrow{EB}$.   105 is assigned to $\overrightarrow{EC}$.

You can subtract *m*∠*AEB* from *m*∠*AEC* to find *m*∠*BEC*.

$$m\angle BEC = |105 - 47| = 58$$

CONTINUED ON THE NEXT PAGE

EXAMPLE 4 CONTINUED

Try It! **4.** Refer to the figure in Example 4.

a. What is $m\angle AEC$? **b.** What is $m\angle BED$?

POSTULATE 1-4 Angle Addition Postulate

If point D is in the interior of $\angle ABC$, then $m\angle ABD + m\angle DBC = m\angle ABC$.

If...

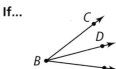

Then... $m\angle ABD + m\angle DBC = m\angle ABC$

APPLICATION

EXAMPLE 5 Use the Angle Addition Postulate to Solve Problems

A lighting designer is finalizing the lighting plan for an upcoming production. The spotlight can rotate 25° to the left or right from the shown starting position. The beam of light from the spotlight forms a 22° angle. Can the designer use the spotlight to light each of the objects on the stage?

Formulate Draw and label a diagram to represent the beam angle, the angles given and the unknown angles.

Use the Angle Addition Postulate to find the angles the light must rotate to the left and right to light the chair and table.

Compute Write and solve equations to find x and y.

$$x + 22 = 57 \qquad y + 57 = 74$$
$$x = 35 \qquad\quad y = 17$$

Interpret The spotlight can rotate 25° to the right or left, so the designer can use the spotlight to light the table but cannot light the chair.

Try It! **5.** Refer to Example 5. Can the lighting designer use a spotlight with a 33° beam angle that can rotate 25° to the left and right to light all of the objects on the stage?

CONCEPT SUMMARY Measuring Segments and Angles

	Ruler Postulate	**Protractor Postulate**
WORDS	Every point on a line can be paired with a unique real number called the *coordinate* of the point. The distance between any two points *X* and *Y* is the absolute value of the difference of their coordinates.	Given $\overrightarrow{KL}$ and a point *J* not on $\overrightarrow{KL}$, a unique real number from 0 to 180 can be paired with $\overrightarrow{KJ}$. This is the measure of $\angle LKJ$.
DIAGRAM		
SYMBOLS	$JK = 5$ $KL = 4$ $JL = 9$ $JK + KL = JL$	$m\angle JKL = 50$ $m\angle JKM = 70$ $m\angle JKL + m\angle JKM = 120$

Do You UNDERSTAND?

1. **ESSENTIAL QUESTION** How are the properties of segments and angles used to determine their measures?

2. **Error Analysis** Ella wrote $AB = |-1 + 5| = 4$. Explain Ella's error. © MP.3

3. **Vocabulary** What does it mean for points to be collinear? How many lines pass through five collinear points?

4. **Make Sense and Persevere** Suppose *M* is a point in the interior of $\angle JKL$. If $m\angle MKL = 42$ and $m\angle JKL = 84$, what is $m\angle JKM$? © MP.1

Do You KNOW HOW?

Find the length of each segment.

5. $\overline{WX}$ 6. $\overline{WY}$

7. Points *A*, *B*, and *C* are collinear and *B* is between *A* and *C*. Given $AB = 12$ and $AC = 19$, what is *BC*?

8. Given $m\angle JML = 80$ and $m\angle KML = 33$, what is $m\angle JMK$?

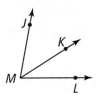

PRACTICE & PROBLEM SOLVING

UNDERSTAND

9. Reason The coordinate of point *M* on a number line is 11. If *MN* = 12, what are the possible coordinates for *N* on the number line? **© MP.2**

10. Construct Arguments How can you use the Segment Addition Postulate to show that *AE* = *AB* + *BC* + *CD* + *DE*? **© MP.3**

11. Higher Order Thinking If points *C*, *D*, and *E* are on a line and *CD* = 20 and *CE* = 32, what are the possible values of *DE*?

12. Error Analysis Point *P* is in the interior of ∠*MNO*. Benito wrote the equation ∠*MNP* + ∠*PNO* = ∠*MNO*. Explain Benito's errors.

13. Make Sense and Persevere Point *Y* is in the interior of ∠*XWZ*. Given that $\overrightarrow{WX}$ and $\overrightarrow{WZ}$ are opposite rays, and *m*∠*XWY* = 4(*m*∠*YWZ*), what is *m*∠*YWZ*? **© MP.1**

14. Mathematical Connections The area of *ABED* is 49 square units. Given *AG* = 9 units and *AC* = 10 units, what fraction of the area of *ACIG* is represented by the shaded region? Give your answer in simplest form.

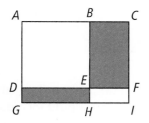

15. Look for Relationships In the diagram below what are the measures of ∠*DBC*, ∠*DBE*, ∠*EBF*, and ∠*DBF*? **© MP.7**

PRACTICE

Find the length of each segment. SEE EXAMPLES 1 AND 2

16. $\overline{DF}$ **17.** $\overline{DE}$ **18.** $\overline{FG}$

19. $\overline{FH}$ **20.** $\overline{GH}$ **21.** $\overline{EH}$

Points *A*, *B*, *C*, *D*, and *E* are collinear and *AC* = 16.
SEE EXAMPLE 3

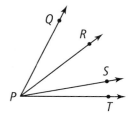

22. What is *x*?   **23.** What is *AB*?

24. What is *BD*?   **25.** What is *CE*?

Use the figure shown for Exercises 26–28.
SEE EXAMPLES 4 AND 5

26. If *m*∠*QPR* = 24 and *m*∠*QPS* = 59, what is *m*∠*RPS*?

27. If *m*∠*QPR* = 4*x* − 8, *m*∠*RPS* = 3*x* + 15, *m*∠*SPT* = *x* + 13, and *m*∠*QPT* = 76, what is the value of *x*?

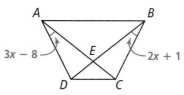

28. If *m*∠*RPT* = 46, *m*∠*QPS* = 61, and *m*∠*QPR* = 28, what is *m*∠*SPT*?

In the figure, *m*∠*DBC* = *m*∠*CAD*, *m*∠*DBA* = *m*∠*CAB*, and *EC* = *ED*. If *m*∠*CBA* = 5*x* + 2, *EC* = 3, and *EB* = 8, find each value. SEE EXAMPLES 3 AND 5

29. *m*∠*DBC*   **30.** *m*∠*CBA*   **31.** *m*∠*CAB*

32. *BD*   **33.** *m*∠*DBA*   **34.** *m*∠*DAB*

35. Points *P*, *Q*, *R*, and *S* are collinear. Point *Q* is between *P* and *R*, *R* is between *Q* and *S*, and *PQ* = *RS*. If *PS* = 18 and *PR* = 15, what is the value of *QR*?

EXAMPLE 3 CONTINUED

Try It!   **3.** Tavon claims that $d = \sqrt{(x_1 - x_2)^2 + (y_1 - y_2)^2}$ can also be used to find the distance between two points. Is he correct? Explain.

CONCEPT Distance Formula

The distance d between two points $P(x_1, y_1)$ and $Q(x_2, y_2)$ is:

$$d(P, Q) = \sqrt{(x_2 - x_1)^2 + (y_2 - y_1)^2}$$

APPLICATION

EXAMPLE 4   Find the Distance

A pitcher throws a ball to a batter, who hits the ball to the shortstop. If the ball travels in a straight line between each, what is the total distance traveled by the ball? **Round your answer to the nearest tenth of a foot.**

Formulate   Represent the pitcher at point $P(5, 5)$, the batter at point $B(0, 0)$, and the shortstop at point $S(5, 10)$.

Compute   Use the Distance Formula to find each distance.

$$d(P, B) = \sqrt{(0 - 5)^2 + (0 - 5)^2}$$

Use the Distance Formula with $P(5, 5)$ and $B(0, 0)$.

$$= \sqrt{(-5)^2 + (-5)^2}$$
$$= \sqrt{25 + 25}$$
$$= \sqrt{50}$$
$$\approx 7.1$$

$$d(B, S) = \sqrt{(5 - 0)^2 + (10 - 0)^2}$$

Use the Distance Formula with $B(0, 0)$ and $S(5, 10)$.

$$= \sqrt{5^2 + 10^2}$$
$$= \sqrt{25 + 100}$$
$$= \sqrt{125}$$
$$\approx 11.2$$

Interpret   The total distance the ball traveled is about $7.1 + 11.2 = 18.3$ units, or about $(18.3)(9) = 164.7$ ft.

Try It!   **4.** How far does the shortstop need to throw the ball to reach the first baseman? Round your answer to the nearest tenth of a foot.

CONCEPT SUMMARY Midpoint and Distance on the Coordinate Plane

MIDPOINT

$$M = \left(\frac{x_1 + x_2}{2}, \frac{y_1 + y_2}{2}\right)$$

DISTANCE

$$d = \sqrt{(x_2 - x_1)^2 + (y_2 - y_1)^2}$$

EXAMPLE

The endpoints of $\overline{PQ}$ are $P(-3, 4)$ and $Q(1, 7)$.

$$M = \left(\frac{-3 + 1}{2}, \frac{4 + 7}{2}\right)$$

$$= \left(-1, \frac{11}{2}\right)$$

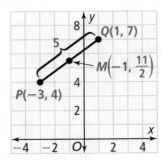

$$d = \sqrt{(-3 - 1)^2 + (4 - 7)^2}$$

$$= \sqrt{(-4)^2 + (-3)^2}$$

$$= \sqrt{25}$$

$$= 5$$

Do You UNDERSTAND?

1. **ESSENTIAL QUESTION** How are the midpoint and length of a segment on the coordinate plane determined?

2. **Error Analysis** Kaleel calculated the midpoint of $\overline{AB}$ with $A(-3, 5)$ and $B(1, 7)$. What is Kaleel's error? Ⓒ **MP.3**

$$M\left(\frac{-3 + 5}{2}, \frac{1 + 7}{2}\right)$$

$$M(1, 4) \quad ✗$$

3. **Vocabulary** If M is the midpoint of $\overline{PQ}$, what is the relationship between PM and MQ? Between PM and PQ?

4. **Reason** Is it possible for $\overline{PQ}$ to have two distinct midpoints, $M_1(a, b)$ and $M_2(c, d)$? Explain. Ⓒ **MP.2**

Do You KNOW HOW?

$\overline{PQ}$ has endpoints at $P(-5, 4)$ and $Q(7, -5)$.

5. What is the midpoint of $\overline{PQ}$?

6. What are the coordinates of the point $\frac{2}{3}$ of the way from P to Q?

7. What is the length of $\overline{PQ}$?

8. A chair lift at a ski resort travels along the cable as shown.

1 unit = 10 ft

How long is the cable? Round your answer to the nearest whole foot.

PRACTICE & PROBLEM SOLVING

UNDERSTAND

9. **Use Structure** Point K is $\frac{1}{n}$ of the way from $J(4, -5)$ to $L(0, -7)$.

   a. What are the coordinates of K if $n = 4$?

   b. What is a formula for the coordinates of K for any n? ⓒ **MP.7**

10. **Error Analysis** Describe and correct the error a student made in finding the midpoint of $\overline{CD}$ with $C(-4, 5)$ and $D(-1, -4)$. ⓒ **MP.3**

$$\left(\frac{-4 - (-1)}{2}, \frac{5 - (-4)}{2}\right)$$
$$\left(-\frac{3}{2}, \frac{9}{2}\right) \quad ✗$$

11. **Mathematical Connections** Point M is the midpoint of $\overline{FG}$. Can you determine the value of a? Explain.

   $G(2a, 3b + 3)$
   $M(3, 5)$
   $F(b + 1, a + 2)$

12. **Reason** Suppose $\overline{PQ}$ has one endpoint at $P(0, 0)$.

   a. If $(2, 5)$ is the midpoint of $\overline{PQ}$, what are the coordinates of point Q?

   b. How would you find Q if $(2, 5)$ is $\frac{1}{4}$ of the way from P to Q? ⓒ **MP.2**

13. **Higher Order Thinking** $\overline{PQ}$ has a length of 17 units with $P(-4, 7)$. If the x- and y-coordinates of Q are both greater than the x- and y-coordinates of P, what are possible integer value coordinates of Q? Explain.

14. **Make Sense and Persevere** Suppose $\overline{PQ}$ has $P(a, b)$ and midpoint $M(c, d)$. What is an expression for PM? Use the expression for PM to find an expression for PQ. ⓒ **MP.1**

PRACTICE

Find the coordinates of each given point on $\overline{AB}$.
SEE EXAMPLE 2

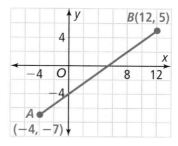

15. The point that partitions $\overline{AB}$ in the ratio 3:7.

16. Point B partitions $\overline{AC}$ in the ratio 1:3. What are the coordinates of C?

Find the midpoint of $\overline{PQ}$. SEE EXAMPLE 1

17. $P(3, 5)$, $Q(-2, 13)$

18. $P(-2, 2.5)$, $Q(1.4, 4)$

19. $P\left(4\frac{1}{3}, 3\frac{1}{6}\right)$, $Q\left(-2\frac{1}{5}, 3\frac{2}{3}\right)$

Cameron, Arthur, and Jamie are playing soccer. Their locations are recorded by a motion tracking system. The distance between gridlines is 5 meters.
SEE EXAMPLES 3 AND 4

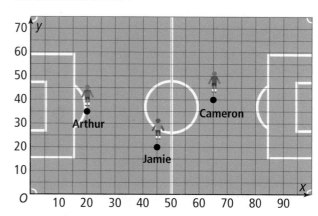

20. How far apart are Arthur and Jamie? Round to the nearest tenth of a meter.

21. Who is closer to Cameron? Explain.

22. The soccer ball is located at the point (35, 60). Who is closest to the soccer ball?

PRACTICE & PROBLEM SOLVING

23. **Model With Mathematics** A university is building a new student center that is two-thirds the distance from the arts center to residential housing. What are the coordinates of the new center? Explain. © MP.4

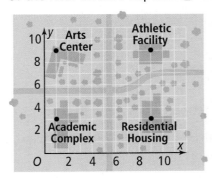

24. **Mathematical Connections** A lighthouse casts a revolving beam of light as far as the pier. What is the area that the light covers?

1 unit = 0.4 mi

25. **Make Sense and Persevere** A ship captain is attempting to contact a deep sea diver. © MP.1

If the maximum range for communication is 60 meters, will he be able to communicate with the diver based on their current positions? Explain.

26. $\overline{AB}$ has an endpoint at $A(1, -2)$ and midpoint $C(3, 2)$. Graph $\overline{AB}$ and point C.

27. **SAT/ACT** $\overline{RS}$ has an endpoint at $R(6, -4)$ and length 17. Which of the following cannot be the coordinates of S?

Ⓐ (14, 11)

Ⓑ (6, 13)

Ⓒ (−9, −12)

Ⓓ (23, 13)

Ⓔ (23, −4)

28. **Performance Task** A parade route must start and end at the intersections shown on the map. The city requires that the total distance of the route cannot exceed 3 miles. A proposed route is shown.

1 unit = 0.25 mi

Part A Why does the proposed route not meet the requirement?

Part B Assuming that the roads used for the route are the same and the end point is the same, at what intersection could the parade start so the total distance is as close to 3 miles as possible?

Part C The city wants to station video cameras halfway down each road in the parade. Using your answer to Part B, what are the coordinates of the locations for the cameras?

1-4

Inductive Reasoning

I CAN... use inductive reasoning to make conjectures about mathematical relationships.

VOCABULARY
• conjecture
• counterexample
• inductive reasoning

© **Common Core State Standards**
Prepares for HSG.CO.C.9, HSG.CO.C.10, HSG.CO.C.11, MP.3, MP.7, MP.8

STUDY TIP
When looking for a pattern, remember to always test subsequent terms to be sure that you have found the correct rule.

EXPLORE & REASON

Powered By **desmos**

When points on a circle are connected, the line segments divide the circle into a number of regions, as shown.

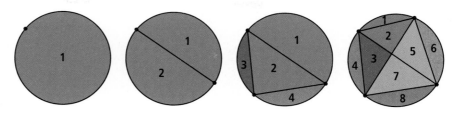

A. How does the number of regions change when another point is added?

B. Look for Relationships Using the pattern you observed, make a prediction about the number of regions formed by connecting 5 points on a circle. Make a drawing to test your prediction. Is your prediction correct? © **MP.7**

ESSENTIAL QUESTION
How is inductive reasoning used to recognize mathematical relationships?

EXAMPLE 1   Use Inductive Reasoning to Extend a Pattern

Inductive reasoning is a type of reasoning that reaches conclusions based on a pattern of specific examples or past events. How can you use inductive reasoning to determine what appears to be the next two terms in each sequence?

A. 88, 82, 76, 70, 64,...

> Look for a pattern. Observe that the terms decrease and the difference of the first two terms is 6.

Test whether the pattern continues with subsequent terms.

$$82 - 6 = 76 \qquad 76 - 6 = 70 \qquad 70 - 6 = 64$$

The rule works. Use the pattern to find the next two terms.

The next two terms in the sequence appear to be 58 and 52.

B. 3, 5, 9, 15, 23,...

> Look for a pattern. Observe that the terms increase by successive multiples of 2.

The next two terms in the sequence appear to be 33 and 45.

Try It!   **1.** What appear to be the next two terms in each sequence?

     a. 800, 400, 200, 100,...   **b.** 18, 24, 32, $\frac{128}{3}$,...

EXAMPLE 2   Use Inductive Reasoning to Make a Conjecture

A **conjecture** is an unproven statement or rule that is based on inductive reasoning. What conjecture can be made about the number of dots in the *n*th term of this geometric pattern?

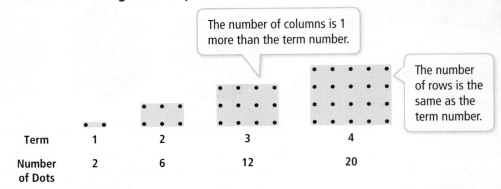

The number of columns is 1 more than the term number.

The number of rows is the same as the term number.

Term	1	2	3	4
Number of Dots	2	6	12	20

Write an algebraic expression to generalize the pattern for the *n*th term. Since the number or rows in the pattern is equivalent to the term number, use *n* to represent the number of rows.

> **MODEL WITH MATHEMATICS**
> You can write an algebraic expression to represent a geometric pattern. What expressions can you write for the *n*th term? © MP.4

n + 1 columns

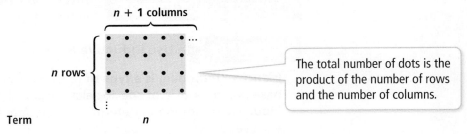

n rows

Term   *n*

The total number of dots is the product of the number of rows and the number of columns.

Conjecture: The *n*th term of the sequence will contain $n(n + 1)$, or $n^2 + n$ dots.

Try It!   **2. a.** How many dots are in the 5th and 6th terms of the pattern?

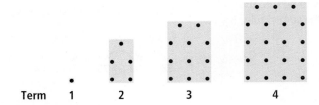

Term   1   2   3   4

b. What conjecture can you make about the number of dots in the *n*th term of the pattern?

EXAMPLE 3 ▶ Use a Conjecture to Make a Prediction

Based on the data in the table, how many residents would you expect to vote in the 7th town council election?

Town Council Elections Voter Turnout

Year	Total Residents	Voters
1	3,511	386
2	3,790	414
3	4,085	451
4	4,907	544
5	5,562	623
6	7,014	767
7	7,786	?

Formulate ◀ Look for a pattern by comparing the ratios $\frac{\text{number of voters}}{\text{number of residents}}$ for each year. Then use the pattern to make a conjecture about the number of residents who will vote in the 7th town election.

Compute ◀

$\frac{386}{3,511} \approx 0.110$ $\frac{414}{3,790} \approx 0.109$

$\frac{451}{4,085} \approx 0.110$ $\frac{544}{4,907} \approx 0.111$

$\frac{623}{5,562} \approx 0.112$ $\frac{767}{7,014} \approx 0.109$

Conjecture: The number of voters each year is about 11% of the total residents.

Use the pattern to predict the number of voters in the 7th election.

$7,786 \cdot 0.11 = 856.46$

Interpret ◀ About 856 people can be expected to vote in the 7th town council election.

Try It! **3.** Based on the data, about how many members would you expect the chess club to have in its 5th year?

Year	1	2	3	4
Club Members	10	13	17	22

EXAMPLE 4 ▶ Find a Counterexample to Show a Conjecture Is False

Powered By
desmos

Why does a *counterexample* show that a conjecture is false?

> A **counterexample** is an example that shows a statement or conjecture is false.

Conjecture: A polygon has two fewer diagonals as sides.

To find a counterexample, you must find a polygon that has a number of diagonals that is not two fewer than the number of its sides.

CONSTRUCT ARGUMENTS
For a conjecture to be true, it must be true for every possible case, so if a counterexample is found, the conjecture is false. Ⓒ MP.3

4 sides
2 diagonals

5 sides
5 diagonals

> You only need to find one counterexample to show that a statement is false. A counterexample exists, so the conjecture is false.

Try It! **4.** What is a counterexample that shows the statement, *the sum of two composite numbers must be a composite number*, is false?

EXAMPLE 5 ▶ Test a Conjecture

For each conjecture, test the conjecture with several more examples or find a counterexample to disprove the conjecture.

A. A polygon with four congruent sides is a square.

A square has four congruent sides and four right angles.

> Think: Is it possible to draw a polygon with four congruent sides but not four right angles?

> This rhombus has four congruent sides and no right angles.

A counterexample exists, so this conjecture is false.

B. If a figure is a convex quadrilateral, then at least one angle is greater than or equal to 90°.

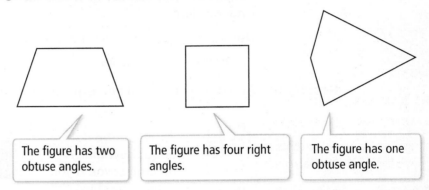

> The figure has two obtuse angles.

> The figure has four right angles.

> The figure has one obtuse angle.

None of the figures are a counterexample to the conjecture. However, just because a counterexample cannot be found, you cannot conclude that the conjecture is true.

COMMUNICATE PRECISELY
Why is a lack of a counterexample not enough to conclude that the conjecture is true? ⒸMP.6

Try It! 5. For each conjecture, test the conjecture with several more examples or find a counterexample to disprove it.

a. For every integer n, the value of n^2 is positive.

b. A number is divisible by 4 if the last two digits are divisible by 4.

CONCEPT SUMMARY Inductive Reasoning

WORDS Inductive Reasoning

- leads to a conjecture by observing patterns.
- uses specific examples to make a generalization.

- does not show that a conjecture is true, so a conjecture could be disproven by a counterexample.

DIAGRAM

Pattern	Generalization	Conjecture

$0^2 + 0 + 11 = 11$
$1^2 + 1 + 11 = 13$
$2^2 + 2 + 11 = 17$
$3^2 + 3 + 11 = 23$
$4^2 + 4 + 11 = 31$

→ As the pattern continues, the sum is a prime number.

→ If n is a whole number, then $n^2 + n + 11$ is a prime number.

Counterexample: If $n = 11$, $11^2 + 11 + 11 = 143$ is divisible by 11, so the sum is not always prime.

Do You UNDERSTAND?

1. **ESSENTIAL QUESTION** How is inductive reasoning used to recognize mathematical relationships?

2. **Error Analysis** Esteban made the following drawing and then stated this conjecture: "The altitude of a triangle always lies inside of or along the side of the triangle." What error did Esteban make? © MP.3

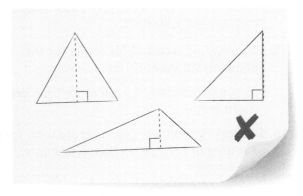

3. **Vocabulary** What type of statement results from inductive reasoning?

Do You KNOW HOW?

4. What appear to be the next three numbers in the pattern?

   4, 11, 18, 25,…

5. What conjecture can you make about the number of regions created by n unique diameters?

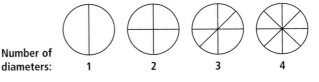

Number of diameters:　1　　2　　3　　4

6. Can you find four examples that are true or a counterexample for the following statement?

   For every integer n, the value of $n^2 + 1$ is odd.

PRACTICE & PROBLEM SOLVING

UNDERSTAND

7. Mathematical Connections Abby notices that for the first twenty perfect squares, each square is either a multiple of 5, one less than a multiple of 5, or one more than a multiple of 5.

1	4	9	16	25
36	49	64	81	100
121	144	169	196	225
256	289	324	361	400

She writes the following statement.

> If n is a natural number, then n^2 can be written as $5k - 1$, $5k$, or $5k + 1$, where k is a whole number.

What type of statement did Abby make? Has she shown that her statement is true for all values of n? Explain.

8. Error Analysis Danielle tests the following conjecture.

> If two angles share a common vertex, then they are adjacent.

Her work is shown below. What error does Danielle make? Ⓒ **MP.3**

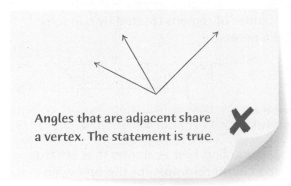

Angles that are adjacent share a vertex. The statement is true. ✗

9. Higher Order Thinking Consider the following conjecture.

> There are no prime numbers between 7,608 and 7,620.

How could you show that this statement is true or false? Would it still be a conjecture if you do not find a counterexample? Explain.

PRACTICE

For each sequence, what appear to be the next three numbers? SEE EXAMPLE 1

10. 101, 89, 77, 65,…

11. 9, 6, 4, $\frac{8}{3}$,…

12. Observe the pattern made by the figures. Can you write a conjecture about the number of triangles formed by connecting one vertex of a polygon with n sides to each of the other vertices? SEE EXAMPLE 2

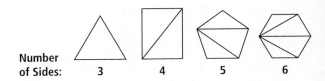

Number of Sides: 3   4   5   6

The table shows the number of students in the senior class and the number of seniors who have their driver's license. SEE EXAMPLE 3

Year	2021	2022	2023	2024
Number of Seniors	341	367	309	382
Seniors With a License	222	240	199	246

13. What pattern can you find between the number of seniors and the seniors who have a driver's license?

14. The class of 2025 has 413 students. How many seniors in the class of 2025 do you think will have a driver's license?

15. Can you find a counterexample for the following statement? SEE EXAMPLE 4

> A trapezoid cannot have more than one right angle.

16. Support the following conjecture with four examples or provide a counterexample. SEE EXAMPLE 5

> The quotient of two rational numbers is a rational number.

17. How can you determine whether the conjecture is true?

> The first and third digits of a three-digit number are the same. If the second digit is equal to the sum of the first and third digits, then the number must be divisible by 11.

PRACTICE & PROBLEM SOLVING

18. Model With Mathematics Data from four identical trials on a new sleep herb are shown in the table.

Group	Number of Subjects	Number Who Reported Better Sleep
A	250	55
B	170	35
C	210	48
D	190	40

a. What conjecture can you make about the effectiveness of the herb?

b. The next trial will have 1,000 subjects. What is a reasonable prediction for the next trial? ⓒ **MP.4**

19. Generalize A graphic designer wants to know the number of regions that are formed when circles overlap in a particular way. Can she find a rule that describes how the number of regions increases when another circle is added to the design? How many regions would a design with 6 circles create? ⓒ **MP.8**

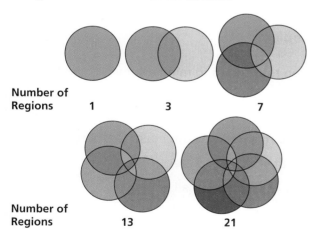

Number of Regions   1   3   7

Number of Regions   13   21

20. Consider the conjecture, "Any number divisible by 2 is also divisible by 4." Is each number a counterexample of the conjecture? Select *Yes* or *No*.

Number	Yes	No
12	☐	☐
19	☐	☐
22	☐	☐
28	☐	☐
30	☐	☐

21. SAT/ACT Which number is next in the following sequence?

1, 2, 2, 4, 8, 32,...

Ⓐ 64   Ⓑ 84   Ⓒ 106   Ⓓ 256

22. SAT/ACT How many dots are in the nth term of the following sequence?

term: 1   2   3   4

Ⓐ $n + 2$ Ⓑ $2n + 1$

Ⓒ $n^2 + 2$ Ⓓ $n + 3$

23. Performance Task The graph shows data from a survey of 300 random voters on whether they support Proposition 3.

Support for Prop 3

Part A Make a conjecture about the likelihood of Proposition 3 passing and explain your reasoning.

Part B If 7,500 people vote in the next election, how many people would you expect to vote for Proposition 3?

ⓒ **Common Core State Standards**
HSG.CO.A.1, HSG.CO.C.9,
HSG.CO.D.12, MP.4

SavvasRealize.com

The Mystery Spokes

Powered By
desmos

Some photos are taken in such a way that it is difficult to determine exactly what the picture shows. Sometimes it's because the photo is a close up part of an object, and you do not see the entire object. Other times, it might be because the photographer used special effects when taking the photo.

You can often use clues from the photo to determine what is in the photo and also what the rest of the object might look like. What clues would you look for? Think about this during the Mathematical Modeling in 3 Acts lesson.

ACT 1 ▶ **Identify the Problem**

1. What is the first question that comes to mind after watching the video?

2. Write down the main question you will answer about what you saw in the video.

3. Make an initial conjecture that answers this main question.

4. Explain how you arrived at your conjecture.

5. Write a number that you know is too small.

6. Write a number that you know is too large.

ACT 2 ▶ **Develop a Model**

7. Use the math that you have learned in this Topic to refine your conjecture.

ACT 3 ▶ **Interpret the Results**

8. Is your refined conjecture between the highs and lows you set up earlier?

9. Did your refined conjecture match the actual answer exactly? If not, what might explain the difference?

1-5
Conditional Statements

I CAN... write conditionals and biconditionals and find their truth values.

VOCABULARY
- biconditional
- conclusion
- conditional
- contrapositive
- converse
- hypothesis
- inverse
- negation
- truth table
- truth value

© **Common Core State Standards**
Prepares for HSG.CO.C.9, HSG.CO.C.10, HSG.CO.C.11, MP.1, MP.6, MP.7

EXPLORE & REASON

If-then statements show a cause and effect. The table shows some if-then statements.

Cause	Effect
If it is raining	then it is spring.
If x and y are whole numbers	then their difference, $x - y$, is a whole number.
If water is heated	then it boils.
If a triangle has a right angle	then it is a right triangle.
If your favorite color is blue	then you are a good speller.

A. Construct Arguments Determine whether each effect is always true for the given cause, or is not necessarily true for the given cause. For the effects that are not necessarily true, how could you change them to make them always true? © **MP.3**

B. Write some if-then statements of your own. Write two statements that are always true and two statements that are not necessarily true.

ESSENTIAL QUESTION
How do if-then statements describe mathematical relationships?

CONCEPT Conditional Statement

A **conditional** is an *if-then* statement that relates a **hypothesis**, the part that follows *if*, to a **conclusion**, the part that follows *then*.

Conditionals can be represented as $p \rightarrow q$, read as "If p, then q," where p represents the hypothesis and q represents the conclusion.

EXAMPLE 1 Write a Conditional Statement

Write each statement as a conditional.

A. You can register to vote if you are at least 18 years old.

Identify the hypothesis and conclusion.

> The conclusion ("**q**") gives the outcome or result.

> The hypothesis ("**p**") follows "if" and gives the condition.

You can register to vote if you are at least 18 years old.

Conditional: If you are at least 18 years old, then you may register to vote.

CONTINUED ON THE NEXT PAGE

COMMON ERROR
Remember that in everyday language, the hypothesis does not necessarily come before the conclusion.

EXAMPLE 1 CONTINUED

B. A square must have four congruent sides.

Identify the hypothesis and conclusion.

> The hypothesis is that a polygon is a square.

> The conclusion is that the polygon has four congruent sides.

A square must have four congruent sides.

Conditional: If a polygon is a square, then it has four congruent sides.

Try It! **1.** Write each statement as a conditional.

a. A triangle with all angles congruent is equilateral.

b. Alberto can go to the movies if he washes the car.

CONCEPTUAL UNDERSTANDING

| EXAMPLE 2 | Find a Truth Value of a Conditional |

The **truth value** of a statement is "true" (T) or "false" (F) according to whether the statement is true or false, respectively. A **truth table** lists all the possible combinations of truth values for two or more statements.

Truth Table for $p \rightarrow q$

Hypothesis p	Conslusion q	Conditional $p \rightarrow q$
T	T	T
T	F	F
F	T	T
F	F	T

> A true hypothesis and a false conclusion has a value of false.

What is the truth value of each conditional?

A. If a number is even, then it is divisible by 2.

An even number is always divisible by two, so when the hypothesis is true, the conclusion is always true. Therefore, the conditional is true.

B. If a quadrilateral has two pairs of congruent angles, then it is a parallelogram.

Assume the hypothesis, a quadrilateral that has two pairs of congruent angles, is true. To decide whether the conclusion is true, determine whether the quadrilateral **must** be a parallelogram.

> An isosceles trapezoid has two pairs of congruent angles, but is not a parallelogram.

Although there are instances in which the hypothesis and conclusion are both true, this counterexample is an instance in which the hypothesis is true but the conclusion is false. Since the truth value of the conditional is not **always** true, the conditional is false.

CONTINUED ON THE NEXT PAGE

EXAMPLE 2 CONTINUED

Try It! **2.** What is the truth value of each conditional? Explain your reasoning.

  a. If a quadrilateral has a right angle, then it is a rectangle.

  b. If X is the midpoint of $\overline{AB}$, then X lies on $\overline{AB}$.

CONCEPT Related Conditional Statements

Definition	Symbols	Words
A conditional has a hypothesis and a conclusion.	$p \rightarrow q$	If p, then q.
The **converse** reverses the hypothesis and the conclusion of a conditional.	$q \rightarrow p$	If q, then p.
The **negation** of a statement has the opposite meaning of the original statement.	$\sim p$	not p
The **inverse** is obtained by negating both the hypothesis and the conclusion of a conditional.	$\sim p \rightarrow \sim q$	If not p, then not q.
The **contrapositive** is obtained by negating and reversing both the hypothesis and the conclusion of a conditional.	$\sim q \rightarrow \sim p$	If not q, then not p.

EXAMPLE 3 Write and Evaluate the Truth Value of a Converse

Write and determine the truth value of the converse of the conditional.

If you play the trumpet, then you play a brass instrument.

To write the converse, reverse the hypothesis and conclusion.

| p: You play the trumpet | q: You play a brass instrument | If you play a brass instrument, then you may play a brass instrument that is **not** a trumpet. |

STUDY TIP
To remember that the converse reverses the order, remember that a *conversation* goes back and forth between two people.

if **you play a brass instrument**, then **you play the trumpet**.

In the converse, the hypothesis can be true while the conclusion is false. Since the converse has a counterexample, the truth value of the converse is false.

Try It! **3.** Write and determine the truth value of the converse of the conditional.

  a. If a polygon is a quadrilateral, then it has four sides.

  b. If two angles are complementary, then their angle measures add to 90.

EXAMPLE 4 Write and Evaluate the Truth Value of an Inverse and a Contrapositive

Write and determine the truth value of the inverse and contrapositive of the conditional.

If two whole numbers are both even, then their sum is even.

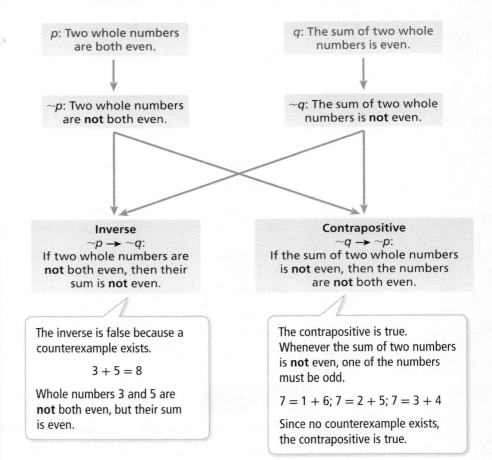

COMMUNICATE PRECISELY

Consider how you can use clear and accurate reasoning to determine a truth value. What can you reason about a conditional if the conclusion is not true? © MP.6

p: Two whole numbers are both even.

q: The sum of two whole numbers is even.

~p: Two whole numbers are **not** both even.

~q: The sum of two whole numbers is **not** even.

Inverse
~p → ~q:
If two whole numbers are **not** both even, then their sum is **not** even.

Contrapositive
~q → ~p:
If the sum of two whole numbers is **not** even, then the numbers are **not** both even.

The inverse is false because a counterexample exists.

$3 + 5 = 8$

Whole numbers 3 and 5 are **not** both even, but their sum is even.

The contrapositive is true. Whenever the sum of two numbers is **not** even, one of the numbers must be odd.

$7 = 1 + 6; 7 = 2 + 5; 7 = 3 + 4$

Since no counterexample exists, the contrapositive is true.

Try It! 4. Write the converse, the inverse, and the contrapositive. What is the truth value of each?

If today is a weekend day, then tomorrow is Monday.

CONCEPT Biconditional Statements

A **biconditional** is the combination of a conditional, $p → q$, and its converse, $q → p$. The resulting compound statement $p ↔ q$ is read as "p if and only if q."

A counterexample to a biconditional statement occurs when the hypothesis is true and the conclusion is false, or when the hypothesis is false and the conclusion is true.

p	q	p ↔ q
T	T	T
T	F	F
F	T	F
F	F	T

EXAMPLE 5 Write and Evaluate a Biconditional

A marine biologist writes this conditional: "If a seahorse gives birth, then it is a male." Since it is true that, among seahorses, only the males can become pregnant and give birth, should the marine biologist state this as a biconditional in a paper she is writing?

Formulate ◄ Identify the hypothesis p and the conclusion q of the conditional.

Combine the conditionals $p \to q$ and $q \to p$ in the form $p \leftrightarrow q$ to write the biconditional.

Then evaluate the truth value of the biconditional.

Compute ◄ p: **A seahorse gives birth.**

     q: **A seahorse is male.**

     Biconditional $p \leftrightarrow q$: A seahorse gives birth if and only if it is male.

Determine the truth value of the biconditional.

     $p \to q$: If a seahorse gives birth, then it is male.   **T**

     $q \to p$: If a seahorse is male, then it gives birth.   **F**

> If each of the combined conditionals is true, then the biconditional is true.

Interpret ◄ The biconditional is not true; the biologist should not include the statement as a biconditional in her paper.

Try It!   **5.** Write a biconditional for the following conditional. What is its truth value?

     If two lines intersect at right angles, then they are perpendicular.

EXAMPLE 6 Identify the Conditionals in a Biconditional

What are the two conditionals associated with the biconditional?

     A triangle is equilateral if and only if it has three congruent sides.

Identify the two statements in the biconditional

     p: A triangle is equilateral.

     q: A triangle has three congruent sides.

Write the two conditionals.

     $p \to q$: If a triangle is equilateral, then it has three congruent sides.

     $q \to p$: If a triangle has three congruent sides, then it is equilateral.

STUDY TIP
Remember that because the conditionals that form a true biconditional are also true, you can choose either part of the biconditional as the hypothesis and the other part as the conclusion.

Try It!   **6.** What are the two conditionals associated with the biconditional?

     The product of two numbers is negative if and only if the numbers have opposite signs.

CONCEPT SUMMARY Conditional Statements

STATEMENT	Conditional	Converse	Inverse	Contrapositive	Biconditional
SYMBOLS	$p \rightarrow q$	$q \rightarrow p$	$\sim p \rightarrow \sim q$	$\sim q \rightarrow \sim p$	$p \leftrightarrow q$
WORDS	If p, then q.	If q, then p.	If not p, then not q.	If not q, then not p.	p if and only if q.

Do You UNDERSTAND?

1. **ESSENTIAL QUESTION** How do if-then statements describe mathematical relationships?

2. **Error Analysis** Alma was asked to write the inverse of the following conditional.

   If it is sunny, then I use sunscreen.

   What error did Alma make? ⓒ MP.3

   If it is not sunny, then I use sunscreen. ✗

3. **Vocabulary** Which term is used to describe the opposite of a statement?

4. **Generalize** How do you write the converse of a conditional? How do you write the contrapositive of a conditional? ⓒ MP.8

5. **Communicate Precisely** Explain how the inverse and the contrapositive of a conditional are alike and how they are different. ⓒ MP.6

Do You KNOW HOW?

6. Write the following statement as a biconditional.

   A prime number has only 1 and itself as factors.

For Exercises 7–9, use the following conditional.

   If a rectangle has an area of 12 m², then it has sides of length 3 m and 4 m.

7. What is the hypothesis? What is the conclusion?

8. What is the truth value of the conditional? What would be a counterexample?

9. What are the converse, the inverse, and the contrapositive? What are their truth values?

10. What two conditionals are associated with the following biconditional?

"The city can build new roads if and only if the sales tax is raised to 8%."

PRACTICE & PROBLEM SOLVING

UNDERSTAND

11. Construct Arguments Why is the following conditional logically true? ⒼMP.3

> If 20 is a multiple of 3, then 101 is a perfect square.

12. Higher Order Thinking Write a true biconditional and show that both associated conditionals are true.

13. Error Analysis Jacy was asked to write the following statement as a conditional.

> Water freezes if it is below 0°C.

What error did she make? What is the correct conditional? ⒼMP.3

If water freezes, then it is below 0°C ✗

14. Higher Order Thinking Write a true biconditional about angle bisectors.

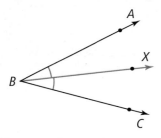

15. Reason Can an inverse and the contrapositive both have false truth values? Explain. ⒼMP.2

16. Reason If a biconditional is true, what are the truth values of the hypothesis and conclusion of the conditional? Explain. ⒼMP.2

17. Look for Relationships Emma found a counterexample to a given conditional. What are the truth values of the hypothesis and the conclusion? Explain. ⒼMP.7

18. Mathematical Connections Write the Pythagorean Theorem as a conditional. Then write a biconditional to include the Converse of the Pythagorean Theorem.

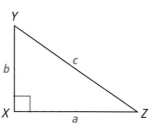

PRACTICE

Write each statement as a conditional.
SEE EXAMPLE 1

19. My hair will be shorter if I cut it.

20. A number that is divisible by 6 is divisible by 3.

21. Movie tickets are half-price on Tuesdays.

Find the truth value of each conditional. Explain your reasoning or show a counterexample.
SEE EXAMPLE 2

22. If a pair of lines is parallel, then they do not intersect.

23. If the product of two numbers is positive, then the numbers are both positive.

Write the negation of the hypothesis and the negation of the conclusion for each conditional.
SEE EXAMPLES 3 and 4

24. If the sum of the interior angle measures of a polygon is 180, then the polygon is a triangle.

25. If one whole number is odd and the other whole number is even, then the sum of the two numbers is odd.

Write each related conditional and determine each truth value for the following conditional.
SEE EXAMPLES 3 and 4

> If an angle measures 100, then it is obtuse.

26. converse   **27.** contrapositive

28. inverse

29. An employee at an animal shelter wrote the true conditional "If 47% of the dogs at the shelter are female, then 53% of the dogs are male." Can he rewrite this as a true biconditional? Explain. SEE EXAMPLE 5

Write two conditionals associated with each biconditional. SEE EXAMPLE 6

30. A month has exactly 28 days if and only if it is February.

31. Two angles are complementary if and only if their measures add up to 90.

32. The area of a square is s^2 if and only if the perimeter of the square is 4s.

PRACTICE & PROBLEM SOLVING

33. Model With Mathematics In general, a person is 1% shorter in the evening than in the morning. Use your height to write a conditional that uses this fact. **© MP.4**

34. Communicate Precisely In the year 1881, three different men were president of the United States—Rutherford B. Hayes, James Garfield, and Chester A. Arthur.

a. Use this fact to write a conditional and a biconditional.

b. There was one other year in which three different men were president of the United States. In 1841, Martin Van Buren, William Henry Harrison, and John Tyler were president. Using this information, determine the truth value of the conditional and the biconditional you wrote for part (a). **© MP.6**

35. Reason The sign shows the hours for an art museum.

MO CA	Museum Of Contemporary Art	HOURS
Monday	Closed	
Tuesday	10:00 AM	8:00 PM
Wednesday	10:00 AM	6:00 PM
Thursday	10:00 AM	8:00 PM
Friday	9:00 AM	6:00 PM
Saturday	9:00 AM	6:00 PM
Sunday	12:00 PM	5:00 PM

a. Write a conditional to describe the hours of the museum on Mondays.

b. Write a conditional to describe the hours of the museum on Thursdays.

c. Write the converse, inverse, and contrapositive of the conditional you wrote in part (b). Then give the truth value for each statement.

d. Can each conditional you wrote for parts (a) and (b) be written as a true biconditional? Why or why not? If so, give each biconditional. **© MP.2**

36. Consider the conditional $p \rightarrow q$, where p is true and q is false. Copy and complete the table to show the truth value of each statement.

Statement	Truth Value
Conditional	F
Converse	
Inverse	
Contrapositive	

37. SAT/ACT Which represents the contrapositive of $p \rightarrow q$?

Ⓐ $p \leftrightarrow q$

Ⓑ $q \rightarrow p$

Ⓒ $\sim p \rightarrow \sim q$

Ⓓ $\sim q \rightarrow \sim p$

Ⓔ $\sim q \leftrightarrow \sim p$

38. Performance Task A group of students drew several different right triangles and found the measures of the two non-right angles. Their findings are shown in the table.

Angle Measure	Angle Measure	Sum
27	63	90
41	49	90
70	20	90
33	57	90

Part A Make a conjecture about the sum of two non-right angles in a right triangle. Write the conjecture in the form of a conditional.

Part B Use a protractor and ruler to draw several right angles with line segments of different lengths. Form right triangles by drawing a side opposite of the right angle. Then, measure the angles of each triangle. Do your measurements support your conjecture, or were you able to find a counterexample?

Part C Write the converse, the inverse, and the contrapositive of your conditional. Then, write a biconditional. Is the biconditional true? Explain.

1-6

Deductive Reasoning

I CAN... use deductive reasoning to draw conclusions.

VOCABULARY
• deductive reasoning
• Law of Detachment
• Law of Syllogism

 Common Core State Standards
Prepares for HSG.CO.C.9, HSG.CO.C.10, HSG.CO.C.11, MP.2, MP.4, MP.7

CRITIQUE & EXPLAIN

A deck of 60 game cards are numbered from 1 to 15 on one of four different shapes (triangle, circle, square, and pentagon). A teacher selects five cards and displays four of the cards.

She tells her class that all of the cards she selected have the same shape and asks them to draw a conclusion about the fifth card.

Chen

The fifth card is 11.

Carolina

The fifth card has a circle.

A. Describe how each student might have reached his or her conclusion. Is each student's conclusion valid? Explain.

B. Make Sense and Persevere What are other possibilities of the fifth card? What could the teacher say to narrow the possibilities? ⒸMP.1

ESSENTIAL QUESTION How can you use given and previously known facts to draw conclusions?

CONCEPTUAL UNDERSTANDING

EXAMPLE 1 Determine Whether a Statement Is True

Given that a conditional and its conclusion are true, can you use deductive reasoning to determine whether the hypothesis is true?

STUDY TIP
Recall that in a conditional $p \rightarrow q$, p is the hypothesis and q is the conclusion.

You are given the facts that $p \rightarrow q$ is true and q is true. Make a truth table for the conditional $p \rightarrow q$.

Deductive reasoning is a process of reasoning using given and previously known facts to reach a logical conclusion.

p	q	$p \rightarrow q$
T	T	T
T	F	F
F	T	T
F	F	T

When $p \rightarrow q$ and q are true, p can be true or false.

You cannot determine whether the hypothesis is true.

Try It! **1.** Given that a conditional and its hypothesis are true, can you determine whether the conclusion is true?

CONCEPT Law of Detachment

The **Law of Detachment** is a law of logic that states if a conditional statement and its hypothesis are true, then its conclusion is also true.

If... $p \rightarrow q$ and p are true.

Then... q is true.

EXAMPLE 2 Apply the Law of Detachment to Draw Real-World and Mathematical Conclusions

Assume that each set of given information is true.

A. If Alicia scores 85 or greater on her test, she will earn an A as her final grade. Alicia scores 89 on her test. What can you logically conclude?

To apply the Law of Detachment, determine the truth value of $p \rightarrow q$ and p.

$p \rightarrow q$: If Alicia scores 85 or greater on her test, then she will earn an A as her final grade.

> This given conditional is true.

p: Alicia scores 85 or greater on her test.

> The hypothesis is true because 89 > 85.

The conditional and its hypothesis are true, so by the Law of Detachment, the conclusion q is true.

You can conclude that Alicia will earn an A as her final grade.

B. If point D is in the interior of $\angle ABC$, then $m\angle ABC = m\angle ABD + m\angle DBC$. What can you logically conclude about $m\angle ABC$?

Determine the truth value of $p \rightarrow q$ and p.

$p \rightarrow q$: If point D is in the interior of $\angle ABC$, then $m\angle ABC = m\angle ABD + m\angle DBC$.

> The conditional is true by the Angle Addition Postulate.

p: Point D is in the interior of $\angle ABC$.

> This given hypothesis is true.

By the Law of Detachment, the conclusion q is true.

You can conclude that $m\angle ABC = m\angle ABD + m\angle DBC$.

REASON
If you cannot assume that given information is true, you can use deductive reasoning to determine whether the conditional and the hypothesis are true. © **MP.2**

Try It! 2. Assume that each set of given information is true.

a. If two angles are congruent, then the measures of the two angles are equal to each other. Angle 1 is congruent to $\angle 2$. What can you logically conclude about the measures of $\angle 1$ and $\angle 2$?

b. If you finish the race in under 30 minutes, then you win a prize. You finished the race in 26 minutes. What can you logically conclude?

CONCEPT Law of Syllogism

The **Law of Syllogism** is a law of logic that states that given two true conditionals with the conclusion of the first being the hypothesis of the second, there exists a third true conditional having the hypothesis of the first and the conclusion of the second.

If... $p \rightarrow q$ and $q \rightarrow r$ are true.

Then... $p \rightarrow r$ is true.

EXAMPLE 3 Apply the Law of Syllogism to Draw Real-World and Mathematical Conclusions

Assume that each set of conditionals is true. What can you conclude using the Law of Syllogism?

A. If Kenji plays the trumpet, then he plays a brass instrument. If he plays a brass instrument, he is a member of the marching band.

To apply the Law of Syllogism, determine whether the conclusion of one statement is the hypothesis of the other statement.

$p \rightarrow q$: If Kenji plays the trumpet, then he plays a brass instrument.

$q \rightarrow r$: If he plays a brass instrument, then he is a member of the marching band.

> The conclusion of one statement is the hypothesis of the other statement.

You can conclude that the following conditional is true: If Kenji plays the trumpet, then he is a member of the marching band.

B. If points A, B, and C are collinear and B is between A and C, then $\overrightarrow{BA}$ and $\overrightarrow{BC}$ are opposite rays. If $\overrightarrow{BA}$ and $\overrightarrow{BC}$ are opposite rays, then $AB + BC = AC$. What can you conclude?

To apply the Law of Syllogism, determine whether the conclusion of one statement is the hypothesis of the other statement.

$p \rightarrow q$: If points A, B, and C are collinear and B is between A and C, then $\overrightarrow{BA}$ and $\overrightarrow{BC}$ are opposite rays.

$q \rightarrow r$: If $\overrightarrow{BA}$ and $\overrightarrow{BC}$ are opposite rays, then $AB + BC = AC$.

> The conclusion of one statement is the hypothesis of the other statement.

You can conclude that the following conditional is true: If points A, B, and C are collinear and B is between A and C, then $AB + BC = AC$.

COMMON ERROR
You may confuse the hypotheses and conclusions of the given conditionals in writing the third conditional. Recall that the identical parts of the given conditionals are not part of the concluding conditional.

Try It! 3. Assume that each set of conditionals is true. Use the Law of Syllogism to draw a conclusion.

a. If an integer is divisible by 6, it is divisible by 2. If an integer is divisible by 2, then it is an even number.

b. If it is a holiday, then you do not have to go to school. If it is Labor Day, then it is a holiday.

EXAMPLE 4 Apply the Laws of Detachment and Syllogism to Draw Conclusions

What conclusions can you draw from the following true statements?

If you are climbing a mountain at an altitude of 28,500 feet or higher, then you are on the tallest mountain above sea level on Earth. If you are on the tallest mountain above sea level on Earth, then you are on Mount Everest. You are climbing a mountain at an altitude of 29,000 feet.

Identify conditional statements and use the laws of logic to draw a conclusion.

Use the Law of Detachment

$p \rightarrow q$: If you are climbing a mountain at an altitude of 28,500 feet or higher, then you are on the tallest mountain above sea level on Earth.

> This given conditional is true.

p: You are climbing a mountain at an altitude of 28,500 feet or higher.

> p is true because 29,000 > 28,500.

By the Law of Detachment, the conclusion q is true.

You are on the tallest mountain above sea level on Earth.

Use the Law of Syllogism and the Law of Detachment

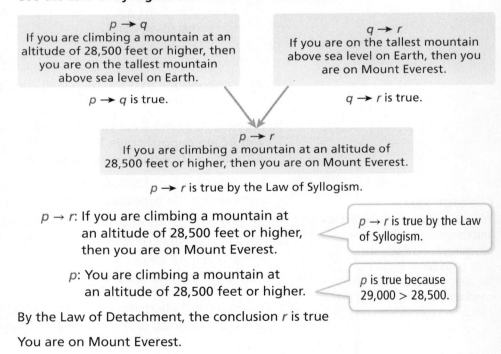

$p \rightarrow q$
If you are climbing a mountain at an altitude of 28,500 feet or higher, then you are on the tallest mountain above sea level on Earth.

$p \rightarrow q$ is true.

$q \rightarrow r$
If you are on the tallest mountain above sea level on Earth, then you are on Mount Everest.

$q \rightarrow r$ is true.

$p \rightarrow r$
If you are climbing a mountain at an altitude of 28,500 feet or higher, then you are on Mount Everest.

$p \rightarrow r$ is true by the Law of Syllogism.

$p \rightarrow r$: If you are climbing a mountain at an altitude of 28,500 feet or higher, then you are on Mount Everest.

> $p \rightarrow r$ is true by the Law of Syllogism.

p: You are climbing a mountain at an altitude of 28,500 feet or higher.

> p is true because 29,000 > 28,500.

By the Law of Detachment, the conclusion r is true

You are on Mount Everest.

LEARN TOGETHER
How do you listen actively as others share ideas?

Try It! 4. If a quadrilateral has four right angles, then it is a rectangle. If a quadrilateral is a rectangle, then it has two sets of parallel sides.

A polygon has four sides and four right angles. Using the Law of Detachment and the Law of Syllogism, what conclusion can you draw?

EXAMPLE 5 Use Geometric Definitions and Mathematical Properties to Draw Conclusions

Suppose ∠1 and ∠3 are both complementary to ∠2. Use deductive reasoning to draw a conclusion.

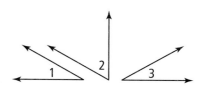

Use geometric definitions and properties of equality to write conditional statements. Then apply the Law of Syllogism.

$p \rightarrow q$: If ∠1 and ∠3 are complementary to ∠2, then $m\angle 1 + m\angle 2 = 90$ and $m\angle 3 + m\angle 2 = 90$.

> $p \rightarrow q$ is true by the definition of complementary angles.

$q \rightarrow r$: If $m\angle 1 + m\angle 2 = 90$ and $m\angle 3 + m\angle 2 = 90$, then $m\angle 1 + m\angle 2 = m\angle 3 + m\angle 2$.

> $q \rightarrow r$ is true by the Substitution Property of Equality.

$r \rightarrow s$: If $m\angle 1 + m\angle 2 = m\angle 3 + m\angle 2$, then $m\angle 1 = m\angle 3$.

> $r \rightarrow s$ is true by the Subtraction Property of Equality.

$s \rightarrow t$: If $m\angle 1 = m\angle 3$, then $\angle 1 \cong \angle 3$.

> $s \rightarrow t$ is true by the definition of congruent angles.

By applying the Law of Syllogism multiple times, the conditional $p \rightarrow t$ is true:

If ∠1 and ∠3 are both complementary to ∠2, then $\angle 1 \cong \angle 3$.

CONSTRUCT ARGUMENTS
Think about properties, theorems, and definitions you have learned in previous lessons. Which ones can be used to lead to a conclusion? ⒼMP.3

Try It! **5.** Suppose point *D* is in the interior of ∠*ABC*. Use deductive reasoning to draw a conclusion about *m*∠*DBC*.

CONCEPT SUMMARY Deductive Reasoning

Law of Detachment

If a conditional statement and its hypothesis are true, then its conclusion is also true.

Law of Syllogism

Given two true conditionals with the conclusion of the first being the hypothesis of the second, there exists a third true conditional having the hypothesis of the first and the conclusion of the second.

If... $p \rightarrow q$ and p are true.

Then... q is true.

If... $p \rightarrow q$ and $q \rightarrow r$ are true.

Then... $p \rightarrow r$ is true.

Do You UNDERSTAND?

1. **ESSENTIAL QUESTION** How can you use given and previously known facts to draw conclusions?

2. **Error Analysis** Dakota writes the following as an example of using the Law of Detachment. What is her error? © **MP.3**

   > If my favorite team wins more than 55 games, they win the championship. My team won the championship, so they won more than 55 games. ✗

3. **Vocabulary** What are the differences between the Law of Detachment and the Law of Syllogism?

4. **Use Structure** How can representing sentences and phrases with symbols help you determine whether to apply the Law of Detachment or the Law of Syllogism? © **MP.7**

Do You KNOW HOW?

Assume that each set of given information is true.

5. If you have a temperature above 100.4°F, then you have a fever. Mario has a temperature of 101.2°F. What can you conclude about Mario? What rule of inference did you use?

6. If points A, B, and C are collinear with B between A and C, then $AB + BC = AC$. Use the information in the figure shown. What can you conclude about AC?

Assume that each set of conditionals is true. Use the Law of Syllogism to write a true conditional.

7. If you eat too much, you get a stomach ache. If you get a stomach ache, you want to rest.

8. If two numbers are odd, the sum of the numbers is even. If a number is even, then the number is divisible by 2.

PRACTICE & PROBLEM SOLVING

UNDERSTAND

9. **Error Analysis** Samantha writes the following as an example of using the Law of Syllogism. Explain Samantha's error. ⓒ MP.3

> If an animal is a dog, then it is a mammal.
> If an animal is a dog, then it has four legs.
>
> I can conclude that if an animal has four legs, then it is a mammal. ✗

10. **Look for Relationships** Make a truth table with statements $p, q, r, p \rightarrow q, q \rightarrow r,$ and $p \rightarrow r$. How does the truth table support the validity of the Law of Syllogism and the Law of Detachment? ⓒ MP.7

11. **Mathematical Connections** Consider the following conditional.

    If all four sides of a quadrilateral are of equal length, then its diagonals intersect at right angles.

    Which of the following figures can you use with the conditional to apply the Law of Detachment to draw the conclusion that its diagonals intersect at right angles?

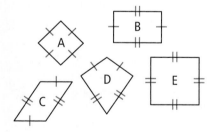

12. **Higher Order Thinking** Suppose you are given that a conditional is true but its conclusion is false. What can you conclude about the hypothesis? Explain your answer using the negation of the hypothesis and the conclusion with the Law of Detachment.

13. **Look for Relationships** To apply the Law of Detachment, a conditional statement and its hypothesis must both be true. Can you draw any conclusions if the conditional is true but the hypothesis is false? Explain. ⓒ MP.7

PRACTICE

14. Given that a conditional is false, what can you determine about the hypothesis and conclusion? SEE EXAMPLE 1

Assume that each set of statements is true. Use the Law of Detachment to write a true statement. If the Law of Detachment cannot be used, explain why. SEE EXAMPLE 2

15. If you can play the piano, then you can play a musical instrument. Kiyo can play a musical instrument.

16. If the endpoints of a segment are $P(x_1, y_1)$ and $Q(x_2, y_2)$, then the coordinates of the midpoint are $M = \left(\frac{x_1 + x_2}{2}, \frac{y_1 + y_2}{2} \right)$. The endpoints of $\overline{CD}$ are $C(2, -4)$ and $D(-3, 5)$.

17. If the graph of a linear function has a positive slope, then the function is not decreasing. The slope of the graph is 0.

Assume that each set of conditionals is true. Use the Law of Syllogism to write a true conditional. If the Law of Syllogism cannot be used, explain why. SEE EXAMPLE 3

18. If $\overrightarrow{BD}$ bisects $\angle ABC$, then $\angle ABD \cong \angle DBC$. If $\angle ABD \cong \angle DBC$, then $m\angle ABD = m\angle DBC$.

19. If a whole number is even, then it is divisible by 2. If the sum of the digits of a whole number is divisible by 3, then the whole number is divisible by 3.

20. If Zachary eats fish for dinner, then he goes to bed early. If it is Tuesday night, then Zachary eats fish for dinner.

Use the Law of Detachment and the Law of Syllogism to draw conclusions from each set of true statements. SEE EXAMPLES 4 AND 5

21. If it is Thursday, then Charles has baseball practice. If Charles has baseball practice, then he eats grilled chicken for dinner. It is the day after Wednesday.

22. If the length of a segment is PQ, then the distance from P to the midpoint of $\overline{PQ}$ is $\frac{1}{2} PQ$. If the endpoints of a segment are $P(x_1, y_1)$ and $Q(x_2, y_2)$, then the length of the segment is $PQ = \sqrt{(x_2 - x_1)^2 + (y_2 - y_1)^2}$. The endpoints of $\overline{PQ}$ are $P(3, -4)$ and $Q(-3, -12)$.

PRACTICE & PROBLEM SOLVING

23. Model With Mathematics Represent each true statement with symbols. Use symbols to write related contrapositives of the conditionals. Then use the Law of Detachment and the Law of Syllogism to draw a conclusion. **Ⓒ MP.4**

If Avery draws a numbered card from 4 to 10, then his game piece moves to home base. If his game piece moves to home base, he wins the game. Avery does not win.

24. Mathematical Connections The chart describes the number of tickets needed to win prizes at a family fun center.

Numbers of Tickets	Prize Level	Sample Prizes
0–100	A	magnet, stickers
101–200	B	keychain, flashlight
201–300	C	T-shirt, soccer ball

a. Write conditionals with sample prizes as the hypothesis and prize level as the conclusion. Write conditionals that relate the prize level to the number of tickets.

b. Ines wins an soccer ball. Use the Law of Detachment and Law of Syllogism to write true statements about Ines based on the conditionals you wrote in part (a).

25. Reason The table shows the main dishes served each day at a cafeteria.

Monday	hamburger, salad, pizza
Tuesday	hamburger, stir fry, pizza
Wednesday	fish and chips, stir fry, salad
Thursday	stir fry, salad, tacos
Friday	fish and chips, tacos, pizza

Suppose you know that Joshua has a salad and Juana has stir fry. Is that enough information to determine what day it is? If not, what other piece of information could help you? **Ⓒ MP.2**

26. The following two statements are true.

- If you are over 54 inches tall, you can ride on the roller coasters.
- If you can ride on the roller coasters, then you can go on the drop tower.

Cindy is 56 inches tall. Which of the following statements must be true?

☐ **A.** Cindy can ride the roller coasters.

☐ **B.** Cindy can go on the drop tower.

☐ **C.** If Cindy rides on the roller coasters, then she goes on the drop tower.

☐ **D.** If a person can go on the drop tower, then they can ride the roller coasters.

☐ **E.** If a person can go on the drop tower, they are over 54 inches tall.

27. SAT/ACT Which statement can you conclude from the given true statements?

If you ride your bike to school, you exercise. If you exercise, you are happy.

Ⓐ If you are happy, you exercise.

Ⓑ You exercise.

Ⓒ If you exercise, you ride your bike.

Ⓓ If you bike to school, you are happy.

28. Performance Task In a game of exploration, rolling a cube numbered from 1 to 6 simulates asset acquisition. Some rules are listed.

- If you roll an even number, you get 1 red chip.
- If you roll a factor of 6, you get 1 blue chip.
- If you roll a number greater than 3, you get 1 green chip.
- If you get 2 green chips, then you exchange the 2 green chips for 1 purple chip.
- If you get 2 red chips, then you exchange the 2 red chips for 1 purple chip.

Note that a roll can earn more than one chip.

Part A Jacinta rolls a 2, 5, 1, and then 3. What chips does she have?

Part B After four rolls, Kimberly has 1 purple chip, 1 green chip, 3 blue chips, and no red chips. What numbers could she have rolled?

1-7

Writing Proofs

I CAN... use deductive reasoning to prove theorems.

VOCABULARY
• paragraph proof
• proof
• theorem
• two-column proof

Common Core State Standards
HSG.CO.C.9, MP.2, MP.3, MP.7

CRITIQUE & EXPLAIN

William solved an equation for *x* and wrote justifications for each step of his solution.

$6(14 + x) = 108$	Given
$84 + 6x = 108$	Distributive Property
$6x = 108 - 84$	Subtraction Property of Equality
$6x = 24$	Simplify
$x = 4$	Multiplication Property of Equality

A. Make Sense and Persevere Are William's justifications valid at each step? If not, what might you change? Explain. **MP.1**

B. Can you justify another series of steps that result in the same solution for *x*?

ESSENTIAL QUESTION
How is deductive reasoning used to prove a theorem?

THEOREM 1-1 Vertical Angles Theorem

Vertical angles are congruent.

If...

PROOF: SEE EXAMPLE 1.

Then... $\angle 1 \cong \angle 2$ and $\angle 3 \cong \angle 4$

CONCEPTUAL UNDERSTANDING

EXAMPLE 1 ▶ **Write a Two-Column Proof**

A theorem is a conjecture that is proven. Prove the Vertical Angles Theorem.

Given: Lines *AE* and *DC* form vertical angles $\angle ABC$ and $\angle DBE$

Prove: $\angle ABC \cong \angle DBE$

The "If..." statement in the theorem is the Given statement for the proof, and the "then..." statement is what you need to Prove.

A **proof** is a convincing argument that uses deductive reasoning. A **two-column proof**, in which the statements and reasons are aligned in columns, is one way to organize and present a proof.

STUDY TIP
It is helpful to use the reasoning laws from previous lessons when writing proofs. In this example, the Law of Syllogism can be applied to connect one statement to another, leading to the conclusion.

Statements	Reasons
1) $\angle ABC$ and $\angle DBE$ are vertical angles	1) Given
2) $m\angle ABE = 180$ and $m\angle DBC = 180$	2) Definition of straight angles
3) $m\angle ABC + m\angle CBE = m\angle ABE$ and $m\angle DBE + m\angle CBE = m\angle DBC$	3) Angle Addition Postulate
4) $m\angle ABC + m\angle CBE = 180$ and $m\angle DBE + m\angle CBE = 180$	4) Substitution

CONTINUED ON THE NEXT PAGE

EXAMPLE 1 CONTINUED

5) $m\angle A\,BC = 180 - m\angle CBE$ and $m\angle DBE = 180 - m\angle CBE$	**5)** Subtraction Property of Equality
6) $m\angle ABC = m\angle DBE$	**6)** Transitive Property of Equality
7) $\angle ABC \cong \angle DBE$	**7)** Definition of congruent angles

Try It! **1.** Write a two-column proof.

Given: $\overrightarrow{BD}$ bisects $\angle CBE$.

Prove: $\angle ABD \cong \angle FBD$

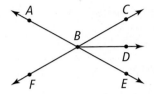

APPLICATION

EXAMPLE 2 **Apply the Vertical Angles Theorem**

The diagram shows how glass lenses change the direction of light rays passing through a telescope. What is the value of x, the angle formed by the crossed outermost light rays through the focal point?

Light Rays

$11°$

$11°$

$x°$

Objective Lens

Focal Point

Eyepiece Lens

Formulate ◀ Draw and label a diagram to represent the telescope.

Use the Angle Addition Postulate to find the measure of $\angle BDC$.

$\angle BDC$ and $\angle EDF$ are vertical angles. Use the Vertical Angles Theorem to determine the measure of $\angle EDF$.

Compute ◀ $m\angle BDC = 11 + 11 = 22$ $\qquad\qquad m\angle EDF = m\angle BDC = 22$

Interpret ◀ The outermost light rays form a 22° angle as they leave the focal point, so the value of x is 22.

Try It! **2.** Find the value of x and the measure of each labeled angle.

a.
$(6x - 45)°$ $(4x + 5)°$

b.
$(8x - 20)°$ $(5x + 37)°$

THEOREM 1-2 Congruent Supplements Theorem

If two angles are supplementary to congruent angles (or to the same angle), then they are congruent.

If... $m\angle 1 + m\angle 2 = 180$ and $m\angle 3 + m\angle 2 = 180$

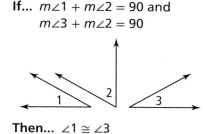

PROOF: SEE EXAMPLE 3.

Then... $\angle 1 \cong \angle 3$

THEOREM 1-3 Congruent Complements Theorem

If two angles are complementary to congruent angles (or to the same angle), then they are congruent.

If... $m\angle 1 + m\angle 2 = 90$ and $m\angle 3 + m\angle 2 = 90$

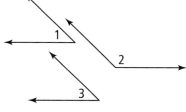

PROOF: SEE EXAMPLE 3 TRY IT.

Then... $\angle 1 \cong \angle 3$

PROOF

EXAMPLE 3 Write a Paragraph Proof

Write a paragraph proof of the Congruent Supplements Theorem.

Given: $\angle 1$ and $\angle 2$ are supplementary.
$\angle 2$ and $\angle 3$ are supplementary.

Prove: $\angle 1 \cong \angle 3$

Another way to write a proof is a paragraph proof. In a **paragraph proof**, the statements and reasons are connected in sentences.

Proof: By the definition of supplementary angles, $m\angle 1 + m\angle 2 = 180$ and $m\angle 2 + m\angle 3 = 180$. Since both sums equal 180, $m\angle 1 + m\angle 2 = m\angle 2 + m\angle 3$. Subtract $m\angle 2$ from each side of this equation to get $m\angle 1 = m\angle 3$. By the definition of congruent angles, $\angle 1 \cong \angle 3$.

> **COMMON ERROR**
> Remember that in order for a proof to be complete, each statement needs a corresponding reason. Because of the format of a paragraph proof, some statements or reasons might unintentionally be omitted. To ensure each statement has a reason, underline each statement and circle each corresponding reason.

Try It! **3.** Write a paragraph proof of the Congruent Complements Theorem.

Given: $\angle 1$ and $\angle 2$ are complementary.
$\angle 2$ and $\angle 3$ are complementary.

Prove: $\angle 1 \cong \angle 3$

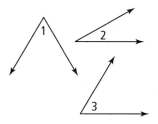

THEOREM 1-4

All right angles are congruent.

If...

PROOF: SEE EXERCISE 9.

Then... $\angle A \cong \angle B$

THEOREM 1-5

If two angles are congruent and supplementary, then each is a right angle.

If... $\angle 1 \cong \angle 2$ and $m\angle 1 + m\angle 2 = 180$

PROOF: SEE EXERCISE 11.

Then... $\angle 1$ and $\angle 2$ are right angles

THEOREM 1-6 Linear Pairs Theorem

The sum of the measures of a linear pair is 180.

If... $\angle 1$ and $\angle 2$ form a linear pair.

PROOF: SEE EXERCISE 12.

Then... $m\angle 1 + m\angle 2 = 180$

PROOF

EXAMPLE 4 Write a Proof Using a Theorem

Write a two-column proof.

Given: $m\angle 1 = m\angle 2$, $m\angle 1 = 105$

Prove: $m\angle 3 = 75$

Statements	Reasons
1) $m\angle 1 = m\angle 2$	1) Given
2) $m\angle 1 = 105$	2) Given
3) $m\angle 2 = 105$	3) Transitive Property of Equality
4) $\angle 2$ and $\angle 3$ are a linear pair	4) Definition of a linear pair
5) $m\angle 2 + m\angle 3 = 180$	5) Linear Pairs Theorem
6) $105 + m\angle 3 = 180$	6) Substitution Property of Equality
7) $m\angle 3 = 75$	7) Subtraction Property of Equality

CONSTRUCT ARGUMENTS
Consider the logical flow for writing a proof. How can you be sure that each step in a proof follows logically from the preceding step or steps? © MP.3

Try It! 4. Write a two-column proof.

Given: $m\angle 4 = 35$, $m\angle 1 = m\angle 2 + m\angle 4$

Prove: $m\angle 3 = 70$

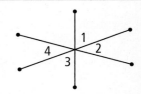

CONCEPT SUMMARY Proofs

Proofs use given information and logical steps justified by **definitions**, **postulates**, **theorems**, and **properties** to reach a conclusion.

Given: ∠1 and ∠2 and are vertical angles

Prove: ∠1 ≅ ∠2

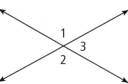

PROOF Two-Column Proof

Statements	Reasons
1) ∠1 and ∠2 are vertical angles	**1)** Given
2) $m\angle 1 + m\angle 3 = 180$ and $m\angle 2 + m\angle 3 = 180$	**2)** Linear Pairs Theorem
3) $m\angle 1 + m\angle 3 = m\angle 2 + m\angle 3$	**3)** Subst. Prop. of Equality
4) $m\angle 1 = m\angle 2$	**4)** Subtr. Prop. of Equality
5) ∠1 ≅ ∠2	**5)** Def. ≅ angles

PROOF Paragraph Proof

By the Linear Pairs Theorem, $m\angle 1 + m\angle 3 = 180$ and $m\angle 2 + m\angle 3 = 180$. By the Substitution Property of Equality, $m\angle 1 + m\angle 3 = m\angle 2 + m\angle 3$. Subtracting $m\angle 3$ from each side of the equation gives $m\angle 1 = m\angle 2$. Then by the definition of congruent angles, ∠1 ≅ ∠2.

Do You UNDERSTAND?

1. **ESSENTIAL QUESTION** How is deductive reasoning used to prove a theorem?

2. **Error Analysis** Jayden states that based on the Congruent Supplements Theorem, if $m\angle 1 + m\angle 2 = 90$ and if $m\angle 1 + m\angle 3 = 90$, then ∠2 ≅ ∠3. What is the error in Jayden's reasoning? © MP.3

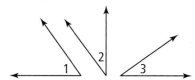

3. **Vocabulary** How is a theorem different from a postulate? How is a theorem different from a conjecture?

4. **Reason** If ∠2 and ∠3 are complementary, how could you use the Vertical Angles Theorem to find $m\angle 1$? © MP.2

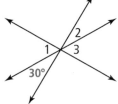

Do You KNOW HOW?

Use the figures to answer Exercises 5–7.

5. What statement could you write in a proof for $m\angle ADC$ using the Angle Addition Postulate as a reason?

6. Could you use the Vertical Angles Theorem as a reason in a proof to state $m\angle ADC = m\angle EDG$ or to state ∠ADC ≅ ∠EDG? Explain.

7. Given $m\angle ADC = 90$, what reason could you give in a proof to state ∠ADC ≅ ∠HJK?

8. The Tower of Pisa, in Italy, began tilting during its construction in the 12th century. It currently leans at an angle of about 4° from the vertical, as shown. What equation for the measure of x, the angle it makes from the horizontal, could you use in a proof?

PRACTICE & PROBLEM SOLVING

UNDERSTAND

9. Construct Arguments Fill in the missing reasons for the proof of Theorem 1-4. Ⓒ MP.3

Given: ∠F and ∠G are right angles.

Prove: ∠F ≅ ∠G

Statements	Reasons
1) ∠F and ∠G are right angles	**1)** Given
2) $m∠F = 90$ and $m∠G = 90$	**2)**
3) $m∠F = m∠G$	**3)**
4) ∠F ≅ ∠G	**4)**

10. Error Analysis A student uses the Vertical Angles Theorem and the definition of complementary angles to conclude $m∠PTR = 50$ in the figure. What mistake did the student make? Ⓒ MP.3

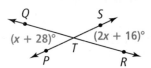

11. Construct Arguments Write a paragraph proof of Theorem 1-5. Given that ∠N and ∠M are congruent and supplementary, prove that ∠N and ∠M are right angles. Ⓒ MP.3

12. Construct Arguments Write a two-column proof of Theorem 1-6. Given that ∠ABC and ∠CBD are a linear pair, prove that ∠ABC and ∠CBD are supplementary. Ⓒ MP.3

13. Higher Order Thinking Explain how the Congruent Complements Theorem applies to the figure shown.

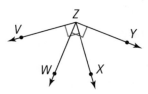

PRACTICE

Find the value of each variable and the measure of each labeled angle. SEE EXAMPLES 1 AND 2

14.

15.

16.

17.

18. Write a paragraph proof. SEE EXAMPLE 3

Given: $m∠ABC = 114$; $m∠DHE = 25$; $m∠EHF = 41$; ∠ABC and ∠GHF are supplementary.

Prove: ∠DHF ≅ ∠GHF

Write a two-column proof for each statement.
SEE EXAMPLE 4

19. Given: ∠1 and ∠2 are complementary.

$m∠1 = 23$

Prove: $m∠3 = 113$

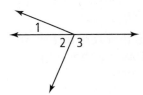

20. Given: $m∠2 = 30$

$m∠1 = 2m∠2$

Prove: $m∠3 + m∠4 = 90$

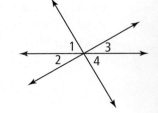

PRACTICE & PROBLEM SOLVING

21. Mathematical Connections The graph shows percentages of sales made by various divisions of a company in one year. The angle at Division A forms a vertical angle with the combined angles of Divisions C and D. What are the missing percentages? What are the angles formed by the segments for each division?

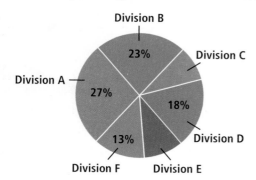

22. Use Structure A type of floor tiling is designed to give the illusion of a three-dimensional figure. Given that $m\angle 1 = 85$ and $m\angle 3 = 45$, what are the measures of the remaining angles? **©MP.7**

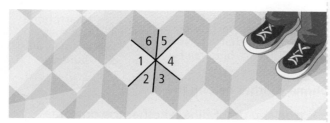

23. Reason Consider the angles formed by the lattice in the garden gate. Using theorems from this lesson, what can you conclude from each of the following statements? State which theorem you applied to reach your conclusion. **©MP.2**

a. $m\angle 1 = 90$ and $m\angle 2 = 90$.

b. $\angle 3$ and $\angle 4$ are vertical angles.

24. Consider the figure shown.

Select the statement that is never true.

Ⓐ $m\angle 1 + m\angle 2 = 180$

Ⓑ $m\angle 1 + m\angle 2 + m\angle 3 = 180$

Ⓒ $m\angle 2 + m\angle 4 = 180$

Ⓓ $m\angle 2 = m\angle 4$

25. SAT/ACT Given $\angle ABC$ and $\angle DEF$ are supplementary and $\angle ABC$ and $\angle GHJ$ are supplementary, what can you conclude about the angles?

Ⓐ $m\angle DEF = m\angle GHJ$

Ⓑ $m\angle DEF + m\angle GHJ = 90$

Ⓒ $m\angle DEF + m\angle GHJ = 180$

Ⓓ $m\angle ABC = m\angle DEF$ and $m\angle ABC = m\angle GHJ$

26. Performance Task The figure shows lines that divide a designer window into different parts.

Part A Copy the figure onto a sheet of paper. Label each of the inner angles, using *A* as a point on the left-center ray, using *B*, *C*, *D*, *E*, and *F* as a point on each following ray going clockwise, and using *G* as the vertex of each angle. Use a protractor to measure any two of the inner angles in the figure. Using your measurements, determine the measurements of the other angles.

Part B Choose two of the inner angles that you did not actually measure. How do you know the angle measures for these two angles? Write a two-column proof to show how you know their measures are correct.

1-8
Indirect Proof

I CAN... use indirect reasoning to write a proof.

VOCABULARY
• indirect proof

Common Core State Standards
HSG.CO.C.9, HSG.CO.C.10,
HSG.CO.C.11, MP.1, MP.2, MP.7

CRITIQUE & EXPLAIN

Philip presents the following number puzzle to his friends.

A. **Make Sense and Persevere**
Philip states that the number must be 7. Explain why this cannot be true. **© MP.1**

B. Write your own number puzzle that has an answer of 5. Your friend says the answer is not 5. How do you use the statements of your puzzle to identify the contradiction?

The number is a prime number.
The square of the number is less than 100 and greater than 10.
The number is not a factor of 21.
What is the number?

ESSENTIAL QUESTION What can you conclude when an assumption leads to a contradiction?

APPLICATION →

EXAMPLE 1   Use Assumptions to Draw a Conclusion

Beth had three friends over for dinner. The next day, Beth realized one of her friends left a smartphone charger with a white wire at her apartment.

 Libby uses a wireless smartphone charger.

 Mercedes' smartphone charger has a black wire.

 Kelly's smartphone was fully charged at dinner.

Who does the smartphone charger belong to?

Assume each scenario is true and determine whether the outcome is possible or not.

```
                        ?

   Libby              Mercedes           Kelly
wireless charger     black wire       fully charged
```

STUDY TIP
Use a flow chart or table to keep track of details if you have difficulty following the logic in an indirect reasoning problem.

✖ It cannot be Libby's charger since the one that was left at Beth's apartment has a wire.

✖ It cannot be Mercedes' charger because her wire is black, not white.

✔ Kelly must have been charging her phone at dinner, and the other options have been proven false.

The smartphone charger must belong to Kelly.

Try It!   1. Draw a conclusion in the following situation.

A bagel shop gives customers a free bagel on their birthday. Thato went to the bagel shop today but did not get a free bagel.

CONCEPT Writing an Indirect Proof by Contradiction

A proof that uses indirect reasoning is an **indirect proof**. Two types of indirect proof are proof by contradiction and proof by contrapositive.

Proof by Contradiction

A statement is given as a conditional $p \rightarrow q$.

Step 1 Assume p and $\sim q$ are true.

Step 2 Show that the assumption $\sim q$ leads to a contradiction.

Step 3 Conclude that q must be true.

PROEF →

EXAMPLE 2 Write an Indirect Proof by Contradiction

Write an indirect proof of the following statement using proof by contradiction.

> **If Alani walks more than 8 kilometers over a two-day period, then she walks more than 4 kilometers on one or both days.**

Identify the hypothesis and conclusion.

p: Alani walks more than 8 kilometers over a two-day period.

q: She walks more than 4 kilometers on one or both days.

The statement has the form $p \rightarrow q$.

Step 1 Assume p and $\sim q$ are true.

$\sim q$: Alani does not walk more than 4 kilometers on either day.

Step 2 Show that the assumption $\sim q$ leads to a contradiction.

If Alani does not walk more than 4 kilometers on either day, then the total distance she walks over the two-day period must be less than or equal to 8 kilometers. This contradicts the hypothesis, p.

Step 3 Conclude that q must be true.

Because the assumption leads to a contradiction, q must be true.

Alani walks more than 4 kilometers on one or both days.

LOOK FOR RELATIONSHIPS
Consider what you can logically conclude from your assumption. What can you conclude from the negation? Ⓒ MP7

Try It! 2. Write an indirect proof for the statement using proof by contradiction.

If $\angle A$ and $\angle B$ are complementary, then $m\angle A < 90$.

CONCEPT Writing an Indirect Proof by Contrapositive

A conditional $p \rightarrow q$ and its contrapositive $\sim q \rightarrow \sim p$ are logically equivalent, so they have the same truth value.

If you prove the contrapositive, you have also proven the conditional.

Proof by Contrapositive

Step 1 Assume $\sim q$ is true.

Step 2 Show that the assumption leads to $\sim p$, which shows $\sim q \rightarrow \sim p$.

Step 3 Conclude that $p \rightarrow q$ must be true.

CONCEPTUAL UNDERSTANDING

EXAMPLE 3 Write an Indirect Proof by Contrapositive

Write an indirect proof of the following statement using proof by contrapositive.

> **For two positive integers n and m, if $nm > 16$, then either n or m is greater than 4 or both are greater than 4.**

Write the negations of p and q.

p: $nm > 16$

$\sim p$: $nm \leq 16$ ← This is the part of the contrapositive you prove.

q: $n > 4$ or $m > 4$ or both are greater than 4

$\sim q$: $n \leq 4$ and $m \leq 4$ ← This is the part of the contrapositive you assume.

COMMON ERROR
Be careful not to make assumptions that are not given in the statements.

Step 1 Assume $\sim q$ is true.

Assume $n \leq 4$ and $m \leq 4$.

Step 2 Show that the assumption leads to $\sim p$.

$n \leq 4 \longrightarrow nm \leq 4m$

$m \leq 4 \longrightarrow 4m \leq 16$

Use properties of inequality to write equivalent expressions of $n \leq 4$ and $m \leq 4$ as $nm \leq 16$.

By the Transitive Property, $nm \leq 16$.

Therefore, $\sim q \rightarrow \sim p$

Step 3 Conclude that $p \rightarrow q$ must be true.

Proving the contrapositive proves the conditional. Therefore, for two positive integers n and m, if $nm > 16$, then either n or m is greater than 4 or both are greater than 4.

Try It! 3. Write an indirect proof of each statement using proof by contrapositive.

    a. If a number is an integer, it is rational.

    b. If a whole number is between 1 and 4, it is a factor of 6.

CONCEPT SUMMARY Indirect Proof of $p \to q$

BY CONTRADICTION

Steps

1. Assume p and $\sim q$ are true.
2. Show that the assumption $\sim q$ leads to a contradiction.
3. Conclude that q must be true.

BY CONTRAPOSITIVE

Steps

1. Assume $\sim q$ is true.
2. Show that the assumption leads to $\sim p$, which shows $\sim q \to \sim p$.
3. Conclude that $p \to q$ must be true.

Do You UNDERSTAND?

1. **ESSENTIAL QUESTION** What can you conclude when an assumption leads to a contradiction?

2. **Vocabulary** What are the two types of indirect proof? How are they similar and how are they different?

3. **Error Analysis** Consider the figure below.

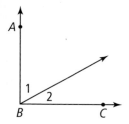

Consider the following conditional.

> If $\angle ABC$ is a right angle and $m\angle 1 < 60$, then $m\angle 2 > 30$.

A student will prove the contrapositive as a way of proving the conditional. The student plans to assume $m\angle 2 < 30$ and then prove $m\angle 1 > 60$. Explain the error in the student's plan. Ⓖ **MP.3**

4. **Make Sense and Persevere** How do truth tables explain why proving the contrapositive also proves the original conditional statement? Ⓖ **MP.1**

5. **Generalize** Explain how you can identify the statement you assume and the statement you try to prove when writing a proof by contrapositive. Ⓖ **MP.8**

Do You KNOW HOW?

Use indirect reasoning to draw a conclusion in each situation.

6. Tamira only cuts the grass on a day that it does not rain. She cut the grass on Thursday.

7. Gabriela works at the library every Saturday morning. She did not work at the library this morning.

Write the first step of an indirect proof for each of the following statements.

8. $m\angle JKM = m\angle JKL - m\angle MKL$

9. $\overline{PQ}$ is perpendicular to $\overline{ST}$.

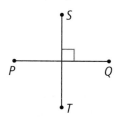

10. What can you conclude from the following situation using indirect reasoning? Explain.

   • Nadeem spent more than $10 but less than $11 for a sandwich and drink.

   • He spent $8.49 on his sandwich.

   • The cost for milk is $1.49.

   • The cost for orange juice is $2.49.

   • The cost for a tropical smoothie is $2.89.

   • The cost for apple juice is $2.59.

PRACTICE & PROBLEM SOLVING

UNDERSTAND

11. Construct Arguments Write an indirect proof for this conditional statement about the given figure. **ⓒ MP.3**

If $\overline{NJ}$ is perpendicular to $\overline{KM}$, then $m\angle MLJ = 90$.

12. Higher Order Thinking Write an indirect proof about the given conditional using either contradiction or contrapositive. What is an advantage of the method you chose?

Given that x is a whole number, if x and $3x$ are both less than 10, then $x \leq 3$.

13. Mathematical Connections Write a proof by contrapositive to prove the following conditional about the figures.

If $\angle TUV \cong \angle WXY$, then $x \neq y$.

14. Error Analysis Consider the conditional, "If x^2 is even, then x is even." Anna uses the contrapositive to prove the conditional. What is Anna's error? **ⓒ MP.3**

> Assume x is even. Then x can be written in the form $2k$, where k is an integer. Substitute this into x^2 to get $(2k)^2$, or $4k^2$. This expression can be written in the form $2m$, where m is an integer, which proves x^2 is even. ✗

PRACTICE

Draw a conclusion in each situation. SEE EXAMPLE 1

15. Every student in Mr. Green's 2nd period class got an A on the math test. Paige got a B on the test.

16. Only students who studied at least 3 hours for the history test got an A on it. Kyrone studied 2 hours for the test.

Write the first step of an indirect proof of each statement. SEE EXAMPLE 2

17. $ST + TU + UV = 150$

18. Ray DE is the angle bisector of $\angle ADC$.

Identify the two statements that contradict each other in each set. SEE EXAMPLE 2

19. I. $m\angle K + m\angle L = 150$

 II. $m\angle K - m\angle L = 20$

 III. $m\angle K = 180$

20. I. $\angle S$ is an acute angle.

 II. $m\angle S = 80$

 III. $m\angle S + m\angle T = 40$

21. Write an indirect proof for the following conditional about the figure. SEE EXAMPLE 2

If $\angle EFG$ and $\angle HFJ$ are vertical angles, then $x \neq 3y$.

22. Write a proof of the contrapositive to prove the following conditional about the figures. SEE EXAMPLE 3

If $AB + CD = EF$, then $EF = 14$.

PRACTICE & PROBLEM SOLVING

APPLY

23. Model With Mathematics The lighthouse forms a right angle with the path of the boat. 🄖 MP.4

a. Write an equation relating *h*, *d*, and *x*.

b. Write an indirect proof of the statement by proving the contrapositive.

If *x* decreases, then *d* decreases.

24. Reason Friends eat all 6 slices of a pie. No slices are left over. No slices are shared. Prove the following conditional by proving the contrapositive for the conditional. 🄖 MP.2

If four friends share the pie, then at most two of the friends will have more than one slice of pie each.

25. Reason The library is at the midpoint between Nicky's home and the museum.

Nicky begins at her home and walks toward the museum. Write an indirect proof for this conditional: When she gets to the library, she will have less than 2 miles left to go. 🄖 MP.2

ASSESSMENT PRACTICE

26. Does this pair of statements contradict each other? Explain.

$\angle P$ and $\angle Q$ are both obtuse angles.

$\angle P$ and $\angle Q$ are supplementary.

27. SAT/ACT If you write a proof of the following conditional by proving the contrapositive, what should your assumption be?

If $\overrightarrow{JK}$ is the angle bisector of $\angle HJL$, then $m\angle HJK + m\angle KJL = 90$.

Ⓐ $\overrightarrow{JK}$ is the angle bisector of $\angle HJL$.

Ⓑ $\overrightarrow{JK}$ is not the angle bisector of $\angle HJL$.

Ⓒ $m\angle HJK + m\angle KJL = 90$

Ⓓ $m\angle HJK + m\angle KJL \neq 90$

28. Performance Task Customers who eat lunch at a diner have the following meal choices:

LUNCH MENU
Jerk chicken, cabbage, dumplings
Stewed beef, beans, plantains
Oxtail, beans, plantains
Stewed beef, cabbage, dumplings
Jerk chicken, peas, plantains
All meals come with coconut rice

Part A Write an indirect proof of the following conditional.

If a customer chooses a meal with peas, then the customer also has jerk chicken.

Part B Write another conditional statement related to which meal a customer has at the diner. Then write an indirect proof of your conditional statement.

Topic Review

1. What are the fundamental building blocks of geometry?

Vocabulary Review

Choose the correct term to complete each sentence.

2. A statement accepted without proof is a _____.

3. Arriving at a conclusion by observing patterns is _____.

4. A _____ is the combination of a conditional and its converse.

5. According to the _____, if a conditional statement and its hypothesis are true, then its conclusion is also true.

6. A conjecture that has been proven is a _____.

7. A statement of the form *if not q, then not p* is a _____ of the conditional *if p, then q*.

8. You use _____ when you logically come to a valid conclusion based on given statements.

- biconditional
- conjecture
- contrapositive
- converse
- deductive reasoning
- inductive reasoning
- Law of Detachment
- Law of Syllogism
- postulate
- theorem

Concepts & Skills Review

LESSON 1-1 ▸ Measuring Segments and Angles

Quick Review

If a **line segment** is divided into parts, the length of the whole segment is the sum of the lengths of its individual parts.

Similarly, if an **angle** is divided into parts, the measure of the whole angle is the sum of the measures of the individual angles.

Example

Given $SU = 60$, find x.

$$ST + TU = SU$$
$$(6x - 24) + (2x + 20) = 60$$
$$8x - 4 = 60$$
$$8x = 64$$
$$x = 8$$

Practice & Problem Solving

Find each value.

9. $LN = 45$. Find x.

$$\overset{3x+2}{\underset{L \qquad M}{\rule{3cm}{0.4pt}}} \overset{x+19}{\underset{\qquad N}{\rule{3cm}{0.4pt}}}$$

10. $RS = 27$. Find QS.

$$\overset{9x}{\underset{Q \qquad R}{\rule{3cm}{0.4pt}}} \overset{12x-21}{\underset{\qquad S}{\rule{3cm}{0.4pt}}}$$

Find the measure of each angle.

11. $m\angle EBG = 60$; $m\angle FBG = 2m\angle EBF$; $m\angle EBF = \blacksquare$

12. $m\angle ABE = 64$; $m\angle ABD = m\angle DBE$; $m\angle DBE = \blacksquare$

13. $m\angle GBH = 28$; $\overline{BH}$ bisects $\angle GBC$; $m\angle GBC = \blacksquare$

14. **Reason** Point K is located at 7 on a number line, and $JK = KL$. If the coordinate of L is 23, what is the coordinate of point J? ⒸMP.2

LESSON 1-2 Basic Constructions

Quick Review

You can use a compass and a straightedge to copy segments and angles, and to construct the **angle bisector** of a given angle.

Any geometric figure that can be constructed using a compass and straightedge is a **construction**.

Example

Construct the angle bisector of ∠A.

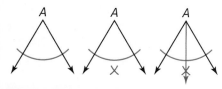

From the vertex, draw an arc that intersects both sides of the angle.

Next, using the same compass setting at each intersection, draw intersecting arcs within the angle.

Finally, draw the angle bisector from the vertex through the intersecting arcs.

Practice & Problem Solving

Copy each segment.

15.

16.

Copy each angle, and construct its bisector.

17.

18.

19. **Make Sense and Persevere** When constructing an angle bisector, why must the compass width be larger than half the distance from the vertex to the intersection point of the first arc and one of the rays? Ⓒ **MP.1**

20. **Model With Mathematics** The sides of a roof meet at a 120° angle. A strip of wood extends down from the vertex so that it bisects the angle. Draw a diagram of the roof with the bisecting strip of wood. Ⓒ **MP.4**

LESSON 1-3 Midpoint and Distance

Quick Review

The midpoint formula gives the coordinates of the **midpoint** between two points.

$$M = \left(\frac{x_1 + x_2}{2}, \frac{y_1 + y_2}{2}\right)$$

The distance formula gives the distance between two points on a coordinate plane.

$$d = \sqrt{(x_2 - x_1)^2 + (y_2 - y_1)^2}$$

Example

What are the coordinates of point K that is $\frac{2}{3}$ the distance from J(8, 3) to L(2, 6)?

Horizontal change: $\frac{2}{3}(x_2 - x_1) = \frac{2}{3}(2 - 8) = -4$

Vertical change: $\frac{2}{3}(y_2 - y_1) = \frac{2}{3}(6 - 3) = 2$

$K(x, y) = (x_1 + (-4), y_1 + 2) = (8 - 4, 3 + 2) = (4, 5)$

Practice & Problem Solving

Find the midpoint and length of each segment.

21. $\overline{EF}$

22. $\overline{FG}$

23. $\overline{GH}$

24. $\overline{EH}$

25. What are the coordinates of the point that partitions $\overline{HE}$ in the ratio 2:3?

26. **Make Sense of Problems** Sadie models her neighborhood on a coordinate plane so that her school is at (8, 12) and a store is at (14, 3). What are the coordinates of the point halfway between the school and the store? Ⓒ **MP.1**

Quick Review

Inductive reasoning is the process of reaching a conclusion by observing patterns. A **conjecture** is a conclusion reached through inductive reasoning.

You can use several examples to support a conjecture, or you can disprove it by finding a **counterexample**.

Example

Make a conjecture about the shape of the *n*th term of the pattern shown.

1st term: 2 blocks down each side, 3 blocks across

2nd term: 3 blocks down each side, 4 blocks across

3rd term: 4 blocks down each side, 5 blocks across

Conjecture: The *n*th term will have *n* + 1 blocks down each side and *n* + 2 blocks across.

Practice & Problem Solving

Use inductive reasoning to find the next two terms in each sequence.

27. 1, 2, 6, 24, 120, ...   **28.** 3, 5, 8, 10, 13, ...

29. 2, 5, 9, 14, 20, ...   **30.** 17, 21, 25, 29, 33, ...

Find a counterexample to disprove each statement, or support it with four examples.

31. All triangles have three congruent angles.

32. If *p* is an even number, then *p* + 12 is even.

33. Construct Arguments Explain why only one counterexample is sufficient to disprove a statement, but one example is not sufficient to prove a statement. © MP.3

34. The table shows how much Jack saves in his bank account each week. At this rate, how much will he save on week 10?

Week	Savings ($)
1	1.75
2	3.50
3	5.25
4	7.00

Quick Review

A **conditional** *p* → *q* relates a **hypothesis** *p* to a **conclusion** *q*. The **converse** is *q* → *p*, the **inverse** is ~*p* → ~*q*, the **contrapositive** is ~*q* → ~*p* and a **biconditional** is *p* ↔ *q*.

Statements are logically equivalent if they have the same **truth value**. A conditional and its contrapositive are logically equivalent. A converse and an inverse are also logically equivalent.

Example

Find the truth value of the following conditional: All quadrilaterals have four congruent angles.

A parallelogram that is not a rectangle is an example of a quadrilateral. It is a counterexample because its angles are not all congruent. The truth value for the conditional is false.

Practice & Problem Solving

For each statement, write a conditional and the converse, inverse, and contrapositive.

35. A number that is a multiple of 4 is a multiple of 2.

36. Kona jogs 5 miles every Saturday morning.

Find the truth value of each conditional. Explain your reasoning or show a counterexample.

37. If a number is less than 4, then it is prime.

38. If 3*x* − 7 < 14, then *x* < 8.

39. If it snows, then school will be cancelled.

40. Communicate Precisely A cafeteria only offers pudding on Tuesdays. Use this fact to write a biconditional about the pudding. © MP.6

LESSON 1-6 Deductive Reasoning

Quick Review

Deductive reasoning uses logical steps based on given facts to reach a conclusion and can be applied through laws of logic, such as the following.

- **Law of Detachment:** If $p \to q$ and p are true, then q is true.
- **Law of Syllogism:** If $p \to q$ and $q \to r$ are true, then $p \to r$ is true.

Example

Given the following, use the Law of Syllogism to write a true conditional.

- If $m\angle A < 90$, then $\angle A$ is acute.
- If $\angle A$ is acute, then it is not a right angle.

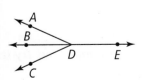

Conditional: If $m\angle A < 90$, then $\angle A$ is not a right angle.

Practice & Problem Solving

Assume the given information is true.

41. If $AB = BC$, then $DE = 2(AB)$. $AB = 6$ and $BC = 6$. What can you conclude?

42. If it is a sunny day, the water park is filled with people. If the water park is filled with people, the lines for each ride are long. Use the Law of Syllogism to write a true conditional.

43. **Communicate Precisely** An advertisement says if you use their toothpaste for more than a week, you will have fresher breath. You use the toothpaste ten days. If the advertisement is true, what can you conclude? © **MP.6**

LESSON 1-7 & 1-8 Writing Proofs and Indirect Proof

Quick Review

A **proof** uses deductive reasoning to explain why a conjecture is true. A conjecture that has been proven is a **theorem**.

For an indirect proof, assume the negation of what is to be proven, and then show that the assumption leads to a contradiction.

Example

Write a paragraph proof.

Given: $m\angle BDC + m\angle ADE = 180$

Prove: $\angle ADB \cong \angle BDC$

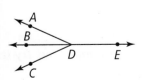

Proof: By definition of supplementary angles, $m\angle ADB + m\angle ADE = 180$. Since it is given that $m\angle BDC + m\angle ADE = 180$, by the Congruent Supplements Theorem, $\angle ADB \cong \angle BDC$.

Practice & Problem Solving

Find the value of each variable and the measure of each labeled angle.

44.

45.

46. **Construct Arguments** Write a proof. © **MP.3**

   Given: $m\angle TUV = 90$

   Prove: $x = 12$

47. **Construct Arguments** Write an indirect proof by proving the contrapositive. © **MP.3**

   Given: $GJ = 48$

   Prove: $x \neq 12$

TOPIC 2

Parallel and Perpendicular Lines

TOPIC ESSENTIAL QUESTION

What properties are specific to parallel lines and perpendicular lines?

Topic Overview

enVision® STEM Project:
  Build a Roof

2-1 Parallel Lines

2-2 Proving Lines Parallel

2-3 Parallel Lines and Triangle Angle Sums

2-4 Slopes of Parallel and
  Perpendicular Lines

Mathematical Modeling in 3 Acts:
  Parallel Paving Company

Topic Vocabulary

• flow proof

Digital Experience

INTERACTIVE STUDENT EDITION
Access online or offline.

ACTIVITIES Complete *Explore & Reason, Model & Discuss*, and *Critique & Explain* activities. Interact with *Examples* and *Try Its.*

CONCEPT SUMMARY Review key lesson content through multiple representations.

ASSESSMENT Show what you've learned.

 Go online | SavvasRealize.com

MATHEMATICAL MODELING IN 3 ACTS

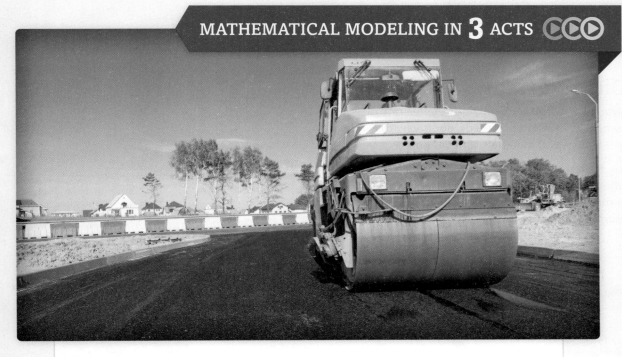

Parallel Paving Company

Building roads consists of many different tasks. Once civil engineers have designed the road, they work with surveyors and construction crews to clear and level the land. Sometimes specialists have to blast away rock in order to clear the land. Once the land is leveled, the crews bring in asphalt pavers to smooth out the hot asphalt.

Sometimes construction crews will start work at both ends of the new road and meet in the middle. Think about this during the Mathematical Modeling in 3 Acts lesson.

TOPIC 2

VIDEOS Watch clips to support *Mathematical Modeling in 3 Acts Lessons* and **enVision®** *STEM Projects.*

TUTORIALS Get help from *Virtual Nerd*, right when you need it.

PRACTICE Practice what you've learned.

ADAPTIVE PRACTICE Practice that is *just right* and *just for you.*

FAMILY ENGAGEMENT Involve family in your learning.

GLOSSARY Read and listen to English and Spanish definitions.

MATH TOOLS Explore math with digital tools and manipulatives.

DESMOS Use Anytime and as embedded Interactives in Lesson content.

Did You Know?

A roof is a critical component of shelter, one of humankind's most basic needs. Roofs vary depending on climate, local materials, and designs.

The front and back panels of a roof require a different, more complex, design than the rest of the roof and include vertical support beams called **gable studs**.

A **roof's pitch** determines the length of the rafters.

The **weight** of the roofing material affects the spacing of a roof's rafters and gable studs.

Bermuda has no fresh water other than falling rain, so roofs are designed to **funnel rain** down into underground holding tanks.

The weight of snow on a roof can be up to **21 lbs per square foot**.

A **green roof** is topped with earth and plants, which cools the building in the summer and insulates it in the winter.

Your Task: Build a Roof

You and your classmates will plan the construction of a roof, including the location and cost of its ridge-board, rafters, and gable studs. How does the cost of the roof change based on on its pitch and the spacing between rafters?

2-1

Parallel Lines

I CAN... determine the measures of the angles formed when parallel lines are intersected by a transversal.

Common Core State Standards
HSG.CO.A.1, HSG.CO.C.9, MP.1, MP.3, MP.8

EXPLORE & REASON

Powered By **desmos**

The diagram shows two parallel lines cut by a transversal.

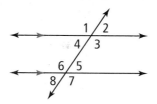

A. Look for Relationships What relationships among the measures of the angles do you see? © **MP.7**

B. Suppose a different transversal intersects the parallel lines. Would you expect to find the same relationships with the measures of those angles? Explain.

ESSENTIAL QUESTION

What angle relationships are created when parallel lines are intersected by a transversal?

EXAMPLE 1 · Identify Angle Pairs

Identify the pairs of angles of each angle type made by the snowmobile tracks.

∠4 and ∠8, ∠1 and ∠5, ∠2 and ∠6, and ∠3 and ∠7 are corresponding angles.

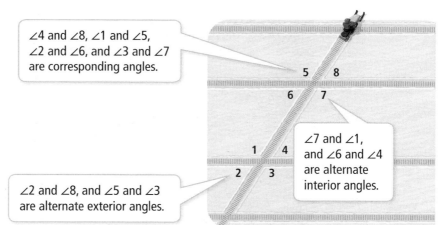

∠7 and ∠1, and ∠6 and ∠4 are alternate interior angles.

∠2 and ∠8, and ∠5 and ∠3 are alternate exterior angles.

STUDY TIP
Transversals can intersect either parallel or nonparallel lines. The types of angle pairs remain the same.

Try It! **1.** Which angle pairs include the named angle?

    a. ∠4   **b.** ∠7

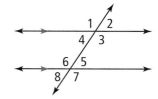

POSTULATE 2-1 Same-Side Interior Angles Postulate

If a transversal intersects two parallel lines, then same-side interior angles are supplementary.

If...

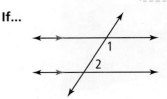

Then... $m\angle 1 + m\angle 2 = 180$

CONCEPTUAL UNDERSTANDING

EXAMPLE 2 Explore Angle Relationships

How can you express each of the numbered angles in terms of *x*?

LOOK FOR RELATIONSHIPS
What patterns do you notice about the angles formed by two parallel lines cut by a transversal?
© MP.7

By Postulate 2-1, $\angle 2$ and the angle with measure *x* are supplementary.

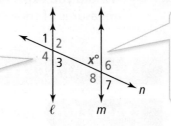

The angle with measure *x* and $\angle 7$ are vertical angles. Both $\angle 6$ and $\angle 8$ form a linear pair with the angle with measure *x*.

You can make conclusions about $\angle 1$, $\angle 3$, and $\angle 4$ as you did with $\angle 6$, $\angle 7$, and $\angle 8$.
The angles with measures equal to *x* are $\angle 1$, $\angle 3$, and $\angle 7$.
The angles that are supplementary to the angle with measure *x* are $\angle 2$, $\angle 4$, $\angle 6$, and $\angle 8$, which have measure $(180 - x)$.

Try It!   **2.** Use the figure at the right.

a. If $m\angle 4 = 118$, what is the measure of each of the other angles?

b. If $m\angle 2 = 9x - 12$ and $m\angle 4 = 6x + 30$, what is $m\angle 5$?

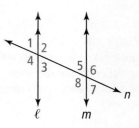

THEOREM 2-1 Alternate Interior Angles Theorem

If a transversal intersects two parallel lines, then alternate interior angles are congruent.

PROOF: SEE EXAMPLE 3.

If...

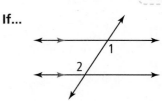

Then... $\angle 1 \cong \angle 2$

THEOREM 2-2 Corresponding Angles Theorem

If a transversal intersects two parallel lines, then corresponding angles are congruent.

PROOF: SEE EXAMPLE 3 TRY IT.

If...

Then... $\angle 1 \cong \angle 2$

THEOREM 2-3 Alternate Exterior Angles Theorem

If a transversal intersects two parallel lines, then alternate exterior angles are congruent.

PROOF: SEE EXERCISE 12.

If...

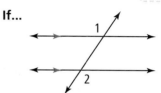

Then... $\angle 1 \cong \angle 2$

PROOF

EXAMPLE 3 Prove the Alternate Interior Angles Theorem

Prove the Alternate Interior Angles Theorem.

Given: $m \parallel n$

Prove: $\angle 1 \cong \angle 2$

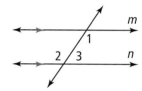

Plan: Use the Same-Side Interior Angles Postulate to show $\angle 1$ is supplementary to $\angle 3$. Then show that angles 1 and 2 are congruent because they are both supplementary to the same angle.

Proof:

Statements	Reasons
1) $m \parallel n$	**1)** Given
2) $\angle 1$ and $\angle 3$ are supplementary	**2)** Same-Side Interior $\angle$s Postulate
3) $m\angle 1 + m\angle 3 = 180$	**3)** Def. of supplementary angles
4) $m\angle 2 + m\angle 3 = 180$	**4)** Angle Addition Postulate
5) $m\angle 1 + m\angle 3 = m\angle 2 + m\angle 3$	**5)** Transitive Property of Equality
6) $m\angle 1 = m\angle 2$	**6)** Subtraction Property of Equality
7) $\angle 1 \cong \angle 2$	**7)** Def. of congruence

COMMON ERROR
Remember that for the proof to be complete, the last statement of the proof must match what you are trying to prove.

Try It! **3.** Prove the Corresponding Angles Theorem.

Given: $m \parallel n$

Prove: $\angle 1 \cong \angle 2$

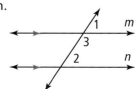

EXAMPLE 4 Use Parallel Lines to Prove an Angle Relationship

Use the diagram to prove the angle relationship.

Given: $\overline{AC} \parallel \overline{DF}$, and $\overline{BE} \perp \overline{DF}$, $\angle AEB \cong \angle CEB$

Prove: $\angle BAE \cong \angle BCE$

Proof:

Statements	Reasons
1) $\overline{AC} \parallel \overline{DF}$, $\overline{BE} \perp \overline{DF}$	1) Given
2) $\angle BED$, $\angle BEF$ are rt. angles	2) Def. of perpendicular
3) $m\angle BED = m\angle BEF = 90$	3) Def. of rt. angles
4) $m\angle AED + m\angle AEB = 90$, $m\angle CEF + m\angle CEB = 90$	4) Angle Addition Postulate
5) $\angle AEB \cong \angle CEB$	5) Given
6) $\angle AED \cong \angle CEF$	6) Congruent Complements Thm.
7) $\angle BAE \cong \angle AED$, $\angle BCE \cong \angle CEF$	7) Alt. Interior $\angle$s Thm.
8) $\angle BAE \cong \angle BCE$	8) Transitive Prop. of Congruence

STUDY TIP
Recall that you can use the Reflexive Property of Congruence, the Symmetric Property of Congruence, and the Transitive Property of Congruence as reasons in a proof.

Try It! **4.** Given $\overline{AB} \parallel \overline{CD}$, prove that $m\angle 1 + m\angle 2 + m\angle 3 = 180$.

EXAMPLE 5 Find Angle Measures

The white trim shown for the wall of a barn should be constructed so that $\overline{AC} \parallel \overline{EG}$, $\overline{JA} \parallel \overline{HB}$, and $\overline{JC} \parallel \overline{KG}$. What should $m\angle 1$ and $m\angle 3$ be?

Formulate ◄ You can create a simple drawing of the wall of the barn so that the angles are easier to visualize. Look for relationships among the angles.

Compute ◄ By the Same-Side Interior Angles Postulate, $m\angle 1 + 68 = 180$.

$$m\angle 1 = 180 - 68 = 112$$

By the Corresponding Angles Theorem, $\angle EAB \cong \angle 2$ and $\angle 2 \cong \angle 3$, so $\angle 3 \cong \angle EAB$ by the Transitive Property of Congruence.

$$m\angle 3 = 68$$

Interpret ◄ So, $m\angle 1 = 112$ and $m\angle 3 = 68$.

Try It! **5.** If $m\angle EJF = 56$, find $m\angle FHK$.

CONCEPT SUMMARY Parallel Lines and Angle Pairs

There are four special angle relationships formed when parallel lines are intersected by a transversal.

POSTULATE 2-1 ▸ **Same-Side Interior Angles Postulate**

If...

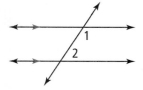

Then... $m\angle 1 + m\angle 2 = 180$

THEOREM 2-1 ▸ **Alternate Interior Angles Theorem**

If...

Then... $\angle 1 \cong \angle 2$

THEOREM 2-2 ▸ **Corresponding Angles Theorem**

If...

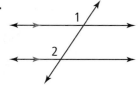

Then... $\angle 1 \cong \angle 2$

THEOREM 2-3 ▸ **Alternate Exterior Angles Theorem**

If...

Then... $\angle 1 \cong \angle 2$

Do You UNDERSTAND?

1. **ESSENTIAL QUESTION** What angle relationships are created when parallel lines are intersected by a transversal?

2. **Vocabulary** When a transversal intersects two parallel lines, which angle pairs are congruent?

3. **Error Analysis** What error did Leah make? Ⓒ MP.3

$m\angle 1 = 88$ by Corresponding Angles Theorem ✗

4. **Generalize** For any pair of angles formed by a transversal intersecting parallel lines, what are two possible relationships? Ⓒ MP.8

Do You KNOW HOW?

Use the diagram for Exercises 5–10.

Classify each pair of angles. Compare angle measures, and give the postulate or theorem that justifies it.

5. $\angle 2$ and $\angle 6$

6. $\angle 3$ and $\angle 5$

If $m\angle 1 = 71$, find the measure of each angle.

7. $\angle 5$ 8. $\angle 7$

If $m\angle 3 = 3x + 12$ and $m\angle 5 = 2x + 3$, find the measure of each angle.

9. $\angle 5$ 10. $\angle 7$

11. Elm St. and Spruce St. are parallel. What is $m\angle 1$?

PRACTICE & PROBLEM SOLVING

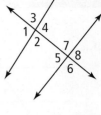

UNDERSTAND

12. Construct Arguments Write a two-column proof of the Alternate Exterior Angles Theorem. **© MP.3**

Given: $m \parallel n$

Prove: $\angle 1 \cong \angle 2$

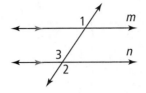

13. Higher Order Thinking Using what you know about angle pairs formed by parallel lines and a transversal, how are $\angle 1$, $\angle 2$, $\angle 3$, and $\angle 4$ related in the trapezoid? Explain.

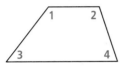

14. Error Analysis What error did Tyler make? **© MP.3**

$m\angle 1 = 72$ by Same-Side Exterior Angles Theorem ✗

15. Generalize In the diagram shown, if $x + y = 180$, label the remaining angles as $x°$ or $y°$. **© MP.8**

16. Mathematical Connections A transversal intersects two parallel lines. The measures of a pair of alternate interior angles are $5v$ and $2w$. The measures of a pair of same-side exterior angles are $10w$ and $5v$. What are the values of w and v?

PRACTICE

Identify a pair of angles for each type. SEE EXAMPLE 1

17. same-side interior

18. corresponding

19. alternate exterior

20. Which angles are supplementary to $\angle 1$? Which are congruent to $\angle 1$? SEE EXAMPLE 2

Find each measure. SEE EXAMPLE 3

21. $m\angle 1$

22. x

23. Opposite sides of a parallelogram are parallel. Prove that opposite angles of a parallelogram are congruent. SEE EXAMPLE 4

Given: $ABCD$ is a parallelogram.

Prove: $\angle A \cong \angle C$, $\angle B \cong \angle D$

24. For safety and strength, the supports of a set of scissor steps form parallelograms. What should the measure of $\angle 1$ be to allow a dog to climb safely into its owner's car? SEE EXAMPLE 5

PRACTICE & PROBLEM SOLVING

25. Model With Mathematics A glazier is setting supports in parallel segments to prevent glass breakage during storms. What are the values of x and y? Justify your conclusions. **© MP.4**

26. Reason In the parking lot shown, all of the lines for the parking spaces should be parallel. If $m\angle 3 = 61$, what should $m\angle 1$ and $m\angle 2$ be? Explain. **© MP.2**

27. Communicate Precisely Margaret is in a boat traveling due west. She turned the boat 50° north of due west for a couple of minutes to get around a peninsula. Then she resumed due west again. **© MP.6**

a. How many degrees would she turn the wheel to resume a due west course?

b. What type of angle pair did she use? Are the angles congruent or supplementary?

28. Parallel lines m and n intersect parallel lines x and y, representing two sets of intersecting railroad tracks. If the minimum measure for $\angle 1$ is 101° and the maximum measure for $\angle 1$ is 106°, what are the minimum and maximum measures for $\angle 2$?

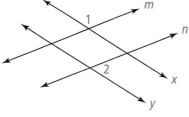

29. Classify each angle as *congruent to* $\angle 1$ or *congruent to* $\angle 2$.

Angle	Congruent to $\angle 1$	Congruent to $\angle 2$
$\angle 3$	☐	☐
$\angle 4$	☐	☐
$\angle 5$	☐	☐
$\angle 6$	☐	☐
$\angle 7$	☐	☐
$\angle 8$	☐	☐

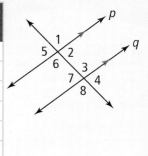

30. SAT/ACT In the diagram, $a \parallel b$. What is $m\angle 1$?

Ⓐ 28   Ⓒ 90

Ⓑ 62   Ⓓ 118

31. Performance Task Students on a scavenger hunt are given the map shown and several clues.

Part A The first clue states the following.

Skyline Trail forms a transversal with Wood Path and Mission Path. Go to the corners that form same side exterior angles north of Skyline Trail.

Which two corners does the clue mean? Use intersections and directions to explain.

Part B If the second clue states the following, what trail marker should they go to?

Wood and Mission Paths are parallel, and the northeast corner of Wood Path and Skyline Trail forms a 131° angle. The measure of the angle formed by the southwest corner of Skyline Trail and Mission Path is equal to the trail marker number on River Trail you must go to.

2-2
Proving Lines Parallel

I CAN... use angle relationships to prove that lines are parallel.

VOCABULARY
• flow proof

 Common Core State Standards
HSG.CO.C.9, HSG.CO.D.12, HSG.MG.A.3, HSG.CO.A.1, MP.2, MP.3, MP.7

CRITIQUE & EXPLAIN

Juan analyzes the diagram to see if line ℓ is parallel to line m. His teacher asks if there is enough information to say whether the lines are parallel.

> Yes, if a transversal intersects two parallel lines, then alternate interior angles are congruent and corresponding angles are congruent. I have both angle relationships here, so the lines are parallel.

A. **Make Sense and Persevere** Why is Juan's statement correct or incorrect? **MP.1**

B. Can you use the Alternate Exterior Angles Theorem to prove that the lines are not parallel?

ESSENTIAL QUESTION

What angle relationships can be used to prove that two lines intersected by a transversal are parallel?

CONCEPTUAL UNDERSTANDING

EXAMPLE 1 Understand Angle Relationships

Suppose two lines are not parallel. Can corresponding angles still be congruent?

Draw two nonparallel lines t and m and a transversal s. Draw line ℓ parallel to m that passes through the intersection of s and t.

Lines t and m are not parallel.

Transversal s intersects line t and line m. The 120° angle corresponds with the angle formed by combining ∠1 and ∠2.

Since $\ell \parallel m$, $m\angle 1 = 120$ by the Corresponding Angles Theorem.
By the Alternate Interior Angles Theorem, $m\angle 2 = x$.
Since $m\angle 1 + m\angle 2 = 120 + x$, $m\angle 1 + m\angle 2 > 120$.

If two lines are not parallel, then corresponding angles are not congruent.

COMMUNICATE PRECISELY
Consider the conclusion in the example. What statement can you write that is logically equivalent to this statement? **MP.6**

Try It! 1. Could ∠3 be supplementary to a 120° angle? Explain.

THEOREM 2-4 Converse of the Corresponding Angles Theorem

If two lines and a transversal form corresponding angles that are congruent, then the lines are parallel.

PROOF: SEE EXERCISE 8.

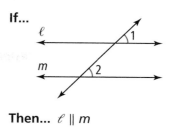

If...

Then... $\ell \parallel m$

THEOREM 2-5 Converse of the Alternate Interior Angles Theorem

If two lines and a transversal form alternate interior angles that are congruent, then the lines are parallel.

PROOF: SEE EXAMPLE 2.

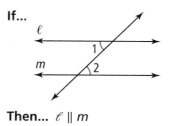

If...

Then... $\ell \parallel m$

PROOF

EXAMPLE 2 ▸ Write a Flow Proof of Theorem 2-5

Write a flow proof to prove the Converse of the Alternate Interior Angles Theorem.

In a **flow proof**, arrows show the logical connections between statements. Reasons are shown below the statements.

Given: $\angle 1 \cong \angle 2$

Prove: $\ell \parallel m$

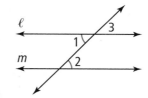

COMMON ERROR
You may incorrectly write all information along one line of the flow proof. Remember that you should have two separate arrows when two statements are needed to justify the next statement in a proof.

Proof:

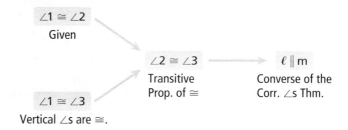

Try It!   **2.** Write a flow proof for Theorem 2-6, the Converse of the Same-Side Interior Angles Postulate.

THEOREM 2-6 Converse of the Same-Side Interior Angles Postulate

If two lines and a transversal form same-side interior angles that are supplementary, then the lines are parallel.

PROOF: SEE EXAMPLE 2 TRY IT.

If... $m\angle 1 + m\angle 2 = 180$

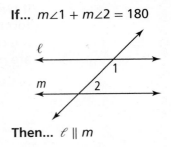

Then... $\ell \parallel m$

THEOREM 2-7 Converse of the Alternate Exterior Angles Theorem

If two lines and a transversal form alternate exterior angles that are congruent, then the lines are parallel.

PROOF: SEE EXERCISE 16.

If...

Then... $\ell \parallel m$

EXAMPLE 3   Determine Whether Lines Are Parallel

In a blueprint, an architect uses trapezoids to represent the exterior of the top three levels of the Smithsonian National Museum of African American History and Culture. How can the architect ensure that the left edges of the trapezoids are parallel to each other?

> By the Alternate Interior Angles Theorem, $m\angle 2 = 67$.

MAKE SENSE AND PERSEVERE
Think about other theorems that could be applied to determine parallel edges. What other measurements could the architect make? © MP.1

If $m\angle 1 = 67$ and $\angle 3 \cong \angle 2$, then the upper-left and lower-left edges are parallel to the middle-left edge by the Converse of the Alternate Interior Angles Theorem.

So, if the architect makes $m\angle 1 = m\angle 3 = 67$, the three edges will be parallel.

Try It! 3. What should $\angle 4$ and $\angle 5$ measure to ensure that the right edges of the trapezoids are parallel to each other?

EXAMPLE 4 **Construct a Parallel Line**

How can you construct a parallel line through a point that is not on the line?

You can use angle relationships to construct a parallel line.

Step 1 Draw point A on the given line. Then, draw a line that connects points A and P.

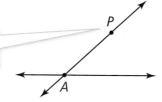

$\overleftrightarrow{AP}$ will be the transversal of the two lines.

Step 2 Construct an angle at P that is corresponding and congruent to the angle at A.

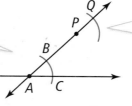

Draw an arc from A, and label B and C.

Draw an arc from p with the same setting, and label Q.

Open the compass to the distance between B and C.

Draw an arc from Q. Label R where the two arcs intersect.

Draw $\overleftrightarrow{PR}$.

MAKE SENSE AND PERSEVERE
Think about other angle relationships that prove lines are parallel. Can you construct a parallel line using a different pair of angles? Ⓒ **MP.1**

Since ∠QPR is congruent to ∠BAC, $\overleftrightarrow{PR}$ is parallel to the given line by the Converse of the Corresponding Angles Theorem.

Try It! **4.** Construct a line parallel to the given line through point P.

THEOREM 2-8

If two lines are parallel to the same line, then they are parallel to each other.

PROOF: SEE EXERCISE 17.

If...

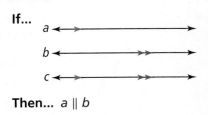

Then... $a \parallel b$

THEOREM 2-9

If two lines in the same plane are perpendicular to the same line, then they are parallel to each other.

PROOF: SEE EXERCISE 18.

If...

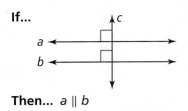

Then... $a \parallel b$

APPLICATION

EXAMPLE 5 Solve a Problem With Parallel Lines

A. The properties of parallel lines can be applied to the boards that Bailey is using to build a gate. How does Bailey know that the vertical boards *v* and *w* are parallel?

By Theorem 2-9, they are parallel.

LOOK FOR RELATIONSHIPS
Look for different ways that parts of a diagram are put together as a whole. How can you use the labeled parts to determine a strategy for solving a problem?
ⓒ MP.7

B. What should ∠1 measure to ensure board *b* is parallel to board *a*?

Apply the Converse of the Same-Side Interior Angles Postulate.

$$35 + m\angle 1 = 180$$
$$m\angle 1 = 145$$

For board *b* to be parallel to board *a*, the measure of ∠1 must be 145°.

LEARN TOGETHER
How can you provide constructive feedback while being aware of the feelings and reactions of others?

Try It! **5. a.** Bailey also needs board *c* to be parallel to board *a*. What should ∠2 measure? Explain.

b. Is *b* ∥ *c* ? Explain.

DIAGRAM

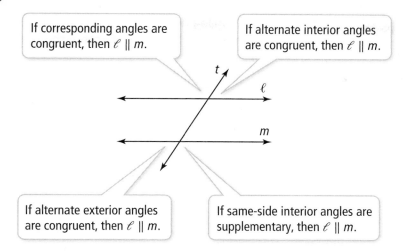

If corresponding angles are congruent, then $\ell \parallel m$.

If alternate interior angles are congruent, then $\ell \parallel m$.

If alternate exterior angles are congruent, then $\ell \parallel m$.

If same-side interior angles are supplementary, then $\ell \parallel m$.

Do You UNDERSTAND?

1. **ESSENTIAL QUESTION** What angle relationships can be used to prove that two lines intersected by a transversal are parallel?

2. **Error Analysis** Noemi wrote, "If $\angle 1 \cong \angle 2$, then by the Converse of the Same-Side Interior Angles Postulate, $\ell \parallel m$." Explain the error in Noemi's reasoning. © MP.3

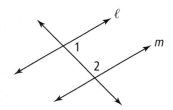

3. **Vocabulary** How does a *flow proof* show logical steps in the proof of a conditional statement?

4. **Reason** How is Theorem 2-9 a special case of the Converse of the Corresponding Angles Theorem? © MP.2

Do You KNOW HOW?

Use the figure shown for Exercises 5 and 6.

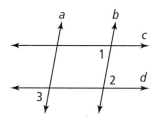

5. If $\angle 1 \cong \angle 2$, which theorem proves that $c \parallel d$?

6. If $m\angle 2 = 4x - 6$ and $m\angle 3 = 2x + 18$, for what value of x is $a \parallel b$? Which theorem justifies your answer?

7. Using the Converse of the Same-Side Interior Angles Postulate, what equation could be used to prove that $g \parallel h$?

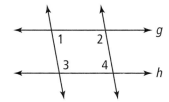

PRACTICE & PROBLEM SOLVING

UNDERSTAND

8. Construct Arguments Write an indirect proof of the Converse of the Corresponding Angles Theorem following the outline below. © MP.3

Given: ∠1 ≅ ∠2

Prove: ℓ ∥ m

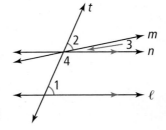

- Assume that lines ℓ and m are not parallel.
- Draw line n parallel to line ℓ.
- Conclude that m∠3 > 0.
- Use the Corresponding Angles Theorem to arrive at the contradiction that m∠1 ≠ m∠2.

9. Error Analysis What is the student's error? © MP.3

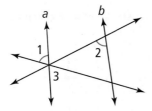

Given ∠1 ≅ ∠2. By the Vertical Angles Thm., ∠1 ≅ ∠3, so by the Transitive Property, ∠2 ≅ ∠3. By the Converse of the Corresponding Angles Thm., a ∥ b. ✗

10. Mathematical Connections Construct a line through P parallel to ℓ. Use a protractor to measure the angles formed by the parallel lines and the transversal. Which theorems can you use to verify that the lines are parallel?

11. Higher Order Thinking The interior angles of a regular hexagon are congruent. Why are any pair of opposite sides parallel?

PRACTICE

For Exercises 12–15, use the given information. Which lines in the figure can you conclude are parallel? State the theorem that justifies each answer. SEE EXAMPLES 1 AND 3

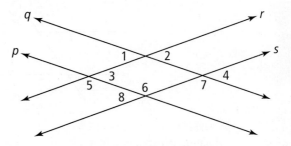

12. ∠2 ≅ ∠3

13. ∠6 ≅ ∠7

14. ∠1 ≅ ∠4

15. m∠5 + m∠8 = 180°

16. Write a flow proof of the Converse of the Alternate Exterior Angles Theorem. SEE EXAMPLE 2

Use the diagram for Exercises 17 and 18. SEE EXAMPLE 2

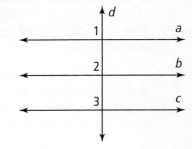

17. Given a ∥ c and b ∥ c, write a flow proof of Theorem 2-8.

18. Given a ⊥ d and b ⊥ d, write a flow proof of Theorem 2-9.

19. For what value of x is f ∥ g? Which theorem justifies your answer? SEE EXAMPLE 5

(10x + 5)°

(12x − 9)°

20. Copy the diagram from Exercise 19. Construct a line parallel to line g. SEE EXAMPLE 4

PRACTICE & PROBLEM SOLVING

21. Look for Relationships To make a puzzle, Denzel draws lines *a* and *b* to cut along on a square piece of posterboard. He wants to draw line *c* so that it is parallel to line *b*. What should the measure of ∠1 be? Explain. © MP.7

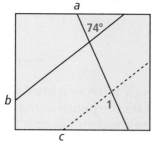

22. Reason A downhill skier is fastest when her skis are parallel. What should ∠1 be in order for the skier to maximize her speed through a gate? Which theorem justifies your answer? © MP.2

23. Make Sense and Persevere Malia makes a fabric design by drawing diagonals between opposite corners. She wants to draw other lines parallel to one of the diagonal lines, as shown by the dashed lines.

a. What should ∠1 be in order for line *b* to be parallel to line *a*? Explain.

b. What should ∠2 be in order for line *c* to be parallel to line *b*? Explain. © MP.1

24. In order for *c* ∥ *d*, ∠2 and ∠7 must be ___?___, and ∠3 and ∠5 must be ___?___.

25. SAT/ACT Which statement must always be true?

Ⓐ If ∠1 ≅ ∠2, then *g* ∥ *h*.

Ⓑ If ∠1 ≅ ∠3, then *g* ∥ *h*.

Ⓒ If ∠2 ≅ ∠4, then *j* ∥ *k*.

Ⓓ If ∠3 ≅ ∠4, then *j* ∥ *k*.

26. Performance Task The diagram shows part of a plan to arrange aisles in a store.

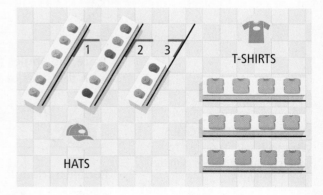

Part A The aisles are arranged so that $m\angle 1 = 117$. What should be the measures of the other labeled angles so that all three aisles will be parallel? Explain.

Part B Describe how theorems can be applied to make sure that the T-shirt aisles are parallel.

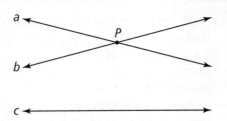

2-3

Parallel Lines and Triangle Angle Sums

I CAN... solve problems using the measures of interior and exterior angles of triangles.

© **Common Core State Standards**
HSG.CO.C.10, MP.2, MP.4, MP.7

CONCEPTUAL UNDERSTANDING

USE APPROPRIATE TOOLS
What tools might you use to confirm that the angles sum to 180°? © **MP.5**

EXPLORE & REASON

Powered By
desmos

Two parallel lines never intersect. But, can two lines that intersect ever be parallel to the same line?

Draw point *P*. Then draw lines *a* and *b* that intersect at point *P* as shown.

A. Place a pencil below the intersecting lines on your paper to represent line *c*. Rotate the pencil so that it is parallel to line *b*. Can you rotate the pencil so that it is parallel to line *a* at the same time as line *b*?

B. **Look for Relationships** Can you adjust your drawing of the two intersecting lines so you can rotate the pencil to be parallel to both lines? © **MP.7**

ESSENTIAL QUESTION What is true about the interior and exterior angle measures of a triangle?

EXAMPLE 1 Investigate the Measures of Triangle Angles

Powered By
desmos

What appears to be the relationship between the angle measures of a triangle?

Using pencil and paper, or scissors and paper, construct several triangles of different types. Number the angles.

Trace the angles from each triangle and place the vertices together with the sides of the angles sharing a vertex and ray.

For each triangle shown, the angles combine to form a straight angle.

So, the sum of the angle measures of a triangle appears to be 180.

Try It! **1.** Given two angle measures in a triangle, can you find the measure of the third angle? Explain.

THEOREM 2-10

Through a point not on a line, there is one and only one line parallel to the given line.

PROOF: SEE EXERCISE 10.

If...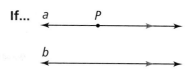

Then... line *a* is the only line parallel to line *b* through *P*.

THEOREM 2-11 Triangle Angle-Sum Theorem

Powered By
desmos

The sum of the measures of all the angles of a triangle is 180.

PROOF: SEE EXAMPLE 2.

If...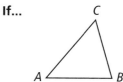

Then... $m\angle A + m\angle B + m\angle C = 180$

PROOF

EXAMPLE 2 Prove the Triangle Angle-Sum Theorem

Prove the Triangle Angle-Sum Theorem.

Given: △*ABC*

Prove: $m\angle 1 + m\angle 2 + m\angle 3 = 180$

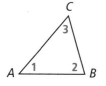

STUDY TIP
When using a geometric figure in a proof, you can construct additional parts to help with the proof, such as parallel lines, angle bisectors, and midpoints.

Plan: Draw a line through *C*, because a straight angle measures 180. This line should be parallel to the line containing $\overline{AB}$ so that an alternate interior angle relationship is formed.

Proof:

Use Theorem 2-10 to justify drawing a line through *C* parallel to $\overleftrightarrow{AB}$.

Apply the Angle Addition Postulate: $m\angle 4 + m\angle 3 + m\angle 5 = 180°$.

By the Alternate Interior Angles Theorem, $\angle 1 \cong \angle 4$, so $m\angle 1 = m\angle 4$.

Also by the Alternate Interior Angles Theorem, $\angle 2 \cong \angle 5$, so $m\angle 2 = m\angle 5$.

By substitution, $m\angle 1 + m\angle 3 + m\angle 2 = 180$. Therefore, using the Commutative Property of Addition, $m\angle 1 + m\angle 2 + m\angle 3 = 180$.

Try It! 2. How does Theorem 2-10 justify the construction of the line through *C* that is parallel to $\overleftrightarrow{AB}$?

EXAMPLE 3 ▸ Use the Triangle Angle-Sum Theorem

What are the values of *x* and *y*?

Write and solve an equation that relates the measures of the angles of △TRS.

$$32 + 78 + x = 180$$

Use the Triangle Angle-Sum Theorem.

$$x = 70$$

To find the value of *y*, notice that ∠QRS is a straight angle.

$$m\angle QRT + m\angle TRS = 180$$

Apply the Angle Addition Postulate.

$$y + 78 = 180$$

$$y = 102$$

The value of *x* is 70 and the value of *y* is 102.

HAVE A GROWTH MINDSET
How can you take on challenges with positivity?

Try It! **3.** What are the values of *x* and *y* in each figure?

a.

b.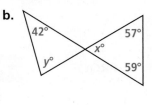

THEOREM 2-12 Triangle Exterior Angle Theorem

The measure of each exterior angle of a triangle equals the sum of the measures of its two remote interior angles.

If...

Then... $m\angle 1 = m\angle 2 + m\angle 3$

PROOF: SEE EXERCISE 13.

EXAMPLE 4 ▸ Apply the Triangle Exterior Angle Theorem

What is the missing angle measure in each figure?

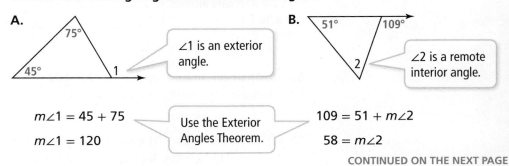

A.

∠1 is an exterior angle.

$$m\angle 1 = 45 + 75$$

Use the Exterior Angles Theorem.

$$m\angle 1 = 120$$

B.

∠2 is a remote interior angle.

$$109 = 51 + m\angle 2$$

$$58 = m\angle 2$$

COMMON ERROR
Be careful when writing an equation to solve for the unknown angle measure. The unknown value can be an addend or the sum.

CONTINUED ON THE NEXT PAGE

EXAMPLE 4 CONTINUED

Try It!   **4.** What is the value of *x* in each figure?

a.

b.

APPLICATION

EXAMPLE 5   Apply the Triangle Theorems

Before starting to weave the Navajo rug shown, Jada made a sketch of her design. The longest sides of the two largest triangles must be parallel. What is the measure of ∠3?

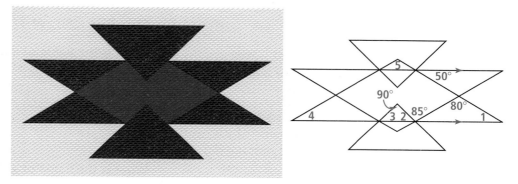

By the Alternate Interior Angles Theorem, $m\angle 1 = 50$. You can use $m\angle 1$ to find $m\angle 2$, and then $m\angle 3$.

Step 1   Find the measure of ∠2.

Together, ∠2 and the 85° angle form an exterior angle to a triangle. Apply the Triangle Exterior Angle Theorem to write an equation using $m\angle 1$ and $m\angle 2$.

$m\angle 2 + 85 = m\angle 1 + 80$ ⟵ The interior angles of the triangle are ∠1 and the 80° angle.

$m\angle 2 + 85 = 50 + 80$

$m\angle 2 = 45$

Step 2   Find the measure of ∠3.

Both ∠2 and ∠3 are in the same triangle. Use the third angle to write an equation.

$m\angle 2 + m\angle 3 + 90 = 180$ ⟵ Apply the Triangle Angle Sum Theorem.

$45 + m\angle 3 + 90 = 180$

$m\angle 3 = 45$

The measure of ∠3 is 45°.

Try It!   **5.** In Jada's sketch, $m\angle 1 = m\angle 4$. What is $m\angle 5$? Explain.

CONCEPT SUMMARY Angle Measures of Triangles

WORDS	**Interior Angle Measures**	**Exterior Angle Measure**

Interior Angle Measures

The sum of the measures of all the angles of a triangle is 180.

Exterior Angle Measure

The measure of each exterior angle of a triangle equals the sum of the measures of its two remote interior angles.

DIAGRAM

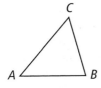

$m\angle A + m\angle B + m\angle C = 180$

$m\angle 1 = m\angle 2 + m\angle 3$

Do You UNDERSTAND?

1. **ESSENTIAL QUESTION** What is true about the interior and exterior angle measures of a triangle?

2. **Error Analysis** Cheng determined that the value of x is 103 and the value of y is 132 in the figure below. What mistake did Cheng make? © MP.3

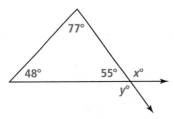

3. **Vocabulary** The word *remote* means distant or far apart. What parts of a figure are *remote interior angles* distant from?

4. **Look for Relationships** Use the Triangle Angle-Sum Theorem to answer the following questions. Explain your answers.

   a. What are the measures of each angle of an equiangular triangle?

   b. If one of the angle measures of an isosceles triangle is 90, what are the measures of the other two angles? © MP.7

Do You KNOW HOW?

What is the value of x in each figure?

5.

6.

What is the value of x in each figure?

7.

8.

9. Write an equation relating the measures of $\angle 1$, $\angle 2$, and $\angle 3$. Write another equation relating the measures of $\angle 1$, $\angle 2$, and $\angle 4$.

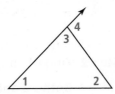

PRACTICE & PROBLEM SOLVING

UNDERSTAND

10. Construct Arguments Write a proof for Theorem 2-10. ⓒ MP.3

11. Higher Order Thinking Marisol claims that each pair of remote interior angles in a triangle has two exterior angles. Do you agree? Use a diagram to support your answer.

12. Error Analysis A student was asked to find the value of x. What error did the student make? ⓒ MP.3

By the Linear Pairs Theorem,
$w + 56 = 180$, so $w = 124$.
By the Triangle Exterior Angle
Theorem, $w = x + 31$, or
$124 = x + 31$, so $x = 93$.

13. Reason Prove the Triangle Exterior Angle Theorem. ⓒ MP.2

14. Mathematical Connections What are the values of x, y, and z? Use theorems to justify each answer.

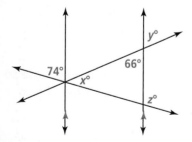

15. Use Structure Write and solve an equation to find the value of x. What is the measure of each labeled angle? ⓒ MP.7

PRACTICE

What are the values of the variables in each figure? SEE EXAMPLES 1–3

16.

17.

18.

19.

What is the value of x in each figure? SEE EXAMPLE 4

20.

21.

22.

23.

For Exercises 24–27, find the measure of each angle. SEE EXAMPLE 4

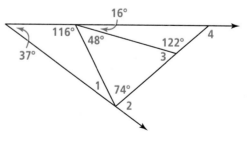

24. ∠1

25. ∠2

26. ∠3

27. ∠4

28. A pennant is in the shape of an isosceles triangle. One leg of the triangle is fastened to a stick. The stick forms an 84° angle with the other leg. What is the measure of each remote interior angle in the triangle? SEE EXAMPLE 5

PRACTICE & PROBLEM SOLVING

29. **Model With Mathematics** Pilar is making a replacement set of sails for a sailboat.

a. What equation can Pilar use that relates the values of *w* and *x*?

b. What equation can Pilar use that relates the values of *y* and *z*? Ⓒ MP.4

30. **Reason** An artist painting from a photo begins with a geometric sketch to match angle measures. What is the value of *z*? Ⓒ MP.2

31. **Look for Relationships** Use the drawing of a beach chair.

a. What is the value of *x*?

b. What is the value of *y*?

c. The chair can lay farther back so that the 70° angle changes to 86° and *x*° changes to 36°. How does this affect the 119° angle? Ⓒ MP.7

32. What are the values of *x*, *y*, and *z*?

33. **SAT/ACT** What is the value of *x*?

Ⓐ 98   Ⓒ 102

Ⓑ 106   Ⓓ 176

34. **Performance Task** A tablet case is supported at the back. The measure of the slant angle of the tablet, ∠1, can be changed, but $m\angle 2 = m\angle 3$ for any slant that is chosen.

Part A A user adjusts the case so that $m\angle 2 = 42$. What are the measures of the other angles?

Part B Is it possible to slant the tablet case so that $m\angle 1 = m\angle 5$? If so, explain how. If not, explain why it is not possible.

Part C A user wants to slant the tablet case so that $m\angle 1 = 2(m\angle 5)$. What should the measure of each of the five angles be?

2-4

Slopes of Parallel and Perpendicular Lines

I CAN... use slope to solve problems about parallel and perpendicular lines.

Common Core State Standards
HSG.GPE.B.4, HSG.GPE.B.5, MP.2, MP.3, MP.4

MODEL & DISCUSS

Pilar and Jake begin climbing to the top of a 100-ft monument at the same time along two different sets of steps at the same rate. The tables show their distances above ground level after a number of steps.

Pilar				
Steps	1	3	17	25
Height (ft)	2	3	10	14

Jake				
Steps	1	7	15	29
Height (ft)	5	8	12	19

$1\frac{1}{2}$ ft $\quad 4\frac{1}{2}$ ft
Ground Level

A. How many feet does each student climb after 10 steps? Explain.

B. Will Pilar and Jake be at the same height after the same number of steps? Explain.

C. **Reason** What would you expect the graphs of each to look like given your answers to parts A and B? Explain. **MP.2**

ESSENTIAL QUESTION

How do the slopes of lines that are parallel to each other compare? How do the slopes of lines that are perpendicular to each other compare?

CONCEPTUAL UNDERSTANDING

EXAMPLE 1 ▸ Slopes of Parallel Lines

A 6-foot-wide scaffolding is used to support workers during the construction of a building. Each flight of stairs rises 8 feet. What is the geometric relationship between the bottom and top flights?

You can represent the flights of stairs using lines in the coordinate plane.

Each point on one line is 16 vertical feet from a corresponding point on the other line. The two lines will never intersect, so they are parallel.

The slope of the line through the origin is $\frac{8 - 0}{6 - 0} = \frac{4}{3}$.

The slope of the other line is $\frac{24 - 16}{6 - 0} = \frac{4}{3}$.

Therefore, the two parallel lines have the same slope.

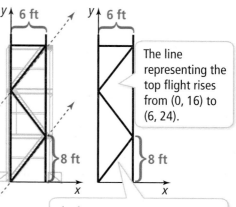

The line representing the top flight rises from (0, 16) to (6, 24).

6 ft   6 ft

8 ft   8 ft

The line representing the bottom flight rises from (0, 0) to (6, 8).

MODEL WITH MATHEMATICS
How would you describe the relationship between the slopes of the parallel lines if the *y*-intercept for the bottom set of stairs were at a point other than (0, 0)? **MP.4**

CONTINUED ON THE NEXT PAGE

EXAMPLE 1 CONTINUED

Try It! 1. A fourth level of scaffolding is 6 feet above the third level. Is the fourth flight of stairs parallel to any of the other flights? Explain.

THEOREM 2-13

Two non-vertical lines are parallel if and only if their slopes are equal.

Any two vertical lines are parallel.

PROOF: SEE LESSON 7-5.

If... p and q are both not vertical	**If...** p and q are both vertical
Then... $p \parallel q$ if and only if the slope of line p = slope of line q	**Then...** $p \parallel q$

EXAMPLE 2 Check Parallelism

Are lines k and n parallel?

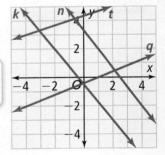

Step 1 Find the slope of line k.

$m = \dfrac{-3 - 2}{2 - (-2)} = -\dfrac{5}{4}$ Line k passes through $(-2, 2)$ and $(2, -3)$.

COMMON ERROR
Be sure that the first numbers in both subtraction expressions are the coordinates of the same point.

Step 2 Find the slope of line n.

$m = \dfrac{-2 - 2}{4 - 1} = -\dfrac{4}{3}$ Line n passes through $(1, 2)$ and $(4, -2)$.

Step 3 Compare the slopes.

Parallel lines have equal slope, but $-\dfrac{5}{4} \neq -\dfrac{4}{3}$. Thus, lines k and n are not parallel.

Try It! 2. Are lines t and q parallel?

THEOREM 2-14

Two non-vertical lines are perpendicular if and only if the product of their slopes is −1.

A vertical line and a horizontal line are perpendicular to each other.

PROOF: SEE LESSON 7-4.

If... p and q are both not vertical

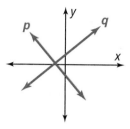

Then... $p \perp q$ if and only if the product of their slopes is −1

If... one of p and q is vertical and the other is horizontal

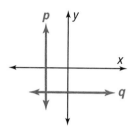

Then... $p \perp q$

EXAMPLE 3 ▶ Check Perpendicularity

Are lines j and k perpendicular?

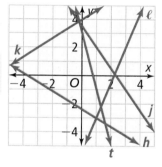

STUDY TIP
Look for two points on each line where you can easily read the coordinates of the points from the graph.

Step 1 Find the slope of line j.

$$m = \frac{2-5}{1-(-1)} = -\frac{3}{2}$$

Line j passes through $(-1, 5)$ and $(1, 2)$.

Step 2 Find the slope of line k.

$$m = \frac{4-2}{0-(-3)} = \frac{2}{3}$$

Line k passes through $(-3, 2)$ and $(0, 4)$.

Step 3 Compare the slopes.

Perpendicular lines have slopes with a product of −1, and $-\frac{3}{2} \cdot \frac{2}{3} = -1$. Thus, lines j and k are perpendicular.

Try It! **3. a.** Are lines h and ℓ perpendicular?

b. Are lines k and t perpendicular?

A. What is an equation of the line through P that is parallel to ℓ?

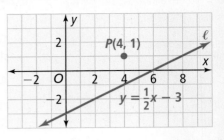

Step 1 Identify the slope of the parallel line.

The slope of ℓ is $\frac{1}{2}$. Parallel lines have equal slope, so the slope of the parallel line is $\frac{1}{2}$.

Step 2 Solve for the y-intercept of the parallel line.

$y = mx + b$

$1 = \frac{1}{2}(4) + b$ Use the point (4, 1).

$b = -1$

Step 3 Write an equation of the line.

$y = \frac{1}{2}x - 1$

The line parallel to ℓ passing through P is $y = \frac{1}{2}x - 1$.

GENERALIZE

If the slope of a line is $\frac{a}{b}$, what is the slope of any line perpendicular to it? How do you know?

B. What is the equation of the line through P that is perpendicular to ℓ?

Step 1 Identify the slope of the perpendicular line.

The slope of ℓ is $\frac{1}{2}$. Perpendicular lines have slopes with a product of -1, so the slope of the perpendicular line is -2.

Step 2 Solve for the y-intercept of the perpendicular line.

$y = mx + b$

$1 = -2(4) + b$ Use the point (4, 1).

$b = 9$

Step 3 Write the equation of the line.

$y = -2x + 9$

The line perpendicular to ℓ passing through P is $y = -2x + 9$.

Try It!   **4.** What are equations of lines parallel and perpendicular to the given line k passing through point T?

   a. $y = -3x + 2$; $T(3, 1)$ **b.** $y = \frac{3}{4}x - 5$; $T(12, -2)$

EXAMPLE 5 ▶ Use Slope to Solve a Problem

A landscape architect is designing her yard, which will have a walkway leading to a shed. She wants the edges of her walkway to be perpendicular to the back of the house. Can she continue using her design, shown below, and add the shed, or will she need to revise the design first?

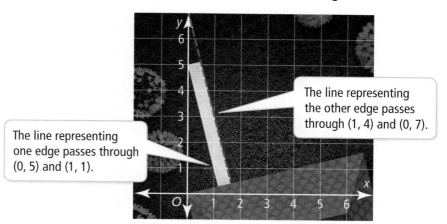

The line representing the other edge passes through (1, 4) and (0, 7).

The line representing one edge passes through (0, 5) and (1, 1).

Assume the edge of the roof of the house is parallel to the back of the house.

Formulate ◀ Find the slopes of each walkway edge to confirm they are parallel. Then find the slope of the edge of the roof to confirm it is perpendicular to the edges of the walkway.

Use the points (0, 5) and (1, 1) to find the slope of one edge of the walkway.

$$m = \frac{1 - 5}{1 - 0} = -4$$

Use the points (0, 7) and (1, 3) to find the slope of the other edge.

$$m = \frac{3 - 7}{1 - 0} = -4$$

The slopes of each edge of the walkway are equal, so the sides are parallel.

Compute ◀ The edge of the roof passes through the points (0, 0) and (4, 1). Use those points to find the slope.

$$m = \frac{1 - 0}{4 - 0} = \frac{1}{4}$$

The line representing the edge of the roof has a slope of $\frac{1}{4}$.

Interpret ◀ Compare the slopes.

Since $-4 \cdot \frac{1}{4} = -1$, the edges of the walkway and the house are perpendicular. The architect can continue using her design.

Try It! 5. The architect wants the front of the shed to be parallel to the back of the house. If one corner of the shed is at (0, 5), can the other corner be at (3, 6.5)? Explain.

CONCEPT SUMMARY Slopes of Parallel and Perpendicular Lines

DIAGRAMS **Parallel Lines**

Perpendicular Lines

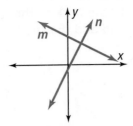

SYMBOLS $j \parallel k$ if and only if the slopes are the same.

$m \perp n$ if and only if the product of the two slopes is -1.

Do You UNDERSTAND?

1. **ESSENTIAL QUESTION** How do the slopes of lines that are parallel to each other compare? How do the slopes of lines that are perpendicular to each other compare?

2. **Error Analysis** Katrina said that the lines $y = -\frac{2}{3}x + 5$ and $y = -\frac{3}{2}x + 2$ are perpendicular. Explain Katrina's error. © MP.3

3. **Reason** Give an equation for a line perpendicular to the line $y = 0$. Is there more than one such line? Explain. © MP.2

4. **Communicate Precisely** What are two different if-then statements implied by Theorem 2-13? © MP.6

5. **Error Analysis** Duante said that $\overleftrightarrow{AB}$ and $\overleftrightarrow{CD}$ for $A(-2, 0)$, $B(2, 3)$, $C(1, -1)$, and $D(5, -4)$ are parallel. Explain and correct Duante's error. © MP.3

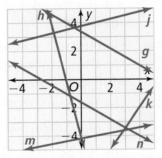

slope of $\overleftrightarrow{AB}$: $\dfrac{3-0}{2-(-2)} = \dfrac{3}{4}$

slope of $\overleftrightarrow{CD}$: $\dfrac{-1-(-4)}{5-1} = \dfrac{3}{4}$

slopes are equal, so $\overleftrightarrow{AB} \parallel \overleftrightarrow{CD}$ ✗

Do You KNOW HOW?

Use the diagram for Exercises 6–9.

6. Are lines g and n parallel?

7. Are lines j and m parallel?

8. Are lines n and k perpendicular?

9. Are lines h and j perpendicular?

10. What is an equation for the line parallel to $y = -x + 7$ that passes through $(7, -2)$?

11. What is an equation for the line perpendicular to $y = 3x - 1$ that passes through $(-9, -2)$?

12. The graph of a roller coaster track goes in a straight line through coordinates $(10, 54)$ and $(42, 48)$, with coordinates in feet. A support beam runs parallel 12 feet below the track. What equation describes the support beam?

PRACTICE & PROBLEM SOLVING

UNDERSTAND

13. Look for Relationships What are the equations of lines *m* and *q*? ⒸMP.7

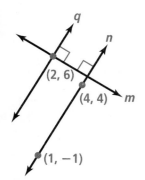

14. Reason Why can you not say that two vertical lines have equal slope? Why can you not say that the product of the slopes of a vertical and horizontal line is −1? ⒸMP.2

15. Higher Order Thinking Lines *k* and *n* intersect on the *y*-axis.

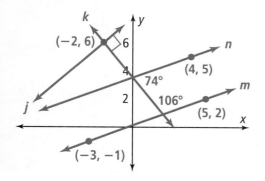

a. What is the equation of line *k* in slope-intercept form?

b. What is the equation of line *j* in slope-intercept form?

16. Construct Arguments Line *m* passes through points *X* and *Y*. Line *n* passes through points *X* and *Z*. If *m* and *n* have equal slope, what can you conclude about points *X*, *Y*, and *Z*? Explain. ⒸMP.3

17. Error Analysis Shaniqua says that the lines $y = -3x - 4$, $y = -\frac{1}{3}x + 6$, $y = -4x - 5$, and $y = \frac{1}{4}x - 5$ could represent the sides of a rectangle. Explain Shaniqua's error. ⒸMP.3

PRACTICE

Compare the slopes of $y = f(x)$ and $y = g(x)$. Is each pair of lines parallel? SEE EXAMPLE 1

18.

x	f(x)	g(x)
0	20	22
1	35	37
2	50	52
3	65	67

19.

x	f(x)	g(x)
0	5	10
1	7	15
2	9	20
3	11	25

Determine if each pair of lines is parallel.
SEE EXAMPLE 2

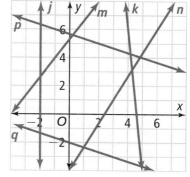

20. *j* and *k*

21. *m* and *n*

22. *p* and *q*

Determine if each pair of lines is perpendicular.
SEE EXAMPLE 3

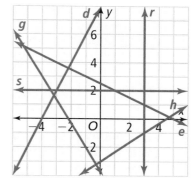

23. *d* and *e*

24. *g* and *h*

25. *r* and *s*

Write equations for the lines that pass through Q and are parallel and perpendicular to the given line. SEE EXAMPLE 4

26. $y = -4x + 1$; $Q(6, -1)$

27. $y = \frac{3}{2}x + 4$; $Q(-1, 1)$

28. A community garden has two faucets. The gardeners want the soaker hoses from the faucets to run parallel to each other. One hose starts at faucet *A*(0, 1) and stretches through point *G*(7, 4.5). The other hose starts at faucet *B*(5, 6). Could the second hose pass through point *F*(−3, 4)? Explain. SEE EXAMPLE 5

PRACTICE & PROBLEM SOLVING

29. **Model With Mathematics** The table shows locations of several sites at a high school campus. A landscaper wants to connect two sites with a path perpendicular to the path connecting the cafeteria and the library. Which two sites should he connect? ⒸMP.4

Locations	
Cafeteria (5, 5)	Library (11, 14)
Office (4, 12)	Gym (15, 8)
Woodshop (11, 6)	Art Studio (3, 16)

30. **Make Sense and Persevere** Are the steepest parts of the two water slides parallel? Explain. ⒸMP.1

31. **Mathematical Connections** Teo rides his bike in a straight line from his location, perpendicular to path A, and Luke rides his bike in a straight line from his location, perpendicular to path B. What are the coordinates of the point where they meet?

ASSESSMENT PRACTICE

32. $\overleftrightarrow{AB} \perp \overleftrightarrow{BC}$ for $A(-3, 2)$ and $C(2, 7)$. Which of the following could be the coordinates of B? Select all that apply.

Ⓐ (8, 0)　　　　　Ⓓ (1, 3)

Ⓑ (−2, 2)　　　　Ⓔ (−1, −1)

Ⓒ (−4, 5)　　　　Ⓕ (−3, 7)

33. **SAT/ACT** Line k passes through $(2, -3)$ and $(8, 1)$. Which equation represents a line that is parallel to k?

Ⓐ $y = -\frac{2}{3}x - \frac{5}{3}$　　Ⓒ $y = \frac{3}{2}x - 6$

Ⓑ $y = \frac{2}{3}x - \frac{13}{3}$　　Ⓓ $y = -\frac{3}{2}x$

34. **Performance Task** A knight travels in a straight line from the starting point to Token 1. The knight can only make right-angle turns to get to Tokens 2 and 3.

Part A Since the knight can only make right-angle turns, what are the slopes of the straight line paths the knight can travel?

Part B What is the fewest number of turns that the knight can take in order to get all three tokens?

MATHEMATICAL MODELING IN 3 ACTS

Common Core State Standards
HSG.CO.C.9, HSG.GPE.B.4, HSG.MG.A.3, MP.4

Parallel Paving Company

Powered By **desmos**

Building roads consists of many different tasks. Once civil engineers have designed the road, they work with surveyors and construction crews to clear and level the land. Sometimes specialists have to blast away rock in order to clear the land. Once the land is leveled, the crews bring in asphalt pavers to smooth out the hot asphalt.

Sometimes construction crews will start work at both ends of the new road and meet in the middle. Think about this during the Mathematical Modeling in 3 Acts lesson.

ACT 1 Identify the Problem

1. What is the first question that comes to mind after watching the video?

2. Write down the main question you will answer about what you saw in the video.

3. Make an initial conjecture that answers this main question.

4. Explain how you arrived at your conjecture.

5. What information will be useful to know to answer the main question? How can you get it? How will you use that information?

ACT 2 Develop a Model

6. Use the math that you have learned in this Topic to refine your conjecture.

ACT 3 Interpret the Results

7. Did your refined conjecture match the actual answer exactly? If not, what might explain the difference?

1. What properties are specific to parallel lines and perpendicular lines?

Vocabulary Review

Choose the correct term to complete each sentence.

2. Angles that are outside the space between parallel lines and that lie on the same side of a transversal are _____.

3. A _____ intersects coplanar lines at distinct points.

4. Two angles inside a triangle that correspond to the nonadjacent exterior angle are the _____.

5. _____ lie on the same side of a transversal of parallel lines and are in corresponding positions relative to the parallel lines.

6. Angles between parallel lines that are nonadjacent and that lie on opposite sides of a transversal are _____.

7. Angles between parallel lines that are on the same side of a transversal are _____.

- alternate exterior angles
- alternate interior angles
- corresponding angles
- exterior angle of a triangle
- remote interior angles
- same-side exterior angles
- same-side interior angles
- transversal

Concepts & Skills Review

LESSON 2-1 & 2-2 **Parallel Lines and Proving Lines Parallel**

Quick Review

When two **parallel lines** are intersected by a **transversal**, the angle pairs that are formed have special relationships. These angle pairs are either congruent or supplementary angles.

Example

Which angles are supplementary to ∠3?

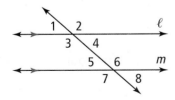

∠1, ∠4, ∠5, ∠8

Practice & Problem Solving

Use the figure for Exercises 8–9.

8. Suppose $\ell \parallel m$. What is the measure of each angle if $m\angle 2 = 138$?

    a. $m\angle 1$ **b.** $m\angle 3$ **c.** $m\angle 4$

9. If $m\angle 1 = 3x - 3$ and $m\angle 5 = 7x + 23$, for what value of x is $\ell \parallel m$?

10. **Reason** The transversal that intersects two parallel lines forms corresponding angles with measures $m\angle 1 = 3x - 7$ and $m\angle 2 = 2x + 12$. What is the measure of each angle? ⓒ **MP.2**

LESSON 2-3 — Parallel Lines and Triangle Angle Sums

Quick Review

The interior and exterior angle measures of a triangle have the following properties.
- The sum of the interior angles of every triangle is 180°.
- The measure of each **exterior angle of a triangle** equals the sum of the measures of the two corresponding **remote interior angles**.

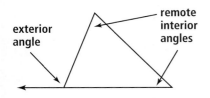

Example

What is $m\angle 1$?

$m\angle 1 = 36 + 127$
$m\angle 1 = 163$

Practice & Problem Solving

What is the value of x in each figure?

11.

12.

13.

14.

15. **Make Sense and Persevere** During a storm, a tree is blown against a building so that it forms a triangle with remote interior angles of 90° and 52°. What is the measure of the corresponding exterior angle formed by the leaning tree? Ⓒ MP.1

LESSON 2-4 — Slopes of Parallel and Perpendicular Lines

Quick Review

Two non-vertical lines are parallel if they have the same slope. Two vertical lines are parallel to each other.

Two non-vertical lines are perpendicular if the product of the slopes is −1. A vertical line is perpendicular to a horizontal line.

Example

What is the equation of a line that is parallel to the line $y = 3x - 9$ and passes through (6, 12)?

The slope of the line is 3.
Solve for the y-intercept of the parallel line:

$$y = mx + b$$
$$12 = (3)(6) + b$$
$$b = -6$$

The equation of the parallel line is $y = 3x - 6$.

Practice & Problem Solving

Use the figure for Exercises 16–17. Show the calculations you use to answer each question.

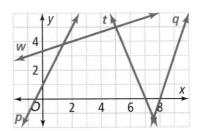

16. Are lines p and q parallel?

17. Are lines w and t perpendicular?

18. **Reason** Theorem 2-4 states that two non-vertical lines are perpendicular if and only if the product of their slopes is −1. Why are vertical lines excluded? Ⓒ MP.2

19. **Use Structure** Write an equation for each line that passes through (2, 7) and is parallel or perpendicular to the line $y = -3x - 6$. Ⓒ MP.7

TOPIC 3

Transformations

What are properties of the four types of rigid motion?

Topic Overview

enVision® STEM Project:
  Create an Animation

Mathematical Modeling in 3 Acts:
  The Perplexing Polygon

Topic Vocabulary

- composition of rigid motions
- glide reflection
- perpendicular bisector
- point symmetry
- reflectional symmetry
- rigid motion
- rotational symmetry

Digital Experience

INTERACTIVE STUDENT EDITION
Access online or offline.

ACTIVITIES Complete *Explore & Reason*, *Model & Discuss*, and *Critique & Explain* activities. Interact with *Examples* and *Try Its.*

CONCEPT SUMMARY Review key lesson content through multiple representations.

ASSESSMENT Show what you've learned.

 Go online | **SavvasRealize.com**

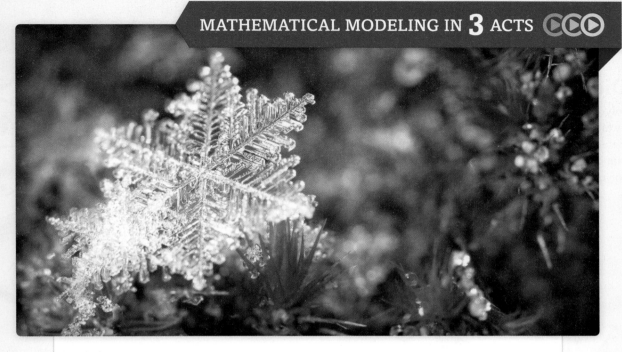

MATHEMATICAL MODELING IN 3 ACTS ◉◉▶

The Perplexing Polygon

Look around and you will see shapes and patterns everywhere you look. The tiles on a floor are often all the same shape and fit together to form a pattern. The petals on a flower often make a repeating pattern around the center of the flower. When you look at snowflakes under a microscope, you can notice that they are made up of repeating three-dimensional crystals. Think about the patterns you have seen during the Mathematical Modeling in 3 Acts lesson.

▶ **VIDEOS** Watch clips to support *Mathematical Modeling in 3 Acts Lessons* and **enVision**® *STEM Projects.*

▶ **TUTORIALS** Get help from *Virtual Nerd*, right when you need it.

✎ **PRACTICE** Practice what you've learned.

✎ **ADAPTIVE PRACTICE** Practice that is *just right* and *just for you.*

🗂 **FAMILY ENGAGEMENT** Involve family in your learning.

A-Z **GLOSSARY** Read and listen to English and Spanish definitions.

🔧 **MATH TOOLS** Explore math with digital tools and manipulatives.

〰 **DESMOS** Use Anytime and as embedded Interactives in Lesson content.

Did You Know?

Polygonal modeling uses polygons to model the surfaces of three-dimensional objects. Animators use vertices and edges to define polygons (usually triangles or quadrilaterals), and they use multiple polygons to create more complex shapes.

The phenakistoscope was invented nearly **200 years ago**. When the viewer looks through a slot, a sequence of images appears to show moving figures.

An animated character represents hundreds of hours of work. An animator builds a *mesh* of polygons connected through shared vertices and edges. A rigger links the mesh to a system of joints and control handles. To represent a curved surface in a realistic way, the animator uses a mesh of many small polygons. Then the animator programs the joints and handles so that the character moves realistically. Finally, an artist provides surface texture and shading.

Your Task: Create an Animation

Starting with the pixels (points) of a simple geometric figure, you and your classmates will use translations and reflections to move the figure through a series of frames.

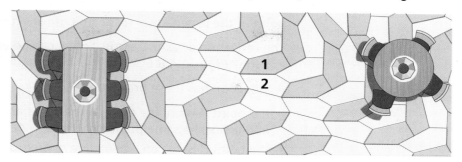
3-1

Reflections

I CAN... draw and describe the reflection of a figure across a line of reflection.

VOCABULARY

- rigid motion
- perpendicular bisector

Common Core State Standards
HSG.CO.A.2, HSG.CO.A.4,
HSG.CO.A.5, MP.2, MP.5, MP.7

EXPLORE & REASON

The illustration shows irregular pentagon-shaped tiles covering a floor.

A. Which tiles are copies of tile 1? Explain.

B. **Communicate Precisely** If you were to move tile 1 from the design, what actions would you have to do so it completely covers tile 2? Ⓒ **MP.6**

C. Which tiles are *not* copies of tile 1? Explain.

ESSENTIAL QUESTION How are the properties of reflection used to transform a figure?

EXAMPLE 1 Identify Rigid Motions

A rigid motion is a transformation that preserves length and angle measure. Does the transformation appear to be a rigid motion? Explain.

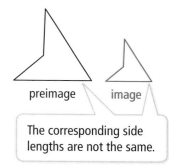

Although angle measure is preserved, the image is smaller than the preimage, so the transformation involves a change in length.

The transformation is not a rigid motion because the length is not preserved.

> The corresponding side lengths are not the same.

STUDY TIP

A transformation can be described as a function that maps each point of a given figure called the preimage onto corresponding points of the resulting figure, the image.

Try It! **1.** Is each transformation a rigid motion? Explain.

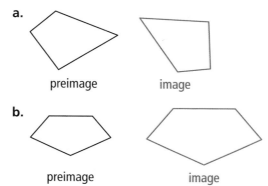

a.
preimage   image

b.
preimage   image

CONCEPT Reflections

A reflection is a transformation that reflects each point in the preimage across a line of reflection.

The reflection of $\triangle ABC$ across line m can be written as $r_m(\triangle ABC) = \triangle A'B'C'$.

A reflection has these properties:

- If a point A is on line m, then the point and its image are the same point (that is, $A' = A$).
- If a point B is not on line m, line m is perpendicular to and bisects $\overline{BB'}$.
- The orientation, or the position of points relative to each other, is not preserved.

A reflection is a rigid motion since length and angle measures are preserved.

CONCEPTUAL UNDERSTANDING

EXAMPLE 2 Reflect a Figure Across a Line

How can you reflect $\triangle FGH$ across line ℓ?

Use the properties of reflections to draw the image of $\triangle FGH$.

VOCABULARY

A *perpendicular bisector* of a segment is a line, segment, or ray that is perpendicular to the segment and divides the segment into two congruent segments.

Step 1 Draw lines through points F, G, and H that are perpendicular to line ℓ.

The line of reflection is the *perpendicular bisector* of the segment connecting corresponding preimage and image points.

Step 2 On each line, mark points F', G', and H', so that $FP = F'P$, $GQ = G'Q$, and $HR = H'R$.

Step 3 Connect the vertices to draw $\triangle F'G'H'$.

Try It! 2. Sketch the reflection of $\triangle LMN$ across line n.

EXAMPLE 3   Reflect a Figure on a Coordinate Plane

Quadrilateral *FGHJ* has coordinates *F*(0, 3), *G*(2, 4), *H*(4, 2), and *J*(−2, 0).

A. Graph and label *FGHJ* and $r_{x\text{-axis}}$(*FGHJ*). What is a general rule for reflecting a point across the *x*-axis?

Step 1 Graph *FGHJ*.

Step 2 Find *F'*, *G'*, *H'*, and *J'* and draw *F'G'H'J'*.

Because *J* is on the line of reflection, *J'* = *J*.

$$r_{x\text{-axis}}(0, 3) = (0, -3)$$

$$r_{x\text{-axis}}(2, 4) = (2, -4)$$

$$r_{x\text{-axis}}(4, 2) = (4, -2)$$

$$r_{x\text{-axis}}(-2, 0) = (-2, 0)$$

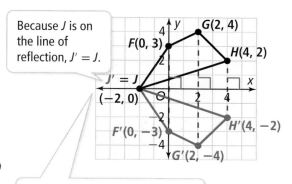

The *x*-axis is the line of reflection, so it is the perpendicular bisector of $\overline{FF'}$, $\overline{GG'}$, and $\overline{HH'}$.

The rule for any point (*x*, *y*) reflected across the *x*-axis is (*x*, *y*) → (*x*, −*y*).

$$r_{x\text{-axis}}(x, y) = (x, -y)$$

B. Graph and label *FGHJ* and $r_{y\text{-axis}}$(*FGHJ*). What is a general rule for reflecting a point across the *y*-axis?

Step 1 Graph *FGHJ*.

Step 2 Find *F'*, *G'*, *H'*, and *J'* and draw *F'G'H'J'*.

$$r_{y\text{-axis}}(0, 3) = (0, 3)$$

$$r_{y\text{-axis}}(2, 4) = (-2, 4)$$

$$r_{y\text{-axis}}(4, 2) = (-4, 2)$$

$$r_{y\text{-axis}}(-2, 0) = (2, 0)$$

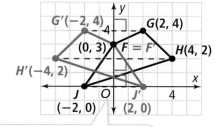

The *y*-axis is the line of reflection, so it is the perpendicular bisector of $\overline{GG'}$, $\overline{HH'}$, and $\overline{JJ'}$.

The rule for any point (*x*, *y*) reflected across the *y*-axis is (*x*, *y*) → (−*x*, *y*).

$$r_{y\text{-axis}}(x, y) = (-x, y)$$

USE APPROPRIATE TOOLS
You can use tracing paper to draw or confirm a reflected image. First, trace the preimage and the line of reflection. Then, flip the tracing paper over and align the traced line of reflection with the actual line of reflection. The tracing paper shows where the image should be located. ⓒ **MP.5**

COMMUNICATE PRECISELY
A reflection can be described as a function that maps every point of the preimage (the input) to a corresponding point of the image (output). ⓒ **MP.6**

Try It!   **3.** Triangle *ABC* has vertices *A*(−5, 6), *B*(1, −2), and *C*(−3, −4). What are the coordinates of the vertices of △*A'B'C'* for each reflection?

a. $r_{x\text{-axis}}$

b. reflection across the *y*-axis

CONCEPT Reflecting Points Across the *x*-axis and *y*-axis

The rule for reflecting any point (x, y) on the coordinate plane across the *x*-axis is:

$$r_{x\text{-axis}}(x, y) = (x, -y)$$

The rule for reflecting any point (x, y) on the coordinate plane across the *y*-axis is:

$$r_{y\text{-axis}}(x, y) = (-x, y)$$

EXAMPLE 4 **Describe a Reflection on the Coordinate Plane**

What reflection maps △*KLM* to its image?

Step 1 Write the coordinates of the preimage and the image.

$K(-3, 5)$ $L(1, 3)$ $M(-5, 1)$

$K'(5, -3)$ $L'(3, 1)$ $M'(1, -5)$

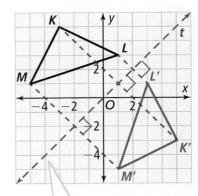

Step 2 Find the midpoints of the segments connecting two pairs of corresponding points.

Midpoint of $\overline{KK'}$:

$$\left(\frac{-3 + 5}{2}, \frac{5 + (-3)}{2}\right) = (1, 1)$$

Midpoint of $\overline{MM'}$:

$$\left(\frac{-5 + 1}{2}, \frac{1 + (-5)}{2}\right) = (-2, -2)$$

> The line of reflection is the perpendicular bisector of the segments that connect corresponding vertices of the preimage and image.

Step 3 Write the equation of the line through the midpoints.

Find the slope.

$$m = \frac{1 - (-2)}{1 - (-2)}$$
$$= 1$$

Use point-slope form.

$$y - 1 = 1 \cdot (x - 1)$$
$$y = x$$

STUDY TIP
When providing a rule, you must clearly define the line of reflection. Be certain that the line of reflection is the perpendicular bisector of segments between preimage and image points.

The transformation is a reflection across the line $y = x$. You can write this reflection rule as $r_{y = x}(\triangle KLM) = (\triangle K'L'M')$, or $r_m(x, y) = (y, x)$, where *m* is the line $y = x$.

Try It! **4.** What is a reflection rule that maps each triangle to its image?

    a. $C(3, 8)$, $D(5, 12)$, $E(4, 6)$ and $C'(-8, -3)$, $D'(-12, -5)$, $E'(-6, -4)$

    b. $F(7, 6)$, $G(0, -4)$, $H(-5, 0)$ and $F'(-5, 6)$, $G'(2, -4)$, $H'(7, 0)$

EXAMPLE 5 Use Reflections

An animator is creating an animation of a billiards game. The animated player must hit the white cue ball so that it hits the red ball without touching the yellow ball. At what point on the top rail should the animator make the cue ball bounce off the top rail so that it hits the red ball?

Consider the top rail to be the line of reflection and reflect the red ball across it.

Draw the segment from the cue ball to the image of the red ball.

The line of reflection is drawn where the cue ball will bounce.

Reflect the segment from the cue ball to the red ball across the line of reflection.

The player should hit point P, where the two segments intersect.

MAKE SENSE AND PERSEVERE
What do you notice about the angles formed by the line of reflection and the path of the cue ball? Which angles are congruent? ⓒ MP.1

Try It! 5. Student A sees the reflected image across the mirror of another student who appears to be at B'. Trace the diagram and show the actual position of Student B.

B'
•

——————————————— mirror

•
A

CONCEPT SUMMARY Reflections

DIAGRAM

The reflection line m is the perpendicular bisector of $\overline{BB'}$ and $\overline{CC'}$.

$r_m(\triangle ABC) = \triangle A'B'C'$

GRAPH

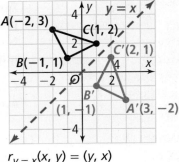

$r_{y\,=\,x}(x, y) = (y, x)$

$r_{x\text{-axis}}(x, y) = (x, -y)$

$r_{y\text{-axis}}(x, y) = (-x, y)$

Do You UNDERSTAND?

1. **ESSENTIAL QUESTION** How are the properties of reflection used to transform a figure?

2. **Error Analysis** Oscar drew the image of a triangle reflected across the line $y = -1$. What mistake did Oscar make? © MP.3

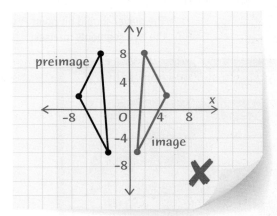

3. **Vocabulary** One meaning of the word *rigid* is "not bendable," and another is "unable to be changed." How do those meanings correspond to the definition of rigid motion?

4. **Communicate Precisely** How can you determine whether the transformation of a figure is a rigid motion? © MP.6

5. **Generalize** Describe the steps you must take to identify the path an object will follow if it bounces off a surface and strikes another object. © MP.8

Do You KNOW HOW?

6. Does the transformation shown appear to be a rigid motion? Explain.

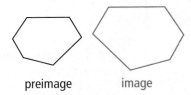

preimage   image

What are the coordinates of each image?

7. $r_{x\text{-axis}}(-5, 3)$ 8. $r_{x\text{-axis}}(1, 6)$

9. Write a reflection rule that maps each triangle to its image.

   a. $J(1, 0)$, $K(-5, 2)$, $L(4, -4)$ and $J'(-9, 0)$, $K'(-3, 2)$, $L'(-12, -4)$

   b. $P(8, 6)$, $Q(-4, 12)$, $R(7, 7)$ and $P'(8, -20)$, $Q'(-4, -26)$, $R'(7, -21)$

10. Squash is a racket sport like tennis, except that the ball must bounce off a wall between returns. Trace the squash court. At what point on the front wall should player 1 aim in order to reach the rear wall as far from player 2 as possible?

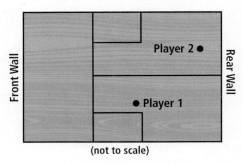

(not to scale)

PRACTICE & PROBLEM SOLVING

UNDERSTAND

11. **Look for Relationships** Becky draws a triangle with vertices $A(6, 7)$, $B(9, 3)$, and $C(4, -2)$ on a coordinate grid. She reflects the triangle across the line $y = 4$ to get $\triangle DEF$. She then reflects the image across the line $x = 3$ to get $\triangle JKL$. ⓒ **MP.7**

    a. What are the coordinates of $\triangle DEF$ and $\triangle JKL$?

    b. Write a rule for each reflection.

12. **Use Structure** Under a transformation, a preimage and its image are both squares with side length 3. Is the transformation a rigid motion? Explain. ⓒ **MP.7**

For Exercises 13 and 14, use the art of the miniature golf hole below.

13. **Error Analysis** Jacob is playing miniature golf. He says that he cannot hit the ball from the start, bounce it off the back wall once, and reach the hole in one shot. Is Jacob correct? Trace and label a diagram to support your answer. ⓒ **MP.3**

14. **Higher Order Thinking** Jacob wants to bounce the ball off the back wall and then the right wall. Draw a diagram to show how Jacob can hit the ball so that it reaches the hole after two bounces.

15. **Mathematical Connection** Talisha reflects point $A(2, 5)$ across line ℓ to get image point $A'(6, 1)$. What is an equation for line ℓ?

16. **Look for Structure** Can a figure be reflected across three lines of reflection so the image is the original figure? Explain. ⓒ **MP.7**

PRACTICE

For Exercises 17 and 18, does each transformation appear to be a rigid motion? Explain. SEE EXAMPLE 1

17.

preimage   image

18.

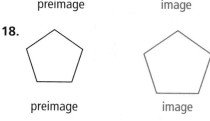

preimage   image

For Exercises 19–24, suppose m is the line with equation $x = -5$, line n is the line with equation $y = 1$, line g is the line with equation $y = x$, and line h is the line with equation $y = -2$. Given $A(9, -3)$, $B(6, 4)$, and $C(-1, -5)$, what are the coordinates of the vertices of $\triangle A'B'C'$ for each reflection? SEE EXAMPLES 2 AND 3

19. $r_{x\text{-axis}}$ 20. $r_{y\text{-axis}}$

21. r_m 22. r_n

23. r_g 24. r_h

For Exercises 25–28, what is a reflection rule that maps each triangle and its image? SEE EXAMPLE 4

25. $D(3, 6)$, $E(-4, -3)$, $F(6, 1)$ and $D'(1, 6)$, $E'(8, -3)$, $F'(-2, 1)$

26. $G(9, 12)$, $H(-2, -15)$, $J(3, 8)$ and $G'(9, -2)$, $H'(-2, 25)$, $J'(3, 2)$

27. $K(7, -6)$, $L(9, -3)$, $M(-4, 6)$ and $K'(7, -4)$, $L'(9, -7)$, $M'(-4, -16)$

28.

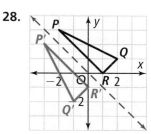

29. Trace the diagram below. Where does the shopper in a dressing room see her image in each mirror? SEE EXAMPLE 5

mirror 2

mirror 1   ● shopper   mirror 3

PRACTICE & PROBLEM SOLVING

APPLY

30. **Look for Relationships** The Moroccan zellij mosaic shown uses tiles of various shapes. Which numbered tiles cannot be mapped to another numbered tile by a rigid motion? Ⓒ MP.7

31. **Use Structure** Laquinta is inside a shop and sees the sign on the window from the back. Draw the letters as they would appear from the outside of the shop. Is the transformation a rigid motion? Ⓒ MP.7

32. **Make Sense and Persevere** Look at the floor plan below. Abdul sees the image of a clock in the mirror on the door. Ⓒ MP.1

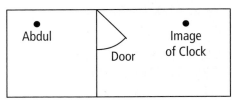

a. Trace the diagram. Where is the line of reflection? Explain.

b. Where is the clock located? Explain.

c. Find where Abdul's image is located relative to the line of reflection. Can Abdul see himself in the mirror? Explain.

ASSESSMENT PRACTICE

33. Classify whether each pair of figures appears to be a *rigid motion* or *not a rigid motion*.

34. **SAT/ACT** $\triangle ABC$ with vertices $A(3, 9)$, $B(2, -7)$, and $C(6, 14)$ is reflected, resulting in $\triangle A'B'C'$ with vertices $A'(-25, 9)$, $B'(-24, -7)$, and $C'(-28, 14)$.

What is the line of reflection?

Ⓐ $x = 11$ Ⓒ $x = -11$

Ⓑ $x = 22$ Ⓓ $x = -22$

35. **Performance Task** Sound echoes from a solid object in the same way that light reflects from a mirror. A hiker at point A shouts the word hello. The hiker at point B first hears the shout directly and later hears the echo.

Part A Trace the diagram. Show the path taken by the sound the hiker at point B hears echoing from the cliff.

Part B Sound travels at about 1,000 feet per second. After how long does the hiker at point B hear the shout directly? After how long does he hear the echo? Show your work.

3-2
Translations

I CAN... draw and describe the translation of a figure.

VOCABULARY
• composition of rigid motions

Common Core State Standards
HSG.CO.A.2, HSG.CO.A.4, HSG.CO.A.5, HSG.CO.B.6, MP.3, MP.6, MP.7

EXPLORE & REASON

Powered By desmos

Draw a copy of *ABCD* on a grid. Using another color, draw a copy of *ABCD* on the grid in a different location with the same orientation, and label it *QRST*.

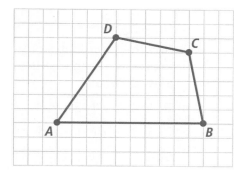

A. On another sheet of paper, write instructions that describe how to move *ABCD* to the location of *QRST*.

B. Exchange instructions with a partner. Follow your partner's instructions to draw a third shape *EFGH* in another color on the same grid. Compare your drawings. Do your drawings look the same? Explain.

C. Communicate Precisely What makes a set of instructions for this Explore & Reason a good set of instructions? **MP.6**

ESSENTIAL QUESTION

What are the properties of a translation?

CONCEPT Translations

STUDY TIP
When *r* is positive, the translation is *r* units to the right. When *r* is negative, the translation is |*r*| units to the left. When *s* is positive, the translation is *s* units up. When *s* is negative, the translation is |*s*| units down.

A translation is a transformation in a plane that maps all points of a preimage the same distance and in the same direction.

The translation $(x, y) \rightarrow (x + r, y + s)$ maps the preimage (x, y) to its image |*r*| units along the *x*-axis and |*s*| units along the *y*-axis. The translation for $\triangle ABC$ can be written as $T_{\langle r, s \rangle}$ $(\triangle ABC) = \triangle A'B'C'$.

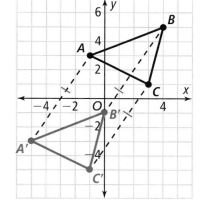

A translation has the following properties:

If $T_{\langle r, s \rangle} (\triangle ABC) = \triangle A'B'C'$, then

• $\overline{AA'} \parallel \overline{BB'} \parallel \overline{CC'}$.
• $\overline{AA'} \cong \overline{BB'} \cong \overline{CC'}$.
• $\triangle ABC$ and $\triangle A'B'C'$ have the same orientation.

A translation is a rigid motion since length and angle measure are preserved.

EXAMPLE 1 **Find the Image of a Translation**

What is the graph of $T_{\langle 7, -4\rangle}(\triangle EFG)$?

Each point of $\triangle EFG$ is translated 7 units right and 4 units down.

$T_{\langle 7, -4\rangle}(x, y) = (x + 7, y - 4)$

Find the coordinates of the vertices of the image. Then plot the points and draw $\triangle E'F'G'$.

$E(-5, 4) \rightarrow E'(-5 + 7, 4 - 4) = E'(2, 0)$

$F(-1, 5) \rightarrow F'(-1 + 7, 5 - 4) = F'(6, 1)$

$G(-2, -1) \rightarrow G'(-2 + 7, -1 - 4) = G'(5, -5)$

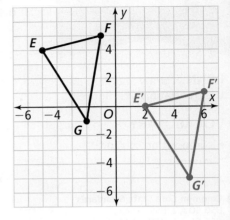

> **COMMON ERROR**
> The translation does not only map the vertices of the preimage to the vertices of the image. The translation maps all points of $\triangle EFG$ onto $\triangle E'F'G'$.

Try It! **1.** What are the vertices of $\triangle E'F'G'$ for each translation?

a. $T_{\langle 6, -7\rangle}(\triangle EFG) = \triangle E'F'G'$

b. $\triangle EFG$ is translated 11 units right and 2 units up

---

EXAMPLE 2 **Write a Translation Rule**

What translation rule maps $STUV$ onto $S'T'U'V'$?

Use one pair of corresponding vertices to determine the change in the horizontal and vertical directions between the preimage to its image.

> Use the vertex $S(-5, 6)$ and its image $S'(-6, 2)$.

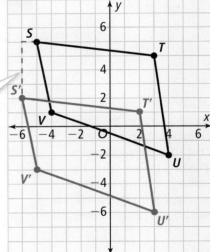

Change in the horizontal direction x:

$-6 - (-5) = -1$

Change in the vertical direction y:

$2 - 6 = -4$

The translation rule for each point is $(x, y) \rightarrow (x - 1, y - 4)$, or $T_{\langle -1, -4\rangle}$. You can verify the rule on the remaining vertices.

> **LEARN TOGETHER**
> What are ways to stay positive and work toward goals?

Try It! **2.** What translation rule maps $P(-3, 1)$ to its image $P'(2, 3)$?

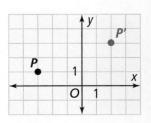

CONCEPT Composition of Rigid Motions

A **composition of rigid motions** is a transformation with two or more rigid motions in which the second rigid motion is performed on the image of the first rigid motion.

Step 1 Translate $\triangle ABC$ left 2 units and up 5 units.

$$(r_\ell \circ T_{\langle -2, 5 \rangle})(\triangle ABC)$$

This notation uses a small open circle to indicate a composition of rigid motions on $\triangle ABC$.

Step 2 Reflect $\triangle A'B'C'$ across line ℓ.

APPLICATION

EXAMPLE 3 Compose Translations

A producer is creating an animation in which a dancer moves from position A to position B and then to position C. What single transformation describes the dancer's move from position A to position C?

Formulate ◀ Let (0, 0) represent position A. The translation from A to B is $T_{\langle 2, 2 \rangle}(x, y)$. The translation from B to C is $T_{\langle 1, -1 \rangle}(x, y)$. The dancer's final position is the composition of those two translations.

Compute ◀ Find $T_{\langle 1, -1 \rangle} \circ T_{\langle 2, 2 \rangle}(x, y)$.

$T_{\langle 2, 2 \rangle}(x, y) = (x + 2, y + 2)$

$T_{\langle 1, -1 \rangle}(x + 2, y + 2) = (x + 3, y + 1)$

First, apply $T_{\langle 2, 2 \rangle}$. Then apply $T_{\langle 1, -1 \rangle}$ to the result.

Interpret ◀ The translation $T_{\langle 3, 1 \rangle}(A)$ represents a single transformation that maps the dancer's move from position A to position C.

Try It! **3.** What is the composition of the transformations written as one transformation?

a. a translation 1 unit right and 1 unit down, then a translation 3 units right and 2 units down

b. $T_{\langle -4, 0 \rangle} \circ T_{\langle -2, 5 \rangle}$

CONCEPTUAL
UNDERSTANDING

EXAMPLE 4 Relate Translations and Reflections

How is a composition of reflections across parallel lines related to a translation?

> **Step 1** Reflect $\triangle ABC$ across the y-axis. The image is $\triangle A'B'C'$.

> **Step 2** Reflect $\triangle A'B'C'$ across line m. The image is $\triangle A''B''C''$.

STUDY TIP
After the first reflection, the orientation of the figure is reversed. After the second reflection, the orientation of the figure returns to that of the preimage.

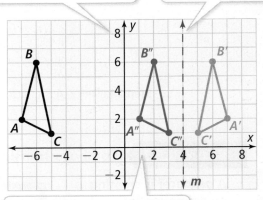

> Notice that the distance between corresponding points on the y-axis and line m is 4 units and $BB'' = AA'' = CC'' = 8$ units.

If $\triangle ABC$ is translated 8 units to the right, its image is also $\triangle A''B''C''$.

So, $(r_m \circ r_{y\text{-axis}})(\triangle ABC) = T_{\langle 8, 0\rangle}(\triangle ABC)$.

Try It!   4. Suppose n is the line with equation $y = 1$. Given $\triangle DEF$ with vertices $D(0, 0)$, $E(0, 3)$, and $F(3, 0)$, what translation image is equivalent to $(r_n \circ r_{x\text{-axis}})(\triangle DEF)$?

THEOREM 3-1

A translation is a composition of reflections across two parallel lines.

- Both reflection lines are perpendicular to the line containing a preimage point and its corresponding image point.

- The distance between the preimage and the image is twice the distance between the two reflection lines.

PROOF: SEE EXAMPLE 5.

If... $T(ABC) = A''B''C''$

$AA'' = BB'' = CC'' = 2d$

Then... $(r_n \circ r_m)(ABC) = A''B''C''$

EXAMPLE 5 ▸ Prove Theorem 3-1

Given: A translation T, with $T(C) = C''$

Prove: There exist parallel lines m and n such that $T = r_n \circ r_m$.

Plan: The given information says the translation T maps C to C''. First find a composition of reflections that maps C to C''. Then show that this composition of reflections is equivalent to the translation T for *any* point. (There are several cases to consider. One case is shown below.)

Proof: Let C' be the midpoint of $\overline{CC''}$, and let $CC' = C'C'' = d$. Let m be the perpendicular bisector of $\overline{CC'}$ and n be the perpendicular bisector of $\overline{C'C''}$.

By the properties of reflections $r_m(C) = C'$ and $r_n(C') = C''$, so $(r_n \circ r_m)(C) = C''$. Also, the distance between n and m is d and the distance between C and C'' is $2d$.

Now pick another point B and show that $(r_n \circ r_m)(B) = T(B)$. To do this, show that $BB'' = CC'' = 2d$, and $\overline{BB''} \parallel \overline{CC''}$.

First reflect across m. Call the image B'. Let the distance from B to m and the distance from m to B' be x.

Now reflect B' across n. Call the image B''. Since the distance between m and n is d, the distance between B' and n is $d - x$. By the properties of reflections, the distance between n and B'' is also $d - x$.

So $BB'' = x + x + (d - x) + (d - x) = 2d$.

Since $\overline{CC''}$ and $\overline{BB''}$ are both perpendicular to m and n, they are parallel to each other.

Therefore $(r_n \circ r_m)(B) = T(B)$.

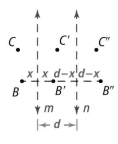

CONSTRUCT ARGUMENTS
The choice of C and C'' were arbitrary. Why does this mean that this proof is valid for any translation? ⒸMP.3

Try It! 5. Suppose the point B you chose in the Proof of Theorem 3-1 was between lines m and n. How would that affect the proof? What are the possible cases you need to consider?

CONCEPT SUMMARY Translations and Compositions of Rigid Motions

WORDS A translation is a transformation that maps all points the same distance and in the same direction.

A composition of two reflections across parallel lines is a translation.

GRAPH

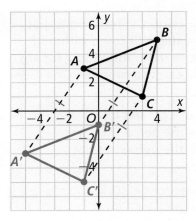

DIAGRAM

SYMBOLS A translation of $\triangle ABC$ 4 units left and 6 units down is $\triangle A'B'C'$:

$$T_{\langle -4, -6 \rangle}(\triangle ABC) = \triangle A'B'C'$$

$\overline{AA'}$, $\overline{BB'}$, and $\overline{CC'}$ are congruent to each other: $\overline{AA'} \cong \overline{BB'} \cong \overline{CC'}$

$$T(ABC) = (r_n \circ r_m)(ABC)$$

$$AA'' = BB'' = CC'' = 2d$$

Do You UNDERSTAND?

1. **ESSENTIAL QUESTION** What are the properties of a translation?

2. **Error Analysis** Nori says that for any $\triangle XYZ$, the reflection over the y-axis composed with the reflection over the x-axis is equivalent to a translation of $\triangle XYZ$. Explain Nori's error. Ⓒ **MP.3**

3. **Vocabulary** Write an example of a composition of rigid motions for $\triangle PQR$.

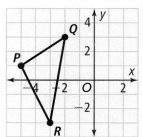

4. **Make Sense and Persevere** What are the values of x and y if $T_{\langle -2, 7 \rangle}(x, y) = (3, -1)$? Ⓒ **MP.1**

Do You KNOW HOW?

For Exercises 5 and 6, the vertices of $\triangle XYZ$ are $X(1, -4)$, $Y(-2, -1)$, and $Z(3, 1)$. For each translation, give the vertices of $\triangle X'Y'Z'$.

5. $T_{\langle -4, -3 \rangle}(\triangle XYZ)$ 6. $T_{\langle 5, -3 \rangle}(\triangle XYZ)$

7. What is the rule for the translation shown?

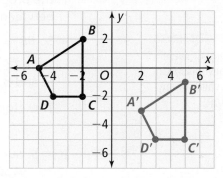

For Exercises 8 and 9, write each composition of translations as one translation.

8. $T_{\langle 7, 8 \rangle} \circ T_{\langle -3, -4 \rangle}$ 9. $T_{\langle 0, 3 \rangle} \circ T_{\langle 4, 6 \rangle}$

10. How far apart are two parallel lines m and n such that $T_{\langle 12, 0 \rangle}(\triangle JKL) = (r_n \circ r_m)(\triangle JKL)$?

PRACTICE & PROBLEM SOLVING

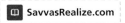
UNDERSTAND

11. Error Analysis Hugo graphed $\triangle PQR$ and $(r_t \circ T_{\langle 3, 1 \rangle})(\triangle PQR)$ where the equation of line t is $y = 2$. His translation and reflection were both correct. What mistake did Hugo make? **© MP.3**

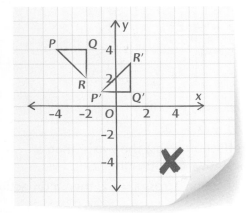

12. Mathematical Connections Suppose line k has equation $x = 3$. Compare the areas of $ABCD$ and $A''B''C''D'' = (T_{\langle 1, 2 \rangle} \circ r_k)(ABCD)$. Justify your answer.

13. Make Sense and Persevere A robot travels from position A to B to C to D. What composition of rigid motions represents those moves? **© MP.1**

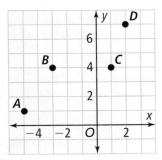

14. Higher Order Thinking How can you describe the complete transformation to a person who cannot see the transformations below?

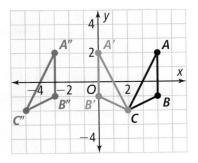

PRACTICE

For Exercises 15–17, give the coordinates of the image. SEE EXAMPLE 1

15. $T_{\langle 3, -1 \rangle}(\triangle ABC)$ for $A(5, 0)$, $B(-1, 2)$, $C(6, -3)$

16. $T_{\langle -4, 0 \rangle}(\triangle DEF)$ for $D(3, 3)$, $E(-2, 3)$, $F(0, 2)$

17. $T_{\langle -10, -5 \rangle}(\triangle GHJ)$ for $G(0, 0)$, $H(3, 6)$, $J(12, -1)$

18. What is the rule for the rigid motion? SEE EXAMPLE 2

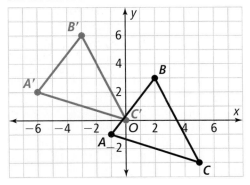

19. Write a composition of translations that is equivalent to $(x, y) \rightarrow (x + 8, y - 5)$. SEE EXAMPLE 3

20. Given $\triangle XYZ$, line n with equation $x = -2$, and line p with equation $x = 2$, write a translation rule that is equivalent to $r_n \circ r_p (\triangle XYZ)$. SEE EXAMPLE 4

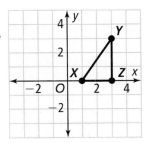

For Exercises 21–24, write each composition of translations as one translation. SEE EXAMPLE 3

21. $T_{\langle -3, 3 \rangle} \circ T_{\langle -2, 4 \rangle}$

22. $T_{\langle -4, -3 \rangle} \circ T_{\langle 3, 1 \rangle}$

23. $T_{\langle 5, -6 \rangle} \circ T_{\langle -7, 5 \rangle}$

24. $T_{\langle 8, -2 \rangle} \circ T_{\langle -4, 9 \rangle}$

For Exercises 25–28, write each composition of reflections as one translation. Suppose k is the line with equation $x = -3$, ℓ is the line with equation $x = -2$, m is the line with equation $x = 1$, n is the line with equation $x = -1$, p is the line with equation $y = 1$, q is the line with equation $y = 3$, s is the line with equation $y = 2$, and t is the line with equation $y = -4$. SEE EXAMPLE 4

25. $r_k \circ r_\ell$ **26.** $r_m \circ r_n$ **27.** $r_p \circ r_q$ **28.** $r_s \circ r_t$

29. The distance between vertical lines a and b is 6 units and a is left of b. If $T_{\langle x, 0 \rangle}(\triangle JKL) = (r_b \circ r_a)(\triangle JKL)$, what is the value of x? SEE EXAMPLE 5

PRACTICE & PROBLEM SOLVING

APPLY

30. **Communicate Precisely** Benjamin walks from his house to Timothy's house and then to school. Describe Benjamin's walk as a composition of translations. If Benjamin walks from his house directly to school, what translation describes his walk? © **MP.6**

1 = 80ft

Use the map for Exercises 31 and 32.

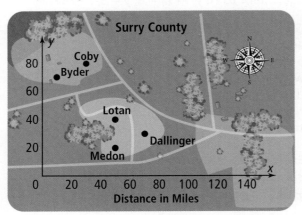

31. **Model With Mathematics** The Surry County sheriff's patrol route starts in Coby. The composition of rigid motions $T_{\langle -20, 10 \rangle} \circ T_{\langle 40, -50 \rangle}$ describes her route. How would you describe the sheriff's route in words? © **MP.4**

32. **Reason** What composition of rigid motions describes a car trip starting in Medon, stopping in Dallinger, and then going on to Byder? © **MP.2**

ASSESSMENT PRACTICE

33. Which rigid motions, when applied to $\triangle ABC$, result in $\triangle A''B''C''$?

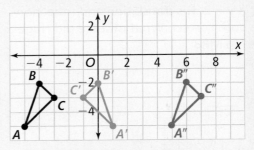

□ **A.** $(x, y) \rightarrow (x, y + 10)$

□ **B.** $(x, y) \rightarrow (x + 10, y)$

□ **C.** a reflection across the y-axis, then a translation 6 units right

□ **D.** a reflection across $x = -2$, then a reflection across $x = 3$

□ **E.** a translation 2 units right, then a reflection across $x = 3$

34. **SAT/ACT** Which transformation or composition of transformations is equivalent to a translation 6 units left and 4 units up, then a translation 1 unit left and 3 units up?

Ⓐ a reflection across the line $x = -7$

Ⓑ a translation 7 units left and 7 units up

Ⓒ a reflection across the line $x = 7$

Ⓓ a translation 5 units left and 1 unit up

35. **Performance Task** Rectangle $WXYZ$ has a perimeter of 16 units and an area of 15 square units.

Part A Graph $WXYZ$ on a sheet of graph paper. Write a composition of rigid motions describing two reflections of $WXYZ$ across parallel lines of your choosing. Graph and label the parallel lines, $W'X'Y'Z'$, and $W''X''Y''Z''$.

Part B Write a single rigid motion that is equivalent to the composition of rigid motions in Part B. Justify your answer.

Part C Compare the perimeter and area of $WXYZ$ and $W''X''Y''Z''$. What can you conclude about the effect of translation on the properties of figures?

3-3

Rotations

I CAN... draw and describe the rotation of a figure about a point of rotation for a given angle of rotation.

Common Core State Standards
HSG.CO.A.2, HSG.CO.A.4,
HSG.CO.A.5, HSG.CO.B.6,
MP.1, MP.6, MP.7

STUDY TIP
Unless otherwise stated, rotations are always performed counterclockwise.

CRITIQUE & EXPLAIN

Filipe says that the next time one of the hands of the clock points to 7 will be at 7:00 when the hour hand points to 7. Nadia says that it will be at 5:35 when the minute hand points to 7.

A. Whose statement is correct? Explain.

B. Communicate Precisely Suppose the numbers on the clock face are removed. Write instructions that another person could follow to move the minute hand from 2 to 6. © MP.6

ESSENTIAL QUESTION What are the properties that identify a rotation?

EXAMPLE 1   Draw a Rotated Image

How can you perform a 75° rotation of △XYZ about point P?

To rotate △XYZ 75° about point P, each point in the triangle must rotate 75° counterclockwise. Then the measure of the angle formed by each preimage point, point P, and the corresponding image point is 75°.

Use a ruler and protractor to draw 75° angles from each vertex on △XYZ with point P, and mark image points that are the same distance from P.

Step 1 To rotate X, draw $\overline{PX}$ to form one side of a 75° angle.

Step 2 Measure the angle and draw the other side, PX′. Mark point X′ so PX′ = PX.

Step 3 Repeat Step 1 and Step 2 for Y and Z in order to locate points Y′ and Z′.

Step 4 Connect the image points to form △X′Y′Z′.

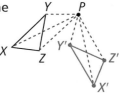

Try It! **1.** Do you think a rotated image would ever coincide with the original figure? Explain.

CONCEPT Rotations

A rotation $R_{(x°, P)}$ is a transformation that rotates each point in the preimage about a point P, called the center of rotation, by an angle measure of $x°$, called the angle of rotation. A rotation has these properties:

- The image of P is P' (that is, $P' = P$).
- For a preimage point A, $PA = PA'$ and $m\angle APA' = x°$.
- Orientation is preserved.

A rotation is a rigid motion, so length and angle measure are preserved. Note that a rotation is counterclockwise for a positive angle measure.

CONCEPT Rotations in the Coordinate Plane

Rules can be used to rotate a figure 90°, 180°, and 270° about the origin O in the coordinate plane.

$R_{(90°, O)} (x, y) = (-y, x)$ $R_{(180°, O)} (x, y) = (-x, -y)$ $R_{(270°, O)} (x, y) = (y, -x)$

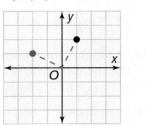

EXAMPLE 2 Draw Rotations in the Coordinate Plane

What is $R_{(90°, O)}$ ABCD?

A rotation of 90° about the origin follows the rule $(x, y) \rightarrow (-y, x)$.

Determine the vertices of the image.

$A(3, 5) \rightarrow A'(-5, 3)$

$B(1, 7) \rightarrow B'(-7, 1)$

$C(-2, 4) \rightarrow C'(-4, -2)$

$D(2, -1) \rightarrow D'(1, 2)$

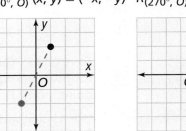

Draw $A'B'C'D'$ on the coordinate plane.

LOOK FOR RELATIONSHIPS
Compare the distance of each vertex from the origin for the preimage and image. What relationships must they have? © MP.7

Try It! 2. The vertices of $\triangle XYZ$ are $X(-4, 7)$, $Y(0, 8)$, and $Z(2, -1)$.

    a. What are the vertices of $R_{(180°, O)}(\triangle XYZ)$?

    b. What are the vertices of $R_{(270°, O)}(\triangle XYZ)$?

EXAMPLE 3 Use Rotations

The first drummer in a drumline is at the 20 yard line and the sixth drummer is at the 35 yard line. The drumline rotates counterclockwise 180° about the sixth drummer and then rotates 135° clockwise about the first drummer. Where does the sixth drummer stand after the rotations? Describe the change in position as a composition of rotations.

Represent the first drummer as point *B* and the sixth drummer as point *A*.

First, rotate the drumline 180° counterclockwise about point *A*.

Second, rotate the drumline 135° clockwise about point *B'*.

The sixth drummer stands at the position labeled *A″*. The drumline is first transformed by the rotation $R_{(180°, A)}$ and then by the rotation $R_{(-135°, B')}$.

Try It! **3. a.** Suppose the drumline instead turns counterclockwise about *B'*. How many degrees must it rotate so that the sixth drummer ends in the same position?

b. Can the composition of rotations be described by $R_{(45°, A)}$ since 180° − 135° = 45°? Explain.

EXAMPLE 4 Investigate Reflections and Rotations

LOOK FOR RELATIONSHIPS
Consider how properties of the
transformations are related. What
properties would you consider
in determining the number of
reflections needed? Ⓒ MP.7

Can you find a sequence of reflections that result in the same image as a rotation?

The image of *JKLM* rotated about point *T* is *WXYZ*. Try to reflect *JKLM* one or more times so that the image aligns with *WXYZ*.

Step 1 Draw line *p* through point *T* and reflect *JKLM* across *p* to form *J′K′L′M′*.

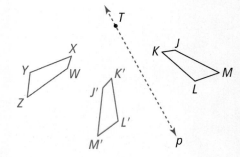

Step 2 Think about how to reflect *J′K′L′M′* to form *WXYZ*. Connect corresponding points in *J′K′L′M′* and *WXYZ* and then find each midpoint.

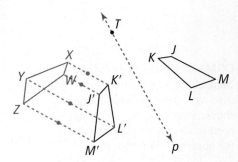

Step 3 The midpoints appear to be collinear with *T*. Draw line *q* through the midpoints and *T*. The reflection of *J′K′L′M′* across *q* is *WXYZ*.

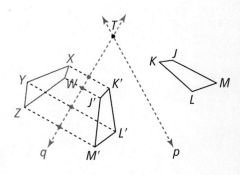

Try It! 4. Perform the same steps shown, except draw line *p* so that it does not pass through *T*. Do you get the same results? Explain.

THEOREM 3-2

Any rotation is a composition of reflections across two lines that intersect at the center of rotation.

The angle of rotation is twice the angle formed by the lines of reflection.

If...

Then...

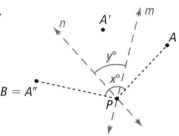

PROOF: SEE EXAMPLE 5.

$$y = \frac{1}{2}x$$

PROOF

EXAMPLE 5   Prove Theorem 3-2

Prove Theorem 3-2.

Given: $R_{(x°, P)}(A) = B$

Prove: There exist two lines m and n such that $(r_n \circ r_m)(A) = R_{(x°, P)}(A)$ equals B, and the measure of the angle formed by lines m and n is $\frac{1}{2}x$.

Proof:

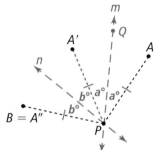

> **LOOK FOR RELATIONSHIPS**
> Think about how to construct lines to help you in the proof. What properties does the angle bisector preserve as a line of reflection? ⒸMP.7

Mark a point Q anywhere except on $\overrightarrow{PA}$. Draw line m through Q and P. Reflect A across m to image A'. The reflection line is an angle bisector of $\angle APA'$. Let $m\angle APQ = m\angle A'PQ = a$.

Construct the angle bisector n of $\angle BPA'$. Reflect A' across n to image A''. Since a reflection is rigid motion, $PA = PA' = PA'' = PB$. So $A'' = B$. The congruent angles formed measure b. Therefore, $R_{(x°, P)}(A) = (r_n \circ r_m)(A)$.

The angle of rotation $x°$ has a measure equal to $a + a + b + b$, or $2(a + b)$. The angle formed by lines m and n has a measure equal to $a + b$, or $\frac{1}{2}x$.

Try It!   **5.** Suppose point Q is closer to point B or even outside of $\angle APB$. Does the relationship still hold for the angle between the reflection lines and the angle between the preimage and the image? Explain.

DIAGRAMS

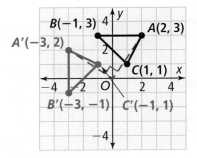

SYMBOLS

$R_{(x°,\ P)}(\triangle ABC) = \triangle A'B'C'$

$PA = PA',\ PB = PB',\ PC = PC'$

$m\angle APA' = m\angle BPB' = m\angle CPC' = x$

$R_{(90°,\ O)}(x, y) = (-y, x)$

$R_{(180°,\ O)}(x, y) = (-x, -y)$

$R_{(270°,\ O)}(x, y) = (y, -x)$

Do You UNDERSTAND?

1. **ESSENTIAL QUESTION** What are the properties that identify a rotation?

2. **Error Analysis** Isabel drew the diagram below to show the rotation of $\triangle DEF$ about point T. What is her error? **© MP.3**

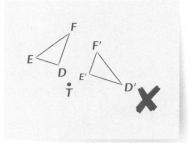

3. **Vocabulary** How is the *center of rotation* related to the *center of a circle*?

4. **Construct Arguments** In the diagram, $\triangle A''B''C''$ is the image of reflections of $\triangle ABC$ across lines p and q. It is also the image of a rotation of $\triangle ABC$ about R. What is the angle of rotation? Explain. **© MP.3**

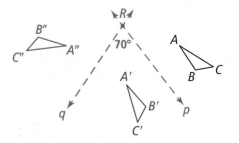

Do You KNOW HOW?

Trace each figure and draw its rotated image.

5. $R_{(90°,\ P)}(\overline{MN})$

6. $R_{(120°,\ T)}(\triangle ABC)$

Give the coordinates of each image.

7. $R_{(180°,\ O)}(\overline{GH})$ for $G(2, -9)$, $H(-1, 3)$

8. a rotation of $\triangle XYZ$ 90° about the origin, for $X(0, 3)$, $Y(1, -4)$, and $Z(5, 2)$

Trace each figure and draw two lines of reflection such that the composition of the reflections across the lines maps onto the image shown.

9.

10.

PRACTICE & PROBLEM SOLVING

UNDERSTAND

11. Construct Arguments When you rotate a figure, does every point move the same distance? Explain. ⒼMP.3

12. Error Analysis Ting says that △X'Y'Z' is a rotation of △XYZ about P. What is the correct transformation from △XYZ to △X'Y'Z'? ⒼMP.3

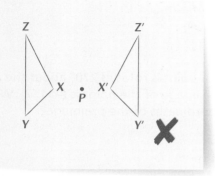

13. Mathematical Connections Points A' and B' are the images of points A and B after a 270° rotation about the origin. If the slope of $\overleftrightarrow{AB}$ is −3, what is the slope of $\overleftrightarrow{A'B'}$? Explain.

14. Use Structure The diagram shows $R_{(90°, O)}(ABCD)$. What are the coordinates of ABCD? ⒼMP.7

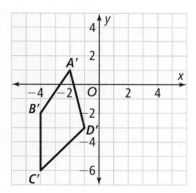

15. Higher Order Thinking In the diagram, $R_{(180°, O)}(\triangle ABC) = \triangle A'B'C'$. Describe a composition of a rotation and a translation that results in the same image.

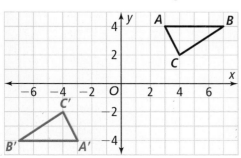

PRACTICE

For Exercises 16–18, trace each figure and draw its rotated image. SEE EXAMPLES 1 AND 3

16. $R_{(80°, P)}(\triangle ABC)$

17. $R_{(110°, Q)}(\triangle DEFG)$

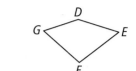

18. $R_{(175°, R)}(\triangle HJK)$

For Exercises 19–22, give the coordinates of each image. SEE EXAMPLE 2

19. $R_{(90°, O)}(\triangle DEF)$ for D(0, 5), E(−2, 8), F(−3, −5)

20. $R_{(270°, O)}(WXYZ)$ for W(4, −2), X(7, 3), Y(1, 11), Z(−4, 6)

21. $R_{(180°, O)}(\triangle STU)$ for S(−2, −6), T(−5, 3), U(1, 0)

22. $R_{(360°, O)}(JKLM)$ for J(−4, 7), K(1, 5), L(6, 1), M(3, −9)

23. Trace the point and triangle. Draw the image $R_{(160°, T)}(\triangle XYZ)$. Then draw two reflections that result in the same image. SEE EXAMPLES 4 AND 5

24. Find the angle of rotation for the rotation about point S that is the composition $r_n \circ r_m$. Then trace the figure and draw the image.

PRACTICE & PROBLEM SOLVING

25. Make Sense and Persevere What rotation must the driver gear make for gear A to rotate 90° clockwise? Explain how you found your answer. Ⓒ **MP.1**

Gear A   Driver Gear

26. Reason Luis is programming an animation during which points flash in sequence, one at a time, around a circle. He calculates that the coordinates of the first four points in his sequence are (6, 0), (5.5, 2.3), (4.2, 4.2), and (2.3, 5.5). He can find the rest of the coordinates by rotating each of the first four points by 90°, 180°, and 270°. What are the coordinates of the points that complete the sequence around the circle? Ⓒ **MP.2**

27. Communicate Precisely Lourdes created the design below by rotating △ABF, quadrilateral BCEF, and △CDE. Describe the rotations she used. How do you determine the angles of rotation? Ⓒ **MP.6**

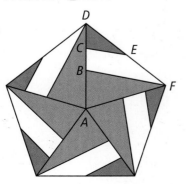

28. Quadrilateral $J'K'L'M'$ is the image of $JKLM$ rotated about point P. Select all true statements that describe the relationship between $JKLM$ and $J'K'L'M'$.

☐ **A.** $m\angle J'K'L' \cong m\angle JKL$

☐ **B.** $\overline{LM} \cong \overline{JK}$

☐ **C.** $m\angle KLM \cong m\angle J'K'L'$

☐ **D.** $\overline{K'L'} \cong \overline{ML}$

☐ **E.** $\overline{J'K'} \cong \overline{JK}$

29. SAT/ACT A point is rotated 270° about the origin. The image of the point is (−11, 7). What are the coordinates of the preimage?

Ⓐ (7, −11)

Ⓑ (−7, −11)

Ⓒ (7, 11)

Ⓓ (11, 7)

30. Performance Task Use graph paper, a protractor, and a straight edge to complete the task.

Part A On a coordinate plane, draw an irregular quadrilateral $ABCD$ at a location of your choice. Draw image $A'B'C'D'$ by rotating $ABCD$ 112° about the origin.

Part B Construct two lines of reflection that map $ABCD$ onto $A'B'C'D'$. Write the equations of these lines in point-slope form.

3-4

Classification of Rigid Motions

I CAN... identify different rigid motions used to transform two-dimensional shapes.

VOCABULARY
• glide reflection

Common Core State Standards
HSG.CO.A.5, HSG.CO.B.6, MP.2, MP.4, MP.7

CRITIQUE & EXPLAIN

Two students are trying to determine whether compositions of rigid motions are commutative. Paula translates a triangle and then reflects it across a line. When she reflects and then translates, she gets the same image. She concludes that compositions of rigid motions are commutative.

Translate. Then reflect.

Reflect. Then translate.

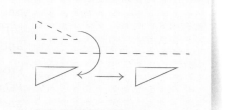

Keenan rotates a triangle and then reflects it. When he changes the order of the rigid motions, he gets a different image. He concludes that compositions of rigid motions are not commutative.

Rotate. Then reflect.

Reflect. Then rotate.

A. Should Paula have used grid paper? Explain.

B. Communicate Precisely Do you agree with Paula or with Keenan? Explain. **MP.6**

ESSENTIAL QUESTION How are properties of the four types of rigid motions similar or different?

THEOREM 3-3

The composition of two or more rigid motions is a rigid motion.

If...

Then...

$(N \circ M)$: $QRST \rightarrow Q''R''S''T''$ is a rigid motion.

M: $QRST \rightarrow Q'R'S'T'$ and
N: $Q'R'S'T' \rightarrow Q''R''S''T''$ are rigid motions.

PROOF: SEE EXAMPLE 1.

PROOF →

EXAMPLE 1 ▸ Prove Theorem 3-3

Write a paragraph proof of Theorem 3-3.

Given: *T* and *S* are rigid motions.

Prove: *S* ∘ *T* is a rigid motion.

Plan: Let *P*, *Q*, and *R* be any three noncollinear points in the preimage. You want to show that length and angle measure are preserved, so it is sufficient to show that $PQ = P''Q''$ and $m\angle PQR = m\angle P''Q''R''$.

Proof: Since *T* and *S* are rigid motions, $PQ = P'Q'$, $P'Q' = P''Q''$, $m\angle PQR = m\angle P'Q'R'$, and $m\angle P'Q'R' = m\angle P''Q''R''$.

By the Transitive Property of Equality, $PQ = P''Q''$ and $m\angle PQR = m\angle P''Q''R''$.

S ∘ *T* is a rigid motion because it preserves length and angle measure.

Try It! 1. Describe how you can use the reasoning used to prove Theorem 3-3 to show that the theorem is true when composing three rigid motions. Can your strategy be extended to include any number of rigid motions?

EXAMPLE 2 ▸ Explore Glide Reflections

A. **Is there a rigid motion that maps △*ABC* to △*A'B'C'*?**

Observe that $m\angle A = m\angle A'$, $m\angle B = m\angle B'$, and $m\angle C = m\angle C'$.

Also, $AB = A'B'$, $AC = A'C'$, and $BC = B'C'$.

Length and angle measure are preserved, so the transformation is a rigid motion.

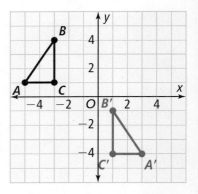

B. **Does a reflection, translation, or rotation map △*ABC* to △*A'B'C'*?**

Since the orientation of △*ABC* is not preserved, the rigid motion is not a translation or rotation.

By observation, the perpendicular bisector of $\overline{BB'}$ is not the perpendicular bisector of $\overline{AA'}$ or $\overline{CC'}$. Therefore, the rigid motion is not a reflection.

CONTINUED ON THE NEXT PAGE

EXAMPLE 2 CONTINUED

C. What composition of two rigid motions maps △ABC to △A′B′C′?

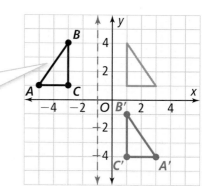

> Because △ABC has a clockwise orientation and △A′B′C′ has a counterclockwise orientation, orientation is not preserved. This means that one of the rigid motions must be a reflection.

Reflect △ABC across k, the line with equation x = −1.

Then translate the image down 5 units.

$(T_{\langle 0, -5 \rangle} \circ r_k)(\triangle ABC) = \triangle A'B'C'$

The composition of a reflection followed by a translation in a direction parallel to the line of reflection is a rigid motion called a **glide reflection**.

USE STRUCTURE
Often there is more than one composition of rigid motions that maps a preimage to its image. What is another composition of rigid motions that maps △ABC to △A′B′C′? © **MP.7**

Try It! **2.** Draw the image of △ABC translated 5 units down followed by a reflection across line k with equation x = −1. What conclusion can you draw about the order of the rigid motions in a glide reflection?

APPLICATION

EXAMPLE 3 **Find the Image of a Glide Reflection**

A digital artist is reproducing a tire tread pattern from a partial tire print at a crime scene by applying a glide reflection. She uses the rule $T_{\langle 0, 0.1 \rangle} \circ r_{y\text{-axis}}$ to generate a pattern. Confirm that her rule can be applied to the partial pattern that was taken from the crime scene.

Step 1 Apply the first rigid motion.

Reflect the outlined preimage across the line x = 0.

Step 2 Apply the second rigid motion.

Translate the reflection 0.1 unit up.

The rule appears to map the pieces of the partial pattern onto itself.

COMMON ERROR
The notation tells you the order in which you should use the transformations. Remember that in the composition $T_{\langle 0, 0.1 \rangle} \circ r_{y\text{-axis}}$, the reflection is performed first.

Try It! **3.** Quadrilateral RSTV has vertices R(−3, 2), S(0, 5), T(4, −4), and V(0, −2). Use the rule $T_{\langle 1, 0 \rangle} \circ r_{x\text{-axis}}$ to graph and label the glide reflection of RSTV.

THEOREM 3-4

Any rigid motion is either a translation, reflection, rotation, or glide reflection.

If... M is a rigid motion

Then... M is a reflection, r_ℓ, or
M is a translation, $T_{\langle x, y \rangle}$, or
M is a rotation, $R_{(n°, P)}$, or
M is a composition of
a reflection and a
translation, $T_{\langle x, y \rangle} \circ r_\ell$

COROLLARY TO THEOREM 3-4

Any rigid motion can be expressed as a composition of reflections.

PROOF: SEE EXERCISE 8.

If... M is a rigid motion

Then... M is either a reflection, r_ℓ, a composition of two reflections, $r_\ell \circ r_m$, or a composition of three reflections, $r_\ell \circ r_m \circ r_n$.

EXAMPLE 4   Determine a Glide Reflection

What is the glide reflection that maps $\triangle JKL$ to $\triangle J''K''L''$?

To determine the glide reflection, you can work backward.

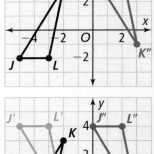

Step 1 Determine the translation.

First determine the translation that vertically aligns J'' with J and L'' with L. It is 5 units horizontally and 0 units vertically.

Step 2 Determine the line of reflection.

The vertices of an image and preimage are the same distance from the line ℓ with equation $y = 1$, so ℓ is the line of reflection. If you reflect $\triangle J'K'L'$ across ℓ, you map back to the original triangle, $\triangle JKL$.

Step 3 Write the complete glide reflection.

Reflecting $\triangle JKL$ across the line $y = 1$, then translating it 5 units right will map it to $\triangle J''K''L''$.

$\left(T_{\langle 5, 0 \rangle} \circ r_\ell \right)(\triangle JKL) = J'K'L'$, where ℓ is the line $y = 1$

> **STUDY TIP**
> The vertices of the preimage and of the image are equidistant from the line of reflection.

Try It!   **4.** What is the glide reflection that maps each of the following?

     a. $\triangle ABC \rightarrow \triangle A'B'C'$ given $A(-3, 4)$, $B(-4, 2)$, $C(-1, 1)$, $A'(1, 1)$, $B'(2, -1)$, and $C'(-1, -2)$.

     b. $\overline{RS} \rightarrow \overline{R'S'}$ given $R(-2, 4)$, $S(2, 6)$, $R'(4, 0)$, and $S'(8, -2)$.

CONCEPT SUMMARY Types of Rigid Motions

Any rigid motion is either a reflection, translation, rotation, or glide reflection.

REFLECTION

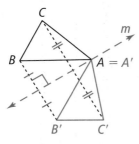

$$r_m(\triangle ABC) = \triangle A'B'C'$$

TRANSLATION

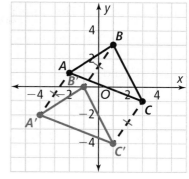

$$T_{\langle -2,\, -3 \rangle}(\triangle ABC) = \triangle A'B'C'$$

ROTATION

$$R_{(x°,\, P)}(\triangle ABC) = \triangle A'B'C'$$

GLIDE REFLECTION

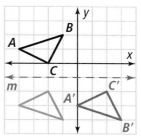

$$\left(T_{\langle 4,\, 0 \rangle} \circ r_m \right)(\triangle ABC) = \triangle A'B'C'$$

Do You UNDERSTAND?

1. **ESSENTIAL QUESTION** How are properties of the four types of rigid motions similar or different?

2. Is it correct to say that the composition of a translation followed by a reflection is a glide reflection? Explain.

3. **Error Analysis** Tamika draws the following diagram as an example of a glide reflection. What error did she make? Ⓒ **MP.3**

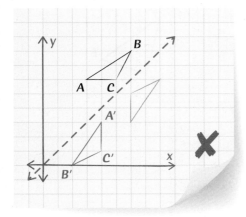

Do You KNOW HOW?

Use the figures for Exercises 4–7. Identify each rigid motion as a translation, a reflection, a rotation, or a glide reflection.

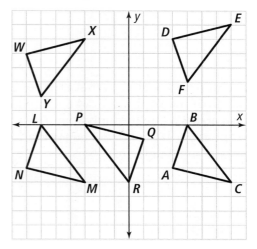

4. $\triangle WYX \rightarrow \triangle NLM$ 5. $\triangle DFE \rightarrow \triangle WYX$

6. $\triangle WYX \rightarrow \triangle ABC$ 7. $\triangle NLM \rightarrow \triangle QRP$

PRACTICE & PROBLEM SOLVING

UNDERSTAND

8. Construct Arguments Write a paragraph proof of the Corollary to Theorem 3-4. Ⓒ **MP.3**

9. Error Analysis Damian draws the diagram for the glide reflection $(T_{\langle 0, 7\rangle} \circ r_{y\text{-axis}})(ABCD)$. What error did he make? Ⓒ **MP.3**

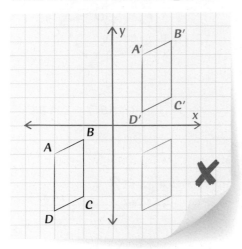

10. Higher Order Thinking What are the reflection and translation for the glide reflection shown? Sketch the intermediate image.

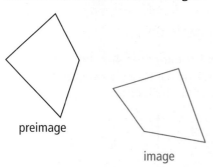

preimage

image

11. Mathematical Connections What are the coordinates of the vertices of △$A'B'C'$ after a reflection across a line through point P with a y-intercept at $y = -2$, followed by translation 3 units right and 3 units up?

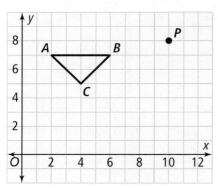

PRACTICE

12. What are two rigid motions with a composition that map △JKL to △$J'K'L'$?

SEE EXAMPLES 1 AND 2

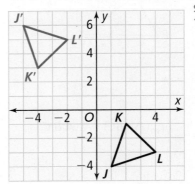

For Exercises 13–17, given $A(6, -4)$, $B(3, 8)$, and $C(-7, 9)$, determine the coordinates of the vertices of △$A'B'C'$ for each glide reflection. Suppose p is the line $x = -3$, q is the line $y = 9$, and r is the line $y = -2$. SEE EXAMPLE 3

13. $(T_{\langle 0, -2\rangle} \circ r_{y\text{-axis}})(\triangle ABC) = \triangle A'B'C'$

14. $(T_{\langle 4, 0\rangle} \circ r_{x\text{-axis}})(\triangle ABC) = \triangle A'B'C'$

15. $(T_{\langle 0, 8\rangle} \circ r_p)(\triangle ABC) = \triangle A'B'C'$

16. $(T_{\langle -5, 0\rangle} \circ r_q)(\triangle ABC) = \triangle A'B'C'$

17. $(T_{\langle 7, 0\rangle} \circ r_r)(\triangle ABC) = \triangle A'B'C'$

For Exercises 18–21, write a rule that maps △DEF to △$D'E'F'$. SEE EXAMPLE 4

18. $D(7, -2)$, $E(3, 9)$, $F(8, 6)$; $D'(-5, 1)$, $E'(-1, 12)$, $F'(-6, 9)$

19. $D(-5, 8)$, $E(1, 4)$, $F(6, 3)$; $D'(-3, 8)$, $E'(3, 12)$, $F'(8, 13)$

20. $D(0, 4)$, $E(6, 3)$, $F(9, 8)$; $D'(-6, -8)$, $E'(0, -7)$, $F'(3, -12)$

21.

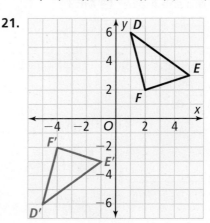

PRACTICE & PROBLEM SOLVING

22. Look for Relationships The graphing software shown is being used to design a quilt. The design can be described by two glide reflections from triangle 1 to triangle 5. Write the rules for each glide reflection. ⓒ MP.7

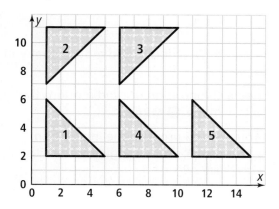

23. Model With Mathematics Each parking space in the figure can be the image of another parking space as a glide reflection. What is the rule that maps the parking space where the red car is parked to the parking space where the blue car is parked? ⓒ MP.4

24. Look for Relationships Rocks shaped like quadrilaterals are embedded into a rock-climbing wall following a pattern of glide reflections. If the pattern starts from tile 1 and continues, what are the shapes and locations of the next two quadrilateral rocks the builder will place in the wall? Explain. ⓒ MP.7

25. For each rigid motion, identify the image.

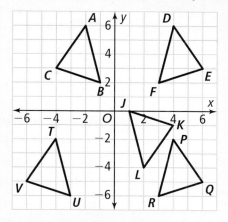

I. △ABC rotated 180° about the point (0, 1)

II. △TUV reflected across the y-axis, then translated 8 units up

III. △DFE reflected across the y-axis, then translated 2 units right

IV. △TUV reflected across the y-axis

26. SAT/ACT If △ABC with vertices A(7, 1), B(2, 9), and C(3, −5), is reflected across the line y = 3, then translated 4 units left, what are the coordinates of its image, △A′B′C′?

Ⓐ A′(11, 4), B′(6, 12), C′(7, −2)

Ⓑ A′(11, 5), B′(−6, −3), C′(7, 11)

Ⓒ A′(3, 4), B′(−2, 12), C′(−1, −2)

Ⓓ A′(3, 5), B′(−2, −3), C′(−1, 11)

27. Performance Task Glide reflections are used to print a design across wrapping paper.

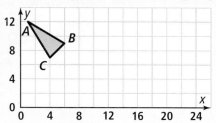

Part A Copy the diagram and draw image △A′B′C′ = $(T_{\langle 0, -2 \rangle} \circ r_\ell)$(△ABC), where ℓ is the line with equation x = 5.

Part B Translate △ABC 7 units right to print △DEF and 14 units right to print △GHJ. What glide reflections of △DEF and △GHJ result in the same arrangement as in Part A? Draw the images to create the pattern.

3-5
Symmetry

I CAN... identify different types of symmetry in two-dimensional figures.

VOCABULARY
• point symmetry
• reflectional symmetry
• rotational symmetry

Ⓒ Common Core State Standards
HSG.CO.A.3, HSG.CO.A.5, HSG.CO.B.6, MP.3, MP.6, MP.7

CONCEPTUAL UNDERSTANDING

STUDY TIP
To identify reflectional symmetry, fold a figure so one half lines up with the other.

EXPLORE & REASON

Look at the kaleidoscope image shown. Then consider pieces A and B taken from the image.

Piece A   Piece B

A. How are piece A and piece B related? Describe a rigid motion that you can use on piece B to produce piece A.

B. **Communicate Precisely** Describe a composition of rigid motions that you can use on piece A to produce the image. Ⓒ **MP.6**

C. How many rigid motions did you need to produce the image from piece A? Can you think of another composition of rigid motions to produce the image starting with piece A?

ESSENTIAL QUESTION ▸ How can you tell whether a figure is symmetric?

EXAMPLE 1 **Identify Transformations for Symmetry**

What transformations can be used to map the figure onto itself? Why can some figures be mapped onto themselves?

A figure has symmetry if a rigid motion can map the figure onto itself.

Reflectional symmetry is a symmetry for which a reflection maps the figure onto itself. The line of reflection for a reflection symmetry is called the line of symmetry.

The reflections r_m and r_n map the figure onto itself. Observe that lines m and n both divide the figure into two pieces with the same size and shape.

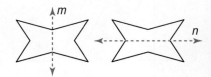

A figure has **rotational symmetry** if its image is mapped onto the preimage after a rotation of less than 360°.

The rotation $R_{(180°, P)}$ maps the figure onto itself.

Try It! **1.** What transformations map each figure onto itself?

a.

b.

EXAMPLE 2 › Identify Lines of Symmetry

How many lines of symmetry does a regular hexagon have?

Each line through opposite vertices creates equal halves.

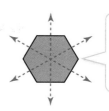

Each line through midpoints of opposite sides creates equal halves.

A regular hexagon has six lines of symmetry.

Try It! **2.** How many lines of symmetry does each figure have? How do you know whether you have found them all?

a.

b.

EXAMPLE 3 › Identify Rotational Symmetry

For what angles of rotation does the figure map onto itself?

A. an equilateral triangle

Find the angles of rotation about the center that map △ABC onto itself.

- A rotation of 120° creates an identical image with vertex B at the top.

- A rotation of 240° creates an identical image with vertex C at the top.

B. a parallelogram

- Only a rotation of 180° maps the figure onto itself.

The type of symmetry for which there is rotation of 180° that maps a figure onto itself is called **point symmetry**. A parallelogram has 180° rotational symmetry, or point symmetry.

Try It! **3.** What are the rotational symmetries for each figure? Does each figure have point symmetry?

a.

b.

c.

d.

EXAMPLE 4 ▸ Determine Symmetries

What type(s) of symmetry does each figure have?

A. Balloon flower

- A line through the center of a petal is a line of reflection. Since there are 5 petals, there are 5 lines of symmetry.

- Since 360° ÷ 5 = 72°, there is rotational symmetry at multiples of 72°.

The flower has reflectional symmetry with 5 lines of symmetry and rotational symmetry for angles of 72°, 144°, 216°, and 288°.

B. Mahjong tile

- No lines of symmetry can be drawn.

- Rotating the tile 180° about its center results in an identical image.

The tile has 180° rotational symmetry, or point symmetry.

COMMON ERROR
You may think a rectangular figure has reflectional symmetry along a diagonal. Recognize that a rectangular shape may only have horizontal or vertical lines of symmetry.

Try It! **4.** What symmetries does a square have?

APPLICATION

EXAMPLE 5 ▸ Use Symmetry

A company CEO wants a new logo that looks the same for each rotation of 30° and uses the three company colors. What are some possible designs?

Formulate ◂ Consider the different elements of the design.

Start with a polygon that has the specified rotational symmetry, which means a polygon that maps to itself at each 30° rotation.

Compute ◂ To find the number of sides for the polygon, find the number of 30° rotations in a full circle.

$$360° ÷ 30° = 12$$

You need a regular 12-gon (dodecagon).

Then, consider how the colors can be used so that each section is the same.

Interpret ◂ Three possible designs are shown.

Try It! **5.** What is a possible design for a circular logo that looks the same for each 60° rotation and uses at least two colors?

140 TOPIC 3 Transformations

CONCEPT SUMMARY Symmetry

	Reflectional Symmetry	**Rotational Symmetry**
WORDS	• A figure that maps onto itself when it is reflected over a line has reflectional symmetry. • A line of symmetry is a line of reflection when a figure is reflected onto itself.	• A figure that maps onto itself when it is rotated about its center by an angle measuring less than 360° has **rotational symmetry**. • A figure with 180° rotational symmetry has **point symmetry**.
DIAGRAMS		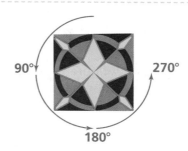

Do You UNDERSTAND?

1. **ESSENTIAL QUESTION** How can you tell whether a figure is symmetric?

2. **Error Analysis** For the figure below, Adam was asked to draw all lines of reflection. His work is shown. What error did Adam make? **ⓒ MP.3**

3. **Vocabulary** What type of symmetry does a figure have if it can be mapped onto itself by being flipped over a line?

4. **Communicate Precisely** What does it mean for a figure to have 60° rotational symmetry? **ⓒ MP.6**

5. **Construct Arguments** Is it possible for a figure to have rotational symmetry and no reflectional symmetry? Explain or give examples. **ⓒ MP.3**

Do You KNOW HOW?

Find the number of lines of symmetry for each figure.

6.

7.

Describe the rotational symmetry of each figure. State whether each has point symmetry.

8.

9.

Identify the types of symmetry of each figure. For each figure with reflectional symmetry, identify the lines of symmetry. For each figure with rotational symmetry, identify the angles of rotation that map the figure onto itself.

10.

11.

PRACTICE & PROBLEM SOLVING

UNDERSTAND

12. **Construct Arguments** Is it possible for a figure to have reflectional symmetry and no rotational symmetry? Explain or give examples. © MP.3

13. **Reason** Explain how you would find the angles of rotational symmetry for the figure shown. © MP.2

14. **Mathematical Connections** A figure that has 180° rotational symmetry also has point symmetry. Write a conditional to relate those facts. Then, write the converse, inverse, and contrapositive.

15. **Look for Relationships** If a figure has 90° rotational symmetry, what other symmetries must it have? © MP.7

16. **Error Analysis** Yumiko's work is shown below. What error did she make? © MP.3

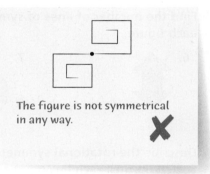

The figure is not symmetrical in any way. ✗

17. **Higher Order Thinking** Three types of rigid motion are translations, rotations, and reflections.

A frieze pattern is a linear pattern that repeats and has translational symmetry. The frieze below is a Zapotec geometric pattern at an archaeological site in Oaxaca, Mexico.

Find and name some other occurrences of frieze patterns in the real world.

PRACTICE

For Exercises 18 and 19, find all transformations that can be used to map each figure onto itself. SEE EXAMPLE 1

18.

19.

20. How many lines of symmetry does a regular five-pointed star have? SEE EXAMPLE 2

For Exercises 21 and 22, describe the rotational symmetries of each figure. SEE EXAMPLE 3

21.

22.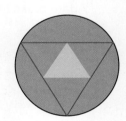

23. What types of symmetry does the figure have? Explain. SEE EXAMPLE 4

24. When drawn in the style shown, the number 808 has horizontal and vertical reflectional symmetry, as well as 180° rotational symmetry.

$\overset{\uparrow}{\underset{\downarrow}{\leftarrow}} 808 \rightarrow$

What are some other combinations of numbers or letters with symmetry? Find at least three other combinations, and identify the types of symmetry for each. SEE EXAMPLE 5

PRACTICE & PROBLEM SOLVING

APPLY

25. **Reason** How would you decide which flags show reflection symmetry? Rotational symmetry? No symmetry? ⓒ **MP.2**

Canada

Jamaica

Sweden

Saint Kitts and Nevis

26. **Look for Relationships** Make observations about the structure of each snowflake, and describe the types of symmetry that a snowflake can have. ⓒ **MP.7**

27. **Make Sense and Persevere** Describe the symmetries of each molecule shown. ⓒ **MP.1**

a. benzene

b. water

c. hydrogen peroxide

28. Which types of symmetry does the figure display? Select all that apply.

☐ **A.** reflectional symmetry across a vertical line

☐ **B.** reflectional symmetry across a horizontal line

☐ **C.** 120° rotational symmetry

☐ **D.** 180° rotational symmetry

☐ **E.** 60° rotational symmetry

29. **SAT/ACT** What is the equation of the line of symmetry for the graph of the quadratic equation shown?

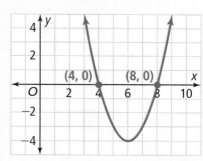

Ⓐ $y = -4$ Ⓒ $x = 4$

Ⓑ $y = 8$ Ⓓ $x = 6$

30. **Performance Task** A client wants a graphic designer to create an emblem that has rotational symmetry of 90° and 180°. The client needs the colors of the emblem to be red, yellow, and blue. The emblem should also include the first letter of the company name, X.

Part A The designer begins his design with a polygon. What polygons can he use?

Part B If a figure has rotational symmetry of 90° and 180°, what type of reflectional symmetry does the figure have?

Part C Create two possible designs for the client.

MATHEMATICAL MODELING IN 3 ACTS

Common Core State Standards
HSG.CO.B.6, HSG.CO.A.5, MP.4

SavvasRealize.com

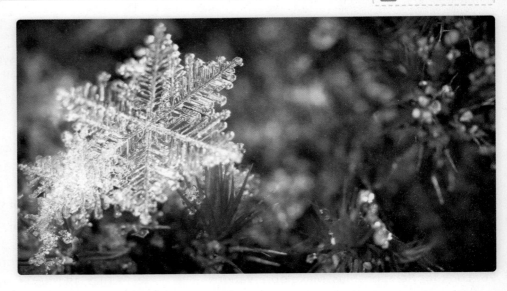

The Perplexing Polygon

Look around and you will see shapes and patterns everywhere you look. The tiles on a floor are often all the same shape and fit together to form a pattern. The petals on a flower often make a repeating pattern around the center of the flower. When you look at snowflakes under a microscope, you'll notice that they are made up of repeating three-dimensional crystals. Think about this during the Mathematical Modeling in 3 Acts lesson.

ACT 1 Identify the Problem

1. What is the first question that comes to mind after watching the video?

2. Write down the main question you will answer about what you saw in the video.

3. Make an initial conjecture that answers this main question.

4. Explain how you arrived at your conjecture.

5. What information will be useful to know to answer the main question? How can you get it? How will you use that information?

ACT 2 Develop a Model

6. Use the math that you have learned in this Topic to refine your conjecture.

ACT 3 Interpret the Results

7. Did your refined conjecture match the actual answer exactly? If not, what might explain the difference?

Topic Review

1. What are properties of the four types of rigid motion?

Vocabulary Review

Choose the correct term to complete each sentence.

2. A(n) _____ is a transformation about a point with a given angle measure.

3. Reflections, translations, rotations, and glide reflections are the four types of _____.

4. A line that a figure is reflected across so that it maps onto itself is called a(n) _____.

5. The composition of a reflection and a translation is called a(n) _____.

6. The set of points that a transformation acts on is called the _____.

7. The result of a transformation is called the _____.

- composition of rigid motions
- glide reflection
- image
- line of reflection
- line of symmetry
- perpendicular bisector
- preimage
- rigid motion
- rotation
- translation

Concepts & Skills Review

LESSON 3-1 ▸ **Reflections**

Quick Review

A **rigid motion** is a transformation that preserves length and angle measure.

A reflection is a transformation that reflects a point across a line of reflection m such that the image of a point A on m is A, and for a point B not on m, line m is the perpendicular bisector $\overline{BB'}$.

A reflection is a rigid motion.

Example

What is the reflection of $\triangle ABC$ across ℓ?

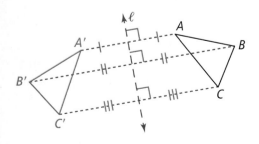

Practice & Problem Solving

8. Does the transformation appear to be a rigid motion?

 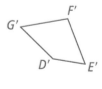

preimage   image

For Exercises 9 and 10, the vertices of $\triangle HJK$ are $H(-3, 2)$, $J(-1, -3)$, and $K(4, 3)$. What are the coordinates of the vertices of $\triangle H'J'K'$ for each reflection?

9. $r_{y\text{-axis}}$

10. $r_{x\text{-axis}}$

11. **Communicate Precisely** Given the coordinates of two points and the equation of a line, how can you check that one point is the image of the other point reflected across the line? ⒼMP.6

Quick Review

A translation is a transformation that maps all points the same distance and in the same direction, so that for any two points A and B, $AA' = BB'$.

A translation is a rigid motion. Any translation can be expressed as a composition of two reflections across two parallel lines.

Example

What is the graph of $T_{\langle 3, -2 \rangle}(\triangle LMN)$?

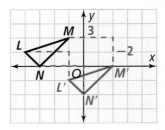

Practice & Problem Solving

For Exercises 12 and 13, the vertices of $\triangle PQR$ are $P(-4, 3)$, $Q(-2, 3)$, and $R(1, -3)$. What are the coordinates of the vertices of $\triangle P'Q'R'$ for each translation?

12. a translation 3 units left and 2 units down

13. $T_{\langle 4, -5 \rangle}$

14. What is the translation shown?

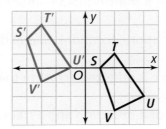

15. **Make Sense and Persevere** Given reflections r_h and r_k, where h is a line with equation $x = -3$ and k is a line with equation $x = 2$, how can you determine the distance of the translation resulting from the composition $r_k \circ r_h$? Ⓒ MP.1

Quick Review

A rotation is a transformation that rotates a point about the center of rotation P by the angle of rotation $x°$ such that the image of P is P, $PA = PA'$, and $m\angle APA' = x$.

A rotation is a rigid motion. Any rotation can be expressed as a composition of reflections across two intersecting lines.

Example

What is the 150° rotation of $\overline{XY}$ about P?

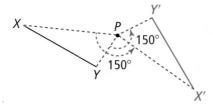

Practice & Problem Solving

For Exercise 16 and 17, the vertices of $\triangle ABC$ are $A(2, -2)$, $B(-3, -2)$, and $C(-1, 3)$. What are the coordinates of the vertices of $\triangle A'B'C'$ for each rotation?

16. a rotation 90° about the origin

17. $R_{(270°, O)}$

18. Draw two lines of reflection so the composition of the reflections across the lines is equivalent to the rotation shown.

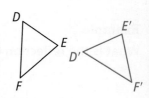

19. **Use Structure** If two lines intersect at a right angle at point P, what rotation is equivalent to the composition of the reflections across the two lines? Ⓒ MP.7

LESSON 3-4 · Classification of Rigid Motions

Quick Review

A **glide reflection** is the composition of a reflection followed by a translation.

Any rigid motion is either a translation, reflection, rotation, or glide reflection. As a result, any rigid motion can be expressed as a combination of reflections.

Example

What is a glide reflection that maps △GHJ to △KLM?

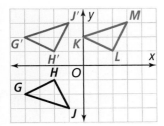

First reflect △GHJ across the x-axis to get △G′H′J′. Then translate △G′H′J′ by 4 units to the right to get △KLM. The glide reflection is $T_{\langle 4, 0\rangle} \circ r_{x\text{-axis}}$.

Practice & Problem Solving

For Exercises 20 and 21, the vertices of △LMN are L(−2, 4), M(1, 2), and N(−3, −5). Suppose j is a line with equation x = 3 and k is a line with equation y = −2. what are the coordinates of the vertices of △L′M′N′ for each glide reflection?

20. $T_{\langle -2, 4\rangle} \circ r_j$

21. a reflection across line k, then a translation 2 units right and 3 units down

22. What is a glide reflection for the transformation shown?

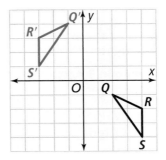

23. Make Sense and Persevere Is there more than one way to describe a glide reflection as a composition of a reflection and then a translation? Explain. ⓒ MP.1

LESSON 3-5 · Symmetry

Quick Review

A figure has **symmetry** if a rigid motion can map the figure to itself. If the rigid motion is a reflection, then the symmetry is reflectional **symmetry**. If the rigid motion is a rotation, then the symmetry is **rotational symmetry**.

When the angle of rotation is 180°, the rotational symmetry is called **point symmetry**.

Example

How many lines of symmetry does the figure have?

You can draw a line of reflection through each vertex and the center of the star. There are six lines of symmetry.

Practice & Problem Solving

24. Describe the transformations that can be used to map the figure onto itself.

For Exercises 25 and 26, describe all the symmetries of each figure. If the figure has reflectional symmetry, identify all the lines of symmetry. If the figure has rotational symmetry, give the angles of rotation.

25. **26.**

27. Communicate Precisely Suppose a figure has at least two lines of symmetry. Explain why the figure must have rotational symmetry. ⓒ MP.6

TOPIC ESSENTIAL QUESTION

What relationships between sides and angles of triangles can be used to prove triangles congruent?

Topic Overview

enVision® STEM Project:
   Design a Bridge

4-1 Congruence

4-2 Isosceles and Equilateral Triangles

Mathematical Modeling in 3 Acts:
   Check It Out!

4-3 Proving and Applying the SAS and SSS Congruence Criteria

4-4 Proving and Applying the ASA and AAS Congruence Criteria

4-5 Congruence in Right Triangles

4-6 Congruence in Overlapping Triangles

Topic Vocabulary

- congruence transformation
- congruent

Digital Experience

📖 **INTERACTIVE STUDENT EDITION**
Access online or offline.

👆 **ACTIVITIES** Complete *Explore & Reason, Model & Discuss*, and *Critique & Explain* activities. Interact with *Examples* and *Try Its.*

👆 **CONCEPT SUMMARY** Review key lesson content through multiple representations.

☑ **ASSESSMENT** Show what you've learned.

Go online | SavvasRealize.com

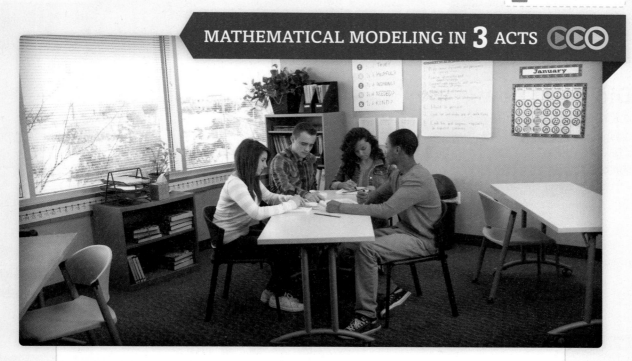

MATHEMATICAL MODELING IN **3** ACTS

Check It Out!

Maybe you've played this game before: you draw a picture. Then you try to get a classmate to draw the same picture by giving step-by-step directions but without showing your drawings.

Try it with a classmate. Draw a map of a room in your house or a place in your town. Then give directions to a classmate to draw the map that you drew. How similar are they? Think about your results during the Mathematical Modeling in 3 Acts lesson.

 VIDEOS Watch clips to support *Mathematical Modeling in 3 Acts Lessons* and **enVision®** *STEM Projects.*

 TUTORIALS Get help from *Virtual Nerd,* right when you need it.

PRACTICE Practice what you've learned.

 ADAPTIVE PRACTICE Practice that is *just right* and *just for you.*

FAMILY ENGAGEMENT Involve family in your learning.

 GLOSSARY Read and listen to English and Spanish definitions.

MATH TOOLS Explore math with digital tools and manipulatives.

DESMOS Use Anytime and as embedded Interactives in Lesson content.

Did You Know?

The **Tacoma Narrows Bridge** in Washington collapsed in high winds a few months after it opened in 1940. The bridge was rebuilt in 1950 using a truss for stabilization.

A bridge works by **balancing compression (pressing inward) and tension (pressing outward)**, distributing the load onto the bridge supports.

The design of a truss is based on the strength of a triangle. It distributes a load from a narrow point to a wider base.

BRIDGE LOAD = Weight of **bridge** + Weight of **people** + Weight of **vehicles** + Weight of **precipitation**

Your Task: Design a Bridge

You and your classmates will analyze different truss bridge designs and how congruent triangles are used in each construction. What type of truss would you use in a bridge design, and why?

4-1
Congruence

I CAN... use a composition of rigid motions to show that two objects are congruent.

VOCABULARY
- congruence transformation
- congruent

Ⓖ Common Core State Standards
HSG.CO.A.5, HSG.CO.B.6, MP.2, MP.6, MP.7

EXPLORE & REASON

Some corporate logos are distinctive because they make use of repeated shapes. Below are some logo mockups for a renewable energy company.

A designer creates two versions of a new logo for the company. Version 1 uses the original image shown at the right and a reflection of it. Version 2 uses reduced copies of the original image.

A. Make a sketch of each version.

B. **Communicate Precisely** The owner of the company says, "I like your designs, but it is important that the transformed image be the same size and shape as the original image." What would you do to comply with the owner's requirements? Ⓖ **MP.6**

C. What transformations can you apply to the original image that would produce logos acceptable to the owner? Explain.

ESSENTIAL QUESTION What is the relationship between rigid motions and congruence?

CONCEPTUAL UNDERSTANDING

EXAMPLE 1 **Understand Congruence**

Suppose there is a rigid motion that maps one figure to another. Why does that show that the two figures are congruent?

Figure *GHIJKL* is the image of *ABCDEF* after the rigid motion $T_{\langle 2, -5 \rangle} \circ r_{\ell}$.

Figure *ABCDEF* has the following lengths and angle measures.

$$AB = 3 \qquad BC = 1 \qquad CD = 1$$
$$DE = 2 \qquad EF = 2 \qquad FA = 3$$

All angles in figure *ABCDEF* are right angles.

Figure *GHIJKL* has the following lengths and angle measures.

$$GH = 3 \qquad HI = 1 \qquad IJ = 1$$
$$JK = 2 \qquad KL = 2 \qquad LG = 3$$

All angles in figure *GHIJKL* are right angles.

Rigid motions preserve length and angle measure. Therefore, if a rigid motion maps one figure to another, the figures are *congruent*.

STUDY TIP
Recall that angles with the same measure are congruent, and segments with the same length are congruent.

Try It! **1.** A 90° rotation about the origin maps △*PQR* to △*LMN*. Are the triangles congruent? Explain.

CONCEPT Congruence

Figures that have the same size and shape are said to be *congruent*. Two figures are **congruent** if there is a rigid motion that maps one figure to the other.

A rigid motion is sometimes called a **congruence transformation** because it maps a figure to a congruent figure.

Use the ≅ symbol to show that two figures are congruent. Since $r_m(\triangle ABC) = \triangle DEF$, $\triangle ABC \cong \triangle DEF$.

EXAMPLE 2   Verify Congruence

Powered By
desmos

Use rigid motions to verify whether $\triangle XYZ \cong \triangle ABC$.

If there is a rigid motion that maps $\triangle XYZ$ to $\triangle ABC$, then $\triangle XYZ \cong \triangle ABC$.

First rotate $\triangle XYZ$ 180° about point Z. Next translate the image three units to the right.

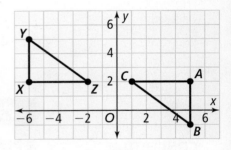

$$(T_{\langle 3, 0 \rangle} \circ R_{(180°, Z)})(\triangle XYZ) = \triangle ABC$$

The composition $T_{\langle 3, 0 \rangle} \circ R_{(180°, Z)}$ maps $\triangle XYZ$ to $\triangle ABC$. Therefore, the triangles are congruent.

LOOK FOR RELATIONSHIPS
Think of other solutions. Can you identify another composition of rigid motions that maps one triangle to the other? Ⓒ **MP.7**

Try It!   **2.** Use the graph shown.

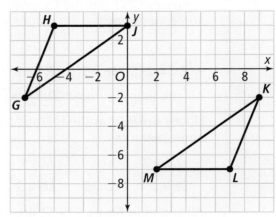

a. Given $\triangle GHJ \cong \triangle KLM$, what is one composition of rigid motions that maps $\triangle GHJ$ to $\triangle KLM$?

b. What is another composition of rigid motions that maps $\triangle GHJ$ to $\triangle KLM$?

EXAMPLE 3 **Identify Congruent Figures**

Given △ABC, △EFG, and △JKL, which triangles are congruent?

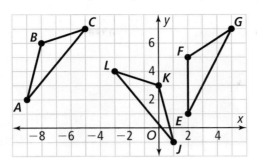

Find a composition of rigid motions to map △ABC to △JKL.

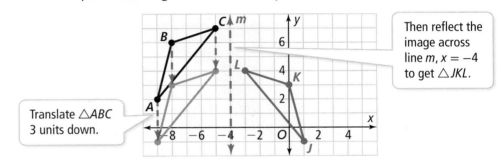

Then reflect the image across line $m, x = -4$ to get △JKL.

Translate △ABC 3 units down.

The composition of rigid motions $r_m \circ T_{\langle 0, -3 \rangle}$ maps △ABC to △JKL. Therefore, △ABC ≅ △JKL.

Observe that $\overline{AC}$ and $\overline{EG}$ are the longest side in each corresponding triangle, and $AC \neq EG$, so there is no single rigid motion or composition of rigid motions that maps △ABC to △EFG. Therefore, they are not congruent.

STUDY TIP
To show that two figures are not congruent, you only need to find one corresponding pair of sides or angles that do not have the same measure.

Try It! **3.** Use the graph shown.

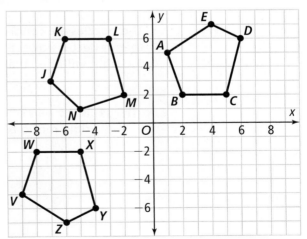

a. Are *ABCDE* and *JKLMN* congruent? If so, describe a composition of rigid motions that maps *ABCDE* to *JKLMN*. If not, explain.

b. Are *ABCDE* and *VWXYZ* congruent? If so, describe a composition of rigid motions that maps *ABCDE* to *VWXYZ*. If not, explain.

EXAMPLE 4   Determine Congruence

Which pairs of objects are congruent? If a pair of objects is congruent, describe a composition of rigid motions that maps one to the other.

A.

The puzzle pieces are congruent. A reflection across a vertical line maps one puzzle piece to the other.

B.

COMMON ERROR
Remember that the composition of rigid motions must map *all* points from the preimage to the image for objects to be congruent.

The frame corners are not congruent. The diagonal segment at the corner of the left frame is longer than the diagonal segment at the corner of the right frame, so the two frame corners are not the same size.

C.

The puzzles are congruent. Rotate the puzzle on the left 90° clockwise, then reflect it across a vertical line through its center. A translation to the right will then map the resulting figure to the figure on the right.

Try It!   **4.** Is the pair of objects congruent? If so, describe a composition of rigid motions that maps one object onto the other.

a.

b.

EXAMPLE 5 Apply Congruence

A boat builder plans to connect two pieces of wood using a puzzle joint as shown. For a successful join, the units must be congruent.

Given Unit A, what composition of rigid motions maps Unit A to Unit B?

Unit B is the result of a rotation and translation of Unit A. Unit B has the same size, shape, and orientation as Unit A. The differences are that Unit B is rotated so that its peak faces the left side instead of the right, and it is shifted down.

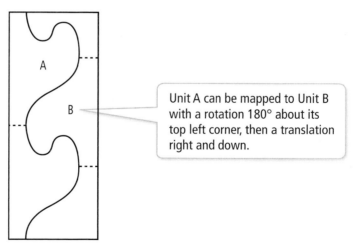

Unit A can be mapped to Unit B with a rotation 180° about its top left corner, then a translation right and down.

Try It! 5. What is another composition of rigid motions that shows Unit A is congruent to Unit B?

CONCEPT SUMMARY Congruent Figures

WORDS If two figures are congruent, a composition of rigid motions maps one figure to another.

DIAGRAM Since $r_n(\triangle PQR) = \triangle P'Q'R'$, $\triangle PQR \cong \triangle P'Q'R'$.

Do You UNDERSTAND?

1. **ESSENTIAL QUESTION** What is the relationship between rigid motions and congruence?

2. **Error Analysis** Taylor says *ABCD* and *EFGH* are congruent because he can map *ABCD* to *EFGH* by multiplying each side length by 1.5 and translating the result to coincide with *EFGH*. What is Taylor's error? © **MP.3**

ABCD ≅ EFGH ✗

3. **Vocabulary** Why is a rigid motion also called a congruence transformation?

4. **Reason** For any two line segments that are congruent, what must be true about the lengths of the segments? © **MP.2**

5. **Construct Arguments** A composition of rigid motions maps one figure to another figure. Is each intermediate image in the composition congruent to the original and final figures? Explain. © **MP.3**

6. **Communicate Precisely** Describe how you can find a rigid motion or composition of rigid motions to map a segment to a congruent segment and an angle to a congruent angle. © **MP.6**

Do You KNOW HOW?

7. Given *ABCD* ≅ *EFGH*, what rigid motion, or composition of rigid motions, maps *ABCD* to *EFGH*?

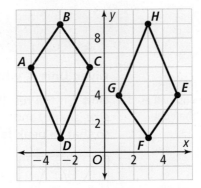

8. Which triangles are congruent?

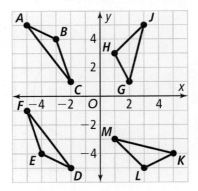

9. Are Figure A and Figure B congruent? If so, describe a composition of rigid motions that maps Figure A to Figure B. If not, explain.

Figure A   Figure B

PRACTICE & PROBLEM SOLVING

UNDERSTAND

10. Reason If △JKL ≅ △RST, give the coordinates for possible vertices of △RST. Justify your answer by describing a composition of rigid motions that maps △JKL to △RST. ⓒ **MP.2**

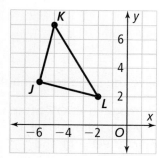

11. Error Analysis Yuki says that if all lines are congruent, then all line segments must be congruent. Is Yuki correct? Explain. ⓒ **MP.3**

$$\overline{AB} \cong \overline{CD} \quad ✗$$

12. Mathematical Connections Square *JKLM* maps to square *RSTU* by a translation 1 unit right and 5 units up, followed by a translation 6 units left and 4 units up. What is the area of *RSTU*? ⓒ **MP.7**

12 cm

13. Higher Order Thinking Are $\overrightarrow{AB}$ and $\overrightarrow{CD}$ congruent? If so, describe a composition of rigid motions that maps any ray to any other ray. If not, explain. Are any two rays congruent? Explain.

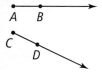

PRACTICE

14. Given $r_m(\triangle PQR) = \triangle P'Q'R'$, do △P'Q'R' and △PQR have equal perimeters? Explain. **SEE EXAMPLE 1**

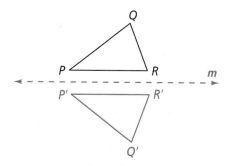

15. Given *WXYZ* ≅ *WTUV*, describe a composition of rigid motions that maps *WXYZ* to *WTUV*. **SEE EXAMPLE 2**

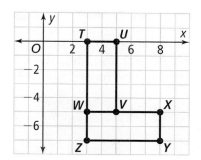

16. Are *ABCD* and *EFGH* congruent? If so, describe a composition of rigid motions that maps *ABCD* to *EFGH*. If not, explain. **SEE EXAMPLE 3**

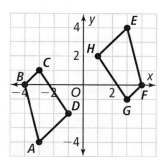

17. Which objects are congruent? For any congruent objects, describe a composition of rigid motions that maps the preimage to the image. **SEE EXAMPLES 4 AND 5**

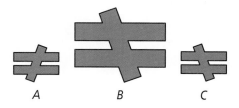

PRACTICE & PROBLEM SOLVING

18. **Communicate Precisely** Using a 3D printer, LaTanya makes the chocolate mold shown by copying different shapes. ⓒ MP.6

    a. Which of the designs in the mold appear to be congruent?

    b. Describe a composition of rigid motions that maps the congruent shapes.

19. **Reason** Are the illustrations of the shoes in the advertisement congruent? If so, describe a rigid motion that maps one shoe to the other. ⓒ MP.2

20. **Use Structure** Describe a rigid motion or a composition of rigid motions that can be used to make sure that each slice of quiche is the same size and shape as the first slice. ⓒ MP.6

21. △GHI can be mapped to △JKL by a rotation 90° about G, followed by a translation 3 units right and 8 units up. Select all true statements.

    ☐ **A.** $GI = JL$

    ☐ **B.** $HI = JK$

    ☐ **C.** $\angle K \cong \angle G$

    ☐ **D.** $\triangle GHI \cong \triangle JKL$

    ☐ **E.** points G and J have the same coordinates

22. **SAT/ACT** △PQR is the image of △XYZ after a reflection across the y-axis followed by a translation 3 units down. If $PQ = 11$ and $PR = 7$, what is XZ?

    Ⓐ 4   Ⓒ 9

    Ⓑ 7   Ⓓ 11

23. **Performance Task** The Aztec fabric pattern shown is based on the original image.

Original Image ⟶

Part A Identify any images in the pattern that appear to be congruent to the original image.

Part B Describe a composition of rigid motions that maps the original image to each congruent image in the pattern.

Part C For any images in the pattern that are not congruent to the original image, explain how you know they are not congruent.

4-2

Isosceles and Equilateral Triangles

I CAN... apply theorems about isosceles and equilateral triangles to solve problems.

© Common Core State Standards
HSG.CO.C.10, MP.2, MP.3, MP.7

EXPLORE & REASON

 Powered By **desmos**

Cut out a triangle with two sides of equal length from a sheet of paper and label its angles 1, 2, and 3. Trace the outline of your triangle on another sheet of paper and label the angles.

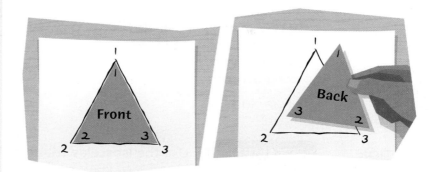

A. In how many different ways can you flip, slide, or turn the triangle so that it fits exactly on the outline?

B. **Look for Relationships** How do the angles and sides of the outline correspond to the angles and sides of the triangle? **© MP.7**

C. How would your answer to Part A change if all three sides of the triangle were of equal length?

ESSENTIAL QUESTION   How are the side lengths and angle measures related in isosceles triangles and in equilateral triangles?

CONCEPTUAL UNDERSTANDING

EXAMPLE 1   **Understand Angles of Isosceles Triangles**

How are the base angles of an isosceles triangle related?

Draw isosceles triangle ABC.

Because $\overline{BC} \cong \overline{BA}$, there is a rigid motion that maps $\overline{BC}$ onto $\overline{BA}$. Draw the angle bisector $\overleftrightarrow{BD}$ of $\angle ABC$, so that $m\angle DBC = m\angle DBA$.

STUDY TIP
A triangle is defined by three points known as its vertices. Since the rigid motion maps each vertex of $\triangle BCD$ to its corresponding vertex in $\triangle BAD$, it is also true that every point in triangle $\triangle BCD$ maps to a corresponding point in $\triangle BAD$.

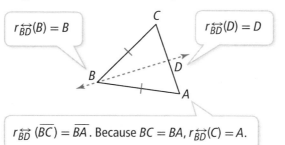

$r_{\overleftrightarrow{BD}}(B) = B$

$r_{\overleftrightarrow{BD}}(D) = D$

$r_{\overleftrightarrow{BD}}(\overline{BC}) = \overline{BA}$. Because $BC = BA$, $r_{\overleftrightarrow{BD}}(C) = A$.

Since the reflection maps $\triangle BCD$ to $\triangle BAD$, $m\angle BCA = m\angle BAC$. Therefore, $\angle BCA \cong \angle BAC$.

Try It!   **1.** Copy isosceles $\triangle ABC$. Reflect the triangle across line BC to create the image $\triangle A'B'C'$. What is another rigid motion that maps $\triangle A'B'C'$ onto $\triangle ABC$? Can you use this to show that $\angle A \cong \angle C$? Explain.

THEOREM 4-1 Isosceles Triangle Theorem and the Converse

If two sides of a triangle are congruent, then the angles opposite those sides are congruent.

If two angles of a triangle are congruent, then the sides opposite those angles are congruent.

PROOF: SEE EXERCISE 17.

If... $\overline{AB} \cong \overline{BC}$,
Then... $\angle ACB \cong \angle BAC$.

If... $\angle ACB \cong \angle BAC$,
Then... $\overline{AB} \cong \overline{BC}$.

APPLICATION →

EXAMPLE 2 Use the Isosceles Triangle Theorem

An architect is designing a community park between N. First St. and S. First St. The pathways along these streets will be equal in length. To protect the landscaping and minimize erosion, the architect will place a triangular section of cobblestones at the corners along Park Plaza. What angle measure should the architect specify for the corners in her design?

The park is in the shape of an isosceles triangle. Find $m\angle F$ and $m\angle E$.

$$m\angle D + m\angle E + m\angle F = 180$$
$$50 + m\angle F + m\angle F = 180$$
$$m\angle F = 65$$

> The base angles of the isosceles triangle are congruent by the Isosceles Triangle Theorem, so $m\angle E = m\angle F$.

STUDY TIP
Confirm your solution by using your original equation. In this example, the three angles of $\triangle ABC$ are 65°, 65°, and 50°, and the sum is 180°.

The landscape architect should specify that the angles at the corners measure 65°.

Try It! **2.** What is the value of x?

a.

$(5x + 9)°$

$28°$

b.

$(-4x + 9)°$ $(8x - 3)°$

EXAMPLE 3 **Use the Converse of the Isosceles Triangle Theorem**

What are the lengths of all three sides of the triangle?

COMMON ERROR
Be careful not to set the expressions for the length of a leg and the length of the base equal to each other. Remember that the congruent legs are opposite the congruent base angles.

Step 1 Find the value of x.

$$x + 20 = \frac{8x}{3}$$

$$3x + 60 = 8x$$

$$12 = x$$

Because $\angle P \cong \angle Q$, the sides opposite $\angle P$ and $\angle Q$ are also congruent.

Step 2 Substitute 12 for x to determine the side lengths.

$$PR = x + 20 \qquad\qquad PQ = 6x - 12 \qquad\qquad QR = \frac{8x}{3}$$

$$= 12 + 20 \qquad\qquad\quad = 6(12) - 12 \qquad\qquad = \frac{8(12)}{3}$$

$$= 32 \qquad\qquad\qquad\quad = 60 \qquad\qquad\qquad\quad = 32$$

Try It! **3.** Use the figure shown.

    a. What is the value of x?

    b. What are the lengths of all three sides of the triangle?

THEOREM 4-2

Powered By
desmos

If a line or line segment bisects the vertex angle of an isosceles triangle, then it is also the perpendicular bisector of the opposite side.

If...   **Then...**

$\overline{AB} \cong \overline{BC}$ and $m\angle ABD = m\angle CBD$ $\overline{BD} \perp \overline{AC}$ and $\overline{AD} \cong \overline{DC}$

PROOF: SEE EXERCISE 13.

EXAMPLE 4 Use Perpendicular Bisectors to Solve Problems

A prefabricated house is delivered to a foundation in two symmetric halves that are assembled on-site. Along the planned route to the site, the truck must pass under a bridge that has a clearance height of 17 feet. Should the trucker plan a different route for delivering the house? Explain.

Draw a diagram to represent the roof.

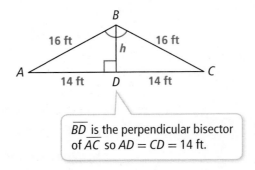

$\overline{BD}$ is the perpendicular bisector of $\overline{AC}$ so $AD = CD = 14$ ft.

Use the Pythagorean Theorem to find the height h.

$$h^2 + 14^2 = 16^2$$
$$h^2 = 60$$
$$h = \sqrt{60} \approx 7.7$$

The house is approximately 17.7 feet tall, so the total height that the truck must clear is greater than 17.7 ft. The trucker should plan a different route to the site.

CONSTRUCT ARGUMENTS
Consider the information the figure provides about △ABC. What other information given in the figure is needed? Ⓒ MP.3

Try It! **4.** Use the figure shown.

a. What is $m\angle RSQ$?

b. What is PR?

Corollary to Theorem 4-1

If a triangle is equilateral, then it is equiangular.

If a triangle is equiangular, then it is equilateral.

If... $\overline{AB} \cong \overline{BC} \cong \overline{AC}$, **then...** $\angle A \cong \angle B \cong \angle C$.

If... $\angle A \cong \angle B \cong \angle C$, **then...** $\overline{AB} \cong \overline{BC} \cong \overline{AC}$.

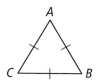

PROOF

EXAMPLE 5 Prove that Equilateral Triangles Are Equiangular

A. Prove that equilateral triangles are equiangular.

Given: $\overline{DE} \cong \overline{EF} \cong \overline{DF}$

Prove: $\angle D \cong \angle E \cong \angle F$

Plan: Use the fact that an equilateral triangle is also an isosceles triangle to show that all three angles are congruent.

Proof:

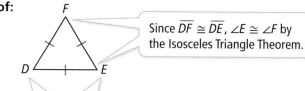

Since $\overline{DF} \cong \overline{DE}$, $\angle E \cong \angle F$ by the Isosceles Triangle Theorem.

Since $\overline{DF} \cong \overline{EF}$, $\angle E \cong \angle D$ by the Isosceles Triangle Theorem.

Since $\angle D \cong \angle E$ and $\angle E \cong \angle F$, $\angle D \cong \angle E \cong \angle F$.

B. Prove that equiangular triangles are equilateral.

Given: $\angle G \cong \angle H \cong \angle J$

Prove: $\overline{GH} \cong \overline{HJ} \cong \overline{GJ}$

Plan: Use a strategy similar to the one in Part A by applying the Converse of the Isosceles Triangle Theorem.

Proof:

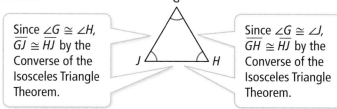

Since $\angle G \cong \angle H$, $\overline{GJ} \cong \overline{HJ}$ by the Converse of the Isosceles Triangle Theorem.

Since $\angle G \cong \angle J$, $\overline{GH} \cong \overline{HJ}$ by the Converse of the Isosceles Triangle Theorem.

Since $\overline{GJ} \cong \overline{HJ}$ and $\overline{GH} \cong \overline{HJ}$, $\overline{GH} \cong \overline{HJ} \cong \overline{GJ}$.

STUDY TIP
When planning a proof, consider proofs that may be parallel in structure.

Try It! **5.** What rotation can be used to show the angles of an equilateral triangle are congruent?

EXAMPLE 6 Use Angles in Isosceles and Equilateral Triangles

A. If $m\angle CBD = 130$, what is $m\angle BAD$?

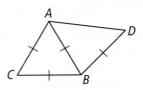

Step 1 Find $m\angle ABD$.

$$m\angle ABC + m\angle ABD = m\angle CBD$$

$$60 + m\angle ABD = 130$$

$$m\angle ABD = 70$$

> Since the measures of the interior angles of any triangle sum to 180° and $\triangle ABC$ is equilateral, $m\angle ABC = 60$.

COMMON ERROR
You may think you have solved the problem after finding one angle measure. Make sure you provide the measure of the angle asked for in the question.

Step 2 Use the Isosceles Triangle Theorem to find $m\angle BAD$.

$$m\angle ABD + m\angle BDA + m\angle BAD = 180$$

$$70 + m\angle BAD + m\angle BAD = 180$$

$$m\angle BAD = 55$$

> Since $\triangle ABD$ is isosceles, $m\angle BDA = m\angle BAD$.

B. What is $m\angle U$?

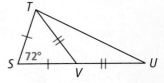

Step 1 Find $m\angle SVT$. Write an equation using the Triangle Angle-Sum Theorem.

$$m\angle S + m\angle STV + m\angle SVT = 180$$

$$72 + m\angle SVT + m\angle SVT = 180$$

$$2m\angle SVT = 108$$

$$m\angle SVT = 54$$

> Since $\triangle STV$ is isosceles, $m\angle STV = m\angle SVT$.

Step 2 Find $m\angle U$. Write an equation using the Triangle Exterior Angle Theorem.

$$m\angle SVT = m\angle VTU + m\angle U$$

$$54 = m\angle U + m\angle U$$

$$54 = 2m\angle U$$

$$m\angle U = 27$$

> Since $\triangle VTU$ is isosceles, $m\angle VTU = m\angle U$.

Try It! **6.** Find each angle measure in the figure.

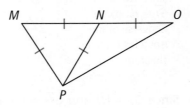

a. $m\angle PNO$ **b.** $m\angle NOP$

ISOSCELES TRIANGLES

If $\overline{AB} \cong \overline{BC}$, then $\angle ACB \cong \angle BAC$.

If $\angle ACB \cong \angle BAC$, then $\overline{AB} \cong \overline{BC}$.

EQUILATERAL TRIANGLES

If $\overline{AB} \cong \overline{BC} \cong \overline{AC}$, then $\angle A \cong \angle B \cong \angle C$.

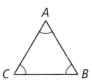

If $\angle A \cong \angle B \cong \angle C$, then $\overline{AB} \cong \overline{BC} \cong \overline{AC}$.

Do You UNDERSTAND?

1. **ESSENTIAL QUESTION** How are the side lengths and angle measures related in isosceles triangles and in equilateral triangles?

2. **Error Analysis** Nate drew the following diagram to represent an isosceles triangle sharing a side with an equilateral triangle. What mistake did Nate make? ⓒ MP.3

3. **Vocabulary** What is the difference between the base and a leg of an isosceles triangle?

4. **Reason** Is it possible for the vertex of an isosceles triangle to be a right angle? Explain why or why not, and state the angle measures of the triangle, if possible. ⓒ MP.2

5. **Communicate Precisely** Describe five rigid motions that map equilateral triangle △PQR onto itself. ⓒ MP.6

Do You KNOW HOW?

For Exercises 6 and 7, find the unknown angle measures.

6.

7.

For Exercises 8 and 9, find the lengths of all three sides of the triangle.

8.

9.

10. What is $m\angle ABD$ in the figure shown?

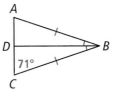

11. A light is attached to a cable and suspended between two poles that are each 9.5 feet tall. How far above the ground is the light? Round to the nearest tenth of a foot.

PRACTICE & PROBLEM SOLVING

 UNDERSTAND

12. Mathematical Connections What are the measures of ∠1 and ∠2? Explain.

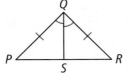

13. Construct Arguments Use the properties of rigid motions to write a proof of Theorem 4-2. Ⓒ **MP.3**

Given: $\overline{PQ} \cong \overline{RQ}$ and $m\angle PQS = m\angle RQS$

Prove: $\overline{QS} \perp \overline{PR}$ and $PS = SR$

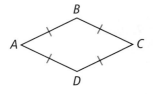

14. Look for Relationships Prove that ∠BAD ≅ ∠BCD and ∠ABC ≅ ∠CDA. Ⓒ **MP.7**

15. Error Analysis Amaya is asked to find the side lengths of the triangle shown. What is her error? Ⓒ **MP.3**

> From the top leg and the base, 2x = 6, so x = 3. Substitute x into the expression for the bottom leg's length to get 3(3) − 5 = 4. ✗

16. Higher Order Thinking Deondra draws points at (1, 5) and (1, −1) on a coordinate plane. Each point will be a vertex of an isosceles right triangle. What are two possible points in the second quadrant that she can specify as a vertex of her triangle? Explain.

PRACTICE

17. Use rigid motions to write a proof of the Converse of the Isosceles Triangle Theorem. SEE EXAMPLE 1

Given: ∠J ≅ ∠L

Prove: $\overline{JK} \cong \overline{KL}$

Find the unknown angle measures in each triangle. SEE EXAMPLE 2

18.

19.

Find the lengths of all three sides of each triangle. SEE EXAMPLE 3

20.

21.

Use the figure shown for Exercises 22 and 23. SEE EXAMPLE 4

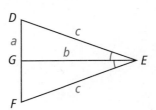

22. What is m∠DEG if m∠DFE = 70?

23. What is the value of b if a = 8 and c = 24?

24. Prove that ∠ABC is a right angle. SEE EXAMPLE 5

Given: $\overline{AD} \cong \overline{BD} \cong \overline{CD}$

Prove: m∠ABC = 90

25. Given m∠PSR = 134, what is the measure of ∠SQR? SEE EXAMPLE 6

PRACTICE & PROBLEM SOLVING

26. Make Sense and Persevere Each of the five points on a star produced for a flag is an isosceles triangle with leg length 6 cm and base length 4.2 cm. What is the total height *h* of each star? Round to the nearest tenth of a centimeter. Ⓒ MP.1

27. Use Structure The front of the tent below has the shape of an equilateral triangle. Ⓒ MP.7

a. What is the side length of the triangle? Round to the nearest tenth of a foot.

b. Explain the method you use to calculate the length.

28. Look for Relationships For a crane to lift the beam shown below, the beam and the two support cables must form an isosceles triangle with height *h*. If the distance between the cables along the beam is 18 ft and the height *h* is 8 ft, what is the total length of the two cables? Round to the nearest tenth of a foot. Ⓒ MP.7

29. Consider the following triangle.

a. Write an equation you can solve to find the value of *y*.

b. What is $m\angle K$?

30. SAT/ACT Given $AB = BD = BC = DC$ and $m\angle ABC = 114$, what is $m\angle BAD$?

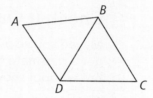

Ⓐ 54   Ⓒ 60

Ⓑ 63   Ⓓ 72

31. Performance Task Emaan designs the birdhouse shown below.

Part A What is the total height of the birdhouse? Show your work.

Part B Emaan decides to change the design by increasing each side of the roof from 12.5 cm to 15.2 cm. To do this, the overall height of the birdhouse must increase. What will be the new height of the birdhouse? All other labeled dimensions on the birdhouse will remain unchanged.

Ⓒ **Common Core State Standards**
HSG.CO.B.7, HSG.CO.B.8, MP.4

▶ SavvasRealize.com

Powered By
desmos

Check It Out!

Maybe you've played this game before: you draw a picture. Then you try to get a classmate to draw the same picture by giving step-by-step directions but without showing your drawings.

Try it with a classmate. Draw a map of a room in your house or a place in your town. Then give directions to a classmate to draw the map that you drew. How similar are they? Think about this during the Mathematical Modeling in 3 Acts lesson.

ACT 1 Identify the Problem

1. What is the first question that comes to mind after watching the video?

2. Write down the main question you will answer about what you saw in the video.

3. Make an initial conjecture that answers this main question.

4. Explain how you arrived at your conjecture.

5. What information will be useful to know in order to answer the main question? How can you get it? How will you use that information?

ACT 2 Develop a Model

6. Use the math that you have learned in this Topic to refine your conjecture.

ACT 3 Interpret the Results

7. Did your refined conjecture match the actual answer exactly? If not, what might explain the difference?

4-3

Proving and Applying the SAS and SSS Congruence Criteria

I CAN... use SAS and SSS congruence criteria to prove triangles are congruent.

© Common Core State Standards
HSG.CO.B.8, HSG.SRT.B.5,
HSG.CO.A.5, HSG.CO.B.6, HSG.CO.B.7
MP.3, MP.7, MP.8

CONCEPTUAL UNDERSTANDING

COMMUNICATE PRECISELY
An *included angle* is the angle between two specific sides of a triangle. For sides $\overline{RS}$ and $\overline{ST}$, the included angle is $\angle S$ and the non-included angles are $\angle R$ and $\angle T$. **© MP.6**

COMMON ERROR
When writing congruence statements, the order of the letters is important, as corresponding parts must be written in the same order. The statement $\triangle RST \cong \triangle ZYX$ is not correct, because the vertices on the left side of the congruence symbol do not correspond to the vertices on the right.

EXPLORE & REASON

Make five triangles that have a 5-inch side, a 6-inch side, and one 40° angle.

A. How many unique triangles can you make?

B. **Construct Arguments** How are the unique triangles different from each other? **© MP.3**

ESSENTIAL QUESTION

How are SAS and SSS used to show that two triangles are congruent?

EXAMPLE 1 Explore the Side-Angle-Side (SAS) Congruence Criterion

Given two triangles with two pairs of sides congruent and the included angles congruent, verify that the triangles are congruent.

To prove that the triangles are congruent, show that a rigid motion maps $\triangle RST$ to $\triangle XYZ$.

Translate $\triangle RST$ so point S maps to point Y.

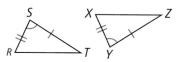

Since the translation maps S to Y, $Y = S'$.

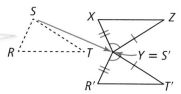

Rotate $\triangle R'S'T'$ about point Y, so $\overrightarrow{S''R''}$ coincides with $\overrightarrow{YX}$.

Since rotation preserves length, $R''S'' = RS = XY$, so $X = R''$.

Then reflect $\triangle R''S''T''$ across $\overleftrightarrow{XY}$.

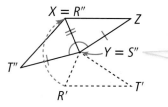

Since reflection preserves angle measure and length, all corresponding sides and angles are congruent. $m\angle R'''S'''T''' = m\angle RST = m\angle XYZ$, so $\overrightarrow{S'''T'''}$ coincides with $\overrightarrow{YZ}$. Additionally, $S'''T''' = ST = YZ$, so Z coincides with T'''.

Because the vertices of $\triangle R'''S'''T'''$ coincide with the vertices of $\triangle XYZ$, there exists a rigid motion that maps $\triangle RST$ to $\triangle XYZ$. By the definition of congruence, $\triangle RST \cong \triangle XYZ$.

CONTINUED ON THE NEXT PAGE

EXAMPLE 1 CONTINUED

Try It! **1.** What rigid motion or composition of rigid motions shows that △UVW maps to △XYZ?

THEOREM 4-3 Side-Angle-Side (SAS) Congruence Criterion

If two sides and the included angle of one triangle are congruent to two sides and the included angle of another triangle, then the two triangles are congruent.

If...

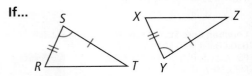

Then... △RST ≅ △XYZ

PROOF: SEE EXAMPLE 1.

THEOREM 4-4 Corresponding Parts of Congruent Triangles are Congruent (CPCTC)

If two triangles are congruent, then each pair of corresponding sides is congruent and each pair of corresponding angles is congruent.

If... △ABC ≅ △XYZ

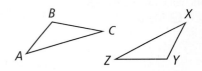

Then... $\overline{AB} \cong \overline{XY}$, $\overline{BC} \cong \overline{YZ}$, $\overline{AC} \cong \overline{XZ}$, ∠A ≅ ∠X, ∠B ≅ ∠Y, and ∠C ≅ ∠Z.

PROOF: SEE EXERCISE 13.

APPLICATION

EXAMPLE 2 Apply the SAS Congruence Criterion

Allie cuts two triangles from a rectangular piece of metal along the dashed line to make earrings. How can Allie show that the earrings are the same size and shape?

LEARN TOGETHER
How can you share your ideas and communicate your thinking with others?

Draw diagrams to represent the earrings.

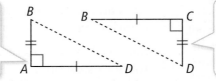

Because the sheet is a rectangle, $m\angle A = m\angle C = 90$, so ∠A ≅ ∠C.

Opposite sides of a rectangle have the same length, so $\overline{AD} \cong \overline{BC}$ and $\overline{AB} \cong \overline{CD}$.

By SAS, △ABD ≅ △CDB. Because the triangles are congruent, the earrings are the same size and shape.

CONTINUED ON THE NEXT PAGE

EXAMPLE 2 CONTINUED

Try It! **2.** Given that $\overline{AB} \parallel \overline{CD}$ and $\overline{AB} \cong \overline{CD}$, how can you show that $\angle B \cong \angle D$?

THEOREM 4-5 Side-Side-Side (SSS) Congruence Criterion

If three sides of one triangle are congruent to three sides of another triangle, then the two triangles are congruent.

If...

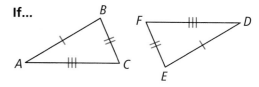

PROOF: SEE EXAMPLE 3.

Then... $\triangle ABC \cong \triangle DEF$

PROOF

EXAMPLE 3 **Prove the Side-Side-Side (SSS) Congruence Criterion**

Prove the SSS Congruence Criterion.

Given: $\overline{AB} \cong \overline{DE}$, $\overline{BC} \cong \overline{EF}$, $\overline{AC} \cong \overline{DF}$

Prove: $\triangle ABC \cong \triangle DEF$

Proof: First, translate $\triangle ABC$ so point B maps to point E. Since the translation maps B to E, $E = B'$.

Then rotate $\triangle A'B'C'$ about point E so the image $\overline{B''C''}$ coincides with $\overline{EF}$. It appears that A'' coincides with D'', but this needs to be proven.

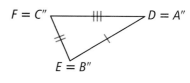

STUDY TIP
Use indirect reasoning to show that A'' must coincide with D.

To show that A'' does coincide with D, assume that A'' does not coincide.

Draw $\overline{A''D}$. Then $\overline{A''D}$ is the base of two isosceles triangles, $\triangle FA''D$ and $\triangle EDA''$.

By the Isosceles Triangle Theorem, $\angle FA''D \cong \angle FDA''$ and $\angle EA''D \cong \angle EDA''$. From the diagram, observe that $m\angle FA''D > m\angle EA''D$ and $m\angle FDA'' < m\angle EDA''$.

$m\angle FA''D > m\angle EA''D$
$m\angle FDA'' > m\angle EA''D$
$m\angle FDA'' > m\angle EDA''$

Substitute $m\angle FDA''$ for $m\angle FA''D$, and substitute $m\angle EDA''$ for $m\angle EA''D$.

This contradicts the observation that $\angle FDA'' < \angle EDA''$. Therefore, A'' must coincide with D. Since $D = A''$, $E = B''$, and $F = C''$, there exists a rigid motion that maps $\triangle ABC$ to $\triangle DEF$, so $\triangle ABC \cong \triangle DEF$.

CONTINUED ON THE NEXT PAGE

EXAMPLE 3 CONTINUED

Try It! **3.** What composition of rigid motions maps △PQR to △STU?

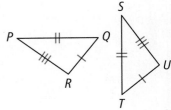

EXAMPLE 4 > **Determine Congruent Triangles**

A. Which of the following pairs are congruent by SAS or SSS?

Congruent by SSS

Congruent by SAS

COMMON ERROR
It may not be enough to identify two pairs of congruent sides and one pair of congruent angles. Recall that to apply SAS, the congruent angle pair must be the included angles.

Cannot be determined

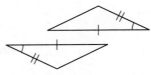

Congruent by SAS

B. What additional information is needed to show △ABC ≅ △DEF by SAS? By SSS?

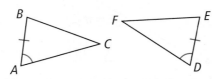

To show △ABC ≅ △DEF by SAS, you need $\overline{AC} \cong \overline{DF}$.

To show △ABC ≅ △DEF by SSS, you need $\overline{AC} \cong \overline{DF}$ and $\overline{BC} \cong \overline{EF}$.

Try It! **4.** Determine if the triangles are congruent. If it cannot be determined, what additional information is needed to show the triangles are congruent?

a.

b.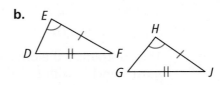

CONCEPT SUMMARY Triangle Congruence Criteria

THEOREM 4-3 — Side-Angle-Side (SAS)

If...

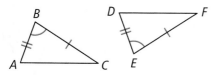

$\overline{AB} \cong \overline{DE}$, $\overline{BC} \cong \overline{EF}$, and $\angle B \cong \angle E$

Then... $\triangle ABC \cong \triangle DEF$

THEOREM 4-5 — Side-Side-Side (SSS)

If...

$\overline{JK} \cong \overline{MN}$, $\overline{JL} \cong \overline{MP}$, and $\overline{KL} \cong \overline{NP}$

Then... $\triangle JKL \cong \triangle MNP$

Do You UNDERSTAND?

1. **ESSENTIAL QUESTION** How are SAS and SSS used to show that two triangles are congruent?

2. **Error Analysis** Elijah says $\triangle ABC$ and $\triangle DEF$ are congruent by SAS. Explain Elijah's error. ⓒ **MP.3**

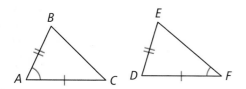

3. **Construct Arguments** Suppose $\overline{PR} \cong \overline{ST}$ and $\angle P \cong \angle S$. Ron wants to prove $\triangle PQR \cong \triangle STU$ by SAS. He says that all he needs to do is show $\overline{RQ} \cong \overline{SU}$. Will this work? Explain. ⓒ **MP.3**

4. **Reason** How would you decide what theorem to use to prove $\angle JKL \cong \angle MNP$? Explain. ⓒ **MP.2**

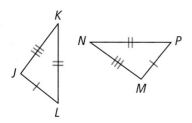

5. **Make Sense and Persevere** Suppose that $\overline{JK}$ and $\overline{LM}$ bisect each other. Is there enough information to show that $\triangle JPM \cong \triangle KPL$? Explain. ⓒ **MP.1**

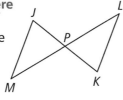

Do You KNOW HOW?

For Exercises 6–8, which pairs of triangles are congruent by SAS? By SSS?

6.

7.

8.

For Exercises 9–11, are the triangles congruent? Explain.

9.

10.

11.

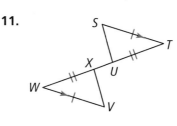

PRACTICE & PROBLEM SOLVING

UNDERSTAND

12. Error Analysis Zhang says △ABC is congruent to △ADC. Explain the error in Zhang's work. © MP.3

$\overline{AD} \cong \overline{CD}$
$\overline{AC} \cong \overline{AC}$
∠DCA ≅ ∠BCA

Therefore,
△ABC ≅ △ADC by SAS ✗

13. Construct Arguments Given △ABC ≅ △XYZ, use a rigid motion to prove Theorem 4-4, Corresponding Parts of Congruent Triangles are Congruent. © MP.3

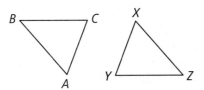

14. Mathematical Connections Is △JKL congruent to △MNL? Explain.

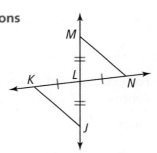

15. Make Sense and Persevere Why is △ABC ≅ △GHJ? © MP.1

16. Higher Order Thinking Given quadrilaterals ABCD and LMNO, and $\overline{AC} \cong \overline{LN}$, how can you show that the corresponding angles of the quadrilaterals are congruent?

PRACTICE

17. Prove △ACE is an isosceles triangle.
SEE EXAMPLES 1 AND 2

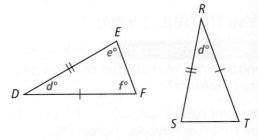

18. What is m∠RTS? Justify your answer.
SEE EXAMPLES 1 AND 2

19. What additional information is needed to show that △PQR ≅ △STU by SSS? SEE EXAMPLE 3

20. What additional information is needed to show that △ABC ≅ △DEF? SEE EXAMPLE 3

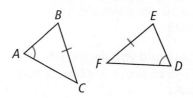

21. Is △RSV ≅ △UTV? Explain.
SEE EXAMPLE 4

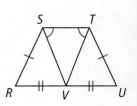

22. Is △PQR ≅ △PSR? Explain.
SEE EXAMPLE 4

PRACTICE & PROBLEM SOLVING

23. Critique Reasoning Yumi runs from the northwest corner to the southeast corner of a rugby field and Mìa runs from the northeast corner to the southwest corner. Mìa says she ran farther. Is she correct? Explain. ⒸMP.3

24. Reason Following the route shown, what is the total distance traveled by the architectural tour if it ends where it started? What properties and theorems did you use to find the distance? ⒸMP.2

25. Make Sense and Persevere Justice and Leah each made a triangular scarf. Do the scarves have the same size and shape? What do you notice about the information that is given? ⒸMP.1

26. Select all the sets of congruent parts that are sufficient to conclude that △FGH ≅ △JKL?

☐ **A.** $\overline{FG} \cong \overline{JK}$, $\overline{GH} \cong \overline{KL}$, $\overline{FH} \cong \overline{JL}$

☐ **B.** $\overline{FG} \cong \overline{JK}$, $\overline{FH} \cong \overline{JL}$, $\angle FHG \cong \angle JLK$

☐ **C.** $\overline{GH} \cong \overline{KL}$, $\overline{FG} \cong \overline{JK}$, $\angle FGH \cong \angle JKL$

☐ **D.** $\overline{GH} \cong \overline{KL}$, $\overline{FH} \cong \overline{JL}$, $\angle FHG \cong \angle JLK$

☐ **E.** $\overline{GH} \cong \overline{KL}$, $\overline{FH} \cong \overline{JL}$, $\angle FGH \cong \angle JKL$

27. SAT/ACT Consider △DEF and △PQR, where $\overline{DF} \cong \overline{PR}$ and $\overline{EF} \cong \overline{QR}$. Which additional piece of information would allow you to conclude that △DEF ≅ △PQR?

Ⓐ $\angle D \cong \angle P$

Ⓒ $\angle D \cong \angle Q$

Ⓑ $\angle E \cong \angle Q$

Ⓓ $\angle F \cong \angle R$

28. Performance Task In a marching band show, Huian and Latoya start 10 yards apart. Huian marches the path in blue and Latoya marches the path in green.

Part A Are the triangles formed by the paths congruent? Explain.

Part B Are the angle measures that Huian and Latoya turn at points A and B the same? Explain.

4-4

Proving and Applying the ASA and AAS Congruence Criteria

I CAN... determine congruent triangles by comparing two angles and one side.

Common Core State Standards
HSG.CO.B.8, HSG.SRT.B.5,
HSG.CO.A.5, HSG.CO.B.6, HSG.CO.B.7,
MP.1, MP.5, MP.7

LOOK FOR RELATIONSHIPS
Think about how change in one part of a figure affects the rest of the figure. Does the result follow a pattern? **MP.7**

EXPLORE & REASON

Are these triangles congruent?

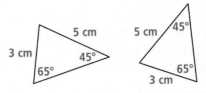

A. **Make Sense and Persevere** Assume the triangles are *not* congruent. What contradictions can you find to contradict your assumption? Explain. **MP.1**

B. Is it sufficient to say that the triangles are congruent because of the contradictions you found? Explain.

ESSENTIAL QUESTION How are ASA and AAS used to show that triangles are congruent?

EXAMPLE 1 Explore the ASA Congruence Criterion

How many possible triangles can you determine when given two angles and the included side of a triangle?

Consider $\overrightarrow{AB}$, $\overrightarrow{AE}$, and $\overrightarrow{BG}$, where $\overrightarrow{AB}$ and $\overrightarrow{AE}$ form a 25° angle.

Let $\overrightarrow{BG}$ rotate counterclockwise about point B to form a 68° angle, a 57° angle, and a 45° angle. The rays will intersect to form some triangles.

When m∠B changes, the second and third side lengths and third angle measure always change.

Notice that, once the 25° angle and the side of length 3 cm are set, there is exactly one way to complete the triangle with a 68° angle, a 57° angle, or a 45° angle. So for each unique combination of AB, m∠A, and m∠B, there exists a unique triangle.

Try It! **1.** What is the relationship between BX and CY? What conclusion can you draw about the relationship of △AXB and △CDY? Explain.

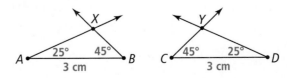

THEOREM 4-6 Angle-Side-Angle (ASA) Congruence Criterion

If two angles of one triangle and the included side are congruent to two angles and the included side of another triangle, then the two triangles are congruent.

PROOF: SEE EXAMPLE 2.

If...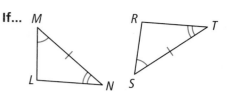

Then... $\triangle MLN \cong \triangle SRT$

PROOF →

EXAMPLE 2 Prove the Angle-Side-Angle (ASA) Congruence Criterion

Given two triangles with two pairs of angles congruent and the included sides congruent, prove the triangles are congruent.

Given: $\angle LMN \cong \angle RST$, $\angle LNM \cong \angle RTS$, $\overline{MN} \cong \overline{ST}$

Prove: $\triangle MLN \cong \triangle SRT$

Translate $\triangle MLN$ to map M to S.   Rotate $\triangle M'L'N'$ about point S to map $\overline{M'N'}$ to $\overline{ST}$.

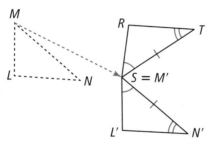

Reflect $\triangle M''L''N''$ across $\overleftrightarrow{ST}$.

STUDY TIP
When all vertices coincide, there exists a rigid motion that maps one triangle to the other. By definition, the triangles are congruent.

Because angle measures are preserved with reflections, $\overrightarrow{M'''L'''}$ coincides with $\overrightarrow{SR}$ and $\overrightarrow{N'''L'''}$ coincides with $\overrightarrow{TR}$. The intersection of $\overrightarrow{SR}$ and $\overrightarrow{TR}$ is at both R and L'''. Since the intersection of two rays is unique, R and L''' coincide.

Therefore, $\triangle MLN \cong \triangle SRT$.

Try It! **2.** Describe a series of transformations that shows $\triangle JKL \cong \triangle MNO$.

EXAMPLE 3 **Apply the Angle-Side-Angle (ASA) Congruence Criterion**

A technician installs cables from a cell phone tower to the ground. To pass inspection, both cables must be the same length. Does this installation meet the cable-length requirement? Explain.

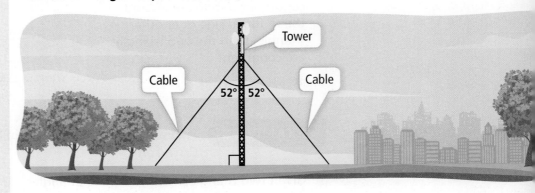

Formulate ◄ The ground, tower, and cables form two triangles, △ABX and △CBX.

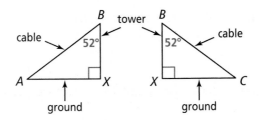

Compute ◄ All right angles are congruent, so ∠AXB ≅ ∠CXB. By the Reflexive Property of Congruence, $\overline{BX} \cong \overline{BX}$. Also, m∠ABX = 52° and m∠CBX = 52°, so ∠ABX ≅ ∠CBX.

Two angles and the included side of △ABX are congruent to two angles and the included side of △CBX. Therefore, △ABX ≅ △CBX by ASA.

By CPCTC, $\overline{AB} \cong \overline{CB}$. So, both cables are the same length.

Interpret ◄ The cable lengths do meet the inspection requirement.

Try It! **3. a.** Are △JKL and △MNO congruent? Explain.

b. Are △JKL and △PQR congruent? Explain.

EXAMPLE 4

Investigate the Angle-Angle-Side (AAS) Congruence Criterion

HAVE A GROWTH MINDSET
What other strategies can you try when you get stuck?

Given △ABC, is the triangle determined by ∠A, ∠B, and the non-included side $\overline{AC}$ unique?

Assume that △ABC is not unique. Then there must exist △DEF such that △ABC ≇ △DEF, ∠A ≅ ∠D, ∠B ≅ ∠E, and $\overline{AC} ≅ \overline{DF}$.

By the Triangle Angle-Sum Theorem, $m∠C = 180 - m∠A - m∠B$ and $m∠F = 180 - m∠D - m∠E$. Since ∠A ≅ ∠D and ∠B ≅ ∠E, $m∠C = 180 - m∠D - m∠E = m∠F$, so ∠C ≅ ∠F.

Therefore, by ASA, △ABC ≅ △DEF, and the assumption is false. A unique triangle is determined by ∠A and ∠B and the non-included side $\overline{AC}$.

Try It! **4.** Using the figures shown, describe a sequence of rigid motions that maps △JKL to △QRP.

THEOREM 4-7 Angle-Angle-Side (AAS) Congruence Criterion

If two angles and a nonincluded side of one triangle are congruent to two angles and a nonincluded side of another triangle, then the two triangles are congruent.

If...

Then... △UVW ≅ △XYZ

PROOF: SEE EXERCISE 16.

EXAMPLE 5

Use Triangle Congruence Criteria

A. State whether each pair of triangles is congruent by SAS, SSS, ASA, or AAS, or if the congruence cannot be determined.

congruent by ASA

congruent by SSS

COMMON ERROR
Be careful not to just assume that triangles are congruent when given two pairs of congruent angles and one pair of congruent sides. The congruent sides must be corresponding sides.

congruent by AAS

cannot be determined

CONTINUED ON THE NEXT PAGE

EXAMPLE 5 CONTINUED

B. Prove that $\overline{FH} \cong \overline{JL}$.

Given: $\overline{GH} \cong \overline{KL}$, $\angle GFH \cong \angle KJL$, and $\angle FGH \cong \angle JKL$

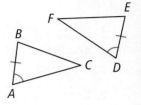

Prove: $\overline{FH} \cong \overline{JL}$

Statements	Reasons
1) $\angle F \cong \angle J$, $\angle G \cong \angle K$, $\overline{GH} \cong \overline{KL}$	1) Given
2) $\triangle FGH \cong \triangle JKL$	2) AAS
3) $\overline{FH} \cong \overline{JL}$	3) CPCTC

Try It! **5. a.** What additional information is needed to show $\triangle ABC \cong \triangle DEF$ by ASA?

b. What additional information is needed to show $\triangle ABC \cong \triangle DEF$ by AAS?

EXAMPLE 6 ▶ **Determine Congruent Polygons**

All sides and angles of *ABCD* are congruent to the corresponding sides and angles of *A'B'C'D'*. Is *ABCD* congruent to *A'B'C'D'*?

Each polygon can be divided into two triangles by the diagonals shown.

$\triangle ABC \cong \triangle A'B'C'$ by SAS. $\triangle ADC \cong \triangle A'D'C'$ by SAS.

Since $\triangle ABC \cong \triangle A'B'C'$, there is a rigid motion that maps $\triangle ABC$ to $\triangle A'B'C'$. Consider this rigid motion applied to $\triangle ADC$. Side $\overline{AC}$ maps to $\overline{A'C'}$ since $\overline{AC}$ is shared by both $\triangle ABC$ and $\triangle ADC$.

Now suppose that this rigid motion maps *D* to some point other than *D'*. Call that point *E*. Since $\triangle A'D'C'$ and $\triangle A'EC'$ are congruent to $\triangle ADC$, $\triangle A'D'C' \cong \triangle A'EC'$. Since $\angle C'A'E \cong \angle C'A'D'$, *E* lies on $\overleftrightarrow{A'D'}$. By a similar argument, *E* lies on $\overleftrightarrow{C'D'}$. So *E* must be the point *D'*.

Since the rigid motion that maps $\triangle ABC$ to $\triangle A'B'C'$ also maps *ABCD* to *A'B'C'D'*, *ABCD* is congruent to *A'B'C'D'*.

Try It! **6.** Given $ABCD \cong EFGH$, what is the value of *x*?

CONCEPT SUMMARY Triangle Congruence

THEOREM 4-6 Angle-Side-Angle (ASA)

If...
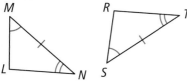

$\overline{MN} \cong \overline{ST}$, $\angle M \cong \angle S$, and $\angle N \cong \angle T$

Then... $\triangle MLN \cong \triangle SRT$

THEOREM 4-7 Angle-Angle-Side (AAS)

If...

$\overline{VW} \cong \overline{YZ}$, $\angle U \cong \angle X$, and $\angle V \cong \angle Y$

Then... $\triangle UVW \cong \triangle XYZ$

Do You UNDERSTAND?

1. **ESSENTIAL QUESTION** How are ASA and AAS used to show that triangles are congruent?

2. **Error Analysis** Why is Terrell's conclusion incorrect? ⓒ **MP.3**

$\overline{AB} \cong \overline{CD}$

$\angle DAB \cong \angle ADC$
$\angle CBA \cong \angle BCD$

Therefore,
$\triangle ABD \cong \triangle CDB$ by AAS

3. **Reason** How can you tell which property of triangle congruence shows $\triangle RST \cong \triangle UVW$? ⓒ **MP.2**

4. **Make Sense and Persevere** Is there a congruence relationship that is sufficient to show that $\triangle MNO \cong \triangle TUV$? Explain. ⓒ **MP.1**

Do You KNOW HOW?

For Exercises 5 and 6, find the value of x.

5.

6.

For Exercises 7 and 8, state whether the triangles are congruent and by which theorem.

7.

8.
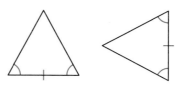

9. Why is $LMNO \cong PQRS$?

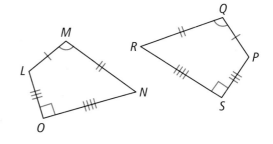

PRACTICE & PROBLEM SOLVING

UNDERSTAND

10. Error Analysis Stacy says there is not enough information to prove △ACX ≅ △BCX. Explain why Stacy's statement is incorrect. ⒸMP.3

Given: ∠AXC ≅ ∠BXC, ∠ACX ≅ ∠BCX
Prove: △ACX ≅ △BCX

Not enough information ✗

11. Mathematical Connections Given $\overleftrightarrow{WZ} \parallel \overleftrightarrow{XY}$ and $\overleftrightarrow{WX} \parallel \overleftrightarrow{ZY}$, write a two-column proof to show $\overline{WX} \cong \overline{YZ}$.

12. Use Structure Given the figure shown, write a two-column proof to prove ∠CAE ≅ ∠CEA. ⒸMP.7

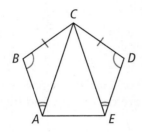

13. Reason How might you decide what additional piece of information you need to prove △JKL ≅ △NOM? ⒸMP.2

14. Higher Order Thinking Describe a composition of rigid motions that maps $\overline{DE}$ to $\overline{JK}$ and ∠D to ∠J. Does this same composition map $\overline{EF}$ to $\overline{KL}$? Explain.

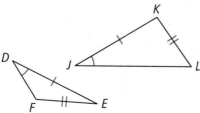

PRACTICE

15. Carpenters build a set of triangular roof supports, each with the measurements shown. How can the carpenters be sure all the slanted beams are the same length? SEE EXAMPLES 1–3

slanted beams
28° 28°

16. Prove the Angle-Angle-Side Congruence Criterion. SEE EXAMPLE 4

Given: ∠P ≅ ∠S, ∠Q ≅ ∠T, $\overline{QR} \cong \overline{TU}$

Prove: △PQR ≅ △STU

17. Write a proof. SEE EXAMPLE 5

Given: ∠A ≅ ∠C, $\overline{BX} \cong \overline{DX}$

Prove: $\overline{AX} \cong \overline{CX}$

18. Is ABCD ≅ GHJK? Explain. SEE EXAMPLE 6

19. If ABCD ≅ EFGH, are all corresponding parts congruent? Explain. SEE EXAMPLE 6

PRACTICE & PROBLEM SOLVING

APPLY

20. Look for Relationships Climbers want to determine a halfway point up a vertical cliff. If the top and bottom are parallel, why is point *P*, where the ropes intersect, halfway up the cliff? **ⓒ MP.7**

21. Use Appropriate Tools Keisha, Dwayne, and Lonzell are planning for a new bridge to replace the old bridge. The new bridge will start at point *B*, where Dwayne is standing, and end at point *C*, where Keisha is standing. Lonzell walks to point *D* and then walks parallel to the river until he reaches point *E*, where he sees Dwayne and Keisha are aligned. Why is the distance from *E* to *B* the length of the new bridge? **ⓒ MP.5**

22. Construct Arguments The Robotics Club wants to divide their robot battle arena into two congruent arenas for a tournament. Nori says that if they build a wall perpendicular to and bisecting $\overline{PO}$ from *M*, then the arenas will be congruent. Is Nori correct? Explain. **ⓒ MP.3**

ASSESSMENT PRACTICE

23. Given the figure shown, list all the pairs of congruent sides and pairs of congruent angles.

24. SAT/ACT Given $\triangle LMN \cong \triangle QRS$, what is the value of *x*?

Ⓐ 30   Ⓑ 35   Ⓒ 45   Ⓓ 60

25. Performance Task Gregory wants to make four congruent triangular flags using the entire rectangular canvas shown.

Part A Draw and label a diagram to show how Gregory should cut the fabric.

Part B Explain why the flags are congruent.

Part C Is there another way Gregory can cut the fabric to make 4 congruent triangular flags using the same amount of fabric? Explain.

4-5

Congruence in Right Triangles

I CAN... identify congruent right triangles.

 Common Core State Standards
HSG.CO.C.10, HSG.SRT.B.5, MP.2, MP.6, MP.7

CRITIQUE & EXPLAIN

Seth and Jae wrote the following explanations of why the two triangles are congruent.

Seth

There are two pairs of congruent sides, $\overline{AB} \cong \overline{DE}$ and $\overline{AC} \cong \overline{DF}$, and a pair of congruent right angles, $\angle C \cong \angle F$. So $\triangle ABC \cong \triangle DEF$ by SSA.

Jae

The lengths of $\overline{BC}$ and $\overline{EF}$ are 3 in., since these are 3-4-5 right triangles. There are three pairs of congruent sides, $\overline{AB} \cong \overline{DE}$, $\overline{AC} \cong \overline{DF}$, and $\overline{BC} \cong \overline{EF}$. So $\triangle ABC \cong \triangle DEF$ by SSS.

A. Do you think either student is correct? Explain.

B. Communicate Precisely Describe when you can state that two right triangles are congruent if you are only given two pairs of congruent sides and a right angle in each triangle. **© MP.6**

ESSENTIAL QUESTION What minimum criteria are needed to show that right triangles are congruent?

CONCEPTUAL UNDERSTANDING

EXAMPLE 1 Investigate Right Triangle Congruence

When any two pairs of corresponding sides are congruent, can you show that two right triangles $\triangle ABC$ and $\triangle DEF$ are congruent? Explain.

Given that right triangles have one pair of congruent corresponding angles with right angles, look to see what else is congruent.

LOOK FOR RELATIONSHIPS
Given two right triangles, which side of one triangle must correspond to the hypotenuse of the other triangle? Why? **© MP.7**

- If both pairs of corresponding legs are congruent, use SAS with $\overline{AC} \cong \overline{DF}$, $\angle C \cong \angle F$, and $\overline{BC} \cong \overline{EF}$.

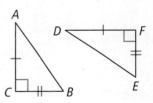

- If one pair of corresponding legs is congruent along with the hypotenuses, apply the Pythagorean Theorem to show that the other pair of corresponding legs is also congruent.

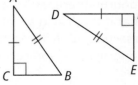

$$BC = \sqrt{AB^2 - AC^2} = \sqrt{DE^2 - DF^2} = EF$$

The right triangles are congruent by SSS.

Try It! **1.** Can you show that two right triangles are congruent when any one pair of corresponding acute angles is congruent and any one pair of corresponding legs is congruent? Explain.

THEOREM 4-8 Hypotenuse-Leg (HL) Theorem

If the hypotenuse and one
leg of a right triangle are
congruent to the hypotenuse
and leg of another right
triangle, then the triangles are
congruent.

PROOF: SEE EXERCISE 9.

If...

Then... $\triangle MNL \cong \triangle PQR$

APPLICATION

EXAMPLE 2 Use the Hypotenuse-Leg (HL) Theorem

**Ashton is washing windows using
a 10-foot ladder. The ladder reaches
the first window when he places it
as shown. The next window is the
same distance above ground as the
first. Where should Ashton place the
foot of the ladder in order to reach
the next window?**

> **COMMON ERROR**
> Remember that the triangles
> must be right triangles in order to
> use the HL Theorem. Be sure the
> situation, like this one, describes
> right triangles.

The ground, the ladder, and the side
of the house form a right triangle,
$\triangle RAH$, where R is the base of the
ladder and A is the top of the ladder.
When Ashton moves the ladder, it will form another right triangle, $\triangle SBK$,
where S is the base of the ladder and B is the top of the ladder.

Since the two windows are the same height above ground, $AH = BK$.
If $RA = SB$ and $AH = BK$, then $\triangle RAH \cong \triangle SBK$ by the HL Theorem.

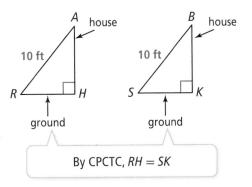

By CPCTC, $RH = SK$

Thus, by placing the base of the ladder the same distance away from the
house as he did for the first window, the ladder will reach the next window.

Try It! **2.** What information is
needed in order to apply
the Hypotenuse-Leg (HL)
Theorem?

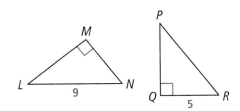

EXAMPLE 3 Write a Proof Using the Hypotenuse-Leg (HL) Theorem

Write a proof to show that a triangle is isosceles.

Given: $\overline{FD} \perp \overline{AB}$, $\overline{FE} \perp \overline{AC}$, $\overline{AE} \cong \overline{AD}$, $\overline{FC} \cong \overline{FB}$

Prove: $\triangle ABC$ is isosceles.

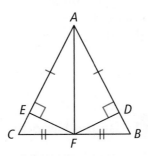

Statement	Reason
1) $\overline{FD} \perp \overline{AB}$, $\overline{FE} \perp \overline{AC}$	1) Given
2) $m\angle FDA = m\angle FDB = 90$, $m\angle FEA = m\angle FEC = 90$	2) Def. of $\perp$
3) $\triangle FEA$, $\triangle FDA$, $\triangle FEC$, and $\triangle FDB$ are rt. triangles	3) Def. of rt. triangle
4) $\overline{AE} \cong \overline{AD}$	4) Given
5) $\overline{AF} \cong \overline{AF}$	5) Refl. Prop. of Congruence
6) $\triangle FEA \cong \triangle FDA$	6) HL Theorem
7) $\overline{EF} \cong \overline{DF}$	7) CPCTC
8) $\overline{FC} \cong \overline{FB}$	8) Given
9) $\triangle FDB \cong \triangle FEC$	9) HL Theorem
10) $\angle ECF \cong \angle DBF$	10) CPCTC
11) $\overline{AC} \cong \overline{AB}$	11) Converse of Isosc. Triangle Thm.
12) $\triangle ABC$ is isosceles.	12) Def. of isosc. triangle

LOOK FOR RELATIONSHIPS
Consider what properties can be used to identify congruent parts in two triangles. What property shows that a common side is congruent to itself? Ⓒ **MP.7**

Try It! **3.** Write a proof to show that two triangles are congruent.

Given: $\overline{JL} \perp \overline{KM}$, $\overline{JK} \cong \overline{LK}$

Prove: $\triangle JKM \cong \triangle LKM$

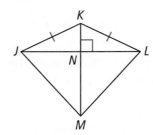

CONCEPT SUMMARY Congruence of Right Triangles

Triangle congruence theorems apply to right triangles.

THEOREM 4-3 Side-Angle-Side (SAS)

If...

$\overline{MN} \cong \overline{PQ}$ and $\overline{NO} \cong \overline{QR}$

Then... $\triangle MNO \cong \triangle PQR$

THEOREM 4-6 Angle-Side-Angle (ASA)

If...

$\overline{BC} \cong \overline{EF}$ and $\angle C \cong \angle F$

Then... $\triangle ABC \cong \triangle DEF$

THEOREM 4-7 Angle-Angle-Side (AAS)

If...

$\overline{GI} \cong \overline{JL}$ and $\angle I \cong \angle L$

Then... $\triangle GHI \cong \triangle JKL$

THEOREM 4-8 Hypotenuse-Leg (HL) Theorem

If...

Then... $\triangle STU \cong \triangle XYZ$

Do You UNDERSTAND?

1. **ESSENTIAL QUESTION** What minimum criteria are needed to show that right triangles are congruent?

2. **Error Analysis** Yama stated that $\triangle KLM \cong \triangle PLN$ by the HL Theorem. What mistake did Yama make? © MP.3

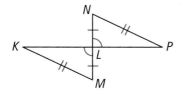

3. **Use Structure** What are the three conditions that two triangles must meet in order to apply the HL Theorem? © MP.7

4. **Reason** The HL Theorem is a side-side-angle theorem for right triangles. Why does it prove congruence for two right triangles but not prove congruence for two acute triangles or for two obtuse triangles? © MP.2

Do You KNOW HOW?

What information is needed to prove the triangles are congruent using the Hypotenuse-Leg (HL) Theorem?

5.

6.

What information would be sufficient to show the two triangles are congruent by the Hypotenuse-Leg (HL) Theorem?

7.

8.

PRACTICE & PROBLEM SOLVING

UNDERSTAND

9. **Construct Arguments** Follow the steps to prove the HL Theorem. **© MP.3**

   Given: Right triangles $\triangle MNL$ and $\triangle PQR$, $\overline{MN} \cong \overline{PQ}$, $\overline{ML} \cong \overline{PR}$

   Prove: $\triangle MNL \cong \triangle PQR$

   - Show that there is a rigid motion that maps L to R and M to P so that N' and Q are on opposite sides of $\overleftrightarrow{PR}$.

   - Then show that $\triangle PQN'$ is isosceles.

   - Show that $\triangle M'N'L' \cong \triangle PQR$, so $\triangle MNL \cong \triangle PQR$.

10. **Mathematical Connections** Consider the figures.

    Describe the steps you would have to take before you could use the HL Theorem to prove $\triangle GHJ \cong \triangle KLM$.

11. **Error Analysis** Mohamed wrote the paragraph proof to show that $\triangle DEG \cong \triangle EFG$. What mistake did he make? **© MP.3**

    $\triangle DEG$ and $\triangle EFG$ are right triangles. The figure shows $\overline{DE} \cong \overline{EF}$, AND $\overline{EG} \cong \overline{EG}$, by the reflexive Property. Therefore, by the HL theorem, $\triangle DEG \cong \triangle EFG$. ✗

12. **Higher Order Thinking** Suppose $\triangle ABC$ is an equilateral triangle. Use the HL Theorem to explain why any segment perpendicular to a side from the opposite vertex produces two congruent triangles. Would the same be true if $\triangle ABC$ were an isosceles triangle that was not equilateral? Explain.

PRACTICE

For Exercises 13–16, you are given a theorem and a congruence statement. What additional information is needed to prove that the triangles are congruent? SEE EXAMPLE 1

13. By using ASA, given $\overline{AC} \cong \overline{EF}$

14. By using AAS, given $\angle B \cong \angle D$

15. By using SAS, given $\overline{AB} \cong \overline{DE}$

16. By using HL, given $\overline{CB} \cong \overline{DF}$

For Exercises 17–18, what information would be sufficient to show that the triangles are congruent by the HL Theorem? SEE EXAMPLE 2

17.

18.

For Exercises 19–20, write a proof using the HL Theorem to show that the triangles are congruent. SEE EXAMPLE 3

19. **Given:** $\overline{AB} \cong \overline{CB}$, $\overline{AC} \perp \overline{DB}$

    Prove: $\triangle ABD \cong \triangle CBD$

    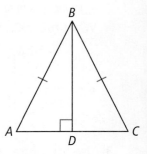

20. **Given:** $\overline{EF} \cong \overline{GH}$, G is the midpoint of $\overline{EJ}$

    Prove: $\triangle EFG \cong \triangle GHJ$

PRACTICE & PROBLEM SOLVING

APPLY

21. Make Sense and Persevere Part of a truss bridge consists of crossbeam $\overline{KM}$ and a perpendicular beam $\overline{LN}$. Which beams could an engineer measure in order to show $\triangle KLN \cong \triangle MLN$? State which theorem the engineer could use. **© MP.1**

22. Construct Arguments Raul wants to verify that the steps built by a carpenter are uniform by checking that $\triangle ABC \cong \triangle CDE$. The carpenter assures him they are because $\overline{AB} \cong \overline{CD}$ and $\overline{BC} \cong \overline{DE}$. **© MP.3**

a. Explain why Raul cannot use the HL Theorem to prove $\triangle ABC \cong \triangle CDE$.

b. Is there another theorem that Raul can apply to prove $\triangle ABC \cong \triangle CDE$? If so, state the theorem. If not, explain why not.

23. Communicate Precisely What are the fewest measurements that a homeowner could make to be certain that the windows shown below are congruent? **© MP.6**

ASSESSMENT PRACTICE

24. For each congruence statement, state the theorem that can be used to prove that the two triangles are congruent.

a. $\overline{PQ} \cong \overline{ST}$ and $\overline{QU} \cong \overline{TR}$

b. $\overline{PU} \cong \overline{SR}$ and $\overline{QU} \cong \overline{TR}$

c. $\overline{QU} \cong \overline{TR}$ and $\angle U \cong \angle R$

d. $\overline{QU} \cong \overline{TR}$ and $\angle P \cong \angle S$

25. SAT/ACT In right triangles ABC and DFE, $\overline{BC} \cong \overline{FE}$. Which statement(s) is(are) sufficient to prove the triangles are congruent?

   I. $\overline{AB} \cong \overline{EF}$ **II.** $\overline{AC} \cong \overline{DE}$

Ⓐ I is sufficient, but II is not

Ⓑ II is sufficient, but I is not

Ⓒ I is sufficient and II is sufficient

Ⓓ Neither I nor II is sufficient

26. Performance Task Wyetta makes the origami figure shown. Assume that every angle that appears to be a right angle is a right angle.

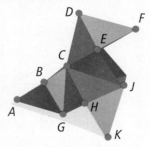

Part A What can Wyetta measure to prove that $\triangle ABG \cong \triangle CBG$?

Part B Wyetta measures to find that $HK = DE$ and $HJ = EC$. Which theorem(s) can she use to prove that $\triangle JHK \cong \triangle CED$? Explain.

Part C Choose two other triangles on the figure. Describe what Wyetta could measure to prove the triangles are congruent by using the HL Theorem.

4-6
Congruence in Overlapping Triangles

I CAN... use triangle congruence to solve problems with overlapping triangles.

© **Common Core State Standards**
HSG.SRT.B.5, MP.1, MP.3, MP.7

EXPLORE & REASON

Look at the painting shown.

A. How many triangles can you find?

B. **Make Sense and Persevere** What strategy did you use to count the triangles? How well did your strategy work? © **MP.1**

ESSENTIAL QUESTION Which theorems can be used to prove that two overlapping triangles are congruent?

EXAMPLE 1 Identify Corresponding Parts in Triangles

Figure *ABCD* is a rectangle with diagonals $\overline{AC}$ and $\overline{BD}$. How can identifying corresponding parts of overlapping triangles help prove they are congruent?

Consider △*ABC* and △*DCB*. Identify the corresponding sides and angles in the two triangles by first determining congruent parts.

Two segments, $\overline{AB}$ and $\overline{DC}$, have the same length.

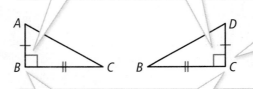

$\overline{BC}$ and $\overline{CB}$ are a common side in both triangles.

Two angles, ∠*ABC* and ∠*DCB,* are right angles.

COMMON ERROR
Be careful to state correspondence correctly. The parts should be named with corresponding vertices in the same order. Since *A* corresponds to *D* and *C* corresponds to *B*, state "$\overline{AC}$ corresponds to $\overline{DB}$" and not "$\overline{AC}$ corresponds to $\overline{BD}$."

Identify the corresponding vertices. Then use the corresponding vertices to identify the corresponding angles and sides.

Corresponding angles:

∠*ACB* and ∠*DBC*
∠*CBA* and ∠*BCD*
∠*BAC* and ∠*CDB*

Corresponding sides:

$\overline{AC}$ and $\overline{DB}$
$\overline{CB}$ and $\overline{BC}$
$\overline{BA}$ and $\overline{CD}$

Once you identify the corresponding angles and sides, you can determine if the triangles are congruent.

CONTINUED ON THE NEXT PAGE

EXAMPLE 1 CONTINUED

Try It! **1.** What are the corresponding sides and angles in △FHJ and △KHG?

EXAMPLE 2 **Use Common Parts of Triangles**

Prove ∠EGD ≅ ∠EFH.

> Since $\overline{DE} \cong \overline{HE}$, △DEH is isosceles, and therefore ∠D ≅ ∠H.

> Since $\overline{FG} \cong \overline{FG}$ and $\overline{DF} \cong \overline{HG}$, $\overline{DG} \cong \overline{HF}$ by the Segment Addition Postulate.

You can draw two separate triangles using the information above.

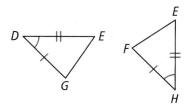

Because $\overline{DE} \cong \overline{HE}$, ∠D ≅ ∠H, and $\overline{DG} \cong \overline{HF}$, △EDG ≅ △EHF by SAS. By CPCTC, ∠EGD ≅ ∠EFH.

Try It! **2.** Are $\overline{VW}$ and $\overline{ZY}$ congruent? Explain.

EXAMPLE 3 **Prove That Two Triangles Are Congruent**

Write a proof to show that △BFE is congruent to △CEF.

Given: $\overline{AB} \cong \overline{DC}$, $\overline{AF} \cong \overline{DE}$, and ∠A ≅ ∠D

Prove: △BFE ≅ △CEF

Proof: Given that $\overline{AF} \cong \overline{DE}$ and $\overline{FE} \cong \overline{FE}$, $\overline{AE} \cong \overline{DF}$ by the Segment Addition Postulate. Since $\overline{AB} \cong \overline{DC}$ and ∠A ≅ ∠D, △ABE ≅ △DCF by SAS.

This means that by CPCTC, $\overline{BE} \cong \overline{CF}$ and ∠BEA ≅ ∠CFD. Therefore, by SAS, △BFE ≅ △CEF.

MAKE SENSE AND PERSEVERE
There are often multiple ways to complete a proof. How could you use SSS triangle congruence in this proof? Ⓖ **MP.1**

Try It! **3.** Write a proof to show that △SRV ≅ △TUW.

EXAMPLE 4   Separate Overlapping Triangles

A city runs three triangular bus routes to various attractions. How can you draw a separate triangle for each route? Are any of the routes the same length?

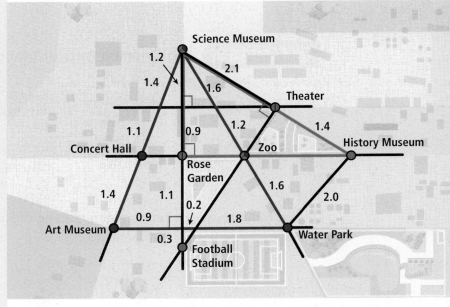

Green Route Stops:
Science Museum
Theater
History Museum
Zoo
Rose Garden
Science Museum

Purple Route Stops:
Water Park
Art Museum
Concert Hall
Science Museum
Zoo
Water Park

Red Route Stops:
Football Stadium
Zoo
Theater
Science Museum
Rose Garden
Football Stadium

Use the map and the list of locations for each route to help you draw the triangles. Add length and angle information to your diagrams.

STUDY TIP
When drawing each triangle, you might find it helpful to cover the parts of the diagram that you are not using.

By HL, the triangles representing the Green Route and the Red Route are congruent. Because the triangles are congruent, their perimeters are equal. Therefore, the Green Route and the Red Route are the same length.

Try It! **4.** A new route will stop at the History Museum, Water Park, Zoo, Science Museum, and Theater. Draw a triangle to represent the new route. Include any length or angle information that is given in the diagram.

CONCEPT SUMMARY Congruence in Overlapping Triangles

All congruence criteria can be applied to overlapping triangles.

THEOREM 4-5

Side-Side-Side (SSS)

If... $\overline{KL} \cong \overline{MJ}$ and $\overline{LM} \cong \overline{JK}$, and by the Reflexive Property, $\overline{KM} \cong \overline{MK}$ and $\overline{LJ} \cong \overline{JL}$,

Then... $\triangle KLM \cong \triangle MJK$ and $\triangle LMJ \cong \triangle JKL$ by SSS.

THEOREM 4-7

Angle-Angle-Side (AAS)

If...
$\angle A \cong \angle C$,
$\overline{FB} \cong \overline{DB}$,
and
$\angle B \cong \angle B$
by the Reflexive Property,

Then... $\triangle ABD \cong \triangle CBF$ by AAS.

THEOREM 4-8

Hypotenuse-Leg (HL) Theorem

If... in right triangles VXT and YWZ, $\overline{VT} \cong \overline{YZ}$ and hypotenuses $\overline{XT} \cong \overline{WZ}$,

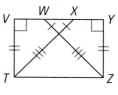

Then... $\triangle VXT \cong \triangle YWZ$ by the HL Theorem.

Do You UNDERSTAND?

1. **ESSENTIAL QUESTION** Which theorems can be used to prove two overlapping triangles are congruent?

2. **Construct Arguments** How could you prove that $\triangle ACD \cong \triangle ECB$?

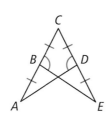

3. **Error Analysis** Nicholas wrote a proof to show that $\triangle EFD \cong \triangle DGE$. Explain Nicholas's error. Is it possible to prove the triangles congruent? Explain.

Since $\overline{EF} \cong \overline{DG}$, $\angle F \cong \angle G$, and $\overline{ED} \cong \overline{ED}$, by SAS, $\triangle EFD \cong \triangle DGE$. ✗

4. **Use Structure** Quadrilateral $JKLM$ is a rectangle. Which triangles are congruent to $\triangle JKL$? Explain.

Do You KNOW HOW?

5. What are the corresponding sides and angles in $\triangle WXV$ and $\triangle XWY$?

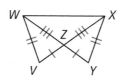

In Exercises 6–9, name a side or angle congruent to each given side or angle.

6. $\angle CDA$

7. $\overline{DB}$

8. $\angle FGH$

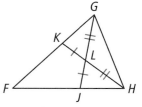

9. $\overline{HJ}$

For Exercises 10 and 11, name a theorem that can be used to prove that each pair of triangles is congruent.

10. $\triangle GJL$ and $\triangle KHL$ 11. $\triangle NQM$ and $\triangle PMQ$

PRACTICE & PROBLEM SOLVING

UNDERSTAND

12. Construct Arguments Write a proof to show that ∠CBH ≅ ∠EFH. **© MP.3**

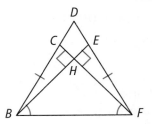

13. Mathematical Connections Explain why △ABF ≅ △GDE.

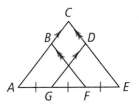

14. Error Analysis Dyani wrote a proof to show that ∠XWY ≅ ∠YZX. What is her error? **© MP.3**

Since ∠WXZ ≅ ∠ZYW, ∠XZW ≅ ∠YWX, and $\overline{XW}$ ≅ $\overline{YZ}$, by AAS, △XWZ ≅ △YWZ. Therefore, by CPCTC, ∠XWY ≅ ∠YZX. ✗

15. Higher Order Thinking Hexagon *ABCDEF* is a regular hexagon with all sides and angles congruent. List all sets of congruent triangles for the triangles in which all three vertices are also vertices of the hexagon.

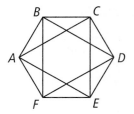

PRACTICE

16. What are the corresponding parts of △*CAE* and △*DAB*? **SEE EXAMPLE 1**

For Exercises 17–20, identify which side or angle is congruent to each given part. SEE EXAMPLE 2

17. ∠*JGK*

18. $\overline{HL}$

19. ∠*WYZ*

20. $\overline{XV}$

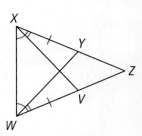

21. Write a proof to show triangles △*MRO* and △*PQN* are congruent. **SEE EXAMPLE 3**

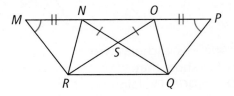

22. Write a proof to show that △*BCE* ≅ △*CBD*. SEE EXAMPLE 3

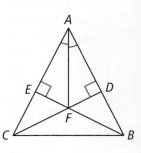

23. Draw separate diagrams showing △*AEC* and △*DBG*. SEE EXAMPLE 4

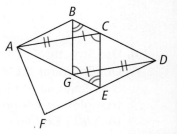

PRACTICE & PROBLEM SOLVING

24. Construct Arguments A park employee wants to place red trim along the seams, $\overline{AC}$ and $\overline{BD}$, of a patio umbrella. He assumes they are the same length. Is he correct? Explain. ⓒ **MP.3**

25. Reason A student is checking whether the design she drew is symmetric. Can she determine whether $\overline{MN}$ and $\overline{PN}$ are the same length? Explain. ⓒ **MP.2**

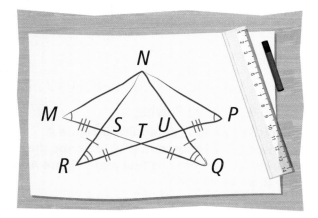

26. Look for Relationships The support for a drop tower ride is shown in the diagram. What is the width of the support? Round to the nearest hundredth. ⓒ **MP.7**

27. Which statement is false?

Ⓐ $\overline{KN} \cong \overline{KL}$ ⓒ $\angle KJN \cong \angle KLM$

Ⓑ $\triangle KMJ \cong \triangle KNL$ Ⓓ $\overline{MJ} \cong \overline{NL}$

28. SAT/ACT Which theorem could you use to prove $\triangle ABD \cong \triangle DCA$?

Ⓐ SAS   ⓒ SSS

Ⓑ AAS   Ⓓ AAA

29. Performance Task The diagram shows running trails at a park.

Part A LiMei ran the triangular route represented by $\triangle BDF$. Kaitlyn starts from point H and wants to run the same distance as LiMei. What triangular route can Kaitlyn run? Explain.

Part B Draw separate triangles to represent LiMei's and Kaitlyn's routes. Label as many side lengths and angle measures as you can determine.

Part C Can you determine the total distances, in kilometers, that each person ran? Explain.

Topic Review

1. What relationships between sides and angles of triangles can be used to prove triangles congruent?

Vocabulary Review

Choose the correct term to complete each sentence.

2. Figures that have the same size and shape are said to be _____.

3. The side of an isosceles triangle that is opposite the vertex is called the _____.

4. A rigid motion is sometimes called a _____ because it maps a figure to a figure with the same shape and size.

5. The legs of an isosceles triangle form an angle called the _____.

- base
- base angle
- congruence transformation
- congruent
- leg
- vertex

Concepts & Skills Review

LESSON 4-1 Congruence

Quick Review

Two figures are **congruent** if there is a rigid motion, or sequence of rigid motions, that maps one figure to the other.

Example

Figure 1 is translated right to form Figure 2. Are the figures congruent?

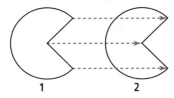

Yes, a translation is a congruence transformation.

Practice & Problem Solving

For Exercises 6 and 7, determine if Figure A and Figure B are congruent. If so, describe the sequence of rigid motions that maps Figure A to Figure B. If not, explain.

6.
A   B

7.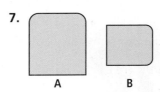
A   B

8. **Reason** If a figure is reflected across the same line twice, is the resulting image congruent to that figure? Explain. ⓖ **MP.2**

LESSON 4-2 ▶ Isosceles and Equilateral Triangles

Quick Review

Two sides of a triangle are congruent if and only if the angles opposite those sides are also congruent.

A line that bisects the **vertex** angle of an isosceles triangle is the perpendicular bisector of the opposite side.

Example

What is the measure of ∠C?

The sides opposite ∠A and ∠C are congruent, so ∠A ≅ ∠C; m∠A is 75°, so m∠C is 75°.

Practice & Problem Solving

Find the unknown angle measures for each triangle.

9.

10.

11. **Use Structure** A zipper bisects the vertex of the front of the tent, which is in the shape of an equilateral triangle, forming two triangles. What are the angle measures of the resulting triangles? Ⓒ **MP.7**

zipper

LESSON 4-3 ▶ Proving and Applying the SAS and SSS Congruence Criteria

Quick Review

Two triangles are congruent if two sides and the included angle of one triangle are congruent to two sides and the included angle of the other triangle (SAS).

Two triangles are congruent if three sides of one triangle are congruent to three sides of the other triangle (SSS).

Corresponding parts of congruent triangles are congruent (CPCTC).

Example

Show that the triangles are congruent.

They are congruent by SAS, because they have two pairs of congruent sides and the included angles are vertical angles and so are congruent.

Practice & Problem Solving

Which pairs of triangles are congruent by SAS or SSS? Explain.

12.

13.
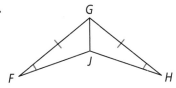

14. **Make Sense and Persevere** The paths of a ping-pong ball during two separate serves intersect at the center of the table. How many pairs of congruent triangles can you find? Ⓒ **MP.1**

Serve 1 ⟶   ⟵ Serve 2

Proving and Applying the ASA and AAS Congruence Criteria

Quick Review

Two triangles are congruent if two angles of one triangle and the included side are congruent to two angles and the included side of the other triangle (ASA).

Two triangles are congruent if two angles and a nonincluded side of one triangle are congruent to two angles and a nonincluded side of the other triangle (AAS).

Example

Show that the triangles are congruent.

They are congruent by ASA because they have two pairs of congruent angles that have a congruent side between the angles.

Practice & Problem Solving

State whether each pair of triangles is congruent by SAS, SSS, ASA, AAS, or the congruence cannot be determined. Justify your answer.

15.   16.

17. **Generalize** Are two triangles with two pairs of congruent angles and one pair of congruent sides always congruent? Explain. © MP.8

18. **Make Sense and Persevere** Are the triangles congruent? If they are, by which congruence criterion? Explain. © MP.1

Congruence in Right Triangles

Quick Review

If the hypotenuse and one leg of a right triangle are congruent to the hypotenuse and leg of another triangle, then the triangles are congruent (HL).

Example

Show that the triangles are congruent.

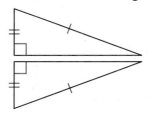

They are congruent by HL because the triangles are right triangles, and the hypotenuses and one pair of legs are congruent.

Practice & Problem Solving

Prove that the pair of triangles is congruent.

19.

20. **Communicate Precisely** Triangle *ABC* is an isosceles triangle with the vertex bisected by a line segment. Draw the triangle and prove that the resulting triangles are congruent. © MP.6

LESSON 4-6 Congruence in Overlapping Triangles

Quick Review

If two triangles are overlapping, all congruence criteria—AAS, ASA, HL, SAS, and SSS—can still be applied.

To identify congruent overlapping triangles, first identify the parts of each triangle. Then test if any of the congruence criteria hold.

Example

Given rectangle ABCD, how can you prove that ∠ADB ≅ ∠BCA?

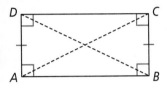

Opposite sides of a rectangle are congruent, so $\overline{AD} \cong \overline{BC}$. All right angles are congruent, so ∠DAB ≅ ∠CBA. By the Reflexive Property, $\overline{AB} \cong \overline{BA}$. Thus, △ADB ≅ △BCA by SAS, and ∠ADB ≅ ∠BCA by CPCTC.

Practice & Problem Solving

For Exercise 21, prove that the pair of triangles is congruent. For Exercise 22, which pairs of triangles are congruent? Explain.

21.

22.

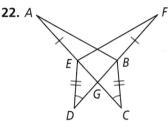

23. **Make Sense and Persevere** Describe where to place point E along $\overline{AC}$ such that △ABD ≅ △CBE. Then explain why the triangles are congruent. Ⓖ MP.1

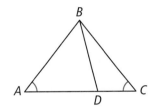

Relationships in Triangles

TOPIC ESSENTIAL QUESTION

How are the sides, segments, and angles of triangles related?

Topic Overview

enVision® STEM Project:
   Find the Center of Mass

5-1 Perpendicular and Angle Bisectors

5-2 Bisectors in Triangles

Mathematical Modeling in 3 Acts:
   Making It Fair

5-3 Medians and Altitudes

5-4 Inequalities in One Triangle

5-5 Inequalities in Two Triangles

Topic Vocabulary

- altitude
- centroid
- circumcenter
- circumscribed
- concurrent
- equidistant
- incenter
- inscribed
- median
- orthocenter
- point of concurrency

Digital Experience

INTERACTIVE STUDENT EDITION
Access online or offline.

ACTIVITIES Complete *Explore & Reason, Model & Discuss*, and *Critique & Explain* activities. Interact with *Examples* and *Try Its*.

CONCEPT SUMMARY Review key lesson content through multiple representations.

ASSESSMENT Show what you've learned.

 Go online | SavvasRealize.com

TOPIC 5

Making It Fair

In rural areas, county planners often work with local officials from a number of small towns to establish a regional medical center to serve all of the nearby communities.

County planners might also establish regional medical evacuation centers to transport patients with serious trauma to larger medical centers. The locations of these regional centers are carefully planned. Think about this during the Mathematical Modeling in 3 Acts lesson.

VIDEOS Watch clips to support *Mathematical Modeling in 3 Acts Lessons* and **enVision® STEM Projects.**

TUTORIALS Get help from *Virtual Nerd*, right when you need it.

PRACTICE Practice what you've learned.

ADAPTIVE PRACTICE Practice that is *just right* and *just for you.*

FAMILY ENGAGEMENT Involve family in your learning.

GLOSSARY Read and listen to English and Spanish definitions.

MATH TOOLS Explore math with digital tools and manipulatives.

DESMOS Use Anytime and as embedded Interactives in Lesson content.

Did You Know?

An object's **center of mass** is the single point at which its mass is evenly dispersed and the object is in balance.

When an object is moving within Earth's gravitational field, the object's center of mass is sometimes called its *center of gravity*.

If the center of mass is too far forward, drag increases and the airplane uses more fuel.

Center of Mass

If the center of mass is too far back, the airplane loses stability.

Athletes adjust their **center of mass** to maximize performance.

Your Task: Find the Center of Mass

In this project, you and your classmates will find the center of mass for a triangular object using mathematics. You will also find the center of mass for an irregular object through experimentation.

5-1

Perpendicular and Angle Bisectors

I CAN... use perpendicular and angle bisectors to solve problems.

VOCABULARY
• equidistant

 Common Core State Standards
HSG.CO.C.9, HSG.CO.D.12, MP.2, MP.3, MP.7

MODEL & DISCUSS

Powered By **desmos**

A new high school will be built for Brighton and Springfield. The location of the school must be the same distance from each middle school. The distance between the two middle schools is 18 miles.

A. Trace the points for the schools on a piece of paper. Locate a new point that is 12 mi from each school. Compare your point with the points of other students. Is there more than one location for the new high school? Explain.

B. **Reason** Can you find locations for the new high school that are the same distance from each middle school for any given distance? Explain. **MP.2**

ESSENTIAL QUESTION

What is the relationship between a segment and the points on its perpendicular bisector? Between an angle and the points on its bisector?

CONCEPTUAL UNDERSTANDING

EXAMPLE 1   Find Equidistant Points

How can you find points that are equidistant from the endpoints of $\overline{AB}$? What do you notice about these points and their relationship with $\overline{AB}$?

A point that is the same distance from two points is **equidistant** from the points.

COMMON ERROR
Be sure not to change the compass setting when drawing each pair of intersecting arcs from each endpoint.

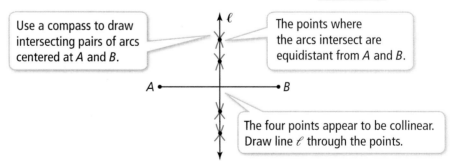

Use a compass to draw intersecting pairs of arcs centered at A and B.

The points where the arcs intersect are equidistant from A and B.

The four points appear to be collinear. Draw line ℓ through the points.

The points that are equidistant from A and B appear to lie on line ℓ. Line ℓ appears to be perpendicular to and bisect $\overline{AB}$ in the same plane as $\overline{AB}$. You can use a ruler and a protractor to support this hypothesis.

Try It!   **1.** Draw a pair of fixed points, and find points that are equidistant from the two fixed points. Draw a line through the set of equidistant points. Repeat this process for several pairs of fixed points. What conjecture can you make about points that are the same distance from a given pair of points?

THEOREM 5-1 Perpendicular Bisector Theorem

If a point is on the perpendicular bisector of a segment, then it is equidistant from the endpoints of the segment.

If...

PROOF: SEE EXAMPLE 2.

Then... $PX = PY$

THEOREM 5-2 Converse of the Perpendicular Bisector Theorem

If a point is equidistant from the endpoints of a segment, then it is on the perpendicular bisector of the segment.

If...

PROOF: SEE EXAMPLE 2 TRY IT.

Then... $XQ = YQ$ and $\overleftrightarrow{PQ} \perp \overline{XY}$

PROOF

EXAMPLE 2 Prove the Perpendicular Bisector Theorem

Prove the Perpendicular Bisector Theorem.

Given: ℓ is the perpendicular bisector of $\overline{XY}$.

Prove: $PX = PY$

Proof:

STUDY TIP
Remember that if a line is a perpendicular bisector of a segment, you can conclude two things: the line is perpendicular to the segment, and it bisects the segment.

All right angles are congruent, so $\angle XQP \cong \angle YQP$.

By the Reflexive Property, $\overline{PQ} \cong \overline{PQ}$.

Since ℓ is the perpendicular bisector of $\overline{XY}$, Q is the midpoint of $\overline{XY}$, and $\overline{XQ} \cong \overline{YQ}$.

By SAS, $\triangle XQP \cong \triangle YQP$. Therefore, $\overline{PX} \cong \overline{PY}$ by CPCTC, so $PX = PY$.

Try It! **2.** Prove the Converse of the Perpendicular Bisector Theorem.

EXAMPLE 3 > **Construct a Perpendicular Bisector**

How can you construct the perpendicular bisector of $\overline{AB}$?

A **perpendicular bisector** of a segment is a line, segment, or ray that is perpendicular to the segment and divides the segment into two congruent segments.

You can use a straightedge and compass to construct the perpendicular bisector of a segment.

Step 1   With a setting greater than $\frac{1}{2}AB$, place the compass point at A. Draw arcs above and below $\overline{AB}$.

Step 2   With the same setting, place the compass point at B. Draw arcs above and below $\overline{AB}$.

Step 3   Label the points of intersection of the arcs E and F. Use a straightedge to draw $\overleftrightarrow{EF}$.

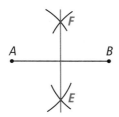

USE APPROPRIATE TOOLS
Consider the tools you can use to verify that a segment bisects another segment. What tool can you use? © **MP.5**

The constructed line, $\overleftrightarrow{EF}$, is the perpendicular bisector of $\overline{AB}$.

Try It!   **3.** Construct the perpendicular bisector of $\overline{JK}$.

EXAMPLE 4 **Construct a Perpendicular Lines**

A. How can you construct a perpendicular line from a point not on the line?

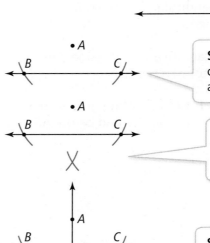

Step 1: With Point *A* as the center, construct an arc that intersects the line at two points. Label the points *B* and *C*.

Step 2: With the same setting, construct arcs from points *B* and *C* that intersect on the opposite side of the line.

Step 3: Label the point of intersection *D*. Use a straightedge to draw $\overleftrightarrow{AD}$. The constructed line $\overleftrightarrow{AD}$ is perpendicular to $\overleftrightarrow{BC}$.

B. Construct a perpendicular line from a point that lies on the line.

Construct a line that is perpendicular to the given line through point *D*.

Step 1: With Point *D* as the center, construct an arc that intersects the line at two points. Label the points *E* and *F*.

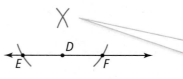

Step 2: Set the compass a little wider. With this setting, construct arcs from points *E* and *F* that intersect on one side of the line.

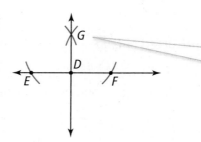

Step 3: Label the point of intersection *G*. Use a straightedge to draw $\overleftrightarrow{GD}$. The constructed line $\overleftrightarrow{GD}$ is perpendicular to $\overleftrightarrow{EF}$.

COMMUNICATE PRECISELY
Compare and contrast the constructions of a perpendicular bisector, a perpendicular line through a point not on the line, and a perpendicular line through a point on the line. How would you describe the similarities and differences to another student? Ⓖ **MP.6**

Try It! **4. a.** Construct a line perpendicular to line *m* through point *A*.

b. Construct a line perpendicular to line *m* through point *B*.

EXAMPLE 5 > Use Constructions of Perpendicular Lines

Mr. Lee wants to locate his ice cream cart along Main Street so that he is equidistant from the entrances of the amusement park and the zoo. How can Mr. Lee determine where to put his cart? Where should that location be?

Mr. Lee can use the perpendicular bisector of the segment that connects the two entrances to find the location.

Step 1 Label the entrances of the amusement park and zoo as points *A* and *Z*, and draw line *m* for Main Street.

Step 2 Draw *AZ*, and construct the perpendicular bisector.

Step 3 Mark point *T* where the perpendicular bisector and line *m* intersect.

Mr. Lee should park his cart at point *T*, because it is equidistant from both entrances.

LEARN TOGETHER
How can you respectfully disagree and manage your emotions?

Try It! 5. Ms. Medina wants to position her souvenir cart on the other side of Main Street so that she is directly across from Mr. Lee's ice cream cart. How can Ms. Medina determine where to put her cart?

EXAMPLE 6 **Apply the Perpendicular Bisector Theorem**

What is the value of AD?

By definition, $\overline{AC}$ is the perpendicular bisector of $\overline{BD}$.

$AB = AD$

The lengths are equal by the Perpendicular Bisector Theorem.

$6x - 10 = 3x + 2$

$3x = 12$

$x = 4$

$AD = 3(4) + 2$

Evaluate the expression for AD.

$AD = 14$

STUDY TIP
Look for relationships in the diagram to help you solve a problem. For example, a right angle marker tells you that two line segments are perpendicular.

Try It! **6. a.** What is the value of WY? **b.** What is the value of OL?

EXAMPLE 7 **Find Equidistant Points from the Sides of an Angle**

An airport baggage inspector is most efficient when he stands equidistant from the two conveyor belts. How can the inspector determine where he should stand?

Use pairs of corresponding points on each conveyor belt that are the same distance away from the vertex of the angle. To be equidistant from the conveyor belts, a point must have the same distance from corresponding points.

Draw the lines perpendicular from each pair of corresponding points.

Each point of intersection of the two perpendicular lines is equidistant from each conveyor belt.

The points are collinear and form ray q.

USE APPROPRIATE TOOLS
Think about the tools you can use to make sure that segments are perpendicular. What tool would you use? **Ⓒ MP.5**

Since the pairs of right triangles formed are congruent by the HL Theorem, the corresponding angles formed by the vertex angle and ray q are congruent by CPCTC. Therefore, ray q is the angle bisector.

The inspector can determine where to stand by choosing a point on the angle bisector.

CONTINUED ON THE NEXT PAGE

EXAMPLE 7 CONTINUED

Try It! **7.** Consider two triangles that result from drawing perpendicular segments from where the inspector stands to the conveyor belts. How are the triangles related? Explain.

THEOREM 5-3 Angle Bisector Theorem

If a point is on the bisector of an angle, then it is equidistant from the two sides of the angle.

If... *D* is on the bisector of ∠*A*

PROOF: SEE EXERCISE 9.

Then... *BD = CD*

THEOREM 5-4 Converse of the Angle Bisector Theorem

If a point is equidistant from two sides of an angle, then it is on the angle bisector.

If... *BD = CD*

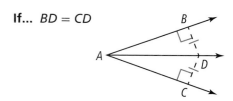

PROOF: SEE EXERCISE 10.

Then... *m∠BAD = m∠CAD*

EXAMPLE 8 **Apply the Angle Bisector Theorem**

What is the value of *KL*?

$\overrightarrow{JL}$ is the angle bisector of ∠*KJM* since *m∠KJL = m∠MJL*.

$KL = ML$

The lengths are equal by the Angle Bisector Theorem.

$2x + 3 = 4x - 11$

$2x = 14$

$x = 7$

$KL = 2(7) + 3$

Evaluate the expression for *KL*.

$KL = 17$

Try It! **8.** Use the figure shown.

  a. If *HI = 7*, *IJ = 7*, and *m∠HGI = 25*, what is *m∠IGJ*?

  b. If *m∠HGJ = 57*, *m∠IGJ = 28.5*, and *HI = 12.2*, what is the value of *IJ*?

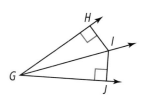

CONCEPT SUMMARY Perpendicular and Angle Bisectors

THEOREM 5-1 Perpendicular Bisector Theorem

If... Then...

$XM = YM$ and $\overline{PM} \perp \overline{XY}$

$PX = PY$

THEOREM 5-2 Converse of Perpendicular Bisector Theorem

If... Then...

$PX = PY$

$XM = YM$ and $\overline{PM} \perp \overline{XY}$

THEOREM 5-3 Angle Bisector Theorem

If... Then...

 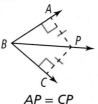

$\angle ABP \cong \angle CBP$

$AP = CP$

THEOREM 5-4 Converse of Angle Bisector Theorem

If... Then...

$AP = CP$

$\angle ABP \cong \angle CBP$

Do You UNDERSTAND?

1. **ESSENTIAL QUESTION** What is the relationship between a segment and the points on its perpendicular bisector? Between an angle and the points on its bisector?

2. **Vocabulary** How can you determine if a point is *equidistant* from the sides of an angle?

3. **Error Analysis** Dionne says that $\overrightarrow{KM}$ is the bisector of $\angle LKJ$ because $LM = MJ$. Explain the error in her reasoning. **© MP.3**

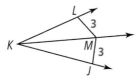

4. **Construct Arguments** You know that $\overline{AB}$ is the perpendicular bisector of $\overline{XY}$, and $\overline{XY}$ is the perpendicular bisector of $\overline{AB}$. What can you conclude about the side lengths of quadrilateral $AXBY$? Explain. **© MP.3**

Do You KNOW HOW?

5. If $JL = 14$, $KL = 10$, and $ML = 7$, what is JK?

Use the figure shown for Exercises 6 and 7.

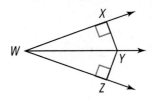

6. If $\angle XWY \cong \angle ZWY$ and $XY = 4$, what is YZ?

7. If $XY = ZY$ and $m\angle ZWY = 18$, what is $m\angle XWZ$?

8. What is an algebraic expression for the area of the square picture and frame?

$x - 2$ in.

PRACTICE & PROBLEM SOLVING

UNDERSTAND

9. Construct Arguments Write a two-column proof for the Angle Bisector Theorem. © MP.3

10. Construct Arguments Write a paragraph proof for the Converse of the Angle Bisector Theorem. © MP.3

11. Reason In the diagram below, $AB = BC$, $DF = EF$, and $m\angle BDF = m\angle BEF = 90°$. Is $\triangle ADF \cong \triangle CEF$? Justify your answer. © MP.2

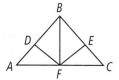

12. Error Analysis A student analyzed the diagram and incorrectly concluded that $AB = 2BC$. Explain the student's error. © MP.3

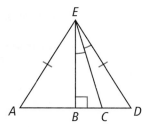

> $\overline{EB}$ is the perpendicular bisector of $\overline{AD}$, so $AB = BD$.
> $\angle BEC \cong \angle DEC$, so
> $BC = CD$.
> $BC + CD = BD = AB$, and
> $BC + CD = BC + BC = 2BC$, ✗
> so $AB = 2BC$.

13. Higher Order Thinking Describe the process of constructing the bisector of an angle. Draw a diagram and explain how this construction relates to the Angle Bisector Theorem.

PRACTICE

14. Construct the perpendicular bisector of $\overline{XY}$.
SEE EXAMPLES 1–3 and 5

15. Construct a line that is perpendicular to $\overline{AB}$ through point P.
SEE EXAMPLE 4

Use the figure shown for Exercises 16 and 17.
SEE EXAMPLE 6

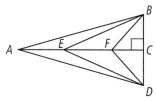

16. If $AD = 21$, $BF = 8$, and $DF = 8$, what is the value of AB?

17. If $ED = 7x + 4$, $BC = 2x + 1$, $CD = 5x - 8$, and $BD = 14$, what is the value of EB?

Use the figure shown for Exercises 18 and 19.
SEE EXAMPLES 7 and 8

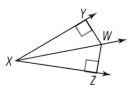

18. If $m\angle YXW = 21$, $YW = 5$, and $WZ = 5$, what is $m\angle ZXY$?

19. If $m\angle YXZ = 38$, $m\angle WXZ = 19$, and $WZ = 8.1$, what is the value of YW?

20. If $CD = 4$ and the perimeter of $\triangle ABC$ is 23, what is the perimeter of $\triangle ABE$?

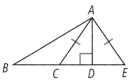

21. Given that $\angle ACF \cong \angle ECF$ and $m\angle ABF = m\angle EDF = 90$, write a two-column proof to show that $\triangle ABF \cong \triangle EDF$.

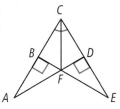

PRACTICE & PROBLEM SOLVING

22. Make Sense and Persevere A farmer paves a 40-foot horizontal path through his garden. He wants to pave a 40-foot vertical path such that he can stand at any point along the vertical path and be equidistant from the endpoints of the horizontal path. Then, he wants to pave another 40-foot horizontal path at the very top of the vertical path. Construct the two paths that the farmer wants to pave.

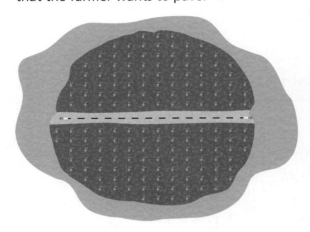

23. Look for Relationships An artist uses colored tape to divide sections of a mural. She needs to cut a piece of paper to cover △EFC while she works on other sections. What angles should she cut so she only covers triangle △EFC? ⓒ MP.7

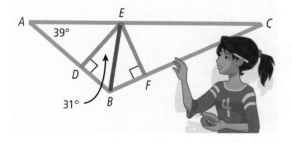

24. Mathematical Connections A surveyor took some measurements of a piece of land. The owner needs to know the area of the land to determine the value. What is the area of the piece of land?

25. $\overleftrightarrow{AB}$ is the perpendicular bisector of $\overline{XY}$. Point P is the midpoint of $\overline{XY}$. Select all statements that are always true.

☐ **A.** $AP = XP$

☐ **B.** $AB = XY$

☐ **C.** $AP = BP$

☐ **D.** $XB = YB$

☐ **E.** $AY = XB$

☐ **F.** $XP = YP$

26. SAT/ACT Points G, J, and K are not collinear, and $GJ = GK$. If P is a point on $\overline{JK}$, which of the following conditions is sufficient to prove that $\overleftrightarrow{GP}$ is the perpendicular bisector of $\overline{JK}$?

Ⓐ $JG = PG$ Ⓒ $\angle GJK \cong \angle GKJ$

Ⓑ $m\angle GPJ = 90$ Ⓓ $PK = PG$

27. Performance Task A manufacturer makes roofing trusses in a variety of sizes. All of the trusses have the same shape with three supports, as shown, with $\overline{ED} \perp \overline{AB}$ and $\overline{FD} \perp \overline{BC}$.

Part A One builder needs $\angle ABD$ and $\angle CBD$ to be congruent for a project. You need to check that a truss meets the builder's requirement. The only tools you have are a measuring tape and a steel square, which is a carpentry tool for measuring right angles. How can you use these tools to verify the angles are congruent?

Part B In addition to the requirement of the first builder, another builder also needs $\overline{AB}$ and $\overline{BC}$ to be congruent as well as $\overline{AD}$ and $\overline{DC}$. Using the same tools, how can you efficiently verify that all three pairs are congruent? Explain.

5-2
Bisectors in Triangles

I CAN... use triangle bisectors to solve problems.

VOCABULARY

- circumcenter
- circumscribed
- concurrent
- incenter
- inscribed
- point of concurrency

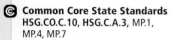
Common Core State Standards
HSG.CO.C.10, HSG.C.A.3, MP.1, MP.4, MP.7

MODEL & DISCUSS

Powered By desmos

A town has three recycling sites. They want to build a parking garage for the recycling trucks so that the distances from the sites to the parking garage are as close to equal as possible.

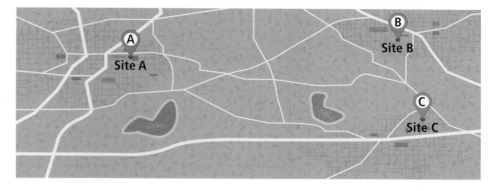

A. Points *A*, *B*, and *C* represent the locations of the three sites. Trace the points on a piece of paper. Locate a point *D* that appears to be the same distance from *A*, *B*, and *C* by sight only.

B. **Communicate Precisely** Measure the lengths from points *A*, *B*, and *C* to point *D* on your diagram. Are the lengths equal? If not, can you find a better location for point *D*? Explain. Ⓒ **MP.6**

C. What do you think is the quickest way to find the best point *D* in similar situations?

ESSENTIAL QUESTION   What are the properties of the perpendicular bisectors in a triangle? What are the properties of the angle bisectors in a triangle?

THEOREM 5-5 Concurrency of Perpendicular Bisectors

Powered By desmos

The perpendicular bisectors of the sides of a triangle are concurrent at a point equidistant from the vertices.

If... *d*, *f*, and *g* are the perpendicular bisectors of $\overline{AB}$, $\overline{BC}$, and $\overline{AC}$, respectively

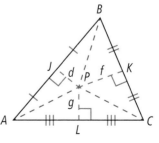

PROOF: SEE EXAMPLE 1.

Then... *d*, *f*, and *g* intersect at *P* and $PA = PB = PC$

EXAMPLE 1 Prove Theorem 5-5

How do you prove the Concurrency of Perpendicular Bisectors Theorem?

Given: △ABC with perpendicular bisectors q, r, and s.

Prove: Lines q, r, and s are concurrent at a point that is equidistant from A, B, and C.

VOCABULARY
When three or more lines intersect at one point, the lines are *concurrent*. The point where the lines intersect is called the *point of concurrency*.

COMMON ERROR
Make sure that you prove everything required to complete the proof. For this proof, you need to show both that the lines are concurrent and that they are equidistant from the vertices.

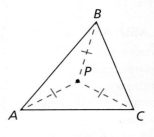

Let P be the point of intersection of q and r. By the Perpendicular Bisector Theorem, PA = PB, and PB = PC. Therefore PA = PC.

By the Converse of the Perpendicular Bisector Theorem, P also lies on the perpendicular bisector of $\overline{AC}$.

P is the point of concurrency of q, r, and s. Since PA = PB = PC, point P is equidistant from A, B, and C.

Try It! 1. Verify the Concurrency of Perpendicular Bisectors Theorem on acute, right, and obtuse triangles using a straightedge and compass or geometry software.

CONCEPTUAL UNDERSTANDING

EXAMPLE 2 Investigate Circumscribed Circles

How can you construct a circle that contains the three vertices of a given triangle?

The circle that contains all three vertices of a triangle is the **circumscribed** circle of the triangle.

All points on a circle are equidistant from the center of the circle.

The vertices of the triangle must be equidistant from the center of the circle.

By the Concurrency of Perpendicular Bisectors Theorem, the perpendicular bisectors intersect at a point that is equidistant from the vertices.

CONTINUED ON THE NEXT PAGE

EXAMPLE 2 CONTINUED

Use the point of concurrency of the perpendicular bisectors to circumscribe the triangle.

First, construct two perpendicular bisectors to find the point of concurrency of the perpendicular bisectors.

Then construct the circle centered on the point of concurrency, passing through any vertex.

Circumcenter

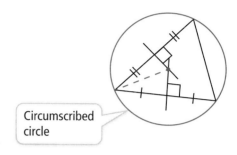

Circumscribed circle

The point of concurrency of the perpendicular bisectors of a triangle is the **circumcenter**. The circumcenter is the center of the circumscribed circle of the triangle.

COMMUNICATE PRECISELY

A point of concurrency is where three or more lines intersect. How would you explain to another student why only two of the three perpendicular bisectors need to be drawn to find the point of concurrency? Ⓒ **MP.6**

Try It!   **2.** What conjecture can you make about the location of the circumcenter for acute, right, and obtuse triangles?

APPLICATION

EXAMPLE 3   Use a Circumcenter

A city manager wants to place a new backup power generator so that it is the same distance from the school, hospital, and recreation center. Where should the generator be placed?

Step 1 Label *S* for the school, *H* for the hospital, and *R* for the recreation center. Connect the points to form a triangle.

Step 2 Construct the perpendicular bisectors of two of the sides.

Step 3 Label point *E* where the perpendicular bisectors intersect.

The city manager should place the backup power generator at point *E*, because it is equidistant to the three locations.

Try It!   **3.** If the city manager decided to place the generator so that it is the same distance from the hospital, school, and grocery store, how can she find the location?

THEOREM 5-6 Concurrency of Angle Bisectors

The angle bisectors of the angles of a triangle are concurrent at a point equidistant from the sides of the triangle.

PROOF: SEE EXERCISE 10.

If... *j*, *k*, and *l* are the angle bisectors of ∠Y, ∠X, and ∠Z, respectively

Then... *j*, *k*, and *l* intersect at Q and QM = QN = QO

EXAMPLE 4 Investigate Inscribed Circles

How can you construct a circle that intersects each side of a given triangle in exactly one point?

The circle that intersects each side of a triangle at exactly one point is the **inscribed** circle of the triangle.

None of the points on the circle are outside the triangle.

The sides of the triangle must be equidistant from the center of the circle.

By the Concurrency of Angle Bisectors Theorem, the angle bisectors of a triangle intersect at a point that is equidistant from the sides of the triangle.

First, construct two angle bisectors to find the point of concurrency of the angle bisectors.

Next, construct a perpendicular segment from the point of concurrency to any side.

Finally, construct the circle centered on the point of concurrency and passing through the point of intersection of the perpendicular segment and the side.

Incenter

Radius of the inscribed circle

Inscribed circle

The point of concurrency of the angle bisectors of a triangle is the **incenter**, so the incenter is the center of the inscribed circle of the triangle.

HAVE A GROWTH MINDSET
In what ways can you be inquisitive and open to learning new things?

Try It! 4. Do you think the incenter of a triangle can ever be located on a side of the triangle? Explain.

EXAMPLE 5 **Identify and Use the Incenter of a Triangle**

If $QP = 3(x + 1)$ and $RP = 5x - 3$, what is the radius of the inscribed circle of $\triangle JKL$?

Since $\overline{KP}$ and $\overline{LP}$ are angle bisectors of $\triangle JKL$, P is the incenter of $\triangle JKL$. Therefore, $QP = RP$.

Step 1 Solve for x.

$$QP = RP$$
$$3(x + 1) = 5x - 3$$
$$3x + 3 = 5x - 3$$
$$6 = 2x$$
$$x = 3$$

Step 2 Find the radius.

$$RP = 5x - 3$$
$$= 5(3) - 3$$
$$= 12$$

> The radius of the inscribed circle is equal to RP.

The radius of the inscribed circle is 12.

STUDY TIP
Remember that $QP = RP$, so evaluating either expression for $x = 3$ gives the value of the radius. Select the expression that is easier to evaluate.

Try It! **5.** Use the figure shown.

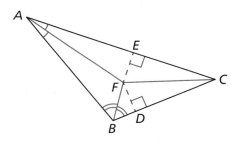

a. If $m\angle BAF = 15$ and $m\angle CBF = 52$, what is $m\angle ACF$?

b. If $EF = 3y - 5$ and $DF = 2y + 4$, what is the distance from F to $\overline{AB}$?

PROPERTIES ▸ **Perpendicular Bisectors**

Perpendicular bisectors intersect at the circumcenter.

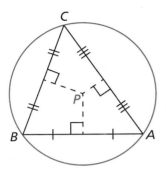

The circumcenter is equidistant from the vertices.

PROPERTIES ▸ **Angle Bisectors**

Angle bisectors intersect at the incenter.

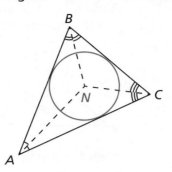

The incenter is equidistant from the sides.

Do You UNDERSTAND?

1. **ESSENTIAL QUESTION** What are the properties of the perpendicular bisectors in a triangle? What are the properties of the angle bisectors in a triangle?

2. **Error Analysis** Terrence constructed the circumscribed circle for △XYZ. Explain Terrence's error. Ⓒ MP.3

3. **Vocabulary** What parts of the triangle is the *circumcenter* equidistant from? What parts of the triangle is the *incenter* equidistant from?

4. **Reason** Is it possible for the circumscribed circle and the inscribed circle of a triangle to be the same? Explain your reasoning. Ⓒ MP.2

Do You KNOW HOW?

The perpendicular bisectors of △ABC are $\overline{PT}$, $\overline{QT}$, and $\overline{RT}$. Find each length.

5. *AT*   6. *RC*

Two of the angle bisectors of △ABC are $\overline{AP}$ and $\overline{BP}$. Find each value.

7. *PK*

8. Perimeter of △APL

9. An artist will place a circular piece of stained glass inside the triangular frame so that the glass touches each side of the frame. What is the diameter of the stained glass? Round to the nearest tenth.

PRACTICE & PROBLEM SOLVING

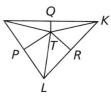

10. Construct Arguments Write a Proof of Theorem 5–6: In △ABC, let the angle bisectors of ∠A and ∠B intersect at point P. Show that P is equidistant from each side of △ABC, and that $\overline{CP}$ bisects ∠C. 🅖 **MP.3**

11. Higher Order Thinking A right triangle has vertices X(0, 0), Y(0, 2a), Z(2b, 0). What is the circumcenter of the triangle? Make a conjecture about the diameter of a circle that is circumscribed about a right triangle.

12. Error Analysis What is the error that a student made in finding the perimeter of △DTM? Correct the error. 🅖 **MP.3**

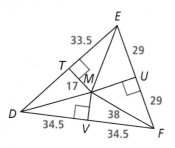

DT = 34.5, TM = 17, DM = 34.5.
The perimeter of △DTM is ✗
34.5 + 17 + 34.5 = 86.

13. Mathematical Connections A triangle with incenter P has side lengths x, y, and z. The distance from P to each side is a. Write an expression for the area of the triangle. Use the distributive property to factor your expression.

14. Reason In a right triangle with side lengths of 3, 4, and 5, what is the radius of the inscribed circle? Show your work. (*Hint:* Let r be the radius. Label the lengths of each segment formed by the perpendiculars to the sides.) 🅖 **MP.2**

PRACTICE

15. The perpendicular bisectors of △JKL are $\overline{PT}$, $\overline{QT}$, and $\overline{RT}$. Name three isosceles triangles. SEE EXAMPLE 1

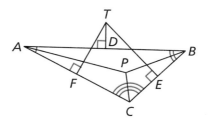

Use the diagram below for Exercises 16–18. Points D, E, and F are the midpoints of the sides of △ABC. SEE EXAMPLES 2 AND 4

16. Which point is the center of a circle that contains A, B, and C?

17. Which point is the center of a circle that intersects each side of △ABC at exactly one point?

18. The perpendicular bisector of $\overline{AB}$ is m and the perpendicular bisector of $\overline{BC}$ is n. Lines m and n intersect at T. If TA = 8.2, what is TC? SEE EXAMPLE 3

Find the values. SEE EXAMPLE 5

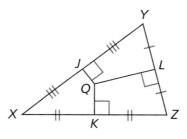

19. EG

20. GF

If XY = 24, XZ = 22, and JQ = 5, find the values. Round to the nearest tenth.

21. The radius of the circumscribed circle of △XYZ

22. QK

PRACTICE & PROBLEM SOLVING

23. **Model With Mathematics** A maintenance crew wants to build a shed at a location that is the same distance from each path. Where should the shed be located? Justify your answer with a diagram. ⊙ MP.4

24. **Reason** The circular patio shown has a sun canopy placed on one side to provide shade. What is the area of the patio **not** covered by the sun canopy? Round to the nearest tenth, and explain how you found your answer. ⊙ MP.2

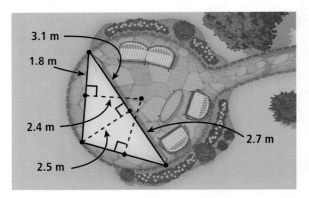

3.1 m
1.8 m
2.4 m
2.7 m
2.5 m

25. **Make Sense and Persevere** A ball manufacturer wants to stack three balls, each with an 8-centimeter diameter, in a box that is an equilateral triangular prism. The diagram shows the dimensions of the bases. Will the balls fit in the box? Explain how you know. ⊙ MP.1

30°
7.8 cm
9 cm
30°

26. In $\triangle ABC$, $\overline{AB}$ has midpoint M, and ℓ is the perpendicular bisector of $\overline{AB}$ and the angle bisector of $\angle ACB$. Which of the following must be true? Select all that apply.

☐ **A.** The radius of the inscribed circle of $\triangle ABC$ is AM.

☐ **B.** $AC = CB$

☐ **C.** Both the circumcenter and incenter of $\triangle ABC$ are on ℓ.

☐ **D.** The circumcenter of $\triangle ABC$ is inside the triangle.

27. **SAT/ACT** Circle O intersects $\overline{AB}$ only at F, $\overline{BC}$ only at G, and $\overline{AC}$ only at H. Which equation is true?

Ⓐ $AH = AC$ Ⓓ $OF = OC$

Ⓑ $m\angle OFB = 90$ Ⓔ $\angle BAO \cong \angle ABO$

Ⓒ $OB = OC$

28. **Performance Task** Edison High School is designing a new triangular pennant. The school mascot will be inside a circle, and the circle must touch each side of the pennant. The circle should fill as much of the pennant as possible.

Part A Using a straightedge and compass, draw at least 4 different types of triangles for the pennant. Construct an inscribed circle in each triangle.

Part B Make a table about your pennants. Include side lengths, type of triangle, circle radius and area, triangle area, and ratio of circle area to triangle area.

Part C What type of triangle do you recommend that they use? Justify your answer.

MATHEMATICAL MODELING IN **3** ACTS

Common Core State Standards
HSG.CO.C.9, HSG.CO.C.10, MP.4

Powered By
desmos

Making It Fair

In rural areas, county planners often work with local officials from a number of small towns to establish a regional medical center to serve all of the nearby communities.

County planners might also establish regional medical evacuation centers to transport patients with serious trauma to larger medical centers. The locations of these regional centers are carefully planned. Think about this during the Mathematical Modeling in 3 Acts lesson.

ACT 1 ▸ Identify the Problem

1. What is the first question that comes to mind after watching the video?

2. Write down the main question you will answer about what you saw in the video.

3. Make an initial conjecture that answers this main question.

4. Explain how you arrived at your conjecture.

5. What information will be useful to know to answer the main question? How can you get it? How will you use that information?

ACT 2 ▸ Develop a Model

6. Use the math that you have learned in this Topic to refine your conjecture.

ACT 3 ▸ Interpret the Results

7. Did your refined conjecture match the actual answer exactly? If not, what might explain the difference?

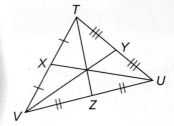
5-3

Medians and Altitudes

I CAN... find the points of concurrency for the medians of a triangle and the altitudes of a triangle.

VOCABULARY

- altitude
- centroid
- median
- orthocenter

CRITIQUE & EXPLAIN

Aisha wrote the following explanation of the relationships in the triangle.

> I can see that ∠TVY ≅ ∠YVU, ∠VUX ≅ ∠XUT, and ∠UTZ ≅ ∠ZTV because TZ, VY, and UX bisect the sides opposite each vertex. By the Concurrency of Angle Bisectors Theorem, VY, UX, and TZ are concurrent.

A. Why is Aisha's explanation not correct?

B. Communicate Precisely What can you do in the future to avoid Aisha's mistake?

ESSENTIAL QUESTION What are the properties of the medians in a triangle? What are the properties of the altitudes in a triangle?

EXAMPLE 1 | Identify Special Segments in Triangles

What are the *altitude* and *median* that are shown in △ADC?

An **altitude** is a perpendicular segment from a vertex of a triangle to the line containing the side opposite the vertex. A **median** of a triangle is a segment that has endpoints at a vertex and the midpoint of the side opposite the vertex.

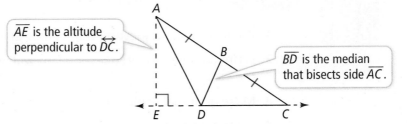

$\overline{AE}$ is the altitude perpendicular to $\overleftrightarrow{DC}$.

$\overline{BD}$ is the median that bisects side $\overline{AC}$.

REASON

Consider an altitude of a triangle that is also a median of the triangle. What properties does it have? What other term can be used to describe this segment?

Try It! **1.** Use the figure shown.

    a. What are the altitude and median that are shown in △ABC?

    b. Copy the triangle and draw the other altitudes and medians of the triangle.

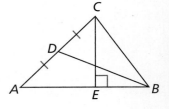

THEOREM 5-7 Concurrency of Medians

The medians of a triangle are concurrent at a point that is two-thirds the distance from each vertex to the midpoint of the opposite side.

If... $\overline{AD}$, $\overline{CF}$, and $\overline{BE}$ are the medians of $\triangle ABC$, and intersect at G

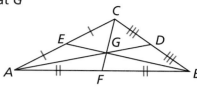

PROOF: SEE LESSON 9-2.

Then...
$AG = \frac{2}{3}AD \quad BG = \frac{2}{3}BE \quad CG = \frac{2}{3}CF$

EXAMPLE 2 Find the Length of a Median

What is the length of $\overline{JN}$ in the figure?

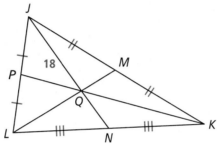

The medians of $\triangle JKL$ are $\overline{JN}$, $\overline{KP}$, and $\overline{LM}$. Point Q is the point of concurrency of the medians. The point of concurrency of the medians of a triangle is called the **centroid**.

COMMON ERROR
Be careful not to confuse which part is $\frac{1}{3}$ of the length of the median and which part is $\frac{2}{3}$ of the length.

$\frac{2}{3}JN = JQ$ ← Use the Concurrency of Medians Theorem.

$\frac{2}{3}JN = 18$

$JN = 27$

Try It! 2. Find AD for each triangle.

a.

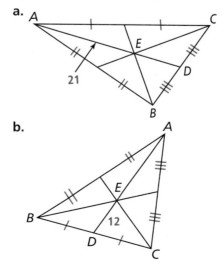

b.

EXAMPLE 3 Locate the Centroid

An artist wants to balance a triangular piece of wood at a single point so that the triangle is parallel to the ground. Where should he balance the triangle?

A triangle is balanced at its *center of gravity*, which is at the centroid of the triangle.

Step 1 Find the midpoint of each side.

Step 2 Draw a median from each midpoint.

Step 3 Label the centroid point *Q*.

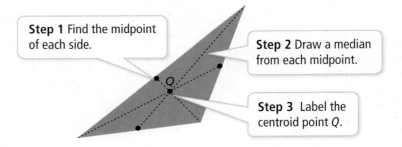

The artist should balance the triangle at point *Q*.

Try It! **3.** Copy the triangle shown.

    a. Use the medians of the triangle to locate its centroid.

    b. Use a ruler to verify the centroid is two-thirds the distance from each vertex to the midpoint of the opposite side.

THEOREM 5-8 Concurrency of Altitudes

The lines that contain the altitudes of a triangle are concurrent.

If...

PROOF: SEE LESSON 9-2.

Then... $\overleftrightarrow{KQ}$, $\overleftrightarrow{LN}$, and $\overleftrightarrow{MP}$ are concurrent at X.

CONCEPTUAL UNDERSTANDING

EXAMPLE 4 Locate the Orthocenter

Powered By **desmos**

How does the type of triangle (obtuse, acute, right) relate to the location of the point of concurrency of its altitudes?

Draw at least two of each type of triangle. Describe any relationship you notice between the type of triangle and the location of the point of concurrency of its altitudes.

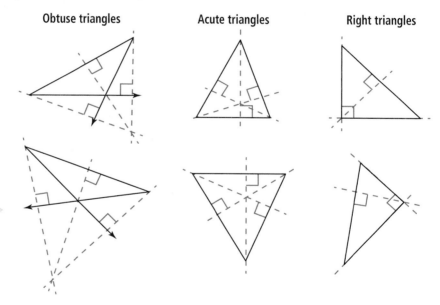

Obtuse triangles   Acute triangles   Right triangles

STUDY TIP
Recall that when you make a conjecture by observing a few examples, you are not actually proving the conjecture.

The point of concurrency of the lines containing the altitudes of a triangle is called the **orthocenter**. The orthocenter is outside an obtuse triangle and inside an acute triangle. For a right triangle, the orthocenter is at the vertex of the right angle.

Try It! **4.** What is the relationship between an isosceles triangle and the location of its orthocenter? Explain your answer.

EXAMPLE 5 Find the Orthocenter of a Triangle

Orthocenters can be found using constructions or coordinate geometry. Where is the orthocenter of △KLM?

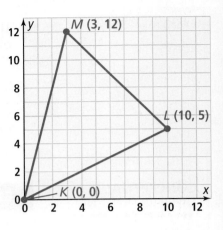

Since the orthocenter is the point of concurrency of the altitudes, find the equations for two altitudes, and solve for the point of intersection.

Step 1 Find the slopes of two sides of the triangle.

$$\text{slope of } \overline{KL} = \frac{5-0}{10-0} = \frac{1}{2}$$

$$\text{slope of } \overline{LM} = \frac{12-5}{3-10} = -1$$

Step 2 Use the point slope form, $y - y_1 = m(x - x_1)$, to write the equations of the altitudes perpendicular to $\overline{KL}$ and $\overline{LM}$.

Equation of the altitude perpendicular to $\overline{KL}$:

$$y - 12 = -2(x - 3)$$
$$y = -2x + 6 + 12$$
$$y = -2x + 18$$

> Point M is the vertex opposite $\overline{KL}$, and the slope of a line perpendicular to $\overline{KL}$ is -2.

Equation of the altitude perpendicular to $\overline{LM}$:

$$y - 0 = 1(x - 0)$$
$$y = x$$

> Point K is the vertex opposite $\overline{LM}$, and the slope of a line perpendicular to $\overline{LM}$ is 1.

STUDY TIP
Remember that since an altitude is perpendicular to a side of the triangle, the product of the slopes of their equations is −1.

Step 3 Solve the system of equations to determine the coordinates of the point of intersection.

$$y = -2x + 18$$
$$y = -2(y) + 18$$
$$y + 2y = 18$$
$$3y = 18$$
$$y = 6$$

> Since $y = x$, substitute y in the equation $y = -2x + 18$. Then solve for y.

Since $y = x$, $x = 6$.

Since all three altitudes intersect at the orthocenter, the intersection of two altitudes is sufficient to determine the orthocenter. The orthocenter of △KLM is (6, 6).

Try It! **5.** Find the orthocenter of a triangle with vertices at each of the following sets of coordinates.

a. (0, 0), (10, 4), (8, 9)   **b.** (0, 0), (6, 3), (8, 9)

MEDIANS

The **centroid** is the point of concurrency of the medians of a triangle.

ALTITUDES

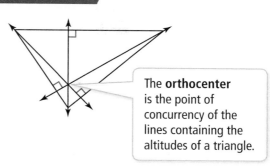

The **orthocenter** is the point of concurrency of the lines containing the altitudes of a triangle.

Do You UNDERSTAND?

1. **ESSENTIAL QUESTION** What are the properties of the medians in a triangle? What are the properties of the altitudes in a triangle?

2. **Vocabulary** The prefix *ortho-* means "upright" or "right." How can this meaning help you remember which segments of a triangle have a point of concurrency at the orthocenter?

3. **Error Analysis** A student labeled *P* as the centroid of the triangle. What error did the student make? Explain. ⓒ **MP.3**

4. **Reason** Why is an orthocenter sometimes outside a triangle but a centroid is always inside? ⓒ **MP.2**

5. **Look for Relationships** Consider the three types of triangles: acute, obtuse, and right. What is the relationship between the type of triangle and the location of the orthocenter? Does the type of triangle tell you anything about the location of the centroid? ⓒ **MP.7**

6. **Generalize** For any right triangle, where is the orthocenter located? ⓒ **MP.8**

Do You KNOW HOW?

7. Find the length of each of the medians of the triangle.

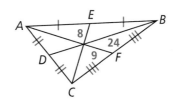

8. Where is the orthocenter of △*ABC*?

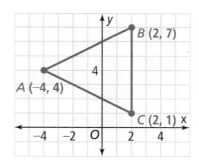

9. A crane operator needs to lift a large triangular piece of plywood at its centroid to keep it balanced. Copy the triangle and use its medians to locate the centroid. ⓒ **MP.4**

PRACTICE & PROBLEM SOLVING

UNDERSTAND

10. Make Sense and Persevere Describe the process for finding the orthocenter of a triangle that is on a coordinate plane. © **MP.1**

11. Look for Relationships Given the midpoints of a triangle, which two points of concurrency can you locate? Which point of concurrency can you locate if you only know the angle bisectors? Which two points of concurrency can you locate by only drawing perpendicular segments? © **MP.7**

12. Error Analysis A student uses the following explanation to identify the triangle's point of concurrency. Explain the student's error. © **MP.3**

> A perpendicular segment bisects each side of the triangle. According to the Concurrency of Altitudes Theorem, the segments are concurrent. The point of concurrency is the orthocenter. ✗

13. Reason Draw several different types of triangles and compare the locations of the centroid and the circumcenter of each triangle. What conjecture can you make about the type of triangle that has a common centroid and circumcenter? Explain. © **MP.2**

14. Mathematical Connections Where is the centroid of △ABC?

- Locate the midpoints of any two sides.

- Find the equations of two medians using the vertex and the opposite midpoint.

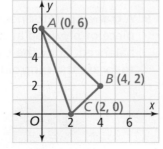

- Solve the system of the two equations to find the coordinates of the centroid.

How can you verify that the coordinates you found are correct?

PRACTICE

15. Identify whether each segment is an altitude, an angle bisector, a median, or a perpendicular bisector. SEE EXAMPLE 1

a. $\overline{BD}$ **b.** $\overline{FJ}$

c. $\overline{CE}$ **d.** $\overline{KL}$

16. What is the value of $\overline{KL}$? SEE EXAMPLE 2

17. Copy the triangle and use its medians to locate the centroid. SEE EXAMPLE 3

18. State whether the orthocenter of each triangle is inside the triangle, outside the triangle, or on the triangle. Explain your reasoning. SEE EXAMPLE 4

a.   **b.**

c.   **d.**

19. Find the coordinates of the orthocenter of a triangle with vertices at each set of points on a coordinate plane. SEE EXAMPLE 5

a. (0, 0), (8, 4), (4, 22)

b. (3, 1), (10, 8), (5, 13)

PRACTICE & PROBLEM SOLVING

APPLY ▶

20. Model With Mathematics A large triangular-shaped table is supported by a single pole at the center of gravity. How far is vertex C from the center of gravity? **ⓒ MP.4**

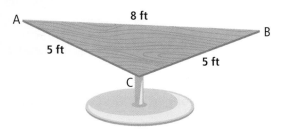

21. Reason To support a triangular kite, Elena attaches thin strips of wood from each vertex perpendicular to the opposite edge. She then attaches the kite's string at the point of concurrency. To calculate the point of concurrency, she determines the coordinates of each vertex on a coordinate plane. What are the coordinates where the wood strips cross? **ⓒ MP.2**

22. Higher Order Thinking A designer wants to place a fountain at the intersection of the shortest distances from each side to the opposite vertex. She drew the model shown. What mistake did she make? At what point of concurrency should the fountain be located?

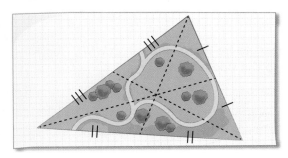

ASSESSMENT PRACTICE ▶

23. Identify the segments and point in △ABC.

The segment $\overline{AD}$ is a(n) ____?____ of the triangle. The segment $\overline{BE}$ is a(n) ____?____ of the triangle. The point X is the ____?____ of the triangle.

24. SAT/ACT A triangle with vertices at (3, 4) and (9, 17) has a centroid at (8, 16). What are the coordinates of the third vertex?

Ⓐ (10, 4) Ⓒ (12, 14)

Ⓑ (10, 7) Ⓓ (12, 27)

25. Performance Task Steve is designing a mobile with triangular pieces of wood. Each piece of wood attaches to a wire at the center of gravity and hangs parallel to the ground. The side lengths of the triangles will be between 4 cm and 8 cm.

Part A Describe how Steve can find the center of gravity for any triangular piece. Then model this process by finding the center of gravity of a triangle with side lengths 5 cm, 5 cm, and 6 cm.

Part B Is it possible for a triangle attached at the orthocenter to hang so that it is parallel to the ground? If it is possible, describe the triangle. What are possible side lengths for such a triangle? If it is not possible, explain why not.

5-4
Inequalities in One Triangle

I CAN... use theorems to compare the sides and angles of a triangle.

Common Core State Standards
HSG.CO.C.10, MP.2, MP.3, MP.7

EXPLORE & REASON

Cut several drinking straws to the sizes shown.

7 cm
6 cm
10 cm
4 cm
3 cm
2 cm

A. Take your two shortest straws and your longest straw. Can they form a triangle? Explain.

B. Try different combinations of three straws to form triangles. Which side length combinations work? Which combinations do not work?

C. **Look for Relationships** What do you notice about the relationship between the combined lengths of the two shorter sides and the length of the longest side? **MP.7**

ESSENTIAL QUESTION How are side lengths and angle measures in a triangle related?

CONCEPTUAL UNDERSTANDING

EXAMPLE 1 Investigate Side and Angle Relationships Powered By desmos

Draw a right triangle and a non-right triangle. How is the largest angle measure of each triangle related to the side lengths?

STUDY TIP
Recall that the non-right angles in a right triangle are acute. This means the right angle is the largest angle.

In the right triangle, $\angle A$ is the largest angle and $\overline{BC}$ is the longest side.

Angle P appears to be obtuse, while $\angle Q$ and $\angle R$ appear to be acute. The largest angle $\angle P$ is across from longest side $\overline{QR}$.

A
5 m
12 m
C
13 m
B

P
6 in.
6 in.
R
10 in.
Q

The largest angle appears to be opposite the longest side.

Try It! **1.** Which angle appears to be the smallest in $\triangle MNP$? How is it related to the side lengths?

M
8 ft
23 ft
P
26 ft
N

THEOREM 5-9

If two sides of a triangle are not congruent, then the larger angle lies opposite the longer side.

If... $b > a$

Then... $m\angle B > m\angle A$

PROOF: SEE EXERCISE 13.

EXAMPLE 2 — Use Theorem 5-9

To support a triangular piece of a float, a brace is placed at the largest angle and a guide wire is placed at the smallest angle. Which angle is the largest? Which angle is the smallest?

REASON

Think about the relationships between pairs of numbers. How can you use the relationships between pairs of numbers to order all the numbers? ⒼMP.2

Compare side lengths to find larger angle measures.

Since 12 > 10, $m\angle A > m\angle B$.
Since 13 > 12, $m\angle C > m\angle A$.

Combining the inequalities of the angle measures, $m\angle C > m\angle A > m\angle B$. Thus, the largest angle is $\angle C$ and the smallest angle is $\angle B$.

Try It!   **2.** Lucas sketched a diagram for a garden box.

a. Which angle is the largest?

b. Which angle is the smallest?

THEOREM 5-10 Converse of Theorem 5-9

If two angles of a triangle are not congruent, then the longer side lies opposite the larger angle.

If... $m\angle B > m\angle A$

Then... $b > a$

PROOF: SEE EXAMPLE 3.

EXAMPLE 3 Prove Theorem 5-10

PROOF

STUDY TIP
Recall that in an indirect proof by contradiction for $p \rightarrow q$, first assume p and $\sim q$ are true. Then, show that the assumption $\sim q$ leads to a contradiction. Conclude that q must be true.

Use indirect reasoning to prove Theorem 5–10.

Given: $m\angle J > m\angle G$

Prove: $GH > HJ$

Assume that $GH \leq HJ$.
This means that $GH = HJ$ or $GH < HJ$.

First show that assuming $GH = HJ$ leads to a contradiction of the given condition that $m\angle J > m\angle G$.

$GH = HJ$	$\overline{GH} \cong \overline{HJ}$	$\triangle GHJ$ is isosceles.	$m\angle J = m\angle G$
Assumption	Def. of congruent	Def. of isosceles	Isosceles Triangle Thm.

By the definition of congruence $m\angle J = m\angle G$, which contradicts $m\angle J > m\angle G$. So the assumption is false. GH cannot be equal to HJ.

Try It! **3.** To complete the proof of Theorem 5-10, show that assuming $GH < HJ$ leads to a contradiction of the given condition that $m\angle J > m\angle G$.

EXAMPLE 4 Use Theorem 5-10

Which side of $\triangle KLM$ is the longest?

By Theorem 5-10, the longest side of the triangle is across from the largest angle. Find the unknown angle measure.

$$m\angle K + m\angle L + m\angle M = 180$$
$$m\angle K + 50 + 62 = 180$$
$$m\angle K = 68$$

Apply the Triangle Angle-Sum Theorem.

STUDY TIP
When needed information is missing from a diagram, you may need to apply properties and theorems to find the needed information.

The largest angle in the triangle is $\angle K$, so the longest side is the side opposite $\angle K$. The longest side is $\overline{LM}$.

Try It! **4.** Identify the sides of $\triangle NOP$.

a. Which side is the longest?

b. Which side is the shortest?

THEOREM 5-11 Triangle Inequality Theorem

The sum of the lengths of any two sides of a triangle is greater than the length of the third side.

PROOF: SEE EXERCISE 14.

If...

Then... $a + b > c$
$a + c > b$
$b + c > a$

EXAMPLE 5 Use the Triangle Inequality Theorem

Powered By
desmos

A. Which of the following sets of segments could be the sides of a triangle?

Set 1

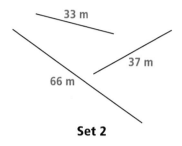

Set 2

Determine if the sum of the two shorter side lengths is longer than the longest side length.

$18 + 19 = 37$

$33 + 37 = 70$

Since $37 < 40$, the segments in Set 1 cannot form a triangle.

Since $70 > 66$, the segments in Set 2 can form a triangle.

COMMON ERROR
You may compare any two sides to a third side, but you must compare the shorter two sides to the longest side to determine whether a triangle is possible.

B. A triangle has sides that measure 11 cm and 16 cm. What are the possible lengths of the third side?

Apply the Triangle Inequality Theorem.

If $x + 11 > 16$, then $x > 5$.

The inequality $x + 16 > 11$ is true for all positive values of x, so this inequality only tells you that $x > 0$.

If $11 + 16 > x$, then $27 > x$.

Therefore, $5 < x < 27$. The third side of the triangle could be between 5 cm and 27 cm long.

Try It! **5. a.** Could a triangle have side lengths 16 m, 39 m, and 28 m?

b. A triangle has side lengths that are 30 in. and 50 in. What are the possible lengths of the third side?

CONCEPT SUMMARY Inequalities in One Triangle

THEOREMS 5-9 AND 5-10

The longest side is opposite the largest angle.

The shortest side is opposite the smallest angle.

$$ZY \; < \; XZ \; < \; XY$$
$$m\angle X < m\angle Y < m\angle Z$$

THEOREMS 5-11 **Triangle Inequality Theorem**

The sum of the lengths of any two sides is greater than the length of the third side.

$5 + 8 \; > 11$
$5 + 11 > 8$
$8 + 11 > 5$

Do You UNDERSTAND?

1. **ESSENTIAL QUESTION** How are side lengths and angle measures in a triangle related?

2. **Reason** If a triangle has three different side lengths, what does that tell you about the measures of its angles? ⓒ **MP.2**

3. **Error Analysis** Ricardo says that $\angle X$ must be the largest angle in $\triangle XYZ$. Explain his error. ⓒ **MP.3**

4. **Use Structure** An isosceles triangle has base angles that each measure 50. How could you determine whether b or s is greater? ⓒ **MP.7**

5. **Generalize** In $\triangle ABC$, $a < c < b$. List the angles in order from smallest to largest. ⓒ **MP.8**

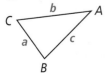

Do You KNOW HOW?

Identify the sides of $\triangle PQR$.

6. Which side is the longest?

7. Which side is the shortest?

Determine whether each set of lengths could form a triangle.

8. 5, 2, and 3

9. 55, 76, and 112

10. 102, 95, and 157

11. 17, 17, and 35

12. Kelsey is welding 3 metal rods to make a triangle. If the lengths of two of the rods are 15 in. and 22 in., what are the possible lengths of a third rod?

PRACTICE & PROBLEM SOLVING

UNDERSTAND

13. Construct Arguments Fill in the missing reasons in the proof of Theorem 5-9. (Hint: The Comparison Property of Inequality states that if $a = b + c$ and $c > 0$, then $a > b$.) Ⓒ **MP.3**

Given: $AB > AC$, $\overline{AC} \cong \overline{AM}$

Prove: $m\angle ACB > m\angle B$

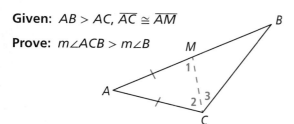

Statements	Reasons
1) $\overline{AC} \cong \overline{AM}$	1) Given
2) $m\angle 1 = m\angle 2$	2) Isosc. Triangle Thm.
3) $m\angle ACB = m\angle 2 + m\angle 3$	3)
4) $m\angle ACB > m\angle 2$	4)
5) $m\angle ACB > m\angle 1$	5)
6) $m\angle 1 = m\angle B + m\angle 3$	6) Ext. Angles Thm.
7) $m\angle 1 > m\angle B$	7)
8) $m\angle ACB > m\angle B$	8)

14. Construct Arguments Write a paragraph proof for Theorem 5-11. First, assume $\overline{AC}$ is the longest side and prove the theorem is true for the other two sides. Then use the figure to prove that $AB + CB > AC$. Ⓒ **MP.3**

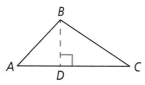

15. Error Analysis A student said that a triangle with side lengths of 3 ft and 4 ft could have a third side with a length of 7 ft. Explain why the student is incorrect. What is a correct statement about the third side of the triangle? Ⓒ **MP.3**

16. Error Analysis Tia says that $\angle Q$ must be the largest angle in $\triangle QRS$ because $150 > 70 > 1.7$. Explain Tia's error. Ⓒ **MP.3**

PRACTICE

17. Which angle measure appears to be the smallest in $\triangle JKL$? What can you conclude about the side opposite that angle? SEE EXAMPLE 1

Identify the angles of $\triangle FGH$. SEE EXAMPLE 2

18. Which angle is the smallest?

19. Which angle is the largest?

Identify the sides of $\triangle NOP$. SEE EXAMPLES 3 AND 4

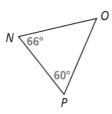

20. Which side is the longest?

21. Which side is the shortest?

Determine whether the side lengths could form a triangle. SEE EXAMPLE 5

22. 13, 15, 9

23. 8, 15, 7

24. 35, 20, 11

25. 65, 32, 40

Given two sides of a triangle, determine the range of possible lengths of the third side. SEE EXAMPLE 5

26. 10 in. and 12 in.

27. 5 ft and 10 ft

28. 200 m and 300 m

29. 90 km and 150 km

PRACTICE & PROBLEM SOLVING

30. **Make Sense and Persevere** It took Ines 2 hours to bicycle the perimeter shown at an average speed of 10 miles per hour. Which two roads form the largest angle? ⒸMP.1

31. **Reason** A jewelry designer plans to make a triangular pendant out of gold wire. The wire costs $31.65 per centimeter. What is the possible range of costs for the wire? ⒸMP.2

32. **Use Structure** A stage manager must use tape to outline a triangular platform on the set. Order the sides of the platform from longest to shortest. ⒸMP.7

33. **Make Sense and Persevere** A dog running an agility course has difficulty making turns. The sharper the angle, the more difficult the turn. Which corner is most difficult for her to turn? ⒸMP.1

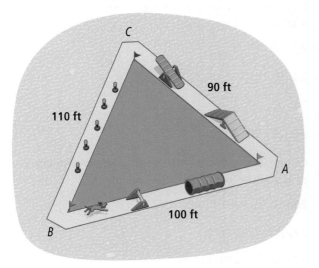

34. The lengths of two sides of a triangle are 13 and 20. What is the range of values for the length x of the third side?

35. **SAT/ACT** Look at △RST.

Which statement is false?

Ⓐ $TS = TR$

Ⓑ $m\angle STR < m\angle TRS$

Ⓒ $TR > SR$

Ⓓ $TS < SR$

Ⓔ $TS + TR > SR$

36. **Performance Task** Teo designed a skateboard ramp.

Part A List the sides of ramp A in order from shortest to longest.

Part B List the angles of ramp B from smallest to largest, and explain how you know.

Part C Ramp B cannot be steeper than 45°. Is it possible to build ramp B so that $\overline{SR}$ is shorter than 6 ft? Explain.

5-5

Inequalities in Two Triangles

I CAN... compare a pair of sides of two triangles when the remaining pairs of sides are congruent.

© **Common Core State Standards**
HSG.CO.C.10, MP.2, MP.3, MP.7

EXPLORE & REASON

A woodworker uses a caliper to measure the widths of a bat to help him determine the widths for a new bat. The woodworker places the open tips of the caliper on the bat. The distance between the tips is a width of the bat.

caliper

A. Suppose a caliper opens to an angle of 25° for one width of a bat and opens to an angle of 35° for another. What can you conclude about the widths of the bat?

B. **Look for Relationships** Next, suppose you use a caliper to measure the width of a narrow part of a bat and a wider part of the bat. What can you predict about the angle to which the caliper opens each time? © **MP.7**

ESSENTIAL QUESTION

When two triangles have two pairs of congruent sides, how are the third pair of sides and the pair of angles opposite the third pair of sides related?

CONCEPTUAL UNDERSTANDING

EXAMPLE 1 ▸ Investigate Side Lengths in Triangles

LOOK FOR RELATIONSHIPS
Consider how multiple diagrams are used to show the relationship between moving parts. What changes and what remains the same between diagrams? © **MP.7**

As a rider pedals a unicycle, how do the measure of ∠A and length *b* change? What does this suggest about the change in the triangle?

seat post →

Side *b* increases.

crank arm

The measure of ∠A increases.

If two sides of a triangle stay the same, but the measure of the angle between them increases, the length of the third side also increases.

Try It! **1.** Compare the measures of the labeled angles and side lengths for the triangles.

acute

obtuse

right

THEOREM 5-12 Hinge Theorem

If two sides of one triangle are congruent to two sides of another triangle, and the included angles are not congruent, then the longer third side is opposite the larger included angle.

PROOF: SEE EXERCISE 9.

If... $m\angle YWX > m\angle CAB$

Then... $XY > BC$

APPLICATION

EXAMPLE 2 Apply the Hinge Theorem

Tension in an exercise band varies proportionally with stretch distance. The tension T is described by the function $T(x) = kx$, where k is a constant that depends on the elasticity of the band and x is the stretch distance. Which position shows greater tension in the band?

Formulate ◄ Model the positions with triangles.

Compute ◄ $T(LK)$ is the tension when the angle is 50°, and $T(MK)$ is the tension when the angle is 80°. Since $m\angle MJK > m\angle LJK$, apply the Hinge Theorem.

$$MK > LK$$
$$\frac{T(MK)}{k} > \frac{T(LK)}{k}$$
$$T(MK) > T(LK)$$

> Since the tension T is equal to the product of k and the stretch distance, we can substitute $\frac{T}{k}$ for each distance.

Interpret ◄ A larger angle corresponds to a larger distance from the person's hands to his feet. The larger distance corresponds to a higher tension.

The tension is greater when the person pulls higher on the tension band.

Try It! **2.** The person keeps his arms extended and the length of the tension band the same. If he wants to make the measure of $\angle L$ smaller, how would the length of $\overline{JK}$, the vertical distance from the person's shoulders to his feet, change?

Do not change

THEOREM 5-13 Converse of the Hinge Theorem

If two sides of one triangle are congruent to two sides of another triangle, and the third sides are not congruent, then the larger included angle is opposite the longer third side.

PROOF: SEE EXAMPLE 3.

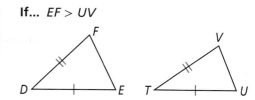

If... $EF > UV$

Then... $m\angle D > m\angle T$

EXAMPLE 3   Prove the Converse of the Hinge Theorem

Use indirect reasoning to prove the Converse of the Hinge Theorem.

Given: $\overline{DF} \cong \overline{TV}$; $\overline{DE} \cong \overline{TU}$; $EF > UV$

Prove: $m\angle FDE > m\angle VTU$

STUDY TIP
If you get stuck when writing a proof, make a list of things you know and what you want to prove.

Assume that $m\angle FDE$ is not greater than $m\angle VTU$. Then, $m\angle FDE = m\angle VTU$, or $m\angle FDE < m\angle VTU$.

Assuming that $m\angle FDE = m\angle VTU$, $\angle FDE \cong \angle VTU$. Applying SAS, $\triangle DEF \cong \triangle TUV$, so by CPCTC, $\overline{EF} \cong \overline{UV}$ and $EF = UV$. But, this contradicts $EF > UV$.

Try It!   **3.** To complete the proof of the Converse of the Hinge Theorem, show that assuming $m\angle FDE < m\angle VTU$ leads to a contradiction of the given statement, $EF > UV$.

EXAMPLE 4   Apply the Converse of the Hinge Theorem

What are the possible values of x?

Since $FG < CD$ and $CD < AB$, apply the Converse of the Hinge Theorem.

COMMON ERROR
Be careful to use the correct inequality sign when comparing triangles. After you write the inequality, check a second time to be sure it indicates that the larger angle is opposite the longer side.

$$m\angle FEG < m\angle CED < m\angle ACB$$
$$36 < 2x - 4 < 60$$
$$40 < 2x < 64$$
$$20 < x < 32$$

The possible values for x are between 20 and 32.

Try It!   **4.** What are the possible values of x for each diagram?

a.

b.

CONCEPT SUMMARY Inequalities in Two Triangles

THEOREM 5-12 Hinge Theorem

If... $\overline{WX} \cong \overline{AB}$, $\overline{WY} \cong \overline{AC}$, and $m\angle W > m\angle A$

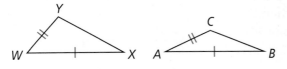

Then... $XY > BC$

THEOREM 5-13 Converse of the Hinge Theorem

If... $\overline{DF} \cong \overline{TV}$, $\overline{DE} \cong \overline{TU}$, and $EF > UV$

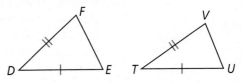

Then... $m\angle D > m\angle T$

Do You UNDERSTAND?

1. **ESSENTIAL QUESTION** When two triangles have two pairs of congruent sides, how are the third pair of sides and the pair of angles opposite the third pair of sides related?

2. **Error Analysis** Venetta applies the Converse of the Hinge Theorem to conclude that $m\angle EKF > m\angle HKG$ for the triangles shown. Is Venetta correct? Explain your answer. © MP.3

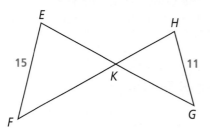

3. **Reason** Why must the angles described in the Hinge Theorem be between the congruent pairs of sides? © MP.2

4. **Communicate Precisely** The Hinge Theorem is also known as the Side-Angle-Side Inequality Theorem or SAS Inequality Theorem. How are the requirements for applying the Hinge Theorem similar to the requirements for applying SAS? How are the requirements different? © MP.6

Do You KNOW HOW?

5. Order AB, BC, and CD from least to greatest.

6. Order the measures of $\angle PTU$, $\angle SQT$, and $\angle QSR$ from least to greatest.

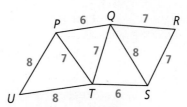

7. Kayak A and kayak B leave a dock as shown. Which kayak is closer to the dock?

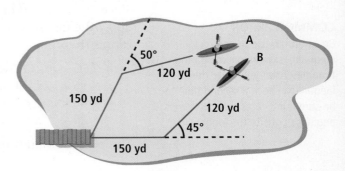

PRACTICE & PROBLEM SOLVING

UNDERSTAND

8. Error Analysis Talisha has the scissors shown.

She describes how she will use the Hinge Theorem with the scissors.

> If you open the right pair of scissors to an angle of 30° and open the left pair of scissors to an angle of 45°, then by the Hinge Theorem, the distance between the blade tips of the left pair of scissors will be larger. ✗

What mistake did she make? Ⓒ MP.3

9. Construct Arguments Write a paragraph proof of the Hinge Theorem. Ⓒ MP.3

Given: $\overline{WX} \cong \overline{AB}$, $\overline{WY} \cong \overline{AC}$, $m\angle W > m\angle A$
Prove: $XY > BC$

Use the following outline.

- Find a point D outside $\triangle ABC$ so $\overline{AD} \cong \overline{WY}$ and $\angle DAB \cong \angle YWX$.

- Show that $\triangle WXY \cong \triangle ABD$.

- Construct the angle bisector of $\angle CAD$. Let point E be the point where the angle bisector intersects $\overline{BD}$.

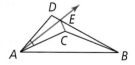

- Show that $\triangle ACE \cong \triangle ADE$ so $\overline{CE} \cong \overline{DE}$.

- Show that $DB = CE + EB$.

- Use the Triangle Inequality Theorem on $\triangle BCE$ to show that $DB > BC$.

- Conclude that $XY > BC$.

PRACTICE

10. Write an inequality describing the range of x for each pair of triangles. SEE EXAMPLES 1 AND 2

a.

b.

11. Write an inequality describing the possible values of x for each pair of triangles. SEE EXAMPLES 3 AND 4

a.

b.

12. Write an inequality describing the possible values of x for each diagram.

a.

b.
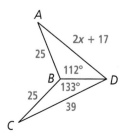

PRACTICE & PROBLEM SOLVING

13. Reason Airplane A flies 300 miles due east of an airport and then flies 200 miles at 15° north of east. Airplane B flies 200 miles due north and then flies 300 miles at 20° west of north. Which airplane is closer to the airport? Explain how you know. © **MP.2**

14. Model With Mathematics According to the Hinge Theorem, is the distance between the tips of the hands greater at 4:00 or at 7:00? Explain how the distance changes throughout a day. © **MP.4**

15. Mathematical Connections Determine the shortest path from start to finish on the obstacle course.

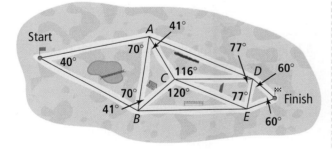

16. Higher Order Thinking When $m\angle 1 = 75$, $d = 43$ in., and when $m\angle 1 = 100$, $d = 54$ in. Quash wants to know how wide a sofa he can buy if he can open the door at most 85°. Using the Hinge Theorem or the Converse of the Hinge Theorem, can you determine the exact value of d when $m\angle 1 = 85$? If you can, explain the method. If not, explain what you can determine about the distance.

17. Which of the following can you conclude from the diagram? Select all that apply.

Ⓐ $x < 7$ Ⓒ $y < 95$

Ⓑ $x > 7$ Ⓓ $y > 95$

18. SAT/ACT Which of the following can you conclude from the diagram?

Ⓐ $m\angle EFG = m\angle GHE$ Ⓒ $m\angle GEF > m\angle EGH$

Ⓑ $m\angle FGE = m\angle HEG$ Ⓓ $m\angle FGE > m\angle EGH$

19. Performance Task Abby, Tamika, and Alma walk from their campsite to get to the lake. The lake is located 3 miles away in the direction of 40° north of west.

Part A Abby walks along a straight path in the direction of 27° east of north for 1 mile to point A. Using the Hinge Theorem, if Tamika walks along a straight path in the direction of 35° south of west for 1 mile to point B, who is closer to the lake?

Part B Alma also walks for 1 mile from the campsite along a different straight path than Abby. Her straight-line distance to the lake is shorter than Abby's distance. What directions could Alma have taken?

Topic Review

1. How are the sides, segments, and angles of triangles related?

Vocabulary Review

Choose the correct term to complete each sentence.

2. The _____ is the point of concurrency of the angle bisectors of a triangle.

3. Three or more lines that intersect at one point are _____.

4. The point of concurrency of the altitudes of a triangle is the _____.

5. A perpendicular segment from a vertex to the line containing the side opposite the vertex is a(n) _____ of a triangle.

6. A point that is the same distance from two points is _____ from the points.

7. A(n) _____ of a triangle has endpoints at a vertex and at the midpoint of the side opposite the vertex.

- altitude
- centroid
- circumcenter
- concurrent
- equidistant
- incenter
- median
- orthocenter

Concepts & Skills Review

| LESSON 5-1 | Perpendicular and Angle Bisectors |

Quick Review

Perpendicular bisectors and angle bisectors are related to the segments or angles they bisect:

- Any point on the perpendicular bisector of a segment is **equidistant** from the endpoints of the segment.

- Any point on the bisector of an angle is equidistant from the two sides of the angle.

Example

Find AB.

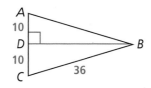

$\overline{DB}$ is the perpendicular bisector of $\overline{AC}$, so $AB = CB$. $AB = 36$.

Practice & Problem Solving

Use the given values to find each unknown.

8. If $PS = 36$, $PQ = 3x + 5$, $QR = 6x - 10$, and $RS = 36$, then $PR = \blacksquare$.

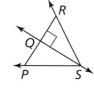

9. If $PS = 4x + 8$, $PQ = 29$, $RS = 5x - 3$, and $QR = 29$, then $PS = \blacksquare$.

10. If $JM = 12$, $LM = 12$, and $m\angle JMK = 25$, then $m\angle KML = \blacksquare$.

11. If $m\angle JML = 49$, $m\angle JMK = 24.5$, and $JK = 17$, then $KL = \blacksquare$.

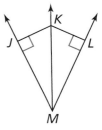

12. **Reason** A point on a perpendicular bisector is 7 cm from each endpoint of the bisected segment and 5 cm from the point of intersection. To the nearest tenth, what is the length of the segment? Ⓒ MP.2

Quick Review

The perpendicular bisectors of a triangle are concurrent at the point equidistant from the vertices of the triangle. This point is called the **circumcenter**.

The angle bisectors of a triangle are concurrent at a point equidistant from the sides of the triangle. This point is called the **incenter**.

Example

For △ABC, what is the radius of the inscribed circle?

$DF = EF$
$3x = 2x + 16$
$x = 16$

The radius is $DF = 3x = 3(16) = 48$.

Practice & Problem Solving

Identify each point of concurrency.

13. incenter

14. circumcenter

Use the diagram to find each unknown quantity.

15. If $m∠GFL = 34$, and $m∠GEL = 36$, what is $m∠FGL$?

16. If $JL = 5$, what is the measure of KL?

17. Reason The circumcenter of a triangle is on one side of the triangle. Explain how to find the area of the circumscribed circle of the triangle given the lengths of the sides. ⓒ **MP.2**

Quick Review

A **median** of a triangle is a line segment from the midpoint of one side to the opposite vertex. The medians of a triangle are concurrent at the **centroid**. The distance from a vertex to the centroid is two-thirds the distance of the median from that vertex.

An **altitude** of a triangle is a line segment perpendicular to one side and ending at the opposite vertex. The lines containing the altitudes of a triangle are concurrent at the **orthocenter**.

Example

Q is the centroid of △XYZ. If DZ = 24, what is QZ?

$QZ = \frac{2}{3} DZ$
$QZ = \frac{2}{3} (24)$
$QZ = 16$

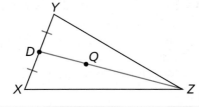

Practice & Problem Solving

Identify each segment type.

18. median

19. altitude

Find the orthocenter of each triangle with the given set of vertices.

20. (2, 0), (2, 12), (8, 6)   **21.** (7, 8), (9, 6), (5, 4)

22. Reason The orthocenter of △ABC is point B. What is the measure of ∠ABC? ⓒ **MP.2**

23. A plastic triangle is suspended parallel to the ground by a string attached at the centroid. Copy the triangle and show where the string should be attached.

| LESSON 5-4 | **Inequalities in One Triangle** |

Quick Review

In a triangle, if two sides are not congruent, then the larger angle is opposite the longer side. If two angles are not congruent, then the longer side is opposite the larger angle.

$XY > XZ > YZ$

$m\angle Z > m\angle Y > m\angle X$

The sum of the lengths of any two sides of a triangle is greater than the length of the third side.

$4 + 5 > 7 \qquad 4 + 7 > 5 \qquad 5 + 7 > 4$

Example

Which side of △TUV is the longest?

$m\angle T + m\angle U + m\angle V = 180$

$52 + 71 + m\angle V = 180$

$m\angle V = 57$

The largest angle is $\angle U$, so the longest side is $\overline{VT}$.

Practice & Problem Solving

Determine if the lengths can form a triangle.

24. 14, 32, 18

25. 14, 25, 29

26. 37, 22, 56

27. 87, 35, 41

Use the figure for Exercises 28 and 29.

28. Which angle has the least measure?

29. Which angle has the greatest measure?

30. Use Structure Why must the sum of two sides of a triangle be greater than the third side? Ⓒ MP.7

31. Reason Two sides of a triangular garden are 6.4 m and 8.2 m. The gardener buys fencing for $29.25 per meter. What is the range of total cost of the fencing? Ⓒ MP.2

| LESSON 5-5 | **Inequalities in Two Triangles** |

Quick Review

The Hinge Theorem states that if two triangles have two congruent sides, and the included angles are not congruent, then the longer third side is opposite the larger included angle.

Example

Order AC, DF, and GJ from greatest to least.

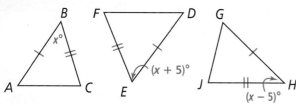

The triangles have two congruent sides.

$\overline{AB} \cong \overline{DE} \cong \overline{GH}$ and $\overline{BC} \cong \overline{EF} \cong \overline{HJ}$

The included angles are not congruent.

$x + 5 > x > x - 5$

Therefore, $DF > AC > GJ$.

Practice & Problem Solving

32. Write an inequality for the possible values of x.

33. Write an inequality for the possible values of x.

34. Construct Arguments Eduardo incorrectly says the Converse of the Hinge Theorem proves that $m\angle S < m\angle W$. Explain his error. Ⓒ MP.3

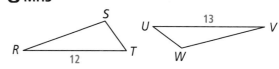

TOPIC 5 REVIEW

6

Quadrilaterals and Other Polygons

How are properties of parallelograms used to solve problems and to classify quadrilaterals?

Topic Overview

enVision® STEM Project:
Design a Quadrilateral Lift

6-1 The Polygon Angle-Sum Theorems

Mathematical Modeling in 3 Acts:
The Mystery Sides

6-2 Kites and Trapezoids

6-3 Properties of Parallelograms

6-4 Proving a Quadrilateral Is a Parallelogram

6-5 Properties of Special Parallelograms

6-6 Conditions of Special Parallelograms

Topic Vocabulary

• midsegment of a trapezoid

Digital Experience

📖 **INTERACTIVE STUDENT EDITION**
Access online or offline.

👆 **ACTIVITIES** Complete *Explore & Reason, Model & Discuss*, and *Critique & Explain* activities. Interact with *Examples* and *Try Its.*

👆 **CONCEPT SUMMARY** Review key lesson content through multiple representations.

☑ **ASSESSMENT** Show what you've learned.

Go online | **SavvasRealize.com**

MATHEMATICAL MODELING IN 3 ACTS

The Mystery Sides

Have you ever looked closely at honeycombs? What shape are they? How do you know? Most often the cells in the honeycombs look like hexagons, but they might also look like circles. Scientists now believe that the bees make circular cells that become hexagonal due to the bees' body heat and natural physical forces.

What are some strategies you use to identify shapes? Think about this during the Mathematical Modeling in 3 Acts lesson.

TOPIC 6

VIDEOS Watch clips to support *Mathematical Modeling in 3 Acts Lessons* and enVision® *STEM Projects.*

TUTORIALS Get help from *Virtual Nerd*, right when you need it.

PRACTICE Practice what you've learned.

ADAPTIVE PRACTICE Practice that is *just right* and *just for you.*

FAMILY ENGAGEMENT Involve family in your learning.

GLOSSARY Read and listen to English and Spanish definitions.

MATH TOOLS Explore math with digital tools and manipulatives.

DESMOS Use Anytime and as embedded Interactives in Lesson content.

Did You Know?

The rhinoceros beetle of Central and South America can lift up to **850 times** its own weight. That's equivalent to a 150-pound human lifting some 120,000 pounds, or **30 cars**.

Cargo bay

The world's largest cargo plane can carry more than half a million pounds. The cargo bay is 142 feet long, which is longer than the length of the first airplane *flight* by the Wright brothers, in 1903.

Your Task: Design a Quadrilateral Lift

A 50,000-pound bus needs to be lifted 6 feet off the ground for engine repairs. You and your classmates will analyze quadrilaterals and design a hydraulic lift for a mechanic to use for those repairs.

6-1

The Polygon Angle-Sum Theorems

I CAN... find the sums of the measures of the exterior angles and interior angles of polygons.

© **Common Core State Standards**
HSG.SRT.B.5, MP.1, MP.3, MP.4

EXPLORE & REASON

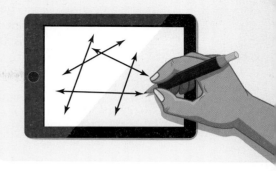
Powered By desmos

Start by drawing a pentagon. Then, for each side of the pentagon, draw the line that includes the side. An example is shown.

A. Choose one pair of lines that intersect at a vertex of the pentagon. Is each of the four angles formed at the vertex an interior angle or an exterior angle of the pentagon?

B. Are the relationships the same for the angles formed by the other pairs of intersecting lines?

C. Make Sense and Persevere If you drew a hexagon and the lines that included the sides of the hexagon, would the relationships between the angles at each vertex be the same as those in the pentagon? © **MP.1**

ESSENTIAL QUESTION ▷ How does the number of sides in convex polygons relate to the sums of the measures of the exterior and interior angles?

CONCEPTUAL UNDERSTANDING

EXAMPLE 1 ▷ Explore Polygon Interior Angle Sums
Powered By desmos

How does the number of sides of a convex polygon, *n*, relate to the sum of measures of its interior angles?

You know that the sum of the interior angle measures of a triangle is 180°. Decompose polygons into triangles and look for a pattern.

COMMON ERROR
Remember that *n* represents the number of sides of the polygon, not the number of triangles.

> To decompose a convex polygon into triangles, construct all diagonals from one vertex.

| *n* = 4 | *n* = 5 | *n* = 6 | *n* = 7 | *n* sides |
| 2 triangles | 3 triangles | 4 triangles | 5 triangles | *n* − 2 triangles |

> An *n*-gon is a polygon with *n* sides.

> Every *n*-sided polygon, or *n*-gon, has *n* − 2 triangles. Each triangle has an angle sum of 180.
>
> Interior angle sum of an *n*-gon = 180 • (*n* − 2)

Try It! **1. a.** How many triangles are formed by drawing diagonals from a vertex in a convex octagon?

b. What is the interior angle sum for a convex octagon?

THEOREM 6-1 Polygon Interior Angle-Sum Theorem

The sum of the measures of the interior angles of a convex n-gon is $180 \cdot (n - 2)$.

If...

$n = 7$

PROOF: SEE EXERCISE 11.

Then... $m\angle 1 + m\angle 2 + m\angle 3 + m\angle 4 + m\angle 5 + m\angle 6 + m\angle 7 = 180 \cdot (7 - 2) = 900$

COROLLARY to Theorem 6-1

The measure of an interior angle of a regular n-gon is $\frac{180 \cdot (n - 2)}{n}$.

If...

$n = 5$

Then... $m\angle 1 = \frac{180 \cdot (5 - 2)}{5} = 108$

APPLICATION

EXAMPLE 2 — Apply the Polygon Interior Angle-Sum Theorem

Jenna is building a cabinet to fit in the corner of a rectangular room. If the two angles marked $x°$ must be congruent, what are their measures?

Formulate ◄ Draw a pentagon to represent the cabinet. Find the sum of interior angle measures of the pentagon and then subtract the known angle measures to calculate the missing angle measures.

Compute ◄ **Step 1** Find the sum of the interior angles.

$(n - 2) \cdot 180 = (5 - 2) \cdot 180$
$= 3 \cdot 180$
$= 540$

Step 2 Find the missing angle measures.

$540 - (90 + 90 + 90) = 2x$
$270 = 2x$
$135 = x$

Interpret ◄ In order for the remaining two angles to be congruent, they must each have a measure of 135.

CONTINUED ON THE NEXT PAGE

EXAMPLE 2 CONTINUED

Try It! **2. a.** What is the interior angle sum of a 17-gon?

b. Each angle of a regular *n*-gon measures 172.8. How many sides does the *n*-gon have?

EXAMPLE 3 Understand Exterior Angle Measures of a Polygon

What is the sum of the exterior angle measures of a convex polygon?

You can use what you know about the sum of the interior angle measures of convex polygons to find the sum of the exterior angle measures.

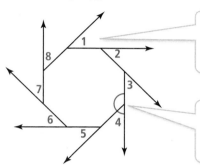

Remember, one side of the polygon and the extension of an adjacent side form an exterior angle.

Each interior and exterior angle pair forms a linear pair, which measures 180°.

GENERALIZE
How do you know that a polygon with *n* sides has *n* angle pairs? **© MP.8**

The sum of the measures of *n* interior and exterior angle pairs is 180 • *n*.

$$\begin{array}{ccc} \text{sum of exterior} & = & \text{sum of interior and} & - & \text{sum of interior} \\ \text{angle measures} & & \text{exterior angle measures} & & \text{angle measures} \end{array}$$

$$\begin{array}{ccc} = & 180n & - & 180(n-2) \end{array}$$

$$= 180n - 180n + 360$$
$$= 360$$

The sum of the exterior angle measures of any convex polygon is 360.

Try It! **3.** What is the sum of exterior angle measures of a convex 17-gon?

THEOREM 6-2 Polygon Exterior Angle-Sum Theorem

The sum of the measures of the exterior angles of a convex polygon, one at each vertex, is 360.

If...

Then... $m\angle 1 + m\angle 2 + m\angle 3 + m\angle 4 + m\angle 5 = 360$

PROOF: SEE EXERCISE 15.

EXAMPLE 4 Find an Exterior Angle Measure

Suppose ∠1 ≅ ∠3, m∠1 = 3x, and m∠2 = 2x. What is the measure of each exterior angle?

Step 1 Find x.

$$m\angle1 + m\angle2 + m\angle3 + m\angle4 + m\angle5 = 360$$
$$m\angle1 + m\angle2 + m\angle1 + 90 + 90 = 360$$
$$3x + 2x + 3x + 180 = 360$$
$$8x = 180$$
$$x = 22.5$$

> The exterior angle sum of a polygon is 360.

MAKE SENSE AND PERSEVERE
Think about how to verify your answers. What must be true if your answers are correct? © **MP.1**

Step 2 Use the value of x to determine the measure of each exterior angle.

m∠1 = 3x	m∠2 = 2x	m∠3 = m∠1	m∠4 = 90
m∠1 = 3(22.5)	m∠2 = 2(22.5)	m∠3 = 67.5	m∠5 = 90
m∠1 = 67.5	m∠2 = 45		

Try It! 4. Suppose ∠1 ≅ ∠3 ≅ ∠4 ≅ ∠6, ∠2 ≅ ∠5, and m∠3 = m∠2 + 30. What is m∠4?

EXAMPLE 5 Find the Measures of Interior Angles

What are the measures of the interior angles of the pentagon shown?

Step 1 Apply the Polygon Interior Angle-Sum Theorem and solve for x.

$$90 + (6x - 3) + (3x + 4) + (7x - 3) + (6x + 12) = 180 \cdot (5 - 2)$$
$$90 + 22x + 10 = 540$$
$$22x = 440$$
$$x = 20$$

Step 2 Substitute the value of x to find each angle measure.

6x − 3 = 6(20) − 3	3x + 4 = 3(20) + 4
= 117	= 64
7x − 3 = 7(20) − 3	6x + 12 = 6(20) + 12
= 137	= 132

The measures of the interior angles are 90, 117, 64, 137, and 132.

Try It! 5. The measure of each interior angle of a regular 100-gon is (3x + 26.4). What is the value of x?

CONCEPT SUMMARY Polygon Angle Sums

> **THEOREM 6-1** **Polygon Interior Angle-Sum Theorem**

The sum of the measures of the interior angles of a convex polygon is 180 • (n − 2), where n is the number of sides of the polygon.

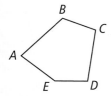

$m\angle A + m\angle B + m\angle C + m\angle D + m\angle E = 180(5 - 2)$
$= 540$

> **THEOREM 6-2** **Polygon Exterior Angle-Sum Theorem**

The sum of the measures of the exterior angles of a convex polygon, one at each vertex, is 360.

$m\angle 1 + m\angle 2 + m\angle 3 + m\angle 4 = 360$

Do You UNDERSTAND?

1. **ESSENTIAL QUESTION** How does the number of sides in convex polygons relate to the sums of the measures of the exterior and interior angles?

2. **Error Analysis** In the calculation shown, what is Valeria's error? Ⓒ MP.3

   > The sum of the measures of the exterior angles of a 25-gon is
   > 180 • (25 – 2) = 4,140.   ✗

3. **Make Sense and Persevere** What is the minimum amount of information needed to find the sum of the interior angles of a regular polygon? Ⓒ MP.1

4. **Reason** A convex polygon can be decomposed into 47 triangles. How many sides does the polygon have? Explain. Ⓒ MP.2

Do You KNOW HOW?

Use Polygon A for Exercises 5 and 6.

5. What is the sum of the measures of the interior angles?

6. What is the sum of the measures of the exterior angles?

Polygon A

Use Polygon B for Exercises 7 and 8.

7. What is the value of y?

8. What is the value of x?

Polygon B

9. What are the measures of the exterior angles of the polygon shown?

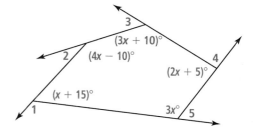

10. The sum of the interior angles of a regular n-gon is 6120°. What is the measure of each interior angle?

PRACTICE & PROBLEM SOLVING

UNDERSTAND

11. **Construct Arguments** Write a proof of the Polygon Interior Angle-Sum Theorem. ⓒ MP.3

12. **Make Sense and Persevere** What are the measures of the angles in the right triangles formed by the two regular pentagons shown? ⓒ MP.1

13. **Reason** Explain why a regular polygon cannot have an interior angle that is 40°. ⓒ MP.2

14. **Error Analysis** Jayesh makes the calculation shown to find the measure of each interior angle of a regular nonagon. What is his error? ⓒ MP.3

> Sum of measure of
> exterior angles:
> $180 \cdot 9 = 1,620$
> Sum of measure of
> interior angles:
> $1,620 \div 7 = 231$ ✗

15. **Construct Arguments** Write a proof of the Polygon Exterior Angle-Sum Theorem. ⓒ MP.3

16. **Higher Order Thinking** The star shown is constructed by extending each side of a regular pentagon. Explain why the surrounding triangles are isosceles and congruent.

PRACTICE

For Exercises 17 and 18, find the sum of the interior angles and the measure of each angle for the given regular polygon. SEE EXAMPLES 1 AND 2

17.   18.

19. How many sides does a regular polygon have if the measure of each interior angle is 160°? SEE EXAMPLES 1 AND 2

20. What is the measure of each exterior angle of a regular polygon with 72 sides? SEE EXAMPLE 3

21. How many sides does a regular polygon with an exterior angle measure of 60° have? SEE EXAMPLE 3

22. What is the value of x? What is the measure of each exterior angle? SEE EXAMPLE 4

For Exercises 23 and 24, find the value of x and the measure of each interior angle. SEE EXAMPLE 5

23.

24.

PRACTICE & PROBLEM SOLVING

APPLY

25. Model With Mathematics An airplane is navigating a polygon-shaped course. Each turn is labeled with the measure of the external angle at the striped post. What is $m\angle 1$? Ⓒ MP.4

26. Use Structure A music producer needs to soundproof a wall with nonoverlapping foam panels consisting of regular polygons. When placed, there cannot be any space between the figures. Which of the regular polygons can she use? Use Theorem 6-1 to explain. Ⓒ MP.7

27. Mathematical Connections Pentagonal building *ABCDE* is shown. Ricardo wants to install two security cameras at point *A* so the parking lot from side $\overline{AE}$ to side $\overline{AB}$ of the building can be monitored. Can he use two cameras, each with a field of view of 110°, installed at point *A*? Explain. If not, what is the minimum field of view that each camera should have?

ASSESSMENT PRACTICE

28. Match the number of sides of a regular polygon with the measure of each interior angle.

Practice and Problem Solving			
	120°	157.5°	160°	90°
4 sides	☐	☐	☐	☐
6 sides	☐	☐	☐	☐
16 sides	☐	☐	☐	☐
18 sides	☐	☐	☐	☐

29. SAT/ACT The figure below is a regular polygon. What is the value of *n*? Round to the nearest whole number.

Ⓐ 45   Ⓑ 51   Ⓒ 129   Ⓓ 135

30. Performance Task A company that manufactures office furniture makes the trapezoidal tables shown. The tables are designed to form a regular polygon when arranged adjacent to each other.

Part A How many tables are needed to form a regular polygon? Explain.

Part B The company wants to make a new model of trapezoidal tables that can be arranged to form a regular pentagon. What must the angle measures of the tables be?

© **Common Core State Standards**
HSG.SRT.B.5, MP.4

The Mystery Sides

Have you ever looked closely at honeycombs? What shape are they? How do you know? Most often the cells in the honeycombs look like hexagons, but they might also look like circles. Scientists now believe that bees make circular cells that become hexagonal due to the bees' body heat and natural physical forces.

What are some strategies you use to identify shapes? Think about this during the Mathematical Modeling in 3 Acts lesson.

ACT 1 ▶ **Identify the Problem**

1. What is the first question that comes to mind after watching the video?

2. Write down the main question you will answer about what you saw in the video.

3. Make an initial conjecture that answers this main question.

4. Explain how you arrived at your conjecture.

5. What information will be useful to know to answer the main question? How can you get it? How will you use that information?

ACT 2 ▶ **Develop a Model**

6. Use the math that you have learned in this Topic to refine your conjecture.

ACT 3 ▶ **Interpret the Results**

7. Did your refined conjecture match the actual answer exactly? If not, how is it different? What might explain the difference?

6-2

Kites and Trapezoids

I CAN... use triangle congruence to understand kites and trapezoids.

VOCABULARY
- midsegment of a trapezoid

© Common Core State Standards
HSG.SRT.B.5, MP.1, MP.2, MP.7

CRITIQUE & EXPLAIN

Manuel is designing kite-shaped key chains for the Debate Team. He draws kite *PQRS* with $\overleftrightarrow{QS}$ as the line of symmetry. He makes a list of conclusions based on the drawing.

- $\overline{PR} \perp \overline{QS}$
- $\overline{QP} \cong \overline{QR}$
- $\overline{SP} \cong \overline{SR}$
- *PR* bisects *QS*.
- △*PQR* is an equilateral triangle.
- △*PSR* is an isosceles triangle.

A. Which of Manuel's conclusions do you agree with? Which do you disagree with? Explain.

B. Use Structure What other conclusions are supported by the diagram? **© MP.7**

ESSENTIAL QUESTION How are diagonals and angle measures related in kites and trapezoids?

CONCEPTUAL UNDERSTANDING

EXAMPLE 1 Investigate the Diagonals of a Kite

How are the diagonals of a kite related?

A kite has two pairs of congruent adjacent sides.

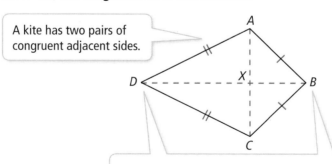

Point *B* is equidistant from the endpoints of $\overline{AC}$, as is *D*, so they lie on the perpendicular bisector of $\overline{AC}$.

The diagonals of a kite are perpendicular to each other. One of the diagonals bisects the other diagonal.

STUDY TIP
Remember that you must show that both *B* and *D* are on the perpendicular bisector in order to show that one diagonal is the perpendicular bisector of the other. It is not sufficient to show that only one is on the perpendicular bisector.

Try It! **1. a.** What is the measure of ∠*AXB*?

b. If *AX* = 3.8, what is *AC*?

c. If *BD* = 10, does *BX* = 5? Explain.

THEOREM 6-3

The diagonals of a kite are perpendicular.

PROOF: SEE EXERCISE 12.

If...

Then... $\overline{WY} \perp \overline{XZ}$

EXAMPLE 2 Use the Diagonals of a Kite

Quadrilateral *PQRS* is a kite with diagonals $\overline{QS}$ and $\overline{PR}$.

A. What is $m\angle 1$?

The diagonals of a kite are perpendicular, so $m\angle 1 = 90$.

COMMON ERROR
You may incorrectly assume angles are congruent just from their appearance. Always check that you can prove congruence first.

B. What is $m\angle 2$?

The sum of the angles of $\triangle PQT$ is 180.

$$m\angle 2 + 35 + 90 = 180$$
$$m\angle 2 = 55$$

C. What is $m\angle 3$?

Since $\triangle PQR$ is an isosceles triangle, $\angle 3 \cong \angle QPT$.

So, $m\angle 3 = 35$.

Try It! 2. Quadrilateral *WXYZ* is a kite.

  a. What is $m\angle 1$?

  b. What is $m\angle 2$?

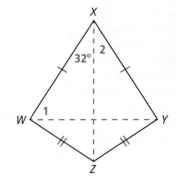

EXAMPLE 3 Explore Parts of an Isosceles Trapezoid

Kiyo is designing a trapezoid-shaped roof. In order for the roof to be symmetric, the overlapping triangles $\triangle DAB$ and $\triangle ADC$ must be congruent. Will the roof be symmetric?

Step 1 Show $\triangle ABE \cong \triangle DCF$.

$\overline{BE} \cong \overline{CF}$, because $\overline{BE}$ and $\overline{CF}$ are altitudes.

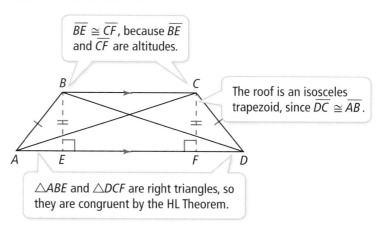

The roof is an isosceles trapezoid, since $\overline{DC} \cong \overline{AB}$.

$\triangle ABE$ and $\triangle DCF$ are right triangles, so they are congruent by the HL Theorem.

HAVE A GROWTH MINDSET
When it takes time to learn something new, how do you stick with it?

Step 1 Show $\triangle DAB \cong \triangle ADC$.

By CPCTC, $\angle DAB \cong \angle ADC$. By the Reflexive Property of Congruency, $\overline{AD} \cong \overline{DA}$. So, $\triangle DAB \cong \triangle ADC$ by SAS.

The overlapping triangles are congruent, so the roof is symmetric.

Try It! **3. a.** Given isosceles trapezoid *PQRS*, what are $m\angle P$, $m\angle Q$, and $m\angle S$?

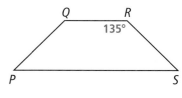

b. Given $\overline{ST} \parallel \overline{RU}$, what is the measure of $\angle TUR$?

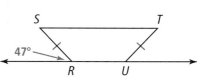

THEOREM 6-4

In an isosceles trapezoid, each pair of base angles is congruent.

If...

PROOF: SEE LESSON 6-3, EXERCISE 17.

Then... $\angle BAD \cong \angle CDA,$
$\angle ABC \cong \angle DCB$

THEOREM 6-5

The diagonals of an isosceles trapezoid are congruent.

If...

PROOF: SEE EXERCISE 18.

Then... $\overline{AC} \cong \overline{DB}$

EXAMPLE 4   Solve Problems Involving Isosceles Trapezoids

All horizontal beams of the high-voltage transmission tower are parallel to the ground.

The center section is an isosceles trapezoid.

The top section is an isosceles trapezoid.

A. If $m\angle 1 = 138$, what is $m\angle 2$?

The sum of the interior angle measures of a quadrilateral is 360.

$$m\angle 1 + m\angle 1 + m\angle 2 + m\angle 2 = 360$$
$$138 + 138 + 2(m\angle 2) = 360$$
$$276 + 2(m\angle 2) = 360$$
$$2(m\angle 2) = 84$$
$$m\angle 2 = 42$$

The base angles are congruent.

The measure of $\angle 2$ is 42.

MAKE SENSE AND PERSEVERE
In a trapezoid, the *bases* are parallel. Using what you know about the angle relationships in parallel lines intersected by a transversal, what other strategy might you use to solve this problem? © **MP.1**

CONTINUED ON THE NEXT PAGE

EXAMPLE 4 CONTINUED

GENERALIZE
Why might this strategy work for isosceles trapezoids but not for trapezoids with noncongruent legs? ⓒ MP.8

B. One cross support in the center of the tower measures $4c + 3$, and the other measures $6c - 5$. What is the length of each cross support?

The cross supports are diagonals of an isosceles trapezoid, so they are congruent.

Step 1 Find the value of c.

$$4c + 3 = 6c - 5$$
$$8 = 2c$$
$$4 = c$$

Step 2 Find the lengths of the diagonals.

$$4c + 3 = 4(4) + 3$$
$$= 19$$
$$6c - 5 = 6(4) - 5$$
$$= 19$$

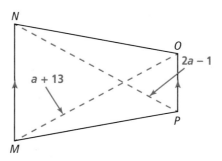

The length of each cross support is 19 ft.

Try It! **4.** Given isosceles trapezoid *MNOP* where the given expressions represent the measures of the diagonals, what is the value of a?

THEOREM 6-6 Trapezoid Midsegment Theorem

In a trapezoid, the segment containing the midpoints of the two legs is parallel to the bases, and its length is half the sum of the lengths of the bases.

PROOF: SEE LESSON 9-2.

If...

Then... $\overline{XY} \parallel \overline{AD}$, $\overline{XY} \parallel \overline{BC}$, and $XY = \frac{1}{2}(AD + BC)$

EXAMPLE 5 Apply the Trapezoid Midsegment Theorem

Paxton designs and makes trapezoidal handbags. She stitches decorative trim along the top, middle, and bottom on both sides of the handbags. How much trim does she need for three handbags?

Formulate ◄ The top and bottom sides of the handbag are the bases of a trapezoid. The left and right sides are the legs. Since the middle segment divides both legs in half, it is the midsegment of the trapezoid. The **midsegment of a trapezoid** is the segment that connects the midpoints of the legs.

Let x represent the length of the midsegment in inches.

Compute ◄ **Step 1** Find the value of x.

$$x = \tfrac{1}{2}(6 + 9)$$

$$x = 7.5$$

> Apply the Trapezoid Midsegment Theorem with the base lengths 6 and 9.

The length of the midsegment is 7.5 in.

Step 2 Find the amount of trim that Paxton needs.

First, find the amount of trim for one side.

$$6 + 9 + 7.5 = 22.5$$

Then, multiply by 2 for the number of sides per handbag and by 3 for the number of handbags.

$$22.5 \cdot 2 \cdot 3 = 135$$

Interpret ◄ Paxton needs 135 inches of trim.

Try It! 5. Given trapezoid *JKLM*, what is *KL*?

WORDS Kites	**Trapezoids**
A kite is a quadrilateral with two pairs of adjacent sides congruent and no pairs of opposite sides congruent. Exactly one diagonal is a perpendicular bisector of the other.	A trapezoid is a quadrilateral with exactly one pair of parallel sides. The length of the midsegment is the average of the lengths of the two bases. A trapezoid with congruent legs is an isosceles trapezoid that has congruent base angles and congruent diagonals.

DIAGRAMS Quadrilateral *ABCD* is a kite.	Quadrilateral *RSTU* is an isosceles trapezoid.

$$\overline{AC} \perp \overline{BD}$$

$$BE = ED$$

$$\overline{SU} \cong \overline{TR}$$

$$AB = \tfrac{1}{2}(ST + RU)$$

$$\overline{AB} \parallel \overline{ST} \parallel \overline{RU}$$

$$m\angle S = m\angle T$$

$$m\angle R = m\angle U$$

Do You UNDERSTAND?

1. **ESSENTIAL QUESTION** How are diagonals and angle measures related in kites and trapezoids?

2. **Error Analysis** What is Nevaeh's error? © **MP.3**

By Theorem 6-5, $\overline{PR} \cong \overline{QS}$ ✗

3. **Vocabulary** If $\overline{XY}$ is the midsegment of a trapezoid, what must be true about point *X* and point *Y*?

4. **Construct Arguments** Emaan says every kite is composed of 4 right triangles. Is he correct? Explain. © **MP.3**

Do You KNOW HOW?

For Exercises 5–7, use kite *WXYZ* to find the measures.

5. $m\angle XQY$

6. $m\angle YZQ$

7. WY

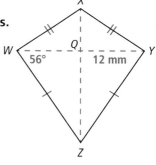

For Exercises 8–10, use trapezoid *DEFG* with $EG = 21$ ft and $m\angle DGF = 77$ to find each measure.

8. ED

9. DF

10. $m\angle DEF$

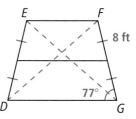

11. What is the length of $\overline{PQ}$?

PRACTICE & PROBLEM SOLVING

UNDERSTAND

12. Construct Arguments Write a two-column proof to show that the diagonals of a kite are perpendicular. ⓒ **MP.3**

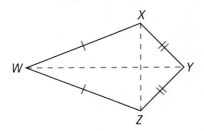

13. Prove that the perpendicular bisector of $\overline{BC}$ is also the perpendicular bisector of $\overline{AD}$. (*Hint:* Extend $\overline{BA}$ and $\overline{CD}$ to meet at point *M*, and show that the perpendicular bisector of $\overline{BC}$ contains *M*.)

14. Error Analysis What is Emily's error? ⓒ **MP.3**

$\overline{BD}$ is the perpendicular bisector of $\overline{AC}$, so *HC* = 8 in. because *AC* = 16 in.

15. Higher Order Thinking Given kite *JKLM* with diagonal $\overline{KM}$, *JK* < *JM*, and *KL* < *LM*, prove that ∠*JMK* is congruent to ∠*LMK*.

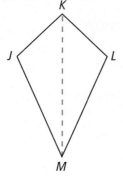

PRACTICE

16. Given kite *ABCD*, in which *AN* = 4.6 m, what is *AC*?
SEE EXAMPLE 1

17. Given kite *RSTU*, what is m∠*RUS*? SEE EXAMPLE 2

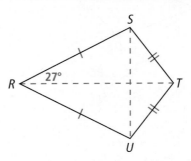

18. Write a two-column proof to show that the diagonals of an isosceles trapezoid are congruent. SEE EXAMPLES 3 AND 4

19. Given trapezoid *MNPQ*, what is m∠*MNP*?
SEE EXAMPLE 4

20. Given trapezoid *WXYZ*, what is *XY*?
SEE EXAMPLE 5

PRACTICE & PROBLEM SOLVING

APPLY

21. Model With Mathematics Legend plans to make a kite like the one shown. He has 700 square inches of plastic sheeting. Does Legend have enough plastic to make the kite? Explain. ⓒ MP.4

22. Reason Coach Murphy uses the map to plan a 2-mile run for the track team. How many times will the team run the trapezoidal route shown? (1 mile = 1,760 yards) ⓒ MP.2

23. Use Structure Abby builds a bench with the seat parallel to the ground. She bends pipe to make the leg and seat supports. At what angles should she bend the pipe? Explain. ⓒ MP.7

ASSESSMENT PRACTICE

24. Choose the word or phrase that completes the sentence: The diagonals of an isosceles trapezoid are always _____.

Ⓐ parallel

Ⓑ perpendicular

Ⓒ congruent

Ⓓ both bisectors of each other

25. SAT/ACT Given trapezoid $ABCD$, what is the length of $\overline{XY}$?

Ⓐ $3\frac{3}{5}$ Ⓑ $4\frac{2}{3}$ Ⓒ 5   Ⓓ 11   Ⓔ 18

26. Performance Task Carlota is a member of a volunteer group that built the play structure shown.

Part A Carlota wants to add three more boards evenly spaced between and parallel to the bottom and top boards of the triangular frame. Based on the lengths of the top and bottom boards shown, what will be the lengths of each of the three additional boards? Explain.

Part B How can Carlota determine where to nail the new boards into the existing frame?

Part C What other measurements should Carlota find to be certain that the boards will fit exactly onto the triangular frame?

6-3

Properties of Parallelograms

I CAN... use the properties of parallel lines, diagonals, and triangles to investigate parallelograms.

CRITIQUE & EXPLAIN

Kennedy lists all the pairs of congruent triangles she finds in quadrilateral *ABCD*.

$\overline{AD} \parallel \overline{CB}$ $\quad$ $\overline{AB} \parallel \overline{CD}$
$\angle ABC \cong \angle CDA$
$\angle DAB \cong \angle BCD$

Congruent triangles:
$\triangle DAB \cong \triangle BCD$ by SAS
$\triangle ABC \cong \triangle CDA$ by SAS

A. Is Kennedy's justification for triangle congruence correct for each pair?

B. **Look for Relationships** Did Kennedy overlook any pairs of congruent triangles? If not, explain how you know. If so, name them and explain how you know they are congruent.

ESSENTIAL QUESTION

What are the relationships of the sides, the angles, and the diagonals of a parallelogram?

CONCEPTUAL UNDERSTANDING

EXAMPLE 1 Explore Opposite Sides of Parallelograms

How do the lengths of the opposite sides of a parallelogram compare to each other?

Quadrilateral *ABCD* is a parallelogram.

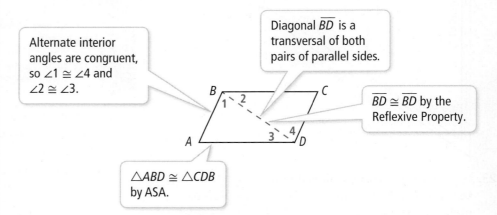

Alternate interior angles are congruent, so $\angle 1 \cong \angle 4$ and $\angle 2 \cong \angle 3$.

Diagonal $\overline{BD}$ is a transversal of both pairs of parallel sides.

$\overline{BD} \cong \overline{BD}$ by the Reflexive Property.

$\triangle ABD \cong \triangle CDB$ by ASA.

USE STRUCTURE
Can you use the same strategy to show other relationships in a parallelogram?

By CPCTC, $\overline{AD} \cong \overline{CB}$ and $\overline{AB} \cong \overline{CD}$, so the lengths of the opposite sides are congruent to each other.

Try It! **1.** Given parallelogram *WXYZ*, what is *YZ*?

THEOREM 6-7

If a quadrilateral is a parallelogram, then its opposite sides are congruent.

If...

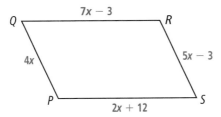

$\overline{WX} \parallel \overline{ZY}$
$\overline{WZ} \parallel \overline{XY}$

PROOF: SEE EXERCISE 13.

Then... $\overline{WX} \cong \overline{YZ}$
$\overline{WZ} \cong \overline{XY}$

EXAMPLE 2 Use Opposite Sides of a Parallelogram

Quadrilateral PQRS is a parallelogram.

Q —— $7x - 3$ —— R
$4x$
$5x - 3$
P —— $2x + 12$ —— S

STUDY TIP
Remember, there is often more than one way to solve a problem. You could also find the value of x by solving the equation $4x = 5x - 3$, since $\overline{QP}$ and $\overline{RS}$ are also opposite sides of the parallelogram.

A. What is the value of x?

$7x - 3 = 2x + 12$

$\overline{QR} \cong \overline{PS}$ because they are opposite sides of a parallelogram.

$5x = 15$

$x = 3$

B. What is the length of each side of PQRS?

$PQ = 4x$	$QR = 7x - 3$	$RS = 5x - 3$	$PS = 2x + 12$
$= 4(3)$	$= 7(3) - 3$	$= 5(3) - 3$	$= 2(3) + 12$
$= 12$	$= 21 - 3$	$= 15 - 3$	$= 6 + 12$
	$= 18$	$= 12$	$= 18$

Try It! **2.** The 600-meter fence around City Park forms a parallelogram. The fence along Chaco Road is twice as long as the fence along Grover Lane. What is the length of the fence along Jones Road?

EXAMPLE 3   Explore Angle Measures in Parallelograms

A. How are consecutive angles in a parallelogram related?

You can use what you know about angle relationships formed when parallel lines are cut by a transversal.

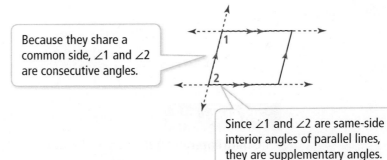

> **STUDY TIP**
> You can visualize a parallelogram as parallel lines intersected by transversals that are also parallel. This may help you determine how the angles are related.

Because they share a common side, ∠1 and ∠2 are consecutive angles.

Since ∠1 and ∠2 are same-side interior angles of parallel lines, they are supplementary angles.

Consecutive angles ∠1 and ∠2 are supplementary.

B. How are opposite angles in a parallelogram related?

Consecutive angles ∠1 and ∠2 are supplementary.

Consecutive angles ∠2 and ∠3 are supplementary.

In the figure, ∠1 and ∠3 are opposite angles. Both angles are supplementary to ∠2, so opposite angles in a parallelogram are congruent.

Try It!   **3. a.** Given parallelogram *ABCD*, what are *m*∠*A* and *m*∠*C*?

     b. What is *m*∠*B*?

THEOREM 6-8

Powered By **desmos**

If a quadrilateral is a parallelogram, then its consecutive angles are supplementary.

PROOF: SEE EXERCISE 15.

If... $\overline{AB} \parallel \overline{DC}$ $\overline{AD} \parallel \overline{BC}$

Then... $m\angle A + m\angle B = 180$
$m\angle B + m\angle C = 180$
$m\angle C + m\angle D = 180$
$m\angle D + m\angle A = 180$

THEOREM 6-9

If a quadrilateral is parallelogram, then opposite angles are congruent.

PROOF: SEE EXERCISE 23.

If... $\overline{AB} \parallel \overline{DC}$
$\overline{AD} \parallel \overline{BC}$

Then... $\angle A \cong \angle C$
$\angle B \cong \angle D$

EXAMPLE 4 Use Angles of a Parallelogram

Anthony is creating stained glass art using parallelogram and triangle pieces, as shown. For the parallelograms that are not squares, the measure of ∠2 must be 3 times the measure of ∠1. What are m∠1, m∠2, and m∠3?

As consecutive angles, $m\angle 1 + m\angle 2 = 180$.

$m\angle 2 = 3m\angle 1$ is given.

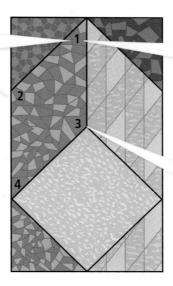

As opposite angles, $\angle 2 \cong \angle 3$.

COMMON ERROR
Be careful to write the relationship of ∠1 and ∠2 correctly.
$m\angle 1 \neq 3m\angle 2$

Find m∠1.	Find m∠2.	Find m∠3.
$m\angle 1 + m\angle 2 = 180$	$m\angle 2 = 3m\angle 1$	$m\angle 3 = m\angle 2$
$m\angle 1 + 3m\angle 1 = 180$	$m\angle 2 = 3(45)$	$m\angle 3 = 135$
$m\angle 1 = 45$	$m\angle 2 = 135$	

The measures of ∠1, ∠2, and ∠3 are 45, 135, and 135, respectively.

Try It! 4. Use the parallelogram shown.

a. Given parallelogram *GHJK*, what is the value of *a*?

b. What are *m∠G*, *m∠H*, *m∠J*, and *m∠K*?

THEOREM 6-10

If a quadrilateral is a parallelogram, then its diagonals bisect each other.

If... $\overline{WX} \parallel \overline{ZY}$
$\overline{WZ} \parallel \overline{XY}$

Then... $\overline{AW} \cong \overline{AY}$
$\overline{AX} \cong \overline{AZ}$

PROOF: SEE EXAMPLE 5.

PROOF

EXAMPLE 5 Explore the Diagonals of a Parallelogram

How are the diagonals of a parallelogram related?

$\overline{AC}$ and $\overline{BD}$ are the diagonals of parallelogram $ABCD$.

Given: $ABCD$ is a parallelogram.

Prove: $\overline{AQ} \cong \overline{CQ}$, $\overline{BQ} \cong \overline{DQ}$

Proof:

STUDY TIP
The given information is usually the best statement to begin a proof.

Try It! 5. Use parallelogram $RSTU$ with $SU = 35$ and $KT = 19$.

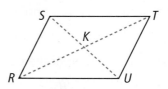

a. What is SK?

b. What is RT?

EXAMPLE 6 Find Unknown Lengths in a Parallelogram

Corey stamps the parallelogram shown on the front of a poster she is making. How many times will she need to stamp the design to make a row 60 cm wide along the dashed line?

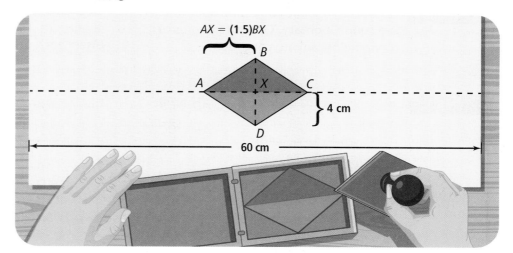

Formulate ◀ By Theorem 6-10, the diagonals $\overline{AC}$ and $\overline{BD}$ bisect each other. So $\overline{BX} \cong \overline{DX}$, and $\overline{AX} \cong \overline{CX}$.

Compute ◀ **Step 1** Determine the length of the diagonal, $\overline{AC}$.

$BX = DX$ — Diagonals bisect each other.

$BX = 4$

$AX = 1.5\ BX$ — Given

$AX = 1.5(4)$

$AX = 6$

$AC = 2(AX)$ — Diagonals bisect each other.

$AC = 2(6)$

$AC = 12$

Step 2 Find the number of times Corey needs to stamp.

$60 \div 12 = 5$

Interpret ◀ Corey will need to stamp the design 5 times to make a row 60 cm wide.

Try It! **6.** Given parallelogram GHJK, if $PK = 4$ and $HK = \frac{2}{3}(GJ)$, what is GP?

CONCEPT SUMMARY Properties of Parallelograms

Angles of Parallelograms	Sides and Diagonals of Parallelograms

WORDS | Consecutive angles of a parallelogram are supplementary. Opposite angles of a parallelogram are congruent. | Opposite sides of a parallelogram are congruent. Diagonals of a parallelogram bisect each other.

SYMBOLS | **If...** $\overline{AD} \parallel \overline{CB}$ $\overline{AB} \parallel \overline{DC}$ | **If...** $\overline{AD} \parallel \overline{CB}$ $\overline{AB} \parallel \overline{DC}$

Then...
$$m\angle A + m\angle B = 180$$
$$m\angle B + m\angle C = 180$$
$$m\angle C + m\angle D = 180$$
$$m\angle D + m\angle A = 180$$
$$m\angle A = m\angle C$$
$$m\angle B = m\angle D$$

Then...
$$AB = CD$$
$$AD = BC$$
$$AX = CX$$
$$BX = DX$$

Do You UNDERSTAND?

1. **ESSENTIAL QUESTION** What are the relationships of the sides, the angles, and the diagonals of a parallelogram?

2. **Error Analysis** What is Pablo's error? ⓒ **MP.3**

$\overline{PR} \cong \overline{QS}$ ✗

3. **Make Sense and Persevere** If you knew the length of $\overline{DF}$ in parallelogram $DEFG$, how would you find the length of $\overline{DK}$? Explain. ⓒ **MP.1**

4. **Reason** Given parallelogram $JKLM$, what could the expression $180 - (3x + 8)$ represent? Explain. ⓒ **MP.2**

Do You KNOW HOW?

For Exercises 5 and 6, use parallelogram $ABCD$ to find each length. The measure of $\overline{DE}$ is $x + 2$.

5. BC

6. BD

For Exercises 7 and 8, use parallelogram $WXYZ$ to find each angle measure.

7. $m\angle WXY$

8. $m\angle XYZ$

For Exercises 9 and 10, use parallelogram $EFGH$ to find each length.

9. EJ

10. FH

For Exercises 11 and 12, use parallelogram $MNPQ$ to find each angle measure.

11. $m\angle NPQ$

12. $m\angle PQM$

PRACTICE & PROBLEM SOLVING

UNDERSTAND

13. Construct Arguments Write a proof of Theorem 6-7. © MP.3

Given: $\overline{WX} \parallel \overline{ZY}, \overline{WZ} \parallel \overline{XY}$

Prove: $\overline{WX} \cong \overline{ZY}, \overline{WZ} \cong \overline{XY}$

14. Error Analysis In the statements shown, explain the student's error. What shape is the quadrilateral? © MP.3

$\overline{JK} \cong \overline{KL}$ and $\overline{LM} \cong \overline{MJ}$.
$\angle MJK \cong \angle KLM$

Therefore, $\triangle MJK \cong \triangle KLM$ by SAS. The triangular halves of JKLM are congruent, so JKLM must be a parallelogram. ✗

15. Construct Arguments Write a proof of Theorem 6-8. © MP.3

Given: $\overline{AB} \parallel \overline{DC}, \overline{AD} \parallel \overline{BC}$

Prove: $m\angle A + m\angle B = 180$
$m\angle B + m\angle C = 180$
$m\angle C + m\angle D = 180$
$m\angle D + m\angle A = 180$

16. Use Appropriate Tools In a parallelogram, opposite sides are congruent, and opposite angles are congruent. If all sides in a parallelogram are congruent, are all angles congruent also? Draw a picture to explain your answer. © MP.5

17. Prove that each pair of base angles of an isosceles trapezoid are congruent. *Hint:* Use the figure below and construct $\overline{AE}$ to be parallel to $\overline{DC}$.

PRACTICE

18. What are the values of *AB* and *DE* in parallelogram *ABCD*? SEE EXAMPLES 1 AND 2

19. Quadrilateral *EFGH* is a parallelogram. What is $m\angle F$? SEE EXAMPLES 3 AND 4

20. Quadrilateral *MNPQ* is a parallelogram. What is *NQ*? SEE EXAMPLES 5 AND 6

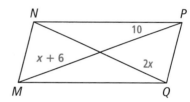

21. The figure below can be divided into two parallelograms. What is the angle measure of the point at the bottom?

22. Find the perimeter of the parallelogram.

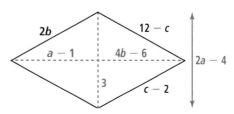

23. Write a proof of Theorem 6-9.

Given: $\overline{AB} \parallel \overline{DC}, \overline{AD} \parallel \overline{BC}$

Prove: $\angle A \cong \angle C, \angle B \cong \angle D$

PRACTICE & PROBLEM SOLVING

24. Model With Mathematics All four arms of a mechanical jack are the same length, and they form a parallelogram. Turning the crank pulls the arms together, raising the top of the jack. How high is the top of the jack when the crank is 5 inches off the ground? Explain. © **MP.4**

25. Use Structure The handrails for a steel staircase form a parallelogram *ABCD*. Additional bars are needed one third and two thirds of the way up the stairs. Explain why the additional bars must be the same length as the end bars. © **MP.7**

26. Higher Order Thinking Serenah designs a pattern consisting of large squares of the same size, small squares of the same size, and some parallelograms. She wants to replicate the pattern using tiles for her bathroom. Are the vertical and horizontal parallelograms congruent? Explain.

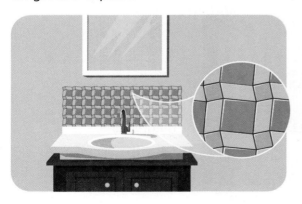

27. Find the values of *a*, *b*, and *c* in the parallelogram.

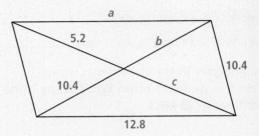

28. SAT/ACT In parallelogram *ABCD*, which angle is congruent to ∠*ABC*?

Ⓐ ∠*ABD*   Ⓒ ∠*BCD*

Ⓑ ∠*CDA*   Ⓓ ∠*DAB*

29. Performance Task A pipe at an amusement park sprays water onto visitors. The cross sections of each pipe shown have the shape of a parallelogram.

Part A Pipe A makes a 120° angle with Pipe B. What are the interior angles of parallelogram B? What is *x*, the measure of the angle that Pipe B makes with the horizontal? Explain.

Part B Park engineers fasten a circular cap onto the end of Pipe B. In the middle of the cap is a nozzle to turn the spray of water into a mist. If the diameter of Pipe A is 3 inches, what is the diameter of the circular cap? Explain.

Part C What are *y* and *z*, the angle measures that the cap makes with Pipe B? Explain.

6-4

Proving a Quadrilateral Is a Parallelogram

I CAN... use the sides, angles, and diagonals of a quadrilateral to determine whether it is a parallelogram.

© Common Core State Standards
HSG.CO.C.11, HSG.SRT.B.5, MP.4, MP.5, MP.6

EXPLORE & REASON

Powered By desmos

Sketch the quadrilaterals as described in the table. Include the diagonals.

	Parallel Sides	Congruent Sides
Quadrilateral 1	0 pairs	2 consecutive pairs
Quadrilateral 2	1 pair	exactly 1 nonparallel pair
Quadrilateral 3	2 pairs	2 opposite pairs

A. Measure the angles of each quadrilateral. How are the angle measures in Quadrilateral 1 related to each other? In Quadrilateral 2? In Quadrilateral 3?

B. Measure the diagonals of each quadrilateral. How are the diagonals in Quadrilateral 1 related to each other? In Quadrilateral 2? In Quadrilateral 3?

C. Communicate Precisely Compare the relationships among the angles and diagonals of Quadrilateral 3 to those of the other two quadrilaterals. Are there any relationships that make Quadrilateral 3 unique? **© MP.6**

ESSENTIAL QUESTION Which properties determine whether a quadrilateral is a parallelogram?

EXAMPLE 1 Investigate Sides to Confirm a Parallelogram

In quadrilateral *ABCD*, $\overline{AC}$ is a diagonal, $\overline{AB} \cong \overline{CD}$, and $\overline{AD} \cong \overline{CB}$. Is *ABCD* a parallelogram? Explain.

STUDY TIP
Recall that any segment is congruent to itself by the Reflexive Property of Congruence.

△*ABC* ≅ △*CDA* by SSS.

By CPCTC, ∠*BAC* ≅ ∠*DCA* and ∠*BCA* ≅ ∠*DAC*.

By the Converse of the Alternate Interior Angles Theorem, $\overline{AB} \parallel \overline{CD}$ and $\overline{AD} \parallel \overline{BC}$. By definition, quadrilateral *ABCD* is a parallelogram.

Try It! **1.** Explain why you cannot conclude that *ABCD* is a parallelogram.

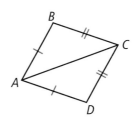

THEOREM 6-11 Converse of Theorem 6-7

If both pairs of opposite sides of a quadrilateral are congruent, then the quadrilateral is a parallelogram.

PROOF: SEE EXAMPLE 1.

If...

$\overline{AB} \cong \overline{CD}$

$\overline{AD} \cong \overline{BC}$

Then... *ABCD* is a parallelogram.

CONCEPTUAL UNDERSTANDING

EXAMPLE 2 ▶ Explore Angle Measures to Confirm a Parallelogram

A. Teo sketches a design of a building with a quadrilateral-shaped base. If ∠1 is supplementary to ∠2 and ∠4, is his design a parallelogram?

> **LEARN TOGETHER**
> How do you value other perspectives and points of view respectfully?

Since ∠1 and ∠2 are same-side interior angles and supplementary, the top and bottom sides are parallel.

Since ∠1 and ∠4 are same-side interior angles and supplementary, the left and right sides are parallel.

The quadrilateral has two pairs of parallel sides, so it is a parallelogram. The design is a parallelogram.

B. Teo sketches a second design in which ∠1 is congruent to ∠3, and ∠2 is congruent to ∠4. Is that design a parallelogram?

The sum of interior angles is 360.

$$m\angle 1 + m\angle 2 + m\angle 3 + m\angle 4 = 360$$

$$m\angle 1 + m\angle 2 + m\angle 1 + m\angle 2 = 360$$

$$2(m\angle 1 + m\angle 2) = 360$$

$$m\angle 1 + m\angle 2 = 180$$

Since ∠1 ≅ ∠3 and ∠2 ≅ ∠4, substitute $m\angle 1$ for $m\angle 3$ and $m\angle 2$ for $m\angle 4$.

Substitute $m\angle 4$ for $m\angle 2$.

$$m\angle 1 + m\angle 4 = 180$$

Because the edges form a quadrilateral with one angle supplementary to both consecutive angles and from the result in Part A, the second design is also a parallelogram.

Try It! **2. a.** Is *DEFG* a parallelogram? Explain.

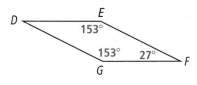

b. Is *LMNO* a parallelogram? Explain.

THEOREM 6-12 Converse of Theorem 6-8

If an angle of a quadrilateral is supplementary to both of its consecutive angles, then the quadrilateral is a parallelogram.

If...

$m\angle A + m\angle B = 180$

$m\angle A + m\angle D = 180$

PROOF: SEE EXERCISE 12.

Then... *ABCD* is a parallelogram.

THEOREM 6-13 Converse of Theorem 6-9

If both pairs of opposite angles of a quadrilateral are congruent, then the quadrilateral is a parallelogram.

If...

$\angle A \cong \angle C$

$\angle B \cong \angle D$

PROOF: SEE EXERCISE 14.

Then... *ABCD* is a parallelogram.

EXAMPLE 3 ▶ Find Values to Make Parallelograms

A. For what values of *r* and *s* is *WXYZ* a parallelogram?

Quadrilateral *WXYZ* is a parallelogram if both pairs of opposite sides are congruent.

$$7r + 1 = 4r + 7 \qquad 2s - 2 = s + 5$$
$$r = 2 \qquad\qquad s = 7$$

If $r = 2$ and $s = 7$, then *WX* and *ZY* are both 15, and *XY* and *WZ* are both 12. So *WXYZ* is a parallelogram if $r = 2$ and $s = 7$.

GENERALIZE
Think about the properties of a parallelogram. What do you know about a quadrilateral that is a parallelogram? © **MP.8**

B. For what values of *a* and *b* is *RSTU* a parallelogram?

Quadrilateral *RSTU* is a parallelogram if both pairs of opposite angles are congruent.

$$5a = 3a + 14 \qquad 4b + 1 = 3b + 37$$
$$2a = 14 \qquad\qquad b = 36$$
$$a = 7$$

If $a = 7$ and $b = 36$, then angles *S* and *U* are both 35° and angles *T* and *R* are both 145°. So *RSTU* is a parallelogram if $a = 7$ and $b = 36$.

Try It! **3. a.** If $x = 25$ and $y = 30$, is *PQRS* a parallelogram?

b. If $g = 14$ and $h = 5$, is *ABCD* a parallelogram?

THEOREM 6-14 Converse of Theorem 6-10

If the diagonals of a quadrilateral bisect each other, then the quadrilateral is a parallelogram.

PROOF: SEE EXAMPLE 4.

If...

$\overline{AX} \cong \overline{CX}$
$\overline{BX} \cong \overline{DX}$

Then... *ABCD* is a parallelogram.

THEOREM 6-15

If one pair of opposite sides of a quadrilateral is both congruent and parallel, then the quadrilateral is a parallelogram.

PROOF: SEE EXERCISE 20.

If...

$\overline{AD} \cong \overline{BC}$
$\overline{AD} \parallel \overline{BC}$

Then... *ABCD* is a parallelogram.

PROOF

EXAMPLE 4 Investigate Diagonals to Confirm a Parallelogram

Given: $\overline{AX} \cong \overline{CX}$ and $\overline{BX} \cong \overline{DX}$

Prove: *ABCD* is a parallelogram

Proof:

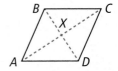

COMMON ERROR
Remember, noncongruent diagonals may bisect each other, just as congruent diagonals do.

Statements	Reasons
1) $\overline{AX} \cong \overline{CX}$ and $\overline{BX} \cong \overline{DX}$	1) Given
2) $\angle AXD \cong \angle CXB$ and $\angle AXB \cong \angle CXD$	2) Vertical Angles Theorem
3) $\triangle AXD \cong \triangle CXB$ and $\triangle AXB \cong \triangle CXD$	3) SAS
4) $\overline{AD} \cong \overline{CB}$ and $\overline{AB} \cong \overline{CD}$	4) CPCTC
5) *ABCD* is a parallelogram.	5) Both pairs of opposite sides of the quadrilateral are congruent.

Try It! **4.** For what values of *p* and *q* is *ABCD* a parallelogram?

EXAMPLE 5 Identify a Parallelogram

A. Is *PQRS* a parallelogram? Explain.

Same-side interior angles *Q* and *R* are supplementary, so $\overline{QP} \parallel \overline{RS}$.

PQRS is a parallelogram by Theorem 6-15.

CONTINUED ON THE NEXT PAGE

EXAMPLE 5 CONTINUED

B. Is WXYZ a parallelogram? Explain.

Although diagonal $\overline{WY}$ bisects $\overline{XZ}$, diagonal $\overline{XZ}$ does not necessarily bisect $\overline{WY}$. Since the diagonals of quadrilateral WXYZ do not bisect each other, WXYZ is not necessarily a parallelogram.

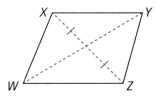

Try It! **5. a.** Is ABCD a parallelogram? Explain.

b. Is EFGH a parallelogram? Explain.

APPLICATION

EXAMPLE 6 **Verify a Parallelogram**

A mechanic raises a truck using a lift. For safety, the floor must be horizontal and the top of the lift must be parallel to the floor. Is the lift shown in a safe position? Explain.

Formulate ◄ The lift and the floor form a quadrilateral. If the quadrilateral is a parallelogram, then the side holding the truck will be parallel to the floor and the lift will be safe.

Compute ◄ Find the sum of the given angles.

$$105 + 75 = 180$$

Since a pair of same-side alternate interior angles are supplementary, the 6-ft sides of the lift are parallel. The lift is a parallelogram by Theorem 6-15.

Interpret ◄ Opposite sides of a parallelogram are parallel, so the side of the lift holding the truck is parallel to the floor. The lift is in a safe position.

Try It! **6.** A carpenter builds the table shown. If the floor is level, how likely is it that a ball placed on the table will roll off?

CONCEPT SUMMARY Identifying Quadrilaterals That Are Parallelograms

SIDES AND DIAGONALS ▶

A quadrilateral is a parallelogram if

- two pairs of opposite sides are congruent

- one pair of opposite sides is congruent and parallel

- the diagonals bisect each other

ANGLES ▶

A quadrilateral is a parallelogram if

- one angle is supplementary to both consecutive angles

- two pairs of opposite angles are congruent

Do You UNDERSTAND?

1. **ESSENTIAL QUESTION** Which properties determine whether a quadrilateral is a parallelogram?

2. **Error Analysis** Explain why Rochelle is incorrect. © MP.3

Given: $AC = BD$

ABCD is a parallelogram, because quadrilaterals with congruent diagonals are parallelograms. ✗

3. **Make Sense and Persevere** Is the information in the diagram enough to show WXYZ is a parallelogram? Explain. © MP.1

Do You KNOW HOW?

What must each angle measure be in order for quadrilateral DEFG to be a parallelogram?

4. $m\angle D$ 5. $m\angle E$

What must each length be in order for quadrilateral JKLM to be a parallelogram?

6. JK

7. JL

Use the diagram for Exercises 8 and 9.

8. If $\overline{AB} \parallel \overline{DC}$, is ABCD a parallelogram? Explain.

9. If ABCD is a parallelogram, how does AC compare to BD? Explain.

PRACTICE & PROBLEM SOLVING

UNDERSTAND

10. Use Appropriate Tools If you are given a drawing of a quadrilateral, how can you determine whether or not it is a parallelogram? What tool or tools can you use? ⒸMP.5

11. Error Analysis Ahmed uses the following explanation to prove that a figure is a parallelogram. What is Ahmed's error? ⒸMP.3

The quadrilateral has a pair of opposite sides congruent and a pair of opposite sides parallel. By Theorem 6-15, the figure is a parallelogram.

12. Construct Arguments Write a proof of Theorem 6-12. ⒸMP.3

Given: $m\angle F + m\angle G = 180$
$m\angle F + m\angle J = 180$

Prove: *FGHJ* is a parallelogram.

13. Mathematical Connections A rectangle is defined as a quadrilateral with four right angles. Which theorem or theorems from the lesson explain why a rectangle is a parallelogram? Explain how the theorem or theorems apply.

14. Construct Arguments Write a proof of Theorem 6-13. ⒸMP.3

Given: $\angle L \cong \angle N$, $\angle M \cong \angle O$

Prove: *LMNO* is a parallelogram.

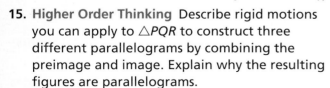

15. Higher Order Thinking Describe rigid motions you can apply to △*PQR* to construct three different parallelograms by combining the preimage and image. Explain why the resulting figures are parallelograms.

PRACTICE

16. Is each quadrilateral a parallelogram? Explain. SEE EXAMPLES 1 AND 2

a.   b.

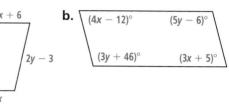

17. In each figure, for what values of *x* and *y* is the figure a parallelogram? SEE EXAMPLE 3

a. b.

18. Given the lengths shown, for what values of *w* and *z* is the figure a parallelogram? SEE EXAMPLE 4

19. Is the figure below a parallelogram? Explain. SEE EXAMPLES 5 AND 6

20. Write a proof of Theorem 6-15.

Given: $\overline{KL} \parallel \overline{JM}$, $\overline{KL} \cong \overline{JM}$

Prove: *JKLM* is a parallelogram.

Hint: Construct diagonal $\overline{JL}$.

PRACTICE & PROBLEM SOLVING

21. **Make Sense and Persevere** A lamp on a wall is suspended from an extendable arm that allows the lamp to slide up and down. When it expands, does the shape shown remain a parallelogram? Explain. ⒼMP.1

22. **Model With Mathematics** In the railway bridge shown, the long horizontal beams on the top and bottom are parallel to each other. How can a bridge inspector confirm that beams 1 and 3 are parallel to each other and that beams 2 and 4 are parallel to each other? Explain. ⒼMP.4

23. **Communicate Precisely** Colorful paper lanterns called Akash Kandil are hung during Diwali celebrations. The lanterns shown are made of quadrilaterals and congruent equilateral triangles. Are the quadrilaterals parallelograms? Explain. ⒼMP.6

24. Copy the graph and plot all possible coordinate pairs for point *Q* on the coordinate plane so that points *P*, *Q*, *R*, and *S* form the vertices of a parallelogram.

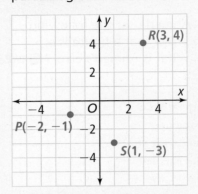

25. **SAT/ACT** In quadrilateral *ABCD*, ∠*A* ≅ ∠*C*. Which additional statement can be used to show that *ABCD* is a parallelogram?

Ⓐ $m\angle A + m\angle C = 180$ 　Ⓒ $m\angle B + m\angle D = 180$
Ⓑ $\overline{BD}$ bisects $\overline{AC}$ 　Ⓓ ∠*B* ≅ ∠*D*

26. **Performance Task** Tabità helps her sister build the baby gate shown using dowels and hinges. This allows the angles of the quadrilateral to stretch and shrink so that the gate can swing upwards and open against the wall along the stairs. They call it the parallelogram gate.

Part A Are they correct to call it a parallelogram gate? Explain.

Part B What are the measurements of the sides of the gate when the gate is open? Explain.

Part C Tabità's father suggests that they add two diagonal slats at the front of the baby gate. What would that do to the gate? Explain.

6-5
Properties of Special Parallelograms

I CAN... use the properties of rhombuses, rectangles, and squares to solve problems.

© **Common Core State Standards**
HSG.CO.C.11, HSG.SRT.B.5, MP.1, MP.3, MP.7

EXPLORE & REASON

Consider these three figures.

Figure 1 Figure 2 Figure 3

A. What questions would you ask to determine whether each figure is a parallelogram?

B. Communicate Precisely What questions would you ask to determine whether Figure 1 is a rectangle? What additional questions would you ask to determine whether Figure 2 is a square? © **MP.6**

C. If all three figures are parallelograms, what is the most descriptive name for Figure 3? How do you know?

ESSENTIAL QUESTION What properties of rhombuses, rectangles, and squares differentiate them from other parallelograms?

CONCEPTUAL UNDERSTANDING

EXAMPLE 1 Investigate the Angles Formed by the Diagonals of a Rhombus

A. Parallelogram *ABCD* is a rhombus. What are the measures of ∠1, ∠2, ∠3, and ∠4?

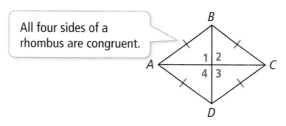

All four sides of a rhombus are congruent.

By the Converse of the Perpendicular Bisector Theorem, *B* and *D* are on the perpendicular bisector of $\overline{AC}$, so $\overline{AC} \perp \overline{BD}$.

All four angles formed by the intersection of the diagonals are right angles, so the measure of ∠1, ∠2, ∠3, and ∠4 is 90.

B. Parallelogram *JKLM* is a rhombus. How are ∠1, ∠2, ∠3, and ∠4 related?

By SSS, △*JKL* ≅ △*JML*, so ∠1 ≅ ∠2 and ∠3 ≅ ∠4.

$\overline{JL} \cong \overline{JL}$

The diagonals of a rhombus bisect the angles at each vertex.

> **STUDY TIP**
> Recall that a rhombus is a parallelogram, so it has all the properties of parallelograms.

Try It! **1. a.** What is *WY*?

b. What is *m∠RPS*?

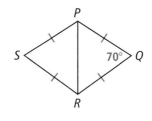

THEOREM 6-16

If a parallelogram is a rhombus, then its diagonals are perpendicular bisectors of each other.

PROOF: SEE EXERCISE 13.

If...

Then... $\overline{WY}$ and $\overline{XZ}$ are perpendicular bisectors of each other.

THEOREM 6-17

If a parallelogram is a rhombus, then each diagonal bisects a pair of opposite angles.

PROOF: SEE EXERCISE 16.

If...

Then... $\angle 1 \cong \angle 2$, $\angle 3 \cong \angle 4$, $\angle 5 \cong \angle 6$, and $\angle 7 \cong \angle 8$.

EXAMPLE 2 Find Lengths and Angle Measures in a Rhombus

A. Quadrilateral *ABCD* is a rhombus. What is $m\angle ADE$?

$\overline{AC}$ bisects $\angle BAD$, so $m\angle DAC = 53$.

$m\angle DAE + m\angle AED + m\angle ADE = 180$

$53 + 90 + m\angle ADE = 180$

$m\angle ADE = 37$

$\overline{AC} \perp \overline{BD}$, so $m\angle AED = 90$.

COMMON ERROR
You may incorrectly state that $m\angle ADE = m\angle DAE$. Remember that consecutive angles are not necessarily congruent.

B. Quadrilateral *GHJK* is a rhombus. What is *GH*?

Step 1 Find *x*.

$\overline{HK}$ bisects $\overline{GJ}$, so $2x + 3 = 4x - 7$

$2x = 10$

$x = 5$

Step 2 Use the value of *x* to find *GH*.

$HJ = 3(5) + 1 = 16$

$GH = HJ$

$GH = 16$

Try It! **2.** Each quadrilateral is a rhombus.

a. What is $m\angle MNO$?

b. What is *QT*?

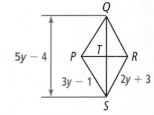

THEOREM 6-18

If a parallelogram is a rectangle, then its diagonals are congruent.

If...

Then... $\overline{AC} \cong \overline{BD}$

PROOF: SEE EXAMPLE 3.

PROOF →

EXAMPLE 3 Prove Diagonals of a Rectangle Are Congruent

Write a proof for Theorem 6-18.

Given: *PQRS* is a rectangle.

Prove: $\overline{PR} \cong \overline{QS}$

Plan: To show that the diagonals are congruent, find a pair of triangles that each diagonal is a part of, and prove the triangles are congruent. Both △*PSR* and △*QRS* have one side that is a diagonal. Draw each triangle separately and label the congruent sides.

Proof:

Statements	Reasons
1) *PQRS* is a rectangle.	1) Given
2) *PQRS* is a parallelogram.	2) Def. of rectangle
3) $\overline{PS} \cong \overline{QR}$	3) Opposite sides of a parallelogram are congruent.
4) ∠*PSR* and ∠*QRS* are right angles.	4) Def. of rectangle
5) ∠*PSR* ≅ ∠*QRS*	5) All right angles are congruent.
6) $\overline{SR} \cong \overline{RS}$	6) Reflexive Prop. of Congruence
7) △*PSR* ≅ △*QRS*	7) SAS Triangle Congruence Thm.
8) $\overline{PR} \cong \overline{QS}$	8) CPCTC

STUDY TIP
When you see triangles in a diagram for a proof, you can often use congruent triangles and CPCTC to complete the proof.

Try It! 3. A carpenter needs to check the gate his apprentice built to be sure it is rectangular. The diagonals measure 52 inches and 53 inches. Is the gate rectangular? Explain.

EXAMPLE 4 Find Diagonal Lengths of a Rectangle

Paul is training his horse to run a course at a pace of 4 meters per second or faster. The horse runs from *D* to *C* to *E* to *B* in 1 minute 30 seconds. *ABCD* is a rectangle. Did Paul reach his goal?

Formulate ◄ Use the Pythagorean Theorem to find *BD*. Then use properties of rectangles to find each segment length and the total distance. Finally, determine the horse's speed.

Compute ◄
$$(BD)^2 = 80^2 + 192^2$$
$$(BD)^2 = 43{,}264$$
$$BD = 208$$

> Apply the Pythagorean Theorem.

Use the properties of rectangles to find the total distance.

$$CE = EB = 104$$

> Diagonals are congruent and bisect each other.

$$DC + CE + EB = 192 + 104 + 104 = 400$$

Determine the pace.

$$400 \div 90 \approx 4.4$$

Interpret ◄ Paul's horse ran at a pace of about 4.4 m/s, so Paul reached his goal.

Try It! 4. A rectangle with area 1,600 m² is 4 times as long as it is wide. What is the sum of the diagonals?

EXAMPLE 5 Diagonals and Angle Measures of a Square

Figure *WXYZ* is a square. If *WY* + *XZ* = 92, what is the area of △*WPZ*?

Since the figure is also a rhombus, $\overline{WY} \perp \overline{XZ}$ and *WP* and *ZP* are the base and height of △*WPZ*.

Step 1 Find the lengths of the diagonals.

$$WY + XZ = 92$$
$$WY = XZ = 46$$

> *WXYZ* is a rectangle, so $\overline{WY} \cong \overline{XZ}$.

USE STRUCTURE
Consider the four triangles formed by the diagonals of a square. What observations do you make about these triangles? © MP.7

Step 2 Find *WP* and *ZP*.

$$WP = \frac{1}{2}(WY) = 23$$
$$ZP = \frac{1}{2}(XZ) = 23$$

> *WXYZ* is a parallelogram, so $\overline{WY}$ and $\overline{XZ}$ bisect each other.

Step 3 Find the area of △*WPZ*.

$$\text{area}(\triangle WPZ) = \frac{1}{2}(23)(23) = 264.5$$

The area of △*WPZ* is 264.5 square units.

Try It! 5. Square *ABCD* has diagonals $\overline{AC}$ and $\overline{BD}$. What is *m*∠*ABD*? Explain.

CONCEPT SUMMARY Properties of Special Parallelograms

	Rectangle	Rhombus	Square
WORDS	If a parallelogram is a rectangle, then the diagonals are congruent.	If a parallelogram is a rhombus, then the diagonals are perpendicular and bisect each pair of opposite angles.	If a parallelogram is a square, the properties of both a rectangle and a rhombus apply.
DIAGRAMS	(rectangle $ABCD$ with diagonals)	(rhombus $PQRS$ with diagonals meeting at T)	(square $WXYZ$ with diagonals meeting)
SYMBOLS	$\overline{AC} \cong \overline{BD}$	$\overline{PR} \perp \overline{QS}$ $\angle QRT \cong \angle SRT \cong \angle QPT \cong \angle SPT$ $\angle PQT \cong \angle RQT \cong \angle PST \cong \angle RST$	$\overline{WY} \cong \overline{XZ}$ $\overline{WY} \perp \overline{XZ}$

Do You UNDERSTAND?

1. **ESSENTIAL QUESTION** What properties of rhombuses, rectangles, and squares differentiate them from other parallelograms?

2. **Error Analysis** Figure $QRST$ is a rectangle. Ramona wants to show that the four interior triangles are congruent. What is Ramona's error? © MP.3

> Diagonals of a rectangle are congruent and bisect each other, so $\overline{RP} \cong \overline{TP} \cong \overline{QP} \cong \overline{SP}$. Because the diagonals are perpendicular bisectors, $\angle RPS$, $\angle SPT$, $\angle TPQ$, and $\angle QPR$ are right angles. Therefore, by SAS, $\triangle RPS \cong \triangle SPT \cong \triangle TPQ \cong \triangle PQR$. ✗

3. **Construct Arguments** Is any quadrilateral with four congruent sides a rhombus? Explain. © MP.3

Do You KNOW HOW?

Find each length and angle measure for rhombus *DEFG*. Round to the nearest tenth.

4. *DF*

5. $m\angle DFG$

6. *EG*

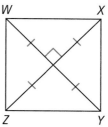

Find each length for rectangle *MNPQ*. Round to the nearest tenth.

7. *MP*

8. *MQ*

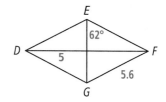

Find each length and angle measure for square *WXYZ*.

9. $m\angle YPZ$

10. $m\angle XWP$

11. *XZ*

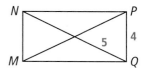

12. What is the value of *x*?

$(4x + 5)°$ $(8x - 6)°$

PRACTICE & PROBLEM SOLVING

UNDERSTAND

13. Construct Arguments Write a proof of Theorem 6-16. © MP.3

Given: *WXYZ* is a rhombus.

Prove: $\overline{WY}$ and $\overline{XZ}$ are perpendicular bisectors of each other.

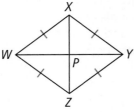

14. Error Analysis Figure *ABCD* is a rhombus. What is Malcolm's error? © MP.3

Since *ABCD* is a rhombus, $\overline{AB} \cong \overline{CD}$. Since the diagonals of a rhombus biscect each other, $\overline{AE} \cong \overline{BE} \cong \overline{CE} \cong \overline{DE}$. So, by SSS △*ABE* ≅ △*CDE*.

15. Mathematical Connections The area of rectangle *WXYZ* is 115.5 in.². What is the perimeter of △*XYZ*? Explain your work.

16. Construct Arguments Write a proof of Theorem 6-17. © MP.3

Given: *ABCD* is a rhombus.

Prove: ∠1 ≅ ∠2, ∠3 ≅ ∠4, ∠5 ≅ 6, ∠7 ≅ ∠8

17. Higher Order Thinking A square is cut apart and reassembled into a rectangle as shown. Which figure has a greater perimeter? Explain.

PRACTICE

For Exercises 18–20, find each angle measure for rhombus *ABCD*. SEE EXAMPLES 1 AND 2

18. m∠*ACD*

19. m∠*ABC*

20. m∠*BEA*

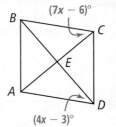

For Exercises 21–23, find each length for rhombus *PQRS*. Round to the nearest tenth.
SEE EXAMPLES 1 AND 2

21. *TR*

22. *QS*

23. *PS*

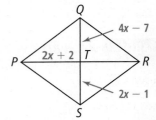

For Exercises 24–27, find each length and angle measure for rectangle *GHJK*. Round to the nearest tenth. SEE EXAMPLES 3 AND 4

24. m∠*GHK*

25. m∠*HLJ*

26. *GJ*

27. *HL*

For Exercises 28–30, find each length and value for square *QRST*. Round to the nearest tenth.
SEE EXAMPLE 5

28. *SV*

29. *RT*

30. perimeter of △*RVS*

31. If *ABCD* is a square, what is *GC*?

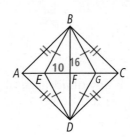

PRACTICE & PROBLEM SOLVING

APPLY

32. **Model With Mathematics** Andrés wants a pen that gives his puppy at least 35 square feet of area and at least 10 feet of diagonal length. Should Andrés buy this pen? Explain. © MP.4

33. **Make Sense and Persevere** Luisa is making a top for a chest with the inlaid pattern shown. © MP.1

   a. What angle should she cut for ∠CDG? Explain.

   b. If she makes the table top correctly, what will the length of the completed top be?

34. **Look for Relationships** A carpenter is building a support for a stage. What should be the measures of ∠1, ∠2, ∠3, and ∠4? Explain your answers.
© MP.7

35. Which statements are true about all rectangles? Select all that apply.

   Ⓐ Diagonals bisect each other.

   Ⓑ Adjacent sides are perpendicular.

   Ⓒ Diagonals are perpendicular.

   Ⓓ Consecutive angles are supplementary.

36. **SAT/ACT** Which expression gives $m\angle DBC$?

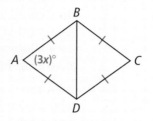

   Ⓐ $\left(180 - \dfrac{3x}{2}\right)^\circ$ Ⓒ $\left(\dfrac{180 - 3x}{2}\right)^\circ$

   Ⓑ $(180 - 3x)^\circ$ Ⓓ $\left(\dfrac{3x}{2} - 180\right)^\circ$

37. **Performance Task** Hina is planning to order tiles for her kitchen floor. She is interested in three types of tiles that are offered at the hardware store. Tile 1 is a square, tile 2 is a rhombus, and tile 3 is a rectangle. Some measurements and the prices for each tile have been provided.

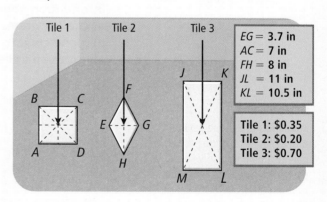

$EG = 3.7$ in
$AC = 7$ in
$FH = 8$ in
$JL = 11$ in
$KL = 10.5$ in

Tile 1: $0.35
Tile 2: $0.20
Tile 3: $0.70

Part A What are the lengths of the sides of each tile?

Part B What is the area of each tile?

Part C Hina needs to cover an area of 50 ft², or 7,200 in.², using only one type of tile. If she wants to spend the least amount of money possible, which tile should she choose? Explain.

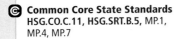

6-6

Conditions of Special Parallelograms

I CAN... identify rhombuses, rectangles, and squares by the characteristics of their diagonals.

Ⓒ **Common Core State Standards**
HSG.CO.C.11, HSG.SRT.B.5, MP.1, MP.4, MP.7

MODEL & DISCUSS

Floating lanterns both in the sky and on water are rooted in ancient cultural traditions. Today, they are used to commemorate cultural and spiritual celebrations across Asia and the US. The sides of the water lantern shown are identical quadrilaterals.

A. Construct Arguments How could you check to see whether a side is a parallelogram? Justify your answer. Ⓒ **MP.3**

B. Does the side appear to be rectangular? How could you check?

C. Do you think that diagonals of a quadrilateral can be used to determine whether the quadrilateral is a rectangle? Explain.

ESSENTIAL QUESTION ▷ Which properties of the diagonals of a parallelogram help you to classify a parallelogram?

CONCEPTUAL UNDERSTANDING

EXAMPLE 1 Use Diagonals to Identify Rhombuses

Information about diagonals can help to classify a parallelogram. In parallelogram *ABCD*, $\overline{AC}$ is perpendicular to $\overline{BD}$. What else can you conclude about the parallelogram?

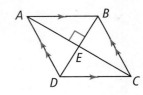

STUDY TIP
Parallelograms have several properties, and some properties may not help you solve a particular problem. Here, the fact that diagonals bisect each other allows the use of SAS.

The diagonals of a parallelogram bisect each other, so $\overline{AE} \cong \overline{CE}$ and $\overline{DE} \cong \overline{BE}$.

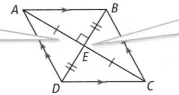

Any angle at *E* either forms a linear pair or is a vertical angle with ∠*AEB*, so all four angles are right angles.

The four triangles are congruent by SAS, so $\overline{AB} \cong \overline{CB} \cong \overline{CD} \cong \overline{AD}$.

Since *ABCD* is a parallelogram with four congruent sides, *ABCD* is a rhombus.

Try It! **1.** If ∠*JHK* and ∠*JGK* are complementary, what else can you conclude about *GHJK*? Explain.

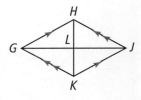

THEOREM 6-19 Converse of Theorem 6-16

If the diagonals of a parallelogram are perpendicular, then the parallelogram is a rhombus.

PROOF: SEE EXERCISE 11.

If...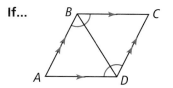

Then... $\overline{JK} \cong \overline{KL} \cong \overline{LM} \cong \overline{MJ}$

THEOREM 6-20 Converse of Theorem 6-17

If a diagonal of a parallelogram bisects two angles of the parallelogram, then the parallelogram is a rhombus.

PROOF: SEE EXAMPLE 2.

If...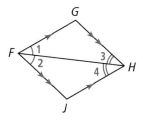

Then... $\overline{AB} \cong \overline{BC} \cong \overline{CD} \cong \overline{DA}$

PROOF

EXAMPLE 2 ▶ Prove Theorem 6-20

Write a proof of Theorem 6-20.

Given: Parallelogram FGHJ with $\angle 1 \cong \angle 2$ and $\angle 3 \cong \angle 4$

Prove: FGHJ is a rhombus.

Proof:

STUDY TIP
Drawing diagonals in parallelograms can help you see additional information that is useful in solving problems.

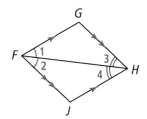

By ASA, $\triangle FHJ \cong \triangle FHG$. So, $\overline{FJ} \cong \overline{FG}$.

By the Alternate Interior Angles Theorem, $\angle 1 \cong \angle 4$, so $\angle 1 \cong \angle 2 \cong \angle 3 \cong \angle 4$.

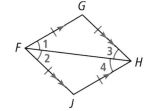

By the Converse of the Isosceles Triangle Theorem, $\overline{FG} \cong \overline{HG}$ and $\overline{FJ} \cong \overline{HJ}$.

Using the Transitive Property of Congruence, $\overline{FG} \cong \overline{HG} \cong \overline{FJ} \cong \overline{HJ}$. Since FGHJ is a parallelogram with congruent sides, it is a rhombus.

Try It! **2.** Refer to the figure FGHJ in Example 2. Use properties of parallelograms to show that if $\angle 1 \cong \angle 2$ and $\angle 3 \cong \angle 4$, then the four angles are congruent.

EXAMPLE 3   Use Diagonals to Identify Rectangles

Ashley measures the diagonals for her deck frame and finds that they are congruent. Will the deck be rectangular?

Since opposite sides are congruent, the supports form a parallelogram. To show that the structure is rectangular, show that the angles are right angles.

Opposite sides and the diagonals are congruent, so $\triangle ACD \cong \triangle BDC$ by SSS. Therefore, $\angle ADC \cong \angle BCD$.

In a parallelogram, consecutive angles are supplementary. Angles that are congruent and supplementary are right angles. In the same way, $\angle DAB$ and $\angle CBA$ are also right angles.

The frame forms a parallelogram with four right angles, which is a rectangle.

Try It!   **3.** If the diagonals of any quadrilateral are congruent, is the quadrilateral a rectangle? Justify your answer.

THEOREM 6-21 Converse of Theorem 6-18

If the diagonals of a parallelogram are congruent, then the parallelogram is a rectangle.

If... X ... Y W ... Z $XZ \cong WY$

PROOF: SEE EXERCISE 13.

Then... $\angle XWZ$, $\angle WZY$, $\angle XYZ$, and $\angle WXY$ are right angles

---

EXAMPLE 4   Identify Special Parallelograms

Can you conclude whether each parallelogram is a rhombus, a square, or a rectangle? Explain.

A. Parallelogram *ABCD*

By SAS, $\triangle ABD \cong \triangle CBD$.

$\angle ADB \cong \angle CDB$ by CPCTC.

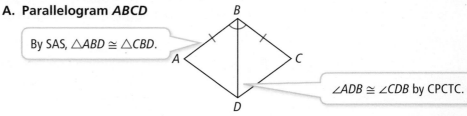

CONSTRUCT ARGUMENTS
There are often several ways to prove something. How could you use properties of parallelograms to show the figure is a rhombus without using the congruent angles shown?

Diagonal $\overline{BD}$ bisects $\angle ABC$ and $\angle ADC$, so parallelogram *ABCD* is a rhombus.

CONTINUED ON THE NEXT PAGE

EXAMPLE 4 CONTINUED

B. Parallelogram PQRS

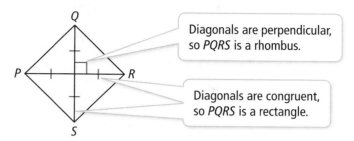

Diagonals are perpendicular, so *PQRS* is a rhombus.

Diagonals are congruent, so *PQRS* is a rectangle.

Since the parallelogram is a rhombus and a rectangle, it is a square.

Try It! 4. Is each parallelogram a rhombus, a square, or a rectangle? Explain.

a.

b.

EXAMPLE 5 Use Properties of Special Parallelograms

Quadrilateral *STUV* is a rhombus. What are the values of *x* and *y*?

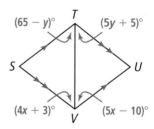

MAKE SENSE AND PERSEVERE
Consider the information given in the diagram. How can you determine whether $\overline{TV}$ bisects the angles? Ⓒ **MP.1**

If a parallelogram is a rhombus then each diagonal bisects opposite angles. So, $\overline{TV}$ bisects $\angle SVU$ and $\angle STU$.

Solve for *x*.

$m\angle SVT = m\angle UVT$ ⟵ $\overline{TV}$ bisects $\angle SVU$ and $\angle STU$. ⟶ $m\angle STV = m\angle UTV$

$4x + 3 = 5x - 10$

$-x = -13$

$x = 13$

Solve for *y*.

$65 - y = 5y + 5$

$-6y = -60$

$y = 10$

Try It! 5. In parallelogram *ABCD*, $AC = 3w - 1$ and $BD = 2(w + 6)$. What must be true for *ABCD* to be a rectangle?

EXAMPLE 6 **Apply Properties of Special Parallelograms**

A group of friends set up a kickball field with bases 60 ft apart. How can they use diagonals to verify that the field is a square?

Opposite sides are congruent, so the field is a parallelogram.

60 ft   60 ft   60 ft   60 ft

All sides are congruent, so the parallelogram is a rhombus.

Home Plate

The field is a rhombus. To show that the rhombus is a square, show that it is also a rectangle.

A parallelogram is a rectangle if the diagonals are congruent.

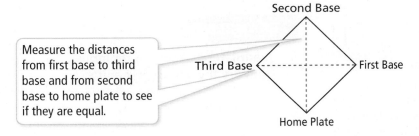

Measure the distances from first base to third base and from second base to home plate to see if they are equal.

Second Base

Third Base ←- - - - - - - - -→ First Base

Home Plate

If the field is a square, then each angle must be a right angle. The friends can use the Pythagorean Theorem to determine that each diagonal should have a length of $\sqrt{60^2 + 60^2}$ ft, or about 84.85 ft. If each diagonal has a length of 84.85 ft, then the field is a square.

Try It!   **6.** Is *MNPQ* a rhombus? Explain.

CONCEPT SUMMARY Conditions of Special Parallelograms

RHOMBUS

A parallelogram is a rhombus if

- diagonals are perpendicular

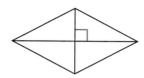

- a diagonal bisects angles

RECTANGLE

A parallelogram is a rectangle if

- diagonals are congruent

SQUARE

A parallelogram is a square if

- diagonals are perpendicular and congruent

- a diagonal bisects angles and diagonals are congruent

Do You UNDERSTAND?

1. **ESSENTIAL QUESTION** Which properties of the diagonals of a parallelogram help you to classify a parallelogram?

2. **Error Analysis** Sergio was asked to classify *DEFG*. What was Sergio's error? Ⓒ **MP.3**

$DF = EG$

Since $DF = EG$, *DEFG* is a rectangle.
Since $\overline{EG} \perp \overline{DF}$, *DEFG* is also a rhombus.
Therefore, *DEFG* is a square. ✗

3. **Construct Arguments** Write a biconditional statement about the diagonals of rectangles. What theorems justify your statement? Ⓒ **MP.3**

4. **Use Appropriate Tools** Make a concept map showing the relationships among quadrilaterals, parallelograms, trapezoids, isosceles trapezoids, kites, rectangles, squares, and rhombuses. Ⓒ **MP.5**

Do You KNOW HOW?

For Exercises 5–8, is the parallelogram a rhombus, a square, or a rectangle?

5.

6.

7.

8.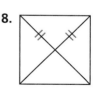

9. What value of *x* will make the parallelogram a rhombus?

10. If $m\angle 1 = 36$ and $m\angle 2 = 54$, is *PQRS* a rhombus, a square, a rectangle, or none of these? Explain.

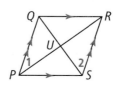

PRACTICE & PROBLEM SOLVING

UNDERSTAND

11. Construct Arguments Write a proof of Theorem 6-19 using the diagram below. © MP.3

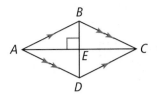

12. Error Analysis Becky is asked to classify *PQRS*. What is her error? © MP.3

$\overline{PR}$ bisects opposite angles ∠SPQ and ∠QRS, so PQRS must be a rhombus. ✗

13. Construct Arguments Write a proof of Theorem 6-21 using the diagram below. © MP.3

14. Construct Arguments Write a proof to show that if *ABCD* is a parallelogram and ∠ABE ≅ ∠BAE, then *ABCD* is a rectangle. © MP.3

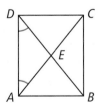

15. Mathematical Connections If *WXYZ* is a rhombus with *W*(−1, 3) and *Y*(9, 11), what must be an equation of $\overleftrightarrow{XZ}$ in order for *WXYZ* to be a rhombus? Explain how you found your answer.

16. Higher Order Thinking The longer diagonal of a rhombus is three times the length of the shorter diagonal. If the shorter diagonal is *x*, what expression gives the perimeter of the rhombus?

PRACTICE

For Exercises 17 and 18, determine whether each figure is a rhombus. Explain your answer.
SEE EXAMPLES 1 AND 2

17.   **18.**

19. What is the perimeter of parallelogram *WXYZ*? SEE EXAMPLE 3

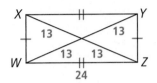

For Exercises 20 and 21, determine the name that best describes each figure: parallelogram, rectangle, square, or rhombus. SEE EXAMPLE 4

20.   **21.**

For Exercises 22–24, give the condition required for each figure to be the specified shape.
SEE EXAMPLES 5 AND 6

22. rectangle

23. rhombus

24. rhombus

PRACTICE & PROBLEM SOLVING

25. **Look for Relationships** Violeta charges $1.50 per square meter for laying sod. She says she can compute the amount to charge for the pentagonal lawn by evaluating $1.50(12^2 + 0.25(12^2))$. Do you agree? Explain. Ⓒ MP.7

26. **Make Sense and Persevere** Tyone is making a wall design with tape. How much tape does he need to put the design shown on his wall? Explain how you used the information in the diagram to find your answer. Ⓒ MP.1

27. **Use Structure** Monisha knits the blanket shown. She plans to sew a ribbon around the edge of the blanket. How much ribbon will she need? Ⓒ MP.7

28. Are the terms below valid classifications for the figure? Select *Yes* or *No*.

Quadrilateral	Yes	No
Square	☐	☐
Rhombus	☐	☐
Parallelogram	☐	☐
Rectangle	☐	☐
Trapezoid	☐	☐

29. **SAT/ACT** Parallelogram *ABCD* has diagonals with lengths $AC = 7x + 6$ and $BD = 9x - 2$. For which value of *x* is *ABCD* a rectangle?

　Ⓐ 2　　Ⓑ 4　　Ⓒ 7　　Ⓓ 9　　Ⓔ 34

30. **Performance Task** Alonso is using the two segments shown as diagonals of quadrilaterals he is making for a decal design for the cover of his phone.

Part A Make a table showing at least four types of different quadrilaterals that Alonso can make using the segments as diagonals. For each type of quadrilateral, draw a diagram showing an example. Label angle measures where the diagonals intersect, and label segment lengths of the diagonals.

Part B Are some types of quadrilaterals not possible using these diagonals? Explain.

Part C Which has the greater area, a square or a rectangle? Explain.

Topic Review

TOPIC ESSENTIAL QUESTION

1. How are properties of parallelograms used to solve problems and to classify quadrilaterals?

Vocabulary Review

Choose the correct term to complete each sentence.

2. A parallelogram is a(n) _____ if its diagonals are perpendicular and congruent.

3. A(n) _____ is a quadrilateral with two pairs of adjacent sides congruent and no pairs of opposite sides congruent.

4. The sum of the measures of the _____ angles of a convex polygon is $180° \cdot (n - 2)$, where n is the number of sides of the polygon.

5. The length of the _____ is the average of its two bases.

- exterior
- interior
- kite
- midsegment of a trapezoid
- rectangle
- rhombus
- square

Concepts & Skills Review

LESSON 6-1 **The Polygon Angle-Sum Theorems**

Quick Review

The sum of the measures of the exterior angles of a convex polygon, one at each vertex, is 360°.

The sum of the measures of the interior angles of a convex polygon is $180° \cdot (n - 2)$, where n is the number of sides of the polygon.

Example

What is the sum of the measures of the interior angles of the regular hexagon?

$180° \cdot (6 - 2) = 720°$

Practice & Problem Solving

Find the sum of the measures of the interior angles and the exterior angles of each figure.

6.

7.

8. **Make Sense and Persevere** Is there enough information to determine the measures of the interior angles of the polygon shown? If so, find the measures. If not, explain. **© MP.1**

LESSON 6-2 — Kites and Trapezoids

Quick Review

A kite is a quadrilateral with two pairs of adjacent sides congruent and no pairs of opposite sides congruent.

A trapezoid is a quadrilateral with exactly one pair of parallel sides. The length of the midsegment of a trapezoid is the average of the two bases.

Example

Given trapezoid ABCD, what is EF?

The midsegment of trapezoid ABCD is $\overline{EF}$, so $EF = \frac{1}{2}(24 + 32) = 28$.

Practice & Problem Solving

Find each measure.

9. $m\angle 1$ **10.** BC

11. Use Structure Shannon wants to hang curtains using a tension rod across the top of the trapezoid-shaped window shown below. Is a 36-inch tension rod long enough to go across the top of her window? Explain. ⓒ MP.7

LESSON 6-3 — Properties of Parallelograms

Quick Review

The sides, diagonals, and angles of parallelograms have special relationships.

- Opposite sides are congruent.
- Diagonals bisect each other.
- Consecutive angles are supplementary.
- Opposite angles are congruent.

Example

Given parallelogram ABCD, if ED = 3 and BD = $\frac{3}{4}$ (AC), what is AC?

Since $ED = BE$, $BD = 6$. Substitute into $BD = \frac{3}{4}(AC)$ to get $6 = \frac{3}{4}(AC)$, and then solve to get $AC = 8$.

Practice & Problem Solving

Use the diagram to find each angle measure.

12. $m\angle W$ **13.** $m\angle X$

14. Construct Arguments The outline of a planned parking lot in the shape of a parallelogram is shown. Tadeo says the north side of the lot is 130 ft and the west side of the lot is 240 ft. What is Tadeo's mistake? ⓒ MP.3

```
        north
  west         east
               130 ft

      240 ft
      south
```

Proving a Quadrilateral Is a Parallelogram

Quick Review

A quadrilateral is a parallelogram if any of the following conditions is true.

- Both pairs of opposite sides are congruent.
- One pair of opposite sides is congruent and parallel.
- An angle is supplementary to both of its consecutive angles.
- Both pairs of opposite angles are congruent.
- The diagonals bisect each other.

Example

Explain why the quadrilateral is a parallelogram.

Two pairs of opposite angles are congruent, so the quadrilateral is a parallelogram.

Practice & Problem Solving

For what value of x is each quadrilateral a parallelogram?

15.

16.

17. Communicate Precisely What measurements can be used to show that each shaded quadrilateral is a parallelogram? Explain. Ⓖ **MP.6**

Properties of Special Parallelograms

Quick Review

The diagonals of a rhombus are perpendicular bisectors of each other. The diagonals of a rectangle are congruent. The diagonals of a square are perpendicular bisectors of each other and congruent.

Example

Given that $WXYZ$ is a rhombus, show that $\overline{PW} \cong \overline{PY}$.

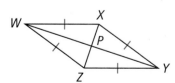

Quadrilateral $WXYZ$ is a rhombus, so it is a parallelogram. Diagonals of parallelograms bisect each other, so $\overline{PW} \cong \overline{PY}$ by definition of bisect.

Practice & Problem Solving

18. Given that $ABCD$ is a rhombus, what is BD?

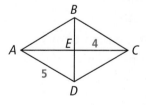

19. Given that $PQRS$ is a rectangle, what is QS?

20. Construct Arguments Is any quadrilateral with four congruent sides a square? Explain. Ⓖ **MP.3**

LESSON 6-6 · Conditions of Special Parallelograms

Quick Review

Suppose a figure is a parallelogram.

- If the diagonals are perpendicular, then the parallelogram is a rhombus.
- If the diagonals are congruent, then the parallelogram is a rectangle.
- If the diagonals are perpendicular and congruent, then the parallelogram is a square.

Example

Show that the parallelogram is a square.

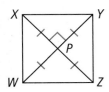

Since $XP = ZP = WP = YP$, $XZ = WY$, the diagonals are congruent. Since the diagonals are congruent, the parallelogram is a rectangle. The diagonals are also given to be perpendicular to each other, so the rectangle is a square.

Practice & Problem Solving

Is the parallelogram a rhombus, a rectangle, or a square?

21.

22.

23. **Make Sense and Persevere** For what value of x is *GHJK* a rhombus? Explain. © **MP.1**

24. **Construct Arguments** Can Trinidad construct a kite with diagonals that bisect each other? Explain. © **MP.3**

TOPIC 7

Similarity

TOPIC ESSENTIAL QUESTION

How are properties of similar figures used to solve problems?

Topic Overview

enVision® STEM Project:
   Design With a 3D Printer

7-1 Dilations

7-2 Similarity Transformations

7-3 Proving Triangles Similar

7-4 Similarity in Right Triangles

Mathematical Modeling in 3 Acts:
   Make It Right

7-5 Proportions in Triangles

Topic Vocabulary

- center of dilation
- geometric mean
- similarity transformation

Digital Experience

INTERACTIVE STUDENT EDITION
Access online or offline.

ACTIVITIES Complete *Explore & Reason, Model & Discuss,* and *Critique & Explain* activities. Interact with *Examples* and *Try Its.*

CONCEPT SUMMARY Review key lesson content through multiple representations.

ASSESSMENT Show what you've learned.

 Go online | SavvasRealize.com

MATHEMATICAL MODELING IN **3** ACTS

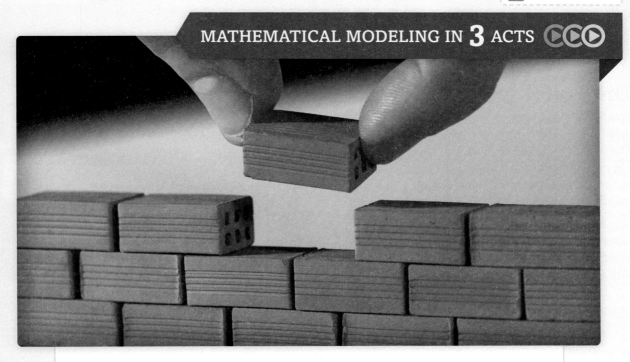

Make It Right

Architects often make a scale physical model of a new building project. The scale model is usually a miniature version of the project it is representing.

When making a model, architects need to make sure that all of the parts of the model are the right size. Think about this during the Mathematical Modeling in 3 Acts lesson.

VIDEOS Watch clips to support *Mathematical Modeling in 3 Acts Lessons* and enVision® *STEM Projects.*

TUTORIALS Get help from *Virtual Nerd*, right when you need it.

PRACTICE Practice what you've learned.

ADAPTIVE PRACTICE Practice that is *just right* and *just for you.*

FAMILY ENGAGEMENT Involve family in your learning.

GLOSSARY Read and listen to English and Spanish definitions.

MATH TOOLS Explore math with digital tools and manipulatives.

DESMOS Use Anytime and as embedded Interactives in Lesson content.

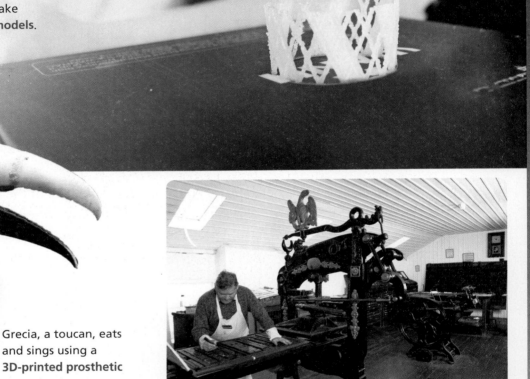

Did You Know?

The **first 3-dimensional printer** was invented in **1983** by Colorado engineer Chuck Hull. Hull's idea was to "print" extremely thin layers of plastic, one atop the other, building up a 3-dimensional object.

3D printers make **toys, replacement parts for machines, and medical prosthetics**. They also make **architectural and scale models**.

Grecia, a toucan, eats and sings using a **3D-printed prosthetic** upper beak.

The **first printing press** was invented by Johannes Gutenberg around the year **1450**. To print a page, Gutenberg made individual letters from metal and arranged the letters **on a block**. Then he inked the letters and **stamped them** on paper.

Your Task: Design With a 3D Printer

An engineer has built a scale model of a part for a rocket engine. Full-size, the part will be mass-produced using 3D printing. You and your classmates will use similarity to scale up the dimensions of the part. Then you'll describe and draw steps for the production of the part.

7-1
Dilations

I CAN... dilate figures and identify characteristics of dilations.

VOCABULARY
• center of dilation

Common Core State Standards
HSG.SRT.A.1.A, HSG.SRT.A.1.B,
HSG.CO.A.2, HSG.CO.A.5,
HSG.MG.A.2, MP.2, MP.3, MP.8

EXPLORE & REASON

Roosevelt High School sells a sticker and a larger car decal with the school logo.

A. Look for Relationships How are the sticker and the car decal alike? How are they different? **MP.7**

B. Suppose the sticker and decal are shown next to each other on a computer screen. If you zoom in to 125%, what would stay the same on the figures? What would be different?

ESSENTIAL QUESTION

How does a dilation affect the side lengths and angle measures of a figure?

CONCEPTUAL UNDERSTANDING

EXAMPLE 1   Dilate a Figure

How can you draw a dilated image?

A dilation produces an image that is a different size than the preimage.

Method 1 The Ratio Method

Dilate $\triangle ABC$ by a scale factor of $\frac{1}{2}$ with fixed center P. This fixed center is called the **center of dilation**.

Step 1 Draw rays from P through each vertex of $\triangle ABC$.

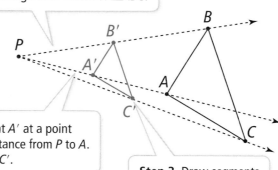

Step 2 Mark point A' at a point that is half the distance from P to A. Repeat for B' and C'.

Step 3 Draw segments to form $\triangle A'B'C'$.

MAKE SENSE AND PERSEVERE
Each line segment in the preimage appears to be parallel to its corresponding segment in the dilated image. How can you confirm whether the corresponding segments are parallel? **MP.1**

Triangle $A'B'C'$ is a copy of $\triangle ABC$ with side lengths that are $\frac{1}{2}$ the lengths of the corresponding sides of $\triangle ABC$.

CONTINUED ON THE NEXT PAGE

EXAMPLE 1 CONTINUED

Method 2 The Parallel Method

Dilate *WXYZ* by a scale factor of 2 with center of dilation *Q*.

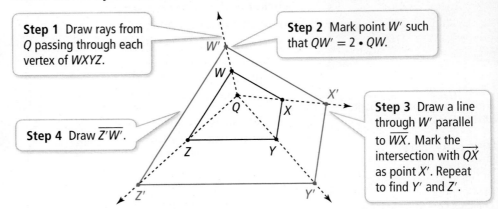

Step 1 Draw rays from *Q* passing through each vertex of *WXYZ*.

Step 2 Mark point *W′* such that *QW′* = 2 • *QW*.

Step 3 Draw a line through *W′* parallel to $\overline{WX}$. Mark the intersection with $\overrightarrow{QX}$ as point *X′*. Repeat to find *Y′* and *Z′*.

Step 4 Draw $\overline{Z'W'}$.

CONSTRUCT ARGUMENTS

Consider the two methods for dilating figures. Why does dilating a preimage with a certain scale factor and center of dilation result in the same image when either method is used? © MP.3

All sides of image *W′X′Y′Z′* are parallel to their corresponding sides in *WXYZ*. In general, if the preimage is a line or line segment that does not pass through the center of dilation, its image is parallel to the preimage.

Quadrilateral *W′X′Y′Z′* is a copy of *WXYZ* with side lengths that are twice the lengths of the corresponding sides of *WXYZ*.

Try It!   **1. a.** Trace △*JKL* and point *R*. Use The Ratio Method to dilate △*JKL* by a scale factor of 3 with center of dilation *R*.

  b. Trace △*PQR* and point *M*. Use The Parallel Method to dilate △*PQR* by a scale factor of $\frac{1}{3}$ with center of dilation *M*.

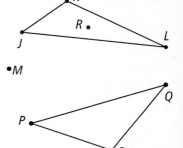

CONCEPT Dilations

A dilation $D_{(n,\ C)}$ is a transformation that has center of dilation *C* and scale factor *n*, where *n* > 0, with the following properties:

• Point *R* maps to *R′* in such a way that *R′* is on $\overrightarrow{CR}$ and *CR′* = *n* • *CR*.

• Each length in the image is *n* times the corresponding length in the preimage (i.e., *X′R′* = *n* • *XR*).

• The image of the center of dilation is the center itself (i.e., *C′* = *C*).

• If *n* > 1, the dilation is an *enlargement*. If 0 < *n* < 1, the dilation is a *reduction*.

• Every angle is congruent to its image under the dilation.

On a coordinate plane, the notation D_n describes the dilation with the origin as the center of dilation. This dilation maps (*x*, *y*) → (*nx*, *ny*).

EXAMPLE 2 **Analyze Dilations**

Rectangle *A′B′C′D′* is a dilation with center *P* of *ABCD*. How are the side lengths and angle measures of *ABCD* related to those of *A′B′C′D′*?

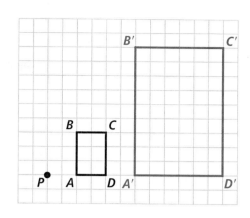

Step 1 Compare the angles.

All angles of rectangles are right angles, so each angle in image *A′B′C′D′* is congruent to the corresponding angle in *ABCD*.

Step 2 Compare the side lengths.

Find the side lengths in the preimage and image.

$AB = 3$	$BC = 2$	$CD = 3$	$DA = 2$
$A'B' = 9$	$B'C' = 6$	$C'D' = 9$	$D'A' = 6$

Find the ratios of the corresponding side lengths.

$$\frac{A'B'}{AB} = \frac{9}{3} = 3 \qquad \frac{B'C'}{BC} = \frac{6}{2} = 3 \qquad \frac{C'D'}{CD} = \frac{9}{3} = 3 \qquad \frac{D'A'}{DA} = \frac{6}{2} = 3$$

The ratios are equal, so the lengths of corresponding sides of the two figures are proportional.

Try It! **2.** Rectangle *W′X′Y′Z′* is a dilation with center *P* of *WXYZ*. How are the side lengths and angle measures of the two figures related?

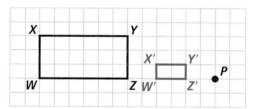

EXAMPLE 3 **Find a Scale Factor**

Quadrilateral *J′K′L′M′* is a dilation of *JKLM*. What is the scale factor?

The scale factor is the ratio of side lengths in the image to the corresponding side lengths in the preimage.

$$\frac{K'L'}{KL} = \frac{18}{12} = \frac{3}{2}$$

The scale factor is $\frac{3}{2}$.

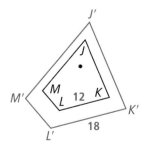

Try It! **3.** Consider the dilation shown.

a. Is △*A′B′C′* an enlargement or a reduction of △*ABC*?

b. What is the scale factor?

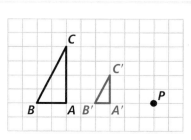

EXAMPLE 4   **Dilate a Figure With Center at the Origin**

What are the vertices of $D_3(\triangle ABC)$?

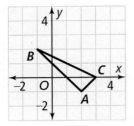

> The notation $D_3(\triangle ABC)$ means the image of $\triangle ABC$ after a dilation centered at the origin, with scale factor 3.

For a dilation with scale factor 3 centered at the origin, each image point is 3 times farther away from the origin than the corresponding preimage point.

Multiply each coordinate of each preimage point by 3 to find the coordinates of the image points.

The dilation D_n maps $(x, y) \rightarrow (nx, ny)$.

$A(2, -1) \rightarrow A'(3 \cdot 2, 3 \cdot -1) = A'(6, -3)$

$B(-1, 2) \rightarrow B'(3 \cdot -1, 3 \cdot 2) = B'(-3, 6)$

$C(3, 0) \rightarrow C'(3 \cdot 3, 3 \cdot 0) = C'(9, 0)$

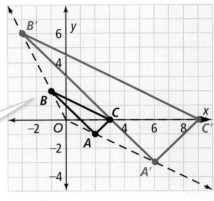

> D_3 maps each point $(x, y) \rightarrow (3x, 3y)$.

The vertices of $D_3(\triangle ABC)$ are $A'(6, -3)$, $B'(-3, 6)$, and $C'(9, 0)$.

Try It!   **4.** Use $\triangle PQR$.

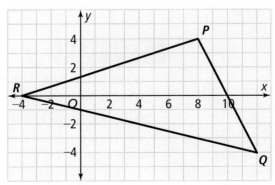

a. What are the vertices of $D_{\frac{1}{4}}(\triangle PQR)$?

b. How can you express this dilation algebraically?

c. How are the distances to the origin from each image point related to the distance to the origin from each corresponding preimage point?

EXAMPLE 5 Dilate a Figure With Center Not at the Origin

What are the vertices of $D_{\left(\frac{1}{2}, R\right)}(QRST)$?

The dilation is centered at $R(-2, 7)$ with a scale factor of $\frac{1}{2}$. So each image point is half the distance from R as the corresponding preimage point is. For each preimage point, multiply the horizontal and vertical changes from R by $\frac{1}{2}$. Then add the horizontal and vertical half-changes to the coordinates of the center of dilation.

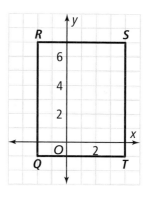

Preimage Point	Change From R(−2, 7)		Half of the Change From R(−2, 7)		Add to R(−2, 7)	Image Point
	horiz	vert.	horiz	vert.		
Q(−2, −1)	0	−8	0	−4	(−2 + 0, 7 − 4)	Q'(−2, 3)
S(4, 7)	6	0	3	0	(−2 + 3, 7 + 0)	S'(1, 7)
T(4, −1)	6	−8	3	−4	(−2 + 3, 7 − 4)	T'(1, 3)

Graph the preimage and image on the same coordinate plane.

Since the center is R, points R and R′ have the same coordinates.

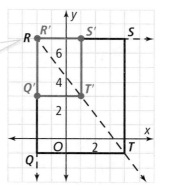

The vertices of $D_{\left(\frac{1}{2}, R\right)}(QRST)$ are $Q'(-2, 3)$, $R'(-2, 7)$, $S'(1, 7)$, and $T'(1, 3)$.

Try It! 5. What are the vertices of $D_{\left(\frac{3}{2}, A\right)}(ABC)$?

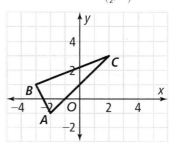

EXAMPLE 6 Solve Population Density Problems

Mott County has a total population of 388,643 people. Within Mott County, the town of Westville is a dilation of the county as a whole with scale factor $\frac{1}{2}$.

According to county planners, Westville is considered overcrowded if its population density exceeds the population density of Mott County as a whole. In order for Westville to not be considered overcrowded, what is its maximum possible population?

Population density is a measure of the number of people in region based on the total area of the region.

Mott County, pop. 388,643

Westville

48 mi

39 mi

Step 1 Find the area of Mott County.

Area of Mott County = (39 mi)(48 mi)

= 1,872 sq. mi

Step 2 Find the population density of Mott County.

Population density = $\frac{388,643}{1,872 \text{ sq. mi}}$

≈ 207.6/sq. mi

Step 3 Find the area of Westville.

Multiply each dimension of the county by $\frac{1}{2}$ to find the dimensions of Westville.

Area of Westville = $\left(\frac{1}{2} \cdot 39 \text{ mi}\right)\left(\frac{1}{2} \cdot 48 \text{ mi}\right)$

= 468 sq. mi

Step 4 Find the population of Westville if its population density is the same as Mott County's.

Population density = $\frac{\text{population}}{\text{area}}$

207.6/sq. mi = $\frac{\text{population}}{468 \text{ sq. mi}}$

> Substitute Mott County's population density and Westville's area. Then solve for population.

population = (207.6/sq. mi)(468 sq. mi)

= 97,156.8

The maximum possible population of Westville should be less than 97,157 in order not to be considered overcrowded.

Try It! **6.** Suppose the population of Westville is 84,106. What is its population density?

CONCEPT SUMMARY Dilations

WORDS > A dilation is a transformation that maps point X to point X' such that X' lies on $\overrightarrow{CX}$ and $CX' = k \cdot CX$ for a center of dilation C and a scale factor k. Dilations preserve angle measures.

DIAGRAM >

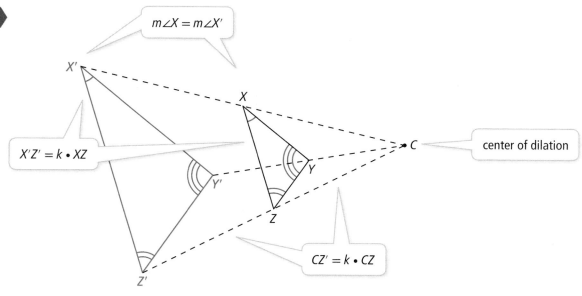

NOTATION > Dilation centered at the origin: $D_k(X)$

Dilation centered at point C: $D_{(k, C)}(X)$

Do You UNDERSTAND?

1. **ESSENTIAL QUESTION** > How does a dilation affect the side lengths and angle measures of a figure?

2. **Error Analysis** Emilia was asked to find the coordinates of $D_2(\triangle ABC)$ for $A(2, 4)$, $B(0, 5)$, and $C(-2, 1)$. What is Emilia's error? ©️ MP.3

   $A(2, 4) \rightarrow A'(4, 6)$
   $B(0, 5) \rightarrow B'(2, 7)$
   $C(-2, 1) \rightarrow C'(0, 3)$ ✗

3. **Vocabulary** In the definition of a dilation D_n, why can't n be equal to 0? What would a transformation like D_0 look like?

4. **Construct Arguments** Compare the vertices of $D_1(\triangle ABC)$ for any points A, B, and C. Justify your answer. ©️ MP.3

Do You KNOW HOW?

5. Trace $\triangle JKL$ and point P. Draw the dilation of $\triangle JKL$ using scale factor 3 and P as the center of dilation.

6. What is the scale factor for the dilation?

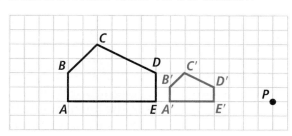

Give the coordinates of the dilation.

7. $(x, y) \rightarrow (5x, 5y)$ for $P(1, -3)$, $Q(-5, -4)$, $R(6, 2)$

8. $D_{(3, B)}(\triangle ABC)$ for $A(0, 4)$, $B(0, 2)$, $C(-3, 2)$

9. $D_{(4, F)}(FGHJ)$ for $F(0, -1)$, $G(4, -1)$, $H(4, -3)$, $J(0, -3)$

PRACTICE & PROBLEM SOLVING

UNDERSTAND

10. Error Analysis Jayden was asked to find the scale factor for the dilation. What is Jayden's error? ⓒ **MP.3**

$$\frac{6}{2} = 3$$

The scale factor is 3.

✗

11. Higher Order Thinking Points $M(a, b)$ and $N(c, d)$ are dilated by scale factor k, with the origin as the center of dilation. Show algebraically that $\overleftrightarrow{MN} \parallel \overleftrightarrow{M'N'}$.

12. Communicate Precisely Suppose you want to dilate a figure on the coordinate plane with a center of dilation at point (a, b) that is not the origin and with a scale factor k. Describe a composition of translations and a dilation centered at the origin to dilate the figure. Then write the transformation rule. ⓒ **MP.6**

13. Reason Rectangle $J'K'L'M'$ is a dilation of $JKLM$ with scale factor k. What are the perimeter and area of $JKLM$? ⓒ **MP.2**

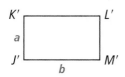

14. Mathematical Connections Carolina says that when a figure is dilated using a scale factor of 2, the angle measures in the image are twice the angle measures in the preimage. How could you use the Triangle Angle Sum Theorem to explain why this cannot be true?

15. Generalize Is it always true that $(D_m \circ D_n)(X) = D_{mn}(X)$? Explain. ⓒ **MP.8**

PRACTICE

16. Trace $ABCD$ and point P. Draw the dilation of $ABCD$ using P as the center of dilation and sides that are two times as long. SEE EXAMPLE 1

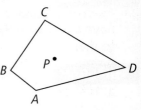

17. How are the side lengths of the preimage and dilated image related? SEE EXAMPLE 2

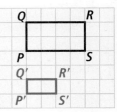

18. What is the scale factor of the dilation shown? SEE EXAMPLE 3

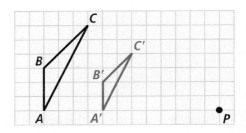

19. What are the coordinates of $(x, y) \to (1.5x, 1.5y)$ for $A(2, 0)$, $B(8, -4)$, $C(4, -6)$, and $D(-5, -10)$? SEE EXAMPLE 4

20. What are the coordinates of $D_{(2, X)}(\triangle XYZ)$ for $X(1, 1)$, $Y(2, 2)$, and $Z(3, 0)$? SEE EXAMPLE 5

21. The population density of the city of Wellington is 12,000 people per square mile. The neighboring city Morrison is a dilation of Wellington with scale factor 1.2. If Morrison has $\frac{3}{4}$ of the population of Wellington, what is the population density of Morrison? SEE EXAMPLE 6

22. What are the coordinates of the center of dilation for the dilation shown?

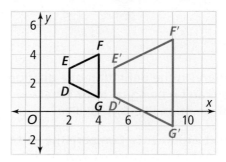

PRACTICE & PROBLEM SOLVING

23. Reason The images on Henry's digital camera have a width-to-length ratio of 2 : 3. He wants to make an 8 in.-by-10 in. print of one of his photographs.

   a. Is this possible? Explain.

   b. How can Henry crop an image so that an 8 in.-by-10 in. print can be made? **ⓒ MP.2**

24. Model With Mathematics Toya draws the scale model shown as a plan for a large wall mosaic.

10 cm

12 cm

   a. The wall is 10 m wide and 7 m high. What are the dimensions of the largest mosaic she can make on that wall? Explain.

   b. The tiles on the wall mosaic will have a mass of 10 kg per square meter. What will be the total mass of the tiles for the entire wall mosaic? Explain how you found your answer. **ⓒ MP.4**

25. Look for Relationships Shadow puppets are flat puppets controlled by sticks and strings. They originated in Asia and are used in many countries to tell folktales and other stories.

How far from the screen should the light be placed in order for the shadow of the puppet to be 30 in. tall? Explain how you found your answer. **ⓒ MP.7**

25 in.

30 in.

2 ft

26. Copy and complete the table to show information about dilations centered at the origin.

Preimage Coordinates	Scale Factor	Image Coordinates
(5, −2)	4	☐
(9, 3)	☐	(3, 1)
☐	1.5	(−6, 0)
(−1, 2)	☐	(−5, 10)

27. SAT/ACT A dilation maps △ABC to △A′B′C′. The area of △ABC is 13 square units, and the area of △A′B′C′ is 52 square units. What is the scale factor?

   Ⓐ 2   Ⓒ 4

   Ⓑ 13   Ⓓ 26

28. Performance Task Alberto wants to make a scale model of the Wright brothers' glider.

Wing Area: 28.3 m²

Wingspan: 9.8 m

Length: 4.9 m

Height: 2.4 m

Part A The wingspan of the scale model must be between 15 cm and 18 cm. What is a possible scale factor he can use? Explain.

Part B Use your scale factor from Part A. What will be the length, wingspan, and height of the model glider?

Part C The wing area is the total area of the two wing sections combined. Using your scale from Part A, what will be the wing area of the model glider? If both wing sections are the same size, what will be the dimensions of each wing section?

7-2

Similarity Transformations

I CAN... determine whether figures are similar.

VOCABULARY
• similarity transformation

© **Common Core State Standards**
HSG.SRT.A.1.B, HSG.SRT.A.2, HSG.C.A.1, MP.3, MP.5, MP.8

CRITIQUE & EXPLAIN

Powered By desmos

Helena and Edwin were asked to apply a composition of transformations to *ABCD*.

Helena

Edwin

A. **Use Appropriate Tools** Is there a composition of transformations that maps *ABCD* to the second figure in each student's work? If so, what is it? © **MP.5**

B. For each student whose work shows a composition of transformations, describe the relationship between the figures.

ESSENTIAL QUESTION

What makes a transformation a similarity transformation? What is the relationship between a preimage and the image resulting from a similarity transformation?

EXAMPLE 1 Graph a Composition of a Rigid Motion and a Dilation

COMMON ERROR
Be careful to use the correct center of dilation. When the notation does not specify the center of dilation, the center of dilation is at the origin.

If line *m* is represented by the equation $x = -3$, what is a graph of the image $(r_m \circ D_{0.5})(\triangle ABC)$?

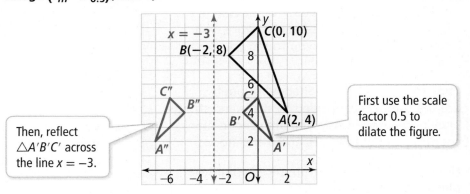

Then, reflect $\triangle A'B'C'$ across the line $x = -3$.

First use the scale factor 0.5 to dilate the figure.

The graph of the image $(r_m \circ D_{0.5})(\triangle ABC)$ is $\triangle A''B''C''$.

Try It! **1.** The vertices of $\triangle XYZ$ are $X(3, 5)$, $Y(-1, 4)$, and $Z(1, 7)$.

a. What is the graph of the image $(D_2 \circ T_{\langle 1, -2 \rangle})(\triangle XYZ)$?

b. What is the graph of the image $(D_3 \circ R_{(90°, O)})(\triangle XYZ)$?

EXAMPLE 2 Describe a Composition of a Rigid Motion and a Dilation

Is there a composition of transformations that maps $\triangle XYZ$ to $\triangle JKL$? Explain.

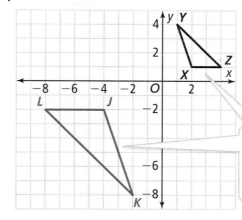

The two triangles appear to be the same shape but different sizes. They are also positioned differently.

MAKE SENSE AND PERSEVERE
Since the orientation of the preimage is not preserved, think about how you could apply a reflection or rotation so that $\triangle XYZ$ has the same orientation as $\triangle JKL$. Which rigid motion would you use? ⒼMP.1

Notice that $\overline{XZ}$ in $\triangle XYZ$ is at the bottom of the triangle, but its corresponding side $\overline{JL}$ in $\triangle JKL$ is at the top of the triangle, so it appears that $\triangle JKL$ is a rotation of $\triangle XYZ$. Since $\triangle JKL$ is larger than $\triangle XYZ$, it is also dilated.

Rotate $\triangle XYZ$ 180° about the origin to produce the image $X'Y'Z'$.

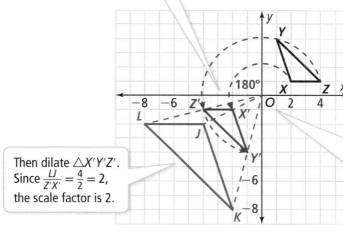

The origin is the center of dilation because the lines connecting the corresponding vertices are concurrent there.

Then dilate $\triangle X'Y'Z'$. Since $\frac{LJ}{Z'X'} = \frac{4}{2} = 2$, the scale factor is 2.

The composition of transformations $D_2 \circ R_{(180°,\ O)}$ maps $\triangle XYZ$ to $\triangle JKL$.

Try It! **2.** If the transformations in Example 2 are performed in the reverse order, are the results the same? Do you think your answer holds for all compositions of transformations? Explain.

EXAMPLE 3 Find Similarity Transformations

Is there a similarity transformation that maps △QRS to △TUV?

A **similarity transformation** is a composition of one or more rigid motions and a dilation. A similarity transformation results in an image that is *similar* to the preimage.

Step 1 Reflect △QRS across *m* to form △Q'R'S'.

Step 2 Translate △Q'R'S' to form △Q"R"S" so that ∠S" maps to ∠V.

Step 3 Using a scale factor of 2, dilate △Q"R"S" centered at S" to form △TUV.

A similarity transformation composed of a reflection, vertical and horizontal translations, and a dilation maps △QRS to △TUV.

In similar figures, the ratios of corresponding side lengths are equal. Check for similarity by calculating those ratios.

$$\frac{TU}{QR} = \frac{26}{13}, \text{ or } \frac{2}{1} \qquad \frac{UV}{RS} = \frac{24}{12}, \text{ or } \frac{2}{1} \qquad \frac{TV}{QS} = \frac{10}{5}, \text{ or } \frac{2}{1}$$

Because the ratios are equal, △QRS ~ △TUV.

The symbol ~ indicates similarity.

> **STUDY TIP**
> Recall that, in a dilation, the ratio of any side length in an image to its corresponding side length in the preimage is equal to the scale factor.

Try It! **3.** Describe a possible similarity transformation for each pair of similar figures shown, and then write a similarity statement.

a.

b.

CONCEPT

For any figures *A*, *B*, and *C*, the following properties hold.

Reflexive Property of Similarity	$A \sim A$
Symmetric Property of Similarity	If $A \sim B$, then $B \sim A$.
Transitive Property of Similarity	If $A \sim B$ and $B \sim C$, then $A \sim C$.

EXAMPLE 4 Determine Similarity

Can the artist copy her sketch to cover an entire wall measuring 15 ft high by 20 ft wide so her wall mural is similar to her sketch? Explain.

20 ft

15 ft

11 in.

14 in.

If the artist can map her sketch onto the wall, then she can place her sketch at the bottom left corner and dilate it.

MAKE SENSE AND PERSEVERE

Why can you compare angle measures and the ratios of the corresponding side lengths to determine whether two figures are similar? © MP.1

Determine whether the sketch can be dilated to fit the wall.

Step 1 Compare the corresponding angles.
Both figures are rectangles, so the corresponding angles are congruent.

Step 2 Compare the ratios of the corresponding side lengths.

vertical sides: $\frac{11}{15}$ horizontal sides: $\frac{7}{10}$

Because $\frac{11}{15} \neq \frac{7}{10}$, the ratios of corresponding side lengths are not equal.

The sketch and the wall are not similar, so the sketch cannot be copied to cover the entire wall.

Try It! 4. Suppose the artist cuts 2 inches from the width of her sketch in Example 4. How much should she cut from the height so she can copy a similar image to cover the wall?

PROOF

EXAMPLE 5 Identify Similar Circles

Write a proof that any two circles are similar.

Given: ⊙P with radius r, ⊙Q with radius s

Prove: ⊙P ~ ⊙Q

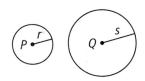

Proof: Translate P to Q, so P' coincides with Q. Then find a scale factor that dilates ⊙P' to the circle with radius s.

Let $k = \frac{s}{r}$. Then the translation followed by a dilation centered at Q with scale factor k maps ⊙P onto ⊙Q. Since a similarity transformation exists, ⊙P ~ ⊙Q.

Try It! 5. Write a proof that any two squares are similar.

CONCEPT SUMMARY Similarity

WORDS
- A similarity transformation is a composition of one or more rigid motions and a dilation.
- Two figures are similar if there is a similarity transformation that maps one to the other. All corresponding sides in the preimage and image of a similarity transformation are proportional.
- All circles are similar to each other.

DIAGRAMS

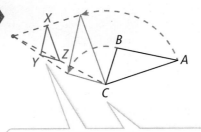

A rotation, followed by a dilation, maps $\triangle ABC$ to $\triangle XYZ$. So, $\triangle ABC \sim \triangle XYZ$.

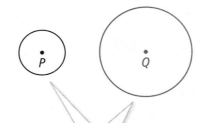

A translation followed by a dilation maps $\odot P$ to $\odot Q$. So, $\odot P \sim \odot Q$.

Do You UNDERSTAND?

1. **ESSENTIAL QUESTION** What makes a transformation a similarity transformation? What is the relationship between a preimage and the image resulting from a similarity transformation?

2. **Error Analysis** Risa described the similarity transformation that maps $\triangle ABC$ to $\triangle XZY$. What is Risa's error? **© MP.3**

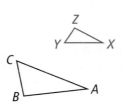

> $\triangle ABC$ is dilated and then rotated to produce the image $\triangle XZY$. ✗

3. **Vocabulary** How are similarity transformations and congruence transformations alike? How are they different?

4. **Construct Arguments** A similarity transformation consisting of a reflection and a dilation is performed on a figure, and one point maps to itself. Describe one way this could happen. **© MP.3**

Do You KNOW HOW?

For Exercises 5 and 6, what are the vertices of each image?

5. $R_{(90°,\ O)} \circ D_{0.5}(ABCD)$ for $A(5, 1)$, $B(-3, 4)$, $C(0, 2)$, $D(4, 6)$

6. $(D_3 \circ r_{x\text{-axis}})(\triangle GHJ)$ for $G(3, 5)$, $H(1, -2)$, $J(-1, 6)$

7. Describe a similarity transformation that maps $\triangle SQR$ to $\triangle DEF$.

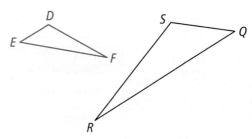

8. Do the two figures appear to be similar? Use transformations to explain.

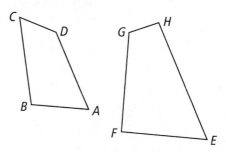

PRACTICE & PROBLEM SOLVING

UNDERSTAND

9. **Construct Arguments** Is it possible to use only translations and dilations to map one circle to another? Explain. **ⓒ MP.3**

10. **Error Analysis** Keegan was asked to graph $(R_{90°} \circ D_2)(\triangle ABC)$. Explain Keegan's error. **ⓒ MP.3**

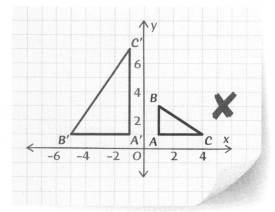

11. **Mathematical Connections** In the diagram, $ABCD \sim A'B'C'D'$. What are the angle measures of $A'B'C'D'$?

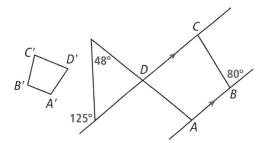

12. **Construct Arguments** Are all squares similar? Use transformations to explain. **ⓒ MP.3**

13. **Generalize** Show whether a composition of a dilation and a translation can be performed in either order and result in the same image. (Hint: Test whether the equation $(D_k \circ T_{\langle a, b \rangle})(x, y) = (T_{\langle a, b \rangle} \circ D_k)(x, y)$ is true.) **ⓒ MP.8**

14. **Higher Order Thinking** Given isosceles triangle ABC with $\overline{AB} \cong \overline{BC}$. Point D is the midpoint of $\overline{AB}$, E is the midpoint of $\overline{BC}$, and F is the midpoint of $\overline{CA}$. Use a similarity transformation and triangle congruence to show that $\triangle ABC \backsim \triangle FEC$.

PRACTICE

What are the vertices of each image? SEE EXAMPLE 1

15. $(T_{\langle 5, -4 \rangle} \circ D_{1.5})(\triangle XYZ)$ for $X(6, -2)$, $Y(4, 1)$, $Z(-2, 3)$

16. $(r_{x\text{-axis}} \circ D_{0.5})(LMNP)$ for $L(2, 4)$, $M(4, 4)$, $N(4, -4)$, $P(2, -4)$

17. $(r_{y\text{-axis}} \circ D_2 \circ R_{270°})(\triangle PQR)$ for $P(1, 3)$, $Q(-4, 2)$, $R(0, 5)$

18. $(D_{0.25} \circ r_{x\text{-axis}})(ABCD)$ for $A(2, 6)$, $B(0, 0)$, $C(-5, 8)$, $D(-2, 10)$

For each black pre-image and red image, describe the similarity transformation and write a similarity statement. SEE EXAMPLES 2 AND 3

19.

20.

Do the figures appear to be similar? Explain. SEE EXAMPLES 4 AND 5

21.

22.

23. One circle has radius 1, and another circle has radius r. Write ratios to compare the lengths of the radii and the circumferences of the two circles. What is the scale factor of $\odot 1$ to $\odot r$? Explain.

PRACTICE & PROBLEM SOLVING

24. Reason Can Bruno use the other sheets of paper shown to make paper cutouts, or *papel picado*, similar to those in the banner? If not, how can he trim the sheets of paper so he can use them? Justify your answer. © **MP.2**

9 in.

12 in.

270 mm

380 mm

44 cm

33 cm

25. Make Sense and Persevere Rachel makes a sketch for a stage set design on a grid. She plans to have a gauze fabric called a scrim drop down from a beam that is 5.5 m wide. Assuming that her sketch is similar to the actual set, how much scrim is needed? Explain. © **MP.1**

5.5 m

Area of scrim

26. Look for Relationships Juanita wants to make a dollhouse following the pattern shown but with a reduced size so that the floor has an area of 25 in.². Make a sketch showing the dimensions of the pieces for the smaller dollhouse. © **MP.7**

Dollhouse Pattern

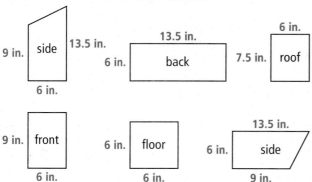

9 in. side 13.5 in.

6 in.

13.5 in.

6 in. back

6 in.

7.5 in. roof

9 in. front

6 in.

6 in. floor

6 in.

13.5 in.

6 in. side

9 in.

27. Graph the image of $(T_{\langle 1, -3\rangle} \circ D_2)(\triangle ABC)$.

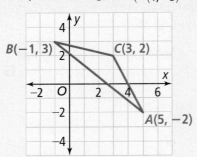

$B(-1, 3)$

$C(3, 2)$

$A(5, -2)$

28. SAT/ACT What are the coordinates of the preimage (8, 2) after a reflection across the *x*-axis, followed by a dilation centered at the origin with a scale factor of 4?

Ⓐ (−32, 8)

Ⓑ (32, 8)

Ⓒ (−32, −8)

Ⓓ (32, −8)

29. Performance Task Natisha makes sketches for her graphic novel using a repeating similar shape as a motif.

Part A On a separate sheet of paper, draw a small simple figure. Label it A.

Part B Use transformations, including similarity transformations, to create at least five images that are similar to the figure A you drew in Part A. Label the images B, C, D, E, and F.

Part C Is it possible to select any two of your figures and find a similarity transformation that maps one to the other? Explain.

7-3

Proving Triangles Similar

I CAN... use dilation and rigid motion to establish triangle similarity theorems.

© Common Core State Standards
HSG.SRT.A.3, HSG.SRT.B.5, HSG.SRT.A.2, MP.1, MP.3, MP.4

CONCEPTUAL UNDERSTANDING

REASON
Think about what it means for figures to be similar. Are congruent triangles similar to the same triangle? **© MP.2**

EXPLORE & REASON

Powered By desmos

The measurements of two triangles are shown.

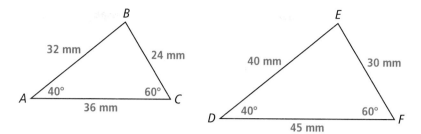

A. Are the triangles similar? Explain.

B. Construct Arguments Would any triangle with 40°- and 60°-angles be similar to △ABC? Explain. **© MP.3**

ESSENTIAL QUESTION How can you use the angles and sides of two triangles to determine whether they are similar?

EXAMPLE 1 Establish the Angle-Angle Similarity (AA ~) Theorem

If $\angle A \cong \angle R$ and $\angle B \cong \angle S$, is $\triangle ABC \sim \triangle RST$? Explain.

To show that the triangles are similar, determine whether there is a similarity transformation that maps △ABC to △RST.

Determine the center of dilation and the scale factor that map △ABC to image △A'B'C' such that A'B' = RS.

Let the scale factor k be $\frac{RS}{AB}$.

Then, $A'B' = k \cdot AB = RS$.

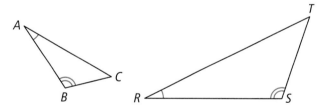

Use vertex A as the center of dilation, so A = A' and $\angle A \cong \angle A' \cong \angle R$.

Dilations preserve angle measure, so $\angle B \cong \angle B' \cong \angle S$.

The dilation $D_{(k, A)}$ maps △ABC to △A'B'C', and △A'B'C' ≅ △RST by ASA, so there is a rigid motion that maps △A'B'C' to △RST. Thus, the composition is a similarity transformation that maps △ABC to △RST. So, △ABC ~ △RST.

Try It! **1.** If $\angle A$ is congruent to $\angle R$, and $\angle C$ is congruent to $\angle T$, how would you prove the triangles are similar?

THEOREM 7-1 Angle-Angle Similarity (AA ~) Theorem

If two angles of one triangle are congruent to two angles of another triangle, then the triangles are similar.

If...

$\angle A \cong \angle D$ and $\angle B \cong \angle E$

PROOF: SEE EXERCISE 10.

Then... $\triangle ABC \sim \triangle DEF$

EXAMPLE 2   Establish the Side-Side-Side Similarity (SSS ~) Theorem

If $\frac{LM}{PQ} = \frac{MN}{QR} = \frac{LN}{PR}$, is there a similarity transformation that maps $\triangle PQR$ to $\triangle LMN$? Explain.

Dilate $\triangle PQR$ by scale factor $k = \frac{LM}{PQ} = \frac{MN}{QR} = \frac{LN}{PR}$ to map $\triangle PQR$ to $\triangle P'Q'R'$.

$$P'R' = k \cdot PR = \frac{LN}{PR} \cdot PR = LN$$

$$Q'R' = k \cdot QR = \frac{MN}{QR} \cdot QR = MN$$

$$P'Q' = k \cdot PQ = \frac{LM}{PQ} \cdot PQ = LM$$

Because $P'R' = LN$, $P'Q' = LM$, and $Q'R' = MN$, $\triangle P'Q'R' \cong \triangle LMN$ by SSS. By the definition of congruence, there is a rigid motion that maps $\triangle P'Q'R'$ to $\triangle LMN$.

So, $\triangle PQR$ was mapped to $\triangle LMN$ by a similarity transformation and $\triangle PQR$ is similar to $\triangle LMN$.

STUDY TIP
Remember, two figures are similar if there is a similarity transformation between them.

Try It!   **2.** If $\frac{DF}{GJ} = \frac{EF}{HJ}$ and $\angle F \cong \angle J$, is there a similarity transformation that maps $\triangle DEF$ to $\triangle GHJ$? Explain.

THEOREM 7-2 Side-Side-Side Similarity (SSS ∼) Theorem

If the corresponding sides of two triangles are proportional, then the triangles are similar.

PROOF: SEE EXERCISE 21.

If...

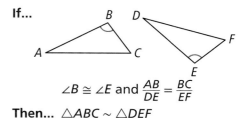

$$\frac{AB}{DE} = \frac{BC}{EF} = \frac{AC}{DF}$$

Then... △ABC ∼ △DEF

THEOREM 7-3 Side-Angle-Side Similarity (SAS ∼) Theorem

If an angle of one triangle is congruent to an angle of a second triangle, and the sides that include the two angles are proportional, then the triangles are similar.

PROOF: SEE EXERCISE 14.

If...

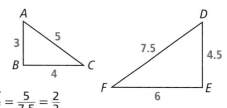

$$\angle B \cong \angle E \text{ and } \frac{AB}{DE} = \frac{BC}{EF}$$

Then... △ABC ∼ △DEF

EXAMPLE 3 ▶ Verify Triangle Similarity

A. Are △ABC and △DEF similar?

Determine whether the ratios of the corresponding side lengths are equal.

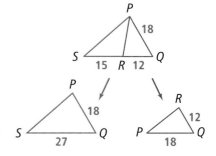

$$\frac{AB}{DE} = \frac{3}{4.5} = \frac{2}{3} \qquad \frac{BC}{EF} = \frac{4}{6} = \frac{2}{3} \qquad \frac{AC}{DF} = \frac{5}{7.5} = \frac{2}{3}$$

The ratios are equal, so the corresponding side lengths are proportional. △ABC ∼ △DEF by SSS ∼.

COMMON ERROR
When setting up ratios to check if triangles are similar, be sure you place sides from the same triangle in the same position in each ratio.

B. Are △PQS and △RQP similar?

The two triangles share an included angle, ∠Q. Separate the triangles and see whether the lengths of the corresponding sides are in proportion.

Since $\frac{SQ}{PQ} = \frac{27}{18} = \frac{3}{2}$ and $\frac{PQ}{RQ} = \frac{18}{12} = \frac{3}{2}$, the lengths of the sides that include ∠Q are proportional. By SAS ∼, △PQS ∼ △RQP.

Try It! **3. a.** Is △ADE ∼ △ABD? Explain.

b. Is △ADE ∼ △BDC? Explain.

EXAMPLE 4 ▶ Find Lengths in Similar Triangles

What is MN?

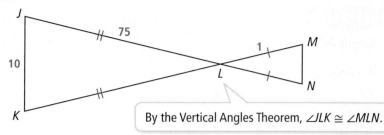

By the Vertical Angles Theorem, $\angle JLK \cong \angle MLN$.

Figure not drawn to scale

Since $\triangle JKL$ and $\triangle MLN$ are isosceles, the sides that include $\angle JLK$ and $\angle MLN$ are proportional.

By SAS ~, $\triangle JLK \sim \triangle MLN$.

Write a proportion using corresponding sides, and solve for MN.

$$\frac{MN}{10} = \frac{1}{75}$$

$$MN = \frac{2}{15}$$

Try It! **4. a.** In Example 4, if the measure of $\overline{JL}$ were 150 instead of 75, how would the value of MN be different?

b. In Example 4, if the measure of $\overline{JK}$ were 20 instead of 10, how would the value of MN be different?

APPLICATION

EXAMPLE 5   Solve Problems Involving Similar Triangles

Avery puts up a radio antenna tower in his yard. Ella tells him that their city has a law limiting towers to 40 ft in height. How can Avery use the lengths of his shadow and the shadow of the tower to determine whether his tower is within the limit without directly measuring it?

You can consider the angles at which the sun hits Avery and the tower to be equal.

Art not drawn to scale.

Since $\angle BAC \cong \angle SRT$ and $\angle ACB \cong \angle RTS$, you can apply the AA ~ Theorem.

$$\frac{ST}{BC} = \frac{RT}{AC}$$

$$\frac{ST}{6} = \frac{40}{5}$$

Corresponding sides of $\triangle ABC$ and $\triangle RST$ are proportional.

$$ST = 48$$

The antenna tower is 48 ft high. Avery's tower is not within the 40-ft limit.

Try It! **5.** If the tower were 39 ft tall, how long would the shadow of the tower be?

CONCEPT SUMMARY Triangle Similarity Theorems

THEOREM 7-1

Angle-Angle Similarity

If...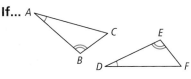

$\angle A \cong \angle D$ and $\angle B \cong \angle E$

Then... $\triangle ABC \sim \triangle DEF$

THEOREM 7-2

Side-Side-Side Similarity

If...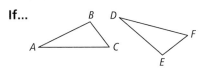

$\dfrac{AB}{DE} = \dfrac{BC}{EF} = \dfrac{AC}{DF}$

Then... $\triangle ABC \sim \triangle DEF$

THEOREM 7-3

Side-Angle-Side Similarity

If...

$\angle B \cong \angle E$ and $\dfrac{AB}{DE} = \dfrac{BC}{EF}$

Then... $\triangle ABC \sim \triangle DEF$

Do You UNDERSTAND?

1. **ESSENTIAL QUESTION** How can you use the angles and sides of two triangles to determine whether they are similar?

2. **Error Analysis** Allie says $\triangle JKL \sim \triangle XYZ$. What is Allie's error? **© MP.3**

$\triangle JKL \sim \triangle XYZ$ by the SAS ~ Theorem. ✗

3. **Make Sense and Persevere** Is any additional information needed to show $\triangle DEF \sim \triangle RST$? Explain. **© MP.1**

4. **Construct Arguments** Explain how you can use triangle similarity to show that $ABCD \sim WXYZ$.

Do You KNOW HOW?

For Exercises 5 and 6, explain whether the two triangles are similar.

5.

6.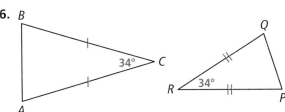

For Exercises 7 and 8, find the value of each variable such that the triangles are similar.

7. *a*

8. *b*

9. Saguaro cacti grow in the Sonoran Desert, which is partly in Arizona and partly in Mexico. When Esteban looks at the puddle, he sees a reflection of the top of the saguaro cactus. How tall is the cactus?

PRACTICE & PROBLEM SOLVING

UNDERSTAND

10. Construct Arguments Write a proof of the Angle-Angle Similarity Theorem. **© MP.3**

Given: $\angle T \cong \angle X$
$\angle U \cong \angle Y$

Prove: $\triangle TUV \sim \triangle XYZ$

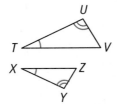

11. Use Structure For each triangle, name the triangle similar to $\triangle ABC$ and explain why it is similar. **© MP.7**

a.

b.

12. Construct Arguments If two triangles are congruent by ASA, are the triangles similar? Explain. **© MP.3**

13. Error Analysis What is Roussel's error? **© MP.3**

$180 - 80 - 60 = 40$,
so the unlabeled angle in each triangle is 40°. So, $m\angle M = 60$, and thus $\triangle FGH \sim \triangle KLM$ by AA ~.

14. Construct Arguments Write a proof of the Side-Angle-Side Similarity Theorem. **© MP.3**

Given: $\dfrac{LM}{QR} = \dfrac{LN}{QS}$
$\angle L \cong \angle Q$

Prove: $\triangle LMN \sim \triangle QRS$

15. Higher Order Thinking Given triangles ABC and DEF, can you determine whether the triangles are similar? Use similarity transformations to explain.

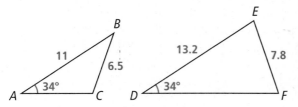

PRACTICE

For Exercise 16–18, explain whether each pair of triangles is similar. SEE EXAMPLES 1–3

16.

17.

18.

19. What is FG? SEE EXAMPLES 4 AND 5

20. What is the value of x? SEE EXAMPLES 4 AND 5

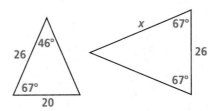

21. Write a proof of the Side-Side-Side Similarity Theorem.

Given: $\dfrac{AB}{EF} = \dfrac{BC}{FG} = \dfrac{AC}{AG}$

Prove: $\triangle ABC \sim \triangle EFG$

PRACTICE & PROBLEM SOLVING

APPLY

22. Communicate Precisely A building manager needs to order 9 replacement panes that are all the same size, each similar to the window itself. At what angles should each pane be cut in order to fit in the window? What are the dimensions of each pane? Explain. © MP.6

23. Use Structure The screen of a surveying device is 0.0026 m wide and is 0.1 m away from the lens. If the surveyor wants the image of the 2-m target to fit on the screen, what distance *d* should the lens be from the target? Explain. © MP.7

24. Mathematical Connections If a light beam strikes the inside of a fiber optic cable, it bounces off at the same angle. In a cable 1,200 micrometers (μm) long, if the beam strikes the wall after 720 μm what distance *x* + *y* does the beam travel? Explain.

ASSESSMENT PRACTICE

25. Which condition is sufficient to show that △*ABC* ~ △*QPR*? Select all that apply.

☐ **A.** *RP* = 4.5

☐ **B.** *m∠Q* = 63

☐ **C.** *m∠P* = 81

☐ **D.** *m∠R* = 63

☐ **E.** *RP* = 4

26. SAT/ACT For which value of *FJ* must △*FGJ* be similar to △*FHG*?

Ⓐ 6　　　Ⓑ 8　　　Ⓒ 9　　　Ⓓ 12

27. Performance Task A rescue helicopter hovering at an altitude of 3.5 km sights a campsite just over the peak of a mountain.

Part A The horizontal distance of the helicopter from the mountain is 2.4 km. If the height of the mountain is 2.8 km, what is the horizontal distance *d* of the helicopter from the campsite? Explain.

Part B The groundspeed (horizontal speed) of the helicopter is 1.6 km/min. When will the helicopter reach the campsite? Explain.

Part C The radio at the campsite can only transmit to a distance of 5 km. If the helicopter begins immediately to descend toward the campsite (along the diagonal line), how far will the pilot be, horizontally, when he first reaches the campsite's radio transmission?

7-4
Similarity in Right Triangles

I CAN... use similarity and the geometric mean to solve problems involving right triangles.

VOCABULARY
• geometric mean

© **Common Core State Standards**
HSG.SRT.B.4, HSG.SRT.B.5, MP.4, MP.5, MP.7

EXPLORE & REASON

Suppose you cut a rectangular sheet of paper to create three right triangles.

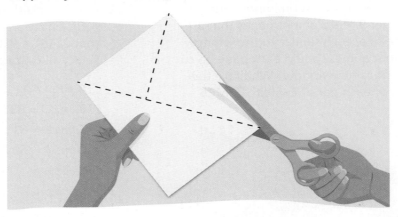

A. **Use Appropriate Tools** How can you compare leg lengths and angle measures among the triangles? © **MP.5**

B. Are any of the triangles similar to each other? Explain.

ESSENTIAL QUESTION
In a right triangle, what is the relationship between the altitude to the hypotenuse, triangle similarity, and the geometric mean?

CONCEPTUAL UNDERSTANDING

EXAMPLE 1   Identify Similar Triangles Formed by an Altitude

When you draw an altitude to the hypotenuse of a right triangle, you create three right triangles. How are the triangles related?

The altitude $\overline{CD}$ divides $\triangle ABC$ into two right triangles, $\triangle ACD$ and $\triangle CBD$. Compare each triangle to $\triangle ABC$.

USE STRUCTURE
Think about an altitude of a triangle. What type of angle does it form with the base? © **MP.7**

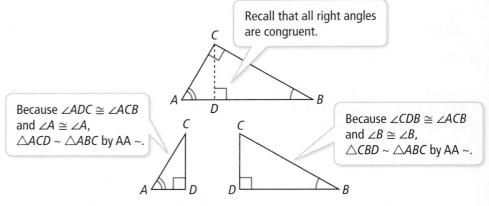

Recall that all right angles are congruent.

Because $\angle ADC \cong \angle ACB$ and $\angle A \cong \angle A$, $\triangle ACD \sim \triangle ABC$ by AA ~.

Because $\angle CDB \cong \angle ACB$ and $\angle B \cong \angle B$, $\triangle CBD \sim \triangle ABC$ by AA ~.

$\triangle ACD$ and $\triangle CBD$ are each similar to $\triangle ABC$.

Try It!   1. In Example 1, how is $\triangle ACD$ related to $\triangle CBD$? Explain.

THEOREM 7-4

The altitude to the hypotenuse of a right triangle divides the triangle into two triangles that are similar to the original triangle and to each other.

If...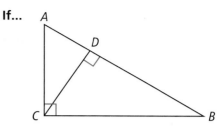

PROOF: SEE EXAMPLE 1

Then... $\triangle CAB \sim \triangle DAC \sim \triangle DCB$

EXAMPLE 2 **Find Missing Lengths Within Right Triangles**

Given that $\triangle QSR \sim \triangle PQR$, what is PQ?

Draw $\triangle QSR$ and $\triangle PQR$. To find PQ, write a proportion using corresponding legs of $\triangle QSR$ and $\triangle PQR$. No side lengths for $\triangle PQR$ are given, but QR can be found by applying the Pythagorean Theorem to $\triangle QSR$.

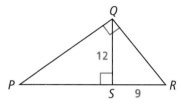

$$QS^2 + SR^2 = QR^2$$
$$12^2 + 9^2 = QR^2$$
$$225 = QR^2$$
$$15 = QR$$

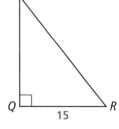

> Because $\triangle QSR \sim \triangle PQR$, $\overline{QS}$ corresponds to $\overline{PQ}$, $\overline{SR}$ corresponds to $\overline{QR}$, and $\overline{QR}$ corresponds to $\overline{PR}$.

$$\frac{QS}{PQ} = \frac{SR}{QR}$$
$$\frac{12}{PQ} = \frac{9}{15}$$
$$180 = 9PQ$$
$$20 = PQ$$

The length of $\overline{PQ}$ is 20.

MAKE SENSE AND PERSEVERE
Consider an alternate method for solving for PQ. Since $\triangle QSR$ is also similar to $\triangle PSQ$, write a proportion that relates two side lengths of $\triangle QSR$ to their corresponding side lengths in $\triangle PSQ$ to solve for PQ. ⓒ **MP.1**

Try It! **2. a.** Using $\triangle PQR$ in Example 2, write a proportion to solve for PS.

b. What is PS?

DEFINITION

The **geometric mean** is the number x such that $\frac{a}{x} = \frac{x}{b}$, where a, b, and x are positive numbers.

EXAMPLE 3 Relate Altitude and Geometric Mean

Given △ACB, what is CD?

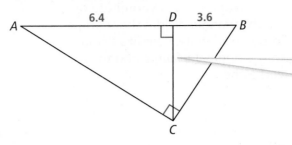

Notice that CD is the length of the longer leg of △CDB and is also the length of the shorter leg of △ADC.

By Theorem 7-4, △ADC ~ △CDB. Use the properties of similar triangles to write a proportion.

STUDY TIP
You can think about the geometric mean in another way. If $x^2 = ab$, then x is the geometric mean of a and b.

$$\frac{AD}{CD} = \frac{CD}{BD}$$

CD is the geometric mean of AD and BD.

$$\frac{6.4}{CD} = \frac{CD}{3.6}$$

$$(CD)^2 = 23.04$$

$$CD = 4.8$$

The length of altitude $\overline{CD}$ is 4.8.

Try It! **3.** Use △ABC.

a. What is CD?

b. Describe how you can use the value you found for CD to find AC and CB.

COROLLARY 1 TO THEOREM 7-4

The length of the altitude to the hypotenuse of a right triangle is the geometric mean of the lengths of the segments of the hypotenuse.

If...

Then... $\frac{AD}{CD} = \frac{CD}{BD}$

PROOF: SEE EXERCISE 14.

EXAMPLE 4 | Relate Side Lengths and Geometric Mean

Given △RST, what is RT?

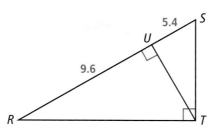

STUDY TIP
If you have difficulty identifying the similar triangles, remember that you can draw them separately as was done in Example 1.

By Theorem 7-4, △RST ~ △RTU. Use the properties of similar triangles to write a proportion.

$$\frac{RS}{RT} = \frac{RT}{RU}$$

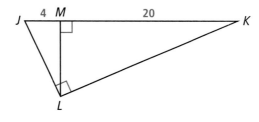

RT is the geometric mean of RS and RU.

$$\frac{15}{RT} = \frac{RT}{9.6}$$

$$(RT)^2 = 144$$

$$RT = 12$$

The length of $\overline{RT}$ is 12.

Try It! **4.** Use △JKL.

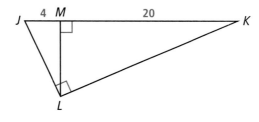

a. What is JL?

b. What is KL?

COROLLARY 2 TO THEOREM 7-4

The altitude to the hypotenuse of a right triangle divides the hypotenuse so that the length of a given leg is the geometric mean of the length of the hypotenuse and the length of the segment of the hypotenuse that is adjacent to the leg.

PROOF: SEE EXERCISE 14.

If...

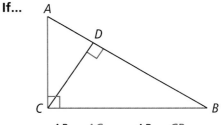

Then... $\frac{AB}{AC} = \frac{AC}{AD}$ and $\frac{AB}{CB} = \frac{CB}{DB}$

EXAMPLE 5 Use the Geometric Mean to Solve Problems

What is the value of x?
Use the formula for the geometric mean.

$$\frac{x+5}{6} = \frac{6}{x}$$

$$x(x+5) = 36$$

$$x^2 + 5x - 36 = 0$$

The geometric mean of x and $x+5$ is 6.

$$(x+9)(x-4) = 0$$

$$x = -9 \text{ or } x = 4$$

Length is always positive.

The value of x is 4.

Try It! **5.** Use the geometric mean and Example 5 to find each unknown.

a. Find the value of y.   **b.** Find the value of z.

APPLICATION

EXAMPLE 6 Apply Geometric Mean to Find a Distance

Zhang is constructing a 4-ft high loading ramp. The length of the back of the base must be 12.8 ft. How long must the entire base be?

Formulate ◀ The ramp and the base form the long leg and the hypotenuse of a right triangle. The height of the ramp is the altitude of the triangle. The base of the ramp is composed of the front base x and the back base 12.8.

Compute ◀ **Step 1** Find the length of the front base x. Use the fact that the height is the geometric mean of the lengths of the front base and the back base.

$$\frac{x}{4} = \frac{4}{12.8}$$

$$12.8x = 16$$

The geometric mean of x and 12.8 is 4.

$$x = 1.25$$

Step 2 Find the length of the base.

$$12.8 + 1.25 = 14.05$$

Interpret ◀ The base of the ramp should be 14.05 feet long.

Try It! **6.** In Example 6, how long should Zhang make the ramp?

CONCEPT SUMMARY   Similarity in Right Triangles

- The altitude to the hypotenuse of a right triangle divides the triangle into two triangles that are similar to the original triangle and to each other.
- The length of the altitude is the geometric mean of the lengths of the segments of the hypotenuse.
- The length of each leg is the geometric mean of the length of the hypotenuse and the length of the segment adjacent to the leg.

DIAGRAMS

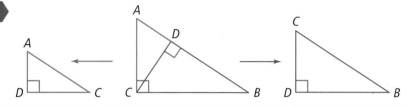

SYMBOLS $\triangle ACD \sim \triangle ABC \sim \triangle CBD$

$$\frac{AB}{AC} = \frac{AC}{AD}, \frac{AD}{CD} = \frac{CD}{DB}, \text{ and } \frac{AB}{CB} = \frac{CB}{DB}$$

Do You UNDERSTAND?

1. **ESSENTIAL QUESTION** In a right triangle, what is the relationship between the altitude to the hypotenuse, triangle similarity, and the geometric mean?

2. **Error Analysis** Pilar is asked to find a geometric mean in $\triangle JKL$. What is her error? ⓒ **MP.3**

$\triangle JKL \sim \triangle MKJ$

$$\frac{KL}{JK} = \frac{JK}{JM}$$ ✗

3. **Vocabulary** Do the altitudes to the legs of a right triangle also create similar triangles? Explain.

Do You KNOW HOW?

For Exercises 4–6, use $\triangle DEF$ to find the lengths.

4. ER

5. DF

6. DE

For Exercises 7–9, use $\triangle PQR$ to find the lengths.

7. QA

8. PQ

9. QR

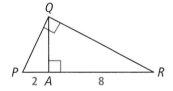

10. Deshawn installs a shelf bracket. What is the widest shelf that will fit without overhang? Explain.

UNDERSTAND

11. Mathematical Connections Consider △XYZ with altitude $\overline{ZW}$.

a. Describe a sequence of transformations that maps △XYZ to △XZW.

b. Describe a sequence of transformations that maps △XYZ to △ZYW.

12. Error Analysis Amaya was asked to find DC. What is Amaya's error? © **MP.3**

△ABC ~ △ACD by Theorem 7-4.

$$\frac{AC}{BC} = \frac{AC}{DC} \rightarrow \frac{7.5}{10} = \frac{7.5}{DC}$$

$7.5 \times DC = 7.5 \times 10$, so $DC = 10$. ✗

13. Make Sense and Persevere Is CD the geometric mean of AD and BD? Explain. © **MP.1**

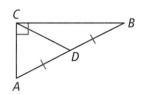

14. Construct Arguments Write proofs of Theorem 7-4 and its corollaries. © **MP.3**

a. **Given:** $m\angle JLK = 90$ and $\overline{LM} \perp \overline{JK}$

Prove: △JKL ~ △JLM ~ △LKM

b. **Given:** △JLM ~ △LKM

Prove: $\frac{JM}{LM} = \frac{LM}{KM}$

c. **Given:** △JKL ~ △JLM ~ △LKM

Prove: $\frac{JK}{JL} = \frac{JL}{JM}$ and $\frac{JK}{LK} = \frac{LK}{MK}$

15. Higher Order Thinking Suppose the altitude to the hypotenuse of a right triangle also bisects the hypotenuse. What type of right triangle is it? Use the similarity of right triangles to explain your answer.

PRACTICE

16. In the figure, what two smaller triangles are similar to △ABC? Explain. SEE EXAMPLE 1

17. What are the values of x and y in the right triangle? Explain. SEE EXAMPLE 2

18. What is the value of y in the right triangle? Explain. SEE EXAMPLE 3

19. What are the values of a and b in each right triangle? Explain. SEE EXAMPLES 4 AND 6

20. What are the values of m and n in each right triangle? Explain. SEE EXAMPLE 5

a.

b.

21. What is the value of w in the right triangle? Explain.

PRACTICE & PROBLEM SOLVING

22. Reason Jake wants the profile of a hotel he is planning to be a right triangle with the dimensions shown. The city prohibits structures over 100 ft at the location where he would like to build. Can the hotel be located there? Explain. ⒸMP.2

23. Look for Relationships Kiyo is repairing a wooden climbing tower.

a. He needs to cut two crossbars. What should the lengths of the two crossbars be? Explain.

b. Kiyo will make a notch in each crossbar in order to fit them together. Where should he make the notch on each crossbar? Explain. ⒸMP.7

24. Higher Order Thinking Write a proof for Theorem 2-14.

Given: Right $\triangle WXY$ with altitude $\overline{XZ}$ to hypotenuse $\overline{WY}$

Prove: The product of the slopes of perpendicular lines is -1.

25. For each figure, write an equation that you could use to find the value of x.

a.

b.

26. SAT/ACT Which triangle is similar to $\triangle ABC$?

Ⓐ $\triangle CBA$ Ⓒ $\triangle CDB$

Ⓑ $\triangle ABD$ Ⓓ $\triangle BDC$

27. Performance Task To estimate the height of a tree, Tia and Felix walk away from the tree until the angle of sight with the top and bottom of the tree is a right angle. Let h represent the height of a person's eyes and d represent the distance away from the tree.

Part A If the height of Tia's eyes is 1.6 m and her distance away from the tree is 2.5 m, what is the height of the tree? Round to the nearest hundredth of a meter.

Part B If the height of Felix's eyes is 1.7 m, about how far from the tree is Felix if his angle of sight is a right angle? Round to the nearest hundredth of a meter.

Part C Suppose Tia and Felix stand the same distance away from another tree and their angles of sight are right angles, what is the height of the tree? Explain.

MATHEMATICAL MODELING IN **3** ACTS

Common Core State Standards
HSG.SRT.A.1.B, HSG.SRT.B.5, MP.4

Make It Right

Architects often make a scale physical model of a new building project. The scale model is usually a miniature version of the project it is representing.

When making a model, architects need to make sure that all of the parts of the model are the right size. Think about this during the Mathematical Modeling in 3 Acts lesson.

ACT 1   Identify the Problem

1. What is the first question that comes to mind after watching the video?

2. Write down the main question you will answer about what you saw in the video.

3. Make an initial conjecture that answers this main question.

4. Explain how you arrived at your conjecture.

5. What information will be useful to know to answer the main question? How can you get it? How will you use that information?

ACT 2   Develop a Model

6. Use the math that you have learned in this Topic to refine your conjecture.

ACT 3   Interpret the Results

7. Did your refined conjecture match the actual answer exactly? If not, what might explain the difference?

7-5

Proportions in Triangles

I CAN... find the lengths of segments using proportional relationships in triangles resulting from parallel lines.

Common Core State Standards
HSG.CO.C.10, HSG.SRT.B.4,
MP.1, MP.3, MP.7

CONCEPTUAL UNDERSTANDING

EXPLORE & REASON

Draw a triangle, like the one shown, by dividing one side into four congruent segments and drawing lines parallel to one of the other sides.

A. How many similar triangles are in the figure? Explain.

B. **Look for Relationships** How are the lengths of the parallel segments related to each other? **MP.7**

ESSENTIAL QUESTION When parallel lines intersect two transversals, what are the relationships among the lengths of the segments formed?

EXAMPLE 1 Explore Proportions from Parallel Lines

In △*JLN*, if *LN* = 9.6, what are *LM* and *MN*? Are the sides divided proportionally? Explain.

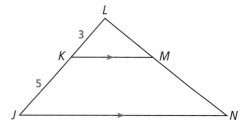

Step 1 Determine how △*JLN* and △*KLM* are related.

The triangles share ∠*L*, and ∠*LJN* ≅ ∠*LKM* by the Corresponding Angles Theorem. Therefore, △*JLN* ~ △*KLM* by AA ~.

Step 2 Write a proportion to relate the corresponding sides.

$$\frac{LK}{LJ} = \frac{LM}{LN}$$

Step 3 Use the proportion to find *LM* and *MN*.

$$\frac{3}{8} = \frac{LM}{9.6}$$

$$LM = 3.6$$

> *LK* = 3, *LJ* = *LK* + *KJ* = 3 + 5 = 8, and *LN* = 9.6

Then *MN* = *LN* − *LM* = 9.6 − 3.6 = 6.

LOOK FOR RELATIONSHIPS
The length of the shorter segments, $\overline{LK}$ and $\overline{LM}$, are each the same fraction of the lengths of the corresponding longer segments, $\overline{KJ}$ and $\overline{MN}$. **MP.7**

Step 4 Find the ratios between the segments of each side divided by $\overline{KM}$.

$$\frac{LK}{KJ} = \frac{3}{5} = 0.6 \text{ and } \frac{LM}{MN} = \frac{3.6}{6} = 0.6$$

Since $\frac{LK}{KJ} = \frac{LM}{MN}$, $\overline{KM}$ divides $\overline{LJ}$ and $\overline{LN}$ proportionally.

Try It! **1.** $\overline{BD}$ bisects sides $\overline{AC}$ and $\overline{CE}$. Is $\overline{AE} \parallel \overline{BD}$? Explain.

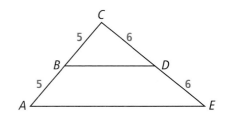

THEOREM 7-5 Side-Splitter Theorem

If a line is parallel to one side of a triangle and intersects the other two sides, then it divides those sides proportionally.

If... $\overline{MN} \parallel \overline{AC}$

PROOF: SEE EXERCISE 14.

Then... $\dfrac{AM}{MB} = \dfrac{CN}{NB}$

THEOREM 7-6 Triangle Midsegment Theorem

Powered By
desmos

If a segment joins the midpoints of two sides of a triangle, then the segment is parallel to the third side and is half as long.

If... $\overline{DG} \cong \overline{GE}$ and $\overline{FH} \cong \overline{HE}$

PROOF: SEE EXERCISE 24.

Then... $\overline{GH} \parallel \overline{DF}$ and $GH = \frac{1}{2}DF$

EXAMPLE 2 Use the Side-Splitter Theorem

What is the value of x in △PQR?

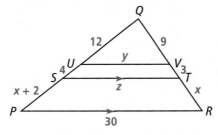

LEARN TOGETHER
How do you value other perspectives and points of view respectfully?

Since $\overline{ST} \parallel \overline{PR}$, $\dfrac{PS}{SQ} = \dfrac{RT}{TQ}$ by the Side-Splitter Theorem. Write a proportion in terms of x and solve.

$$\frac{PS}{SQ} = \frac{RT}{TQ} \qquad \text{SQ} = 4 + 12 = 16 \text{ and } TQ = 3 + 9 = 12$$

$$\frac{x+2}{16} = \frac{x}{12}$$

$$48\left(\frac{x+2}{16}\right) = 48\left(\frac{x}{12}\right)$$

$$3x + 6 = 4x$$

$$x = 6$$

Try It! 2. Refer to △PQR in Example 2.

   a. What is the value of y? Explain.

   b. What is the value of z? Explain.

COROLLARY TO THE SIDE-SPLITTER THEOREM

If three parallel lines intersect two transversals, then the segments intercepted on the transversals are proportional.

If... $\ell \parallel m \parallel n$

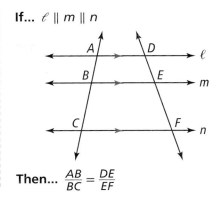

PROOF: SEE EXERCISE 25.

Then... $\dfrac{AB}{BC} = \dfrac{DE}{EF}$

APPLICATION

EXAMPLE 3 Use the Corollary to the Side-Splitter Theorem

An architect is designing a new building. The windows on the second floor will be made up of three window panes that form a trapezoid. To prevent leaks, the trim along the top of the window must be one continuous piece. How long should the piece of trim, z, be?

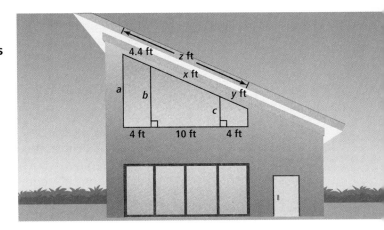

Formulate ◄ Since the window panes are perpendicular to the horizontal, the vertical segments of the window panes are parallel to each other by Theorem 2-9. The value of z is the sum of 4.4, x, and y.

Compute ◄ Write equations to find x and y. Then, find z.

$\dfrac{x}{10} = \dfrac{4.4}{4}$

$x = 10\left(\dfrac{4.4}{4}\right)$ Apply the Corollary to the Side-Splitter Theorem.

$x = 11$

Since $\dfrac{y}{4} = \dfrac{4.4}{4}$, $y = 4.4$.

Since $z = 4.4 + x + y$, substitute the values for x and y to find z.

$z = 4.4 + 11 + 4.4$

$z = 19.8$

Interpret ◄ The piece of trim for the top of the window frame should be 19.8 ft long.

Try It! **3.** How long are segments r and s? Round your answers to the nearest tenth. What theorem(s) can you apply to find the lengths?

EXAMPLE 4 **Investigate Proportionality with an Angle Bisector**

In △KLM, $\overline{NL}$ bisects ∠KLM. Compare the ratios $\frac{KN}{MN}$ and $\frac{KL}{ML}$. Is △LKN ~ △LMN? Explain.

Compute the ratios of the corresponding sides for the given measures.

$$\frac{KN}{MN} = \frac{10.5}{7.5} = 1.4 \qquad \frac{KL}{ML} = \frac{14}{10} = 1.4$$

The ratios $\frac{KN}{MN}$ and $\frac{KL}{ML}$ are equal. However, the third pair is $\overline{NL}$ and $\overline{NL}$, and that ratio is 1. So, the two triangles are not similar.

Try It! 4. Draw $\overrightarrow{ML}$ and a line through K parallel to $\overline{NL}$. Let P be the point of intersection.

a. Is △MNL ~ △MKP? Explain.

b. Is ∠LKP ≅ ∠LPK? Explain.

THEOREM 7-7 Triangle-Angle-Bisector Theorem

If a ray bisects an angle of a triangle, then it divides the opposite side into two segments such that the ratio between the segments is the same as the ratio between the sides adjacent to each segment.

PROOF: SEE EXERCISE 16.

If... ∠UVX ≅ ∠WVX

Then... $\frac{UX}{WX} = \frac{UV}{WV}$

EXAMPLE 5 Use the Triangle-Angle-Bisector Theorem

What are the values of AD and DC?

Since $\overline{BD}$ bisects ∠ABC, use the Triangle-Angle-Bisector Theorem to write a proportion.

$$\frac{AD}{CD} = \frac{AB}{CB}$$

$$\frac{x}{13 - x} = \frac{10}{16}$$

$$16x = 130 - 10x$$

$$26x = 130$$

$$x = 5$$

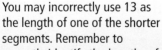

CD = AC − AD or
CD = 13 − x

In the figure, AD = 5 and CD = 13 − 5 = 8.

Try It! 5. a. What is the value of x?

b. What are the values of GH and GK?

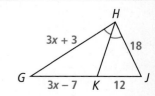

CONCEPT SUMMARY Proportions in Triangles

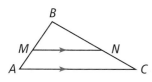

THEOREM 7-5

Side-Splitter Theorem

If... $\overline{MN} \parallel \overline{AC}$

Then... $\dfrac{AM}{MB} = \dfrac{CN}{NB}$

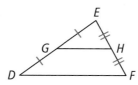

THEOREM 7-6

Triangle Midsegment Theorem

If... $\overline{DG} \cong \overline{GE}$ and $\overline{FH} \cong \overline{HE}$

Then... $\overline{GH} \parallel \overline{DF}$ and $GH = \dfrac{1}{2}DF$

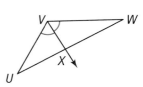

THEOREM 7-7

Triangle-Angle-Bisector Theorem

If... $\angle UVX \cong \angle WVX$

Then... $\dfrac{UX}{WX} = \dfrac{UV}{WV}$

Do You UNDERSTAND?

1. **ESSENTIAL QUESTION** When parallel lines intersect two transversals, what are the relationships among the lengths of the segments formed?

2. **Error Analysis** Carmen thinks that $AD = BD$. What is Carmen's error? © MP.3

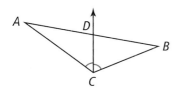

3. **Make Sense and Persevere** What information is needed to determine if x is half of y? © MP.1

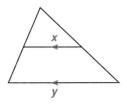

4. **Look for Relationships** If $\overline{RS} \cong \overline{QS}$, what type of triangle is $\triangle PQR$? Use the Triangle-Angle-Bisector Theorem to explain your reasoning. © MP.7

5. **Construct Arguments** Explain why LP must be less than LM. © MP.3

Do You KNOW HOW?

For Exercises 6–11, find each value of x.

6.

7.

8.

9.

10.

11.

PRACTICE & PROBLEM SOLVING

UNDERSTAND

12. Error Analysis What is Benson's error? © MP.3

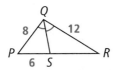

$$\frac{5}{10} = \frac{x}{7}$$
$$10x = 35$$
$$x = 3.5 \quad ✗$$

13. Mathematical Connections What percent of the area of △PQR is the area of △QRS? Explain.

14. Construct Arguments Write a proof of the Side-Splitter Theorem. © MP.3

Given: $\overline{MN} \parallel \overline{AC}$

Prove: $\frac{AM}{MB} = \frac{CN}{NB}$

15. Higher Order Thinking Suppose O, P, and Q are midpoints of the sides of △LMN. Show that △LOQ, △OMP, △QPN, and △PQO are congruent to each other.

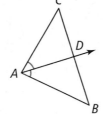

16. Construct Arguments Write a proof for the Triangle-Angle-Bisector Theorem. © MP.3

Given: $\overrightarrow{AD}$ bisects ∠A.

Prove: $\frac{CA}{AB} = \frac{CD}{DB}$

Use the following outline.

- Extend $\overrightarrow{CA}$ and draw a line through point B parallel to $\overrightarrow{AD}$ that intersects $\overrightarrow{CA}$ at point E.
- Show that $\frac{CA}{AE} = \frac{CD}{DB}$.
- Then show that △AEB is isosceles.

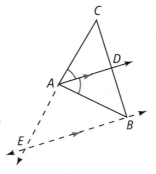

PRACTICE

For Exercises 17–19, find each value.
SEE EXAMPLES 1 AND 2

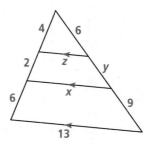

17. x   **18.** y   **19.** z

20. What is the value of x? SEE EXAMPLE 3

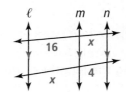

For Exercises 21–23, find each value of x for the given value of y. Round to the nearest tenth.
SEE EXAMPLES 4 AND 5

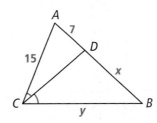

21. y = 16   **22.** y = 20   **23.** y = 18

24. Write a proof of the Triangle Midsegment Theorem.

Given: $\overline{DG} \cong \overline{GE}$, $\overline{FH} \cong \overline{HE}$

Prove: $\overline{GH} \parallel \overline{DF}$, $GH = \frac{1}{2}DF$

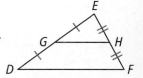

25. Write a proof of the Corollary to the Side-Splitter Theorem.

Given: $\ell \parallel m \parallel n$

Prove: $\frac{AB}{BC} = \frac{DE}{EF}$

Hint: Draw $\overline{AF}$. Label the intersection of $\overline{AF}$ and $\overrightarrow{BE}$ point G.

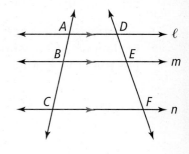

PRACTICE & PROBLEM SOLVING

26. Use Structure The Palace of Peace and Reconciliation, in Kazakhstan, is in the shape of a pyramid with five stories of triangular windows. The face of the building is an equilateral triangle. What are the lengths of parallel supports $\overline{KO}$ and $\overline{LN}$? **© MP.7**

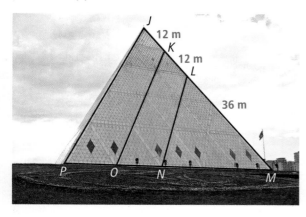

27. Higher Order Thinking Use the figure to prove Theorem 2-13: Two non-vertical lines are parallel if and only if they have the same slope.

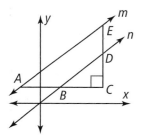

a. Assume the slopes of lines m and n are equal. Use proportions in $\triangle ACE$ and $\triangle BCD$ to show that $m \parallel n$.

b. Now assume that $m \parallel n$. Show that the slopes of m and n are equal.

28. Use Structure Aisha is building a roof and needs to determine the lengths of $\overline{CG}$ and $\overline{CF}$ from the design shown. How can she determine CG and CF? What are CG and CF? **© MP.7**

29. What is the measure of side CB?

Ⓐ 4.57   Ⓑ 6.4   Ⓒ 8.96   Ⓓ 9.4

30. SAT/ACT What is the value of x?

31. Performance Task Emilia is programming a shuffleboard computer game. She needs to determine measurements on the screen to simulate the distances.

Part A The horizontal lines must be parallel and in proportion so that each zone of the shuffleboard appears to be the same length. What are the lengths w, x, and y?

Part B What is the length of each horizontal segment?

Part C Which horizontal segment is closest to the midsegment of the triangle that extends off of the screen? How do you know?

1. How are properties of similar figures used to solve problems?

Vocabulary Review

Choose the correct term to complete each sentence.

2. Two triangles that are _____ have two pairs of corresponding congruent angles.

3. A _____ is a composition of a dilation and one or more rigid motions.

4. A point that is its own image in a dilation is the _____.

5. As a result of a dilation, if $A'B' = n \cdot AB$, then n is the _____.

- center of dilation
- dilation
- geometric mean
- scale factor
- similar
- similarity transformation

Concepts & Skills Review

LESSONS 7-1 & 7-2   **Dilations and Similarity Transformations**

Quick Review

A **dilation** is a transformation that maps a point X to X' such that X' lies on $\overrightarrow{CX}$ and $CX' = k \cdot CX$, with **center of dilation** C and **scale factor** k.

Two figures are **similar** if there is a **similarity transformation** that maps one figure onto the other.

Example

Are △ABC and △DEF similar? Explain.

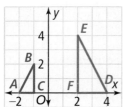

The reflection $r_{y\text{-axis}}$ maps △ABC to a triangle with vertices $A'(2, 0)$, $B'(1, 2)$ and $C'(1, 0)$. The dilation D_2 maps the image to △DEF. Since the composition $D_2 \circ r_{y\text{-axis}}$ maps △ABC to △DEF, the triangles are similar.

Practice & Problem Solving

Give the coordinates of each image.

6. $D_{\frac{1}{2}}(\triangle FGH)$ for $F(5, -2)$, $G(-2, -4)$, $H(0, 6)$

7. $D_{(3, K)}(\triangle KLM)$ for $K(0, 4)$, $L(3, 0)$, $M(-2, 4)$

8. What is a similarity transformation from *PQRS* to *WXYZ*?

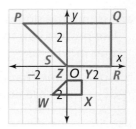

9. **Construct Arguments** Andrés says that the scale factor in the similarity transformation that maps △ABC to △PQR is 2. Is he correct? Explain. **MP.3**

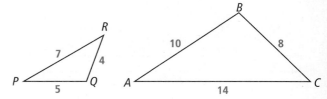

LESSON 7-3 ▸ Proving Triangles Similar

Quick Review

A pair of triangles can be shown to be similar by using the following criteria.

- Two pairs of corresponding angles are congruent.
- All corresponding sides are proportional.
- Two pairs of corresponding sides are proportional and the included angles are congruent.

Example

Explain whether △ABE and △DBC are similar.

By the Alternate Interior Angles Theorem, $\angle A \cong \angle D$ and $\angle E \cong \angle C$. Since two pairs of corresponding angles are congruent, △ABE ~ △DBC.

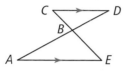

Practice & Problem Solving

For Exercises 10 and 11, explain whether each triangle similarity is true.

10. △FGJ ~ △JGH

11. △KLN ~ △NLM

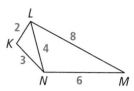

12. **Communicate Precisely** Explain what additional information is needed to use AA ~ to show that △TUV ~ △XZY. © MP.6

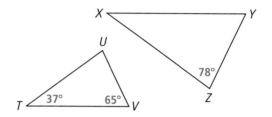

LESSONS 7-4 & 7-5 ▸ Similarity in Right Triangles and Proportions in Triangles

Quick Review

For right triangle △ABC, △ABC ~ △ACD ~ △CBD.

Also, CD is the **geometric mean** of AD and BD, AC is the geometric mean of AB and AD, and CB is the geometric mean of AB and DB.

For △FGH, $\dfrac{FJ}{HJ} = \dfrac{FG}{HG}$.

Example

For △LMN, what is x?

By the Side-Splitter Theorem, $\dfrac{LP}{PM} = \dfrac{NQ}{QM}$, so $\dfrac{6}{9} = \dfrac{4}{x}$. Solve for x to get $x = \dfrac{9}{6}(4) = 6$.

Practice & Problem Solving

For Exercises 13–15, use △RST to find each length.

13. RS

14. ST

15. SU

For Exercises 16–19, find the value of x.

16.

17.

18.

19.

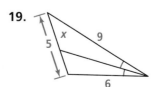

20. **Use Structure** Given right triangle △GHJ with $\overline{JK}$ the altitude to hypotenuse $\overline{GH}$, what is GJ the geometric mean of? Explain. © MP.7

TOPIC 8

Right Triangles and Trigonometry

TOPIC ESSENTIAL QUESTION

How are the Pythagorean Theorem and trigonometry useful?

Topic Overview

enVision® STEM Project:
   Measure a Distance

8-1 Right Triangles and the Pythagorean Theorem

8-2 Trigonometric Ratios

8-3 The Law of Sines

8-4 The Law of Cosines

Mathematical Modeling in 3 Acts:
   The Impossible Measurement

8-5 Problem Solving With Trigonometry

Topic Vocabulary

- angle of depression
- angle of elevation
- cosine
- Law of Cosines
- Law of Sines
- Pythagorean triple
- sine
- tangent
- trigonometric ratios

Digital Experience

INTERACTIVE STUDENT EDITION Access online or offline.

ACTIVITIES Complete *Explore & Reason, Model & Discuss*, and *Critique & Explain* activities. Interact with *Examples* and *Try Its.*

CONCEPT SUMMARY Review key lesson content through multiple representations.

ASSESSMENT Show what you've learned.

Go online | **SavvasRealize.com**

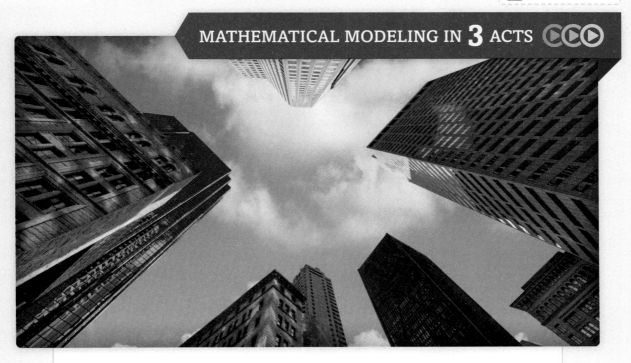

The Impossible Measurement

Tall buildings are often some of the most recognizable structures of cities. The Empire State Building in New York City, the Transamerica Pyramid in San Francisco, and the JPMorgan Chase Tower in Houston are all famous landmarks in those cities.

Cities around the world compete for the tallest building bragging rights. Which city currently has the tallest building? This Mathematical Modeling in 3 Acts lesson will get you thinking about the height of structures, including tall buildings such as these.

TOPIC 8

VIDEOS Watch clips to support *Mathematical Modeling in 3 Acts Lessons* and **enVision® *STEM Projects*.**

TUTORIALS Get help from *Virtual Nerd*, right when you need it.

PRACTICE Practice what you've learned.

ADAPTIVE PRACTICE Practice that is *just right* and *just for you.*

FAMILY ENGAGEMENT Involve family in your learning.

GLOSSARY Read and listen to English and Spanish definitions.

MATH TOOLS Explore math with digital tools and manipulatives.

DESMOS Use Anytime and as embedded Interactives in Lesson content.

Did You Know?

A **laser rangefinder** measures the distance to an object indirectly. The instrument measures the time it takes a laser pulse to travel to the object and return, at a speed of approximately **186,000 miles per second**.

SONAR is used to measure distances underwater. The speed of sound in the ocean depends on the **temperature**, **pressure**, and **salt content** of the water. Once you know the speed of sound, you can bounce SONAR waves off an underwater object, measure the time it takes to return, and calculate the distance to the object.

In the 3rd Century B.C., the Greek mathematician **Eratosthenes** calculated the circumference of the Earth indirectly. He couldn't actually measure the distance foot by foot. So he used **geometry and the shadow of the sun** to make a determination of the circumference.

Your Task: Measure a Distance

Trigonometry is a powerful tool for measuring lengths and distances indirectly. You and your classmates will use trigonometry and indirect measurement to find the height of an object that is too tall to measure directly.

8-1

Right Triangles and the Pythagorean Theorem

I CAN... prove the Pythagorean Theorem using similarity and establish the relationships in special right triangles.

VOCABULARY
• Pythagorean triple

© **Common Core State Standards**
HSG.SRT.B.4, HSG.SRT.C.8, MP.2, MP.6, MP.7

EXPLORE & REASON

Consider △ABC with altitude $\overline{CD}$ as shown.

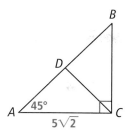

A. What is the area of △ABC? Of △ACD? Explain your answers.

B. Find the lengths of $\overline{AD}$ and $\overline{AB}$.

C. **Look for Relationships** Divide the length of the hypotenuse of △ABC by the length of one of its sides. Divide the length of the hypotenuse of △ACD by the length of one of its sides. Make a conjecture that explains the results. © **MP.7**

ESSENTIAL QUESTION
How are similarity in right triangles and the Pythagorean Theorem related?

Remember that the Pythagorean Theorem and its converse describe how the side lengths of right triangles are related.

THEOREM 8-1 Pythagorean Theorem

If a triangle is a right triangle, then the sum of the squares of the lengths of the legs is equal to the square of the length of the hypotenuse.

If... △ABC is a right triangle.

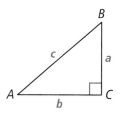

PROOF: SEE EXAMPLE 1.

Then... $a^2 + b^2 = c^2$

THEOREM 8-2 Converse of the Pythagorean Theorem

If the sum of the squares of the lengths of two sides of a triangle is equal to the square of the length of the third side, then the triangle is a right triangle.

If... $a^2 + b^2 = c^2$

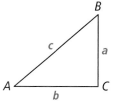

PROOF: SEE EXERCISE 17.

Then... △ABC is a right triangle.

EXAMPLE 1 Use Similarity to Prove the Pythagorean Theorem

Use right triangle similarity to write a proof of the Pythagorean Theorem.

Given: $\triangle XYZ$ is a right triangle.

Prove: $a^2 + b^2 = c^2$

Plan: To prove the Pythagorean Theorem, draw the altitude to the hypotenuse. Then use the relationships in the resulting similar right triangles.

Proof:

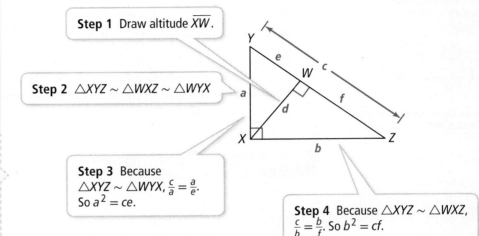

Step 1 Draw altitude $\overline{XW}$.

Step 2 $\triangle XYZ \sim \triangle WXZ \sim \triangle WYX$

LOOK FOR RELATIONSHIPS
Think about how you can apply properties of similar triangles. What is the relationship between corresponding sides of similar triangles? Ⓒ MP.7

Step 3 Because $\triangle XYZ \sim \triangle WYX$, $\frac{c}{a} = \frac{a}{e}$. So $a^2 = ce$.

Step 4 Because $\triangle XYZ \sim \triangle WXZ$, $\frac{c}{b} = \frac{b}{f}$. So $b^2 = cf$.

Step 5 Write an equation that relates a^2 and b^2 to ce and cf.

$$a^2 + b^2 = ce + cf$$
$$a^2 + b^2 = c(e + f)$$
$$a^2 + b^2 = c(c)$$
$$a^2 + b^2 = c^2$$

Try It! **1.** Find the unknown side length of each right triangle.

a. *AB*

b. *EF*

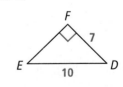

EXAMPLE 2 Use the Pythagorean Theorem and Its Converse

A. To satisfy safety regulations, the distance from the wall to the base of a ladder should be at least one-fourth the length of the ladder. Did Drew set up the ladder correctly?

The floor, the wall, and the ladder form a right triangle.

Step 1 Find the length of the ladder.

$$a^2 + b^2 = c^2$$

$$2.5^2 + 9^2 = c^2$$

$$87.25 = c^2$$

$$9.34 \approx c$$

Use the Pythagorean Theorem with $a = 2.5$ and $b = 9$.

Step 2 Find $\frac{1}{4}$ the length of the ladder.

$$\frac{1}{4}c \approx \frac{1}{4}(9.34)$$

$$\approx 2.335$$

The length of the ladder is 9.34 ft.

The distance from the wall to the base of the ladder is 2.5 ft, which is greater than one-fourth the length of the ladder. Drew set up the ladder correctly.

B. A rancher is building a fence using a crosspiece that is 10 ft long. Why would the rancher build this fence with the measurements shown?

The numbers 6, 8, and 10 form a *Pythagorean triple*. A **Pythagorean triple** is a set of three nonzero whole numbers that satisfy the equation $a^2 + b^2 = c^2$.

Since $6^2 + 8^2 = 10^2$, the posts, the ground, and the crosspieces form right triangles.

By using those measurements, the rancher knows that the fence posts are perpendicular to the ground, which stabilizes the fence.

> **STUDY TIP**
> Learn and recognize common Pythagorean triples such as 3, 4, and 5; and 5, 12, and 13 to speed calculations.

Try It! **2. a.** What is *KL*?

b. Is $\triangle MNO$ a right triangle? Explain.

EXAMPLE 3 Investigate Side Lengths in 45°-45°-90° Triangles

Is there a relationship between the lengths of $\overline{AB}$ and $\overline{AC}$ in △ABC? Explain.

Draw altitude $\overline{CD}$ to form similar right triangles △ABC, △ACD, and △CBD.

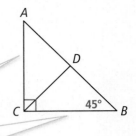

> Notice that △ABC is a 45°-45°-90° triangle. Therefore, $AC = BC$.

REASON
Think about the properties of a triangle with two congruent angles. How do the properties of the triangle help you relate the side lengths? **© MP.2**

Use right-triangle similarity to write an equation.

> Since △ABC ~ △ACD, AC is the geometric mean of AB and AD.

$$\frac{AB}{AC} = \frac{AC}{AD}$$

$$\frac{AB}{AC} = \frac{AC}{\frac{1}{2}AB}$$

$$\frac{1}{2}AB^2 = AC^2$$

$$AB^2 = 2AC^2$$

$$AB = \sqrt{2} \cdot AC$$

> Because △ABC is isosceles, $\overline{CD}$ bisects $\overline{AB}$.

The length of $\overline{AB}$ is $\sqrt{2}$ times the length of $\overline{AC}$.

Try It! **3.** Find the side lengths of each 45°-45°-90° triangle.

a. What are XZ and YZ?

b. What are JK and LK?

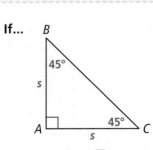

THEOREM 8-3 45°-45°-90° Triangle Theorem

In a 45°-45°-90° triangle, the legs are congruent and the length of the hypotenuse is $\sqrt{2}$ times the length of a leg.

If...

Then... $BC = s\sqrt{2}$

PROOF: SEE EXERCISE 18.

EXAMPLE 4 **Explore the Side Lengths of a 30°-60°-90° Triangle**

Using an equilateral triangle, show how the lengths of the short leg, the long leg, and the hypotenuse of a 30°-60°-90° triangle are related.

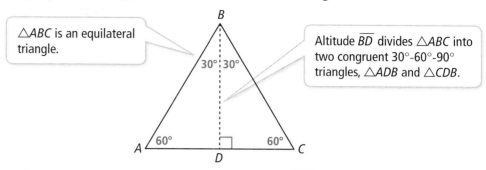

△ABC is an equilateral triangle.

Altitude $\overline{BD}$ divides △ABC into two congruent 30°-60°-90° triangles, △ADB and △CDB.

Look at △ADB. Let the length of the short leg $\overline{AD}$ be s.

Find the relationship between AD and AB.

$AD = CD = s$

$\overline{BD}$ bisects $\overline{AC}$.

$AC = AD + CD$

$AC = 2s$

$AB = 2s$

△ABC is equilateral, so AB = AC = 2s.

Find the relationship between AD and BD.

$AD^2 + BD^2 = AB^2$

Use the Pythagorean Theorem.

$s^2 + BD^2 = (2s)^2$

$BD^2 = 3s^2$

$BD = s\sqrt{3}$

In △ADB, the length of hypotenuse $\overline{AB}$ is twice the length of the short leg $\overline{AD}$. The length of the long leg $\overline{BD}$ is $\sqrt{3}$ times the length of the short leg.

Try It! **4. a.** What are PQ and PR?   **b.** What are UV and TV?

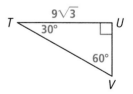

THEOREM 8-4 30°-60°-90° Triangle Theorem

In a 30°-60°-90° triangle, the length of the hypotenuse is twice the length of the short leg. The length of the long leg is $\sqrt{3}$ times the length of the short leg.

If...

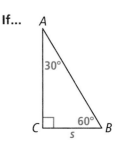

PROOF: SEE EXERCISE 19.   **Then...** $AC = s\sqrt{3}$, $AB = 2s$

EXAMPLE 5 Apply Special Right Triangle Relationships

A. Alejandro needs to make both the horizontal and vertical supports, $\overline{AC}$ and $\overline{AB}$, for a ramp. Is one 12-foot board long enough for both supports? Explain.

The ramp and supports form a 30°-60°-90° triangle.

$BC = 2AB$ $AC = AB\sqrt{3}$

$10 = 2AB$ $AC = 5\sqrt{3}$ ft

$AB = 5$ ft

Find the total length of the supports.

$AB + AC = 5 + 5\sqrt{3}$

≈ 13.66 ft

Since $13.66 > 12$, the 12-foot board will not be long enough for Alejandro to make both supports.

B. Olivia starts an origami paper crane by making the 200-mm diagonal fold. What are the side length and area of the paper square?

Step 1 Find the length of one side of the paper.

$s\sqrt{2} = 200$

$s = \dfrac{200}{\sqrt{2}}$

$s \approx 141.4$ mm

Step 2 Find the area of the paper square.

$A = s^2$

$A = \left(100\sqrt{2}\right)^2$

$A = 20{,}000$ mm^2

The paper square has side length 141.4 mm and area 20,000 mm^2.

Try It! **5. a.** What are AB and BC?

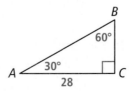

b. What are AC and BC?

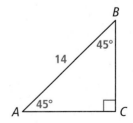

CONCEPT SUMMARY The Pythagorean Theorem and Special Right Triangles

THEOREM 8-1 ▶ **Pythagorean Theorem**

If... $\triangle ABC$ is a right triangle

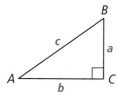

Then... $a^2 + b^2 = c^2$

THEOREM 8-2 ▶ **Converse of the Pythagorean Theorem**

If... $a^2 + b^2 = c^2$

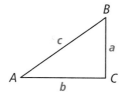

Then... $\triangle ABC$ is a right triangle.

THEOREM 8-3 ▶ **45°-45°-90° Triangle Theorem**

If...

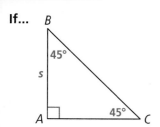

Then... $BC = s\sqrt{2}$

THEOREM 8-4 ▶ **30°-60°-90° Triangle Theorem**

If...

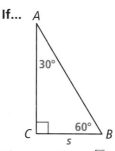

Then... $AC = s\sqrt{3}$, $AB = 2s$

Do You UNDERSTAND?

1. **ESSENTIAL QUESTION** ▶ How are similarity in right triangles and the Pythagorean Theorem related?

2. **Error Analysis** Casey was asked to find XY. What is his error? Ⓖ **MP.3**

$XY = YZ\sqrt{3}$
$XY = 4\sqrt{3}$

3. **Reason** A right triangle has leg lengths 4.5 and $4.5\sqrt{3}$. What are the measures of the angles? Explain. Ⓖ **MP.2**

Do You KNOW HOW?

For Exercises 4 and 5, find the value of x.

4.

5.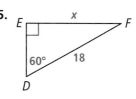

For Exercises 6–8, is $\triangle RST$ a right triangle? Explain.

6. $RS = 20$, $ST = 21$, $RT = 29$

7. $RS = 35$, $ST = 36$, $RT = 71$

8. $RS = 40$, $ST = 41$, $RT = 11$

9. Zaid wants to hang the pennant shown vertically between two windows that are 19 inches apart. Will the pennant fit? Explain.

PRACTICE & PROBLEM SOLVING

UNDERSTAND

10. Mathematical Connections Which rectangular prism has the longer diagonal? Explain.

Prism *P*   Prism *Q*

11. Error Analysis Angeni is asked to find *EF*. What is her error? © **MP.3**

There is not enough information to find *EF* because you need to know either the length of $\overline{DF}$ or one of the other angle measures.

✗

12. Make Sense and Persevere What are expressions for *MN* and *LN*? *Hint*: Construct the altitude from *M* to $\overline{LN}$. © **MP.1**

13. Higher Order Thinking Triangle *XYZ* is a right triangle. For what kind of triangle would $XZ^2 + XY^2 > YZ^2$? For what kind of triangle would $XZ^2 + XY^2 < YZ^2$? Explain.

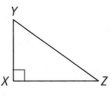

14. Look for Relationships Write an equation that represents the relationship between *JK* and *KL*. © **MP.7**

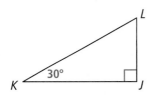

PRACTICE

For Exercises 15 and 16, find the unknown side length of each triangle. SEE EXAMPLE 1

15. *RS*

16. *XY*

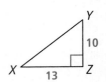

17. Given △*ABC* with $a^2 + b^2 = c^2$, write a paragraph proof of the Converse of the Pythagorean Theorem. SEE EXAMPLE 2

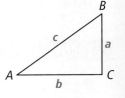

18. Write a two-column proof of the 45°-45°-90° Triangle Theorem. SEE EXAMPLE 3

19. Write a paragraph proof of the 30°-60°-90° Triangle Theorem. SEE EXAMPLE 4

For Exercise 20 and 21, find the side lengths of each triangle. SEE EXAMPLES 3 AND 4

20. What are *GJ* and *HJ*?   **21.** What are *XY* and *YZ*?

22. What is *QS*? SEE EXAMPLE 5

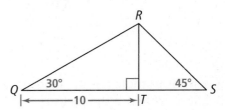

PRACTICE & PROBLEM SOLVING

23. Reason Esteban wants marble bookends cut at a 60° angle, as shown. If Esteban wants his bookends to be between 7.5 in. and 8 in. tall, what is the range of possible values for *d*, the length of the base of the bookends? Explain.
ⓒ **MP.2**

24. Communicate Precisely Tayesha finds an antique dinner bell that appears to be in the shape of an isosceles right triangle, but the only measurement given is the longest side. Tayesha wants to display the bell and wand in a 5.5-in. by 7.5-in. picture frame. Assuming that the bell is an isosceles right triangle, can Tayesha display the bell and wand within the frame? Explain. ⓒ **MP.6**

25. Construct Arguments When Carmen parks on a hill, she places chocks behind the wheels of her car. The height of the chocks must be at least one-fourth of the height of the wheels to hold the car securely in place. The chock shown has the shape of a right triangle. Is it safe for Carmen to use? Explain. ⓒ **MP.3**

26. A kite is flying at the end of a 200 foot-long string. The wind pulls the kite and the string taut, making the string form a line. The line makes a 60-degree angle with the ground. About how high above the ground is the kite?

27. SAT/ACT What is *GJ*?

Ⓐ 18.7   Ⓑ $18.7\sqrt{2}$ Ⓒ $18.7\sqrt{3}$ Ⓓ 74.8

28. Performance Task Emma designed two triangular sails for a boat.

Sail A   Sail B

Part A What is the area of Sail A?

Part B What is the area of Sail B?

Part C Is it possible for Emma to cut both sails from one square of sailcloth with sides that are 9 meters in length? Draw a diagram to explain.

8-2
Trigonometric Ratios

I CAN... use trigonometric ratios to find lengths and angle measures of right triangles.

VOCABULARY
- cosine
- sine
- tangent
- trigonometric ratios

ⓒ **Common Core State Standards**
HSG.SRT.C.6, HSG.SRT.C.7, HSG.SRT.C.8, MP.1, MP.4, MP.6

CRITIQUE & EXPLAIN

A teacher asked students to write a proportion using the lengths of the legs of the two right triangles.

Two students' responses are shown.

Diego

$$\frac{JK}{MN} = \frac{JL}{MO}$$

Rebecca

$$\frac{JK}{JL} = \frac{MN}{MO}$$

A. Do you think that the proportion that Diego wrote is correct? Explain.

B. Do you think that the proportion that Rebecca wrote is correct? Explain.

C. Use Structure If $\frac{a}{b} = \frac{c}{d}$, how can you get an equivalent equation such that the left side of the equation is $\frac{a}{c}$? ⓒ **MP.7**

ESSENTIAL QUESTION

How do trigonometric ratios relate angle measures to side lengths of right triangles?

CONCEPT Trigonometric Ratios

The **trigonometric ratios**, or functions, relate the side lengths of a right triangle to its acute angles.

sine of $\angle A$

$$\sin A = \frac{\text{length of leg opposite } \angle A}{\text{length of hypotenuse}}$$

$$= \frac{BC}{AB}$$

cosine of $\angle A$

$$\cos A = \frac{\text{length of leg adjacent to } \angle A}{\text{length of hypotenuse}}$$

$$= \frac{AC}{AB}$$

tangent of $\angle A$

$$\tan A = \frac{\text{length of leg opposite } \angle A}{\text{length of leg adjacent to } \angle A}$$

$$= \frac{BC}{AC}$$

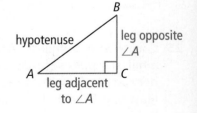

EXAMPLE 1 Understand Trigonometric Ratios Using Similarity

How are the sines of two different angles with the same measure related?

Let △ABC and △DEF be right triangles with $m\angle B = m\angle E$.

Since $\angle C \cong \angle F$ and $\angle B \cong \angle E$, △ABC ~ △DEF by AA.

You can use properties of similarity to determine the relationship between sin B and sin E.

By the definition of the sine ratio, $\sin B = \frac{AC}{AB}$ and $\sin E = \frac{DF}{DE}$.

MAKE SENSE AND PERSEVERE
There are many proportional relationships in similar triangles. Look for one that uses all the side lengths in the expressions for sin B and sin E. © MP.1

Because △ABC ~ △DEF, you know that corresponding side lengths are proportional. In particular, $\frac{AC}{DF} = \frac{AB}{DE}$. Rewrite this equation to compare the sides in △ABC to the sides in △DEF.

$$\frac{AC}{DF} \cdot \frac{DF}{AB} = \frac{AB}{DE} \cdot \frac{DF}{AB}$$

$$\frac{AC}{AB} = \frac{DF}{DE}$$

Substitute sin B for $\frac{AC}{AB}$ and sin E for $\frac{DF}{DE}$.

$$\sin B = \sin E$$

Any two acute angles with the same measure have the same sine.

Try It! 1. Show that any two acute angles with the same measure have the same cosine.

EXAMPLE 2 Write Trigonometric Ratios

What are the sine, cosine, and tangent ratios for ∠H?

Use the definitions of the trigonometric ratios.

COMMON ERROR
You may incorrectly assume that the value of the trigonometric ratio is the measure of the angle. Remember that the trigonometric ratio relates the side lengths of a right triangle to its acute angles. You will learn how to use this ratio to determine the measure of the angle later on in this lesson.

$$\sin H = \frac{\text{length of leg opposite } \angle H}{\text{length of hypotenuse}} = \frac{12}{15}$$

$$\cos H = \frac{\text{length of leg adjacent } \angle H}{\text{length of hypotenuse}} = \frac{9}{15}$$

$$\tan H = \frac{\text{length of leg opposite } \angle H}{\text{length of leg adjacent } \angle H} = \frac{12}{9}$$

Try It! 2. In Example 2, what are the sine, cosine, and tangent ratios of ∠F?

EXAMPLE 3 **Trigonometric Ratios of Special Angles**

A. What are the sine, cosine, and tangent ratios for 30°, 45°, and 60° angles?

You can use what you know about 45°-45°-90° and 30°-60°-90° right triangles to find the ratios.

$$\sin 45° = \frac{1}{\sqrt{2}} = \frac{\sqrt{2}}{2}$$ $$\sin 30° = \frac{1}{2}$$ $$\sin 60° = \frac{\sqrt{3}}{2}$$

$$\cos 45° = \frac{1}{\sqrt{2}} = \frac{\sqrt{2}}{2}$$ $$\cos 30° = \frac{\sqrt{3}}{2}$$ $$\cos 60° = \frac{1}{2}$$

$$\tan 45° = \frac{1}{1} = 1$$ $$\tan 30° = \frac{1}{\sqrt{3}} = \frac{\sqrt{3}}{3}$$ $$\tan 60° = \frac{\sqrt{3}}{1} = \sqrt{3}$$

> **LOOK FOR RELATIONSHIPS**
> Notice that sin 45° = cos 45°, sin 30° = cos 60°, and sin 60° = cos 30°. Before moving on to Part B, use inductive reasoning to make a conjecture about the relationship between the sine and cosine of complementary angles. ⓒ MP.7

B. How are the sine and cosine of complementary angles related?

By the Triangle Angle-Sum Theorem, the two acute angles in any right triangle are complementary.

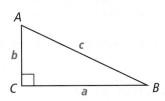

$$m\angle A + m\angle B + m\angle C = 180$$
$$m\angle A + m\angle B + 90 = 180$$
$$m\angle A + m\angle B = 90$$

Find the sine and cosine of the complementary angles ∠A and ∠B.

$$\sin A = \frac{a}{c} \qquad \sin B = \frac{b}{c}$$

$$\cos A = \frac{b}{c} \qquad \cos B = \frac{a}{c}$$

$$\sin A = \cos B = \frac{a}{c}$$
$$\sin B = \cos A = \frac{b}{c}$$

The sine of an angle is equal to the cosine of its complement, and vice versa. For any angle with measure x°, where 0 < x < 90:

$$\sin x = \cos (90 - x) \qquad \text{and} \qquad \cos x = \sin (90 - x)$$

> **VOCABULARY**
> Recall that two angles are *complementary* if the sum of their measures is 90. If an angle has measure x, its complement has measure 90 − x.

Try It! **3. a.** In △FGH, what is the value of y?

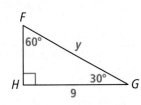

b. How can you write an equivalent expression for cos 70° using sine? An equivalent expression for sin 34° using cosine?

c. Given sin 65° ≈ 0.91, what is the approximate value of cos 25°?

EXAMPLE 4 Use Trigonometric Ratios to Find Distances

A plane takes off 12.5 miles from an 11,088-foot mountain and climbs at a 12° angle. Is that angle sufficient enough to fly over the mountain, or does the pilot need to increase the plane's angle of ascent?

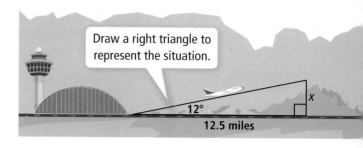

Draw a right triangle to represent the situation.

12°
12.5 miles

Step 1 You know the length of the side adjacent to the 12° angle, so use the tangent ratio to find the altitude of the plane as it passes the mountain.

$$\tan 12° = \frac{x}{12.5}$$
$$x = 12.5 \cdot \tan 12°$$
$$\approx 2.66$$

Use a calculator.

12.5 [TAN] 12 [ENTER]

The altitude of the plane is about 2.66 miles.

Step 2 Compare the altitude of the plane to the height of the mountain.

$$11{,}088 \text{ ft} \cdot \frac{1 \text{ mi}}{5{,}280 \text{ ft}} = 2.1 \text{ mi}$$

Write the height of the mountain in miles.

A 12° angle is sufficient because 2.1 mi < 2.66 mi.

Try It! **4.** If a plane climbs at 5° and flies 20 miles through the air as it climbs, what is the altitude of the airplane, to the nearest foot?

EXAMPLE 5 Use Trigonometric Inverses to Find Angle Measures

What are $m\angle A$ and $m\angle B$?

If you know the sine, cosine, or tangent of an angle, you can use a *trigonometric inverse* ($\sin^{-1}$, $\cos^{-1}$, or $\tan^{-1}$) to find the angle measure.

Since you know that $\cos A = \frac{1}{4}$, use $\cos^{-1}$ to find $m\angle A$.

$$m\angle A = \cos^{-1}\left(\frac{1}{4}\right)$$
$$\approx 75.5$$

Since you know that $\sin B = \frac{1}{4}$, use $\sin^{-1}$ to find $m\angle B$.

$$m\angle B = \sin^{-1}\left(\frac{1}{4}\right)$$
$$\approx 14.5$$

Try It! **5. a.** What is $m\angle P$?

b. What is $m\angle Q$?

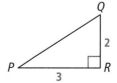

CONCEPT SUMMARY Trigonometric Ratios

WORDS For a right triangle, **the trigonometric ratios sine, cosine,** and **tangent** relate the measure of an acute angle of the triangle to the lengths of the sides.

DIAGRAM Triangle *ABC* is a right triangle.

hypotenuse

leg opposite ∠A

leg adjacent to ∠A

SYMBOLS

$$\sin A = \frac{\text{length of leg opposite } \angle A}{\text{length of hypotenuse}}$$

$$\cos A = \frac{\text{length of leg adjacent to } \angle A}{\text{length of hypotenuse}}$$

$$\tan A = \frac{\text{length of leg opposite } \angle A}{\text{length of leg adjacent to } \angle A}$$

Do You UNDERSTAND?

1. **ESSENTIAL QUESTION** How do trigonometric ratios relate angle measures to side lengths of right triangles?

2. **Error Analysis** What is the error in this equation for a trigonometric ratio? © **MP.3**

$$\sin A = \frac{2}{4.5}$$

3. **Vocabulary** How is finding the inverses of trigonometric ratios similar to using inverse operations?

4. **Communicate Precisely** How is the sine ratio similar to the cosine ratio? How is it different? © **MP.6**

5. **Look for Relationships** If $\sin A = \frac{a}{c}$, how could you use *a* and *c* to find cos *A*? © **MP.7**

6. **Reason** What is an expression for *d* using $x°$, $y°$, and *h*? © **MP.2**

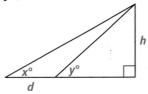

Do You KNOW HOW?

For Exercises 7–12, use △*ABC* to find each trigonometric ratio or angle measure.

7. tan *B*
8. cos *B*
9. sin *A*
10. tan *A*
11. $m\angle B$
12. $m\angle A$

13. What are the sine and cosine of the smallest angle in the right triangle shown?

14. What is the measure of the largest acute angle in the right triangle shown?

15. In the figure shown, what are $m\angle S$ and $m\angle T$?

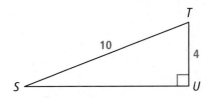

PRACTICE & PROBLEM SOLVING

UNDERSTAND

16. Error Analysis Jacinta's teacher asks her to find the tangent of ∠Y. What is her error? © MP.3

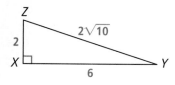

$$\tan Y = \frac{XY}{XZ}$$
$$\tan Y = \frac{6}{2}$$
$$\tan Y = 3$$

17. Make Sense and Persevere If sin B = 0.5 in the triangle shown, what is an expression for AB? © MP.1

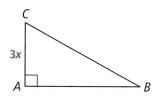

18. Reason Every tread of a staircase is 8 in. deep, and every riser is 6 in. high. How would you find the angle the staircase makes with the floor? Explain. © MP.2

19. Mathematical Connections Find the values.

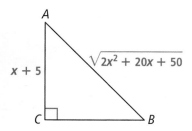

a. sin B   **b.** m<B

20. Higher Order Thinking Why are the sine and cosine ratios of x° never greater than one? Use the triangle below to explain your reasoning. © MP.3

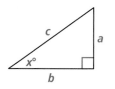

PRACTICE

For Exercises 21–23, write each ratio. SEE EXAMPLE 1

21. sin x°   **22.** cos x°   **23.** tan x°

For Exercises 24–29, find each value. SEE EXAMPLE 2

24. sin x°   **25.** cos x°   **26.** tan x°

27. sin y°   **28.** cos y°   **29.** tan y°

For Exercises 30–35, find each value. SEE EXAMPLE 3

30. sin 30°   **31.** cos 60°   **32.** sin 45°

33. tan 45°   **34.** cos 30°   **35.** tan 60°

36. Write an expression for cos 68° using sine.

37. Write an expression for sin 44° using cosine.

For Exercises 38 and 39, find each length.
SEE EXAMPLE 4

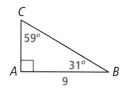

38. AC   **39.** BC

For Exercises 40–43, find the angle measures in each triangle. SEE EXAMPLE 5

40. m∠B

41. m∠C

42. m∠K

43. m∠L

LESSON 8-2 Trigonometric Ratios   363

PRACTICE & PROBLEM SOLVING

APPLY

44. Make Sense and Persevere Workers need to make repairs on a building. A boom lift has maximum height of 60 ft at an angle of 48°. If the bottom of the boom lift is 60 ft from the building, can the boom reach the top of the building? Explain. ⒸMP.1

45. Model With Mathematics A coach draws up a play so a quarterback throws the football at the same time as a receiver runs straight down the field. The quarterback throws the football at a speed of 40 ft/s and the receiver runs at a speed of 24 ft/s. At what angle $x°$ to the horizontal must the quarterback throw the ball for the receiver to catch it? Explain. ⒸMP.4

46. Use Structure Kelsey puts up an inflatable gorilla to advertise a sale. She realizes that she needs to secure the figure with rope. She estimates she needs to attach three pieces at the angles shown. How much rope does Kelsey need? Round to the nearest foot. ⒸMP.7

ASSESSMENT PRACTICE

47. Match each expression to a trigonometric ratio.

I. cos ∠ACD	**A.** $\frac{12}{13}$
II. tan ∠ABC	**B.** $\frac{4}{5}$
III. sin ∠BAC	**C.** $\frac{3}{5}$
IV. cos ∠CAD	**D.** $\frac{5}{12}$

48. SAT/ACT What is the value of cos $x°$?

Ⓐ $\frac{\sqrt{5}}{2}$ Ⓑ $\frac{3}{2}$ Ⓒ $\frac{\sqrt{5}}{3}$ Ⓓ $\frac{2}{3}$

49. Performance Task Jamar anchors a retractable leash to a tree and attaches the leash to his dog's collar. When the dog fully extends the leash, the angle between the leash and the tree is 84°.

Part A If a neighbor's yard is 18 feet away from the tree, can Jamar's dog get into the neighbor's yard? If so, how far into the yard can the dog go? Round to nearest tenth of a foot.

Part B If Jamar wants to make sure his dog cannot get within 1 foot of the neighbor's yard, how high up the tree must he anchor the leash? Round to the nearest tenth of a foot.

8-3

The Law of Sines

I CAN... use the Law of Sines to solve problems.

VOCABULARY
• Law of Sines

Ⓒ Common Core State Standards
HSG.SRT.D.10 (+), HSG.SRT.D.11 (+), MP.1, MP.2, MP.4

EXPLORE & REASON

Consider the 30°-60°-90° triangle shown.

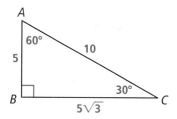

A. Calculate the values of the ratios $\frac{\sin A}{BC}$ and $\frac{\sin C}{AB}$. How are the values of the ratios related?

B. **Make Sense and Persevere** Do you think the ratios would have the same relationship in any 30°-60°-90° right triangle? Explain your answer. **Ⓒ MP.1**

ESSENTIAL QUESTION

How can the Law of Sines be used to determine side lengths and angle measures in acute and obtuse triangles?

CONCEPTUAL UNDERSTANDING

EXAMPLE 1   Explore the Sine Ratio

How can you use the sine ratio to relate the lengths and angle measures in △ABC?

Construct the altitude $\overline{AD}$ from vertex A.

The altitude intersects $\overline{BC}$ at point D, forming right triangles △ADB and △ADC.

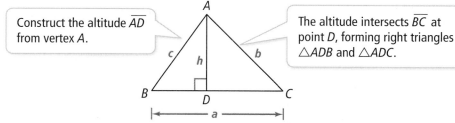

Write equations for sin B and sin C using the right triangles.

$$\sin B = \frac{h}{c} \qquad \sin C = \frac{h}{b}$$
$$c \sin B = h \qquad b \sin C = h$$

Solve each equation for h.

Set the two expressions for h equal to each other.

$$c \sin B = b \sin C$$
$$\frac{\sin B}{b} = \frac{\sin C}{c}$$

The definition of the sine ratio only includes acute angles. For triangles with right and obtuse angles, you can extend the definition of sine and cosine to include these angles.

STUDY TIP
Recall that the sine ratio relates the length of the opposite side to the length of the hypotenuse.

Try It!   **1.** For Example 1, show that $\frac{\sin A}{a} = \frac{\sin B}{b} = \frac{\sin C}{c}$.

CONCEPT Law of Sines

For any $\triangle ABC$ with side lengths a, b, and c opposite angles A, B, and C, respectively, the **Law of Sines** relates the sine of each angle to the length of the opposite side.

$$\frac{\sin A}{a} = \frac{\sin B}{b} = \frac{\sin C}{c}$$

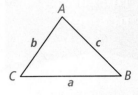

EXAMPLE 2 Use the Law of Sines to Find a Side Length

For $\triangle XYZ$, what is YZ to the nearest tenth?

Identify pairs of known sides and angles.

- The measure of $\angle Z$ and the length of its opposite side $\overline{XY}$ are known.
- The measure of $\angle X$ is known. The length of $\overline{YZ}$ is the unknown quantity.

COMMON ERROR
Be careful to correctly write the ratio of the sine of an angle and its opposite side length. It may be helpful to draw an arrow from each angle that points to its opposite side.

Use the Law of Sines to write and solve an equation for YZ.

$$\frac{\sin 77°}{7} = \frac{\sin 51°}{YZ} \qquad \boxed{\frac{\sin Z}{XY} = \frac{\sin X}{YZ}}$$

$$YZ = \frac{7 \sin 51°}{\sin 77°}$$

$$YZ \approx 5.6 \qquad \boxed{\text{Use a calculator.} \\ 7 \;\fbox{×}\; \fbox{SIN}\; 51 \;\fbox{÷}\; \fbox{SIN}\; 77}$$

Try It! 2. In Example 2, what is XZ to the nearest tenth?

EXAMPLE 3 Use Law of Sines to Find the Measure of an Angle

What are $m\angle R$ and $m\angle S$ in $\triangle RST$?

HAVE A GROWTH MINDSET
In what ways do you give your best effort and persist?

Step 1 Use the Law of Sines to write and solve an equation to find $\sin S$.

$$\frac{\sin S}{RT} = \frac{\sin T}{RS}$$

$$\frac{\sin S}{12.7} = \frac{\sin 74°}{12.3}$$

$$\sin S = \frac{12.7 \sin 74°}{12.3}$$

$$\sin S \approx 0.9925$$

> You know $m\angle T$ and the length of the side opposite $\angle T$. You also know the length of the side opposite $\angle S$.

Step 2 Use the inverse function $\sin^{-1}$ to find $m\angle S$.

$$\sin^{-1}(\sin S) = \sin^{-1}(0.9925)$$

$$m\angle S \approx 83$$

Step 3 Find $m\angle R$.

$$m\angle R \approx 180 - 74 - 83$$

$$\approx 23$$

CONTINUED ON THE NEXT PAGE

EXAMPLE 3 CONTINUED

Try It! **3. a.** What is $m\angle N$?

b. What is $m\angle O$?

APPLICATION

EXAMPLE 4 Apply the Law of Sines

The map shows the path a pilot flew between Omaha and Chicago in order to avoid a thunderstorm. How much longer is this route than the direct route to Chicago?

MAKE SENSE AND PERSEVERE
Think about what the problem is asking. Which distances are you supposed to find? © MP.1

STUDY TIP
So far, you have found the sine and cosine of angles with measures less than 90°. You can also find the sine and cosine of an angle with measure greater than 90°.

Step 1 Let x represent the distance from the turning point to Omaha. Find x.

Use the Law of Sines.

$$\frac{\sin 113°}{471} = \frac{\sin 22°}{x}$$

$$x = \frac{471 \sin 22°}{\sin 113°}$$

$$x \approx 191.7$$

Step 2 Let y represent the distance from Chicago to the turning point. Find y.

First determine the measure of the angle opposite y.

$$180° - 113° - 22° = 45°$$

Then use the Law of Sines.

$$\frac{\sin 113°}{471} = \frac{\sin 45°}{y}$$

$$y = \frac{471 \sin 45°}{\sin 113°}$$

$$y \approx 361.8$$

Step 3 Find the total distance the pilot flew.

$$191.7 \text{ mi} + 361.8 \text{ mi} = 553.5 \text{ mi}$$

The pilot flew 553.5 mi − 471 mi = 82.5 mi farther.

Try It! **4.** Suppose the pilot chose to fly north of the storm. How much farther is that route than the direct route?

CONCEPT SUMMARY Law of Sines

WORDS For any △*ABC* with side lengths *a*, *b*, and *c* opposite angles *A*, *B*, and *C*, respectively, the Law of Sines relates the sine of each angle to the length of the opposite side.

DIAGRAM

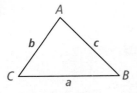

SYMBOLS

$$\frac{\sin A}{a} = \frac{\sin B}{b} = \frac{\sin C}{c}$$

Do You UNDERSTAND?

1. **ESSENTIAL QUESTION** How can the Law of Sines be used to determine side lengths and angle measures in acute and obtuse triangles?

2. **Error Analysis** Amelia is asked to find a missing side length in △*RST*. What is her error? Ⓒ **MP.3**

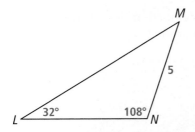

3. **Vocabulary** What are the pairs of opposite angles and side lengths in △*LMN*? What does the Law of Sines help you find?

Figure for Exercise 3 (△LMN with M, 5, L 32°, 108° N)

4. **Reason** Can you find all the missing parts of a triangle using the Law of Sines if you know the lengths of all three sides? Explain. Ⓒ **MP.2**

Do You KNOW HOW?

For Exercises 5 and 6, list the parts of each triangle you can determine using the Law of Sines.

5.

6.

For Exercises 7 and 8, use △*QRS*.

7. What are *m∠Q* and *m∠R*?

8. What is the perimeter of △*QRS*?

For Exercises 9 and 10, use △*XYZ*.

9. What is *XY*?

10. What is *XZ*?

11. What are *AB* and *BC*?

12. What is the perimeter of △*TUV*?

PRACTICE & PROBLEM SOLVING

UNDERSTAND

13. Error Analysis Andrés is asked to find $m\angle M$. What is his error? ☉ **MP.3**

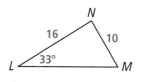

$$\frac{\sin M}{16} = \frac{\sin L}{10}$$

$$\sin M = \frac{16 \cdot \sin 33°}{10}$$

$$m\angle M = 0.8714$$

14. Construct Arguments Suppose you only know the lengths and angle measures of two triangles used to show they are congruent by SAS. Can you find the missing angle measures and side lengths of the triangles using the Law of Sines? Explain. ☉ **MP.3**

15. Communicate Precisely The measures of two angles are given along with the measure of the side opposite the third angle of a triangle. How can the Law of Sines be used to find missing angle measures and side lengths of the triangle? Explain. ☉ **MP.6**

16. Mathematical Connections What is AC? Use both the Distance Formula and the Law of Sines. How do the values compare? Explain.

17. Reason Explain how to use the Law of Sines to find the perimeter of $\triangle PQR$. Then write an expression for the perimeter. ☉ **MP.2**

PRACTICE

For Exercises 18–23, find each length x. Round to the nearest tenth. SEE EXAMPLES 1 AND 2

18.

19.

20.

21.

22.

23.

For Exercises 24–29, find each angle measure $x°$. Round to the nearest tenth. SEE EXAMPLE 3

24.

25.

26.

27.

28.

29.

For Exercises 30–33, find the perimeter of each triangle. Round to the nearest tenth. SEE EXAMPLE 4

30.

31.

32.

33.

PRACTICE & PROBLEM SOLVING

34. Make Sense and Persevere To find the height of a tree, a forester uses a clinometer to measure the angle to the top of the tree. She then measures again at a distance 8 feet farther away. What is the height of the tree? Round to the nearest foot. © MP.1

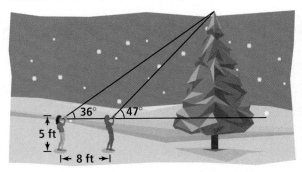

35. Model With Mathematics At point *A*, the pilot of a plane looks down at an angle of 7° at the landing strip. After flying up to point *B*, the pilot looks down at an angle of 9° to see the landing strip. What is the distance from point *B* to the landing strip if the distance from point *A* to point *B* is 1,100 ft? Round to the nearest foot.

© MP.4

36. Higher Order Thinking A boat is cruising due east. At point *X*, the captain measures the angle east of north to a pier. At point *Y*, he again measures the angle east of north to the pier. A restricted area with radius 2.5 miles is centered at the end of the pier. Does the boat enter the restricted area? Explain.

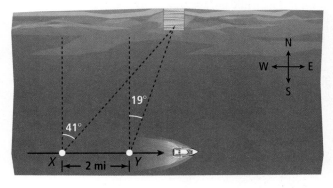

ASSESSMENT PRACTICE

37. What is the value of *x*? Round to the nearest tenth.

38. SAT/ACT What is the measure of the angle made by the roads at Bigville?

Ⓐ 55.10°   Ⓒ 49.60°

Ⓑ 72.28°   Ⓓ 40.40°

39. Performance Task An engineer is designing a walkway for an aquarium, but she only receives the partial information shown for the supports of the walkway. She must determine the lengths of the remaining supports to complete the design.

AC = 21.4 ft
BD = 15.2 ft

Part A What is *AB* to the nearest tenth of a foot?

Part B The engineer decides she wants beams from point *A* to the left end of the walkway and from point *D* to the right end of the walkway. Is there enough information given to find the lengths? If so, find the lengths. If not, explain what other information she needs.

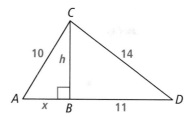
8-4

The Law of Cosines

I CAN... use the Law of Cosines to solve problems.

VOCABULARY
• Law of Cosines

© **Common Core State Standards**
HSG.SRT.D.10 (+), HSG.SRT.D.11 (+),
MP.2, MP.4, MP.7

EXPLORE & REASON

Use △ACD to answer the questions.

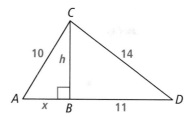

A. Write equations for the side lengths of △ABC and △CBD using the Pythagorean Theorem.

B. Use a system of equations to solve for x.

C. Use Structure How can you use the information you found to determine m∠A? © **MP.7**

| **ESSENTIAL QUESTION** | How can the Law of Cosines be used to determine side lengths and angle measures of acute and obtuse triangles? |

CONCEPTUAL UNDERSTANDING

EXAMPLE 1 Develop the Law of Cosines with Trigonometry

Triangle ABC is not a right triangle. How can you use a cosine ratio to write an equation relating the side lengths a, b, and c?

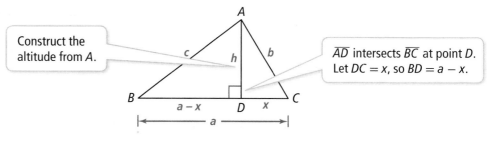

Construct the altitude from A.

$\overline{AD}$ intersects $\overline{BC}$ at point D. Let $DC = x$, so $BD = a - x$.

Use the Pythagorean Theorem with △ABD. Then distribute and combine like terms.

$$c^2 = (a - x)^2 + h^2$$
$$c^2 = a^2 - 2ax + x^2 + h^2$$
$$c^2 = a^2 - 2ax + b^2$$
$$c^2 = a^2 - 2ab(\cos C) + b^2$$
$$c^2 = a^2 + b^2 - 2ab \cos C$$

△ACD is a right triangle, so $x^2 + h^2 = b^2$. Substitute b^2 for $x^2 + h^2$.

Since $\cos C = \frac{x}{b}$, $x = b(\cos C)$. Substitute $b(\cos C)$ for x.

Thus, given side lengths a and b of a triangle and the included angle measure, you can find the length c of the third side by taking the square root of the expression on the right side of the equation.

Try It! **1.** Use the same method as in Example 1 to write equations for a^2 using cos A and b^2 using cos B.

CONCEPT Law of Cosines

For any $\triangle ABC$, the **Law of Cosines** relates the cosine of each angle to the side lengths of the triangle.

$$a^2 = b^2 + c^2 - 2bc \cos A$$

$$b^2 = a^2 + c^2 - 2ac \cos B$$

$$c^2 = a^2 + b^2 - 2ab \cos C$$

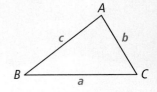

EXAMPLE 2 Use the Law of Cosines to Find a Side Length

What is BC to the nearest tenth?

> The side length opposite $\angle A$ is unknown. You know two side lengths and the measure of their included angle, $\angle A$.

USE STRUCTURE
What information does the Law of Cosines provide that the Law of Sines does not? © MP.7

Use the Law of Cosines to write and solve an equation for BC.

$$BC^2 = AB^2 + AC^2 - 2(AB)(AC) \cos A$$

$$BC^2 \approx 8^2 + 10^2 - 2(8)(10)(0.5446)$$

$$BC^2 \approx 76.864$$

$$BC \approx 8.8$$

Try It! **2. a.** What is DE?

b. What is GH?

EXAMPLE 3 Use the Law of Cosines to Find an Angle Measure

The optimal tilt for Keenan's solar panel is between 58° and 60° to the horizontal. Has Keenan placed his solar panel at an optimal angle?

Write an equation using the Law of Cosines. Then use the inverse cosine to find $m\angle P$.

COMMON ERROR
In applying the Law of Cosines, be sure to correctly place the included angle measure and the length of the side opposite the include angle on opposite sides of the equation.

$$QR^2 = PR^2 + PQ^2 - 2(PQ)(QR)\cos P$$

$$19^2 = 18^2 + 20^2 - 2(18)(20)\cos P$$

$$\cos P = \frac{-363}{-720}$$

$$\cos P \approx 0.5042$$

$$m\angle P \approx 59.72°$$

Keenan has placed his solar panel at an optimal angle.

CONTINUED ON THE NEXT PAGE

EXAMPLE 3 CONTINUED

Try It! **3. a.** What is $m\angle X$?   **b.** What is $m\angle P$?

 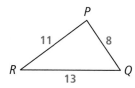

APPLICATION

EXAMPLE 4 Use the Law of Cosines to Solve a Problem

The district ranger wants to build a new ranger station at the location of the fire tower because it would be closer to Bald Mountain than the old station is. Is the district ranger correct? Explain.

Formulate ◄ The ranger station, Bald Mountain, and the fire tower form the vertices of a triangle. Label the ranger station vertex A, Bald Mountain vertex B, and the fire tower vertex C. Draw the triangle.

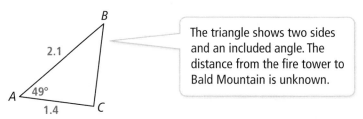

The triangle shows two sides and an included angle. The distance from the fire tower to Bald Mountain is unknown.

Compute ◄ Use the Law of Cosines to write an equation for the unknown.

$$BC^2 = AC^2 + AB^2 - 2(AC)(AB)\cos A$$

$$BC^2 = 1.4^2 + 2.1^2 - 2(1.4)(2.1)(\cos 49°)$$

Substitute the known values and solve.

$$BC^2 \approx 2.512$$

$$BC \approx 1.6$$

Interpret ◄ The distance from the fire tower to Bald Mountain is about 1.6 miles, so the district ranger is correct that a new station at the fire tower would be closer.

Try It! **4.** In Example 4, what is the angle that the new path forms with the old path at Bald Mountain?

CONCEPT SUMMARY Law of Cosines

WORDS For any △ABC, the Law of Cosines relates the cosine of each angle to the side lengths of the triangle.

SYMBOLS
$a^2 = b^2 + c^2 - 2bc \cos A$
$b^2 = a^2 + c^2 - 2ac \cos B$
$c^2 = a^2 + b^2 - 2ab \cos C$

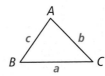

Do You UNDERSTAND?

1. **ESSENTIAL QUESTION** How can the Law of Cosines be used to determine side lengths and angle measures of acute and obtuse triangles?

2. **Error Analysis** Cameron is asked to find *DE*. What is his error? ⒸMP.3

$DE^2 = DF^2 + EF^2 - 2(DF)(EF)\cos F$
$DE^2 = 8^2 + 6^2 - 2(8)(6)\cos 62°$
$DE^2 = 54.930...$
$DE = 7.411...$ ✗

3. **Vocabulary** How would you describe the Law of Cosines in words?

4. **Construct Arguments** With the Law of Sines and the Law of Cosines, can you find the missing side lengths and angle measures of any triangle for which you know any three parts? Explain. ⒸMP.3

5. **Reason** Use the Law of Cosines and the Pythagorean Theorem with △ABC to show that cos 90° = 0. ⒸMP.2

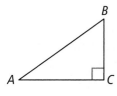

Do You KNOW HOW?

For Exercises 6–9, list the parts of each triangle you can determine using the Law of Cosines.

6.

7.

8.

9.

10. What is *PR* to the nearest tenth?

11. What is *m∠B* to the nearest tenth of a degree?

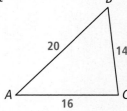

12. Use the Law of Cosines to find the diagonal of the parallelogram.

PRACTICE & PROBLEM SOLVING

UNDERSTAND

13. Construct Arguments How is the Law of Cosines used to find missing angle measures if the side lengths of a triangle are given? Explain. ⓒ **MP.3**

14. Error Analysis Tavon is asked to find *EF*. What error does Tavon make? ⓒ **MP.3**

$$EF^2 = DF^2 + DE^2 - 2(DF)(DE)\cos D$$
$$EF^2 = 8^2 + 10^2 - 2(8)(10)\cos 44°$$
$$EF^2 \approx 64 + 100 - 160 \cdot 0.7193$$
$$EF \approx 48.91$$

✗

15. Higher Order Thinking Use the diagram to show that for acute angle $x°$, $\cos(180 - x)° = -\frac{a}{c}$. *Hint:* Apply the Law of Cosines to $\triangle ABD$ and write an equation involving $\cos(180 - x)°$. Then, for $\triangle ABC$, use the relationship $a^2 + b^2 = c^2$.

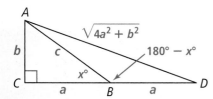

16. Generalize Suppose you know two of the side lengths of a triangle and the measure of one of the angles. How do you choose whether to find the third side length using the Law of Sines or the Law of Cosines? Explain. ⓒ **MP.8**

17. Look for Relationships Consider $\triangle ABC$.

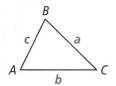

a. How would you find $m\angle A$ if you were given a, b, and c? Include an equation in your explanation.

b. How would you find a if you were given $m\angle A$, b, and c? Include an equation in your explanation. ⓒ **MP.7**

PRACTICE

For Exercises 18 and 19, use $\triangle DEF$. Find an equation for each length. SEE EXAMPLE 1

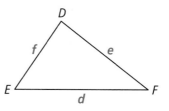

18. length e **19.** length f

For Exercises 20–23, find x to the nearest tenth. SEE EXAMPLE 2

20.   **21.**

22.   **23.**

For Exercises 24–27, find x to the nearest tenth. SEE EXAMPLE 3

24.   **25.**

26.   **27.**

28. A golfer hits a ball from a tee that is 300 yards from the hole. The ball lands 275 yards from the tee, but is 13° off line from the hole. How much farther must the golfer now hit the ball to reach the hole? SEE EXAMPLE 4

PRACTICE & PROBLEM SOLVING

29. Model With Mathematics Alejandro, Camilla, and Damian are practicing for a game that is played on a field and uses a flying disc. Alejandro has the disc and Camilla is in the end zone, but Alejandro can only throw accurately for distances of 7.5 m or less. He throws the disc to Damian, because Damian can throw with accuracy up to 9.5 m. Is Camilla within Damian's range of accuracy? Explain. ⒼMP.4

30. Mathematical Connections Two rescue workers leave at the same time to find an injured hiker. The first walks 25° west of north at 3.5 mi/h, and the second walks 36° east of north at 2.5 mi/h.

After 2 hours, the second worker finds the hiker and radios the first worker for help. If the first worker jogs directly to the second worker at 6 mi/h, how long will it take for her to arrive?

31. Make Sense and Persevere An architect proposes the plan shown for a new roof with a 40° incline on one side. The owner of the house thinks that 40° is not steep enough and wants the incline to be 50°. If the length of the adjacent side does not change, by how much does the length, x ft, of the opposite side increase? What is the new angle of incline for the opposite side? ⒼMP.1

32. Which equations are true for the triangle shown? Select all that apply.

- ☐ **A.** $a^2 = 16 + 49 - 28 \cos 30°$
- ☐ **B.** $16 = a^2 + 49 - (14a)\cos 30°$
- ☐ **C.** $49 = a^2 + 16 - (4a)\cos 67°$
- ☐ **D.** $a^2 = 49 + 16 - 56 \cos 67°$
- ☐ **E.** $49 = a^2 + 16 - (8a)\cos 83°$

33. SAT/ACT A triangle has sides with lengths 12 cm and 15 cm. The measure of the included angle is 46°. What is the length of the third side, to the nearest tenth of a centimeter?

- Ⓐ 24.9 cm
- Ⓒ 13.0 cm
- Ⓑ 10.5 cm
- Ⓓ 10.9 cm

34. Performance Task A medical supply drone leaves Port A traveling 40 degrees east of north. After flying 32 mi on that course to point C, the drone turns 50° to the right to fly due east. It then flies another 8 mi, where it makes a drop at Island Port.

Part A The drone can fly a total distance of 75 miles before it needs to recharge. Can it fly directly back to Port A from Island Port? Explain.

Part B Port B is 24 miles due north of Port A. What is the distance from Island Port to Port B? Can the drone fly to Port B?

Part C Port B appears to be directly west of Island Port. Is it? If so, explain. If not, what direction is it from Island Port?

Ⓒ **Common Core State Standards**
HSG.SRT.C.8, MP.4

Ⓥ SavvasRealize.com

The Impossible Measurement

Tall buildings are often some of the most recognizable structures of cities. The Empire State Building in New York City, the Transamerica Pyramid in San Francisco, and the JPMorgan Chase Tower in Houston are all famous landmarks in those cities.

Cities around the world compete for the tallest building bragging rights. Which city currently has the tallest building? This Mathematical Modeling in 3 Acts lesson will get you thinking about the height of structures, including tall buildings such as these.

ACT 1 ▷ **Identify the Problem**

1. What is the first question that comes to mind after watching the video?

2. Write down the main question you will answer about what you saw in the video.

3. Make an initial conjecture that answers this main question.

4. Explain how you arrived at your conjecture.

5. What information will be useful to know to answer the main question? How can you get it? How will you use that information?

ACT 2 ▷ **Develop a Model**

6. Use the math that you have learned in the topic to refine your conjecture.

ACT 3 ▷ **Interpret the Results**

7. Did your refined conjecture match the actual answer exactly? If not, what might explain the difference?

8-5
Problem Solving With Trigonometry

I CAN... use trigonometry to solve problems.

VOCABULARY
- angle of depression
- angle of elevation

© Common Core State Standards
HSG.SRT.D.11 (+), HSG.SRT.C.8, HSG.SRT.D.9 (+), MP.3, MP.5, MP.6

MODEL & DISCUSS

A search-and-rescue team is having a nighttime practice drill. Two members of the team are in a helicopter that is hovering at 2,000 feet above ground level.

2,000 ft

B   A   C

1,800 ft
3,200 ft
4,500 ft

A. The team first tries to locate object A. At what angle from the horizontal line even with the helicopter should they position the spotlight so that it shines on object A?

B. Next, they shine the spotlight on object B. How does the angle of the spotlight from the horizontal line change?

C. **Use Structure** In general, how does the angle of the spotlight from the horizontal change as the light moves from object A to object B? From object A to object C? **© MP.7**

ESSENTIAL QUESTION   How can trigonometry be used to solve real-world and mathematical problems?

EXAMPLE 1   Identify Angles of Elevation and Depression

Identify ∠2 as an angle of elevation or an angle of depression. Do the same for ∠3. Explain your reasoning.

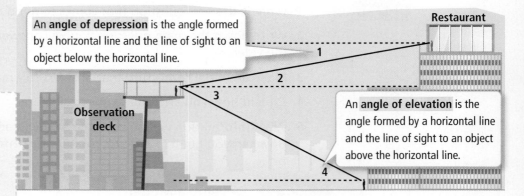

An **angle of depression** is the angle formed by a horizontal line and the line of sight to an object below the horizontal line.

Restaurant

1

2

3

Observation deck

An **angle of elevation** is the angle formed by a horizontal line and the line of sight to an object above the horizontal line.

4

STUDY TIP
When solving problems involving an angle of elevation or an angle of depression, it may help to use a diagram and look for right triangles.

To see the person above, the person on the observation deck is looking up from the horizontal, so ∠2 is an angle of elevation.

To see the person below, the person on the observation deck is looking down from the horizontal, so ∠3 is an angle of depression.

Try It!   **1.** In Example 1, how does the angle of depression, ∠1, compare with the angle of elevation, ∠2? Explain your reasoning.

EXAMPLE 2 ▶ Use Angles of Elevation and Depression

For a reverse bungee ride, Reagan stands halfway between two posts. Two bungee cords extend from the top of the posts to Reagan's waist, 1 m above the ground, and at a 70°-angle of elevation. How tall are the posts?

The post, the ground, and a bungee cord form a right triangle. Write an equation to determine x, the vertical distance in meters from the top of a post to a point 1 meter above the ground.

$$\tan 70° = \frac{x}{4}$$

$$x = 4 \tan 70°$$

$$x \approx 10.9899, \text{ or } 11$$

> The unknown length and the 4-m length are opposite and adjacent to a 70° angle. Use the tangent ratio.

COMMON ERROR
Be careful not to forget the distance between Reagan's waist and the ground.

Find the height of the posts.

$$11 + 1 = 12$$

The posts are about 12 meters tall.

Try It! **2.** Nadeem is standing 180 feet above the ground on top of a tower. He looks down at a tour bus at an angle of depression of 23°. To the nearest foot, how far is the bus from the base of the tower?

EXAMPLE 3 ▶ Use Trigonometry to Solve Problems

An instructor holds a safety rope at point C for a student to rappel from the anchor point T. The rope between them measures 61 ft. How much more rope should the instructor let out so the student can make it to a resting point at R?

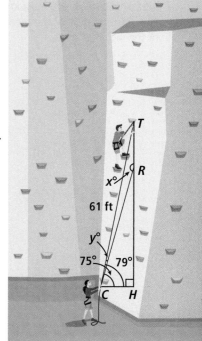

A side length and two angle measures are known for △TRC. So, use the Law of Sines to solve for TR.

Step 1 Write the Law of Sines in terms of the figure.

$$\frac{\sin x°}{CT} = \frac{\sin y°}{TR}$$

Step 2 Find y and x.

$$y = 79 - 75 = 4$$

$$m\angle CRH = 90 - 75 = 15$$

$$x = 180 - 15 = 165$$

LEARN TOGETHER
How do you listen actively as others share ideas?

Step 3 Use the proportion to solve for TR.

$$\frac{\sin 165°}{61} = \frac{\sin 4°}{TR}$$

$$TR = \frac{61(\sin 4°)}{\sin 165°} \approx 16$$

The instructor should let out about 16 ft of rope.

CONTINUED ON THE NEXT PAGE

EXAMPLE 3 CONTINUED

Try It! **3.** In Example 3, how far is the student from the instructor at the resting point?

<title>CONCEPTUAL UNDERSTANDING</title>

EXAMPLE 4 Use Trigonometry to Find Triangle Area

A. How can you use trigonometry to find the area of △ABC?

Draw altitude $\overline{BD}$ with length h.

To write a formula with side lengths b and c and included $\angle A$, apply the area formula for a triangle.

$$\text{area} = \frac{1}{2}bh$$
$$= \frac{1}{2}b(c \sin A)$$
$$= \frac{1}{2}bc \sin A$$

In △ABD, $\sin A = \frac{h}{c}$, so $h = c \sin A$.

You can apply the same reasoning to $\angle B$ and $\angle C$ to write the following area formulas.

$$\text{area} = \frac{1}{2}ac \sin B \qquad\qquad \text{area} = \frac{1}{2}ab \sin C$$

B. What is the area of △FEG?

In the triangle, the lengths of sides g and f are 3 cm and 4 cm, respectively, and the measure of the included angle is 116°.

STUDY TIP
In order to use the formula area $= \frac{1}{2}bc \sin A$, you must know two side lengths and the measure of the included angle.

$$\text{area} = \frac{1}{2}gf \sin E$$
$$= \frac{1}{2}(3)(4) \sin 116°$$
$$= 6 \sin 116°$$
$$\approx 5.4$$

The area of the triangle is about 5.4 cm^2.

Try It! **4. a.** What is the area of △JKL?   **b.** What is the area of △PQR?

CONCEPT SUMMARY Using Trigonometry to Solve Problems

Angles of Elevation or Depression	Area Formulas

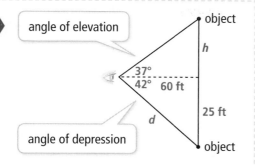

angle of elevation

object

h

37°
42° 60 ft

25 ft

d

angle of depression

object

B

c h a

A D C

b

SYMBOLS

$\tan 37° = \dfrac{h}{60}$

$\sin 42° = \dfrac{25}{d}$

$\text{area} = \dfrac{1}{2} bc \sin A$

$\text{area} = \dfrac{1}{2} ac \sin B$

$\text{area} = \dfrac{1}{2} ab \sin C$

Do You UNDERSTAND?

1. **ESSENTIAL QUESTION** How can trigonometry be used to solve real-world and mathematical problems?

2. **Error Analysis** What error does Rashon make in finding the area? ⓒ MP.3

21 in.

122° 10 in.

14 in.

$A = \dfrac{1}{2} bc \sin A$

$A = \dfrac{1}{2} \cdot 210 \cdot 0.8480$

Area is about 89 in.^{2}

3. **Vocabulary** A person on a balcony and a person on a street look at each other. Draw a diagram to represent the situation and label the angles of elevation and depression.

4. **Make Sense and Persevere** How do you find the area of a triangle when given only the lengths of three sides? ⓒ MP.1

Do You KNOW HOW?

5. A person rides a glass elevator in a hotel lobby. As the elevator goes up, how does the angle of depression to a fixed point on the lobby floor change?

6. A person observes the top of a radio antenna at an angle of elevation of 5°. After getting 1 mile closer to the antenna, the angle of elevation is 10°. How tall is the antenna to the nearest tenth of a foot?

5° 10°

5,280 ft

7. Triangle ABC has $AB = 13$, $AC = 15$, and $m\angle A = 59$. What is the area of the triangle to the nearest tenth?

8. Triangle DEF has $DE = 13$, $DF = 15$, and $EF = 14$. What is the area of the triangle to the nearest tenth?

9. A temporary pen for cattle is built using 10-foot sections of fence arranged in a triangle. One side of the pen has 4 sections, one has 5 sections, and the last has 6 sections. What is the area enclosed by the pen?

UNDERSTAND

10. **Construct Arguments** How is the area of a triangle determined if the lengths of two sides and the measure of the included angle are given? Ⓒ **MP.3**

11. **Error Analysis** Leah is asked to find *AC*. What is her error? Ⓒ **MP.3**

$$AC^2 = AB^2 + BC^2 - 2(AB)(BC)\sin A$$
$$AC^2 = 18^2 + 16^2 - 2(18)(16)\sin 30°$$
$$AC^2 = 292$$
$$AC \approx 17.1$$

✗

12. **Mathematical Connections** Find the length of the diagonal of the isosceles trapezoid. Then find the length of the fourth side.

13. **Look for Relationships** For each triangle, write an equation for *x* using a trigonometric function. Ⓒ **MP.7**

a.

b.

14. **Higher Order Thinking** What is a formula for the area of the parallelogram in the figure? Explain.

15. **Use Appropriate Tools** What is the angle of elevation to the top of a building that is 1,000 m away and is 300 m high? Ⓒ **MP.5**

PRACTICE

16. Identify each numbered angle as an angle of elevation or an angle of depression. **SEE EXAMPLE 1**

17. To what angle of depression should the security camera be adjusted in order to have the lens aimed at point *P* on the ground? **SEE EXAMPLE 2**

18. An angle of elevation to the sun is 21.5°. What is the length of the shadow cast by a person 5 ft 6 in. tall? **SEE EXAMPLE 2**

19. Libby's eyes are 5 ft above the ground, and the angle of elevation of her line of sight to the top of the Washington Monument is 74°. How far is she from the monument? **SEE EXAMPLE 3**

20. Triangle *GHJ* has *GH* = 13, *GJ* = 15, and *m∠G* = 74. What is the area of the triangle? **SEE EXAMPLE 4**

21. What is the area of each triangle? **SEE EXAMPLE 4**

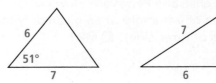

22. Triangle *KLM* has *KL* = 22, *KM* = 27, and *LM* = 29. What is the area of the triangle? **SEE EXAMPLE 4**

PRACTICE & PROBLEM SOLVING

23. Model With Mathematics A research submarine dives at a speed of 100 ft/min directly toward the research lab. How long will it take the submarine to reach the lab from the surface of the ocean to the nearest tenth of a minute? Ⓒ MP.4

24. Make Sense and Persevere Benito aims for the center of the target from a distance of 70 meters. If Benito shoots an arrow at a 0.055° angle of depression below the center, will he hit the yellow circle? Explain. Ⓒ MP.1

25. Reason Ramona is climbing a hill with a 10° incline and wants to know the height of the rock formation. She walks 100 ft up the hill and uses a clinometer to measure the angle of elevation to the top of the formation. She then walks another 229.4 ft to the top of the hill. What is the height h of the rock formation? Ⓒ MP.2

26. What is the area of the triangle? Round to the nearest one hundredth of a square unit.

27. SAT/ACT Which of the following equations is true?

  I. $\tan B = \frac{4}{3}$

  II. $AD = 2\sqrt{7}$

  III. $AB^2 = BD^2 + AD^2 - 2 \bullet (BD) \bullet (AD)\cos 30°$

Ⓐ I only   Ⓒ III only

Ⓑ II only   Ⓓ II and III only

28. Performance Task An amateur astronomer sets up his telescope in the center of a circular field. The field is surrounded by trees 20 m tall. The tripod holding the telescope pivots 1 m above the ground.

Part A What is the lowest angle of elevation at which the astronomer can observe a star?

Part B If the astronomer wants to observe a star 15° above the horizon to the east, how far west must the astronomer move the telescope to see the star?.

Part C If the astronomer sets up the telescope in the center of the field on the bed of a truck 1.5 meters above the ground, what is the lowest angle at which he can observe?

Topic Review

1. How are the Pythagorean Theorem and trigonometry useful?

Vocabulary Review

Choose the correct term to complete each sentence.

2. The ratio of the length of the leg adjacent to an acute angle in a right triangle to the length of the hypotenuse is the _____ of the angle.

3. The _____ gives a relationship between the sine of each angle in a triangle and the length of the side opposite the angle.

4. The angle formed by a horizontal line and a line of sight to an object above the line is a(n) _____.

5. A(n) _____ is a set of three nonzero whole numbers that satisfies the equation $a^2 + b^2 = c^2$.

- angle of depression
- angle of elevation
- cosine
- Law of Cosines
- Law of Sines
- Pythagorean triple
- sine
- tangent
- trigonometric ratio

Concepts & Skills Review

LESSONS 8-1 & 8-2 **Right Triangles and The Pythagorean Theorem, and Trigonometric Ratios**

Quick Review

Given △ABC, the Pythagorean Theorem states $a^2 + b^2 = c^2$.

The **trigonometric ratios** are

$\sin A = \frac{a}{c}$ $\cos A = \frac{b}{c}$ $\tan A = \frac{a}{b}$.

Example

Given △DEF, what is sin D?

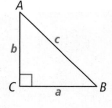

Step 1 Use the Pythagorean Theorem to find x.

$8^2 + 6^2 = x^2$
$10 = x$

Step 2 Use a trigonometric ratio to find sin D.

$\sin D = \frac{8}{10} = \frac{4}{5}$

Practice & Problem Solving

For Exercises 6–8, use △ABC to find each value.

6. BC   7. cos B

8. $m\angle A$ to the nearest tenth

9. Kendis has 16 feet of rope to stake out the front part of her tent. Does she have enough rope? Explain.

10. **Make Sense and Persevere** Given △XYZ, what additional information do you need to find YZ? Explain. **© MP.1**

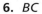

LESSONS 8-3 & 8-4 — The Law of Sines and The Law of Cosines

Quick Review

Given $\triangle ABC$, The **Law of Sines** states
$$\frac{(\sin A)}{a} = \frac{(\sin B)}{b} = \frac{(\sin C)}{c}.$$

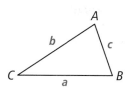

The **Law of Cosines** states
$$a^2 = b^2 + c^2 - 2bc(\cos A)$$
$$b^2 = a^2 + c^2 - 2ac(\cos B)$$
$$c^2 = a^2 + b^2 - 2ab(\cos C).$$

Example

Given $\triangle DEF$, what is EF to the nearest tenth?

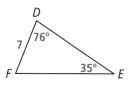

By the Law of Sines,

$$\frac{(\sin 35°)}{7} = \frac{(\sin 76°)}{EF}$$

$$EF = \frac{7(\sin 76°)}{(\sin 35°)}$$

$$EF \approx 11.8$$

Practice & Problem Solving

For Exercises 11 and 12, use $\triangle RST$ to find each measure to the nearest tenth.

11. $m\angle T$ 12. RT

For Exercises 13 and 14, use $\triangle JKL$ to find each measure to the nearest tenth.

13. JK 14. $m\angle J$

15. How wide is the gate shown, to the nearest inch?

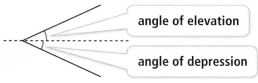

16. **Reason** How can the Law of Sines be applied to show that the expression is equivalent to the perimeter of $\triangle ABC$? **MP.2**

$$\frac{AB \sin A}{\sin C} + \frac{BC \sin B}{\sin A} + \frac{BC \sin C}{\sin A}$$

LESSON 8-5 — Problem Solving With Trigonometry

Quick Review

Many problems, such as those with angles of elevation or depression, can be modeled with triangles.

angle of elevation

angle of depression

You can use trigonometric ratios, the Law of Sines, or the Law of Cosines to solve those problems.

Example

The angle of depression from the top to the bottom of a well is 62°. If the well is 4.5 feet in diameter, how deep is it?

$$\tan 62° = \frac{x}{4.5 \text{ ft}}$$

$$x \approx 8.5 \text{ ft}$$

Practice & Problem Solving

For Exercises 17 and 18, find the area of each triangle.

17.

18.

19.

20.

21. **Communicate Precisely** A hiker whose eyes are $5\frac{1}{2}$ feet above ground looks down at a kayaker on the far side of the river below. How could you find the approximate width of the river? **MP.6**

Coordinate Geometry

How can geometric relationships be proven by applying algebraic properties to geometric figures represented in the coordinate plane?

Topic Overview

enVision® STEM Project:
Design a Solar Collector

9-1 Polygons in the Coordinate Plane

Mathematical Modeling in 3 Acts:
You Be the Judge

9-2 Proofs Using Coordinate Geometry

9-3 Circles in the Coordinate Plane

9-4 Parabolas in the Coordinate Plane

Topic Vocabulary

- directrix
- focus
- parabola

Digital Experience

INTERACTIVE STUDENT EDITION
Access online or offline.

ACTIVITIES Complete *Explore & Reason*, *Model & Discuss*, and *Critique & Explain* activities. Interact with *Examples* and *Try Its*.

CONCEPT SUMMARY Review key lesson content through multiple representations.

ASSESSMENT Show what you've learned.

Go online | SavvasRealize.com

MATHEMATICAL MODELING IN 3 ACTS

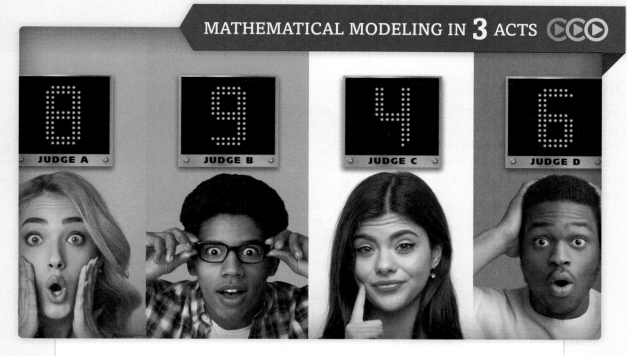

JUDGE A | JUDGE B | JUDGE C | JUDGE D

You Be the Judge

Have you ever been a judge in a contest or competition? What criteria did you use to decide the winner? If you were one of many judges, did you all agree on who should win?

Often there is a set of criteria that judges use to help them score the performances of the contestants. Having criteria helps all of the judges be consistent regardless of the person they are rating. Think of this during the Mathematical Modeling in 3 Acts lesson.

VIDEOS Watch clips to support *Mathematical Modeling in 3 Acts Lessons* and **enVision® STEM Projects.**

TUTORIALS Get help from *Virtual Nerd*, right when you need it.

PRACTICE Practice what you've learned.

ADAPTIVE PRACTICE Practice that is *just right* and *just for you.*

FAMILY ENGAGEMENT Involve family in your learning.

A-Z GLOSSARY Read and listen to English and Spanish definitions.

MATH TOOLS Explore math with digital tools and manipulatives.

DESMOS Use Anytime and as embedded Interactives in Lesson content.

Did You Know?

Solar reflectors are made of mirrors or pieces of glass in many shapes and sizes. **Parabolic reflectors** collect the sun's rays from a wide area and **focus them on a small area**, concentrating the energy.

258,048
mirrors

100
megawatts

20,000
homes

Sunlight

Focal
Point

Parabolic
Reflector

The world's largest power station, the SHAMS 1 in the United Arab Emirates, uses **258,048 mirrors**. That's enough to generate **100 megawatts** of electricity per day and power **20,000 homes**.

In 2016, the United States produced more than 40 billion kilowatt-hours of **solar energy**, 40 times more than it did a decade earlier.

Your Task: Design a Solar Collector

Giant solar power plants are not the only place to see parabolic trough collectors—you might find a water purifier made from a single 6 ft-x-4 ft mirror in a neighbor's back yard! You and your classmates will analyze parabolas and design a solar collector for use in your school or community.

9-1

Polygons in the Coordinate Plane

I CAN... use the coordinate plane to analyze geometric figures.

© **Common Core State Standards**
HSG.GPE.B.4, HSG.GPE.B.7, MP.3, MP.4, MP.5

EXPLORE & REASON

Players place game pieces on the board shown and earn points from the attributes of the piece placed on the board.

- 1 point for a right angle
- 2 points for a pair of parallel sides
- 3 points for the shortest perimeter

A. Which game piece is worth the greatest total points? Explain.

B. **Make Sense and Persevere** Describe a way to determine the perimeters that is different from the way you chose. Which method do you consider better? Explain. © **MP.1**

ESSENTIAL QUESTION

How are properties of geometric figures represented in the coordinate plane?

CONCEPTUAL UNDERSTANDING

EXAMPLE 1   Connect Algebra and Geometry Through Coordinates

What formulas can you use to identify properties of figures on the coordinate plane?

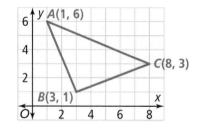

A. Which formula can you use to find *AB*?

Use the Distance Formula to find segment length.

$$AB = \sqrt{(3-1)^2 + (1-6)^2} = \sqrt{29}$$

B. What point bisects $\overline{AB}$?

Use the Midpoint Formula to find a segment bisector.

$$\text{midpoint of } \overline{AB} = \left(\frac{1+3}{2}, \frac{6+1}{2}\right) = \left(2, \frac{7}{2}\right)$$

COMMON ERROR
Recall that the slope of a line is the ratio of the difference in the *y*-coordinates to the difference in the *x*-coordinates. Be careful not to reverse the ratio.

C. Why do slopes of $\overline{AB}$ and $\overline{BC}$ show that $m\angle ABC = 90°$?

Use the slopes of the two segments to show that they are perpendicular.

$$\text{slope of } \overline{AB} = \frac{1-6}{3-1} = -\frac{5}{2}$$

$$\text{slope of } \overline{BC} = \frac{3-1}{8-3} = \frac{2}{5}$$

The product of the slopes is −1. So $\overline{AB} \perp \overline{BC}$, and $m\angle ABC = 90°$.

Try It!   **1.** Given △*ABC* in Example 1, what is the length of the line segment connecting the midpoints of $\overline{AC}$ and $\overline{BC}$?

EXAMPLE 2 ▶ Classify a Triangle on the Coordinate Plane

A. Is △XYZ equilateral, isosceles, or scalene?

Find the length of each side.

$$XY = \sqrt{(5-1)^2 + (8-2)^2} = \sqrt{52}$$

$$YZ = \sqrt{(8-5)^2 + (6-8)^2} = \sqrt{13}$$

$$XZ = \sqrt{(8-1)^2 + (6-2)^2} = \sqrt{65}$$

No two sides are congruent. The triangle is scalene.

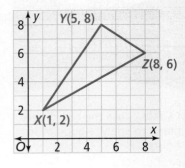

B. Is △XYZ a right triangle?

If △XYZ is a right triangle, then $\overline{XZ}$ is the hypotenuse because it is the longest side, and XY, YZ, and XZ satisfy the Pythagorean Theorem.

$$\left(\sqrt{52}\right)^2 + \left(\sqrt{13}\right)^2 \overset{?}{=} \left(\sqrt{65}\right)^2$$

$$65 = 65 \checkmark$$

Triangle XYZ is a right triangle.

Try It! **2.** The vertices of △PQR are P(4, 1), Q(2, 7), and R(8, 5).

a. Is △PQR equilateral, isosceles, or scalene? Explain.

b. Is △PQR a right triangle? Explain.

EXAMPLE 3 ▶ Classify a Parallelogram on the Coordinate Plane

What type of parallelogram is RSTU?

Determine whether RSTU is a rhombus, a rectangle, or a square. First calculate ST and SR:

$$ST = \sqrt{(2-8)^2 + (8-4)^2} = \sqrt{52}$$

$$RS = \sqrt{(2-1)^2 + (8-5)^2} = \sqrt{10}$$

Since not all side lengths are equal, RSTU is not a rhombus or a square.

Check for right angles by finding the slopes.

$$\text{slope of } \overline{ST} = \frac{4-8}{8-2} = -\frac{2}{3}$$

$$\text{slope of } \overline{RS} = \frac{8-5}{2-1} = 3$$

The product of the slopes is not −1, so $\overline{ST}$ and $\overline{RS}$ are not perpendicular. At least one angle is not a right angle, and RSTU is not a rectangle. Therefore, quadrilateral RSTU is a parallelogram that is neither a square, nor a rhombus, nor a rectangle.

Try It! **3.** The vertices of a parallelogram are A(−2, 2), B(4, 6), C(6, 3), and D(0, −1).

a. Is ABCD a rhombus? Explain.

b. Is ABCD a rectangle? Explain.

LEARN TOGETHER
Do you seek help when needed? Do you offer help and support others?

MAKE SENSE AND PERSEVERE
Consider other formulas you use on the coordinate plane. What are some ways to show that a quadrilateral is not a rectangle or a rhombus? ⒸMP.1

EXAMPLE 4 Classify Quadrilaterals as Trapezoids and Kites on the Coordinate Plane

A. Is *ABCD* a trapezoid?

A trapezoid has exactly one pair of parallel sides. Use the slope formula to determine if one pair of opposite sides is parallel.

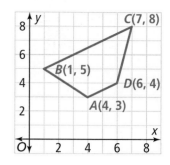

$$\text{slope of } \overline{AB} = \frac{5-3}{1-4} = -\frac{2}{3}$$

$$\text{slope of } \overline{BC} = \frac{8-5}{7-1} = \frac{1}{2}$$

$$\text{slope of } \overline{CD} = \frac{4-8}{6-7} = \frac{4}{1}$$

$$\text{slope of } \overline{AD} = \frac{4-3}{6-4} = \frac{1}{2}$$

Since only the slopes of $\overline{BC}$ and $\overline{AD}$ are equal, $\overline{BC} \parallel \overline{AD}$, and only one pair of opposite sides is parallel. Therefore, quadrilateral *ABCD* is a trapezoid.

COMMUNICATE PRECISELY
Think about the properties of a trapezoid. Why do you need to find the slopes for all four sides? ⓒ **MP.6**

B. Is *JKLM* a kite?

A kite has two pairs of consecutive congruent sides and no opposite sides congruent. Use the Distance Formula to find the lengths of the sides.

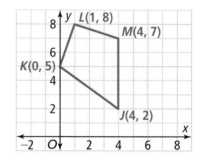

$$JK = \sqrt{(0-4)^2 + (5-2)^2} = 5$$

$$KL = \sqrt{(1-0)^2 + (8-5)^2} = \sqrt{10}$$

$$LM = \sqrt{(4-1)^2 + (7-8)^2} = \sqrt{10}$$

$$MJ = \sqrt{(4-4)^2 + (2-7)^2} = 5$$

Consecutive pair $\overline{KL}$ and $\overline{LM}$ and consecutive pair $\overline{JK}$ and $\overline{MJ}$ are congruent. No opposite pair is congruent, so *JKLM* is a kite.

Try It! **4.** Is each quadrilateral a kite, a trapezoid, or neither?

a.

b.
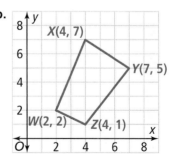

EXAMPLE 5 Find Perimeter and Area

Dylan draws up a plan to fence in a yard for his chickens. The distance between grid lines is 1 foot.

A. Is 30 feet of fencing enough to enclose the yard?

Find the lengths of the sides.

$$AB = \sqrt{(2-10)^2 + (6-12)^2} = 10 \text{ ft}$$
$$BC = \sqrt{(10-10)^2 + (12-2)^2} = 10 \text{ ft}$$
$$AC = \sqrt{(2-10)^2 + (6-2)^2} = \sqrt{80} \text{ ft}$$

Find the perimeter of the yard.

$$P = 10 + 10 + \sqrt{80}$$
$$\approx 28.9 \text{ ft}$$

The perimeter is about 28.9 feet, which is less than 30 feet. Dylan has enough fencing.

CONSTRUCT ARGUMENTS
Consider the properties of an isosceles triangle. What property of an isosceles triangle justifies that $\overline{BX}$ is a height of the triangle? Ⓖ MP.3

B. **For a healthy flock, each chicken needs at least 8 square feet of space. What is the maximum number of chickens Dylan can put in the yard?**

The yard is an isosceles triangle. To find the area, you need the height of the triangle. The height of $\triangle ABC$ is BX, where X is the midpoint of $\overline{AC}$.

Find the midpoint of $\overline{AC}$.

$$X = \left(\frac{2+10}{2}, \frac{6+2}{2}\right) = (6, 4)$$

Find the height of $\triangle ABC$.

$$BX = \sqrt{(10-6)^2 + (12-4)^2} = \sqrt{80} \text{ ft}$$

Then find the area of the yard.

$$\text{area of } \triangle ABC = \frac{1}{2}(\sqrt{80})(\sqrt{80}) = 40 \text{ ft}^2$$

Divide 40 by 8 to find the allowable number of chickens.

$$40 \div 8 = 5$$

Dylan can keep as many as 5 chickens in the yard.

Try It! 5. The vertices of $WXYZ$ are $W(5, 4)$, $X(2, 9)$, $Y(9, 9)$, and $Z(8, 4)$.

   a. What is the perimeter of $WXYZ$?

   b. What is the area of $WXYZ$?

CONCEPT SUMMARY Connecting Algebra and Geometry

	Distance Formula	Slope Formula	Midpoint Formula
WORDS	Use the Distance Formula to find the lengths of segments to classify figures.	Use the Slope Formula to determine whether two lines or segments are parallel or perpendicular.	Use the Midpoint Formula to determine if a point bisects a segment.
GRAPH		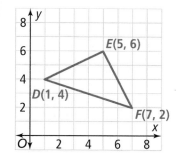	
NUMBERS	$DE = \sqrt{(5-1)^2 + (6-4)^2}$ $= \sqrt{20}$	slope of $\overline{DE} = \dfrac{6-4}{5-1}$ $= \dfrac{1}{2}$	midpoint of $\overline{DF}$ $= \left(\dfrac{1+7}{2}, \dfrac{4+2}{2}\right)$, or (4, 3)

Do You UNDERSTAND?

1. **ESSENTIAL QUESTION** How are properties of geometric figures represented in the coordinate plane?

2. **Error Analysis** Chen is asked to describe two methods to find BC. Why is Chen incorrect? ⓒ **MP.3**

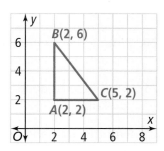

> The only possible method is to use the Distance Formula because you only know the endpoints of $\overline{BC}$.

3. **Communicate Precisely** Describe three ways you can determine whether a quadrilateral is a parallelogram given the coordinates of the vertices. ⓒ **MP.6**

Do You KNOW HOW?

Use JKLM for Exercises 4–6.

4. What is the perimeter of JKLM?

5. What is the relationship between $\overline{JL}$ and $\overline{KM}$? Explain.

6. What type of quadrilateral is JKLM? Explain.

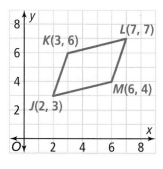

Use △PQR for Exercises 7 and 8.

7. What kind of triangle is PQR? Explain.

8. What is the area of PQR?

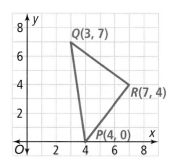

PRACTICE & PROBLEM SOLVING

UNDERSTAND

9. **Error Analysis** What error did Kelley make in finding the area of △PQR? © MP.3

Area $= \frac{1}{2} bh = \frac{1}{2} (PR)(PQ) = \frac{1}{2} \sqrt{26} \sqrt{40}$

The area of △PQR is about 16.12 square units. ✗

10. **Mathematical Connections** Find the equation of the line that passes through point R and is perpendicular to line m.

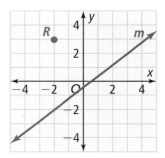

11. **Construct Arguments** Prove △ABC ≅ △DEF. © MP.3

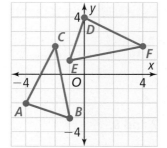

12. **Communicate Precisely** Given the coordinates of the vertices, how can you show that a quadrilateral is a kite without using the Distance Formula? © MP.6

13. **Higher Order Thinking** Let line p be the perpendicular bisector of $\overline{AB}$ that has endpoints and $A(x_1, y_1)$ and $B(x_2, y_2)$. Describe the process for writing a general equation in slope-intercept form for line p.

PRACTICE

Use the figure shown for Exercises 14–17.
SEE EXAMPLE 1

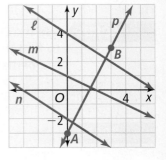

14. Which lines are parallel?

15. Which lines are perpendicular?

16. What is the length of $\overline{AB}$?

17. What is the midpoint of $\overline{AB}$?

Use the figure for Exercises 18–23.

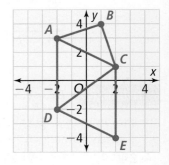

18. Is △ABC a scalene, isosceles, or equilateral triangle? Is it a right triangle? Explain. SEE EXAMPLE 2

19. Is △ADC a scalene, isosceles, or equilateral triangle? Is it a right triangle? Explain. SEE EXAMPLE 2

20. What type of parallelogram is ACED? Explain. SEE EXAMPLE 3

21. What type of quadrilateral is ABCD? How do you know? SEE EXAMPLE 4

22. Find the area and perimeter of △ABC. SEE EXAMPLE 5

23. Find the area and perimeter of ABCD. SEE EXAMPLE 5

Three vertices of a quadrilateral are P(−2, 3), Q(2, 4), and R(1, 0). SEE EXAMPLE 3

24. Suppose PQRS is a parallelogram. What are the coordinates of vertex S? What type of parallelogram is PQRS?

25. Suppose PQSR is a parallelogram. What are the coordinates of vertex S? What type of parallelogram is PQSR?

PRACTICE & PROBLEM SOLVING

26. Use Appropriate Tools An architect is designing a trapezoidal greenhouse *ABCD* for the side of a house. She wants to locate point *D* so that $\overline{CD}$ is perpendicular to the house. What should the coordinates of point *D* be? How can she use the slopes of $\overline{AD}$ and $\overline{CD}$ to verify that point *D* is in the correct location? **© MP.5**

27. Model with Mathematics A gardener is installing a fence around a triangular garden as shown below. Each unit on the axes represents 1 yard. How much fencing, in yards, does the gardener need? **© MP.4**

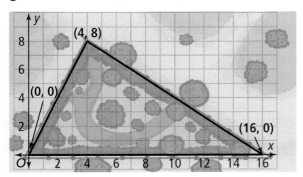

28. Construct Arguments To receive a certificate for a deep sea diving class, Anna and Richard each need to explore at least 25 square meters underwater. Who is closer to reaching the goal and receiving the certificate? Explain. **© MP.3**

29. Triangle *ABC* has vertices *A*(2, 5), *B*(6, 8), and *C*(5, 1). Determine whether each statement about △*ABC* is true. Select *Yes* or *No*.

	Yes	No
$\overline{AB} \cong \overline{AC}$	☐	☐
$BC = AB\sqrt{2}$	☐	☐
The midpoint of *BC* is (5.5, 4).	☐	☐
The perimeter is 12.5 units.	☐	☐

30. SAT/ACT Quadrilateral *JKLM* has vertices *J*(1, −2), *K*(7, 1), *L*(8, −1), and *M*(2, −4). Which is the most precise classification of *JKLM*?

Ⓐ rectangle

Ⓑ rhombus

Ⓒ trapezoid

Ⓓ kite

31. Performance Task Kyan draws the side view of a TV stand that has slanted legs. Each unit in his plan equals half of a foot.

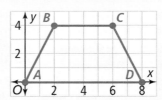

Part A Kyan thinks his TV stand is in the shape of an isosceles trapezoid. Is he correct? Explain.

Part B Kyan adds an additional support by connecting the midpoints of the legs. How long is the support?

Part C Kyan decides he wants to make the TV stand a half foot higher by placing *B* at (2, 5) and *C* at (6, 5). How much longer will the legs and support connecting the midpoints be?

MATHEMATICAL MODELING IN 3 ACTS

Common Core State Standards
HSG.GPE.B.4, HSG.GPE.B.6, MP.4

You Be the Judge

Have you ever been a judge in a contest or competition? What criteria did you use to decide the winner? If you were one of many judges, did you all agree on who should win?

Often there is a set of criteria that judges use to help them score the performances of the contestants. Having criteria helps all of the judges be consistent regardless of the person they are rating. Think of this during the Mathematical Modeling in 3 Acts lesson.

ACT 1 ⟩ Identify the Problem

1. What is the first question that comes to mind after watching the video?

2. Write down the main question you will answer about what you saw in the video.

3. Make an initial conjecture that answers this main question.

4. Explain how you arrived at your conjecture.

5. What information will be useful to know to answer the main question? How can you get it? How will you use that information?

ACT 2 ⟩ Develop a Model

6. Use the math that you have learned in this Topic to refine your conjecture.

ACT 3 ⟩ Interpret the Results

7. Did your refined conjecture match the actual answer exactly? If not, what might explain the difference?

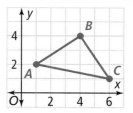

9-2

Proofs Using Coordinate Geometry

I CAN... prove geometric theorems using algebra and the coordinate plane.

Ⓒ **Common Core State Standards**
HSG.CO.C.10, HSG.GPE.B.4, MP.2, MP.6, MP.7

CRITIQUE & EXPLAIN

Dakota and Jung are trying to show that △*ABC* is a right triangle. Each student uses a different method.

Dakota

slope of $\overline{AB} = \frac{2}{3}$, slope of $\overline{BC} = -\frac{3}{2}$

slope of $\overline{AB}$ • slope of $\overline{BC} = -1$

Triangle *ABC* is a right triangle.

Jung

$AB = BC = \sqrt{13}$, $AC = \sqrt{26}$

$(\sqrt{13})^2 + (\sqrt{13})^2 = (\sqrt{26})^2$

Triangle *ABC* is a right triangle.

A. Did Dakota and Jung both show △*ABC* is a right triangle? Explain.

B. **Reason** If the coordinates of △*ABC* were changed to (2, 3), (5, 5), and (7, 2), how would each student's method change? Explain. Ⓒ **MP.2**

ESSENTIAL QUESTION

How can geometric relationships be proven algebraically in the coordinate plane?

CONCEPTUAL UNDERSTANDING

EXAMPLE 1 — Plan a Coordinate Proof

How can you use coordinates to prove geometric relationships algebraically? Plan a proof for the Trapezoid Midsegment Theorem.

Draw and label a diagram that names all points to be used in the proof.

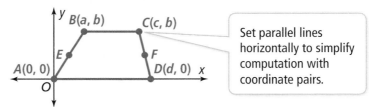

Set parallel lines horizontally to simplify computation with coordinate pairs.

Restate the Trapezoid Midsegment Theorem so the statement can be proved using algebra on the coordinate plane.

Theorem: The midsegment of a trapezoid is parallel to each base and its length is one half the sum of the lengths of the bases.

USE STRUCTURE
Variables are used according to the properties of trapezoids. Why is the proof valid for all trapezoids? Ⓒ **MP.7**

Restatement: If $\overline{EF}$ is the midsegment of trapezoid *ABCD*, then slope $\overline{EF}$ = slope $\overline{AD}$ = slope $\overline{BC}$ and $EF = \frac{AD + BC}{2}$.

Plan: To show that the midsegment is parallel to the bases, show that their slopes are equal. Then show that the mean of the base lengths is the length of the midsegment.

Try It! **1.** Plan a proof to show that the diagonals of a square are congruent and perpendicular.

EXAMPLE 2 ▶ Write a Coordinate Proof

Write a coordinate proof of the Trapezoid Midsegment Theorem. Use the conditional statement from Example 1 to decide what is given and what is to be proved.

Given: Trapezoid *ABCD*, with midpoints *E* and *F*

Prove: $\overline{EF} \parallel \overline{AD} \parallel \overline{BC}$ and $EF = \dfrac{AD + BC}{2}$

Plan: Apply the plan and diagram from Example 1. Use the coordinates in the diagram to show that slope $\overline{EF}$ = slope $\overline{AD}$ = slope $\overline{BC}$, and $EF = \dfrac{AD + BC}{2}$.

Proof:

Step 1 Use the Midpoint Formula to find the coordinates of points *E* and *F*.

$$E = \left(\frac{0+a}{2}, \frac{0+b}{2}\right) \qquad\qquad F = \left(\frac{c+d}{2}, \frac{b+0}{2}\right)$$

$$= \left(\frac{a}{2}, \frac{b}{2}\right) \qquad\qquad\qquad = \left(\frac{c+d}{2}, \frac{b}{2}\right)$$

Step 2 The slopes of $\overline{AD}$, $\overline{BC}$, and $\overline{EF}$ all equal zero, because the segments are horizontal.

Therefore, $\overline{EF} \parallel \overline{AD} \parallel \overline{BC}$.

Step 3 Determine *AD*, *BC*, and *EF*.

Since the segments are horizontal lines, the lengths are differences of the *x*-coordinates.

$$AD = d - 0 \qquad\qquad BC = c - a \qquad\qquad EF = \frac{c+d}{2} - \frac{a}{2}$$

$$= d \qquad\qquad\qquad\qquad\qquad\qquad\qquad = \frac{c+d-a}{2}$$

Step 4 Use algebra to show that $\dfrac{AD + BC}{2} = EF$.

$$\frac{AD + BC}{2} = \frac{d + (c - a)}{2} = \frac{c + d - a}{2} = EF$$

The bases and the midsegment are parallel, and the length of the midsegment is equal to the mean of the base lengths.

Therefore, $\overline{EF} \parallel \overline{AD} \parallel \overline{BC}$ and $EF = \dfrac{AD + BC}{2}$.

Try It! 2. Use coordinate geometry to prove that the diagonals of a rectangle are congruent.

EXAMPLE 3 Plan and Write a Coordinate Proof

Write a coordinate proof of the Concurrency of Medians Theorem.

Given: $\triangle ABC$ with medians $\overline{AD}$, $\overline{BE}$, and $\overline{CF}$

Prove: The medians are concurrent at point P such that

$$AP = \tfrac{2}{3}AD,\ BP = \tfrac{2}{3}BE,\ \text{and}\ CP = \tfrac{2}{3}CF.$$

Plan: Draw and label a triangle in the coordinate plane. Then use the Midpoint Formula to locate the midpoints. Draw two medians and locate the point of intersection P. Use algebra to determine that the medians are concurrent at P. Finally, find the distance from P to each vertex.

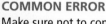

COMMON ERROR
Make sure not to confuse the Midpoint and Distance Formulas. The x-coordinate of a midpoint is the average of the x-coordinates of the endpoints, and the y-coordinate is the average of the y-coordinates.

Proof: Draw the triangle with the coordinates shown.

Find the coordinates of D, E, and F using the Midpoint Formula.

$$D = (a + c,\ b) \qquad E = (c,\ 0) \qquad F = (a,\ b)$$

Then find the slopes of the lines containing the medians $\overline{AD}$ and $\overline{CF}$.

$$\text{slope of } \overline{AD} = \frac{b - 0}{a + c - 0} = \frac{b}{a + c} \qquad\qquad \text{slope of } \overline{CF} = \frac{b - 0}{a - 2c} = \frac{b}{a - 2c}$$

Write equations for $\overleftrightarrow{AD}$ and $\overleftrightarrow{CF}$ using point-slope form.

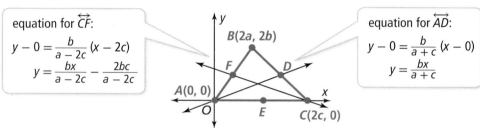

equation for $\overleftrightarrow{CF}$:
$$y - 0 = \frac{b}{a - 2c}(x - 2c)$$
$$y = \frac{bx}{a - 2c} - \frac{2bc}{a - 2c}$$

equation for $\overleftrightarrow{AD}$:
$$y - 0 = \frac{b}{a + c}(x - 0)$$
$$y = \frac{bx}{a + c}$$

Set the expressions for y equal to each other. Solve for x to get $x = \dfrac{2(a + c)}{3}$. Then substitute the expression for x into $y = \dfrac{bx}{a + c}$ to get $y = \dfrac{2b}{3}$.

Let point P be $\left(\dfrac{2(a + c)}{3},\ \dfrac{2b}{3} \right)$.

To show that point P is on $\overline{BE}$, find an equation for the line containing $\overline{BE}$. Start by finding the slope of $\overline{BE}$.

$$\text{slope of } \overline{BE} = \frac{0 - 2b}{c - 2a} = -\frac{2b}{c - 2a}$$

Then, using point-slope form, an equation for $\overleftrightarrow{BE}$ is $y = -\dfrac{2bx}{c - 2a} + \dfrac{2bc}{c - 2a}$.

Substituting $\dfrac{2(a + c)}{3}$ for x into the equation results in $y = \dfrac{2b}{3}$, so point P is on $\overline{BE}$. The three medians are concurrent at P.

Use the Distance Formula to complete the proof in the Try It.

Try It! **3.** Complete the proof in Example 3. Use the Distance Formula to show that $AP = \tfrac{2}{3}AD$, $BP = \tfrac{2}{3}BE$, and $CP = \tfrac{2}{3}CF$.

EXAMPLE 4 Use Coordinate Proofs to Solve Problems

An interior designer wants the center of a circular fountain to be equidistant from the corners of a triangular lobby. Where should he place the center of the fountain?

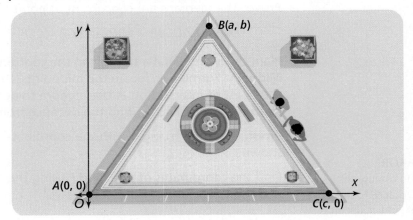

Formulate ◄ The center of the fountain must be at the circumcenter of the triangle. Find the point of intersection of the perpendicular bisectors of two sides of the triangle.

Compute ◄ Determine the intersection of the perpendicular bisectors of $\overline{AC}$ and $\overline{AB}$.

An equation of the perpendicular bisector of $\overline{AC}$ is $x = \frac{c}{2}$.

The perpendicular bisector of $\overline{AB}$ contains the point $\left(\frac{a}{2}, \frac{b}{2}\right)$ and has slope $-\frac{a}{b}$. Its point-slope equation is $y - \frac{b}{2} = -\frac{a}{b}\left(x - \frac{a}{2}\right)$, which simplifies to $y = -\frac{a}{b}x + \frac{a^2 + b^2}{2b}$.

Calculate the intersection of the two lines.

$$y = -\frac{a}{b}x + \frac{a^2 + b^2}{2b}$$
$$y = -\frac{a}{b} \cdot \frac{c}{2} + \frac{a^2 + b^2}{2b}$$
$$y = \frac{a^2 - ac + b^2}{2b}$$

> Substitute $\frac{c}{2}$ for x, then solve for y.

Interpret ◄ The center of the fountain should be at the point $\left(\frac{c}{2}, \frac{a^2 - ac + b^2}{2b}\right)$.

Try It! **4.** A table has a top that is a right triangle and a single support leg. Where should the center of the leg be placed so it corresponds with the center of gravity of the table top? Plan a coordinate geometry proof to find its location.

CONCEPT SUMMARY Writing a Coordinate Proof

WORDS
- Determine which numerical relationships you must calculate to show the statement is true.
- Draw and label a figure on a coordinate plane. Choose coordinates that simplify computations.
- Calculate the numerical values needed to prove a statement or solve a problem.

DIAGRAMS

Choose coordinates so parallel lines are horizontal.

Choose coordinates so the line of symmetry is the y-axis.

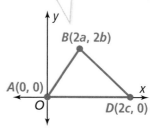
Choose coordinates so the coordinates of midpoints are convenient.

Do You UNDERSTAND?

1. **ESSENTIAL QUESTION** How can geometric relationships be proven algebraically in the coordinate plane?

2. **Error Analysis** Venetta tried to find the slope of $\overline{AB}$. What is her error? Ⓒ MP.3

$$\text{slope } \overline{AB} = \frac{a - 0}{b - 0}$$

$$\text{slope } \overline{AB} = \frac{a}{b}$$ ✗

3. **Communicate Precisely** What is a coordinate geometry proof? Ⓒ MP.6

4. **Reason** Describe why it is important to plan a coordinate proof. Ⓒ MP.2

5. **Use Structure** What coordinates would you use to describe an isosceles triangle on a coordinate plane? Explain. Ⓒ MP.7

Do You KNOW HOW?

For Exercises 6–8, write a plan for a coordinate proof.

6. The diagonals of a rhombus are perpendicular.

7. The area of a triangle with vertices $A(0, 0)$, $B(0, a)$ and $C(b, c)$ is $\frac{ab}{2}$.

8. The lines that contain the altitudes of a triangle are concurrent.

For Exercises 9–12, plan and write a coordinate proof.

9. A point on the perpendicular bisector of a segment is equidistant from the endpoints.

10. The diagonals of a kite are perpendicular.

11. All squares are similar.

12. The area of a rhombus is half the product of the lengths of its diagonals.

PRACTICE & PROBLEM SOLVING

UNDERSTAND

13. **Communicate Precisely** What coordinates would you use to describe an equilateral triangle in the coordinate plane? Explain. Ⓒ **MP.6**

14. **Error Analysis** Tanya drew a diagram to prove the Perpendicular Bisector Theorem using coordinate geometry. What error did she make in her choice of coordinates? Ⓒ **MP.3**

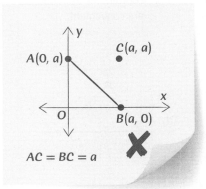

For Exercises 15 and 16, use the graph.

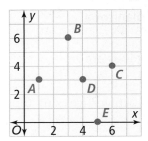

15. **Make Sense and Persevere** Write a plan for a coordinate proof to show that $\triangle ABC$ is a right triangle. Ⓒ **MP.1**

16. **Make Sense and Persevere** Describe how you would prove points B, D, and E are collinear. Ⓒ **MP.1**

17. **Mathematical Connections** What is the equation of the line containing the perpendicular bisector of $\overline{AB}$?

PRACTICE

For Exercises 18–21, write a plan for a coordinate proof. SEE EXAMPLE 1

18. The diagonals of a parallelogram that is not a rectangle are not congruent.

19. The length of a diameter of a circle is twice that of its radius.

20. The diagonals of a parallelogram bisect each other.

21. The area of $\triangle XYZ$ is twice the area of $\triangle XWZ$, where W is the midpoint of $\overline{YZ}$.

For Exercises 22–25, plan and write a coordinate proof. SEE EXAMPLES 2 AND 3

22. The length of a diagonal of a rectangle is the square root of the sum of the squares of the lengths of two adjacent sides.

23. All right triangles with one acute angle measuring 30° are similar.

24. One and only one diagonal of a kite bisects the other.

25. The length of the median to the hypotenuse of a right triangle is half the length of the hypotenuse.

26. Find the centroid of the triangle by finding the point two thirds of the distance from the vertex on one median. SEE EXAMPLE 4

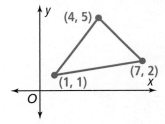

27. Show that the centroid and circumcenter of an equilateral triangle are the same point.

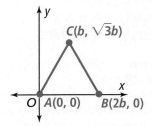

PRACTICE & PROBLEM SOLVING

28. Model With Mathematics Each student in a woodworking class inlays brass wire along the lines connecting the midpoints of adjacent sides of a square trivet. If the wire costs $0.54 per inch, what is the cost of the wire for making 12 trivets? ⓒ MP.4

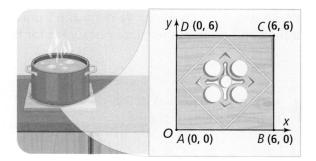

29. Make Sense and Persevere The owner of an animal park wants a quadrilateral trail that connects the four sides of the iscosceles-trapezoid-shaped park, with all sides of the trail the same length. Deon says that if the trail connects the midpoint of each side to the midpoints of the adjacent sides, the trail will be a rhombus. Write a coordinate proof to show that Deon is correct. ⓒ MP.1

30. Higher Order Thinking In the sculpture, $\triangle ABC$ is symmetric about the y-axis. Point A is located at $(-3, 0)$, and $\overline{AC}$ is the longest side of $\triangle ABC$. The perimeter of $\triangle ABC$ is 16. What is the value of a?

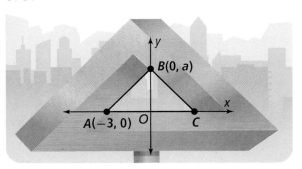

31. An isosceles right triangle is placed on a coordinate plane. Which set of vertices makes it easiest to calculate the length of the sides of the triangle?

Ⓐ $(0, 0)$, $(a, 0)$, $\left(\frac{a}{2}, \frac{a}{2}\right)$

Ⓑ $(0, a)$, $(0, -a)$, (a, a)

Ⓒ $(0, 0)$, $(a, 0)$, $(0, a)$

Ⓓ $(0, 0)$, $(0, a)$, $\left(\frac{a}{2}, \frac{a}{2}\right)$

32. SAT/ACT Which statements are true?

I. $AB = BC$
II. $\overline{AB} \perp \overline{BC}$
III. $AC = 2a^2 + 2b^2$

Ⓐ I only

Ⓑ II only

Ⓒ I and II only

Ⓓ I, II, and III

33. Performance Task Consider $\triangle ABC$ on the coordinate plane. Points D, E, and F are the midpoints of the sides.

Part A What are the coordinates of D, E, and F?

Part B Prove that the coordinates of the point of concurrency of the medians is the average of the x and y coordinates of the vertices.

$$\left(\frac{x_1 + x_2 + x_3}{3}, \frac{y_1 + y_2 + y_3}{3}\right)$$

Hint: Apply the Concurrency of Medians Theorem and find the point $\frac{2}{3}$ of the way from A to D.

Part C Explain why it does not make sense to place one of the coordinates at the origin for this proof.

9-3

Circles in the Coordinate Plane

I CAN... use the equations and graphs of circles to solve problems.

Common Core State Standards
HSG.GPE.A.1, HSG.GPE.B.4,
HSG.CO.A.1, MP.2, MP.4, MP.8

CONCEPTUAL UNDERSTANDING

GENERALIZE
What other formula or formulas compares the sum of two squares to a third square? How are these formulas related? **© MP.8**

MODEL & DISCUSS

Damian uses an app to find all pizza restaurants within a certain distance of his current location.

A. What is the shape of the region that the app uses to search for pizza restaurants? Explain how you know.

B. What information do you think the app needs to determine the area to search?

C. Construct Arguments If Damian's friend is using the same app from a different location, could the app find the same pizza restaurant for both boys? Explain. **© MP.3**

ESSENTIAL QUESTION

How is the equation of a circle determined in the coordinate plane?

EXAMPLE 1   Derive the Equation of a Circle

What equation defines a circle in the coordinate plane?

Draw a circle with point (h, k) as the center of the circle. Then select any point (x, y) on the circle.

Use variables that can apply to any circle on the coordinate plane.

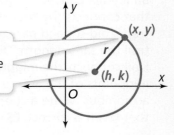

Use the Distance Formula to find the distance r between the two points.

$$d = \sqrt{(x_2 - x_1)^2 + (y_2 - y_1)^2}$$
$$r = \sqrt{(x - h)^2 + (y - k)^2}$$

Because the radius is the same from the center to any point (x, y) on the circle, the equation $r^2 = (x - h)^2 + (y - k)^2$, or $(x - h)^2 + (y - k)^2 = r^2$, satisfies all points of the circle.

Try It!   **1.** What are the radius and center of the circle with the equation $(x - 2)^2 + (y - 3)^2 = 25$?

THEOREM 9-1 Equation of a Circle

An equation of a circle with center (h, k) and radius r is

$(x - h)^2 + (y - k)^2 = r^2$.

If...

Then... $(x - h)^2 + (y - k)^2 = r^2$

PROOF: SEE EXERCISE 13.

EXAMPLE 2 **Write the Equation of a Circle**

What is the equation for ⊙A?

The notation ⊙A means a circle with center at point A.

Step 1 Find the radius r.

The radius is the distance from P to A.

$$r = \sqrt{(-1 - 1)^2 + (2 - 5)^2} = \sqrt{13}$$

The radius of the circle is $\sqrt{13}$.

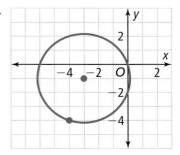

Step 2 Use the radius and center of the circle to write the equation.

$$(x - h)^2 + (y - k)^2 = r^2$$

Use the equation of a circle.

$$(x - (-1))^2 + (y - 2)^2 = (\sqrt{13})^2$$

$$(x + 1)^2 + (y - 2)^2 = 13$$

Substitute values for h, k, and r.

The equation for ⊙A is $(x + 1)^2 + (y - 2)^2 = 13$.

> **COMMON ERROR**
> Be careful with the signs of coordinates. Coordinates of the center are subtracted, so if a coordinate is negative, the expression will convert to addition.

Try It! **2.** What is the equation for each circle?

a.
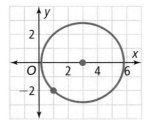

b.

EXAMPLE 3 **Determine Whether a Point Lies on a Circle**

Circle Q has radius 7 and is centered at the origin. Does the point $(-3\sqrt{2}, 5)$ lie on ⊙Q?

Step 1 Write the equation for ⊙Q.

$$(x - h)^2 + (y - k)^2 = r^2$$

$$(x - 0)^2 + (y - 0)^2 = 7^2$$

$$x^2 + y^2 = 49$$

Step 2 Test the point $(-3\sqrt{2}, 5)$ in the equation.

$$(-3\sqrt{2})^2 + 5^2 \stackrel{?}{=} 49$$

$$18 + 25 \stackrel{?}{=} 49$$

$$43 \neq 49$$

The point $(-3\sqrt{2}, 5)$ does not lie on ⊙Q.

> **STUDY TIP**
> Remember that to square an expression $a\sqrt{b}$, you square both factors: $(a\sqrt{b})^2 = a^2(\sqrt{b})^2$.

Try It! **3.** Determine whether each point lies on the given circle.

a. $(-3, \sqrt{11})$; circle with center at the origin and radius $2\sqrt{5}$

b. $(6, 3)$; circle with center at $(2, 4)$ and radius $3\sqrt{3}$

EXAMPLE 4 | **Complete the Square to Find the Center and Radius of a Circle**

The equation $x^2 + y^2 - 6x + 8y + 16 = 0$ represents a circle. How can you rewrite the equation to identify the center and radius of the circle? Graph the circle.

Write the equation in the form $(x - h)^2 + (y - k)^2 = r^2$ by using the method of completing the square. Start by grouping terms by variable.

$$(x^2 - 6x) + (y^2 + 8y) = -16$$

$$(x^2 - 6x + 9) + (y^2 + 8y + 16) = -16 + 9 + 16$$

Add 9 and 16 to each side to complete the squares.

$$(x - 3)^2 + (y + 4)^2 = 9$$

$$(x - 3)^2 + (y - (-4))^2 = 3^2$$

The center (h, k) is $(3, -4)$. The radius r is 3.

Draw the circle. | Plot the center at $(3, -4)$. Then plot points 3 units above, below, left, and right of the center and use the points to draw the circle.

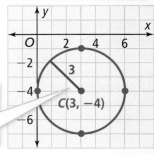

Try It!   **4.** What is the graph of each circle?

     a. $x^2 + 4x + y^2 = 21$ **b.** $x^2 + 2x + y^2 - 4y = -4$

APPLICATION

EXAMPLE 5 | **Use the Graph and Equation of a Circle to Solve Problems**

Doppler radar technology helps detect precipitation. The equation $(x - 90)^2 + (y - 180)^2 = 8100$ defines the outer range for a Doppler station. Which cities are covered by the station?

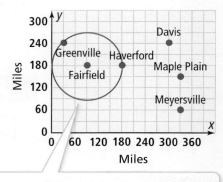

Graph the equation to find the area covered by the Doppler station. Since $8100 = 90^2$, rewrite the equation:

$$(x - 90)^2 + (y - 180)^2 = 90^2$$

The equation is for a circle with radius 90 miles and center $(90, 180)$, or Fairfield.

Fairfield, Greenville, and Haverford are inside or on the circle, so they are covered by the Doppler station. You can verify the distances from Greenville and Haverford to Fairfield are at most 90 miles.

Distance from Fairfield to Greenville: $\sqrt{(90 - 30)^2 + (180 - 240)^2} \approx 85$ miles

Distance from Fairfield to Haverford: $\sqrt{(90 - 180)^2 + (180 - 180)^2} = 90$ miles

Try It!   **5.** The range of a second Doppler station is defined by $(x - 330)^2 + (y - 150)^2 = 8100$. Will the station cover the remaining three cities? Explain.

CONCEPT SUMMARY Equations and Graphs of Circles

WORDS A circle is the set of points equidistant from a fixed point. The fixed point is the center.

ALGEBRA $(x - h)^2 + (y - k)^2 = r^2$ where (h, k) is the center and r is the radius.

GRAPH

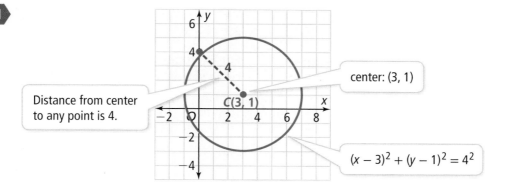

Distance from center to any point is 4.

center: (3, 1)

$C(3, 1)$

$(x - 3)^2 + (y - 1)^2 = 4^2$

Do You UNDERSTAND?

1. **ESSENTIAL QUESTION** How is the equation of a circle determined in the coordinate plane?

2. **Error Analysis** Leo says that the equation for the circle is $(x - 1)^2 + (y - 2)^2 = 3$. What is his error? Ⓒ **MP.3**

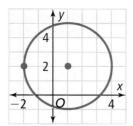

3. **Construct Arguments** If you are given the coordinates of the center and one point on a circle, can you determine the equation of the circle? Explain. Ⓒ **MP.3**

4. **Make Sense and Persevere** How could you write the equation of a circle given only the coordinates of the endpoints of its diameter? Ⓒ **MP.1**

Do You KNOW HOW?

5. What are the center and radius of the circle with equation $(x - 4)^2 + (y - 9)^2 = 1$?

6. What is the equation for the circle with center $(6, 2)$ and radius 8?

7. What are the center and radius of the circle with equation $(x + 7)^2 + (y - 1)^2 = 9$?

8. What is the equation for the circle with center $(-9, 5)$ and radius 4?

For Exercises 9 and 10, write an equation for each circle shown.

9. 　　10.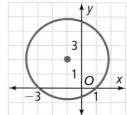

11. Is point $(5, -2)$ on the circle with radius 5 and center $(8, 2)$?

12. What is the equation for the circle with center $(5, 11)$ that passes through $(9, -2)$?

PRACTICE & PROBLEM SOLVING

UNDERSTAND

13. Construct Arguments Write a proof of Theorem 9-1. Ⓒ MP.3

14. Mathematical Connections What are the point(s) of intersection of $x^2 + y^2 = 25$ and $y = 2x - 5$? Graph both equations to check your answer.

15. Error Analysis LaTonya was asked to determine if $(3\sqrt{5}, 4)$ lies on the circle with radius 7 centered at $(0, -2)$. What is her error? Ⓒ MP.3

$$x^2 + (y - 2)^2 = 49$$
$$(3\sqrt{5})^2 + (4 - 2)^2 \overset{?}{=} 49$$
$$45 + 4 = 49$$

The point $(3\sqrt{5}, 4)$ lies on the circle with radius 7 and center $(0, -2)$.

16. Communicate Precisely Describe the graph of $(x - a)^2 + (y - b)^2 = 0$. Ⓒ MP.6

17. Reason If the area of square $ABCD$ is 50, what is the equation for ⊙R? Ⓒ MP.2

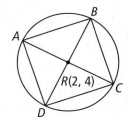

18. Construct Arguments The points (a, b) and (c, d) are the endpoints of a diameter of a circle. What are the center and radius of the circle? Ⓒ MP.3

19. Higher Order Thinking Isabella says the graph shows the circle with center $(-2, 2)$ and radius 3. Tamyra says the graph shows all possible centers for a circle that passes through $(-2, 2)$ with radius 3. Which student is correct? Explain.

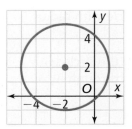

PRACTICE

For Exercises 20–23, find the center and radius for each equation of a circle. SEE EXAMPLE 1

20. $(x - 4)^2 + (y + 3)^2 = 64$

21. $(x + 2)^2 + y^2 = 13$

22. $(x + 5)^2 + (y + 11)^2 = 32$

23. $(x - 8)^2 + (y - 12)^2 = 96$

For Exercises 24 and 25, write the equation for the circle shown in each graph. SEE EXAMPLE 2

24.   **25.**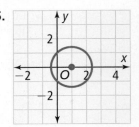

For Exercises 26–29, write the equation for each circle with the given radius and center. SEE EXAMPLE 2

26. radius: 4, center: $(5, 1)$

27. radius: 9, center: $(-3, 8)$

28. radius: $5\sqrt{5}$, center: $(2, -4)$

29. radius: $\sqrt{13}$, center: $(-5, -9)$

For Exercises 30–32, determine whether each given point lies on the circle with the given radius and center. SEE EXAMPLE 3

30. $(2, 4)$; radius: 4, center: $(-1, 1)$

31. $(\sqrt{17}, 8)$; radius: 9, center: $(0, 0)$

32. $(2, 0)$; radius: $\sqrt{10}$, center: $(3, -9)$

For Exercises 33–35, graph each equation.
SEE EXAMPLES 4 AND 5

33. $x^2 - 10x + y^2 + 2y = -22$

34. $x^2 + y^2 - 2y = 15$

35. $x^2 + 6x + y^2 + 8y = -16$

36. The point $(2, b)$ lies on the circle with radius 5 and center $(-1, -1)$. What are the possible values of b?

37. Is $(7, 2)$ inside, outside, or on the circle $(x - 4)^2 + y^2 = 25$? Explain.

PRACTICE & PROBLEM SOLVING

APPLY

38. Model With Mathematics After an earthquake, a circle-shaped tsunami travels outward from the epicenter at an average speed of 420 miles per hour. If the earthquake with the epicenter shown occurred at 5:48 A.M., at what time will the tsunami reach Port Charles? Justify your answer. Ⓒ **MP.4**

39. Make Sense and Persevere A cell phone tower is attached to the ground as shown. A circular security fence must be placed around the tower 10 feet from where the guy wires are attached to the ground. Can a cell phone tower be placed in the region enclosed by the red border? If so, what are possible coordinates of the tower? Ⓒ **MP.1**

Dimensions in Feet

40. Reason Semitrailer trucks can be up to 14 feet tall. Should they be allowed in the outer lanes of the semicircular tunnel? Explain. Ⓒ **MP.2**

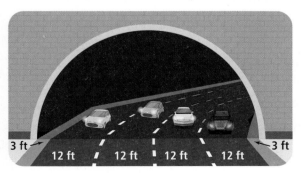

ASSESSMENT PRACTICE

41. A circle has center (0, 0) and passes through the point (−5, 2). Which other points lie on the circle? Select all that apply.

- ☐ **A.** (0, 6)
- ☐ **D.** (−5, −2)
- ☐ **B.** ($\sqrt{11}$, 3$\sqrt{2}$)
- ☐ **E.** (4, −$\sqrt{13}$)
- ☐ **C.** (2, 5)
- ☐ **F.** (−$\sqrt{29}$, 0)

42. SAT/ACT Which equation represents the circle with center (−3, 7) and radius 9?

- Ⓐ $(x + 3)^2 + (y − 7)^2 = 3^2$
- Ⓑ $(x − 3)^2 + (y + 7)^2 = 9^2$
- Ⓒ $(x − 7)^2 + (y + 3)^2 = 9^2$
- Ⓓ $(x + 3)^2 + (y − 7)^2 = 9^2$
- Ⓔ $(x + 7)^2 + (y − 3)^2 = 3^2$

43. Performance Task A farmer can use up to four rotating sprinklers for the field shown. He has ten 50-meter sections that can be combined to form rotating arms with lengths from 50 m to 500 m. The irrigation circles cannot overlap and must not extend beyond the edges of the field. The distance between grid lines is 50 m.

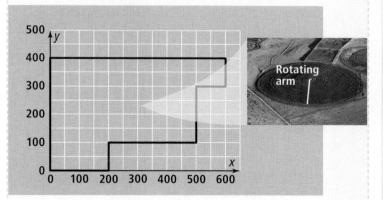

Rotating arm

Part A Design an irrigation system for the field that irrigates as much of the field as possible. Draw a sketch of your system. For each sprinkler, give the coordinates of the center of the sprinkler, the radius, and the equation.

Part B What is the total area of the field? What is the total area irrigated by your system? What percent of the field does your system irrigate?

9-4

Parabolas in the Coordinate Plane

I CAN... use the equations and graphs of parabolas to solve problems.

VOCABULARY
- directrix
- focus
- parabola

Common Core State Standards
HSG.GPE.A.2, MP.1, MP.2, MP.6

CONCEPTUAL UNDERSTANDING

MAKE SENSE AND PERSEVERE
Think about the relationship between the point and line. How would the shape of the parabola change if the line and point were closer together or farther apart? **MP.1**

EXPLORE & REASON

Consider two points and two intersecting lines.

A. Describe the set of points that is equidistant from two points. Draw a diagram to support your answer.

B. Describe the set of points that is equidistant from each of two intersecting lines. Draw a diagram to support your answer.

C. **Look for Relationships** What do you think a set of points that is equidistant from a line and a point would look like? Draw a diagram to support your answer. **MP.7**

ESSENTIAL QUESTION
How does the geometric description of a parabola relate to its equation?

EXAMPLE 1 | Explore the Graph of a Parabola

What is the set of points that are equidistant from the graph of the equation $y = -2$ and the point $(0, 2)$?

Graph the line and the point.

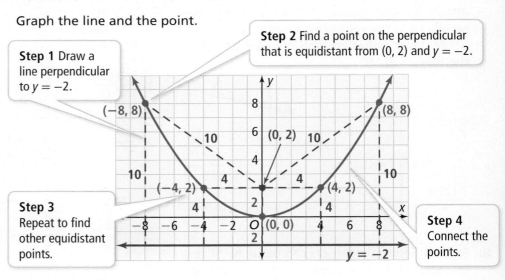

The set of points equidistant from $(0, 2)$ and $y = -2$ is a curve called a *parabola*.

Try It! 1. The set of points equidistant from $(3, 5)$ and the line $y = 9$ is also a parabola.

  a. What is the vertex of the parabola?

  b. Describe the graph of the parabola.

EXAMPLE 2 **Derive the Equation of a Parabola**

What is the equation of a parabola?

A **parabola** is the set of all points in a plane that are the same distance from a fixed point F, the **focus**, as they are from a line d, the **directrix**.

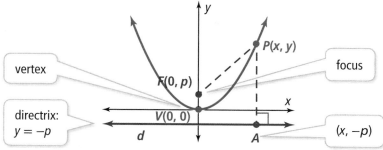

Every point on the parabola is equidistant from F and line d.

$$PF = PA$$

$$\sqrt{(x-0)^2 + (y-p)^2} = \sqrt{(x-x)^2 + (y-(-p))^2}$$ Use the Distance Formula.

$$\sqrt{x^2 + (y-p)^2} = \sqrt{(y+p)^2}$$

$$x^2 + (y-p)^2 = (y+p)^2$$

$$x^2 + y^2 - 2py + p^2 = y^2 + 2py + p^2$$

$$x^2 - 2py = 2py$$

$$x^2 = 4py$$

$$y = \frac{1}{4p}x^2$$ Solve for y in terms of x.

The equation for a parabola with vertex at the origin is $y = \frac{1}{4p}x^2$.

If the vertex is at (h, k), then the parabola is translated h units horizontally and k units vertically, and the equation is $y - k = \frac{1}{4p}(x - h)^2$.

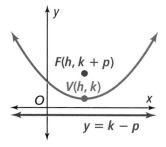

Try It!   2. What expression represents the distance between the focus and the directrix?

CONCEPT Equation of a Parabola

Vertex at origin:

$$y = \frac{1}{4p}x^2$$

Vertex at (h, k):

$$y - k = \frac{1}{4p}(x - h)^2$$

The variable p represents the distance between the focus and the vertex.

EXAMPLE 3 ▸ Write the Equation of a Parabola

A. What equation represents the parabola with focus (5, 5) and directrix $y = 1$?

Graph the focus and directrix to determine the vertex and p.

The vertex is the midpoint of the segment connecting the focus and the directrix.

The value of p is the distance between the focus and the vertex.

Write the equation for the parabola with vertex (5, 3) and $p = 2$.

$$y - k = \frac{1}{4p}(x - h)^2$$

Write the formula for a parabola with vertex (h, k).

$$y - 3 = \frac{1}{4(2)}(x - 5)^2$$

$$y = \frac{1}{8}(x - 5)^2 + 3$$

COMMON ERROR
When substituting values into the equation of a parabola, be sure to use the coordinates of the vertex, not the coordinates of the focus.

B. Graph the parabola from part A.

Use the equation to make a table of values to help you sketch the graph.

x	y	(x, y)
1	$\frac{1}{8}(1 - 5)^2 + 3$	$(1, 5)$
3	$\frac{1}{8}(3 - 5)^2 + 3$	$(3, 3\frac{1}{2})$
8	$\frac{1}{8}(8 - 5)^2 + 3$	$(8, 4\frac{1}{8})$

Try It! **3. a.** What equation represents the parabola with focus $(-1, 4)$ and directrix $y = -2$?

b. What equation represents the parabola with focus (3, 5) and vertex (3, −1)?

EXAMPLE 4 Apply the Equation of a Parabola

The cross section of a satellite dish is a parabola, with the feed horn at the focus. How long do the braces holding the feed horn need to be?

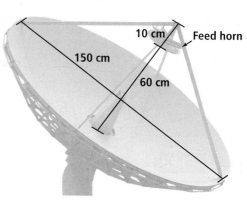

Formulate ◄ Place the parabola on a coordinate plane. Parabolas are symmetric, so computations are easier for a parabola with its vertex at the origin.

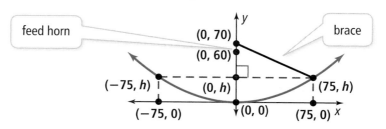

Write an equation for the parabola, and then use the equation to find the height h of the dish. Finally, use the Pythagorean Theorem to find the length of the brace.

Compute ◄ **Step 1** Write the equation.

$y = \dfrac{1}{4p} x^2$ — Write the equation for a parabola with vertex at the origin, where p is the distance between the focus and the vertex.

$y = \dfrac{1}{4(60)} x^2$ — Substitute 60 for p.

$y = \dfrac{1}{240} x^2$

Step 2 Evaluate for $x = 75$ to find the height h of the dish.

$h = \dfrac{1}{240}(75)^2 \approx 23.4$ cm

Step 3 Use the Pythagorean Theorem to find the length of the brace.

$(70 - 23.4)^2 + 75^2 = b^2$

$7{,}796.56 = b^2$

$b \approx 88.3$

Interpret ◄ The braces need to be 88.3 cm long.

Try It! **4.** On a different satellite dish, the feed horn is 38 inches above the vertex. If the height of the dish is 22 inches, what is its width?

CONCEPT SUMMARY Parabolas

WORDS ⟩ A parabola is the set of points equidistant from a focus and a directrix.

ALGEBRA ⟩ $y - k = \frac{1}{4p}(x - h)^2$

where (h, k) is the vertex and p is the distance from the vertex to the focus

GRAPH ⟩

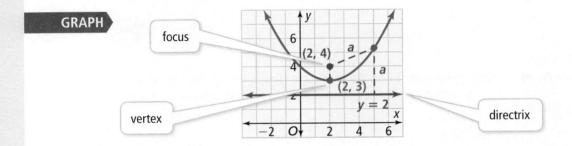

focus

vertex

directrix

Do You UNDERSTAND?

1. **ESSENTIAL QUESTION** ⟩ How does the geometric description of a parabola relate to its equation?

2. **Error Analysis** Arthur says that an equation of the parabola with directrix $y = 0$ and focus $= (0, 6)$ is $y - 3 = \frac{1}{24}x^2$. What is his error? © **MP.3**

3. **Vocabulary** How could the word *direction* help you remember that the directrix is a line?

4. **Reason** What are the coordinates of point *P*? Show your work. © **MP.2**

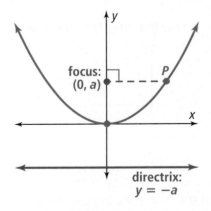

5. **Communicate Precisely** Given vertex (a, b) and focus (a, c), describe how you would write an equation for the parabola. © **MP.6**

Do You KNOW HOW?

For Exercises 6 and 7, write an equation of each parabola with the given focus and directrix.

6. focus: $(5, 1)$; directrix: $y = -5$

7. focus: $(4, 0)$; directrix: $y = -4$

For Exercises 8 and 9, give the vertex, focus, and directrix of each parabola.

8. $y - 2 = \frac{1}{6}x^2$ 9. $y + 3 = \frac{1}{20}(x - 9)^2$

For Exercises 10 and 11, write an equation of each parabola with the given focus and vertex.

10. focus: $(6, 2)$; vertex: $(6, -4)$

11. focus: $(-1, 8)$; vertex: $(-1, 7)$

12. What is the equation of the parabola graphed on the coordinate plane?

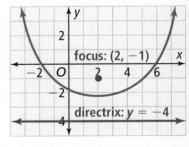

13. Consider the parabola $y = \frac{1}{36}x^2$.

    a. What are the focus and directrix?

    b. The parabola passes through $(12, 4)$. Show that this point is equidistant from the focus and the directrix.

PRACTICE & PROBLEM SOLVING

UNDERSTAND

14. Communicate Precisely Use the graph to answer the questions. Line m is the directrix of the parabola.

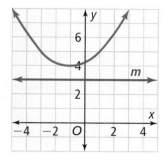

a. How would you find the vertex of the parabola? Explain. © MP.6

b. How would you find the focus of the parabola? Explain.

c. How would you find an equation of the parabola? Explain.

15. Communicate Precisely Define a parabola as a set of points. What is the relationship of the points to the lines and points associated with the parabola? © MP.6

16. Mathematical Connections The general form of the equation of a parabola is $y = x^2 - 6x + 9$. What are the focus, vertex, and directrix of the parabola?

17. Reason How does changing the distance from the focus to the directrix change the shape of a parabola in the coordinate plane? Explain. © MP.2

18. Construct Arguments The parabola has its focus at $\left(0, \frac{1}{4}\right)$ and vertex at $(0, 0)$. How would you find the equation of the parabola? © MP.3

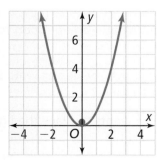

PRACTICE

For Exercises 19–22, find the vertex of each parabola. SEE EXAMPLE 1

19. focus: $(3, 7)$; directrix: $y = -1$

20. focus: $(6, 2)$; directrix: $y = -4$

21. focus: $(-4, 3)$; directrix: $y = 0$

22. focus: $(-2, -1)$; directrix: $y = -6$

For Exercises 23–26, find the vertex, focus and directrix of each parabola. SEE EXAMPLE 2

23. $y - 7 = \frac{1}{8}(x - 3)^2$ **24.** $y + 4 = \frac{1}{36}(x - 1)^2$

25. $y - 3 = \frac{1}{16}(x + 6)^2$ **26.** $y + 5 = \frac{1}{2}(x - 10)^2$

For Exercises 27–29, write an equation of each parabola with the given focus and directrix. SEE EXAMPLE 3

27. focus: $(0, 4)$; directrix: $y = 0$

28. focus: $(5, 1)$; directrix: $y = -9$

29. focus: $(-4, 5)$; directrix: $y = 2$

For Exercises 30–32, write an equation of each parabola with the given focus and vertex. SEE EXAMPLE 3

30. focus: $(4, 5)$; vertex: $(4, -1)$

31. focus: $(-4, 9)$; vertex: $(-4, 5)$

32. focus: $(2, 4)$; vertex: $(2, 0)$

For Exercises 33–35, use the graph of the parabola to answer each question. SEE EXAMPLE 4

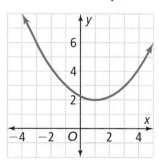

33. What is the vertex of the parabola?

34. Using a point on the parabola and the equation $y - k = \frac{1}{4p}(x - h)^2$, what is p?

35. What is the focus of the parabola?

PRACTICE & PROBLEM SOLVING

APPLY

36. Reason Enzo is building a model of the Clifton Suspension Bridge in Bristol, UK, using a scale factor of 100 ft : 1 in. The cable between the towers is in the shape of a parabola. Enzo writes an equation for the parabola and uses the equation to find the distance from the cable to the deck of the bridge. Suppose the deck of the bridge lies on the x-axis and the vertex of the parabola is on the y-axis. What equation did Enzo write? ⓒ **MP.2**

702 ft

86 ft

37. Model With Mathematics Voshon builds a solar hot dog cooker for the science fair. Suppose the base of the cooker is the x-axis and the hot dog is on the y-axis at the focus. What is the equation of the parabola that models the cooker? ⓒ **MP.4**

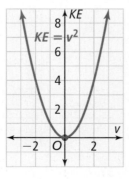

38. Higher Order Thinking
An engineer is making an impact analysis on a car bumper. He graphs the kinetic energy of a 2-kg steel ball as a function of the velocity of the ball. Kinetic energy is measured in joules (J) and velocity is measured in meters per second.

(graph) KE, $KE = v^2$, axis values 8, 6, 4, 2, −2, O, 2, v

a. What are the vertex, focus, and directrix of the parabola?

b. The bumper has to withstand an impact of 25 J from the ball without any damage. How fast is the ball moving when it strikes the bumper with that amount of energy?

ASSESSMENT PRACTICE

39. An equation of a parabola is $y - 5 = \frac{1}{8}(x - 4)$. Select all that apply.

☐ **A.** The vertex of the parabola is (5, 4).

☐ **B.** $p = 2$

☐ **C.** The focus of the parabola is (4, 7).

☐ **D.** The directrix of the parabola is $y = 3$.

40. SAT/ACT Which is the vertex of the parabola represented by the equation $y + 5 = 6(x - 6)^2$?

Ⓐ (6, 5) Ⓒ (6, −5)

Ⓑ (−6, −5) Ⓓ (−6, 25)

41. Performance Task Some flashlights are designed so that a parabolic mirror reflects light forward from a light source.

h

d

For the flashlight to work best, the light source is placed at the focus of the parabola. Wyetta designs a flashlight so $d = 4$ in. and $h = 3$ in.

Part A How could Wyetta model the mirror on the coordinate plane? What is an equation for the mirror?

Part B At what point above the vertex would Wyetta place the light source?

Part C Suppose Wyetta wants to place the light source $\frac{1}{2}$ in. farther from the vertex with the same $h = 3$ in. Will the mirror be narrower or wider? Explain.

Topic Review

1. How can geometric relationships be proven by applying algebraic properties to geometric figures represented in the coordinate plane?

Vocabulary Review

Choose the correct term to complete each sentence.

- circle
- directrix
- focus
- parabola
- radius
- vertex

2. All the points on a parabola are the same distance from a fixed point, the _____ as they are from a line, the _____.

3. A _____ is a set of points equidistant from a point.

4. A _____ is the highest or lowest point on the graph of a function.

Concepts & Skills Review

LESSON 9-1 **Polygons in the Coordinate Plane**

Quick Review

When a geometric figure is represented in a coordinate plane, you can use slope, distance, and midpoints to analyze properties of the figure.

Example

Is △ABC an isosceles triangle? Explain.

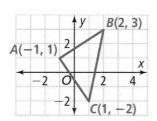

A triangle is isosceles if two sides are congruent. Use the Distance Formula to find the side lengths.

$$AB = \sqrt{(2 - (-1))^2 + (3 - 1)^2} = \sqrt{13}$$
$$BC = \sqrt{(1 - 2)^2 + (-2 - 3)^2} = \sqrt{26}$$
$$CA = \sqrt{(1 - (-1))^2 + (-2 - 1)^2} = \sqrt{13}$$

Since $AB = CA$, △ABC is isosceles.

Practice & Problem Solving

For Exercises 5–8, determine whether each figure is the given type of figure.

5. $F(-2, 4)$, $G(0, 0)$, $H(3, 1)$; right triangle

6. $A(7, 2)$, $B(3, -1)$, $C(3, 4)$; equilateral triangle

7. $J(-4, -4)$, $K(-7, 0)$, $L(-4, 4)$, $M(-1, 0)$; rhombus

8. What are the area and perimeter of $PQRS$?

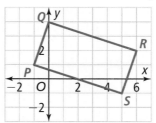

9. **Make Sense and Persevere** Parallelogram $WXYZ$ has coordinates $W(a, b)$, $X(c, d)$, $Y(f, g)$, and $Z(h, j)$. What equation can you use to determine whether $WXYZ$ is a rhombus? Explain. **© MP.1**

Proofs Using Coordinate Geometry

Quick Review

To prove theorems using coordinate geometry, place the figure on the coordinate plane. Use slope, midpoint, and distance to write an algebraic proof.

Example

Prove that the diagonals of a rectangle are congruent.

Place a rectangle on a coordinate plane with one vertex at the origin and two sides along the axes.

$$WY = \sqrt{(a - 0)^2 + (b - 0)^2} = \sqrt{a^2 + b^2}$$
$$XZ = \sqrt{(a - 0)^2 + (0 - b)^2} = \sqrt{a^2 + b^2}$$

Since $WY = XZ$, the diagonals of a rectangle are congruent.

Practice & Problem Solving

For Exercises 10–12, give the coordinates of each missing vertex.

10. $ABCD$ is a parallelogram; $A(0, 0)$, $B(p, q)$, $D(t, 0)$

11. $JKLM$ is a kite; $J(0, 0)$, $K(a, b)$, $L(0, c)$

12. $WXYZ$ is a rhombus; $W(0, 0)$, $Y(0, h)$, $Z(j, k)$

13. **Communicate Precisely** If you are given the coordinates of a quadrilateral, how can you prove that the quadrilateral is an isosceles trapezoid? **MP.6**

14. The diagram shows a fenced garden area, where $PX = PY$. The gardener is dividing the garden with a fence from P to the midpoint of $\overline{XY}$. Will the new fence be perpendicular to $\overline{XY}$? Use coordinate geometry to explain.

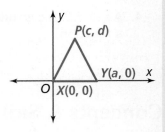

Circles in the Coordinate Plane

Quick Review

The equation of a circle in the coordinate plane is

$$(x - h)^2 + (y - k)^2 = r^2$$

where (h, k) is the center of the circle and r is the radius.

Example

What is the equation of $\odot Q$?

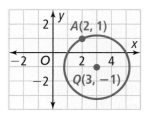

The center of the circle is $(3, -1)$, and the radius is QA.

$$QA = \sqrt{(2 - 3)^2 + (1 - (-1))^2} = \sqrt{5}$$

So, the equation of $\odot Q$ is $(x - 3)^2 + (y + 1)^2 = 5$.

Practice & Problem Solving

For Exercises 15–17, write the equation for the circle with the given center and radius.

15. center: $(0, 0)$, radius: 9

16. center: $(-2, 3)$, radius: 5

17. center: $(-5, -8)$, radius: $\sqrt{13}$

For Exercises 18 and 19, determine whether the given point lies on the circle with the given center and radius.

18. $(-3, 0)$; center: $(-5, 2)$, radius: $2\sqrt{2}$

19. $(11, -1)$; center: $(4, 4)$, radius: $6\sqrt{2}$

20. Suppose that $\overline{AB}$, with $A(1, 15)$ and $B(13, -1)$, and $\overline{CD}$, with $C(15, 13)$ and $D(-1, 1)$, are diameters of $\odot T$. What is the equation of $\odot T$?

21. **Construct Arguments** Is it possible to write the equation of a circle given only two points on the circle? Explain. **MP.3**

Parabolas in the Coordinate Plane

Quick Review

A **parabola** is the set of points that are equidistant from a fixed point, the **focus**, and a line, the **directrix**. The equation for a parabola in the coordinate plane is

$$y - k = \frac{1}{4p}(x - h)^2$$

where (h, k) is the vertex and p is the distance between the vertex and focus.

Example

What is the equation of the parabola with focus (4, 2) and directrix $y = 0$?

The vertex is the midpoint of the segment connecting the focus and the directrix, so the vertex is (4, 1). Since p is the distance between the focus and the vertex, $p = 1$. So, the equation of the parabola is

$$y - 1 = \frac{1}{4}(x - 4)^2.$$

Practice & Problem Solving

For Exercises 22 and 23, write the equation for the parabola with the given focus and directrix.

22. focus: (0, 0), directrix: $y = -6$

23. focus: (−1, −3), directrix: $y = -4$

24. **Reason** Point F is the focus and $y = -p$ is the directrix of the parabola shown. What is AB? Explain how you found your answer. ⓒ MP.2

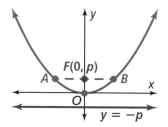

25. The cables for a suspension bridge are parabolic. The support towers are 40 m tall and 100 m apart. At its lowest point, a cable is 15 m above the bridge deck. If the bridge deck lies on the x-axis and a vertex lies on the y-axis, what equation represents the bridge cable?

Circles

TOPIC ESSENTIAL QUESTION

When a line or lines intersect a circle how are the figures formed related to the radius, circumference, and area of the circle?

Topic Overview

enVision® STEM Project:
Design Space Cities

10-1 Arcs and Sectors

10-2 Lines Tangent to a Circle

Mathematical Modeling in 3 Acts:
Earth Watch

10-3 Chords

10-4 Inscribed Angles

10-5 Secant Lines and Segments

Topic Vocabulary

- arc length
- central angle
- chord
- inscribed angle
- intercepted arc
- major arc
- minor arc
- point of tangency
- radian
- secant
- sector of a circle
- segment of a circle
- tangent to a circle

Digital Experience

INTERACTIVE STUDENT EDITION
Access online or offline.

ACTIVITIES Complete *Explore & Reason, Model & Discuss*, and *Critique & Explain* activities. Interact with *Examples* and *Try Its.*

CONCEPT SUMMARY Review key lesson content through multiple representations.

ASSESSMENT Show what you've learned.

 Go online | SavvasRealize.com

MATHEMATICAL MODELING IN 3 ACTS

Earth Watch

Scientists estimate that there are currently about 3,000 operational man-made satellites orbiting Earth. These satellites serve different purposes, from communication to navigation and global positioning. Some are weather satellites that collect environmental information.

The International Space Station is the largest man-made satellite that orbits Earth. It serves as a space environment research facility, and it also offers amazing views of Earth. Think about this during the Mathematical Modeling in 3 Acts lesson.

VIDEOS Watch clips to support *Mathematical Modeling in 3 Acts Lessons* and **enVision® STEM Projects.**

TUTORIALS Get help from *Virtual Nerd*, right when you need it.

PRACTICE Practice what you've learned.

ADAPTIVE PRACTICE Practice that is *just right* and *just for you.*

FAMILY ENGAGEMENT Involve family in your learning.

A-Z GLOSSARY Read and listen to English and Spanish definitions.

MATH TOOLS Explore math with digital tools and manipulatives.

DESMOS Use Anytime and as embedded Interactives in Lesson content.

Did You Know?

Astronauts, six at a time, have lived and worked in the International Space Station (ISS) since 2000. As of April 2022, residents of 20 countries have visited the ISS.

The size of a football field, ISS circles the Earth every 90 minutes at an **altitude of 248 miles** and a speed of about **17,500 miles per hour**.

At its closest, the planet Mars is **150 times as far from Earth** as the Moon is. Despite the distance, the United States and Russia have been landing spacecraft and scientific instruments on Mars for several decades.

Your Task: Design Space Cities

Suppose it's 500 years in the future. Space stations the size of small cities are journeying through space. Use trigonometry and the geometry of circles to calculate the measurements of two of these stations, then design, measure, and describe a group of three "space cities."

10-1

Arcs and Sectors

I CAN... find arc length and sector area of a circle and use them to solve problems.

VOCABULARY
- arc length
- central angle
- intercepted arc
- major arc
- minor arc
- radian
- sector of a circle
- segment of a circle

Common Core State Standards
HSG.CO.A.1, HSG.C.B.5, MP.2, MP.6, MP.7

STUDY TIP
A minor arc may be written with just two letters, as in $\overset{\frown}{AB}$. Use the third point between the endpoints of an arc to name a major arc, as in $\overset{\frown}{ACB}$.

EXPLORE & REASON

Darren bends a piece of wire using a circular disc to make the shape as shown.

22 cm

100 cm

A. How long does the piece of wire need to be to make the shape? Explain.

B. Construct Arguments What information do you think is needed to find part of the circumference of a circle? Justify your answer. **MP.3**

ESSENTIAL QUESTION
How are arc length and sector area related to circumference and area of a circle?

EXAMPLE 1   Relate Central Angles and Arc Measures

What are $m\overset{\frown}{AB}$ and $m\overset{\frown}{ACB}$?

A **central angle** of a circle is an angle formed by two radii with the vertex at the center of the circle. Angle APB is a central angle.

A central angle divides a circle into two arcs. An **intercepted arc** is the part of a circle that lies between two segments, rays, or lines that intersect the circle.

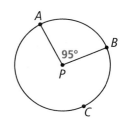

A central angle and its intercepted minor arc have equal measure.

∠APB is a central angle, and $\overset{\frown}{AB}$ is its corresponding intercepted arc.

A **minor arc** of a circle is an arc that is smaller than a semicircle. $\overset{\frown}{AB}$ is a minor arc.

A **major arc** of a circle is an arc that is larger than a semicircle. $\overset{\frown}{ACB}$ is a major arc.

Find $m\overset{\frown}{AB}$.

$$m\overset{\frown}{AB} = m\angle APB = 95$$

The degree measure of $\overset{\frown}{AB}$ is equal to the measure of its corresponding central angle ∠APB.

Find $m\overset{\frown}{ACB}$.

$$m\overset{\frown}{ACB} = 360 - 95 = 265$$

Try It!   1. Use ⊙W.

a. What is $m\overset{\frown}{XZ}$?

b. What is $m\overset{\frown}{XYZ}$?

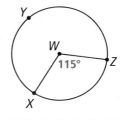

CONCEPT Arc Measure

The measure of an arc is equal to the measure of its corresponding central angle.

$$m\widehat{JM} = m\angle JPM$$

Congruent central angles intercept congruent arcs, and congruent arcs are intercepted by congruent central angles.

$$\angle JPK \cong \angle KPL \qquad \widehat{JK} \cong \widehat{KL}$$

**CONCEPTUAL
UNDERSTANDING**

EXAMPLE 2 Relate Arc Length to Circumference

A. How do you find the length _s_ of an arc measured in degrees?

The *measure* of an arc is a fraction of 360°.

The **arc length** is a fraction of the circumference.

$$\frac{\text{arc length}}{\text{circumference}} = \frac{\text{arc measure (degrees)}}{360}$$

$$\frac{s}{2\pi r} = \frac{n}{360}$$

$$s = \frac{n}{360} \cdot 2\pi r$$

Use a proportion to represent the relationships among arc length *s*, radius *r*, and arc measure *n*.

The formula to find the length of an arc is $s = \frac{n}{360} \cdot 2\pi r$.

B. How do you find the length _s_ of an arc measured in radians?

Besides degrees, angle measures can be expressed in *radians*.

A **radian** is equal to the measure of a central angle that intercepts an arc with length equal to the radius of the circle.

Circumference is $2\pi r$, which is 2π arcs of length *r*. Since each arc of length *r* corresponds to 1 radian, there are 2π radians in a circle. So, 2π radians is equivalent to 360°.

STUDY TIP
Remember that the circumference measures the distance around all of the circle and the arc length is the distance around part of the circle.

To find the arc length, use the following proportion.

$$\frac{\text{arc length}}{\text{circumference}} = \frac{\text{arc measure (radians)}}{2\pi}$$

$$\frac{s}{2\pi r} = \frac{\theta}{2\pi}$$

$$s = \frac{\theta}{2\pi} \cdot 2\pi r = \theta r$$

The variable theta (θ) is often used for angles measured in radians.

Arc length is proportional to radius, with θ as the constant of proportionality.

To find the length of an arc measured in radians, use the formula $s = \theta r$.

CONTINUED ON THE NEXT PAGE

EXAMPLE 2 CONTINUED

Try It! **2.** The two circles share center O. The larger circle is a dilation of the smaller circle with scale factor 1.5. The measure of $\angle AOB$ is 60° and the measure of arc CD is 2π.

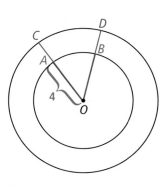

   a. What is the length of arc AB? Round to the nearest tenth.

   b. Show that the measures of $\angle AOB$ and $\angle COD$, in radians, are equal.

CONCEPT Arc Length

The length s of an arc of a circle is the product of the ratio relating the measure of the central angle in degrees to 360 and the circumference of the circle. The length of the arc is also the product of the radius and the central angle measure in radians.

Central angle in degrees:

$$s = \frac{n}{360} \cdot 2\pi r$$

Central angle in radians:

$$s = \theta r$$

EXAMPLE 3 **Apply Arc Length**

What is the length of $\overset{\frown}{AD}$? Express the answer in terms of π.

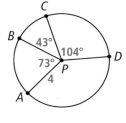

Step 1 Find the arc measure.

$$m\overset{\frown}{AD} = 360 - m\overset{\frown}{AB} - m\overset{\frown}{BC} - m\overset{\frown}{CD}$$

$$= 360 - 73 - 43 - 104$$

$$= 140$$

> Each arc measure is equal to the measure of the corresponding central angle.

MAKE SENSE AND PERSEVERE
Think about when you should express arc lengths in terms of π and when you should give approximate answers. How would you decide? ⓒ **MP.1**

Step 2 Find the arc length.

$$s = \frac{n}{360} \cdot 2\pi r$$

$$= \frac{140}{360} \cdot 2\pi(4) = \frac{28}{9}\pi$$

> Use the formula for arc length for angles given in degrees.

The length of $\overset{\frown}{AD}$ is $\frac{28}{9}\pi$.

Try It! **3.** Use $\odot Q$. Express answers in terms of π.

   a. What is the length of $\overset{\frown}{JK}$?

   b. What is the length of $\overset{\frown}{HK}$?

EXAMPLE 4   Relate the Area of a Circle to the Area of a Sector

A sector of a circle is the region bounded by two radii and the intercepted arc. What is the area of sector *MQN*?

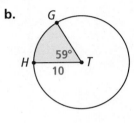

To find the area of the sector, find $\frac{78}{360}$ of the area of the circle.

$$A = \frac{78}{360} \cdot \pi r^2$$

$$= \frac{78}{360} \cdot \pi(10)^2 = \frac{65}{3}\pi$$

In general, the area of a sector is $A = \frac{n}{360} \cdot \pi r^2$, where $n°$ is the measure of the intercepted arc and r is the radius of the circle.

The area of sector *MQN* is $\frac{65}{3}\pi$ cm².

GENERALIZE
Compare the formulas for arc length and sector area. What relationships do you see between the arc length and sector area for any given arc? Ⓖ MP.8

Try It!   4. What is the area of each shaded sector?

a.

b.

EXAMPLE 5   Find the Area of a Segment of a Circle

A segment of a circle is the part of a circle bounded by an arc and the segment joining its endpoints. What is the area of the shaded region?

To find the area of the segment, subtract the area of the triangle from the area of the sector.

Step 1 Find the area of the sector.

$$A = \frac{n}{360} \cdot \pi r^2 = \frac{32}{3}\pi$$

Use the formula for area of a sector.

Step 2 Find the area of the triangle.

Since $\overline{RX}$ and $\overline{RY}$ are both radii and the angle between them is 60°, $\triangle RYX$ is equilateral.

Use the Pythagorean Theorem to find h.

$$4^2 + h^2 = 8^2$$

$$h^2 = 8^2 - 4^2$$

$$h = \sqrt{48} = 4\sqrt{3}$$

Find the area of the triangle.

$$A = \frac{1}{2}bh$$

$$= \frac{1}{2}(8)(4\sqrt{3}) = 16\sqrt{3}$$

MAKE SENSE AND PERSEVERE
Think about other strategies you can use. How could you use trigonometric ratios to find the base and height of $\triangle RXY$? Ⓖ MP.1

Step 3 Find the area of the segment.

$$\text{area of segment} = \text{area of sector} - \text{area of triangle}$$

$$= \frac{32}{3}\pi - 16\sqrt{3} \approx 5.8$$

The area of the shaded region is about 5.8 cm².

CONTINUED ON THE NEXT PAGE

EXAMPLE 5 CONTINUED

Try It!   **5.** What is the area of each segment?

a.

10 ft

b.
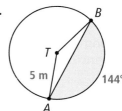
5 m   144°

APPLICATION

EXAMPLE 6   **Solve Problems Involving Circles**

Chen uses sectors cut from circular corkboards to make 18 watermelon coasters to sell at a craft fair.

8 in.   72°

A. **He paints one side of each coaster with special paint. Each jar of paint covers 200 in.^{2}. Will one jar of paint be enough to paint all the coasters?**

COMMON ERROR
Be careful not to confuse the formula for the area of a sector with the formula for arc length. Remember that the area of a sector is proportional to the area of the circle, and the arc length is proportional to the circumference.

Find the area of one watermelon coaster. Use 3.14 for π.

$A = \dfrac{n}{360} \cdot \pi r^2$

$= \dfrac{72}{360} \cdot \pi(4)^2$

≈ 10.0

Use the formula for area of a sector.

The area of one watermelon coaster is about 10 in.^{2}.

Chen can paint $200 \div 10 = 20$ coasters with one jar of paint, so he has enough paint for 18 coasters.

B. **He puts decorative tape around the edge of each coaster. How much tape does he need for each coaster?**

The perimeter of the coaster consists of two radii and an arc.

$P = r + r + \dfrac{n}{360} \cdot 2\pi r$

$= 4 + 4 + \dfrac{72}{360} \cdot 2\pi(4)$

≈ 13.0

4 in.
72°
4 in.

Chen needs about 13 inches of tape for each coaster.

Try It!   **6.** What are the area and perimeter of sector *QNR*? Round to the nearest tenth.

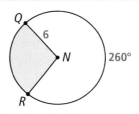
6   260°

CONCEPT SUMMARY Arc Length and Sector Area

WORDS	DIAGRAMS

Arc Length

The arc length is a fraction of the circumference.

Degrees

$$s = \frac{n}{360} \cdot 2\pi r$$

Radians

$$s = \theta r$$

Sector

A sector of a circle is the region bounded by two radii and the intercepted arc.

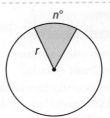

$$A = \frac{n}{360} \cdot \pi r^2$$

Segment

A segment of a circle is the part of a circle bounded by an arc and the segment joining its endpoints.

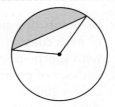

segment area = sector area − triangle area

Do You UNDERSTAND?

1. **ESSENTIAL QUESTION** How are arc length and sector area related to circumference and area of a circle?

2. **Error Analysis** Luke was asked to compute the length of $\widehat{AB}$. What is Luke's error? Ⓒ MP.3

$$S = \frac{n}{360} \cdot 2\pi r$$
$$= \frac{1.5}{360} \cdot 2\pi(3)$$
$$= 0.0785 \quad ✗$$

3. **Vocabulary** How can the word *segment* help you remember what a *segment of a circle* is?

4. **Reason** Mercedes says that she can find the area of a quarter of a circle using the formula $A = \frac{1}{4}\pi r^2$. Using the formula for the area of a sector, explain why Mercedes is correct. Ⓒ MP.2

Do You KNOW HOW?

For Exercises 5 and 6, find the measures and lengths of each arc. Express the answers in terms of π.

5. $\widehat{BC}$

6. $\widehat{ABC}$

7. Circle P has radius 8. Points Q and R lie on circle P, and the length of $\widehat{QR}$ is 4π. What is $m\angle QPR$ in radians?

8. What is the area of sector *EFG*? Express the answer in terms of π.

9. What is the area of the segment? Express the answer in terms of π.

PRACTICE & PROBLEM SOLVING

UNDERSTAND

10. Error Analysis Jamaal is asked to compute the area of the shaded region. What is his error? ⓒ **MP.3**

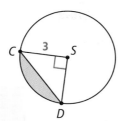

Segment area = sector area − triangle area

$= \dfrac{90}{360} \cdot 2\pi(3) - \dfrac{1}{2}(3)(3)$

≈ 0.21

11. Mathematical Connections The equation $(x - 2)^2 + (y - 3)^2 = 25$ represents $\odot T$. Points $X(-2, 6)$ and $Y(-1, -1)$ lie on $\odot T$. What is $m\widehat{XY}$? Explain how you know.

12. Reason Figure *GHJKL* is a regular pentagon. To the nearest tenth, what percent of the area of $\odot T$ is *not* part of the area of *GHJKL*? Explain. ⓒ **MP.2**

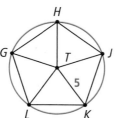

13. Use Structure Explain why the length of an arc with arc measure $a°$ is proportional to the radius of the circle. ⓒ **MP.7**

14. Higher Order Thinking The areas of sectors *ACB* and *DEF* are equal. What expression gives the value of *x*? Show your work.

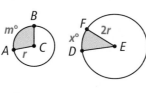

15. A regular octagon is inscribed in a circle.

  a. Write an expression for the area of one triangle.

  b. Write an expression for the area of the octagon.

  c. Write an expression for the area of a regular polygon with *n* sides.

  d. Generalize As the number of sides increases, *h* approaches *r*, and the perimeter of the polygon, *P*, approaches the circumference of the circle, *C*. Use that information to justify the formula $A = \pi r^2$. ⓒ **MP.8**

PRACTICE

For Exercises 16–19, find each arc measure.
SEE EXAMPLE 1

16. $m\widehat{FE}$

17. $m\widehat{BC}$

18. $m\widehat{CE}$

19. $m\widehat{CFE}$

For Exercises 20 and 21, find each arc length in terms of π. SEE EXAMPLES 2 AND 3

20. length of $\widehat{JK}$

21. length of $\widehat{XYZ}$

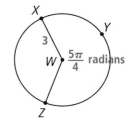

For Exercises 22 and 23, find the area of each sector. Round to the nearest tenth. SEE EXAMPLES 4 AND 6

22. sector *DEF*

23. sector *GHJ*

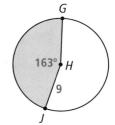

For Exercises 24 and 25, find the area of each segment. Round to the nearest tenth. SEE EXAMPLE 5

24.

25.

26. The length of $\widehat{ABC}$ is 110 ft. What is the radius of $\odot D$? Round to the nearest tenth.

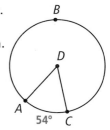

PRACTICE & PROBLEM SOLVING

APPLY

27. Make Sense and Persevere Kanesha and Fatima will each run 150 m on the two inside lanes of the track, so the end markers need to be placed correctly. To the nearest hundredth, what are *x* and *y*? ⓒ **MP.1**

28. Reason Charlie is designing a dart board and wants the red sections to be 25% of the total area. What should be the radius of the inner circle? Round to the nearest tenth. ⓒ **MP.2**

29. Look for Relationships Enrique is selling the drop-leaf table and wants to include the area of the table when the leaves are down in his ad. What is the area of the center section when the leaves are down? Round to the nearest square inch. Explain how you found your answer. ⓒ **MP.7**

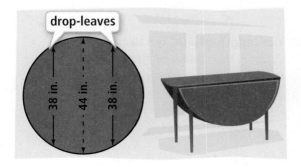

ASSESSMENT PRACTICE

30. What is the diameter of ⊙*T*?

Sector Area = $\frac{64}{5}\pi$

31. SAT/ACT An arc has a central angle of $\frac{2}{5}\pi$ radians and a length of 6π. What is the circumference of the circle?

Ⓐ 12π　　Ⓑ 15π　　Ⓒ 30π　　Ⓓ 36π

32. Performance Task A carpenter is constructing the stage for a concert.

Part A What is the total amount of flooring needed to cover the stage? Round to the nearest square foot. Explain how you found your answer.

Part B A string of lights will be strung along the sides and front of the stage. What is the total length of light string needed? Show your work.

Part C One portion of the stage can be raised during the concert. The lift mechanism can lift a maximum area of 180 ft², but the band needs the width *w* of the raised area to be at least 20 ft. What could be the value of *x*? Justify your answer.

10-2

Lines Tangent to a Circle

I CAN... use properties of tangent lines to solve problems.

VOCABULARY
• point of tangency
• tangent to a circle

© Common Core State Standards
HSG.C.A.2, HSG.C.A.4 (+), MP.1, MP.2, MP.5

CRITIQUE & EXPLAIN

 Powered By desmos

Alicia and Renaldo made conjectures about the lines that intersect a circle only once.

Alicia

• Many lines intersect the circle once at the same point.
• Two lines that intersect the circle once and the segment connecting the points form an isosceles triangle.

Renaldo

• Parallel lines intersect the circle at opposite ends of the same diameter.
• The lines intersecting the circle at one point are perpendicular to a diameter of the circle.

A. Use Appropriate Tools Which of the four conjectures do you agree with? Which do you disagree with? Draw sketches to support your answers. **© MP.5**

B. What other conjectures can you make about lines that intersect a circle at one point?

ESSENTIAL QUESTION How is a tangent line related to the radius of a circle at the point of tangency?

CONCEPTUAL UNDERSTANDING

EXAMPLE 1 Understand Tangents to a Circle

 Powered By desmos

What is the relationship between a circle and a tangent to the circle?

A **tangent to a circle** is a line in the plane of the circle that intersects the circle in exactly one point. That point is the **point of tangency**.

Circle C has tangent line m with point of tangency X. Point Y is any other point on m.

GENERALIZE
Point Y represents any point other than the point of tangency. Would the result be true no matter where point Y is located on m? **© MP.8**

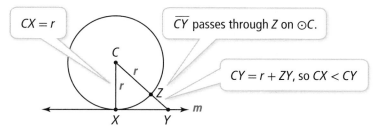

$CX = r$

$\overline{CY}$ passes through Z on $\odot C$.

$CY = r + ZY$, so $CX < CY$

So, $\overline{CX}$ is the shortest segment from C to line m. Since the shortest segment from a point to a line is perpendicular to the line, $\overline{CX} \perp m$.

Try It! 1. Does Example 1 support Renaldo's conjecture that parallel lines intersect the circle at opposite ends of the same diameter? Explain.

THEOREM 10-1 AND THE CONVERSE

Theorem

If $\overleftrightarrow{AB}$ is tangent to $\odot C$ at P, then $\overleftrightarrow{AB}$ is perpendicular to $\overline{CP}$.

PROOF: SEE EXERCISES 12 AND 13.

Converse

If $\overleftrightarrow{AB}$ is perpendicular to radius $\overline{CP}$ at P, then $\overleftrightarrow{AB}$ is tangent to $\odot C$.

If...

Then... $\overleftrightarrow{AB} \perp \overline{CP}$

If...

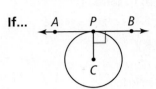

Then... $\overleftrightarrow{AB}$ is tangent to $\odot C$.

EXAMPLE 2 Use Tangents to Solve Problems

A. Is $\overline{KJ}$ tangent to $\odot P$ at J?

A segment or ray that intersects a circle in one point is tangent to the circle if it is part of a tangent line.

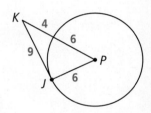

If $\overline{KJ}$ is part of a line that is tangent to $\odot P$ at J, then $\overline{PJ} \perp \overline{JK}$ and $\triangle PJK$ is a right triangle.

$$9^2 + 6^2 \stackrel{?}{=} (4 + 6)^2$$

> Use the Converse of the Pythagorean Theorem to determine whether $\triangle PJK$ is a right triangle.

$$117 \neq 100$$

So, $\overline{PJ}$ is not perpendicular to $\overline{KJ}$.

Therefore, $\overline{KJ}$ is not tangent to $\odot P$ at J.

B. Segment ST is tangent to $\odot R$. What is the radius of $\odot R$?

Since $\overline{ST}$ is tangent to $\odot R$, $\triangle RST$ is a right triangle.

$$x^2 + 24^2 = (x + 18)^2$$

> Use the Pythagorean Theorem with length of the hypotenuse $x + 18$.

$$x^2 + 576 = x^2 + 36x + 324$$

$$252 = 36x$$

$$7 = x$$

The radius of $\odot R$ is 7.

CONTINUED ON THE NEXT PAGE

LEARN TOGETHER

What are ways to stay positive and work toward goals?

COMMON ERROR

To find $(x + 18)^2$, it may be helpful to write $(x + 18)(x + 18)$ as a first step. This helps avoid the common error of squaring each term within the parentheses instead of squaring the binomial.

EXAMPLE 2 CONTINUED

C. Line *m* is tangent to ⊙*T* at *B*, and line *n* is tangent to ⊙*T* at *C*. What is the value of *x*?

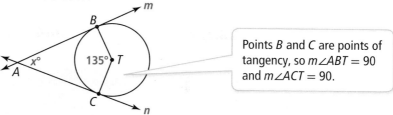

Points *B* and *C* are points of tangency, so $m\angle ABT = 90$ and $m\angle ACT = 90$.

STUDY TIP
Remember that for any convex polygon, the sum of the interior angles is $(n - 2)180°$, where *n* is the number of sides.

Use the Polygon Angle-Sum Theorem to find *x*.

$$m\angle BAC + m\angle ACT + m\angle CTB + m\angle TBA = 360$$
$$x + 90 + 135 + 90 = 360$$
$$x = 45$$

Try It! **2.** Use ⊙*N*.

a. Is $\overleftrightarrow{MP}$ tangent to ⊙*N*? Explain.

b. If $\overline{LK}$ is tangent to ⊙*N* at *L*, what is *KN*?

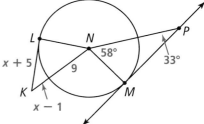

EXAMPLE 3 **Find Lengths of Segments Tangent to a Circle**

What is the relationship between $\overline{YZ}$ and $\overline{XZ}$?

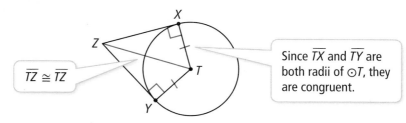

$\overline{TZ} \cong \overline{TZ}$

Since $\overline{TX}$ and $\overline{TY}$ are both radii of ⊙*T*, they are congruent.

By HL, $\triangle TXZ \cong \triangle TYZ$, so $\overline{YZ} \cong \overline{XZ}$ by CPCTC.

Try It! **3.** If $TX = 12$ and $TZ = 20$, what are *XZ* and *YZ*?

THEOREM 10-2 Segments Tangent to a Circle Theorem

Powered By **desmos**

If two segments with a common endpoint exterior to a circle are tangent to the circle, then the segments are congruent.

If...

Then... $\overline{AB} \cong \overline{AC}$

PROOF: SEE EXERCISE 14.

EXAMPLE 4 Find Measures Involving Tangent Lines

A satellite requires a line of sight for communication. Between the ground stations farthest from the satellite, what is the amount of time needed for a signal to go from one station up to the satellite, and then down to the other station?

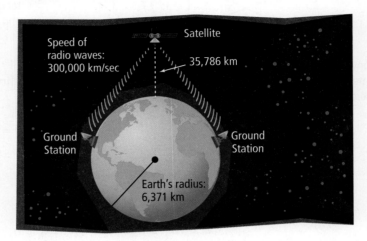

Speed of radio waves: 300,000 km/sec

35,786 km

Satellite

Ground Station

Ground Station

Earth's radius: 6,371 km

Formulate The lines from the satellite to the farthest ground stations are tangent to Earth's surface.

Use the Pythagorean Theorem to compute the distance to the ground stations. Then compute the time for radio waves to travel twice this distance.

Compute **Step 1** Find the distance from the farthest ground stations to the satellite.

$$x^2 + 6,371^2 = (6,371 + 35,786)^2$$

$$x^2 + 40,589,641 = 1,777,212,649$$

$$x^2 = 1,736,623,008$$

$$x \approx 41,673$$

Satellite

35,786 km

x

Ground Station

6,371 km

Center of Earth

6,371 km

Step 2 Find the time for radio waves to travel this distance twice.

$$(41,673 \times 2) \text{ km} \div 300,000 \text{ km/sec} \approx 0.28 \text{ sec}$$

Interpret The amount of time for a signal to travel from one of the farthest ground stations to the satellite and back to the other ground station is about 0.28 second.

Try It! **4.** What is the perimeter of *ABCD*?

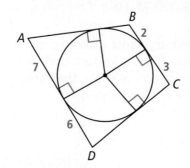

EXAMPLE 5 **Construct Tangent Lines**

How do you construct a tangent to ⊙P passing through point T?

Step 1 Use a straightedge to draw $\overline{PT}$. Label point A where $\overline{PT}$ intersects the circle.

Step 2 Use a compass to construct a circle with center P and passing through T. Construct a perpendicular to $\overline{PT}$ at A. Label point B where the perpendicular intersects the outer circle.

> **COMMON ERROR**
> You may think that A is the midpoint of $\overline{PT}$. However, the construction of a perpendicular line here is different from constructing the perpendicular bisector of $\overline{PT}$.

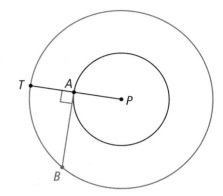

Step 3 Use a straightedge to construct $\overline{BP}$. Label point C where $\overline{BP}$ intersects the inner circle.

Step 4 Use a straightedge to construct $\overline{TC}$.

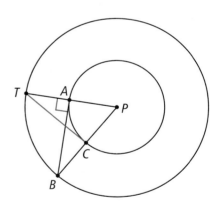

The tangent to ⊙P passing through T is $\overline{TC}$.

Try It! **5.** Prove that $\overline{TC}$ is tangent to ⊙P.

Given: Two circles share center P, points A and C on the smaller circle, points T and B on the larger circle, $\overline{AB} \perp \overline{PT}$

Prove: $\overline{TC}$ is tangent to ⊙P at C.

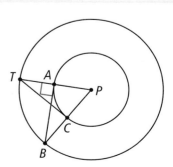

CONCEPT SUMMARY Tangents to a Circle

WORDS A tangent to a circle intersects the circle at exactly one point. The radius that contains the point of tangency is perpendicular to the tangent.

DIAGRAM

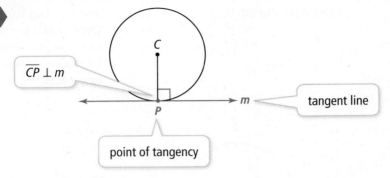

$\overline{CP} \perp m$

tangent line

point of tangency

Do You UNDERSTAND?

1. **ESSENTIAL QUESTION** How is a tangent line related to the radius of a circle at the point of tangency?

2. **Error Analysis** Kona looked at the figure shown and said that $\overline{AB}$ is tangent to ⊙G at A because it intersects ⊙G only at A. What was Kona's error? ⓒ MP.3

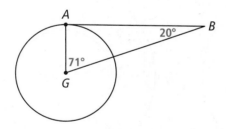

3. **Vocabulary** Can any point on a circle be a *point of tangency*? Explain.

4. **Reason** Lines m and n are tangent to circles A and B. What are the relationships between ∠PAS, ∠PQS, ∠RQS, and ∠RBS? Explain. ⓒ MP.2

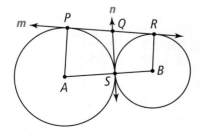

Do You KNOW HOW?

Tell whether each line or segment is a tangent to ⊙B.

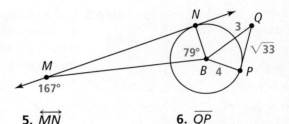

5. $\overleftrightarrow{MN}$

6. $\overline{QP}$

Segment AC is tangent to ⊙D at B. Find each value.

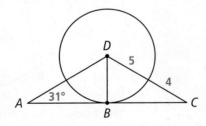

7. m∠ADB

8. BC

Segment FG is tangent to ⊙K at F and $\overline{HG}$ is tangent to ⊙K at H. Find each value.

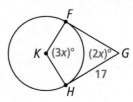

9. FG

10. m∠FGH

PRACTICE & PROBLEM SOLVING

UNDERSTAND

11. Error Analysis Segments $\overline{DF}$, $\overline{DH}$, and $\overline{GF}$ are tangent to the circle. Andrew was asked to find DF. Explain Andrew's error. ⒼMP.3

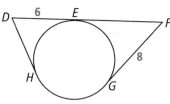

$DF = DE + EF$
By Theorem 10-2, $DE = EF$.
So, $DF = 6 + 6 = 12$. ✗

12. Construct Arguments Use the following outline to write an indirect proof of Theorem 10-1. ⒼMP.3

Given: Line m is tangent to $\odot T$ at G.

Prove: $\overline{GT} \perp m$

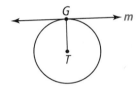

- Assume that $\overline{GT}$ is not perpendicular to m.
- Draw $\overline{HT}$ such that $\overline{HT} \perp m$.
- Use triangles to show that $GT > HT$.
- Show that this is a contradiction, since H is in the exterior of $\odot T$.

13. Construct Arguments Prove the Converse of Theorem 10-1. ⒼMP.3

Given: $\overline{QR} \perp n$

Prove: n is tangent to $\odot Q$ at R

Hint: Select any other point S on line n. Show that $\overline{QS}$ is the hypotenuse of $\triangle QRS$, so $QS > QR$ and therefore S lies outside $\odot Q$.

14. Construct Arguments Prove Theorem 10-2. ⒼMP.3

Given: $\overline{DE}$ and $\overline{DF}$ are tangent to $\odot T$.

Prove: $\overline{DE} \cong \overline{DF}$

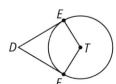

15. Higher Order Thinking If $AC = x$, what is the perimeter of $\triangle BCE$? Explain.

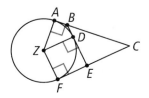

PRACTICE

The segments $\overline{AB}$ and $\overline{CD}$ are tangent to $\odot T$. Find each value. SEE EXAMPLES 1 AND 2

16. AB

17. $m\angle TDC$

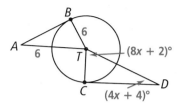

For Exercises 18–20, the segments are tangent to the circle. Find each value. SEE EXAMPLES 3 AND 4

18. DG

19. Perimeter of $JLNQ$

20. AC

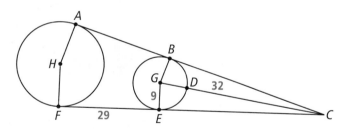

21. Trace $\odot P$ and point A. Construct a tangent to $\odot P$ that passes through A. SEE EXAMPLE 5

22. The diameter of $\odot F$ is 8; $AB = 10$; and $\overline{AB}$, $\overline{BC}$, and $\overline{AC}$ are tangent to $\odot F$. What is the perimeter of $\triangle ABC$?

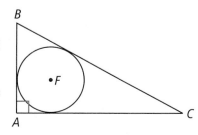

PRACTICE & PROBLEM SOLVING

23. Make Sense and Persevere Yumiko is shopping for a stand for a decorative glass ball with an 8-inch diameter. She is considering the stand shown and wants to know the height h of the portion of the ball that will be visible if the sides of the stand are tangent to the sphere. What is the value of h? ⓒ MP.1

h

5 in.

24. Use Structure Neisha is looking out from the 103rd floor of the Willis Tower, in Chicago, on a clear day. How far away is the horizon? Earth's radius is about 6,400 km. ⓒ MP.7

412 m

25. Mathematical Connections Rail planners want to connect the two straight tracks with a curved track as shown. Any curves must have a radius of at least 450 m.

to Arville: 5 km

106°

to Bremen: 3.5 km

450 m

P 450 m

a. Explain how engineers can locate point P, the center of the curved section of track.

b. Once the curved track is constructed, what distance will trains travel between Arvillle and Bremen? Justify your answer.

26. Circle P is described by the equation $(x + 3)^2 + (y - 2)^2 = 25$. Which of the following lines are tangent to ⊙P? Select all that apply.

☐ **A.** $y = x + 3$

☐ **B.** $y = 5$

☐ **C.** $y = x$

☐ **D.** $x = 2$

☐ **E.** $y = -3$

☐ **F.** $y = x - 3$

27. SAT/ACT Line m is tangent to ⊙A at B. What is the area of △ABC?

m

B

A

4

5

C

Ⓐ 10

Ⓑ 18

ⓒ $2\sqrt{65}$

Ⓓ $\dfrac{5\sqrt{65}}{2}$

28. Performance Task The African art design below is based on circles that are tangent to each other.

r

Part A If the radius of the larger circles is r, what is the radius of the smaller circles?

Part B Choose a value for the larger radius and draw the pattern. Measure the radii of the small and large circles. Are the values related in the way you described in Part A?

Part C In your diagram for Part B, mark the points where the small and large circles are tangent to each other. Add lines that are tangent to the circles at these points. Describe how the tangent lines you drew illustrate Theorems 10-1 and 10-2.

▶ SavvasRealize.com

Earth Watch

Scientists estimate that there are currently about 3,000 operational man-made satellites orbiting Earth. These satellites serve different purposes, from communication to navigation and global positioning. Some are weather satellites that collect environmental information.

The International Space Station is the largest man-made satellite that orbits Earth. It serves as a space environment research facility, and it also offers amazing views of Earth. Think about this during the Mathematical Modeling in 3 Acts lesson.

ACT 1 ▶ Identify the Problem

1. What is the first question that comes to mind after watching the video?

2. Write down the main question you will answer about what you saw in the video.

3. Make an initial conjecture that answers this main question.

4. Explain how you arrived at your conjecture.

5. What information will be useful to know to answer the main question? How can you get it? How will you use that information?

ACT 2 ▶ Develop a Model

6. Use the math that you have learned in this Topic to refine your conjecture.

ACT 3 ▶ Interpret the Results

7. Did your refined conjecture match the actual answer exactly? If not, what might explain the difference?

10-3
Chords

CONCEPTUAL
UNDERSTANDING

STUDY TIP
Refer to the diagram as you read the proof. Note which parts of the triangles are congruent.

EXPLORE & REASON

Use the diagram to answer the questions.

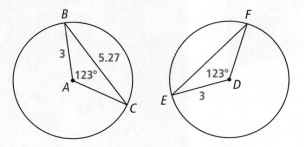

A. What figures in the diagram are congruent? Explain.

B. **Look for Relationships** How can you find *EF*? © **MP.7**

ESSENTIAL QUESTION How are chords related to their central angles and intercepted arcs?

EXAMPLE 1   Relate Central Angles and Chords

A chord is a segment whose endpoints are on a circle.
Why is $\overline{RS} \cong \overline{UT}$?

∠RQS ≅ ∠UQT because they are vertical angles.

$\overline{SQ} \cong \overline{TQ} \cong \overline{UQ} \cong \overline{RQ}$ because all radii of a circle are ≅.

By the SAS Congruence Theorem, △QRS ≅ △QUT. Therefore $\overline{RS} \cong \overline{UT}$ because they are corresponding parts of congruent triangles.

Try It!   **1.** Why is ∠BAC ≅ ∠DAE?

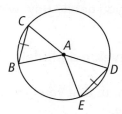

THEOREM 10-3 AND THE CONVERSE

Theorem

If two chords in a circle or in congruent circles are congruent, then their central angles are congruent.

Converse

If two central angles in a circle or in congruent circles are congruent, then their chords are congruent.

PROOF: SEE EXERCISES 12 AND 13.

If... $\overline{MN} \cong \overline{PQ}$

Then... $\angle MTN \cong \angle PTQ$

If... $\angle MTN \cong \angle PTQ$

Then... $\overline{MN} \cong \overline{PQ}$

THEOREM 10-4 AND THE CONVERSE

Theorem

If two arcs in a circle or in congruent circles are congruent, then their chords are congruent.

Converse

If two chords in a circle or in congruent circles are congruent, then their arcs are congruent.

PROOF: SEE EXAMPLE 2 AND EXAMPLE 2 TRY IT.

If... $\overset{\frown}{MN} \cong \overset{\frown}{PQ}$

Then... $\overline{MN} \cong \overline{PQ}$

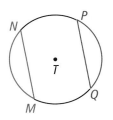

If... $\overline{MN} \cong \overline{PQ}$

Then... $\overset{\frown}{MN} \cong \overset{\frown}{PQ}$

PROOF →

EXAMPLE 2 Relate Arcs and Chords

Write a proof of Theorem 10-4.

Given: $\overset{\frown}{AB} \cong \overset{\frown}{CD}$

Prove: $\overline{AB} \cong \overline{CD}$

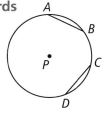

Plan: Use the relationship between central angles and arcs by drawing the radii $\overline{PA}$, $\overline{PB}$, $\overline{PC}$, and $\overline{PD}$.

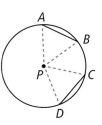

Proof: Since $\overset{\frown}{AB} \cong \overset{\frown}{CD}$, you know that $m\overset{\frown}{AB} = m\overset{\frown}{CD}$. And since the measure of a central angle is equal to the measure of its arc, $m\angle APB = m\overset{\frown}{AB}$ and $m\angle CPD = m\overset{\frown}{CD}$. By substitution, $m\angle APB = m\angle CPD$ and $\angle APB \cong \angle CPD$. So, by the Converse of Theorem 10-3, $\overline{AB} \cong \overline{CD}$.

MAKE SENSE AND PERSEVERE
Think about other strategies you can use. How could you use congruent triangles to prove the relationship? ⓒ **MP.1**

Try It! **2.** Write a flow proof of the Converse of Theorem 10-4.

THEOREM 10-5 AND THE CONVERSE

Theorem

If chords are equidistant from the center of a circle or the centers of congruent circles, then they are congruent.

Converse

If chords in a circle or in congruent circles are congruent, then they are equidistant from the center or centers.

PROOF: SEE EXAMPLE 3 AND EXAMPLE 3 TRY IT.

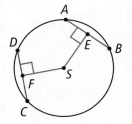

If... $\overline{SE} \cong \overline{SF}$, Then... $\overline{AB} \cong \overline{CD}$

If... $\overline{AB} \cong \overline{CD}$, Then... $\overline{SE} \cong \overline{SF}$

PROOF →

EXAMPLE 3 Relate Chords Equidistant from the Center

Write a proof of Theorem 10-5.

Given: ⊙P with $\overline{AB} \perp \overline{PE}$,
$\overline{CD} \perp \overline{PF}$,
$\overline{PE} \cong \overline{PF}$

Prove: $\overline{AB} \cong \overline{CD}$

COMMON ERROR
Be sure to construct the triangles with corresponding parts that yield the desired conclusion.

Plan: Construct triangles by drawing the radii $\overline{PA}$, $\overline{PB}$, $\overline{PC}$, and $\overline{PD}$. Then show that the triangles are congruent in order to apply CPCTC.

Proof:

Try It! **3.** Write a flow proof of the Converse of Theorem 10-5.

EXAMPLE 4 **Construct a Regular Hexagon Inscribed in a Circle**

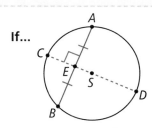

STUDY TIP

Remember, a regular polygon is both equilateral and equiangular.

How do you draw a regular hexagon inscribed in ⊙P?

Step 1 Mark point Q on the circle.

Step 2 Set the compass the radius of the circle. Place the compass point at Q and draw an arc through the circle.

Step 3 Keep the compass setting. Move the compass point to the intersection of the arc and the circle. Draw another arc through the circle. Each point of intersection is a vertex of the hexagon. Continue this way until you have five arcs.

Step 4 Draw chords connecting consecutive points on the circle.

The side lengths of the resulting figure are all congruent because they have the same length as the radius of the circle.

Connecting the center of the circle with the six vertices of the inscribed polygon forms six equilateral triangles, so each angle measures 120. The figure is a regular hexagon.

Try It! **4.** Construct an equilateral triangle inscribed in a circle.

THEOREM 10-6 AND THE CONVERSE

Theorem

If a diameter is perpendicular to a chord, then it bisects the chord.

Converse

If a diameter bisects a chord (that is not a diameter), then it is perpendicular to the chord.

PROOF: SEE EXERCISES 15 AND 16.

If... $\overline{CD}$ is a diameter, $\overline{AB} \perp \overline{CD}$

Then... $\overline{AE} \cong \overline{BE}$

If... $\overline{CD}$ is a diameter, $\overline{AE} \cong \overline{BE}$

Then... $\overline{AB} \perp \overline{CD}$

THEOREM 10-7

The perpendicular bisector of a chord contains the center of the circle.

PROOF: SEE EXERCISE 28.

If...

Then... S is on $\overline{CD}$

EXAMPLE 5 Solve Problems Involving Chords of Circles

An engineer is designing a service tunnel to accommodate two trucks simultaneously. If the tunnel can accommodate a width of 18 ft, what is the greatest truck height that the tunnel can accommodate? Subtract 0.5 ft to account for fluctuations in pavement.

Formulate ◀ Draw and label a sketch to help solve the problem.

9 ft

13.5 ft

x ft

C

6 ft

Let x be the distance from the center to the greatest height. The radius is 13.5 ft.

Compute ◀ Write and solve an equation for x.

$$9^2 + x^2 = 13.5^2$$

Use the Pythagorean Theorem.

$$x^2 = 13.5^2 - 9^2$$

$$x = \sqrt{13.5^2 - 9^2}$$

$$x \approx 10.06$$

Add the distance from the ground to the center $13.5 - 6 = 7.5$ to x and subtract 0.5 ft to account for fluctuations in pavement.

$$7.5 + 10.06 - 0.5 = 17.06$$

Interpret ◀ The greatest height that the tunnel can accommodate is about 17.06 ft.

Try It! **5.** Fresh cut flowers need to be in at least 4 inches of water. A spherical vase is filled until the surface of the water is a circle 5 inches in diameter. Is the water deep enough for the flowers? Explain.

CONCEPT SUMMARY Chords

	Chords and Central Angles	**Chords and Arcs**
WORDS	Two chords in a circle or in congruent circles are congruent if and only if the central angles of the chords are congruent.	Two chords in a circle or in congruent circles are congruent if and only if the chords intercept congruent arcs.
DIAGRAMS		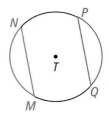
	∠MTN ≅ ∠PTQ if and only if $\overline{MN} \cong \overline{PQ}$.	$\overarc{MN} \cong \overarc{PQ}$ if and only if $\overline{MN} \cong \overline{PQ}$.

Do You UNDERSTAND?

1. **ESSENTIAL QUESTION** How are chords related to their central angles and intercepted arcs?

2. **Error Analysis** Aquene writes a proof to show that two chords are congruent. What is her error? **ⓒ MP.3**

∠APB ≅ ∠CPD	Vert. ∠s ≅
$\overarc{AB} \cong \overarc{CD}$	Intercepted by ≅ ∠s
$\overline{AB} \cong \overline{DC}$	Chords intercept ≅ ares

3. **Vocabulary** Explain why all diameters of circles are also chords of the circles.

4. **Reason** Given $\overarc{RS} \cong \overarc{UT}$, how can you find UT? **ⓒ MP.2**

Do You KNOW HOW?

For Exercises 5–10, in ⊙P, $m\overarc{AB} = 43°$, and AC = DF. Find each measure.

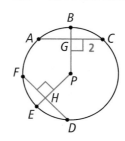

5. DF

6. $m\overarc{AC}$

7. FH

8. $m\overarc{DE}$

9. AC

10. $m\overarc{DF}$

11. For the corporate headquarters, an executive wants to place a company logo that is six feet in diameter with the sides of the H five feet tall on the front wall. What is the width x of the crossbar for the H?

PRACTICE & PROBLEM SOLVING

UNDERSTAND

12. Construct Arguments Write a paragraph proof of Theorem 10-3. ⒼMP.3

Given: $\overline{AB} \cong \overline{CD}$

Prove: $\angle AEB \cong \angle CED$

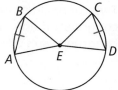

13. Construct Arguments Write a two-column proof of the Converse of Theorem 10-3. ⒼMP.3

Given: $\angle AEB \cong \angle CED$

Prove: $\overline{AB} \cong \overline{CD}$

14. Error Analysis What is Quan's error? ⒼMP.3

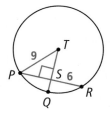

$$TS = \sqrt{PR^2 - PS^2}$$
$$= \sqrt{12^2 - 9^2}$$
$$\approx 7.9 \quad ✗$$

15. Construct Arguments Write a proof of Theorem 10-6. ⒼMP.3

Given: $\overline{LN}$ is a diameter of $\odot Q$; $\overline{LN} \perp \overline{KM}$

Prove: $\overline{KP} \cong \overline{MP}$

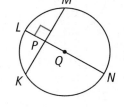

16. Construct Arguments Write a proof of the Converse of Theorem 10-6. ⒼMP.3

Given: $\overline{LN}$ is a diameter of $\odot Q$; $\overline{KP} \cong \overline{MP}$

Prove: $\overline{LN} \perp \overline{KM}$

17. Higher Order Thinking $\triangle ABP \sim \triangle CDE$. How do you show that $\widehat{AB} \cong \widehat{CD}$?

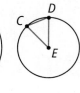

PRACTICE

For Exercises 18–21, in $\odot B$, $m\angle VBT = m\widehat{PR} = 90$, and $QR = TU$. SEE EXAMPLES 1 AND 2

18. Find $m\angle PBR$.

19. Find $m\widehat{TV}$.

20. Which angle is congruent to $\angle QBR$?

21. Which segment is congruent to $\overline{TV}$?

22. Construct a square inscribed in a circle. How is drawing an inscribed square different from drawing an inscribed hexagon or triangle? SEE EXAMPLE 4

23. Find CD. SEE EXAMPLE 3

24. Find FG. SEE EXAMPLE 3

25. A chord is 12 cm long. It is 30 cm from the center of the circle. What is the radius of the circle? SEE EXAMPLE 5

26. The diameter of a circle is 39 inches. The circle has two chords of length 8 inches. What is the distance from each chord to the center of the circle?

27. A chord is 4 units from the center of a circle. The radius of the circle is 5 units. What is the length of the chord?

28. Write a proof of Theorem 10-7.

Given: $\overline{QR}$ is a chord in $\odot P$; $\overline{AB}$ is the perpendicular bisector of $\overline{QR}$.

Prove: $\overline{AB}$ contains P.

PRACTICE & PROBLEM SOLVING

APPLY

29. **Mathematical Connections** Nadia designs a water ride and wants to use a half-cylindrical pipe in the construction. If she wants the waterway to be 8 ft wide when the water is 2 ft deep, what is the diameter of the pipe?

30. **Model With Mathematics** A bike trail has holes up to 20 in. wide and 5 in. deep. If the diameter of the wheels of Ana's bike is 26 in., can she ride her bike without the wheels hitting the bottom of the holes? Explain. ⓖ **MP.4**

31. **Make Sense and Persevere** The bottom of a hemispherical cake has diameter 8 in.

a. If the cake is sliced horizontally in half so each piece has the same height, would the top half fit on a plate with diameter 6 in.? Explain.

b. If the cake is sliced horizontally in thirds so each piece has the same height, would the top third fit on a plate with diameter 5 in.? Explain. ⓖ **MP.1**

32. Which must be true? Select all that apply.

☐ **A.** $\overset{\frown}{QR} \cong \overset{\frown}{TU}$

☐ **B.** $PR = TV$

☐ **C.** $VW = AS$

☐ **D.** $PS = SR$

☐ **E.** $\overset{\frown}{PR} \cong \overset{\frown}{TV}$

33. **SAT/ACT** The radius of the semicircle is r, and $CD = \frac{3}{4} \cdot AB$. What is the distance from the chord to the diameter?

Ⓐ $\frac{5}{4}r$ Ⓑ $\frac{\sqrt{7}}{4}r$ Ⓒ $\frac{\sqrt{7}}{4}\pi r$ Ⓓ $\frac{5}{4}\pi r$

34. **Performance Task** The radius of the range of a radar is 50 miles. At 1:00 P.M., a plane enters the radar screen flying due north. At 1:04 P.M. the aircraft is due east of the radar. At 1:08 P.M., the aircraft leaves the screen. The plane is moving at 8 miles per minute.

Part A What distance does the plane fly on the controller's screen?

Part B What is the distance of the plane from the radar at 1:04 P.M.?

Part C Another plane enters the screen at point A at 1:12 P.M. and flies in a straight line at 9 miles per minute. If it gets no closer than 40 miles from the radar, at what time does it leave the screen? Explain.

10-4

Inscribed Angles

I CAN... use the relationships between angles and arcs in circles to find their measures.

VOCABULARY
- inscribed angle

© **Common Core State Standards**
HSG.C.A.2, MP.1, MP.6, MP.7

CONCEPTUAL UNDERSTANDING

STUDY TIP
There are infinitely many inscribed angles that intercept the arc. These inscribed angles all have the same angle measure.

EXPLORE & REASON

Consider ⊙*T*.

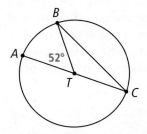

A. Make Sense and Persevere List at least seven things you can conclude about the figure. © **MP.1**

B. How is ∠*ACB* related to ∠*ATB*? Explain.

ESSENTIAL QUESTION How is the measure of an inscribed angle related to its intercepted arc?

EXAMPLE 1 Relate Inscribed Angles to Intercepted Arcs

What is the relationship between $\overset{\frown}{AB}$ and ∠*ACB*?

An **inscribed angle** has its vertex on a circle and its sides contain chords of the circle.

$\overset{\frown}{AB}$ is intercepted by ∠*C*.

△*QCB* is isosceles, so ∠*QBC* ≅ ∠*QCB*.

∠*C* is inscribed in ⊙*Q*.

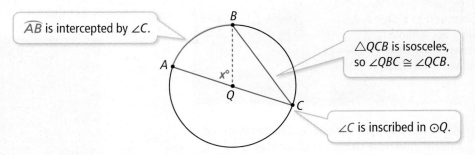

Draw radius $\overline{QB}$ to form △*QCB* and central angle ∠*AQB*.

$m\angle QBC + m\angle QCB = x$ — Apply the Triangle Exterior Angle Theorem.

$2(m\angle QCB) = x$ — $m\angle QBC = m\angle QCB$ since ∠*QBC* ≅ ∠*QCB*.

$m\angle QCB = \frac{1}{2}x$

$m\angle ACB = \frac{1}{2}m\overset{\frown}{AB}$ — $m\angle QCB = m\angle ACB$ and $x = m\overset{\frown}{AB}$.

The measure of an inscribed angle ∠*ACB* is half the measure of the intercepted arc $\overset{\frown}{AB}$.

Try It! **1.** Given ⊙*P* with inscribed angle ∠*S*, if $m\overset{\frown}{RT} = 47$, what is *m*∠*S*?

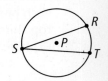

THEOREM 10-8 Inscribed Angles Theorem

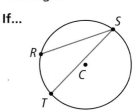
Powered By
desmos

The measure of an inscribed angle is half the measure of its intercepted arc.

Case 1

The center is on one side of the angle.

If...

Then... $m\angle S = \frac{1}{2}m\widehat{RT}$

Case 2

The center is inside the angle.

If...

Then... $m\angle S = \frac{1}{2}m\widehat{RT}$

Case 3

The center is outside the angle.

If...

Then... $m\angle S = \frac{1}{2}m\widehat{RT}$

PROOF: SEE EXERCISES 19, 32, AND 33.

EXAMPLE 2 Use the Inscribed Angles Theorem

A. If $m\widehat{DG} = 45.6$, what are $m\angle E$ and $m\angle F$?

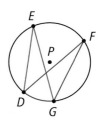

$$m\angle E = \frac{1}{2}m\widehat{DG} \qquad\qquad m\angle F = \frac{1}{2}m\widehat{DG}$$
$$= \frac{1}{2}(45.6) = 22.8 \qquad\qquad = \frac{1}{2}(45.6) = 22.8$$

> **LOOK FOR RELATIONSHIPS**
> The diameter of a circle is a straight angle. What is the measure of the arc intercepted by a diameter? **ⓒ MP.7**

B. If $\widehat{RT}$ is a semicircle, what is $m\angle RST$?

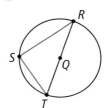

$$m\angle S = \frac{1}{2}m\widehat{RT}$$
$$= \frac{1}{2}(180) = 90$$

C. If $m\widehat{ABC} = 184$ and $m\widehat{BCD} = 242$, what are the measures of the angles of quadrilateral $ABCD$?

$$m\angle A = \frac{1}{2}m\widehat{BCD} \qquad\qquad m\angle B = \frac{1}{2}m\widehat{ADC}$$
$$= \frac{1}{2}(242) = 121 \qquad\qquad = \frac{1}{2}(360 - 184) = 88$$
$$m\angle D = \frac{1}{2}m\widehat{ABC} \qquad\qquad m\angle C = 360 - (121 + 88 + 92)$$
$$= \frac{1}{2}(184) = 92 \qquad\qquad = 59$$

Try It! 2. a. If $m\widehat{RST} = 164$, what is $m\angle RVT$?

b. If $m\angle SPU = 79$, what is $m\widehat{STU}$?

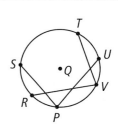

COROLLARIES TO THE INSCRIBED ANGLES THEOREM

Corollary 1

Two inscribed angles that intercept the same arc are congruent.

If...

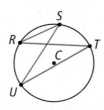

Then... $\angle S \cong \angle T$

Corollary 2

An angle inscribed in a semicircle is a right angle.

If... $m\overset{\frown}{RS} = 180$

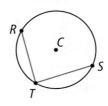

Then... $m\angle T = 90$

Corollary 3

The opposite angles of an inscribed quadrilateral are supplementary.

If...

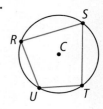

Then...

$m\angle R + m\angle T = 180$

$m\angle S + m\angle U = 180$

EXAMPLE 3 Explore Angles Formed by a Tangent and a Chord

Given chord $\overline{FH}$ and $\overleftrightarrow{HJ}$ tangent to $\odot E$ at point H, what is the relationship between $\angle FHJ$ and $\overset{\frown}{FGH}$?

Consider the angles and arcs formed by the chord, tangent line, and diameter.

Let $m\angle FHJ = x$, so $m\angle FHD = 90 - x$.

$m\angle FHD = \frac{1}{2}m\overset{\frown}{DF}$

$90 - x = \frac{1}{2}m\overset{\frown}{DF}$ *Use the Inscribed Angles Theorem.*

$m\overset{\frown}{DF} = 180 - 2x$

Since $\overline{DH}$ is a diameter, $m\overset{\frown}{DFH} = 180$.

$m\overset{\frown}{DF} + m\overset{\frown}{FGH} = m\overset{\frown}{DFH}$

$180 - 2x + m\overset{\frown}{FGH} = 180$

$m\overset{\frown}{FGH} = 2x$

$m\overset{\frown}{FGH} = 2m\angle FHJ$

$m\angle FHJ = \frac{1}{2}m\overset{\frown}{FGH}$

$m\angle DHJ = 90$

COMMON ERROR
Be careful not to make assumptions about arc measure relationships, such as assuming $m\overset{\frown}{DF} = m\overset{\frown}{FH}$. Think about concepts and theorems you can apply when writing mathematical statements.

Try It! **3. a.** Given $\overleftrightarrow{BD}$ tangent to $\odot P$ at point C, if $m\overset{\frown}{AC} = 88$, what is $m\angle ACB$?

b. Given $\overleftrightarrow{EG}$ tangent to $\odot P$ at point F, if $m\angle GFC = 115$, what is $m\overset{\frown}{FAC}$?

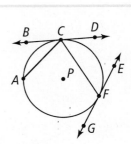

THEOREM 10-9

The measure of an angle formed by a tangent and a chord is half the measure of its intercepted arc.

If...

PROOF: SEE EXERCISE 34.

Then... $m\angle AED = \frac{1}{2}m\widehat{ABE}$

APPLICATION

EXAMPLE 4 ▶ Use Arc Measure to Solve a Problem

A backdrop in the shape of a circular arc is placed behind two newscasters. A director wants to position two cameras to capture the entire backdrop. Where should he position the cameras?

16 ft

45°

Camera

Formulate ◀ Represent the set as a chord $\overline{AB}$ of a circle that intercepts an arc measuring 90°.

Any point on the major arc $\widehat{AB}$ is the vertex of a 45° angle that intercepts arc $\widehat{AB}$.

To find the size of the circle, find the radius of the circle.

Compute ◀ Let P be the center of the circle.

$m\angle APB = m\widehat{AB} = 90$

Find r.

$$\sqrt{2} \cdot r = 16$$

$\triangle APB$ is a 45°-45°-90° triangle, and the length of the hypotenuse is 16.

$$r = \frac{16}{\sqrt{2}}$$
$$r = 8\sqrt{2}$$

Center P is on the perpendicular bisector of $\overline{AB}$, so P is 8 ft from the midpoint of $\overline{AB}$.

Interpret ◀ Position a camera on any point of the circle with radius $8\sqrt{2}$ ft and center 8 ft from the midpoint of the set.

Try It! **4. a.** Given $\overleftrightarrow{WY}$ tangent to $\odot C$ at point X, what is $m\widehat{XZ}$?

b. What is $m\angle VXW$?

CONCEPT SUMMARY Inscribed Angles and Intercepted Arcs

	Inscribed Angles	Angles Formed by a Tangent and a Chord
WORDS	The measure of an inscribed angle is one-half the measure of its intercepted arc.	The measure of an angle formed by a tangent and a chord is one-half the measure of its intercepted arc.
DIAGRAMS	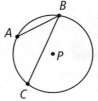	
SYMBOLS	$m\angle ABC = \frac{1}{2}m\widehat{AC}$	$m\angle ABD = \frac{1}{2}m\widehat{BCD}$

Do You UNDERSTAND?

1. **ESSENTIAL QUESTION** How is the measure of an inscribed angle related to its intercepted arc?

2. **Error Analysis** Darren is asked to find $m\widehat{XZ}$. What is his error? © MP.3

$$m\widehat{XZ} = \frac{1}{2}m\angle XYZ$$
$$= \frac{1}{2}(51) \quad ✗$$
$$= 25.5$$

3. **Reason** Can the measure of an inscribed angle be greater than the measure of the intercepted arc? Explain. © MP.2

4. **Make Sense and Persevere** Is there enough information in the diagram to find $m\widehat{RST}$? Explain. © MP.1

Do You KNOW HOW?

For Exercises 5–8, find each measure in $\odot Q$.

5. $m\widehat{JL}$

6. $m\widehat{MJ}$

7. $m\angle KJM$

8. $m\angle KLM$

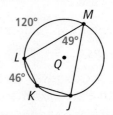

For Exercises 9–12, $\overleftrightarrow{DF}$ is tangent to $\odot Q$ at point E. Find each measure.

9. $m\widehat{EH}$

10. $m\widehat{EJ}$

11. $m\angle HEJ$

12. $m\angle DEJ$

For Exercises 13–16, find each measure in $\odot M$.

13. $m\angle PRQ$

14. $m\angle PTR$

15. $m\angle RST$

16. $m\angle SRT$

PRACTICE & PROBLEM SOLVING

UNDERSTAND

17. Mathematical Connections Given $m\overset{\frown}{ABC} = x$, what is an expression for $m\overset{\frown}{DAB}$ in terms of x? Explain.

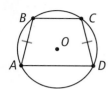

18. Error Analysis Cathy is asked to find $m\overset{\frown}{WVZ}$. What is Cathy's error? ⒢ MP.3

$m\overset{\frown}{WVZ} = 360° - 71°$
$= 289°$ ✗

19. Higher Order Thinking Write a proof of the Inscribed Angles Theorem, Case 2.

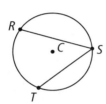

Given: Center C is inside $\angle RST$.

Prove: $m\angle RST = \frac{1}{2}m\overset{\frown}{RT}$

20. Construct Arguments Tandice measures $\angle HGK$ with a protractor and says that it is 98°. Is her answer reasonable? Explain. ⒢ MP.3

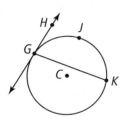

21. Use Structure Given $\odot Q$ with diameter $\overline{AC}$, if point B is located on $\odot Q$, can $\angle ABC$ ever be less than 90°? Can it ever be greater than 90°? Explain. ⒢ MP.7

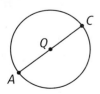

PRACTICE

For Exercises 22–25, find each measure in $\odot P$.
SEE EXAMPLES 1 AND 2

22. $m\overset{\frown}{AD}$

23. $m\overset{\frown}{BDC}$

24. $m\angle ADC$

25. $m\angle BAD$

For Exercises 26–28, $\overrightarrow{SU}$ is tangent to $\odot P$ at point T. Find each measure. SEE EXAMPLES 2 AND 3

26. $m\overset{\frown}{TW}$

27. $m\angle TWX$

28. $m\angle TWV$

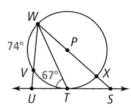

For Exercises 29–31, $\overrightarrow{HK}$ is tangent to $\odot C$ at point J. Find each measure. SEE EXAMPLES 3 AND 4

29. $m\angle KJM$

30. $m\angle MJN$

31. $m\angle HJN$

32. Write a proof of the Inscribed Angles Theorem, Case 1.

Given: Center C is on $\overline{ST}$.

Prove: $m\angle RST = \frac{1}{2}m\overset{\frown}{RT}$

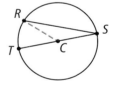

33. Write a proof of the Inscribed Angles Theorem, Case 3.

Given: Center C is outside $\angle RST$.

Prove: $m\angle RST = \frac{1}{2}m\overset{\frown}{RT}$

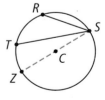

34. Write a two-column proof of Theorem 10-9.

Given: $\overleftrightarrow{AB}$ tangent to $\odot P$ at point B.

Prove: $m\angle ABD = \frac{1}{2}m\overset{\frown}{BCD}$

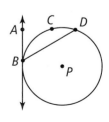

PRACTICE & PROBLEM SOLVING

35. Construct Arguments Deondra needs to know the angle measure for each notch in the 16-notch socket wrench she is designing. The notches will be the same size. What is the angle measure? ⒼMP.3

36. Use Structure Archaeologists in Turkey discovered the fragment of an ancient sun dial. Is there enough information for them to determine the diameter of the entire sundial? Explain. ⒼMP.7

37. Use Appropriate Tools Javier sets up chairs for a home theater showing on his television. His optimal viewing angle is 50°. Besides at chair A, where else could he sit with the same viewing angle? Draw a diagram and explain. ⒼMP.5

38. Write an expression that represents $m\angle DGF$.

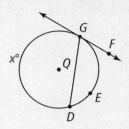

39. SAT/ACT Segment AB is tangent to $\odot M$ at Point A. What is $m\angle DAC$?

Ⓐ 25

Ⓑ 65

Ⓒ 50

Ⓓ 90

Ⓔ 100

40. Performance Task Triangle DEF is inscribed in $\odot G$, and $\overline{AB}$, $\overline{BC}$, and $\overline{AC}$ are tangent to $\odot G$.

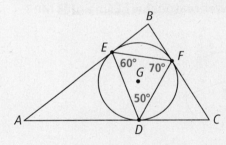

Part A Are there any isosceles triangles in the diagram? If so, explain why the triangles are isosceles. If not, explain why not.

Part B Are △ABC and △DEF similar? Explain.

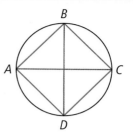
10-5

Secant Lines and Segments

I CAN... use angle measures and segment lengths formed by intersecting lines and circles to solve problems.

VOCABULARY
• secant

Common Core State Standards
HSG.C.A.2, MP.1, MP.3, MP.6

CONCEPTUAL UNDERSTANDING

MAKE SENSE AND PERSEVERE
Consider other relationships in the diagram. What is an alternate plan you could use to solve the problem? © **MP.1**

EXPLORE & REASON

Skyler made the design shown. Points *A*, *B*, *C*, and *D* are spaced evenly around the circle.

A. Using points *A*, *B*, *C*, and *D* as vertices, what congruent angles can you find? How can you justify that they are congruent?

B. **Make Sense and Persevere** What strategy did you use to make sure you found all congruent angles? © **MP.1**

ESSENTIAL QUESTION > How are the measures of angles, arcs, and segments formed by intersecting secant lines related?

EXAMPLE 1   Relate Secants and Angle Measures

A secant is a line, ray, or segment that intersects a circle at two points. Secants $\overleftrightarrow{AC}$ and $\overleftrightarrow{BD}$ intersect to form ∠1. How can you use arc measures to find $m\angle 1$?

> Draw $\overline{AB}$ to form $\triangle AEB$.

> Since ∠BAC is an inscribed angle, $m\angle BAC = \frac{1}{2}m\widehat{BC}$.

> Since ∠ABD is an inscribed angle, $m\angle ABD = \frac{1}{2}m\widehat{AD}$.

Apply the Triangle Exterior Angle Theorem.

$$m\angle 1 = m\angle ABD + m\angle BAC$$

$$= \frac{1}{2}m\widehat{AD} + \frac{1}{2}m\widehat{BC}$$

So the measure of the angle is half the sum of the measures of the two intercepted arcs.

Try It!   **1.** If $m\widehat{AD} = 155$ and $m\widehat{BC} = 61$, what is $m\angle 1$?

THEOREM 10-10

Powered By **desmos**

The measure of an angle formed by two secant lines that intersect inside a circle is half the sum of the measures of the intercepted arcs.

If...

Then... $m\angle 1 = \frac{1}{2}(x + y)$

PROOF: SEE EXERCISE 18.

THEOREM 10-11

The measure of an angle formed by two lines that intersect outside a circle is half the difference of the measures of the intercepted arcs.

Case 1	Case 2	Case 3
If...	**If...**	**If...**
		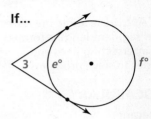
Then...	**Then...**	**Then...**
$m\angle 1 = \frac{1}{2}(b - a)$	$m\angle 2 = \frac{1}{2}(d - c)$	$m\angle 3 = \frac{1}{2}(f - e)$

PROOF: SEE EXAMPLE 2, TRY IT 2, AND EXERCISE 19.

EXAMPLE 2 ▶ Prove Theorem 10-11, Case 1

Write a proof for Theorem 10-11, Case 1.

Given: Secants $\overrightarrow{PS}$ and $\overrightarrow{PT}$

Prove: $m\angle P = \frac{1}{2}(m\widehat{ST} - m\widehat{QR})$

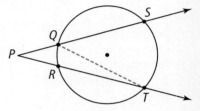

Proof:

Statement	Reason
1) $\overrightarrow{PS}$ and $\overrightarrow{PT}$ are secants.	1) Given
2) Draw $\overline{QT}$.	2) Two points determine a segment.
3) $m\angle QTP = \frac{1}{2}m\widehat{QR}$	3) Inscribed Angles Theorem
4) $m\angle SQT = \frac{1}{2}m\widehat{ST}$	4) Inscribed Angles Theorem
5) $m\angle SQT = m\angle P + m\angle QTP$	5) Triangle Exterior Angle Theorem
6) $m\angle P = m\angle SQT - m\angle QTP$	6) Subtraction Property of Equality
7) $m\angle P = \frac{1}{2}m\widehat{ST} - \frac{1}{2}m\widehat{QR}$	7) Substitution
8) $m\angle P = \frac{1}{2}(m\widehat{ST} - m\widehat{QR})$	8) Distributive Property

STUDY TIP
Remember to look for helpful relationships that you can draw on the given figure when completing a proof. Drawing $\overline{QT}$ forms inscribed angles, which are needed for this proof.

Try It! 2. Prove Theorem 10-11, Case 2.

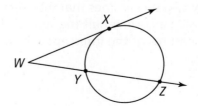

EXAMPLE 3   **Use Secants and Tangents to Solve Problems**

A. What is $m\angle ABD$?

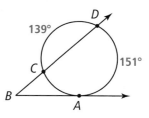

Step 1 Find $m\widehat{AC}$.

$$m\widehat{AC} = 360 - m\widehat{AD} - m\widehat{CD}$$
$$= 360 - 151 - 139$$
$$= 70$$

Step 2 Find $m\angle ABD$.

$$m\angle ABD = \frac{1}{2}(m\widehat{AD} - m\widehat{AC})$$
$$= \frac{1}{2}(151 - 70)$$
$$= 40.5$$

> Since the angle is formed outside the circle by a secant and a tangent, apply Theorem 10-11, Case 2.

B. What is $m\widehat{LM}$?

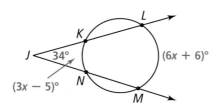

COMMON ERROR
Remember to add the arc measures when the vertex is inside the circle and to subtract them when the vertex is outside the circle.

Step 1 Find x.

$$m\angle LJM = \frac{1}{2}(m\widehat{LM} - m\widehat{KN})$$
$$34 = \frac{1}{2}((6x + 6) - (3x - 5))$$
$$34 = \frac{1}{2}(3x + 11)$$
$$68 = 3x + 11$$
$$19 = x$$

> Since the angle is formed outside the circle by two secants, apply Theorem 10-11, Case 1.

Step 2 Find $m\widehat{LM}$.

$$m\widehat{LM} = 6x + 6$$
$$= 6(19) + 6$$
$$= 120$$

> Substitute the value of x found in Step 1.

Try It!   **3. a.** What is $m\widehat{WX}$?

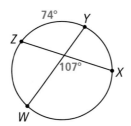

b. What is $m\angle PSQ$?

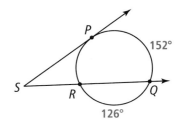

EXAMPLE 4 ▸ Develop Chord Length Relationships

What is the value of x?

∠A and ∠B are inscribed angles that intercept the same arc.

∠C and ∠D are inscribed angles that intercept the same arc.

By the Angle-Angle Similarity Theorem, $\triangle AED \sim \triangle BEC$.

$$\frac{ED}{EC} = \frac{EA}{EB}$$

$$\frac{x}{5} = \frac{6}{4}$$

The ratios of corresponding sides of similar triangles are equal.

$$4 \cdot x = 6 \cdot 5$$

$$x = 7.5$$

The value of x is 7.5.

HAVE A GROWTH MINDSET
In what ways can you be inquisitive and open to learning new things?

Try It! **4.** What is the value of y?

THEOREM 10-12

Powered By desmos

For a given point and circle, the product of the lengths of the two segments from the point to the circle is constant along any line through the point and circle.

Case 1	Case 2	Case 3
If...	If...	If...

  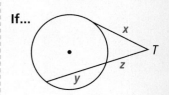

Then...	Then...	Then...
$ab = cd$	$(n + m)n = (q + p)q$	$x^2 = (z + y)z$

PROOF: SEE EXERCISES 11, 23, and 24.

EXAMPLE 5 Use Segment Relationships to Find Lengths

Archaeologists found part of the circular wall that surrounds an ancient city. They measure the distances shown. The 272-m segment lies on a line through the center of the circular wall. What was the diameter of the circular wall?

Draw a diagram to represent the situation.

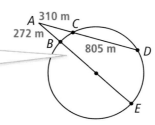

The line through $\overline{AB}$ continues to the center of the circle, so $\overline{BE}$ is a diameter.

MAKE SENSE AND PERSEVERE
Are there other measurements that archaeologists could have taken to help find the diameter using another method? © **MP.1**

Write an equation to relate the segment lengths.

$$(AB + BE)AB = (AC + CD)AC$$

$$(272 + BE)(272) = (310 + 805)(310)$$

Apply Theorem 10-12 and substitute known segment lengths.

$$73{,}984 + 272 \cdot BE = 345{,}650$$

$$272 \cdot BE = 271{,}666$$

$$BE \approx 998.8$$

The diameter of the circular wall was about 998.8 meters.

Try It! **5. a.** What is the value of a?   **b.** What is EC?

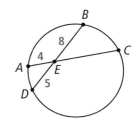

CONCEPT SUMMARY Angle and Segment Relationships in a Circle

	Vertex Inside the Circle	Vertex Outside the Circle
ANGLES	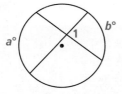 $m\angle 1 = \frac{1}{2}(a + b)$	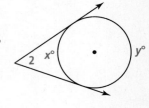 $m\angle 2 = \frac{1}{2}(y - x)$
SEGMENTS	$wx = yz$	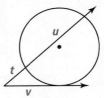 $(a + b)a = (c + d)c$ $(t + u)t = v^2$

Do You UNDERSTAND?

1. **ESSENTIAL QUESTION** How are the measures of angles, arcs, and segments formed by intersecting secant lines related?

2. **Error Analysis** Massimo is asked to find the value of x. What is his error? ⓒ MP.3

   $GK \cdot FK = HK \cdot JK$
   $12 \cdot 9 = 8 \cdot x$
   $x = 13\frac{1}{2}$ ✗

3. **Vocabulary** How are *secants* and *tangents* to a circle alike and different?

4. **Construct Arguments** The rays shown are tangent to the circle. Show that $m\angle 1 = (x - 180)$. ⓒ MP.3

   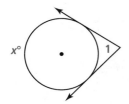

Do You KNOW HOW?

For Exercises 5 and 6, find each angle measure. Rays *QP* and *QR* are tangent to the circle in Exercise 6.

5. $m\angle BEC$

6. $m\angle PQR$

For Exercises 7 and 8, find each length. Ray *HJ* is tangent to the circle in Exercise 7.

7. *GF*

8. *LM*

   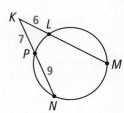

For Exercises 9 and 10, $\overline{AE}$ is tangent to ⊙*P*. Find each length.

9. *BC*

10. *EF*

   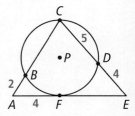

PRACTICE & PROBLEM SOLVING

UNDERSTAND

11. Construct Arguments Given ⊙X, write a two-column proof of Theorem 10-12, Case 2. ⓒ MP.3

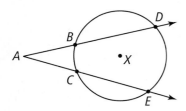

12. Error Analysis Cindy is asked to find m∠VXZ. What is her error? ⓒ MP.3

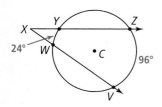

$$m\angle VXZ = \frac{1}{2}\left(m\widehat{WY} + m\widehat{VZ}\right)$$
$$= \frac{1}{2}(24 + 96)$$
$$= 60 \quad ✗$$

13. Mathematical Connections Given ⊙P, secant $\overrightarrow{CA}$, and tangent $\overrightarrow{CD}$, what is the area of ⊙P?

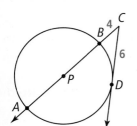

14. Higher Order Thinking Given ⊙T, and tangents $\overline{AD}$ and $\overline{CD}$, what is the measure of ∠ADC?

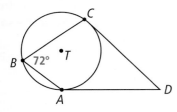

15. Communicate Precisely How would you describe each case of Theorem 10-11? ⓒ MP.6

PRACTICE

For Exercises 16 and 17, find each measure.
SEE EXAMPLE 1

16. m∠1

17. x

18. Given ⊙A and secants $\overline{PR}$ and $\overline{QS}$, write a paragraph proof of Theorem 10-10. SEE EXAMPLE 1

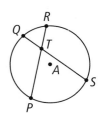

19. Given ⊙Q and tangents $\overrightarrow{AB}$ and $\overrightarrow{AC}$, write a two-column proof of Theorem 10-11, Case 3. SEE EXAMPLE 2

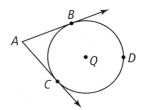

20. Given ⊙C, inscribed angle ∠RWV, and secants $\overrightarrow{TR}$ and $\overrightarrow{TV}$, what is the measure of ∠RTV? SEE EXAMPLE 3

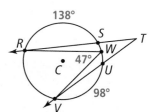

For Exercises 21 and 22, find each length.
SEE EXERCISE 4

21. a

22. b

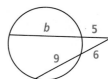

23. Given ⊙T and secants $\overline{JK}$ and $\overline{LM}$ intersecting at point N, write a paragraph proof of Theorem 10-12, Case 1. SEE EXAMPLE 4

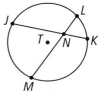

24. Given ⊙C, secant $\overrightarrow{QS}$ and tangent $\overline{PQ}$, write a two-column proof of Theorem 10–12, Case 3. SEE EXAMPLE 5

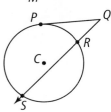

PRACTICE & PROBLEM SOLVING

APPLY

25. Use Structure Mykal stands in the position shown to take a picture of a sculpture with a circular base.

5 ft 4 ft

a. Mykal is deciding on which lens to use. What is the minimum view angle from where he stands so he can get as much of the base as possible in his picture?

b. If Mykal uses a lens with a view angle of 40°, what is the shortest distance he could stand from the sculpture? **© MP.7**

26. Reason A satellite orbits above the equator of Mars as shown and transmits images back to a scientist in the control room. What percent of the equator is the scientist able to see? Explain. **© MP.2**

42° x°

27. Use Structure Carolina wants to etch the design shown onto a circular piece of glass. At what measure should she cut ∠1? Explain. **© MP.7**

ASSESSMENT PRACTICE

28. For what measure of $\overset{\frown}{UW}$ does $m\angle TVX = 34$?

$m\overset{\frown}{UW} =$ _____

29. SAT/ACT Given $\odot P$ and secants $\overline{FH}$ and $\overline{FK}$, what is FG?

3x
G
H
x − 5
•P
F   x − 6   J   K
4x

Ⓐ 3 Ⓑ 4 Ⓒ 9 Ⓓ 27 Ⓔ 36

30. Performance Task Alberto, Kwamin, Charles, and Jorge sit at a round lunch table with diameter 54 inches. The salt shaker is 27 inches from Charles, 18 inches from Kwamin, 20 inches from Jorge, and 30 inches from Alberto.

salt shaker

Part A In what order around the table are they seated? Explain.

Part B Alberto, Kwamin, Charles, and Jorge change the positions of their seats and sit evenly spaced around the table. If the location of the salt shaker does not change, what is the closest that one of them could be from the salt shaker? What is the farthest?

Topic Review

1. When a line or lines intersect a circle how are the figures formed related to the radius, circumference, and area of the circle?

Vocabulary Review

Choose the correct term to complete each sentence.

2. A(n) _____ is a region of a circle with two radii and an arc of the circle as borders.

3. A(n) _____ is an angle with its vertex on the circle.

4. A(n) _____ and the corresponding circle have exactly one point in common.

5. When both rays of an angle intersect a circle, the _____ is the portion of the circle between the rays.

- central angle
- chord
- inscribed angle
- intercepted arc
- secant
- sector of a circle
- segment of a circle
- tangent to a circle

Concepts & Skills Review

LESSON 10-1 ▶ Arcs and Sectors

Quick Review

Arc length and the area of a **sector of a circle** are proportional to the corresponding central angle.

The length of an arc is $\frac{n}{360}$ of the circumference, where n is the measure of the central angle in degrees, and the area of a sector is $\frac{n}{360}$ of the area of the circle.

Example

Circle J has a radius of 6 cm. What is the area of a sector with a central angle of 80°?

Write the formula for the area of a sector:

$$A = \frac{n}{360} \cdot \pi r^2$$

$$= \frac{80}{360} \cdot \pi(6)^2$$

$$\approx 25.1$$

The area of the sector is about 25.1 cm².

Practice & Problem Solving

Find each arc length in terms of π.

6. $\overset{\frown}{JK}$

7. $\overset{\frown}{ABC}$

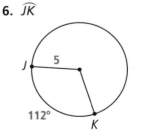

Find the area of each sector in terms of π.

8. sector NRM

9. sector DSE

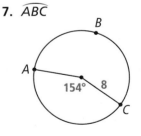

10. **Reason** If you know the circumference of a circle and the area of a sector of the circle, how could you determine the central angle of the sector? Explain. ⒼMP.2

Lines Tangent to a Circle

Quick Review

A **tangent to a circle** is perpendicular to the radius of the circle at the **point of tangency**. You can use properties of right triangles to solve problems involving tangents.

Example

Lines *m* and *n* are tangent to ⊙*T*. What is *m*∠*ATB*?

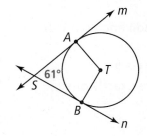

Since lines *m* and *n* are tangent lines, *m*∠*SAT* = *m*∠*SBT* = 90. Points *A*, *T*, *B*, and *S* form a quadrilateral, so use the angle sum of a quadrilateral to solve the problem.

$$m\angle SAT + m\angle ASB + m\angle SBT + m\angle ATB = 360$$
$$90 + 61 + 90 + m\angle ATB = 360$$
$$m\angle ATB = 119$$

So, *m*∠*ATB* = 119.

Practice & Problem Solving

For Exercises 11–12, $\overleftrightarrow{QR}$ and $\overleftrightarrow{AB}$ are tangent to the circle. Find each value.

11. *QR*

12. *m*∠*CAB*

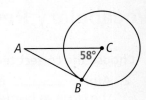

13. Construct Arguments If $\overline{GH}$ is a diameter of ⊙*T*, is it possible to draw tangents to *G* and *H* from the same point external to ⊙*T*? Explain. **ⓒ MP.3**

14. Segment *MN* is tangent to ⊙ *L*. What is the radius of the circle? Explain.

Chords

Quick Review

Chords in a circle have the following properties:

• Two chords in the same circle with the same length have congruent central angles, have congruent arcs, and are equidistant from the center of the circle.

• Chords are bisected by the diameter of the circle that is perpendicular to the chord.

Example

What is the radius of ⊙*T*?

Since $\overline{CT} \perp \overline{AB}$, $\overline{CT}$ bisects $\overline{AB}$. So, *CB* = 7. Use the Pythagorean Theorem to find the radius.

$$(CT)^2 + (CB)^2 = (BT)^2$$
$$3^2 + 7^2 = (BT)^2$$
$$BT \approx 7.6$$

The radius of ⊙*T* is about 7.6.

Practice & Problem Solving

For Exercises 15–17, the radius of ⊙*T* is 7. Find each value. Round to the nearest tenth.

15. *FH*

16. *CD*

17. *m*∠*BTA*

18. Look for Relationships Circles *T* and *S* intersect at points *A* and *B*. What is the relationship between $\overline{AB}$ and $\overleftrightarrow{TS}$? Explain. **ⓒ MP.7**

19. A contractor cuts off part of a circular countertop so that it fits against a wall. What is the length of the cut, *x*? Round to the nearest tenth.

LESSON 10-4   Inscribed Angles

Quick Review

The measure of an **inscribed angle** is half the measure of its intercepted arc. As a result:

• Opposite angles of an inscribed quadrilateral are supplementary.

• The measure of an angle formed by a tangent and chord is half the measure of the intercepted arc.

Example

What are the angle measures of △ABC?

Use inscribed angles:

$m\angle BAC = \frac{1}{2}(84) = 42$

$m\angle BCA = \frac{1}{2}(116) = 58$

$m\angle ABC = 180 - 42 - 58 = 80$

Practice & Problem Solving

Find each value.

20. $m\widehat{EF}$

21. $m\angle MNP$

22. $m\angle WZY$

23. $m\angle QPR$

24. **Generalize** If a rectangle is inscribed in a circle, what must be true about the diagonals of the rectangle? Explain. Ⓒ MP.8

LESSON 10-5   Secant Lines and Segments

Quick Review

Secant lines form angles with special relationships:

• The measure of an angle formed by secants intersecting inside a circle is half the sum of the measures of the intercepted arcs.

• The measure of an angle formed by secants intersecting outside a circle is half the difference of the measures of the intercepted arcs.

Example

What is the value of x?

Use secant segment relationships.

$(AE)(AE + ED) = (AB)(AB + BC)$

$6(6 + 12) = 4(4 + x)$

$108 = 16 + 4x$

$92 = 4x$

$23 = x$

The value of x is 23.

Practice & Problem Solving

For Exercises 25 and 26, find each value in the figure shown.

25. QR

26. $m\angle NRP$

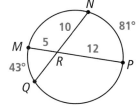

For Exercises 27 and 28, find each value in the figure shown. The segment $\overline{WZ}$ is tangent to the circle.

27. WZ

28. $m\widehat{XZ}$

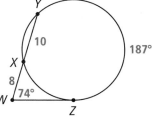

29. **Construct Arguments** A student said that if ∠A is formed by two secants intersecting outside of a circle, then m∠A < 90. Do you agree? Explain. ⒸMP.3

TOPIC 11

Two- and Three-Dimensional Models

TOPIC ESSENTIAL QUESTION

How is Cavalieri's Principle helpful in understanding the volume formulas for solids?

Topic Overview

enVision® STEM Project:
Design a Rigid Package

11-1 Three-Dimensional Figures and Cross Sections

11-2 Volumes of Prisms and Cylinders

Mathematical Modeling in 3 Acts:
Box 'Em Up

11-3 Pyramids and Cones

11-4 Spheres

Topic Vocabulary

- Cavalieri's Principle
- hemisphere
- oblique cylinder
- oblique prism

Digital Experience

INTERACTIVE STUDENT EDITION
Access online or offline.

ACTIVITIES Complete *Explore & Reason, Model & Discuss*, and *Critique & Explain* activities. Interact with *Examples* and *Try Its.*

CONCEPT SUMMARY Review key lesson content through multiple representations.

ASSESSMENT Show what you've learned.

Go online | **SavvasRealize.com**

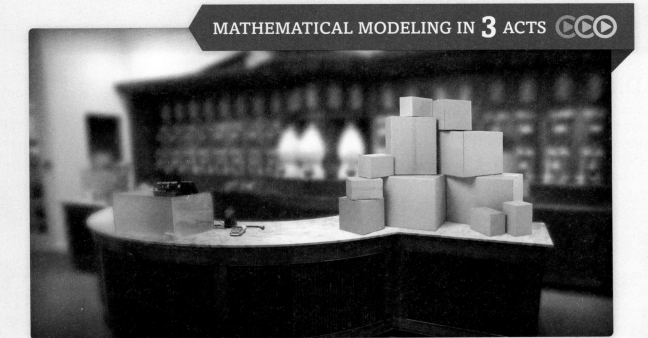

MATHEMATICAL MODELING IN 3 ACTS ▶▶▶

Box 'Em Up

With so many people and businesses shopping online, retailers, and especially e-retailers, ship more and more packages every day. Some of the products people order have unusual sizes and shapes and need custom packaging. Imagine how you might package a surfboard, or a snow blower, or even live crawfish to ship to someone's house!

Think about this during the Mathematical Modeling in 3 Acts lesson.

TOPIC 11

VIDEOS Watch clips to support *Mathematical Modeling in 3 Acts Lessons* and enVision® *STEM Projects.*

TUTORIALS Get help from *Virtual Nerd*, right when you need it.

PRACTICE Practice what you've learned.

ADAPTIVE PRACTICE Practice that is *just right* and *just for you.*

FAMILY ENGAGEMENT Involve family in your learning.

GLOSSARY Read and listen to English and Spanish definitions.

MATH TOOLS Explore math with digital tools and manipulatives.

DESMOS Use Anytime and as embedded Interactives in Lesson content.

Did You Know?

Cardboard boxes look simple, but the machines that make them are not. This **cartoning machine** is capable of making **15,000 boxes per day.**

Packages come in many shapes. The familiar milk carton shape is called a **gable-top carton** because of its resemblance to a house gable. **Cylindrical** packaging is often used for sugar, tea and grains that don't have rigid shapes.

Manufacturers consider many factors when designing a package.

✓ Marketing appeal
✓ Cost of materials
✓ Simplicity
✓ Safety
✓ Recyclability

Your Task: Design a Rigid Package

You will design a rigid package for a product of your choice. Your design will address factors such as attractiveness, protection for the product, and cost. You will then draw two- and three-dimensional representations of your package and build a prototype.

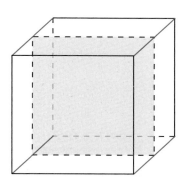
11-1

Three-Dimensional Figures and Cross Sections

I CAN... identify three-dimensional figures and their relationships with polygons to solve problems.

Ⓒ **Common Core State Standards**
HSG.GMD.B.4, MP.1, MP.2, MP.6

CONCEPTUAL UNDERSTANDING

EXPLORE & REASON

Consider a cube of cheese. If you slice straight down through the midpoints of four parallel edges of the cube, the outline of the newly exposed surface is a square.

A. How would you slice the cube to expose a triangular surface?

B. Communicate Precisely How would you slice the cube to expose a triangular surface with the greatest possible area? Ⓒ **MP.6**

ESSENTIAL QUESTION

How are three-dimensional figures and polygons related?

EXAMPLE 1   Develop Euler's Formula

How many faces, vertices, and edges does each prism contain? Do you notice any patterns in these quantities?

Make a table of the number of vertices, edges, and faces for each prism. Look for patterns and relationships.

Type of Prism	Faces (*F*)	Vertices (*V*)	Edges (*E*)
triangular	5	6	9
rectangular	6	8	12
pentagonal	7	10	15
hexagonal	8	12	18

For each additional face on the prism, the prism gains 2 vertices and 3 edges.

Look at the sum of the faces and vertices. Compare it to the number of edges.

$$5 + 6 = 9 + 2$$
$$6 + 8 = 12 + 2$$
$$7 + 10 = 15 + 2$$
$$8 + 12 = 18 + 2$$

The sum of the faces and vertices is always 2 more than the number of edges.

MODEL WITH MATHEMATICS
Look at the relationships among the numbers of vertices, faces, and edges. How might you represent these relationships in an equation? Ⓒ **MP.4**

Try It! **1.** How many faces, vertices, and edges do the pyramids have? Name at least three patterns you notice.

CONCEPT Euler's Formula

The sum of the number of faces (F) and vertices (V) of a polyhedron is 2 more than the number of its edges (E).

$$F + V = E + 2$$

$$F + V = E + 2$$
$$4 + 4 = E + 2$$
$$E = 6$$

APPLICATION

EXAMPLE 2 Apply Euler's Formula

To make polyhedron-shaped game pieces using a 3D printer, Juanita enters the number of faces, edges, and vertices into a program. If she wants a game piece with 20 faces and 30 edges, how many vertices does the piece have?

COMMON ERROR
Remember to add the number of faces and vertices on one side of the equation and to add the number of edges plus 2 on the other side of the equation.

$$F + V = E + 2$$
$$20 + V = 30 + 2$$
$$V = 12$$

Apply Euler's Formula.

The game piece has 12 vertices.

Try It! **2. a.** A polyhedron has 12 faces and 30 edges. How many vertices does it have?

b. Can a polyhedron have 4 faces, 5 vertices, and 8 edges? Explain.

EXAMPLE 3 Describe a Cross Section

Plane *M* and plane *N* intersect the regular octahedron as shown. What is the shape of each cross section?

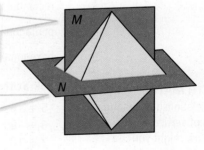

STUDY TIP
Recall that a *cross section* is the intersection of a solid and a plane.

Plane *M* slices the octahedron in half through the top and bottom vertices. The cross section is a rhombus.

Plane *N* slices horizontally between the bases of two square pyramids. The cross section is a square.

Try It! **3. a.** What shape is the cross section shown?

b. What shape is the cross section if the plane is perpendicular to the base and passes through the vertex of the pyramid?

EXAMPLE 4 > Draw a Cross Section

A plane intersects a tetrahedron parallel to the base. How do you draw the cross section?

Step 1 Visualize the plane intersecting the tetrahedron.

Step 2 Draw lines where the plane cuts the surface of the polyhedron.

STUDY TIP
It is not possible for a polyhedron with *n* faces to have a cross section with more than *n* sides.

Step 3 Shade the cross section.

Try It! **4. a.** Draw the cross section of a plane intersecting the tetrahedron through the top vertex and perpendicular to the base.

b. Draw the cross section of a plane intersecting a hexagonal prism perpendicular to the base.

EXAMPLE 5 > Rotate a Polygon to Form a Three-Dimensional Figure

If you rotate an isosceles triangle about the altitude, what three-dimensional figure does the triangle form?

As the triangle rotates, each point on the sides traces out a circle about the axis of rotation.

The line containing the altitude is the axis of rotation.

The rotation forms a stack of circles.

The three-dimensional figure is a cone.

Try It! **5. a.** What three-dimensional figure is formed by rotating equilateral triangle △ABC about $\overline{BD}$?

b. What three-dimensional figure is formed by rotating △ABC about $\overline{BC}$?

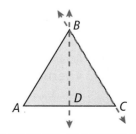

CONCEPT SUMMARY Polyhedrons, Cross Sections, and Rotating a Polygon

WORDS	DIAGRAMS

Euler's Formula The faces of a polyhedron are polygons. The sum of the number of faces *F* and vertices *V* of a polyhedron is 2 more than the number of its edges *E*.

$$F + V = E + 2$$

$$F + V = E + 2$$
$$5 + 6 \stackrel{?}{=} 9 + 2$$
$$11 = 11$$

Cross Sections A cross section is the intersection of a plane and a solid. The cross section of a plane and a convex polyhedron is a polygon.

A cross section perpendicular to the base of the triangular prism is a rectangle.

Rotation of Polygons Rotating a polygon about an axis forms a three-dimensional figure with at least one circular cross section.

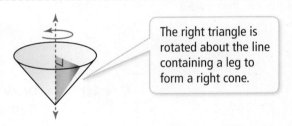

The right triangle is rotated about the line containing a leg to form a right cone.

Do You UNDERSTAND?

1. **ESSENTIAL QUESTION** How are three-dimensional figures and polygons related?

2. **Error Analysis** Nicholas drew a figure to find a cross section of an icosahedron, a polyhedron with 20 faces. What is Nicholas's error? ⓒ **MP.3**

Because the plane that intersects the icosahedron is a rectangle, the cross section is rectangle. ✗

3. **Reason** Can a polyhedron have 3 faces, 4 vertices, and 5 edges? Explain. ⓒ **MP.2**

Do You KNOW HOW?

For Exercises 4–7, copy and complete the table.

	Faces	Vertices	Edges
4.	5	6	
5.	8		18
6.		12	20
7.	22	44	

8. What polygon is formed by the intersection of plane *N* and the octagonal prism shown?

9. Describe the three-dimensional figure that is formed from rotating the isosceles right triangle about the hypotenuse.

10. **Mathematical Connections** If you rotate rectangle *ABCD* about $\overleftrightarrow{CD}$, what is the volume of the resulting three-dimensional figure?

11. **Error Analysis** Marcos was asked to find the number of vertices of a polyhedron with 32 faces and 60 edges. What is his error? Ⓒ MP.3

$$F + E = V + 2$$
$$32 + 60 = V + 2$$
$$90 = V \quad ✗$$

12. **Make Sense and Persevere** A tetrahedron is a polyhedron with four triangular faces. Can a plane intersect the tetrahedron shown to form a cross section with four sides? Explain. Ⓒ MP.1

13. **Use Appropriate Tools** Can the intersection of a plane and a triangular prism produce a rectangular cross section? Draw a diagram to explain. Ⓒ MP.5

14. What is true about all the cross-sections formed by the intersection of a plane and a sphere? Explain. Ⓒ MP.2

15. **Communicate Precisely** Is it possible to rotate a polygon to form a cube? Explain. Ⓒ MP.6

16. **Higher Order Thinking** Does the figure have a cross section with five sides? Copy the figure and draw the cross section or explain why not.

For Exercises 17–20, find the missing number for each polyhedron. SEE EXAMPLES 1 AND 2

17. A polyhedron has 24 edges and 12 vertices. How many faces does it have?

18. A polyhedron has 20 faces and 12 vertices. How many edges does it have?

19. A polyhedron has 8 faces and 15 edges. How many vertices does it have?

20. A polyhedron has 16 edges and 10 vertices. How many faces does it have?

21. Draw the cross section formed by the intersection of plane *A* and the polyhedron shown. What type of polygon is the cross section? SEE EXAMPLE 3

For Exercises 22 and 23, use the square pyramid shown. SEE EXAMPLE 4

22. Visualize a plane intersecting the square pyramid parallel to the base. Describe the cross section.

23. Visualize a plane intersecting the square pyramid through the vertex and perpendicular to opposite edges of the base. Describe the cross section.

24. Describe the three-dimensional figure that is formed from by rotating the rectangle about the side. SEE EXAMPLE 5

25. Describe the three-dimensional figure that is formed by rotating the pentagon about the line shown. SEE EXAMPLE 5

26. Describe the three-dimensional figure that is formed by rotating the circle about a diameter.

PRACTICE & PROBLEM SOLVING

27. Model With Mathematics Sineah cuts 12 pentagons and 20 hexagons out of fabric to make the pillow shown. The pillow has 60 vertices. If it takes 20 inches of thread per seam to connect the edges of the polygons, how many inches of thread does Sineah need to make the pillow? Ⓒ **MP.4**

28. Reason A gem cutter cuts a polyhedral crystal from a garnet gemstone. The crystal has 10 fewer vertices than edges and twice as many edges as faces. How many faces, vertices, and edges does the crystal have? Ⓒ **MP.2**

29. Communicate Precisely Duante wants to install a safety mat under the path of a revolving door. What shape should he make the mat? Explain. Ⓒ **MP.6**

30. Select all true statements regarding rotated two-dimensional figures.

☐ **A.** A circle rotated about its diameter forms a cylinder.

☐ **B.** A right triangle rotated about its height forms a cone.

☐ **C.** A rectangle rotated about its edge forms a cylinder.

☐ **D.** A semicircle rotated about its straight edge forms a sphere.

☐ **E.** A right triangle rotated about its hypotenuse forms a square pyramid.

31. SAT/ACT Which best describes the cross section of plane X and the polyhedron shown?

Ⓐ hexagon

Ⓑ pentagon

Ⓒ rectangle

Ⓓ trapezoid

Ⓔ triangle

32. Performance Task Draw a polyhedron with the fewest possible faces, vertices, and edges. Choose the faces from the polygons shown. You may use a polygon more than once.

Part A Explain why the polygon or polygons you chose minimize the number of vertices and edges.

Part B How do you know that there is no polyhedron with fewer faces, vertices, or edges than the one you drew?

11-2
Volumes of Prisms and Cylinders

I CAN... use the properties of prisms and cylinders to calculate their volumes.

VOCABULARY
- Cavalieri's Principle
- oblique cylinder
- oblique prism

Common Core State Standards
HSG.GMD.A.1, HSG.GMD.A.2 (+), HSG.GMD.A.3, HSG.MG.A.1, HSG.MG.A.2, MP.2, MP.3, MP.4

CONCEPTUAL UNDERSTANDING →

VOCABULARY
Remember that in a right prism, the sides are perpendicular to the bases. In an *oblique prism*, one or more sides are not perpendicular to the bases.

MODEL & DISCUSS

The Environmental Club has a piece of wire mesh that they want to form into an open-bottom and open-top compost bin.

60 in.

100 in.

A. Using one side as the height, describe how you can form a compost bin in the shape of a rectangular prism using all of the mesh with no overlap.

B. Construct Arguments Which height would result in the largest volume? Explain. **MP.3**

C. Suppose you formed a cylinder using the same height as a rectangular prism. How would the volumes compare?

ESSENTIAL QUESTION > How does the volume of a prism or cylinder relate to a cross section parallel to its base?

EXAMPLE 1 **Develop Cavalieri's Principle**

How are the volumes of the two different stacks of index cards related?

The first stack forms a right prism. The second stack forms an *oblique prism*. An **oblique prism** is a prism such that some or all of the lateral faces are nonrectangular.

The heights of the stacks are the same.

Each index card has the same area and represents the rectangular cross section of the prisms.

The volumes of the two stacks are the same because the sums of the areas of the cards are the same.

Try It! **1.** Do you think that right and oblique cylinders that have the same height and cross-sectional area also have equal volume? Explain.

CONCEPT Cavalieri's Principle

Cavalieri's Principle states that if two three-dimensional figures have the same height and the same cross-sectional area at every level, then they have the same volume.

If...

Then... the volumes are equal.

CONCEPT Volumes of Prisms and Cylinders

The volume of a prism is the product of the area of the base and the height of the prism.

$V = Bh$

The volume of a cylinder is the product of the area of the base and the height of the cylinder.

$V = Bh$

$V = \pi r^2 h$

EXAMPLE 2 > **Find the Volumes of Prisms and Cylinders**

A. Lonzell needs to store 20 ft³ of firewood. Could he use the storage rack shown?

4 ft
6 ft
2 ft

The rack is a triangular prism.

$V = Bh$
$= \left[\frac{1}{2}(4)(6)\right](2) = 24$

The volume of the storage rack is 24 ft³, so Lonzell can store his firewood in the rack.

B. Keisha is deciding between the two canisters shown. Which canister holds more? What is the volume of the larger canister?

20 cm   20 cm
27 cm   25 cm

This canister is an *oblique cylinder*. An **oblique cylinder** is a cylinder such that the segment joining the centers of the bases is not perpendicular to the planes of the bases.

COMMON ERROR
The height of an oblique cylinder or prism is the length perpendicular to the bases, not the length of the sides of the figure.

The canisters have the same cross-sectional area at every height. So, by Cavalieri's Principle, the canisters have the same volume.

Use the volume formula to find the volume of the canister on the left.

$V = \pi r^2 h$

$= \pi (10)^2 (25) \approx 7,854$ ← The diameter is 20 cm, so the radius is 10 cm.

The volume of both canisters is about 7,854 cm³.

Try It! **2. a.** How would the volume of the storage shed change if the length of the triangular base is reduced by half?

b. How would the volume of the canisters change if the diameter is doubled?

EXAMPLE 3 ▶ **Apply Volume of a Prism to Solve Problems**

A gardener is building a raised bed for vegetables in a community garden. Estimate the number of bags of soil needed to fill the raised bed.

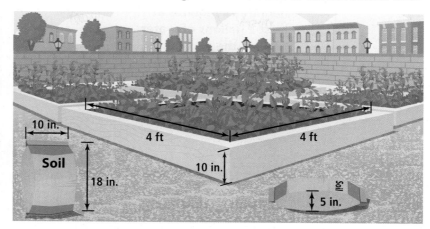

Step 1 Determine the volume of soil needed.

Compute the volume of the raised bed in cubic inches.

$V = Bh$

$\quad = (48 \cdot 48)(10)$ ◁───── Use 4 ft = 48 in.

$\quad = 23{,}040$

The raised bed requires 23,040 in.³ of soil.

Step 2 Estimate the volume of soil in each bag by modeling the bag of soil as a rectangular prism.

The height of the bag is tapered on the ends, but it is thicker in the middle, so use 5 inches as the average height.

$V = Bh$

$\quad = (10 \cdot 18)(5) = 900$

The volume of one bag of soil is about 900 in.³.

MODEL WITH MATHEMATICS
Think about other ways to model the bag. Is a rectangular prism with the values used a reasonable model? ⓒ MP.4

Step 3 Estimate the number of bags needed.

$23{,}040 \div 900 \approx 26$

The gardener needs 26 bags of soil to fill the raised bed.

Try It! **3.** Kathryn is using cans of juice to fill a cylindrical pitcher that is 11 in. tall and has a radius of 4 in. Each can of juice is 6 in. tall with a radius of 2 in. How many cans of juice will Kathryn need?

EXAMPLE 4   Solve Density Problems

Benito has 15 neon tetras in his aquarium. Each neon tetra requires at least 2 gallons of water. What is the maximum number of neon tetras that Benito should have in his aquarium?
(*Hint:* 1 gal = 231 in.^{3})

You can solve this problem using a unit rate called *density*, a measure of one quantity, in this case the number of tetras, per unit of area or volume.

Step 1   Compute the volume of water in cubic inches.

$$V = \pi r^2 h$$
$$= \pi(8)^2(32)$$

> The radius is half the diameter.

$$\approx 6{,}434$$

The volume of the water in the aquarium is about 6,434 in.^{3}.

Step 2   Find the volume of water in gallons.

$$6{,}434 \text{ in.}^3 \cdot \frac{1 \text{ gal}}{231 \text{ in.}^3} \approx 27.85 \text{ gal}$$

The volume of the water in the aquarium is about 27.85 gal.

STUDY TIP
You can also find the number of tetras by solving the following proportion:
$$\frac{x \text{ tetras}}{27.85 \text{ gal}} = \frac{1 \text{ tetra}}{2 \text{ gal}}$$

Step 3   Find the density of tetras per gallon.

$$\frac{1 \text{ tetras}}{2 \text{ gal}} = 0.5 \text{ tetras/gal}$$

Step 4   Compute the number of neon tetras that Benito's tank should hold.

Multiply the number of gallons in the aquarium by the density of tetras per gallon.

$$(27.85 \text{ gal}) \cdot (0.5 \text{ tetras/gal}) = 13.925 \text{ tetras}$$

Since he must have a whole number of tetras, Benito should have no more than 13 neon tetras in his aquarium.

Try It!   **4.** Benito is considering switching to the aquarium shown. What is the maximum number of neon tetras that this aquarium can hold?

EXAMPLE 5 Determine Whether Volume or Surface Area Best Describes Size

A forester surveys giant sequoias by gathering data about the heights and circumferences of the trees.

	A	B	C
Height	270 ft	258 ft	248 ft
Circumference (measured at 4.5 ft)	101 ft	109 ft	106 ft

A. Should the forester use surface area or volume to describe the sizes of the sequoias? Explain.

The amount of wood in a tree is determined by its volume, so she should use volume to determine the size of a giant sequoia.

MODEL WITH MATHEMATICS
Think about other shapes you could use to represent the tree. What is another mathematical model you could use for this problem? ⓒ MP.4

B. What are the sizes of the sequoias shown? Rank them by size from largest to smallest.

Although the sequoias have branches and the trunk tapers gradually toward the top of the tree, each tree can be modeled as a cylinder. Find the volume of each cylinder to estimate the volume of each tree.

	Radius (ft)	Volume of Trunk (ft³)
Tree A 270 ft	$r = \dfrac{101}{2\pi} \approx 16.1$	$V = \pi r^2 h$ $= \pi(16.1)^2(270)$ $\approx 219{,}870$
Tree B 258 ft	$r = \dfrac{109}{2\pi} \approx 17.3$	$V = \pi r^2 h$ $= \pi(17.3)^2(258)$ $\approx 242{,}584$
Tree C 248 ft	$r = \dfrac{106}{2\pi} \approx 16.9$	$V = \pi r^2 h$ $= \pi(16.9)^2(248)$ $\approx 222{,}523$

LEARN TOGETHER
Do you seek help when needed? Do you offer help and support others?

In order from largest to smallest, the three trees are: Tree B, Tree C, Tree A.

Try It! 5. Describe a situation for which surface area might be a better measure of size than volume.

CONCEPT SUMMARY Volumes of Prisms and Cylinders

WORDS **Cavalieri's Principle** Figures with the same height and same cross-sectional area at every level have the same volume.

As a result, right and oblique prisms and cylinders with the same base area and height have the same volume.

DIAGRAMS

$$V = Bh$$
$$V = 30 \cdot 14$$
$$V = 420 \text{ cubic inches}$$

$$V = Bh$$
$$V = \pi r^2 h$$
$$= \pi \cdot 5^2 \cdot 11$$
$$= 863.9 \text{ cubic meters}$$

Do You UNDERSTAND?

1. **ESSENTIAL QUESTION** How does the volume of a prism or cylinder relate to a cross section parallel to its base?

2. **Error Analysis** Juliana says that Cavalieri's Principle proves that the two prisms shown have the same volume. Explain her error. ⒸMP.3

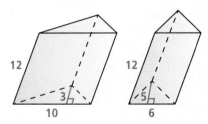

3. **Vocabulary** How are an oblique prism and an oblique cylinder alike and different?

4. **Reason** The circumference of the base of a cylinder is x, and the height of the cylinder is x. What expression gives the volume of the cylinder? ⒸMP.2

5. **Construct Arguments** Denzel kicks a large dent into a trash can and says that the volume does not change because of Cavalieri's Principle. Do you agree with Denzel? Explain. ⒸMP.3

Do You KNOW HOW?

For Exercises 6–11, find the volume of each figure. Round to the nearest tenth.

6.

7.

8.

9.

10.

11.

12. Which figures have the same volume? Explain.

PRACTICE & PROBLEM SOLVING

UNDERSTAND

13. Error Analysis Dylan compares the volumes of two bottles. What is Dylan's error? Ⓒ **MP.3**

The volume of the rectangular prism is equal to the volume of the cylinder because they have the same dimensions. ✗

14. Higher Order Thinking Does Cavalieri's Principle apply to the volumes of the cones shown? Explain.

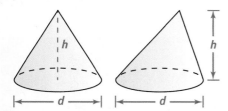

15. Mathematical Connections Does rotating the rectangle about line *m* result in a cylinder with the same volume as rotating the rectangle about line *n*? Explain.

16. Use Appropriate Tools Do the prisms shown have equivalent volumes? Explain. Ⓒ **MP.5**

PRACTICE

17. Laila buys the two vases shown. How do the volumes of the vases compare? Explain. SEE EXAMPLE 1

18. Talisa plans a 6-foot deep pond. While digging, she hits rock 5 feet down. How can Talisa modify the radius to maintain the original volume of the pond? SEE EXAMPLE 2

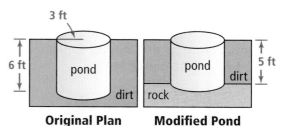

Original Plan   **Modified Pond**

19. The instructions for plant food say to use 0.25 gram per cubic inch of soil. How many grams of plant food should Bastián use if the planter box shown is full of soil? SEE EXAMPLE 3

20. If a stack of 40 nickels fits snugly in the coin wrapper shown, how thick is 1 nickel? Round to the nearest hundredth. SEE EXAMPLE 4

nickel   wrapper
$d = 21.21$ mm $V = 27,560$ mm^3

21. Sections of two flood-control ditches are shown. Which one holds the greater volume of water? Explain. SEE EXAMPLE 5

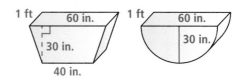

PRACTICE & PROBLEM SOLVING

22. Use Appropriate Tools How many 3-inch-thick bags of mulch should Naomi buy to cover 100 square feet at a depth of 4 inches? ⓒ **MP.5**

3.2 ft

2.5 ft

23. Reason Laia's younger brother will be home in a half hour. If her garden hose flows at a rate 24 gal/min, does she have enough time to fill the pool before he gets home? Explain. (*Hint:* 1 ft³ = 7.48 gal) ⓒ **MP.2**

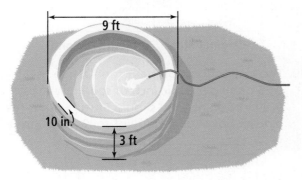

9 ft

10 in.

3 ft

24. Model With Mathematics The ABC Cookie Company wants to promise an average of "12 chocolate chips per cookie." Assuming that the cookies fill about 80% of the box below by volume, will 600 chocolate chips for each box of cookies be sufficient to make the claim? Explain. ⓒ **MP.4**

Cookie
$d = 3$ in.
$h = 0.5$ in.

9.25 in.

3.5 in.

6.5 in.

Box

25. Cylinders A, B, and C have the same volume. Cylinder A has diameter 12 cm and height 8 cm.

  a. If the diameter of cylinder B is 16 cm, what is the height?

  b. If the height of cylinder C is 32 cm, what is the diameter?

26. SAT/ACT If the volume of the prism shown is 70 cubic yards, what is its length?

5 yd

ℓ

3.5 yd

Ⓐ 4 yd   Ⓑ 8 yd   ⓒ 16 yd   Ⓓ 28 yd

27. Performance Task A candle company uses wax that has a density of 0.0325 lb/in.³ to make small candles with a diameter of 2 inches and a height of 4 inches and large candles with a diameter of 4 inches and a height of 8 inches. The company uses two sizes of cardboard boxes to package orders. A customer places an order for 4 large candles and 2 small candles.

16 in.
Max. 20 lb. Candle
12 in.   12 in.

Max. 12 lb. Candle   12 in.
10 in.   10 in.

Part A What is the smallest box the company can use to package the order? Explain how the candles could be organized within the box.

Part B The remaining space in the box is filled with lightweight packing paper to protect the candles. Estimate the volume of packing paper that is needed for the order.

© **Common Core State Standards**
HSG.MG.A.3, HSG.GMD.B.4, MP.4

SavvasRealize.com

Box 'Em Up

With so many people and businesses shopping online, retailers, and especially e-retailers, ship more and more packages every day. Some of the products people order have unusual sizes and shapes and need custom packaging. Imagine how you might package a surfboard, or a snow blower, or even live crawfish to ship to someone's house!

Think about this during the Mathematical Modeling in 3 Acts lesson.

ACT 1 ▶ **Identify the Problem**

1. What is the first question that comes to mind after watching the video?

2. Write down the main question you will answer about what you saw in the video.

3. Make an initial conjecture that answers this main question.

4. Explain how you arrived at your conjecture.

5. What information will be useful to know to answer the main question? How can you get it? How will you use that information?

ACT 2 ▶ **Develop a Model**

6. Use the math that you have learned in this Topic to refine your conjecture.

ACT 3 ▶ **Interpret the Results**

7. Did your refined conjecture match the actual answer exactly? If not, what might explain the difference?

11-3
Pyramids and Cones

I CAN... use the volumes of right and oblique pyramids and cones to solve problems.

Ⓒ **Common Core State Standards**
HSG.GMD.A.1, HSG.GMD.A.2 (+), HSG.GMD.A.3, HSG.MG.A.1, MP.2, MP.6, MP.7

CONCEPTUAL UNDERSTANDING

EXPLORE & REASON

Consider the cube and pyramid.

A. How many pyramids could you fit inside the cube? Explain.

B. Write an equation that shows the relationship between C and P.

C. **Look for Relationships** Make a conjecture about the volume of any pyramid. Explain your reasoning. Ⓒ **MP.7**

Volume = C   Volume = P

ESSENTIAL QUESTION How are the formulas for volume of a pyramid and volume of a cone alike?

EXAMPLE 1 Apply Cavalieri's Principle to Pyramids and Cones

How are the volumes of pyramids and cones with the same base area and height related?

Imagine a set of cardboard discs, each with a slightly smaller radius than the previous disc. You can stack the discs in different ways.

GENERALIZE
Think about the shape formed by the stacks. What would happen if the number of discs increases while the difference in the radii and the thickness of each disc decreases? Ⓒ **MP.8**

The heights of the stacks are the same, and the area at each level is the same. The total volume of cardboard in each stack is the same.

The stacks approximate cones. You can apply Cavalieri's Principle to cones and pyramids.

If two figures have the same height and equal area at every cross section, they have equal volumes.

Try It! **1.** Is it possible to use only Cavalieri's Principle to show that a cone and a cylinder have equal volumes? Explain.

CONCEPT Volumes of Pyramids and Cones

The volume of a pyramid is one-third the product of the area of the base and the height of the pyramid.

$$V = \frac{1}{3} Bh$$

The volume of a cone is one-third the product of the area of the base and the height of the cone.

$$V = \frac{1}{3} Bh$$
$$V = \frac{1}{3} \pi r^2 h$$

EXAMPLE 2 > Find the Volumes of Pyramids and Cones

A. Kyle's truck can haul 1.75 tons of corn per load. One cubic meter of corn weighs 0.8 ton. How many loads will Kyle haul to move this pile of corn?

$$V = \frac{1}{3}\pi r^2 h$$

$$= \frac{1}{3}\pi (2)^2(1.5) \approx 6.3 \text{ m}^3$$

The pile is shaped like a cone, so use the volume formula for cones.

Since 6.3 m³ • 0.8 ton/m³ = 5.04 tons, Kyle will need to haul 5.04 ÷ 1.75 = 2.88 or 3 loads.

B. Jason is using a mold to make 12 candles. How many cubic inches of wax does he need?

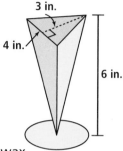

$$V = \frac{1}{3}Bh$$

$$= \frac{1}{3}\left[\frac{1}{2}(4)(3)\right](6) = 12 \text{ in.}^3$$

Use the volume formula for a pyramid.

Use the area formula for a triangle to find the base.

For 12 candles, Jason needs 12 in.³ • 12, or 144 in.³ of wax.

STUDY TIP
The base of a pyramid can be any polygon, so the formula you use to determine the area of the base *B* depends on the shape of the base.

Try It! **2. a.** What is the volume of a cone with base diameter 14 and height 16?

  b. What is the volume of a pyramid with base area 10 and height 7?

EXAMPLE 3 > Apply the Volumes of Pyramids to Solve Problems

Dyani is 1.8 m tall and wants to be able to stand inside her new tent. Should she buy the tent shown?

Tent Features:
- 3.4 cubic meters
- Square floor with 8.4 m perimeter
- Height:

CLEARANCE
$59

Step 1 Draw and label a square pyramid to represent the tent.

Since the perimeter of the square floor is 8.4 m, s = 2.1 m.

HAVE A GROWTH MINDSET
After receiving constructive feedback, how do you use it as an opportunity to improve?

Step 2 Find the height of the pyramid.

$$V = \frac{1}{3}Bh$$

$$3.4 = \frac{1}{3}(2.1)^2 h$$

$$h \approx 2.3$$

The height of the pyramid is approximately 2.3 m.

Dyani will be able to stand in the tent, so she should buy the tent.

CONTINUED ON THE NEXT PAGE

EXAMPLE 3 CONTINUED

Try It! **3.** A rectangular pyramid has a base that is three times as long as it is wide. The volume of the pyramid is 75 ft³ and the height is 3 ft. What is the perimeter of the base?

APPLICATION

EXAMPLE 4 Apply the Volumes of Cones to Solve Problems

A restaurant sells smoothies in two sizes. Which size is a better deal?

Formulate ◄ Compare the prices by determining the cost per cubic centimeter for each size.

The volume of fruit smoothie in each glass can be approximated as the volume of a cone.

10 cm
7 cm
15 cm
12 cm

Large: $5.89   Small: $3.49

Compute ◄ **Step 1** Calculate the height of each cone using the Pythagorean Theorem.

Large	**Small**
$5^2 + h^2 = 15^2$	$3.5^2 + h^2 = 12^2$
$h^2 = 200$	$h^2 = 131.75$
$h \approx 14.1$	$h \approx 11.5$

The height of the large cone is approximately 14.1 cm.

The height of the small cone is approximately 11.5 cm.

Step 2 Calculate the volume of each cone.

Large	**Small**
$V = \frac{1}{3}\pi r^2 h$	$V = \frac{1}{3}\pi r^2 h$
$= \frac{1}{3}\pi(5)^2(14.1)$	$= \frac{1}{3}\pi(3.5)^2(11.5)$
≈ 369.1	≈ 147.5

The volume of the large cone is approximately 369.1 cm³.

The volume of the small cone is approximately 147.5 cm³.

Step 3 Calculate the cost per cubic centimeter for each size.

Large	**Small**
$\frac{\$5.89}{369.1 \text{ cm}^3} \approx \$0.016$ per cm³	$\frac{\$3.49}{147.5 \text{ cm}^3} \approx \$0.024$ per cm³

Interpret ◄ The large size smoothie costs less per cubic centimeter, so the large size smoothie is a better deal.

CONTINUED ON THE NEXT PAGE

EXAMPLE 4 CONTINUED

Try It! **4.** A cone has a volume of 144π and a height of 12.

      a. What is the radius of the base?

      b. If the radius of the cone is tripled, what is the new volume? What is the relationship between the volumes of the two cones?

APPLICATION

EXAMPLE 5   Measure a Composite Figure

Kaitlyn is making a concrete animal sculpture. Each bag of concrete mix makes 0.6 ft³ of concrete. How many bags of concrete mix does Kaitlyn need?

16 in.

20 in.   16 in.

18 in.

15 in.

22 in.

16 in. 4 in.

Calculate the volume of each part.

Step 1 Calculate the volume of one of the legs.

$$V = \pi r^2 h$$

$$= \pi(2)^2(16)$$

> The legs are oblique cylinders.

$$\approx 201 \text{ in.}^3$$

Step 2 Calculate the volume of the body.

$$V = Bh$$

$$= (22 \cdot 18)(15)$$

> The body is a rectangular prism.

$$= 5{,}940 \text{ in.}^3$$

Step 3 Calculate the volume of the head.

$$V = \frac{1}{3}Bh$$

$$= \frac{1}{3}(16 \cdot 16)(20)$$

> The head is a square pyramid.

$$\approx 1{,}707 \text{ in.}^3$$

COMMON ERROR
When multiple parts of a composite figure have the same volume, make sure you account for each part in your total.

Step 4 Calculate the total volume.

$$V = 4(201) + 5{,}940 + 1{,}707$$

> Add the volumes of the parts of the sculpture.

$$= 8{,}451$$

The total volume is 8,451 in.³. Convert to cubic feet to determine the amount of concrete needed.

$$8{,}451 \cdot \frac{1}{1{,}728} = 4.9$$

> $1 \text{ ft}^3 = (12 \text{ in.})^3 = 1{,}728 \text{ in.}^3$

To make the sculpture, 4.9 ft³ of concrete is needed. Kaitlyn needs $4.9 \div 0.6 \approx 8.2$ or 9 bags of concrete mix.

Try It! **5.** A cone-shaped hole is drilled into a prism. The height of the triangular base of the prism is 12 cm. What is the volume of the remaining figure? Round to the nearest tenth.

3 cm

8 cm

22 cm

CONCEPT SUMMARY Pyramids and Cones

WORDS The volume of a pyramid is one-third the volume of a prism with the same base area and height.

The volume of a cone is one-third the volume of a cylinder with the same base area and height.

DIAGRAMS

$$V = \tfrac{1}{3}Bh$$

$$V = \tfrac{1}{3}Bh \text{ or } V = \tfrac{1}{3}\pi r^2 h$$

Do You UNDERSTAND?

1. **ESSENTIAL QUESTION** How are the formulas for volume of a pyramid and volume of a cone alike?

2. **Error Analysis** Zhang is finding the height of a square pyramid with a base side length of 9 and a volume of 162. What is his error? **© MP.3**

$$V = Bh$$
$$162 = 9^2(h)$$
$$h = 2$$
✗

3. **Reason** A cone and cylinder have the same radius and volume. If the height of the cone is h, what is the height of the cylinder? **© MP.2**

4. **Construct Arguments** Do you have enough information to compute the volume of the cone? Explain. **© MP.3**

Do You KNOW HOW?

For Exercises 5–10, find the volume of each figure. Round to the nearest tenth. Assume that all angles in each polygonal base are congruent.

5.

6.

7.

8.

9.

10.

11. A solid metal square pyramid with a base side length of 6 in. and height of 9 in. is melted down and recast as a square pyramid with a height of 4 in. What is the base side length of the new pyramid?

PRACTICE & PROBLEM SOLVING

UNDERSTAND

12. Construct Arguments A stack of 39 pennies is exactly as tall as a stack of 31 nickels. Do the two stacks have the same volume? Explain. © MP.3

13. Error Analysis Miguel is finding the volume of the cylinder. What is his error? © MP.3

$V = B \cdot h$
$V = 3\pi^2 \cdot 2$
$V \approx 59.2$ cubic units

14. Communicate Precisely How would you find the volume of a right square pyramid with a base side length of 10 cm, and the altitude of a triangular side is 13 cm? Explain. © MP.6

15. Mathematical Connections In terms of the radius r, what is the volume of a cone whose height is equal to its radius?

16. Higher Order Thinking A plane slices a cone parallel to the base at one-half of the height of the cone. What is the volume of the part of the cone lying below the plane?

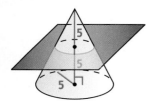

PRACTICE

17. The plane intersects sections of equal area in the two solids. Are the volumes equal?
SEE EXAMPLE 1

For Exercises 18–21, find the volume of each solid. Assume that all angles in each polygonal base are congruent. SEE EXAMPLE 2

18.

19.

20.

21.

22. A cone is inscribed in a right square pyramid. What is the remaining volume if the cone is removed? SEE EXAMPLES 3 AND 4

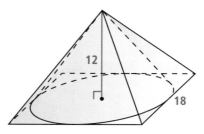

For Exercises 23 and 24, find the volume of each composite figure. SEE EXAMPLE 5

23.

24.

PRACTICE & PROBLEM SOLVING

25. **Make Sense and Persevere** Chiang makes gift boxes in the shape of a right square pyramid. She fills each box with chocolate cubes with $\frac{7}{8}$-in. sides. She can fill about 75% of a box. How many pieces can she fit in each box? ⓒ **MP.1**

4 in.

4 $\frac{1}{2}$ in.

26. **Reason** A pile of snow is plowed into the shape of a right cone. How many trucks with a capacity of 10 yd³ per truck will be needed to move the pile? ⓒ **MP.2**

12 ft

21 ft

27. **Use Structure** The basin beneath a fountain is a right cone that is 7 m across and 1 m deep at the center. After the fountain is cleaned, the pool is refilled at a rate of 300 L/min. One cubic meter is 1,000 L. How long does it take to refill the pool? ⓒ **MP.7**

7 m

1 m

Basin

28. **Model With Mathematics** A physicist wants to know what percentage of gas is empty space. A molecule of methane can be modeled by a regular tetrahedron with side length 0.154 nm (1 nm = 1×10^{-9} m). The altitude of each triangular side is 0.133 nm. If 6.022×10^{23} molecules make up 0.0224 m³ of gas, how does the volume of the molecules compare to the volume of the gas? ⓒ **MP.7**

0.133 nm

0.154 nm

29. Cavalieri's Principle states that if two solids have the same _____?_____ and the same _____?_____ at every cross section, then the solids have the same _____?_____.

30. **SAT/ACT** What is the volume of the largest cone that will fit entirely within the right square prism?

4

8

8

Ⓐ $\frac{16\pi}{3}$　　Ⓑ $\frac{32\pi}{3}$　　Ⓒ $\frac{64\pi}{3}$　　Ⓓ $\frac{128\pi}{3}$

31. **Performance Task** A designer is working on a design for two goblets. Design A is based on a cylinder and design B is based on a cone. The client wants both goblets to be the same height and width.

3 in.　3 in.

6 in.　A　B

Part A The client wants the smaller goblet to hold at least 10 fl oz. One fluid ounce is 1.8 in.³. Will design B be large enough to meet the client's requirements? Explain.

Part B The client wants the larger goblet to hold 20 fl oz. Does design A meet the client's requirement? Explain.

Part C How could design B be changed if the client wants the smaller goblet to hold at least 12 fl oz?

11-4

Spheres

I CAN... calculate the volume of a sphere and solve problems involving the volumes of spheres.

VOCABULARY

• hemisphere

Common Core State Standards
HSG.GMD.A.2 (+), HSG.GMD.A.3, HSG.MG.A.1, MP.1, MP.2, MP.5

CONCEPTUAL UNDERSTANDING

USE APPROPRIATE TOOLS
Think about how you can draw the section of the cylinder with the cone removed. What does the cross section look like? **© MP.5**

CRITIQUE & EXPLAIN

Ricardo estimates the volume of a sphere with radius 2 by placing the sphere inside a cylinder and placing two cones inside the sphere. He says that the volume of the sphere is less than 16π and greater than $\frac{16}{3}\pi$.

A. Do you agree with Ricardo? Explain.

B. Reason How might you estimate the volume of the sphere? **© MP.2**

ESSENTIAL QUESTION How does the volume of a sphere relate to the volumes of other solids?

EXAMPLE 1 Explore the Volume of a Sphere

What is the volume of a sphere? Why does the volume formula for a sphere make sense?

A plane, parallel to the bases, intersects half of a sphere with radius r and a cylinder with radius r and height r. The cylinder has a cone with radius r and height r removed from its center.

By the Pythagorean Theorem, the cross section is a circle with radius $\sqrt{r^2 - h^2}$.

The cross section of the cylinder has radius r. The cross section of the cone has radius h.

Area of the cross section is $\pi\left(\sqrt{r^2 - h^2}\right)^2 = \pi(r^2 - h^2)$.

Area of the cross section is $(\pi \cdot r^2) - (\pi \cdot h^2) = \pi(r^2 - h^2)$.

Once the cone is removed, the areas of the cross sections of the solids are equal at any height. Therefore, by Cavalieri's Principle, the two solids have the same volume.

volume of half a sphere = volume of cylinder − volume of cone

$$= \pi r^2 \cdot r - \frac{1}{3}\pi r^2 \cdot r$$

$$= \frac{2}{3}\pi r^3$$

The volume of a sphere is twice the volume of half of the sphere, so the volume of a sphere with radius r is $\frac{4}{3}\pi r^3$.

CONTINUED ON THE NEXT PAGE

EXAMPLE 1 CONTINUED

Try It! **1.** Find the volumes of the three solids. What do you notice?

CONCEPT Volume of a Sphere

The volume of a sphere is four-thirds of the product of π and the cube of the radius of the sphere.

$$V = \frac{4}{3}\pi r^3$$

APPLICATION

EXAMPLE 2 Use the Volumes of Spheres to Solve Problems

The drama club makes a big foam ball to hang above the stage during a play. They plan to cover the surface of the ball with metallic fabric. What is the minimum number of square meters of fabric that the club needs?

$V = 1.8\ m^3$

Use the volume formula to determine the radius of the ball. Then use the surface area formula of a sphere.

First find r from the volume of the ball.

$$V = \frac{4}{3}\pi r^3$$ — Use the volume formula.

$$1.8 = \frac{4}{3}\pi r^3$$

$$r^3 = \frac{1.35}{\pi}$$ — Use a calculator to find the cube root.

$$r \approx 0.75$$

STUDY TIP
Remember that the surface area of a sphere is four times the area of a circle with the same radius.

The radius of the ball is about 0.75 m. Next, calculate the surface area.

The surface area of a sphere with radius r is S.A. $= 4\pi r^2$.

$$S.A. = 4\pi r^2$$

$$S.A. = 4\pi(0.75)^2$$ — Substitute the radius into the surface area formula.

$$S.A. \approx 7.1$$

The club needs at least 7.1 m² of fabric.

Try It! **2.** What is the largest volume a sphere can have if it is covered by 6 m² of fabric?

EXAMPLE 3 **Find the Volumes of Hemispheres**

What is the volume of the hemisphere?

A *great circle* is the intersection of a sphere and a plane containing the center of the sphere.

VOCABULARY
The prefix *hemi* is from the Greek and means *half*. Thus, hemisphere means half-sphere.

A great circle divides a sphere into two **hemispheres**.

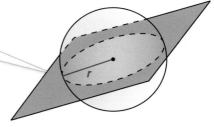

The volume of a hemisphere is one-half the volume of a sphere with the same radius.

$$V = \frac{2}{3}\pi r^3$$
$$V = \frac{2}{3}\pi \cdot 4^3 \approx 134.04$$

Try It! **3. a.** What is the volume of a hemisphere with radius 3 ft?

b. What is the volume of a hemisphere with diameter 13 cm?

EXAMPLE 4 **Find the Volumes of Composite Figures**

A solid is composed of a right cylinder and a hemisphere as shown. If the density of the solid is 100 kg/m³, what is the mass of the solid?

Find the volume of the solid.

volume of solid = volume of cylinder
+ volume of hemisphere

$$= \pi r^2 h + \frac{2}{3}\pi r^3$$

$$= \pi(1)^2(3) + \frac{2}{3}\pi(1)^3$$

$$\approx 11.5$$

COMMON ERROR
As you break a composite figure into figures or parts of figures you are familiar with, be careful not to mix up the measurements of each figure.

The volume of the solid is about 11.5 m³. Next, find the mass of the solid.

11.5 • 100 = 1,150

The mass of the solid is about 1,150 kg.

Try It! **4.** What is the volume of the space between the sphere and the cylinder?

CONCEPT SUMMARY Volume of Spheres

WORDS Cavalieri's Principle can be used to show how the volume of the sphere is related to the volumes of a cylinder and cone. The area of a cross section of a hemisphere is the same as the area of a cross section of a cylinder with height equal to the radius minus the cross section of a cone with height equal to the radius.

DIAGRAMS

 = −

$$\frac{2}{3}\pi r^3 \quad = \quad \pi r^2 \cdot r \quad - \quad \frac{1}{3}\pi r^2 \cdot r$$

Do You UNDERSTAND?

1. **ESSENTIAL QUESTION** How does the volume of a sphere relate to the volumes of other solids?

2. **Error Analysis** Reagan is finding the volume of the sphere. What is her error? **© MP.3**

$$S.A. = \frac{4}{3}\pi r^3$$

$$S.A. = \frac{4}{3} \cdot \pi \cdot 3^3$$

$$S.A. \approx 113.1 \text{ square units}$$

✗

3. **Vocabulary** How does a great circle define a hemisphere?

4. **Reason** The radius of a sphere, the base radius of a cylinder, and the base radius of a cone are r. What is the height of the cylinder if the volume of the cylinder is equal to the volume of the sphere? What is the height of the cone if the volume of the cone is equal to the volume of the sphere? **© MP.2**

Do You KNOW HOW?

For Exercises 5 and 6, find the surface area of each solid.

5.

6.

For Exercises 7 and 8, find the volume of each solid.

7.

8.

9. Find the volume of the largest sphere that can fit entirely in the rectangular prism.

5 cm

4 cm

4 cm

10. Find the volume and surface area of a sphere with radius 1.

PRACTICE & PROBLEM SOLVING

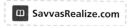

UNDERSTAND

11. Construct Arguments How does Cavalieri's Principle apply to finding the volume of a hemisphere? Explain. ©️ MP.3

12. Error Analysis Destiny is finding the surface area of the sphere. What is her error? ©️ MP.3

$$\text{S.A.} = 4\pi r^2$$
$$\text{S.A.} = 4 \cdot \pi \cdot 14^2$$
$$\text{S.A.} \approx 2{,}463.0 \text{ square units} \quad ✗$$

13. Mathematical Connections Given the surface area of a sphere, write a formula for the volume of a sphere in terms of the surface area.

14. Construct Arguments Fifteen cylinders and 15 rectangular prisms are stacked. Each cylinder has the same top surface area and height as each rectangular prism. What can you determine about the volumes of the two stacks of 15 solids? Explain. ©️ MP.3

15. Reason A sphere is divided by two great circles that are perpendicular to each other. How would you find the surface area and volume of each part of the sphere between the two planes containing the great circles? Explain. ©️ MP.2

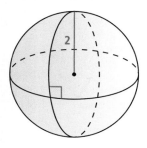

PRACTICE

For Exercises 16–18, find the area of each cross section. SEE EXAMPLE 1

16.   **17.**

18.

For Exercises 19–22, find the surface area of each solid to the nearest tenth. SEE EXAMPLE 2

19.   **20.**

21. sphere with volume 35 cm³

22. sphere with volume 100 in.³

For Exercises 23–26, find the volume of each solid to the nearest tenth. SEE EXAMPLES 2 AND 3

23.   **24.**

25. hemisphere with radius 12 ft

26. sphere with radius 25 m

For Exercises 27 and 28, find the volume of each composite figure to the nearest tenth.
SEE EXAMPLE 4

27.   **28.**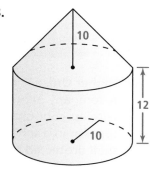

PRACTICE & PROBLEM SOLVING

29. Make Sense and Persevere To reach the regulation pressure for a game ball, the amount of air pumped into a ball is 1.54 times the volume of the ball. A referee adds 15 in.³ of air for each pump of air. How many pumps of air will it take the referee to fill an empty ball? **ⓒ MP.1**

9.55 in.

30. Reason Jayden uses a block of clay to make round beads. How many beads can he make from the block? **ⓒ MP.2**

6 cm 3 cm 1 cm 1 cm

31. Felipe places a spherical round-bottom flask in a cylindrical beaker containing hot water. The flask must fit into the beaker with 2 cm of space around the flask. What is the minimum diameter, *d*, of the beaker?

$V = 250$ cm³ 2 cm 2 cm *d*

32. Higher Order Thinking A company packs each wireless cube-shaped speaker in a spherical shell protected by foam. How much foam does the company use for each speaker?

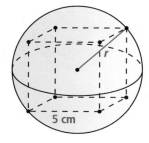

r 5 cm

33. Match each description with its expression.

    I. volume of a sphere with radius 1   **A.** $\frac{4}{3}\pi$

    II. surface area of a sphere with radius 2   **B.** $\frac{16}{3}\pi$

    III. circumference of a great circle for a sphere with radius 3   **C.** 6π

    IV. volume of a hemisphere with radius 2   **D.** 16π

34. SAT/ACT The surface area of a sphere is 64π ft². What is the radius of the sphere?

    Ⓐ 64 ft

    Ⓑ 16 ft

    Ⓒ 8 ft

    Ⓓ 4 ft

35. Performance Task Jayesh is to fill the tank shown with liquid propane.

4 m 1.2 m

Part A The liquid propane expands and contracts as the temperature changes, so a propane tank is never filled to more than 80% capacity with liquid propane. How much liquid propane should Jayesh put in the tank?

Part B If Jayesh has 20 m³ of liquid propane to fill another tank, what are the dimensions of the tank if the length of the cylindrical part is three times the diameter?

Topic Review

TOPIC ESSENTIAL QUESTION

1. How is Cavalieri's Principle helpful in understanding the volume formulas for solids?

Vocabulary Review

Choose the correct term to complete each sentence.

2. A prism is _____ if one or more faces are not perpendicular to the bases.

3. _____ describes the relationship between the volumes of three-dimensional figures that have the same height and the same cross sectional area at every level.

4. A great circle divides a sphere into two _____.

- Cavalieri's Principle
- cones
- cylinders
- hemispheres
- oblique
- right
- spheres

Concepts & Skills Review

LESSON 11-1 ▶ **Three-Dimensional Figures and Cross Sections**

Quick Review

The faces of a polyhedron are polygons. Euler's Formula states that the relationship between the number of faces *F*, number of vertices *V*, and number of edges *E* is

$$F + V = E + 2$$

The cross section of a plane and a convex polyhedron is a polygon.

Rotating a polygon about an axis forms a three-dimensional figure.

Example

A triangular prism has 5 faces and 9 edges. How many vertices does it have?

$$F + V = E + 2$$
$$5 + V = 9 + 2$$
$$V = 6$$

The prism has 6 vertices.

Practice & Problem Solving

For Exercises 5 and 6, use the pyramid shown.

5. The pyramid has 6 vertices and 10 edges. How many faces does it have?

6. Visualize a plane intersecting the pyramid parallel to the base. Describe the cross section.

7. Describe the three-dimensional figure that is formed by rotating the rectangle about the line shown.

8. **Reason** Can a polyhedron have the same number of faces, edges, and vertices? Explain. © **MP.2**

Quick Review

Cavalieri's Principle states that figures with the same height and same area at every horizontal cross section have the same volume.

$V = Bh$
$V = (\ell \cdot w)h$
$V = (9\pi)(20)$
$V = 180\pi$

$V = Bh$
$V = (\pi r^2)h$
$V = (9\pi)(20)$
$V = 180\pi$

Example

Do the cylinders have the same volume? Explain.

Yes, cylinders with the same base area and height have the same volume. The height of each cylinder is 11. The area of the base of each cylinder is $\pi(4)^2$, or 16π.

Practice & Problem Solving

For Exercises 9 and 10, find the volume of each figure. Round to the nearest tenth.

9.   10.

11. **Reason** What does the expression $\frac{3}{4}xyz$ represent for the prism shown? Ⓒ MP.2

12. Malia pours wax in molds to make candles. Compare the amount of wax each mold holds.

Quick Review

The volume of a pyramid is one-third the volume of a prism with the same base area and height. $V = \frac{1}{3}Bh$

The volume of a cone is one-third the volume of a cylinder with the same base area and height. $V = \frac{1}{3}Bh$

Example

What is the volume?

$V = \frac{1}{3}Bh = \frac{1}{3} \cdot \frac{1}{2}(6 \cdot 3)(9)$
$= 27$

The volume of the pyramid is 27 cubic units.

Practice & Problem Solving

For Exercises 13 and 14, find the volume of each figure. Round to the nearest tenth.

13.   14.

15. A sculptor cuts a pyramid from a marble cube with volume t^3 ft³. The pyramid is t ft tall. The area of the base is t^2 ft². Write an expression for the volume of marble removed.

16. A company cuts 2 in. from the tops of the solid plastic cones. How much less plastic is used in the new design?

LESSON 11-4 ▶ Spheres

Quick Review

The volume of a sphere is
$V = \frac{4}{3}\pi r^3$.

The volume of a hemisphere is one-half the volume of a sphere with the same radius, $V = \frac{2}{3}\pi r^3$.

Example

What is the volume of the sphere shown?

$$V = \frac{4}{3}\pi r^3$$
$$= \frac{4}{3}\pi(3)^3 = 36\pi$$

The volume of the sphere is 36π m^3.

Practice & Problem Solving

For Exercises 17 and 18, find the volume of each figure. Round to the nearest tenth.

17.

2.4 in.

18.

1.8 cm

19. **Use Structure** A golf ball has a radius of r centimeters. What is the least possible volume of a rectangular box that can hold 2 golf balls? Ⓖ **MP.7**

20. A capsule of liquid cold medicine is shown. If 1 dose is about 23 ml, how many capsules make up 1 dose? (*Hint:* 1 ml = 1 cm^3)

1 cm
0.5 cm

TOPIC ESSENTIAL QUESTION

How can you find the probability of events and combinations of events?

Topic Overview

enVision® STEM Project:
Simulate Weather Conditions

12-1 Probability Events

12-2 Conditional Probability

Mathematical Modeling in 3 Acts:
Place Your Guess

12-3 Permutations and Combinations

12-4 Probability Distributions

12-5 Expected Value

12-6 Probability and Decision Making

Topic Vocabulary

- binomial distribution
- binomial experiment
- combination
- complement
- conditional probability
- dependent events
- expected value
- factorial
- Fundamental Counting Principle
- independent events
- mutually exclusive
- permutation
- probability distribution
- uniform probability distribution

Digital Experience

INTERACTIVE STUDENT EDITION
Access online or offline.

ACTIVITIES Complete *Explore & Reason, Model & Discuss*, and *Critique & Explain* activities. Interact with *Examples* and *Try Its.*

CONCEPT SUMMARY Review key lesson content through multiple representations.

ASSESSMENT Show what you've learned.

 Go online | **SavvasRealize.com**

MATHEMATICAL MODELING IN 3 ACTS

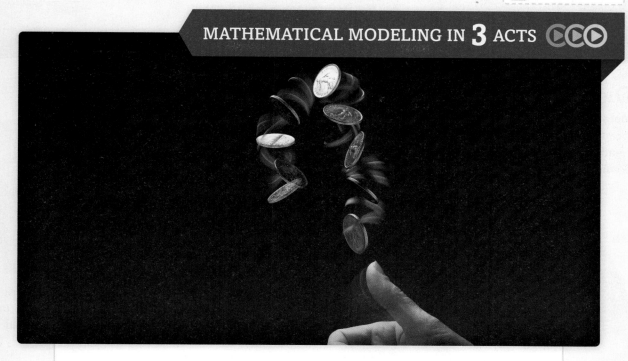

Place Your Guess

A coin toss is a popular way to decide between two options or settle a dispute. The coin toss is popular because it is a simple and unbiased way of deciding. Assuming the coin being tossed is a fair coin, both parties have an equally likely chance of winning.

What other methods could you use to decide between two choices fairly? Think about this during the Mathematical Modeling in 3 Acts lesson.

TOPIC 12

VIDEOS Watch clips to support *Mathematical Modeling in 3 Acts Lessons* and **enVision®** *STEM Projects.*

TUTORIALS Get help from *Virtual Nerd*, right when you need it.

PRACTICE Practice what you've learned.

ADAPTIVE PRACTICE Practice that is *just right* and *just for you.*

FAMILY ENGAGEMENT Involve family in your learning.

GLOSSARY Read and listen to English and Spanish definitions.

MATH TOOLS Explore math with digital tools and manipulatives.

DESMOS Use Anytime and as embedded Interactives in Lesson content.

⚙enVision® STEM

Did You Know?

Meteorologists use past climate data for a particular location and date as well as **weather models** to make weather predictions. Some regions in the U.S. are more predictable than others.

The **greatest temperature change** in a one-day period occurred in Loma, Montana, in 1972. The temperature rose an incredible **103 degrees**, from −54 to 49 °F, in 24 hours.

Weather events can surprise experts, and can vary greatly even within a few miles.

Climate is the long-term average of weather conditions. So the difference between weather and climate is a measure of time.

Your Task: Simulate Weather Conditions

You and your classmates will research climate data for a specific location for one month. You'll use probability to simulate a plausible set of weather conditions for each day of February, including temperature and precipitation, and whether the precipitation will be rain or snow.

12-1
Probability Events

I CAN... use relationships among events to find probabilities.

VOCABULARY
- complement
- independent events
- mutually exclusive

Common Core State Standards
HSS.CP.A.1, HSS.CP.A.2, HSS.CP.A.5, HSS.CP.B.7, MP.2, MP.3, MP.7

EXPLORE & REASON

Allie spins the spinner and draws one card without looking. She gets a 3 on the spinner and the 3 card. Then she sets the card aside, spins again, and draws another card.

A. Is it possible for Allie to get a 3 on her second spin? On her second card? Explain.

B. **Construct Arguments** How does getting the 3 card on her first draw affect the probability of getting the 2 card on her second draw? Explain. © **MP.3**

> **ESSENTIAL QUESTION** How does describing events as mutually exclusive or independent affect how you find probabilities?

EXAMPLE 1 Find Probabilities of Mutually Exclusive Events

You roll a standard number cube once. Let *E* represent the event "roll an even number." Let *T* represent the event "roll a 3 or 5."

A. What is the probability that you roll an even number or roll a 3 or 5?

Show the outcomes of events *E* and *T* as a subset of the sample space *S*.

Events *E* and *T* are **mutually exclusive** because there is no outcome in both sets.

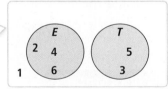

There are 5 outcomes that are even numbers or a 3 or 5. {2, 3, 4, 5, 6} There are a total of 6 possible outcomes in the sample space.

$$P(E \text{ or } T) = \frac{\text{number of favorable outcomes}}{\text{number of total possible outcomes}}$$

$$= \frac{3+2}{6}$$

There are 3 outcomes in event *E* and 2 outcomes in event *T*.

$$= \frac{3}{6} + \frac{2}{6}$$

This is equivalent to $P(E) + P(T)$.

$$= \frac{5}{6}$$

The probability of rolling an even number or rolling a 3 or a 5 is $\frac{5}{6}$.

B. You roll a standard number cube once. What is the probability that you roll an even number and a 3 or 5?

$$P(E \text{ and } T) = \frac{\text{number of favorable outcomes}}{\text{number of total possible outcomes}}$$

$$= \frac{0}{6}$$

Because events *E* and *T* are mutually exclusive, there are no outcomes that are in both sets.

$$= 0$$

The probability of rolling an even number and rolling a 3 or a 5 is 0.

VOCABULARY
A *favorable* outcome is an outcome that is being tested or observed and not necessarily a desirable result. A "favorable" outcome may be a loss for the home team or testing positive for a disease.

CONTINUED ON THE NEXT PAGE

EXAMPLE 1 CONTINUED

GENERALIZE
Notice that *E* and *not E* are mutually exclusive events. What would the sum of $P(E)$ and $P(not\ E)$ be equal to? **ⓒ MP.8**

C. **You roll a standard number cube once. What is the probability that you do not roll an even number?**

$$P(\text{not } E) = \frac{3}{6} \text{ or } \frac{1}{2}$$

There are 3 outcomes that are not even numbers.

The probability of not rolling an even number is $\frac{1}{2}$.

Try It! **1.** A box contains 100 balls. Thirty of the balls are purple and 10 are orange. If you select one of the balls at random, what is the probability of each of the following events?

    a. The ball is purple or orange.

    b. The ball is not purple and not orange.

CONCEPT **Probabilities of Mutually Exclusive Events**

If *A* and *B* are mutually exclusive events, then

- $P(A \text{ or } B) = P(A) + P(B)$
- $P(A \text{ and } B) = 0$

The **complement** of an event is the set of all outcomes in a sample space that are not included in the event.

If *C* is the event that *A* does not occur, then

$$P(C) = 1 - P(A).$$

APPLICATION

EXAMPLE 2 **Find the Probabilities of Non-Mutually Exclusive Events**

A student-made target includes two overlapping squares. Assume that a sticky ball thrown at the target is equally likely to land anywhere on the target. What is the probability that the ball lands inside one or both of the squares?

Step 1 Find the area of the squares, and their overlapping area.

Total area = 1200 cm²

CONTINUED ON THE NEXT PAGE

EXAMPLE 2 CONTINUED

Step 2 Find the probabilities.

One method: $75 \text{ cm}^2 + 25 \text{ cm}^2 + 75 \text{ cm}^2 = 175 \text{ cm}^2$

$$P(A \text{ or } B) = \frac{175}{1,200} = \frac{7}{12}$$

Another method: $P(A \text{ or } B) = \frac{100}{1,200} + \frac{100}{1,200} - \frac{25}{1,200}$

$$= \frac{175}{1,200} = \frac{7}{48}$$

> Subtract the probability of the overlapping area because it was included twice, once for each large square.

The probability that the ball will land inside one or both squares is $\frac{7}{48}$, or about 15%.

USE STRUCTURE
To avoid counting the overlapping region twice, you need to subtract $P(A \text{ and } B)$ from the sum of $P(A)$ and $P(B)$. © MP.7

Try It! **2.** A video game screen is a rectangle with dimensions 34 cm and 20 cm. A starship on the screen is made of two circles with radius 6 cm, and overlapping area of 20 cm². A black hole appears randomly on the screen. What is the probability that it appears within the starship?

CONCEPT **Probabilities of Non-Mutually Exclusive Events**

If A and B are not mutually exclusive events, then
$P(A \text{ or } B) = P(A) + P(B) - P(A \text{ and } B)$.

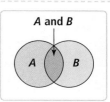

CONCEPTUAL UNDERSTANDING

EXAMPLE 3 **Identify Independent Events**

A jar contains 12 green marbles and 8 violet marbles.

A. **A marble is chosen at random from the jar and replaced. Another marble is chosen at random from the jar. Does the color of the first marble chosen affect the possible outcomes for the second marble chosen?**

Determine the probabilities for each choice to decide whether the first marble chosen affects the possibilities for the second marble.

First Choice-Sample Space
12 Green
8 Violet

Second Choice-Sample Space
12 Green
8 Violet

$$P(G) = \frac{12}{20} = \frac{3}{5}$$
$$P(V) = \frac{8}{20} = \frac{2}{5}$$

$$P(G) = \frac{12}{20} = \frac{3}{5}$$
$$P(V) = \frac{8}{20} = \frac{2}{5}$$

> The probabilities are the same.

The color of the first marble chosen does not affect the possible outcomes for the second marble chosen.

Two events are **independent events** if and only if the occurrence of one event does not affect the probability of a second event.

LEARN TOGETHER
How can you provide constructive feedback while being aware of the feelings and reactions of others?

CONTINUED ON THE NEXT PAGE

EXAMPLE 3 CONTINUED

B. **A marble is chosen at random from the jar and not replaced. Another marble is chosen at random from the jar. Does the color of the first marble chosen affect the possible outcomes for the second marble chosen?**

Determine whether the events are independent.

First Choice-Sample Space
12 Green
8 Violet

COMMON ERROR
When two or more items are selected from the same set, you must determine whether the first item(s) is replaced before the next item is selected. Then find the probabilities.

$P(G) = \frac{12}{20} = \frac{3}{5}$ $P(V) = \frac{8}{20} = \frac{2}{5}$

Assume a green marble was chosen first.

Assume a violet marble is chosen first.

Second Choice-Sample Space
11 Green
8 Violet

Second Choice-Sample Space
12 Green
7 Violet

$P(G) = \frac{11}{19}$ $P(V) = \frac{8}{19}$ $P(G) = \frac{12}{19}$ $P(V) = \frac{7}{19}$

When the first marble is not replaced in the jar, the color of the first marble chosen does affect the possible outcomes for the second marble chosen. These events are not independent.

Try It! 3. There are 10 cards in a box, 5 black and 5 red. Two cards are selected from the box, one at a time.

a. A card is chosen at random and then replaced. Another card is chosen. Does the color of the first card chosen affect the possibilities of the second card chosen? Explain.

b. A card is chosen at random and *not* replaced. Another card is chosen. Does the color of the first card chosen affect the possibilities of the second card chosen? Explain.

CONCEPT Probability of Independent Events

If A and B are independent events, then $P(A \text{ and } B) = P(A) \cdot P(B)$.

If $P(A \text{ and } B) = P(A) \cdot P(B)$, then A and B are independent events.

Example: When rolling a die and tossing a coin, the result of the die roll and the result of the coin toss are independent events.

$P(4) = \frac{1}{6}$ $P(H) = \frac{1}{2}$

$P(4 \text{ and } H) = \frac{1}{6} \cdot \frac{1}{2} = \frac{1}{12}$

EXAMPLE 4 Find Probabilities of Independent Events

Alex cannot decide which shirt to wear today, so she chooses one at random.

The probability of rain today is 40%, or $\frac{2}{5}$.

A. **What is the probability that Alex chooses a solid-colored shirt and it does not rain today?**

Let S represent the event "solid-colored shirt." Let N represent "no rain."

S and N are independent because Alex's choice of shirt does not affect the weather, and the weather does not affect Alex's choice of shirt. Use the formula to find $P(S \text{ and } N)$.

Step 1 Find $P(N)$ and $P(S)$.

$$P(N) = 1 - \frac{2}{5} = \frac{3}{5}$$

> Subtract the probability that it will rain, $\frac{2}{5}$, from 1 to find the probability that it will *not* rain.

$$P(S) = \frac{\text{number of favorable outcomes}}{\text{total number of outcomes}} = \frac{3}{4}$$

Step 2 Apply the formula and multiply the probabilities of S and N.

$$P(S \text{ and } N) = P(S) \cdot P(N) = \frac{3}{4} \cdot \frac{3}{5} = \frac{9}{20} = 45\%$$

> Use the rule for the probability of independent events.

The probability that Alex chooses a solid-colored shirt and it does not rain is 45%.

B. **What is the probability that Alex chooses a solid-colored shirt and it does not rain today or that Alex chooses a striped shirt and it rains today?**

Let T represent "striped shirt."   Let R represent "rain."

The events "S and N" and "T and R" are mutually exclusive because no outcomes are in both events.

Step 1 Find $P(T \text{ and } R)$.

$$P(T \text{ and } R) = P(T) \cdot P(R) = \frac{1}{4} \cdot \frac{2}{5} = \frac{2}{20} = \frac{1}{10} = 10\%$$

> Add to find the probability that either event will occur.

Step 2 Find $P((S \text{ and } N) \text{ or } (T \text{ and } R))$.

$$P((S \text{ and } N) \text{ or } (T \text{ and } R)) = P(S \text{ and } N) + P(T \text{ and } R)$$

$$= 45\% + 10\% = 55\%$$

The probability that Alex chooses a solid-colored shirt and it does not rain or that Alex chooses a striped shirt and it rains is 55%.

Try It! 4. You spin the spinner two times. Assume that the probability of Blue (B) each spin is $\frac{1}{3}$ and the probability of Orange (O) each spin is $\frac{2}{3}$. What is the probability of getting the same color both times? Explain.

CONCEPT SUMMARY Probability Events

	Mutually Exclusive Events	Independent Events
WORDS	A and B are mutually exclusive because no outcome is in both A and B.	D and M are independent because the occurrence of one does not affect the probability of the other.
ALGEBRA	If A and B are mutually exclusive events, then $P(A \text{ or } B) = P(A) + P(B)$. If C is the event that A does not occur, then $P(C) = 1 - P(A)$.	If D and M are independent events, then $P(D \text{ and } M) = P(D) \cdot P(M)$. If $P(D \text{ and } M) = P(D) \cdot P(M)$, then D and M are independent events.
EXAMPLES	Experiment: Spin the spinner.	Experiment: Spin the spinner and roll a number cube.

Event A: number less than 3

Event B: number greater than 5

$P(A \text{ or } B) = P(A) + P(B) = \frac{2}{6} + \frac{1}{6} = \frac{1}{2}$

Event D: odd number on spinner

Event M: number greater than 4 on number cube

$P(D \text{ and } M) = P(D) \cdot P(M) = \frac{1}{2} \cdot \frac{1}{3} = \frac{1}{6}$

Do You UNDERSTAND?

1. **ESSENTIAL QUESTION** How does describing events as independent or mutually exclusive affect how you find probabilities?

2. **Reason** Two marbles are chosen, one at a time, from a bag containing 6 marbles, 4 red marbles and 2 green marbles. Suppose the first marble chosen is green. Is the probability that the second marble will be red greater if the first marble is returned to the bag or if it is not returned to the bag? Explain. ⓒ MP.2

3. **Error Analysis** The probability that Deshawn plays basketball (event B) after school is 20%. The probability that he talks to friends (event T) after school is 45%. He says that $P(B \text{ or } T)$ is 65%. Explain Deshawn's error. ⓒ MP.3

4. **Vocabulary** What is the difference between mutually exclusive events and independent events?

Do You KNOW HOW?

5. A bag contains 40 marbles. Eight are green and 2 are blue. You select one marble at random. What is the probability of each event?

   a. The marble is green or blue.

   b. The marble is not green and not blue.

6. A robot at a carnival booth tosses a dart at a square target with 8-inch sides and a circle with a 3-inch radius in the middle. To the nearest whole percent, what is the probability that the dart will land in the circle?

For Exercises 7 and 8, assume that you roll a standard number cube twice.

7. What is the probability of rolling an even number on the first roll and a number less than 3 on the second roll?

8. What is the probability of rolling an odd number on the first roll and a number greater than 3 on the second roll?

PRACTICE & PROBLEM SOLVING

UNDERSTAND

9. Construct Arguments Let *S* be a sample space for an experiment in which every outcome is both equally likely and mutually exclusive. What can you conclude about the sum of the probabilities for all of the outcomes? Give an example. © MP.3

10. Error Analysis At Lincoln High School, 6 students are members of both the Chess Club and the Math Club. There are 20 students in the Math Club, 12 students in the Chess Club, and 400 students in the entire school.

Daniela calculated the probability that a student chosen at random belongs to the Chess Club or the Math Club. Explain her error. © MP.3

Event *C*: Student is in Chess Club
Event *M*: Student is in Math Club

$P(C \text{ or } M) = P(C) + P(M)$
$= \frac{12}{400} + \frac{20}{400}$
$= \frac{32}{400} = 0.08$

11. Higher Order Thinking Murphy's math teacher sometimes wears a scarf to class. Murphy has been documenting the relationship between his teacher wearing a scarf and when the class has a math quiz. The probabilities are as follows:

- *P*(wearing a scarf) = 10%
- *P*(math quiz) = 15%
- *P*(wearing a scarf and math quiz) = 5%

Are the events "the teacher is wearing a scarf" and "there will be a quiz" independent events? Explain.

Reason **A card is drawn from a box containing 5 cards, each showing a different number from 1 to 5. Consider the events "even number," "odd number," "less than 3," and "greater than 3." Determine whether each pair of events mutually exclusive.** © MP.2

12. <3, >3   **13.** odd, >3

14. even, >3   **15.** odd, even

PRACTICE

16. Isis is playing a virtual reality game in which she must toss a disc to land on the largest triangular section of the board. If the disc is equally likely to land anywhere on the board, what is the probability that she will succeed? Explain. SEE EXAMPLE 1

In a class of 25 students, 8 students have heights less than 65 inches and 10 students have heights of 69 inches or more. For Exercises 17–19, find the probabilities described. SEE EXAMPLE 1

17. *P*(less than 65 inches or greater than 69 inches)

18. *P*(greater than or equal to 65 inches)

19. *P*(greater than or equal to 65 inches and less than or equal to 69 inches)

20. A skydiver is equally likely to land at any point on a rectangular field. Two overlapping circular targets of radius 5 meters are marked on the field. To the nearest percent, what is the probability that the sky diver will land in one or both of the circles? SEE EXAMPLE 2

21. Two marbles are chosen at random, one at a time from a box that contains 7 marbles, 5 red and 2 green. SEE EXAMPLES 3 AND 4

   a. Find the probability of drawing 2 red marbles when the first marble is replaced before the second marble is chosen.

   b. Determine whether the situation described is independent.

PRACTICE & PROBLEM SOLVING

22. **Mathematical Connections** For a science fair project, Elena wants to test whether ants prefer certain colors. She releases ants on the colored surface shown. If the ants are randomly distributed across the entire surface, what is the probability that any given ant will be within the blue circle, but not within the yellow circle? Round to the nearest whole percent.

23. **Use Structure** A city issues 3-digit license plates for motorized scooters. The digits 0–9 are chosen at random by a computer program. What is the probability that a license plate issued meets each set of criteria? ⓒ **MP.7**

a. The three-digit number formed is even.

b. The first number is not 7.

c. The first two digits are the same.

d. All three digits are the same.

24. **Model With Mathematics** During a football game, a kicker is called in twice to kick a field goal from the 30 yard line. Suppose that for each attempt, the probability that he will make the field goal is 0.8. ⓒ **MP.4**

a. What is the probability that the kicker will make both field goals?

b. What is the probability that he will make neither field goal?

25. The probability of events A and B both occurring is 15%. The probability of event A or B occurring is 60%. The probability of B occurring is 50%. What is the probability of A occurring?

26. **SAT/ACT** A robot spins the spinner shown twice. Assume that the outcomes 1, 2, 3, and 4 are equally likely for each spin. What is the probability that the sum of the two outcomes will be 6?

Ⓐ $\frac{1}{16}$ Ⓓ $\frac{1}{4}$

Ⓑ $\frac{1}{8}$ Ⓔ $\frac{3}{4}$

Ⓒ $\frac{3}{16}$

27. **Performance Task** Paula is packing to visit a friend in another city for a long weekend. She looks at the weather forecast shown below to find the chance of rain. Assume that whether it rains on each day is independent of whether it rains on any other day.

Weather Forecast		
SAT	SUN	MON
high 70°	63°	65°
low 59°	49°	48°
10%	50%	20%

Part A What is the probability that it will not rain on any of the three days to the nearest percent?

Part B What is the probability that it will rain at least one of the three days to the nearest percent

Part C Do you think Paula should pack an umbrella? Explain.

12-2
Conditional Probability

I CAN... find the probability of an event given that another event has occurred.

VOCABULARY
• conditional probability
• dependent events

Common Core State Standards
HSS.CP.A.3, HSS.CP.A.4, HSS.CP.B.6, HSS.CP.B.8 (+), HSS.CP.A.5, MP.1, MP.3, MP.7

COMMON ERROR
Avoid confusing $P(A \mid B)$ with $P(B \mid A)$. In the first case the prior event is B, but in the second case the prior event is A.

EXPLORE & REASON

At Central High School, 85% of all senior girls and 65% of all senior boys attended the Spring Dance. Of all attendees, 20% won a prize.

A. Assuming that the number of senior girls at Central High School is about equal to the number of senior boys, estimate the probability that a randomly selected senior won a prize at the dance. Explain.

B. **Construct Arguments** If you knew whether the selected student was a boy or a girl, would your estimate change? Explain. **© MP.3**

ESSENTIAL QUESTION How are conditional probability and independence related in experiments?

EXAMPLE 1 Understand Conditional Probability

A student committee is being formed to decide how after-school activities will be funded. The committee members are selected at random from current club members. The frequency table shows the current club membership data.

Monday Club Memberships by Grade

	Drama	Science	Art	Total
Sophomore	3	9	24	36
Junior	6	18	16	40
Senior	8	13	18	39
Total	17	40	58	115

What is the probability that a member of the art club selected at random is a junior?

One Method Use the frequency table to find the probability that the student chosen is a junior given that the student is a member of the art club.

> The probability that an event B will occur given that another event A has already occurred is called a **conditional probability** and is written as $P(B \mid A)$.

$$P(\text{junior} \mid \text{member of the art club}) = \frac{\text{number of juniors in art club}}{\text{total number of art club members}}$$

$$= \frac{16}{58} = \frac{8}{29}$$

Another Method Use the formula for conditional probability.

For any two events A and B, with $P(A) \neq 0$, $P(B \mid A) = \frac{P(B \text{ and } A)}{P(A)}$.

$$P(\text{junior} \mid \text{art}) = \frac{P(\text{junior and art})}{P(\text{art})} = \frac{\frac{16}{115}}{\frac{58}{115}} = \frac{8}{29}$$

> Of the 115 Monday club members and 58 art club members, 16 are juniors and in the art club.

The probability that the student chosen is a junior member from the art club is $\frac{8}{29}$.

CONTINUED ON THE NEXT PAGE

EXAMPLE 1 CONTINUED

Try It! **1. a.** What is the probability that a member of the drama club is a sophomore, $P(\text{sophomore} \mid \text{drama})$?

b. What is the probability that a sophomore is a member of the drama club, $P(\text{drama} \mid \text{sophomore})$? Is $P(\text{sophomore} \mid \text{drama})$ the same as $P(\text{drama} \mid \text{sophomore})$? Explain.

CONCEPT Conditional Probability and Independent Events

Let A and B be events with $P(A) \neq 0$ and $P(B) \neq 0$.

If events A and B are independent, then the conditional probability of B given A equals the probability of B and the conditional probability of A given B equals the probability of A.

If the conditional probability of B given A equals the probability of B and the conditional probability of A given B equals the probability of A, then events A and B are independent.

If events A and B are independent, then $P(B \mid A) = P(B)$ and $P(A \mid B) = P(A)$.

If $P(B \mid A) = P(B)$ and $P(A \mid B) = P(A)$, then events A and B are independent.

CONCEPTUAL UNDERSTANDING

EXAMPLE 2 Use the Test for Independence

The table below shows the vehicles in a parking garage one afternoon. A vehicle in the garage will be selected at random. Let B represent "the vehicle is black" and V represent "the vehicle is a van." Are the events B and V independent or dependent?

STUDY TIP
When looking at a table of probabilities, consider events that are impossible or guaranteed to occur. For example, it is impossible to select a red van.

	Car	Van	Pickup	Totals
Red	5	0	2	7
White	0	0	2	2
Black	6	3	4	13
Totals	11	3	8	22

One Method

Since $P(B) = \frac{13}{22} \neq 0$ and $P(V \text{ and } B) = \frac{3}{22}$,

$$P(V \mid B) = \frac{P(V \text{ and } B)}{P(B)} = \frac{\frac{3}{22}}{\frac{13}{22}} = \frac{3}{13}$$

Since $P(V \mid B) \neq P(V)$, B and V are not independent events, they are **dependent events**.

CONTINUED ON THE NEXT PAGE

EXAMPLE 2 CONTINUED

Another Method

Since $P(V) = \frac{3}{22} \neq 0$, $P(B) = \frac{13}{22}$, and $P(B \text{ and } V) = P(V \text{ and } B)$,

$$P(B \mid V) = \frac{P(B \text{ and } V)}{P(V)}$$

$$= \frac{\frac{3}{22}}{\frac{3}{22}} = 1$$

> A probability of 1, or 100%, indicates that the event is certain. Given that a van is selected, it must be black.

Again, Since $P(B \mid V) \neq P(B)$, the events B and V are dependent events.

Try It! 2. Let R represent "the vehicle is red" and C represent "the vehicle is a car." Are the events R and C independent or dependent? Explain.

EXAMPLE 3 Apply the Conditional Probability Formula

A band's marketing agent conducted a survey to determine how many high school fans the band has. What is the probability that a surveyed student plans to attend the band's concert and is a fan of the group?

> **Concert Survey Results**
>
> **Students who plan to attend concert**
> - 70% of students plan to attend,
> - 80% of students who plan to attend are fans of the band.
>
> **Students who do not plan to attend**
> - 30% of students do not plan to attend,
> - 25% are fans of the band.

Use the conditional probability formula to find the combined probability.

Rewrite $P(B \mid A) = \frac{P(A \text{ and } B)}{P(A)}$ as $P(A \text{ and } B) = P(A) \cdot P(B \mid A)$.

$$P(A \text{ and } B) = P(A) \cdot P(B \mid A)$$

$$P(\text{attend and fan}) = P(\text{attend}) \cdot P(\text{fan} \mid \text{attend})$$

> Event A is "attend."
> Event B is "fan."

$$= 0.7 \cdot 0.8$$

> Substitute 0.7 for $P(\text{attend})$ and 0.8 for $P(\text{fan} \mid \text{attend})$.

$$= 0.56, \text{ or } 56\%$$

LOOK FOR RELATIONSHIPS
Why might $P(\text{fan} \mid \text{attend})$ not equal $P(\text{attend} \mid \text{fan})$ in this situation? Ⓒ MP.7

The probability that a surveyed student plans to attend the concert and is a fan of the group is 0.56, or 56%.

Try It! 3. What is the probability that a surveyed student plans to attend but is not a fan of the group?

EXAMPLE 4 Use Conditional Probability to Make a Decision

A marketer is looking at mobile phone statistics to help plan an online advertising campaign. She wants to find out which of her company's products is most likely to be purchased after a related search for that product on a mobile phone.

Mobile Phone Search and Buying Behavior		
Product	Search (S)	Search & Buy (S and B)
W	46%	16%
X	32%	14%
Y	35%	12%
Z	40%	15%

Find the probability a mobile phone customer buys, given that they performed a related search. Use the formula $P(B \mid S) = \dfrac{P(S \text{ and } B)}{P(S)}$.

Product	$P(B \mid S)$
W	$\dfrac{0.16}{0.46} = 0.348$ or about 34.8%
X	$\dfrac{0.14}{0.32} = 0.4375$ or 43.75%
Y	$\dfrac{0.12}{0.35} = 0.343$ or 34.3%
Z	$\dfrac{0.15}{0.40} = 0.375$ or 37.5%

Product X has the highest probability of being purchased given that a related search was performed.

MAKE SENSE AND PERSEVERE
Product W has the highest $P(S \text{ and } B)$ of 16% but not the highest $P(B \mid S)$. Can you explain why? ⓒ **MP.1**

Try It! 4. The marketer also has data from desktop computers. Which product is most likely to be purchased after a related search?

Computer Search and Buying Behavior
(% of computer-based site visitors)

Product	Search	Search & Buy
J	35%	10%
K	28%	9%
L	26%	8%
M	24%	5%

CONCEPT SUMMARY Conditional Probability

	Conditional Probability Formula	Conditional Probability and Independent Events
WORDS	The probability that an event *B* will occur given that another event *A* has already occurred is called a **conditional probability**.	Events *A* and *B* are independent events if and only if the conditional probability of *A* given *B* is the same as the probability of *A*, and the conditional probability of *B* given *A* is the same as the probability of *B*.
ALGEBRA	For any two events *A* and *B*, with $P(A) \neq 0$, $$P(B \mid A) = \frac{P(A \text{ and } B)}{P(A)}$$	For any events *A* and *B* with $P(A) \neq 0$ and $P(B) \neq 0$, *A* and *B* are independent if and only if $P(B \mid A) = P(B)$ and $P(A \mid B) = P(A)$.

Do You UNDERSTAND?

1. **ESSENTIAL QUESTION** How are conditional probability and independence related in experiments?

2. **Vocabulary** How is the sample space for $P(B \mid A)$ different from the sample space for $P(B)$?

3. **Vocabulary** Why does the definition of $P(B \mid A)$ have the condition that $P(A) \neq 0$?

4. **Use Structure** Why is $P(A) \cdot P(B \mid A) = P(B) \cdot P(A \mid B)$? **ⓒ MP.7**

5. **Error Analysis** Jamal knows that $P(R) = 0.8$, $P(B) = 0.2$, and $P(R \text{ and } B) = 0.05$. Explain Jamal's error. **ⓒ MP.3**

$$P(B \mid R) = \frac{0.05}{0.2}$$
$$= 0.25 \quad \textbf{✗}$$

6. **Reason** At a sports camp, a coach wants to find the probability that a soccer player is a local camper. Because 40% of the students in the camp are local, the coach reasons that the probability is 0.4. Is his conclusion justified? Explain. **ⓒ MP.2**

Do You KNOW HOW?

7. Let $P(A) = \frac{3}{4}$, $P(B) = \frac{2}{3}$, and $P(A \text{ and } B) = \frac{1}{2}$. Find each probability.

   a. What is $P(B \mid A)$?

   b. What is $P(A \mid B)$?

8. Students generate two digits from 0 to 9 at random to write a number between 0 and 99. Are the events "first digit 5" and "second digit 6" independent or dependent in each case below? What is $P(56)$ in each experiment?

   a. The digits may not be repeated.

   b. The digits may be repeated.

9. Suppose that you select one card at random from the set of 6 cards below.

   Let *B* represent the event "select a blue card" and *T* represent the event "select a card with a 3." Are *B* and *T* independent events? Explain your reasoning.

PRACTICE & PROBLEM SOLVING

UNDERSTAND

10. **Mathematical Connections** How can the formula $P(A \text{ and } B) = P(A) \cdot P(B \mid A)$ be simplified to find the probability of A and B when the events are independent? Explain.

11. **Error Analysis** From a bag containing 3 red marbles and 7 blue marbles, 2 marbles are selected without replacement. Esteban calculated the probability that two red marbles are selected. Explain Esteban's error. Ⓒ MP.3

$$P(\text{red}) = 0.3$$
$$P(\text{red and red}) = P(\text{red}) \cdot P(\text{red})$$
$$= 0.3 \cdot 0.3$$
$$= 0.09 \quad \textbf{✗}$$

12. **Generalize** Kiyo is decorating a table using mosaic tiles chosen and placed at random. She is picking tiles without looking. How does $P(\text{yellow second} \mid \text{blue first})$ compare to $P(\text{yellow second} \mid \text{yellow first})$ if the tiles are selected without replacement? If the tiles are selected and returned to the pile because Kiyo wants a different color? Ⓒ MP.8

13. **Use Structure** At a fundraiser, a participant is asked to guess the contents of an unlabeled can for a possible prize. If there are two crates to choose from, each holding cans of vegetables and cans of soup, what is the probability that the first participant selected a can from the left crate if they selected a can of vegetables? Ⓒ MP.7

    a. The left crate has 2 cans of vegetables and 8 cans of soup, and the right crate has 7 cans of vegetables and 3 cans of soup.

    b. The left crate has 8 cans of vegetables and 2 cans of soup, and the right crate has 5 cans of vegetables and 5 cans of soup.

PRACTICE

For Exercises 14–18, use the data in the table to find the probability of each event. SEE EXAMPLE 1

Technology Class Enrollment by Year

	Sophomore	Junior
Robotics	16	24
Game Design	18	22

14. $P(\text{Junior} \mid \text{Robotics})$

15. $P(\text{Robotics} \mid \text{Junior})$

16. $P(\text{Game Design} \mid \text{Sophomore})$

17. $P(\text{Sophomore} \mid \text{Game Design})$

18. Are year and technology class enrollment dependent or independent events? Explain. SEE EXAMPLE 2

19. At a high school, 40% of the students play an instrument. Of those students, 20% are freshmen. Of the students who do not play an instrument, 30% are freshmen. What is the probability that a student selected at random is a freshman who plays an instrument? SEE EXAMPLE 3

In a study of an experimental medication, patients were assigned at random to take either the medication or a placebo.

Effectiveness of New Medication As Compared to a Placebo

	Medication	Placebo
Health Improved	53	47
Health Did Not Improve	65	35

20. What is the probability that a patient taking the medication showed improvement? Round to the nearest whole percent. SEE EXAMPLE 1

21. Are taking the medication and having improved health independent or dependent events? SEE EXAMPLE 2

22. Based on the data in the table, would you recommend that the medication be made available to doctors? Explain. SEE EXAMPLE 4

PRACTICE & PROBLEM SOLVING

23. Reason In a recreation center with 1,500 members, 200 are high-school students. Of the members, 300 regularly swim. The 45 students of the high-school swim team are all members and practice at the pool every week. What is the probability that a high-school member selected at random is on the swim team? ⓒ **MP.2**

24. Use Structure At the school fair, 5% of students will win a prize. A winner has an equally likely chance to win each prize type shown. What is the probability that a student at the fair will win a comic book? Explain. ⓒ **MP.7**

PRIZES

25. Make Sense and Persevere A box contains 50 batteries, of which 10 are dead and 5 are weak. Suppose you select batteries at random from the box and set them aside for recycling if they are dead or weak. If the first battery you select is dead and the second one is weak, what is the probability that the next battery you select will be weak? ⓒ **MP.1**

26. Higher Order Thinking An inspector at a factory has determined that 1% of the flash drives produced by the plant are defective. If Assembly Line A produces 20% of all the flash drives, what is the probability that a defective flash drive chosen at random is from the corresponding Conveyor Belt A? Explain.

Conveyor Belt A
Defective Rate: 1.5%

27. Which of the following pairs of events are independent? Select all that apply.

☐ **A.** A student selected at random has a backpack. A student selected at random has brown hair.

☐ **B.** Events A and B, where $P(B \mid A) = \frac{1}{3}$, $P(A) = \frac{3}{5}$ and $P(B) = \frac{5}{9}$

☐ **C.** A student selected at random is a junior. A student selected at random is a freshman.

☐ **D.** Events A and B, where $P(A) = 0.30$, $P(B) = 0.25$ and $P(A \text{ and } B) = 0.075$

☐ **E.** Events A and B, where $P(A) = 0.40$, $P(B) = 0.3$ and $P(A \text{ and } B) = 0.012$

28. SAT/ACT The table shows student participation in the newspaper and yearbook by year. A student on the newspaper staff is selected at random to attend a symposium. What is the probability that the selected student is a senior?

Journalism Club Members

	Junior	Senior
Newspaper	16	9
Yearbook	8	17

Ⓐ $\frac{9}{50}$ Ⓓ $\frac{9}{17}$

Ⓑ $\frac{9}{26}$ Ⓔ $\frac{9}{16}$

Ⓒ $\frac{9}{25}$

29. Performance Task In a survey of 50 male and 50 female high school students, 60 students said they exercise daily. Of those students, 32 were female.

Part A Use the data to make a two-way frequency table.

Part B What is the probability that a surveyed student who exercises daily is female? What is the probability that a surveyed student who exercises regularly is male?

Part C Based on the survey, what can you conclude about the relationship between exercise and gender? Explain.

MATHEMATICAL MODELING IN 3 ACTS

Common Core State Standards
HSS.CP.A.1, HSS.CP.A.2, MP.4

Place Your Guess

A coin toss is a popular way to decide between two options or settle a dispute. The coin toss is popular because it is a simple and unbiased way of deciding. Assuming the coin being tossed is a fair coin, both parties have an equally likely chance of winning.

What other methods could you use to decide between two choices fairly? Think about this during the Mathematical Modeling in 3 Acts lesson.

ACT 1 Identify the Problem

1. What is the first question that comes to mind after watching the video?

2. Write down the main question you will answer about what you saw in the video.

3. Make an initial conjecture that answers this main question.

4. Explain how you arrived at your conjecture.

5. What information will be useful to know to answer the main question? How can you get it? How will you use that information?

ACT 2 Develop a Model

6. Use the math that you have learned in this Topic to refine your conjecture.

ACT 3 Interpret the Results

7. Did your refined conjecture match the actual answer exactly? If not, what might explain the difference?

12-3

Permutations and Combinations

I CAN... use permutations and combinations to find the number of outcomes in a probability experiment.

VOCABULARY
- combination
- factorial
- Fundamental Counting Principle
- permutation

Common Core State Standards
HSS.CP.B.9 (+), MP.3, MP.4, MP.7

EXPLORE & REASON

Holly, Tia, Kenji, and Nate are eligible to be officers of the Honor Society. Two of the four students will be chosen at random as president and vice-president. The table summarizes the possible outcomes.

Honor Society Officers

		Vice-President			
		Holly	Tia	Kenji	Nate
President	**Holly**	–	HT	HK	HN
	Tia	TH	–	TK	TN
	Kenji	KH	KT	–	KN
	Nate	NH	NT	NK	–

A. Holly wants to be an officer with her best friend Tia. How many outcomes make up this event?

B. How many outcomes show Holly as president and Tia as vice-president?

C. Generalize How many outcomes have only one of them as an officer? Explain. **© MP.8**

ESSENTIAL QUESTION How are permutations and combinations useful when finding probabilities?

EXAMPLE 1   Use the Fundamental Counting Principle

Manuel wants to advertise the number of one-topping pizzas he offers to his customers. How many different one-topping pizzas are available at Manuel's Pizzeria?

MANUEL'S PIZZERIA
Choose a Size:
large, medium
Choose a Crust:
deep dish or thin
Choose One Topping:
sausage, pepperoni, cheese

Make a tree diagram to find the number of pizzas.

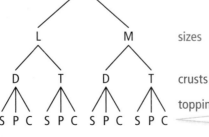

Each path represents a pizza. There are 12 different pizzas.

sizes × crusts × toppings = number of pizzas
2 × 2 × 3 = 12

COMMON ERROR
When you compare a tree diagram to the Fundamental Counting Principle, remember to count the total number of paths from the beginning to the end of the tree diagram, not the number of branches in each section.

This example illustrates the **Fundamental Counting Principle**. If there are m ways to make the first selection and n ways to make the second selection, then there are $m \times n$ ways to make the two selections. If there are p ways to make a third selection, then there are $m \times n \times p$ ways to make all three selections, and so on.

CONTINUED ON THE NEXT PAGE

EXAMPLE 1 CONTINUED

Try It!   1. The car that Ms. Garcia is buying comes with a choice of 3 trim lines (standard, sport, or luxury), 2 types of transmission (automatic or manual), and 8 colors. How many different option packages does Ms. Garcia have to choose from? Explain.

CONCEPTUAL UNDERSTANDING

EXAMPLE 2   Find the Number of Permutations

A. **Gabriela is making a playlist with her 3 favorite songs. How many possible orders are there for the songs?**

Method 1 Use an organized list.

Let A, B, and C represent the 3 songs.
There are 6 different possible orders for the songs.

ABC	ACB
BAC	BCA
CAB	CBA

Method 2 Use the Fundamental Counting Principle.

$3 \cdot 2 \cdot 1$ There are 3 choices for the first song, 2 choices for the second song, and 1 choice for the third song.

The **factorial** of a positive integer n is the product of all positive integers less than or equal to n. It is written $n!$ and is read as n *factorial*. By definition, 0! equals 1.

$$n! = n \cdot (n - 1) \cdot (n - 2) \cdot \ldots \cdot 2 \cdot 1$$

The number of different possible orders for the songs is 3!

$$3! = 3 \cdot 2 \cdot 1 = 6$$

There are 6 different possible orders for the 3 songs.

REASON
How many ways are there to make a playlist with 0 songs?
Ⓒ MP.2

B. **Gabriela wants to make another playlist using 5 of the 8 songs from her favorite artist's latest album. How many playlists are possible?**

Method 1 Use the Fundamental Counting Principle.

There are 8 choices for the first song, 7 choices for the second song, and so on.

$$8 \cdot 7 \cdot 6 \cdot 5 \cdot 4 = 6{,}720$$

There are 6,720 possible playlists with 5 of the 8 songs.

Method 2 Use factorials.

To count the number of ways to order 5 songs from A, B, C, D, E, F, G, and H, consider the list ABCDE. The diagram shows all the possible ways that sequence appears among the 8! ways to list all songs.

For any sequence of 5 songs, there are $(8 - 5)! = 3!$ ways that sequence appears as the first 5 songs when listing all 8! lists. So divide 8! by 3! to find the number of 5-song playlists.

ABCDEFGH	ABCDEFHG
ABCDEGFH	ABCDEGHF
ABCDEHFG	ABCDEHGF

$$\frac{8!}{3!} = \frac{8 \cdot 7 \cdot 6 \cdot 5 \cdot 4 \cdot 3 \cdot 2 \cdot 1}{3 \cdot 2 \cdot 1} = 6{,}720$$

There are 6,720 possible playlists with 5 of the 8 songs.

CONTINUED ON THE NEXT PAGE

EXAMPLE 2 CONTINUED

Try It! **2.** How many possibilities are there for each playlist?

      a. Gabriela's 4 favorite songs   **b.** 5 of the 10 most popular songs

CONCEPT Permutations

A **permutation** is an arrangement of objects in a specific order.

The number of permutations of r objects taken from a set of n objects is

$$_nP_r = \frac{n!}{(n-r)!} \text{ for } 0 \leq r \leq n.$$

CONCEPTUAL UNDERSTANDING

EXAMPLE 3   Find the Number of Combinations

Aaliyah is planning to be a counselor at a summer day camp. She will be supervising 3 activities during the first week of camp. How many different combinations of 3 activities are possible?

Use the formula to write an expression for the number of permutations of 3 objects chosen from a group of 10.

$$_{10}P_3 = \frac{10!}{(10-3)!} = 720$$

In this situation, the order of the 3 chosen activities does not matter, so you must adjust the formula.

A **combination** is a set of objects with no specific order.

3! Permutations   1 Combination

ABC	ACB
BAC	BCA
CAB	CBA

$\rightarrow$ {A, B, C}

A group of 3 items can be arranged in 3! ways, so you must divide the the number of permutations, $_{10}P_3$, by the number of arrangements of each group of 3 items, 3!.

USE APPROPRIATE TOOLS
Most scientific and graphing calculators can calculate permutations ($_nP_r$) and combinations ($_nC_r$). They often use the notation P(n, r) and C(n, r).
© MP.5

The notation $_nC_r$ indicates the number of combinations of r items from a set of n items.

$$_{10}C_3 = \frac{_{10}P_3}{3!} = \frac{10!}{3!(10-3)!}$$

$$= \frac{720}{6}$$

$$= 120$$

$_{10}C_3$ denotes the number of combinations of 3 items from a set of 10 items.

There are 120 different combinations of activities that Aaliyah could be supervising.

Try It! **3.** How many ways can a camper choose 5 activities from the 10 available activities at the summer camp?

CONCEPT Combinations

A **combination** is a set of objects with no specific order.

The number of combinations of r objects taken from a set of n objects is

$$_nC_r = \frac{n!}{r!(n-r)!} \text{ for } 0 \leq r \leq n.$$

APPLICATION

EXAMPLE 4 | Use Permutations and Combinations to Find Probabilities

A teacher chooses 5 students at random from the names shown to work together on a group project. What is the probability that the 5 students' names begin with a consonant?

Formulate ◄ Determine if the problem is about permutations or combinations.

Since the order in which the students are chosen does not matter, use combinations to find the numbers of possible outcomes and desirable outcomes to calculate the probability.

Compute ◄ **Step 1** Find the total number of possible outcomes.

$$_{18}C_5 = \frac{18!}{5!(18-5)!} = 8{,}568$$

There are 8,568 ways the teacher could choose 5 students.

Step 2 Find the number of possible outcomes in which all the names begin with a consonant and none of the names begin with a vowel.

$$_{13}C_5 = \frac{13!}{5!(13-5)!} = 1{,}287 \qquad \qquad _5C_0 = \frac{5!}{0!(5-0)!} = 1$$

> Choose 5 out of 13 names.   Choose 0 out of 5 names.

Use the Fundamental Counting Principle. Multiply the number of possible outcomes for the two subsets to find the total number of outcomes.

$$_{13}C_5 \cdot {_5C_0} = 1{,}287 \cdot 1 = 1{,}287$$

There are 1,287 outcomes with all the names beginning with consonants.

Step 3 Find the probability.

$$P(\text{all consonants}) = \frac{\text{number of outcomes with all consonants}}{\text{total number of possible outcomes}}$$
$$= \frac{1{,}287}{8{,}568} \approx 0.15$$

Interpret ◄ The probability that all 5 names begin with a consonant is about 0.15, or 15%.

Try It!   **4.** Using the data from Example 4, what is the probability that the 5 students' names end with a vowel?

CONCEPT SUMMARY Permutations and Combinations

	Permutation	Combination
WORDS	A selection of items in which the order of the items is important	A selection of items in which the order of the items is not important
	$_nP_r$ represents the number of permutations of r objects taken from a set of n objects.	$_nC_r$ represents the number of combinations of r objects taken from a set of n objects.
ALGEBRA	$_nP_r = \dfrac{n!}{(n-r)!}$ for $0 \le r \le n$	$_nC_r = \dfrac{n!}{r!(n-r)!}$ for $0 \le r \le n$
NUMBERS	The number of permutations of 3 objects taken from a set of 6 objects is $$_6P_3 = \frac{6!}{3!} = \frac{6 \cdot 5 \cdot 4 \cdot 3 \cdot 2 \cdot 1}{3 \cdot 2 \cdot 1} = 120$$	The number of combinations of 4 objects taken from a set of 6 objects is $$_6C_4 = \frac{6!}{4!2!} = \frac{6 \cdot 5 \cdot 4 \cdot 3 \cdot 2 \cdot 1}{(4 \cdot 3 \cdot 2 \cdot 1)(2 \cdot 1)} = 15$$

Do You UNDERSTAND?

1. **ESSENTIAL QUESTION** How are permutations and combinations useful when finding probabilities?

2. **Use Structure** How is the formula for combinations related to the formula for permutations? Ⓒ **MP.7**

3. **Vocabulary** Why is it important to distinguish between a *permutation* and a *combination* when counting possible outcomes?

4. **Look for Relationships** How is $_9C_2$ related to $_9C_7$? Explain. How can you generalize this observation for any values of n and r? Ⓒ **MP.7**

5. **Error Analysis** Explain Beth's error. Ⓒ **MP.3**

$$\frac{_3P_3}{_5P_3} = \frac{3!}{\frac{5!}{(5-3)!}} = \frac{3!}{5!2!} = \frac{1}{40}$$

   ✗

6. **Construct Arguments** A company wants to form a committee of 4 people from its 12 employees. How can you use combinations to find the probability that the 4 people newest to the company will be selected? Ⓒ **MP.3**

Do You KNOW HOW?

Do the possible outcomes represent permutations or combinations?

7. Tamisha will invite 3 of her 10 friends to a concert.

8. Tamisha must decide how she and her 3 friends will sit at the concert.

9. Find the number of permutations: How many ways can 12 runners in a race finish first, second, and third?

Find the number of combinations.

10. In how many ways can 11 contestants for an award be narrowed down to 3 finalists?

11. How many different ways can a 4-person team be chosen from a group of 8 people?

Students will be chosen at random for school spirit awards. There are 6 athletes and 8 non-athletes who are eligible for 2 prizes. What is each probability?

12. P(both prizes are awarded to athletes)

13. P(both prizes are awarded to non-athletes)

14. P(no prize is awarded to an athlete)

15. P(no prize is awarded to a non-athlete)

16. Explain how Exercises 12 and 13 are like Exercises 14 and 15.

PRACTICE & PROBLEM SOLVING

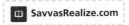

UNDERSTAND

17. Use Structure Dwayne bought a new bike lock, and the lock came with instructions to choose 3 out of 30 numbers on a circular dial to keep his bike secure. The numbers cannot be repeated. How many possible arrangements can Dwayne choose for his lock? Do the arrangements represent permutations or combinations? Explain. ⓒ MP.7

18. Construct Arguments Sofia volunteers to read and play with sick children in a hospital. She selects some erasers from a bag at random to use as prizes. There are 8 alien erasers and 10 flying-saucer erasers. ⓒ MP.3

    a. How many groups of 6 erasers can be formed from the 18 erasers? Explain.

    b. In how many ways can 3 aliens be selected? Explain.

    c. In how many ways can 3 aliens and 3 flying saucers be selected? Explain.

    d. What is the probability that 3 aliens and 3 flying saucers will be selected? Explain.

19. Error Analysis There are 6 tiles numbered 1 to 6 in a box. Two tiles are selected at random without replacement to form a 2-digit number. Jeffrey found the probability that the number selected is 16. Explain his error. ⓒ MP.3

The number of ways to select 1 and 6 is given by $_6C_2 = 15$
$$P(16) = \frac{1}{_6C_2} = \frac{1}{15}$$ ✗

20. Mathematical Connections How many lines are determined by the points, P, Q, R, and S? Explain.

S •
Q •
P •   • R •

21. Higher Order Thinking There are 11! different ways for a group of people to sit around a circular table. How many people are in the group? Explain.

PRACTICE

For Exercises 22–27, determine whether the possible outcomes represent permutations or combinations, then state the number of possible outcomes. SEE EXAMPLES 1, 2, AND 3

22. A student chooses 4 books at random from a reading list of 11 books.

23. At the end of a season, 10 soccer teams are ranked by the state.

24. A committee of 5 people is being selected from a group of 9 to choose the food for a sport's banquet.

25. Hugo displays his 8 model planes in a single row.

26. A class president, secretary, and treasurer are chosen from 12 students running for office.

27. A food truck has a lunch special on tacos. Customers choose a shell, three toppings, and two sides for one price.

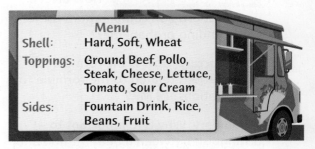

Menu	
Shell:	Hard, Soft, Wheat
Toppings:	Ground Beef, Pollo, Steak, Cheese, Lettuce, Tomato, Sour Cream
Sides:	Fountain Drink, Rice, Beans, Fruit

28. There are 4 comedians and 5 musicians performing in a variety show. The order in which the performers are chosen is random. SEE EXAMPLE 4

    a. What is the probability that the first 3 performers are comedians?

    b. What is the probability that the first two performers are comedians followed by a musician?

29. A jewelry maker chooses three beads at random from a bag with 10 beads labeled A, B, C, D, E, F, G, H, I, and J. SEE EXAMPLES 2, 3, AND 4

    a. How can you use permutations or combinations to find P(selected beads spell the initials DEB)? What is the probability?

    b. How can you use permutations or combinations to find P(selected beads are all vowels)? What is the probability?

PRACTICE & PROBLEM SOLVING

APPLY

30. Make Sense and Persevere Imani's wallet contains three $1 bills, two $5 bills, and three $10 bills. If she pulls two bills without looking, what is the probability that she draws a $1 bill and a $10 bill? Explain. © **MP.1**

31. Model with Mathematics Raul's favorite restaurant is running a prize game. Five of each of the winning tickets shown are available, and a customer must collect three winning tickets to receive the prize. What is the probability Raul will receive the prize for the baseball cap with his first 3 tickets? © **MP.4**

WIN A...
WIN A...
WIN A...
WIN A...

32. Look for Relationships Smart Phones, Inc. chooses a 5-digit security code at random from the digits 0–9. © **MP.7**

  a. Suppose the digits cannot be repeated. What is the probability that the security code is 30429? Explain.

  b. Suppose the digits can be repeated. What is the probability that the security code is 30429? Explain.

33. Make Sense and Persevere Edwin randomly plays 6 different songs from his playlist. © **MP.1**

  a. What is the probability that Edwin hears his 6 favorite songs?

  b. What is the probability that he hears the songs in order from his most favorite to his sixth-most favorite?

ASSESSMENT PRACTICE

34. Consider an arrangement of 8 items taken 3 at a time in which order is not important. Does each expression give the correct number of arrangements? Select *Yes* or *No*.

	Yes	No
$_8P_3$	☐	☐
$_8C_3$	☐	☐
$\dfrac{_8P_3}{3!}$	☐	☐
$8! \cdot 3!$	☐	☐
$\dfrac{8!}{3!}$	☐	☐
$\dfrac{8!}{5!}$	☐	☐
$\dfrac{8!}{3!5!}$	☐	☐
$8 \cdot 7$	☐	☐

35. SAT/ACT Fifteen students enter a Safety Week poster contest in which prizes will be awarded for first through fourth place. In how many ways could the prizes be given out?

Ⓐ 4

Ⓑ 60

Ⓒ 1,365

Ⓓ 32,760

Ⓔ 50,625

36. Performance Task Use the word shown on the tiles below to find each probability.

S U R F B O A R D

Part A Two tiles are chosen at random without replacement. Use conditional probability to find the probability that both letters are vowels. Then find the probability using permutations or combinations. Explain.

Part B Four of the tiles are chosen at random and placed in the order in which they are drawn. Use conditional probability to find the probability the tiles spell the word SURF. Then find the probability using permutations or combinations. Explain.

12-4

Probability Distributions

I CAN... define probability distributions to represent experiments and solve problems.

VOCABULARY
- binomial experiment
- probability distribution
- uniform probability distribution

Common Core State Standards
HSS.CP.B.9 (+), HSS.MD.A.1 (+), HSS.MD.A.3 (+), HSS.MD.A.4 (+), MP.2, MP.4, MP.6

MODEL & DISCUSS

Mr. and Mrs. Mason have three children. Assume that the probability of having a baby girl is 0.5 and the probability of having a baby boy is also 0.5.

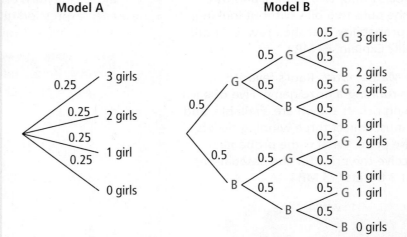

Model A   Model B

A. Reason Which model represents the situation correctly, Model A or Model B? Explain. **MP.2**

B. What is the probability that Mr. and Mrs. Mason have 3 girls?

C. Compare the probability that the Masons' first child was a boy and they then had two girls to the probability that their first two children were girls and they then had a boy. Does the order affect the probabilities? Explain.

> **ESSENTIAL QUESTION** What does a probability distribution tell you about an experiment?

CONCEPTUAL UNDERSTANDING

EXAMPLE 1 Develop a Theoretical Probability Distribution

COMMUNICATE PRECISELY
The sample space {0, 1} represents the number of Teo buttons you can select in one trial. **MP.6**

A. Teo and Henry are running for President of the Student Council. You will select a campaign button at random from the box containing 3 Teo buttons and 3 Henry buttons. You will record the number of Teo buttons that you get. What is the theoretical probability distribution for the sample space {0, 1}?

A **probability distribution** for an experiment is a function that assigns a probability to each outcome of a sample space for the experiment.

Since you are selecting a button at random, you are equally likely to get 0 buttons or 1 button for Teo.

The theoretical probability distribution for this experiment is the function P, defined on the set {0, 1}, such that $P(0) = \frac{1}{2}$ and $P(1) = \frac{1}{2}$.

> A theoretical probability is based upon assumptions rather than on experimentation.

CONTINUED ON THE NEXT PAGE

EXAMPLE 1 CONTINUED

B. Now you plan to select a button at random, put it back in the box, and then select another button at random. You will record the total number of times that you get a Teo button during the experiment. Define the theoretical probability distribution for the sample space {0, 1, 2}. How does this probability distribution differ from the distribution in Part A?

Make a tree diagram for the experiment.

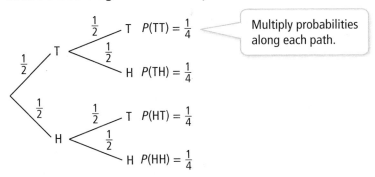

Add the probabilities of TH and HT to find the probability of getting one Teo button.

$$P(1) = \frac{1}{4} + \frac{1}{4} = \frac{1}{2}$$

The theoretical probability distribution is the function P, defined on the set {0, 1, 2}, such that $P(0) = \frac{1}{4}$, $P(1) = \frac{1}{2}$, and $P(2) = \frac{1}{4}$.

Compare this probability distribution to the one in Part A.

A **uniform probability distribution** assigns the same probability to each outcome.

Comparing Probability Distributions		
Select one button	$P(0) = \frac{1}{2}, P(1) = \frac{1}{2}$	uniform
Select two buttons	$P(0) = \frac{1}{4}, P(1) = \frac{1}{2}, P(2) = \frac{1}{4}$	not uniform

The probability distribution in Part A is a uniform probability distribution. The probability distribution in Part B is not.

STUDY TIP
One way to check your work is to check that the sum of the probabilities of all the outcomes is 1.

Try It! **1.** You select two marbles at random from the bowl. For each situation, define the theoretical probability distribution for selecting a number of red marbles on the sample space {0, 1, 2}. Is it a uniform probability distribution?

a. You select one marble and put it back in the bowl. Then you select a second marble.

b. You select one marble and do not put it back in the bowl. Then you select a second marble.

EXAMPLE 2 Develop an Experimental Probability Distribution

A cell phone company surveyed 500 households about the number of smartphones they have that are in use.

Number of Smartphones per Household							
Number	0	1	2	3	4	5	6 or more
Frequency	10	66	120	144	79	37	44

Would you recommend that the company concentrate on selling data plans for individuals or plans for families with three or more smartphones? Explain.

Step 1 Define an experimental probability distribution on the sample space {0, 1, 2, 3, 4, 5, 6 or more}.

Divide each frequency by 500 to find each relative frequency. Round each relative frequency to the nearest whole percent.

Number of Smartphones per Household							
Number	0	1	2	3	4	5	6 or more
Frequency	10	66	120	144	79	37	44
Relative Frequency	2%	13%	24%	29%	16%	7%	9%

Each relative frequency represents the experimental probability that a household selected at random from the 500 households has a given number of smartphones.

> An experimental probability is based upon collecting real-world data and finding relative frequencies.

An experimental probability distribution for the experiment is the function P such that if n is an outcome of the sample space, then $P(n)$ is the probability of that outcome. For example, $P(0) = 2\%$.

Step 2 Graph the probability distribution.

COMMON ERROR
When graphing a probability distribution, the heights of the bars represent the probabilities of each outcome, not their frequencies.

Step 3 Interpret the results.

The probability that a household has 3 or more cell phones is 61%.

Therefore, the company should focus on family plans rather than on individual plans.

CONTINUED ON THE NEXT PAGE

EXAMPLE 2 CONTINUED

Try It! **2.** Suppose that you selected a student at random from the Drama Club and recorded the student's age.

Ages of Students in Drama Club					
Age	14	15	16	17	18
Students	4	7	10	7	9

a. Define an experimental probability distribution on the sample space {14, 15, 16, 17, 18}.

b. Graph the probability distribution you defined.

CONCEPT Binomial Experiments

A **binomial experiment** is an experiment that consists of a fixed number of trials, with the following features.

- Each trial has two possible outcomes, one of which is denoted as "success."
- The results of the trials are independent events.
- The probability of "success" is the same for every trial.

EXAMPLE 3 Binomial Experiments

Is the experiment a binomial experiment?

A. **This spinner is spun 3 times. Assume that the spinner is equally likely to stop in any of the sections. Success is landing on a section marked "Go Forward 2 Spaces."**

Compare the experiment to the requirements for a binomial experiment.

- There are two possible outcomes for each trial, landing on a section labeled "Go Forward 2 Spaces" (success) and not landing on one of those sections.
- The outcome of one spin does not affect the probability of success on any other spin.
- The probability of success is 0.25 for every trial.

The experiment is a binomial experiment.

B. **In a class of 23 students, 7 students completed the term project. Two students selected at random must give presentations. Success is that the student has completed the project.**

The probability that the first student has completed the project is $\frac{7}{23}$.

If the first student completed the project, the probability that the second student did is $\frac{6}{22}$. If the first student is not, the probability is $\frac{7}{22}$.

Because the probabilities for each trial are different, the experiment is not a binomial experiment.

GENERALIZE
Would the experiment be a binomial experiment if there were 25 students in the class? Some other number? Ⓖ **MP.8**

CONTINUED ON THE NEXT PAGE

EXAMPLE 3 CONTINUED

Try It!   3. Is the experiment a binomial experiment? If so, find the probability of success. Explain.

    a. You select one card at random from a set of 7 cards, 4 labeled A and 3 labeled B. Then you select another card at random from the cards that remain. For each selection, success is that the card is labeled A.

    b. You roll a standard number cube 4 times. Assume that each time you roll the number cube, each number is equally likely to come up. For each roll, success is getting an even number.

CONCEPT Binomial Probability Formula

For a binomial experiment consisting of n trials with the probability of success p for each trial, the probability of exactly r successes out of the n trials is given by the following formula:

$$P(r) = \text{(ways to get } r \text{ successes in } n \text{ trials)} \cdot P(r \text{ successes}) \cdot P(n - r \text{ failures})$$

$$P(r) = {}_nC_r \cdot p^r(1 - p)^{n-r}$$

EXAMPLE 4   Probabilities in a Binomial Experiment

A grocery store gives away scratch-off cards with a purchase of more than $100.

Terrell has 5 scratch-off cards. What is the probability that he has exactly 3 winning cards if each card has a 30% chance of being a winner?

Step 1 Determine whether the situation is a binomial experiment.

- Terrell's 5 cards represent 5 trials.
- Each card is either a winning card (success) or not.
- Whether one card is a winning card does not affect the probability that another card is a winning card.
- The probability of success, 0.3, is the same for every trial.

So this is a binomial experiment.

REASON
In the formula for binomial probability, what probability does $1 - p$ represent? ⓒ **MP.2**

Step 2 Find the probability of 3 successes.

The formula $P(r) = {}_nC_r \cdot p^r(1 - p)^{n-r}$ gives the probability of r successes out of n trials. Use $n = 5$, $r = 3$, and $p = 0.3$.

$$\begin{aligned} {}_5C_3 &= \frac{5!}{3!(5-3)!} \\ &= \frac{5 \cdot 4}{2 \cdot 1} \\ &= 10 \end{aligned}$$

$$\begin{aligned} P(3) &= {}_5C_3 \cdot (0.3)^3(1 - 0.3)^{5-3} \\ &= 10(0.3)^3(0.7)^2 \\ &= 10(0.027)(0.49) \\ &= 0.1323 \end{aligned}$$

The probability of having exactly 3 winning cards is about 13%.

Try It!   4. To the nearest tenth of a percent, what is the probability that Terrell has more than 3 winning cards? Explain.

CONCEPT SUMMARY Probability Distributions

TYPES OF DISTRIBUTIONS

A probability distribution for an experiment is a function that assigns a probability to each outcome of a sample space for the experiment.

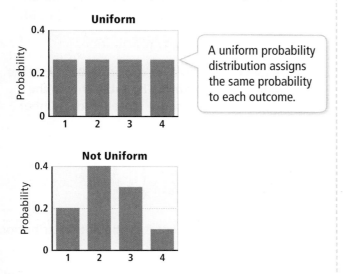

A uniform probability distribution assigns the same probability to each outcome.

BINOMIAL EXPERIMENT

A binomial experiment is an experiment that consists of a fixed number of trials, in which:

- each trial has two possible outcomes, one of which is denoted as "success";
- the results of the trials are independent events; and
- the probability of "success" is the same for every trial.

If the probability of success is p for each trial, then the probability of exactly r successes out of n trials is $P(r) = {}_nC_r \cdot p^r(1 - p)^{n-r}$.

Do You UNDERSTAND?

1. **ESSENTIAL QUESTION** What does a probability distribution tell you about an experiment?

2. **Vocabulary** What are the characteristics of a *binomial experiment*?

3. **Error Analysis** A regular tetrahedron has four triangular sides, with one of the letters A, B, C, and D on each side. Assume that if you roll the tetrahedron, each of the letters is equally likely to end up on the bottom. {A, B, C, D} is a sample space for the experiment. Rochelle was asked to find the theoretical probability distribution for the experiment. Explain and correct the error. © MP.3

$$P(A) = 0.3$$
$$P(B) = 0.3$$
$$P(C) = 0.3 \quad ✗$$
$$P(D) = 0.3$$

Do You KNOW HOW?

Graph each probability distribution P.

4. Theoretical probabilities from selecting a student at random from a group of 3 students: Jack, Alani, and Malik.

5. Probabilities from flipping a fair coin 3 times and counting the number of heads. The sample space is the set of numbers 0, 1, 2, 3. $P(0) = 0.125$, $P(1) = 0.375$, $P(2) = 0.375$, $P(3) = 0.125$.

A bag contains 5 balls: 3 green, 1 red, and 1 yellow. You select a ball at random 4 times, replacing the ball after each selection. Calculate the theoretical probability of each event to the nearest whole percent.

6. getting a green ball exactly 3 times

7. getting a green ball exactly 4 times

8. getting a green ball at least 3 times

9. getting a yellow ball twice

10. getting only red and green balls

PRACTICE & PROBLEM SOLVING

UNDERSTAND

11. Communicate Precisely Explain what it means for a coin to be a fair coin. ⒸMP.6

12. Reason You spin the spinner shown.

Describe a theoretical probability distribution for the experiment. ⒸMP.2

13. Communicate Precisely Five students in a class of 27 students ate chicken lo mein for lunch. Suppose the teacher selects a student in the class at random and then selects another student at random. Success for each selection is selecting a student who ate chicken lo mein. Is this a binomial experiment? Explain. ⒸMP.6

14. Error Analysis A standard number cube is rolled 7 times. Success for each roll is defined as getting a number less than 3. Abby tried to calculate the probability of 5 successes. Describe and correct her error. ⒸMP.3

$$P(5) = \left(\frac{1}{3}\right)^5 \left(\frac{2}{3}\right)^2 \approx 0.002 \quad ✗$$

15. Mathematical Connections A marble is selected 4 times from the bowl shown. The marble is returned to the bowl after each selection.

a. Show that there are exactly ₄C₂ ways to get exactly 2 green marbles.

b. How are ₅C₃ and ₅C₂ related? Explain.

PRACTICE

A card is chosen at random from a box containing 10 cards: 3 yellow, 4 red, 2 green, and 1 blue.
SEE EXAMPLES 1 AND 2

16. Define a probability distribution for this experiment on the sample space {Y, R, G, B}.

17. Graph the probability distribution.

In a certain game, a player can score 0, 1, 2, 3, or 4 points during a turn. The table shows the number of times Alejandra scored each number of points the last time she played the game.
SEE EXAMPLE 2

Score	0	1	2	3	4
Frequency	3	7	9	6	5

18. Define an experimental probability distribution based on Alejandra's scores.

19. Graph the probability distribution you defined in Exercise 18.

Is the experiment a binomial experiment? Explain.
SEE EXAMPLE 3

20. A quality control specialist tests 50 LED light bulbs produced in a factory. Success is that a tested light bulb burns for at least 2,000 hours without dimming. For each light bulb, the probability of success is 0.9.

21. There are 10 black and 10 red cards face down on the table. One card is selected at random. Then another card is selected at random. Success is getting a red card.

22. A basketball player is shooting 2 free throws. The probability of her making the first free throw is 0.86. The probability of her making the second free throw is 0.92.

Each time Joaquin is at bat, the probability that he gets a hit is 0.250. If he bats 10 times in the course of two games, what is the probability of each result? Round to the nearest tenth of a percent. SEE EXAMPLE 4

23. He gets no hits.

24. He gets exactly 1 hit.

25. He gets exactly 2 hits.

26. He gets fewer than 3 hits.

PRACTICE & PROBLEM SOLVING

27. Model with Mathematics The circle graph shows the result of a survey of the most popular types of music in the U.S., based on sales, downloads, and streaming. ⒸMP.4

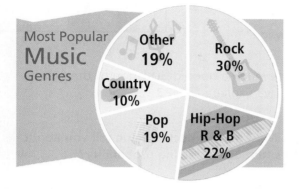

Most Popular **Music** Genres

- Other 19%
- Rock 30%
- Country 10%
- Pop 19%
- Hip-Hop R & B 22%

a. Define a probability distribution for the sample space.

b. Graph the probability distribution.

c. According to the survey, which is the most popular type of music in the United States?

28. Higher Order Thinking A pharmaceutical company is testing a new version of a medication. In a clinical trial of the old version of the medication, 18% of the subjects taking the old medication experienced headaches.

a. Suppose that 18% of the people taking the new medications will experience headaches. If 8 subjects are selected at random and given the new medication, what is the probability that less than two of them will experience headaches?

b. Suppose that two of the eight subjects experience headaches after taking the new medication. Is that cause for concern? Explain your reasoning.

29. Communicate Precisely In a quiz show, a contestant is asked 6 questions. Each question has 5 answer choices. Assume that the contestant picks an answer at random for each question and the probability of guessing the correct answer is 20%. What is the probability of guessing correctly on at least 4 of the questions? Round your answer to the nearest tenth of a percent. ⒸMP.6

30. You are going to roll a game piece two times. The game piece has 10 sides of equal area, each with one of the numbers 0 through 9. Assume that it is equally likely to land with any of the sides on top. Success is defined as getting a 3 on top.

Let P be the function defined on {0, 1, 2} such that $P(n)$ is the probability of n successes. Select all that apply.

☐ **A.** This is a binomial experiment.

☐ **B.** P is a probability distribution for the sample space {0, 1, 2}.

☐ **C.** $P(0) = 0.81$

☐ **D.** $P(1) = 0.09$

☐ **E.** $P(2) = 0.01$

31. SAT/ACT A standard number cube is rolled 6 times. Success is defined as getting a number greater than 4. Rounded to the nearest percent, what is the probability of exactly 2 successes?

Ⓐ 2%   Ⓑ 8%   Ⓒ 2%   Ⓓ 33%   Ⓓ 50%

32. Performance Task Get 5 index cards. Draw a picture on one side and no picture on the other side of each card.

Part A You are going to throw all 5 cards up in the air and count the number of cards that land face up. Assume that it is equally likely that each card will land face up and face down. Define a theoretical probability distribution for the sample space {0, 1, 2, 3, 4, 5}.

Part B Perform the experiment 20 times. Each time you perform the experiment, record the number of cards that land face up. Find the experimental probability for each outcome in the sample space {0, 1, 2, 3, 4, 5} and define an experimental probability distribution the sample space.

Part C Compare the results of Part A and B. If they are different, explain why you think they are different.

12-5

Expected Value

I CAN... calculate, interpret, and apply expected value.

VOCABULARY
• binomial distribution
• expected value

Common Core State Standards
HSS.MD.A.2 (+), HSS.MD.B.5.a (+),
HSS.MD.B.5.b (+), MP.1, MP.2, MP.3

CONCEPTUAL UNDERSTANDING

COMMON ERROR
Note that average profit from each meal is not simply the average of the cost of 1 serving of each of the 4 meals because the number of each kind of meal varies.

EXPLORE & REASON

A company has 20 employees whose hourly wages are shown in the bar graph.

Employee Hourly Wages

A. An employee is chosen at random. What is the probability that his or her hourly wage is $12? $25? $50?

B. What is the mean hourly wage? Explain your method.

C. Construct Arguments Is the mean a good description of the typical hourly wage at this company? Explain. © MP.3

ESSENTIAL QUESTION   What does expected value tell you about situations involving probability?

EXAMPLE 1   Evaluate and Apply Expected Value

The table shows data on sales in one month for each item on a restaurant menu. To estimate future profits, the owner evaluates the average profit from each meal.

Meal	Profit per Serving	Percent Sold
Stew	$0.34	12%
Soup	$0.41	7%
Lasagna	$0.64	45%
Chili	$0.73	36%

A. Based on the data, what is the average profit that the owner can expect to make from each meal?

Expected value is the sum of the value of each outcome multiplied by the probability of the outcome.

$$E = x_1 P(x_1) + x_2 P(x_2) + x_3 P(x_3) + \ldots + x_n P(x_n)$$

The outcomes are the profits for each meal. The percent-sold column shows the probability distribution. Multiply each outcome by its probability. Then add.

$$E = 0.34(0.12) + 0.41(0.07) + 0.64(0.45) + 0.73(0.36) = 0.6203$$

Use the expected value formula when the probability of at least one outcome differs from any of the others.

If this expected value continues, the owner can expect to earn about $0.62 per meal.

B. What is the expected profit for the next 200 meals ordered?

$$\$0.6203 \times 200 = \$124.06$$

The owner can expect to net about $124.06 for the next 200 meals.

CONTINUED ON THE NEXT PAGE

EXAMPLE 1 CONTINUED

Try It! **1. a.** What would happen to the expected value if fewer people ordered chili and more people ordered stew? Explain.

   b. Suppose the restaurant's profit on an order of stew increased by $0.05 and the profit on an order of chili decreased by $0.05. How would these changes affect the expected profit per meal?

EXAMPLE 2 **Find Expected Payoffs**

A charity is considering a fundraising event in which donors will pay $1 to spin the wheel 3 times. What is the expected payoff for the charity for each game?

EVEN THREES

Spin 3 times.
Get 3 even numbers.
Win an item worth $4.

There are 6 possible outcomes. 3 of the possible outcomes are even numbers.

MAKE SENSE AND PERSEVERE
Think about methods used to find probabilities. What do you need to identify to find the probabilities for each situation? Ⓒ **MP.1**

Step 1 Find the probability distribution for the donor.

There are 6^3, or 216 outcomes for spinning the wheel 3 times.

There are 3^3, or 27, ways to spin 3 even numbers in a row, so the probability of a donor winning a $4 prize is $\frac{27}{216}$, or $\frac{1}{8}$.

So, the probability of a donor not winning is $1 - \frac{1}{8}$, or $\frac{7}{8}$.

Step 2 Find the probability distribution for the charity.

The probability that the charity gains $1 is $P(1) = \frac{7}{8}$.

The probability that the charity loses $3 is $P(-3) = \frac{1}{8}$.

Step 3 Find the expected value of each game for the charity.

$$E(x) = 1\left(\frac{7}{8}\right) + (-3)\left(\frac{1}{8}\right)$$
$$= \frac{4}{8}$$
$$= \frac{1}{2}$$

The charity can expect to earn $0.50 each game.

Try It! **2.** What is the expected payoff for the person making the donation?

EXAMPLE 3 Use Expected Values to Evaluate Strategies

You are considering options for an auto insurance policy. The insurance company offers new car replacement insurance, in the case your car is totaled. There is a 1% annual chance of the car being totaled.

Plan	Premium ($)	Deductible ($)
A	50	500
B	60	0

> The deductible is the portion of the cost that the car owner pays.

A. Which of the two plans has the lower expected cost?

The total expected cost is the sum of the known costs and the expected value of the unknown cost. The cost of a new car is higher than the deductible, so you would pay the full deductible if the car needs to be replaced.

CONSTRUCT ARGUMENTS
If the expected costs were the same, what other criteria could the car owner use to decide? Why might the insurance company offer two different plans with the same expected cost? Ⓒ **MP.3**

	Known cost		Expected value of unknown cost		
	Premium	+	Deductible • Probability of replacement	=	Expected cost of insurance
Plan A:	$50	+	$500 • 0.01	=	$55
Plan B:	$60	+	$0 • 0.01	=	$60

Plan A has the lower expected cost.

B. How can you decide whether or not to purchase replacement insurance?

The cost of a new car is very high, so purchasing replacement insurance can be a good idea. Solve an inequality to determine when having no insurance is more costly than having insurance.

	Known cost		Expected value of unknown cost		
	Premium	+	Cost of a new car • Probability of replacement	>	Expected cost of insurance
	$50	+	x • 0.01	>	$55
			$0.01x$	>	$55
			x	>	$5,500

> With or without insurance, you have the same chance of needing a new car.

You should buy replacement insurance if the cost of a new car is greater than $5,500.

Try It! 3. The insurance company also offers safety glass coverage. There is a 50% chance of no repairs ($0), a 30% chance of minor repairs ($50), and a 20% chance of full replacement ($300). Which plan, C or D, has the lower expected cost?

Plan	Premium ($)	Deductible ($)
C	50	200
D	100	0

EXAMPLE 4 ▸ Use Binomial Probability to Find Expected Value

According to the weather app on Talisha's smartphone, there is a 40% chance of rain for each of the 5 days of her vacation. How many rainy days should Talisha expect during her vacation?

Days of Rain	Probability
0	$_5C_0(0.4)^0(0.6)^5 \approx 0.0778$
1	$_5C_1(0.4)^1(0.6)^4 = 0.2592$
2	$_5C_2(0.4)^2(0.6)^3 = 0.3456$
3	$_5C_3(0.4)^3(0.6)^2 = 0.2304$
4	$_5C_4(0.4)^4(0.6)^1 = 0.0768$
5	$_5C_5(0.4)^5(0.6)^0 \approx 0.0102$

Apply the binomial probability formula with $n = 5$, $p = 0.4$, and $1 - p = 0.6$ to find the probability of rain for each number of days of Talisha's vacation.

To find the expected number of rainy days, multiply each probability by the number of rainy days it corresponds to, and add those values together.

Expected number of rainy days

$$= 0 \cdot P(0) + 1 \cdot P(1) + 2 \cdot P(2) + 3 \cdot P(3) + 4 \cdot P(4) + 5 \cdot P(5)$$

$$= 0(0.0776) + 1(0.2592) + 2(0.3456) + 3(0.2304) + 4(0.0768) + 5(0.0102)$$

$$\approx 2$$

Talisha should expect 2 rainy days during her vacation.

The table shows the probability of every outcome of a binomial experiment. This probability distribution is called a **binomial distribution**. A special relationship exists for the expected value for any binomial distribution.

$$E = np$$
$$2 = 5(0.4)$$

E expected value n trials p probability

Try It!   **4.** A carnival game has 4 orange lights and 1 green light that flash rapidly one at a time in a random order. When a player pushes a button, the game stops, leaving one light on. If the light is green, the player wins a prize. Copy and complete the table, then determine the number of prizes that a player can expect to win if the game is played 4 times.

Number of Green Lights	Probability
0	$_4C_0(0.2)^0(0.8)^4 = $ ▦
1	$_4C_\blacksquare(0.2)^\blacksquare(0.8)^\blacksquare = $ ▦
2	$_\blacksquare C_\blacksquare(0.2)^\blacksquare(0.8)^\blacksquare = $ ▦
3	$_\blacksquare C_\blacksquare(0.2)^\blacksquare(0.8)^\blacksquare = $ ▦
4	$_\blacksquare C_\blacksquare(0.2)^\blacksquare(0.8)^\blacksquare = $ ▦

CONCEPT SUMMARY Expected Value

WORDS

Expected value is the average outcome that will occur with many trials of an experiment. It is the sum of the value of each outcome times the probability of the outcome.

ALGEBRA

Let $x_1, x_2, x_3, \ldots x_n$ represent the values of the outcomes of a set of trials.

You can find the expected value, E, with this formula.

$$E = x_1 P(x_1) + x_2 P(x_2) + \ldots + x_n P(x_n)$$

Do You UNDERSTAND?

1. **ESSENTIAL QUESTION** What does expected value tell you about situations involving probability?

2. **Error Analysis** Benjamin is finding the expected value of the number of heads when tossing a fair coin 10 times. What is Benjamin's error? Ⓒ **MP.3**

   > Toss a coin 10 times
   > $E = 50\%$
   >
   > ✗

3. **Construct Arguments** A carnival game costs $1 to play. The expected payout for each play of this game is $1.12. Should the carnival operators modify the game in any way? Explain. Ⓒ **MP.3**

4. **Reason** The students in Ms. Kwan's class are raising money to help earthquake victims. They expect to raise $0.52 for each raffle ticket they sell. If each raffle ticket is sold for $2, what can you conclude? Ⓒ **MP.2**

5. **Reason** A spinner is divided into 6 equal-sized sectors, numbered 1, 1, 1, 4, 7, and 10. Is the expected value of a spin the same as the mean of the numbers? Explain. Ⓒ **MP.2**

Do You KNOW HOW?

6. What is the expected value when rolling a standard number cube?

7. What is the expected value of the sum when rolling two standard number cubes?

8. A travel website reports that in a particular South American city, the probability of rain on any day in April is 40%. What is the expected number of rainy days in this city during the month of April?

9. You buy an airplane ticket for $900. You discover that if you cancel or rebook your vacation flight to Europe, you will be charged an extra $300. There is a 20% chance that you will have to rebook your flight.

   a. What is the expected value of the cost of the ticket?

   b. Is the expected value the amount you will pay to book the ticket whether or not you have to rebook? Explain.

10. A child-care service charges families an hourly rate based upon the age of the child. Their hourly rate per child is $20 per hour for infants less than 1 year old, $18 for toddlers 1 to 3 years old, $15 per hour children 3 or more years old. The ratios of infants : toddlers : 3+ years is 2 : 3 : 5. What is the expected charge per child per hour?

PRACTICE & PROBLEM SOLVING

UNDERSTAND

11. Error Analysis For the dartboard shown, Kyrone calculated the expected number of points per dart. Explain Kyrone's error. What is the correct expected value? Ⓒ MP.3

$$\text{Expected value} = \frac{2}{7}(4) + \frac{5}{7}(1)$$
$$= \frac{8}{7} + \frac{5}{7}$$
$$= \frac{13}{7} \approx 1.86 \quad ✗$$

12. Reason A nonrefundable plane ticket costs $600, while a refundable ticket costs $900. A traveler estimates there is a 20% chance he will have to cancel his upcoming trip. Should the traveler purchase a refundable or nonrefundable ticket? Explain. Ⓒ MP.2

13. Construct Arguments A person choosing a health-insurance plan determines that the expected cost for Option B is $528 per year. Ⓒ MP.3

Option	Annual Premium	Deductible
A	$600	$0
B	$500	$1,000

a. Why might this consumer select the policy with the $1000 deductible?

b. Why might this consumer select the policy with no deductible?

14. Mathematical Connections How is *expected value* related to *mean*?

PRACTICE

A farmer estimates her hens will produce 3,000 dozen more eggs this year than last year. She estimates the probability of her net profit or loss on each dozen eggs based on her costs. SEE EXAMPLE 1

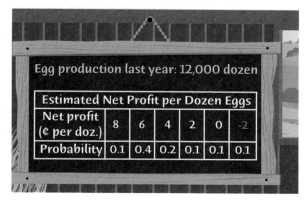

Egg production last year: 12,000 dozen

Estimated Net Profit per Dozen Eggs

Net profit (¢ per doz.)	8	6	4	2	0	-2
Probability	0.1	0.4	0.2	0.1	0.1	0.1

15. What is her expected profit per dozen eggs?

16. What is her expected profit on the total egg production?

17. A baseball team sponsors 50-50 raffles at home games. They sell tickets for $5, and the winning ticket holder gets half the money taken in that day. Last week, the team sold 15 tickets. What was the expected payoff for ticket purchasers? SEE EXAMPLE 2

18. An insurance company offers three policy options. The probability a car will be damaged in a given year is 5%, and if a car is damaged, the cost of the repairs will be $1000. Which option has the least expected annual cost for the car owner? Explain. SEE EXAMPLE 3

Insurance Policy Options

Option	Annual Premium ($)	Deductible ($)
A	900	0
B	800	400
C	700	1000

On a tropical island, the probability of sunny weather is 90% each day. SEE EXAMPLE 4

19. What is the expected number of sunny days in a non-leap year?

20. What is the expected number of sunny days during the month of June?

PRACTICE & PROBLEM SOLVING

21. Model With Mathematics A solar panel company has found that about 1% of its panels are defective. The company's cost to replace each defective panel is $600. A consultant recommends changes to the manufacturing process that will cost $200,000 and reduce the defective rate to 0.2%. The company estimates that it will sell 30,000 panels next year and that sales will increase by 5,000 panels per year for the next 10 years. Should the company follow the consultant's recommendation? Explain. ⓒ **MP.4**

22. Reason A student tosses a coin 4 times and the results are heads, tails, heads, and heads. The student concludes that the expected number of heads for 100 tosses is 75. How did the student find this number? Do you agree with the student's reasoning? Explain. ⓒ **MP.2**

23. Higher Order Thinking Your family wants to buy a new TV set for $599. You find out that the probability that the TV set will need to be serviced in the second year is 0.05 and the probability that the TV set will need to be serviced in the third year is 0.08. A 2-year warranty costs $55, and a 3-year warranty costs $80. The average cost of repairing the TV set is $278. What would you advise your family to do, get a 2-year extended warranty, a 3-year extended warranty or not to get any extended warranty? Explain your reasoning.

24. Make Sense and Persevere A company makes tablets that are guaranteed for one year. On average, one out of every 200 tablets needs to be repaired or replaced within the first year. If a tablet needs to be repaired, the company loses an average of $140. If the company sells 2,600,000 of the tablets in a year, what is their net profit on the sale of the tablets in that year? ⓒ **MP.1**

If no repairs or replacement is needed for a tablet, the company makes a $24 profit on that tablet.

25. A commuter recorded data on the arrival time of his morning train each weekday for 5 weeks. According to the data, he should expect the train to be 1.16 minutes late on any given day. What are the missing values in the commuter's table?

Arrival Time for Train

Minutes Late	0	1	2	3	4	5
Number of Days	▪	5	1	▪	1	3

26. SAT/ACT What is the expected total for 20 spins?

Ⓐ 100
Ⓑ 105
Ⓒ 110
Ⓓ 115
Ⓔ 120

27. Performance Task A toy company is designing a children's game in which players toss chips onto a board. The square board will contain a smaller square at its center.

20 points

Part A Write design instructions for the board so that a chip tossed randomly onto the board is 8 times more likely to land in the outer region than in the inner square. Explain your reasoning.

Part B Assign a whole number of points to the outer region so that the expected score on a single toss is as close as possible to 5. Explain your reasoning.

Part C If the area of the inner square is doubled and the overall size of the board remains the same, how does the expected score change? Is it also doubled? Explain.

12-6

Probability and Decision Making

I CAN... use probability to make decisions.

© **Common Core State Standards**
HSS.CP.B.9 (+), HSS.MD.B.6 (+),
HSS.MD.B.7 (+), MP.1, MP.2, MP.5

CRITIQUE & EXPLAIN

Your friend offers to play the following game with you: "If the product of the roll of two number cubes is 10 or less, I win. If not, you win!"

A. If you were to play the game many times, what percent of the games would you expect to win?

B. Is the game fair? Should you take the offer? Explain.

C. **Make Sense and Persevere** Suggest a way to change the game from fair to unfair, or vice versa, while still using the product of the two number cubes. Explain. © **MP.1**

ESSENTIAL QUESTION How can you use probability to make decisions?

APPLICATION ➡

EXAMPLE 1 Use Probability to Make Fair Decisions

Sadie, Tamira, River, Victor, and Jae are candidates to represent their school at an event. How can you use random integers to select 2 students from the 5 candidates, so that each one is equally likely to be selected?

There are 5 students. Assign a number to each student.

1	2	3	4	5
Sadie	Tamira	River	Victor	Jae

To select a student, use a calculator or other random number generator to generate a random integer from 1 to 5. Repeat to select the second student.

Ignore the duplicate 5. Some calculators may have a function that eliminates duplicates.

Jae (5) and Sadie (1) are selected.

MAKE SENSE AND PERSEVERE
Consider how you would assign integers from 1 to 10 among the 5 students. How do you adjust this for a random number generator that gives a number r from the interval $0 \leq r < 1$? © **MP.1**

Try It! 1. Your trainer creates training programs for you. How can you use index cards to randomly choose the following: Strength training 1 day per week; Cardio training 2 days per week, with no consecutive days; Swimming 1 day per week.

EXAMPLE 2 Determine Whether a Decision Is Fair or Unfair

Thato places three cards in a hat and challenges Helena to a game.

A. Thato says, "If you draw a number greater than 2, you earn 2 points. Otherwise, I earn 2 points." Is the game fair, or unfair? If it is unfair, which player has the advantage? Explain.

In each round, Thato either wins 2 points or loses 2 points.

> If Helena draws a "3" and gets 2 points, Thato considers this a loss of 2 points for himself.

Find the probability of each outcome. Then find the expected value.

$$P(-2) = \frac{1}{3} \text{ and } P(+2) = \frac{2}{3}$$

$$E = -2 \cdot \left(\frac{1}{3}\right) + 2 \cdot \left(\frac{2}{3}\right)$$

$$= \frac{2}{3}$$

> A game is considered "fair" if and only if the expected value is 0.

COMMON ERROR
Recall that the expected value is the sum of the products of the outcomes' values by their respective probabilities. Be careful not to use the sum of the probabilities.

The game is unfair and is skewed to Thato's advantage. The probability of his scoring 2 points is twice the probability of Helena scoring 2 points.

B. Helena proposes a change to the scoring of the game. She says, "If I draw a number greater than 2, I get 2 points. Otherwise, you get 1 point." Is the game fair, or unfair? If it is unfair, which player has the advantage? Explain.

In each round, Thato either scores 1 point or he loses 2 points.

Find the probability of each outcome. Then find the expected value.

$$P(-2) = \frac{1}{3} \text{ and } P(+1) = \frac{2}{3}$$

$$E = -2 \cdot \left(\frac{1}{3}\right) + 1 \cdot \left(\frac{2}{3}\right)$$

$$= -\frac{2}{3} + \frac{2}{3} = 0$$

This is a fair game because the expected value is 0. Neither player has an advantage over the other.

Try It! 2. Justice and Tamika use the same 3 cards but change the game. In each round, a player draws a card and replaces it, and then the other player draws. The differences between the two cards are used to score each round. Order matters, so the difference can be negative. Is each game fair? Explain.

a. If the difference between the first and second cards is 2, Justice gets a point. Otherwise Tamika gets a point.

b. They take turns drawing first. Each round, the first player to draw subtracts the second player's number from her own and the result is added to her total score.

EXAMPLE 3 Make a Decision Based on Expected Value

The Silicon Valley Company manufactures tablets and computers. Their tablets are covered by a warranty for one year, so that if the tablet fails, the company replaces it. Since the failure rate of their model TAB5000 tablet is high, the head of production has a plan for replacing certain components inside the TAB5000 and calling the new model TAB5001.

Model TAB5000
- Cost to produce: $100
- Price: $150
- 5% fail within first year
- Replacement cost to company: $130

Model TAB5001
- Cost to produce: $105
- Price: $150
- 1% fail within first year (estimate)
- Replacement cost to company: $135

If you were the head of production, would you recommend switching to selling the TAB5001?

Formulate ◀ Find the expected profit for each model.

Expected profit = price − cost − (cost to replace)(failure rate)

Compute ◀ Expected profit of TAB5000 = $150 − $100 − ($130)(0.05)

$$= \$50 - \$6.50$$

$$= \$43.50$$

Expected profit of TAB5001 = $150 − $105 − ($135)(0.01)

$$= \$45 - \$1.35$$

$$= \$43.65$$

Interpret ◀ The expected profit of the TAB5001 is more than the expected profit of the TAB5000. It makes sense to sell the TAB5001 instead of the TAB5000. Also, customers who bought a tablet would be more likely to be pleased with their purchase and buy from the same company in the future.

Try It! **3.** Additional data is collected for the TAB5000 and TAB5001. The production and replacement costs for the TAB5001 remain unchanged.

    a. The production and replacement costs for the TAB5000 increased by $10. What would the expected profit be for the TAB5000?

    b. The failure rate for the TAB5001 increased by 1%. What would the expected profit be for the TAB5001?

    c. As a consultant for the company, what would you recommend they do to maximize their profit?

EXAMPLE 4 | Use a Binomial Distribution to Make Decisions

An airport shuttle company takes 8 reservations for each trip because 25% of their reservations do not show up. Is this a reasonable policy?

Capacity: 6 passengers

Find the probability that more passengers show up than the van can carry.

For 8 reservations, the graph shows the number of possible combinations of passengers showing up.

Airport Shuttle

Too many passengers!

8 ways that 7 people show up ($_8C_7 = 8$); 1 way that 8 people show up ($_8C_8 = 1$)

Number of Passengers That Show Up

Number of Combinations

USE APPROPRIATE TOOLS
How does the graph of the number of combinations help you think about the situation? How might it be misleading? ⓒ **MP.5**

To find the probability that too many reservations show up, compute the probability that either 7 or 8 passengers show up. Each reservation has a 75% chance of showing up and a 25% chance of not showing up. Use $P(r) = {_nC_r} \, p^r (1 - p)^{n - r}$.

Find the probability that 7 reservations show up.

$$P(7) = {_8C_7}(0.75)^7(0.25)^1 \approx 8(0.1335)(0.25) \approx 0.267$$

Find the probability that 8 reservations show up.

$$P(8) = {_8C_8}(0.75)^8(0.25)^0 \approx 1(0.1001)(1) \approx 0.100$$

The probability that more reservations will show up than the van can carry is $P(7) + P(8)$, or about $0.267 + 0.100 = 0.367$.

Over one third of the trips will have passengers who cannot get a seat in the van. This will result in dissatisfied customers, so this is not a reasonable policy.

Try It! **4.** A play calls for a crowd of 12 extras with non-speaking parts. Because 10% of the extras have not shown up in the past, the director selects 15 students as extras. Find the probabilities that 12 extras show up to the performance, 15 extras show up to the performance, and more than 12 extras show up to the performance.

EXAMPLE 5 **Understanding False Positive and False Negative Results**

Over several months, a veterinary clinic tests terriers for diabetes. The table shows the results.

Diabetes Test Results

	Positive Test	Negative Test	Totals
Terrier without diabetes	63	327	390
Terrier with diabetes	181	39	220
Totals	244	366	610

A **false positive** result is a positive test result even though the condition is not present.

A **false negative** result is a negative test result even though the condition is present.

A. **What is the probability that a positive test result indicates the presence of diabetes? How likely is a false positive?**

Out of 244 terriers who tested positive, 181 have diabetes.

$P(\text{has diabetes} \mid \text{positive test}) = \frac{181}{244} \approx 74\%$

$P(\text{does not have diabetes} \mid \text{positive test})$ is the complement and equals 26%.

Therefore, a terrier that with a positive test for diabetes has a 74% probability of actually having the condition. The chance of a false positive result is 26%.

B. **What is the risk that a terrier with a negative test result actually has diabetes? How can that risk be reduced?**

Out of 366 terriers who tested negative, 39 have diabetes.

$P(\text{does have diabetes} \mid \text{negative test}) = \frac{39}{366} \approx 11\%$

Approximately 1 terrier in 10 has diabetes even when the test results are negative. If the dog is overweight or has other symptoms, repeating the test could reduce the risk of misdiagnosis.

COMMUNICATE PRECISELY
The probability of a terrier having diabetes is $\frac{220}{610} \approx 36\%$. This differs from the probability of a false positive or a false negative. **MP.6**

REASON
Analyzing risk, the exposure to danger, harm, or loss, can help determine whether false results are acceptable or not. **MP.2**

Try It! 5. A Chemistry teacher gives a pop quiz to see if the students read last night's assignment. The teacher expects a student to pass the quiz if the reading has been completed.

Chemistry Quiz Results

	Passed	Failed	Totals
Completed Reading	95	1	96
Incomplete Reading	7	7	14
Totals	102	8	110

a. What represents false positives and false negatives for the data? What percents are false positives and negatives?

b. What risk does a false value present?

CONCEPT SUMMARY Using Probability to Make Decisions

METHOD	DESCRIPTION	APPLICATIONS
Simple Probability	Find the probability of random events.	• Select the most favorable among random events.
Expected Value	Multiply the probability of each outcome by its value. Add to find the expected value.	• Compare expected values to choose the best of several options. • Compare expected values to decide if a game is fair.
Probability Distribution	Find the probability distribution of all possible outcomes.	• Compare probabilities of outcomes in a binomial experiment. • Create a graph of a probability distribution to present the distribution visually.

Do You UNDERSTAND?

1. **ESSENTIAL QUESTION** How can you use probability to make decisions?

2. **Reason** How can you use random numbers to simulate rolling a standard number cube? Ⓒ **MP.2**

3. **Error Analysis** Explain the error in Diego's reasoning. Ⓒ **MP.3**

If a game uses random numbers, it is always fair. ✗

4. **Use Structure** Describe what conditions are needed for a fair game. Ⓒ **MP.7**

5. **Use Appropriate Tools** Explain how you can visualize probability distributions to help you make decisions. Ⓒ **MP.5**

6. **Reason** Why must the expected value of a fair game of chance equal zero? Ⓒ **MP.2**

Do You KNOW HOW?

7. A teacher assigns each of 30 students a unique number from 1 to 30. The teacher uses the random numbers shown to select students for presentations. Which student was selected first? second?

randInt (1,30) 9
randInt (1,30) 9
randInt (1,30) 4

8. Three friends are at a restaurant and they all want the last slice of pizza. Identify three methods involving probability that they can use to determine who gets the last slice. Explain mathematically why each method will guarantee a fair decision.

9. Edgar rolls one number cube and Novia rolls two. If Edgar rolls a 6, he wins a prize. If Novia rolls a sum of 7, she gets a prize. Is this game fair? Explain.

10. The 10 parking spaces in the first row of the parking lot are reserved for the 12 members of the Student Council. Usually an average of ten percent of the Student Council does not drive to school dances. What is the probability that more members of the Student Council will drive to a dance than there are reserved parking spaces?

PRACTICE & PROBLEM SOLVING

UNDERSTAND

11. Reason Suppose Léon has a pair of 4-sided dice, each numbered from 1 to 4, and Carolina has a pair of 10-sided dice, each numbered from 1 to 10. They decide to play a series of games against each other, using their own dice. © MP.2

  a. Describe a game that would be fair. Explain.

  b. Describe an unfair game. Explain.

12. Construct Arguments Mr. and Ms. Mitchell have 3 children: Luke, Charlie, and Aubrey. All 3 children want to sit in the front seat. Charlie suggests that they flip a coin two times to decide who will sit in the front seat. The number of heads determines who sits in the front seat. Is this a fair method? Explain. © MP.3

Number of Heads	Front Seat Passenger
0	Luke
1	Charlie
2	Aubrey

13. Error Analysis Mercedes is planning a party for 10 people. She knows from experience that about 20% of those invited will not show up. If she invites 12 people, how can she calculate the probability that more than 10 people will show up. What error did she make? What is the correct probability? © MP.3

> Use the binomial distribution for 12 trials, with a 20% probability, and more than 10 show up.
> $(12)(0.80)^1(0.20)^1 +$
> $(1)(0.80)^0(0.20)^{12}$ ✗

14. Use Appropriate Tools How does a two-way frequency table help you organize test results and determine false positive or false negative results? © MP.5

PRACTICE

15. How can you use random integers to select 3 students from a group of 8 to serve as student body representatives, so that each student is equally likely to be selected? SEE EXAMPLE 1

16. Is this game fair or unfair? Explain. SEE EXAMPLE 2

  When it is your turn, roll a standard number cube. If the number is even, you get a point. If it is odd, you lose a point.

Fatima is a contestant on a game show. So far, she has won $34,000. She can keep the $34,000 or spin the spinner shown below and add or subtract the amount shown from $34,000. SEE EXAMPLE 3

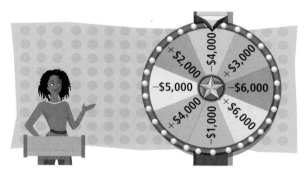

17. If Fatima spins the spinner, what are her expected total winnings?

18. Would you advise Fatima to keep the $34,000 or to spin the spinner? Explain your reasoning.

19. Suppose 0.5% of people who file federal tax returns with an adjusted gross income (AGI) between $50,000 and $75,000 are audited. If 5 people with an AGI between $50,000 and $75,000 are selected at random from all the people who filed federal tax returns, what is the probability that at least 2 people are audited? SEE EXAMPLE 4

The table below shows results for a cancer screening test with rats. SEE EXAMPLE 5

Cancer in Rats Results

	Positive	Negative	Total
Rats with cancer	690	22	712
Rats without cancer	20	130	150
Total	710	152	862

20. What is the likelihood of getting false positives and false negatives for the data in the table? What risk does a false value present? Explain.

PRACTICE & PROBLEM SOLVING

21. Model With Mathematics For $5.49 per month, insurance covers the cost of repairing a leak in the natural gas lines inside Ms. Corchado's house. She estimates a 3% chance that she will need such repairs next year. © MP.4

   a. What is the expected cost of a gas leak, if Ms. Corchado does not buy insurance? Use the cost shown in the middle of the graph.

   b. With more recent information, Ms. Corchado learns that repair costs could be as much as $1,200 dollars with an 8% probability of a leak. What is the expected cost of a gas leak with these assumptions?

   c. Would you advise Ms. Corchado to buy the insurance? Explain.

Average Reported Costs
$657

Low Cost $150   Most Spent Between $387 to $951   High Cost $1,200

22. Higher Order Thinking You are a consultant to a company that manufactures components for cell phones. One of the components the company manufactures has a 4% failure rate. Design changes have improved the quality of the component. A test of 50 of the new components found that only one of the new components is defective.

   a. Before the design improvements what was the probability that among 50 of the items, at most one of the items was defective?

   b. Is it reasonable to say the new components have a failure rate below 4%?

   c. Would you recommend further testing to determine whether the new parts have a lower failure rate than 4%? Explain.

23. Reasoning A helmet manufacturer tests the force needed to make a helmet crack or break. The safety team finds that an acceptable risk for a false positive must be less than 1% and for a false negative must be less than 5%. Interpret the risk levels as related to the safety and development of the helmets. What might explain the difference in criteria? © MP.2

24. Paola, Sasha, and Yumiko live together. They want a system to determine who will wash the dinner dishes on any given night. Select all of the methods that are fair.

  Ⓐ Roll a standard number cube. If the result is 1 or 2, Paola does the dishes; if 3 or 4, Sasha; if 5 or 6, Yumiko.

  Ⓑ Roll a standard number cube. If the result is 1, Paola does the dishes; if 2, Sasha; if 4, Yumiko. If the result is 3, 5, or 6, roll again.

  Ⓒ Roll two standard number cubes. If the sum of the numbers that come up is less than 6, Paola washes the dishes; if the sum is 8, 9, or 12, Sasha; if the sum is 6 or 7, Yumiko. If the sum is 10 or 11, roll again.

  Ⓓ Write the name of each girl on a slip of paper, place the slips in a box, mix them up, and select one at random. The person whose name is selected does the dishes.

25. SAT/ACT A fair choice among a group of students may be made by flipping three coins in sequence, and noting the sequences of heads and tails. If each student is assigned one of these sequences, how many students can be selected fairly by this method?

  Ⓐ 4   Ⓑ 5   Ⓒ 6   Ⓓ 7   Ⓔ 8

26. Performance Task Acme Tire Company makes two models of steel belted radial tires, Model 1001 and Model 1002.

Model	1001
Blowouts per 200,000 tires	2
Profits before any lawsuits	$60

Model	1002
Blowouts per 200,000 tires	1
Profits before any lawsuits	$56

If one of these tires fails and the company is sued, the average settlement is $1,200,000.

Part A Find the expected profit for both models of tires after any potential lawsuits. Explain.

Part B Would you recommend that the company continue selling both models? Explain.

Topic Review

1. How can you find the probability of events and combinations of events?

Vocabulary Review

Choose the correct term to complete each sentence.

2. An arrangement of items in a specific order is called a(n) _____.

3. Two events are _____ if there is no outcome that is in both events.

4. Two events are _____ if the occurrence of one event affects the probability of the other event.

5. An arrangement of items in which order is not important is called a(n) _____.

6. The predicted average outcome of many trials in an experiment is called the _____.

- combination
- complement
- conditional probability
- dependent events
- expected value
- independent events
- mutually exclusive
- permutation
- probability distribution

Concepts & Skills Review

LESSONS 12-1 and 12-2   **Probability Events and Conditional Probability**

Quick Review

Two events are **mutually exclusive** if and only if there is no outcome that lies in the sample space of both events. Two events are **independent events** if and only if the occurrence of one event does not affect the probability of a second event.

For any two events A and B, with $P(A) \neq 0$, $P(A \text{ and } B) = P(A) \cdot P(B \mid A)$. Events A and B are independent if and only if $P(B \mid A) = P(B)$.

Example

Let A represent the event "even number," or $A = \{2, 4, 6, 8\}$.

Let B represent the event "odd number," or $B = \{1, 3, 5, 7\}$.

Are A and B mutually exclusive? Explain.
    Yes; all of their elements are different.

Practice & Problem Solving

Ten craft sticks lettered A through J are in a coffee cup. Consider the events "consonant," "vowel," "letter before D in the alphabet," "letter after A in the alphabet," and "letter after E in the alphabet." State whether each pair of events is mutually exclusive.

7. vowel, letter before D

8. letter before D, letter after E

9. letter after A, letter before D

10. **Error Analysis** One card is selected at random from five cards numbered 1 to 5. A student says that drawing an even number and drawing a prime number are dependent events because $P(\text{prime} \mid \text{even}) = 0.5$ and $P(\text{even}) = 0.4$. Describe and correct the error the student made. Ⓒ **MP.3**

Permutations and Combinations

Quick Review

The number of permutations of r items from a set of n items is $_nP_r = \frac{n!}{(n-r)!}$ for $0 \le r \le n$.

The number of combinations of r items from a set of n items is $_nC_r = \frac{n!}{r!(n-r)!}$ for $0 \le r \le n$.

Example

A bag contains 4 blue tiles and 4 yellow tiles. Three tiles are drawn from the bag at random without replacement. What is the probability all three tiles are blue?

Use combinations since order does not matter. Select 3 blue from 4 blue tiles $_4C_3$, or 4, ways.

Select 0 yellow from 4 yellow tiles $_4C_0$, or 1, way.
Select 3 tiles from 8 total tiles $_8C_3$, or 56, ways.

$P(3 \text{ blue}) = \frac{4 \cdot 1}{56} = \frac{1}{14} \approx 0.07 = 7\%$

Practice & Problem Solving

In Exercises 11 and 12, determine whether the situation involves finding permutations or combinations. Then find the number.

11. How many ways can a team choose a captain and a substitute captain from 8 players?

12. How many ways can 3 numbers be selected from the digits 0–9 to set a lock code if the digits cannot be repeated?

13. **Error Analysis** A student computed $_5C_2$, and said that it is equal to 20. Describe and correct the error the student made. **Ⓖ MP.3**

14. **Look for Relationships** The formulas for permutations and combinations must always evaluate to a natural number. Explain why. **Ⓖ MP.7**

Probability Distributions

Quick Review

For a binomial experiment consisting of n trials, the probability of r successes out of n trials is given by the **binomial probability formula**:

$$P(r) = {}_nC_r \cdot p^r(1-p)^{n-r}$$

Example

Amir scores a touchdown 24% of the time he receives the ball. If Amir receives the ball 7 times, what is the probability he scores a touchdown 4 of those times?

$$P(4 \text{ touchdowns}) = {}_7C_4 \cdot 0.24^4(1 - 0.24)^{7-4}$$

$$= 35 \cdot 0.24^4(0.76)^3$$

$$\approx 0.051 = 5.1\%$$

Practice & Problem Solving

Rhoda finds that every seed she plants has a 56% chance to grow to full height. If she plants 10 seeds, what is the probability each number of plants grows to full height? Round to the nearest hundredth of a percent.

15. 1 plant   16. 3 plants

17. 5 plants   18. 10 plants

19. **Error Analysis** Using the Example, Akasi tried to calculate Amir's probable success rate of 3 touchdowns if he received the ball 5 times, but could not get an answer. Find and correct her mistake. **Ⓖ MP.3**

$$P(3) = {}_3C_5 \cdot 0.24^5 (1 - 0.24)^{3-5}$$
$$= ?$$ ✗

LESSON 12-5 ▸ Expected Value

Quick Review

The **expected value** E of a trial of an experiment is the sum of the value of each possible outcome times its probability or
$E = x_1P(x_1) + x_2P(x_2) + \ldots + x_nP(x_n)$.

Example

The outer ring on a dartboard is worth 10 points, the middle ring is worth 25 points, and the bullseye is worth 100 points. When throwing darts, Ravi has a 45% chance of hitting the outer ring, a 40% chance of hitting the inner ring, a 5% chance of hitting the bullseye, and a 10% chance of missing the board. What is the expected value of a single dart throw?

$E = 10(0.45) + 25(0.4) + 100(0.05) + 0(0.1)$

$= 4.5 + 10 + 5 + 0$

$= 19.5$

Practice & Problem Solving

Use the information in the Example to find the expected value of 15 throws from each of the following people.

20. Rosa: 20% outer ring; 65% inner ring, 10% bullseye, 5% miss

21. Deion: 60% outer ring; 20% inner ring, 12% bullseye, 8% miss

22. **Higher Order Thinking** A basketball player takes 2 shots from the 3-point line and misses them both. She calculates the expected value of taking a shot from the 3-point line is 0 points. Do you agree with the player's calculation? Her reasoning? How could the player improve the accuracy of her estimate?

LESSON 12-6 ▸ Probability and Decision Making

Quick Review

Combined with probability, expected value can be used to help make decisions.

Example

Frederica is playing a game tossing 20 beanbags from a choice of three lines. Frederica has a 90% chance of success from the 5-point line, a 65% chance of success from the 10-point line, and a 20% chance from the 20-point line. Frederica wants to toss every beanbag from the same line, and thinks she should toss from the 5-point line. Is Frederica correct?

Find the expected points per toss, or expected value.

5-point line:
5 points • 0.90 = 4.5 points per toss

10-point line:
10 points • 0.65 = 6.5 points per toss

20-point line:
20 points • 0.20 = 4 points per toss

Frederica should toss the beanbag from the 10-point line.

Practice & Problem Solving

Both situations have the same expected value. Find the missing information.

23. Situation 1: Paul hits a dart target worth 15 points 45% of the time.

    Situation 2: He hits a dart target worth 10 points x% of the time.

24. Situation 1: Lenora has a success rate of 25% when selling bracelets at $15 each.

    Situation 2: She has a success rate of 20% when selling bracelets at $x each.

25. **Make Sense of Problems** Use the information from the Example. Frederica practices her shots and increases her chances from the 20-point line to 30%. Should she now toss the beanbag from the 20-point line? Explain your reasoning. Ⓒ **MP.1**

Visual Glossary

English	Spanish

A

Acute angle   An acute angle is an angle whose measure is between 0 and 90.

Example

17°

Ángulo agudo   Un ángulo agudo es un ángulo que mide entre 0 y 90.

Acute triangle   An acute triangle has three acute angles.

Example

75°
60°   45°

Triángulo acutángulo   Un triángulo acutángulo tiene los tres ángulos agudos.

Adjacent angles   Adjacent angles are two coplanar angles that have a common side and a common vertex but no common interior points.

Example

∠1 and ∠2 are adjacent.   ∠3 and ∠4 are *not* adjacent.

Ángulos adyacentes   Los ángulos adyacentes son dos ángulos coplanarios que tienen un lado común y el mismo vértice, pero no tienen puntos interiores comunes.

Alternate interior (exterior) angles   Alternate interior (exterior) angles are nonadjacent interior (exterior) angles that lie on opposite sides of the transversal.

Example

5   t
1   3
4   2   ℓ
6   m

∠1 and ∠2 are alternate interior angles, as are ∠3 and ∠4. ∠5 and ∠6 are alternate exterior angles.

Ángulos alternos internos (externos)   Los ángulos alternos internos (externos) son ángulos internos (externos) no adyacentes situados en lados opuestos de la transversal.

Altitude   *See* **cone; cylinder; parallelogram; prism; pyramid; trapezoid; triangle.**

Altura   *Ver* **cone; cylinder; parallelogram; prism; pyramid; trapezoid; triangle.**

Altitude of a triangle   An altitude of a triangle is the perpendicular segment from a vertex to the line containing the side opposite that vertex.

Example

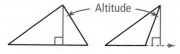

Altitude

Altura de un triángulo   Una altura de un triángulo es el segmento perpendicular que va desde un vértice hasta la recta que contiene el lado opuesto a ese vértice.

English

Angle   An angle is formed by two rays with the same endpoint. The rays are the *sides* of the angle and the common endpoint is the *vertex* of the angle.

Example

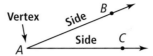

This angle could be named ∠*A*, ∠*BAC*, or ∠*CAB*.

Angle bisector   An angle bisector is a ray that divides an angle into two congruent angles.

Example

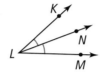

$\overrightarrow{LN}$ bisects ∠*KLM*.
∠*KLN* ≅ ∠*NLM*.

Angle of elevation or depression   An angle of elevation (depression) is the angle formed by a horizontal line and the line of sight to an object above (below) the horizontal line.

Example

Angle of rotation   *See* **rotation.**

Arc   *See* **major arc; minor arc.** *See also* **arc length; measure of an arc.**

Arc length   The length of an arc of a circle is the product of the circumference of the circle and the ratio of the corresponding central angle measure in degrees and 360. The length of the arc is also the product of the radius and central angle measure in radians.

Example

$s = \dfrac{60}{360} \cdot 2\pi(4) = \dfrac{4\pi}{3}$

$s = \dfrac{\pi}{4}(4) = \pi$

Spanish

Ángulo   Un ángulo está formado por dos semirrectas que convergen en un mismo extremo. Las semirrectas son los *lados* del ángulo y los extremos en común son el *vértice.*

Bisectriz de un ángulo   La bisectriz de un ángulo es una semirrecta que divide al ángulo en dos ángulos congruentes.

Ángulo de elevación o depresión   Un ángulo de elevación (depresión) es el ángulo formado por una línea horizontal y la recta que va de esa línea a un objeto situado arriba (debajo) de ella.

Ángulo de rotación   *Ver* **rotation.**

Arco   *Ver* **major arc; minor arc.** *Ver también* **arc length; measure of an arc.**

Longitud de un arco   La longitud del arco de un círculo es el producto de la circunferencia del círculo y la razón de la medida del ángulo central correspondiente en grados y 360. La longitud del arco es también el producto del radio y de la medida del ángulo central en radianes.

English

Spanish

Area The area of a plane figure is the number of square units enclosed by the figure.

Área El área de una figura plana es la cantidad de unidades cuadradas que contiene la figura.

Example The area of the rectangle is 12 square units, or 12 units^2.

Axes *See* **coordinate plane.**

Ejes *Ver* **coordinate plane.**

Base(s) *See* **cone; cylinder; isosceles triangle; parallelogram; prism; pyramid; trapezoid; triangle.**

Base(s) *Ver* **cone; cylinder; isosceles triangle; parallelogram; prism; pyramid; trapezoid; triangle.**

Base angles *See* **trapezoid; isosceles triangle.**

Ángulos de base *Ver* **trapezoid; isosceles triangle.**

Biconditional A biconditional statement is the combination of a conditional statement, $p \rightarrow q$, and its converse, $q \rightarrow p$. A biconditional contains the words "if and only if."

Bicondicional Un enunciado bicondicional es la combinación de un enunciado condicional, $p \rightarrow q$, y su recíproco, $q \rightarrow p$. El enunciado bicondicional incluye las palabras "si y solo si".

Example This biconditional statement is true: Two angles are congruent *if and only if* they have the same measure.

Binomial experiment A binomial experiment is one in which the situation involves repeated trials. Each trial has two possible outcomes (success or failure), and the probability of success is constant throughout the trials.

Experimento binomial Un experimento binomial es un experimento que requiere varios ensayos. Cada ensayo tiene dos resultados posibles (éxito o fracaso), y la probabilidad de éxito es constante durante todos los ensayos.

Binomial probability For a binomial experiment consisting of n trials with probability of success p for each trial, the binomial probability is the probability of r successes out of n trials given by the function $P(r) = {}_nC_r \cdot p^r(1-p)^{n-r}$.

Probabilidad binomial En un experimento que incluye n ensayos con una probabilidad p de cada ensayo, la probabilidad binomial es la probabilidad de r éxitos de n ensayos dados por la función $P(r) = {}_nC_r \cdot p^r(1-p)^{n-r}$.

Example Suppose you roll a standard number cube and that you call rolling a 1 a success. Then $p = \frac{1}{6}$. The probability of rolling nine 1s in twenty rolls is $_{20}C_9 \left(\frac{1}{6}\right)^9 \left(1 - \frac{1}{6}\right)^{20-9} \approx 0.022$.

Bisector *See* **segment bisector; angle bisector.**

Bisectriz *Ver* **segment bisector; angle bisector.**

Cavalieri's Principle If two space figures have the same height and the same cross-sectional area at every level, then they have the same volume.

Principio de Cavalieri Si dos figuras sólidas tienen la misma altura y la misma área transversal en todos los niveles, entonces también tienen el mismo volumen.

Example

Both figures are prisms with height 5 units and horizontal cross-sectional area 6 square units. $V = B \cdot h = (6)(5) = 30$ cubic units

---

Center *See* **circle; dilation; regular polygon; rotation; sphere.**

Centro *Ver* **circle; dilation; regular polygon; rotation; sphere.**

English

Central angle of a circle A central angle of a circle is an angle formed by two radii with the vertex at the center of the circle.

Example

$\angle ROK$ is a central angle of $\odot O$.

Centroid of a triangle The centroid of a triangle is the point of concurrency of the medians of the triangle.

Example P is the centroid of $\triangle ABC$.

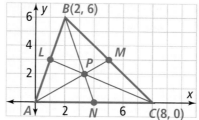

Chord A chord of a circle is a segment whose endpoints are on the circle.

Example

$\overline{HD}$ and $\overline{HR}$ are chords of $\odot C$.

Circle A circle is the set of all points in a plane that are a given distance, the radius, from a given point, the center. The standard form for an equation of a circle with center (h, k) and radius r is $(x - h)^2 + (y - k)^2 = r^2$.

Example

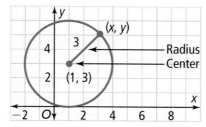

The equation of the circle whose center is $(1, 3)$ and whose radius is 3 is $(x - 1)^2 + (y - 3)^2 = 9$.

Circumcenter of a triangle The circumcenter of a triangle is the point of concurrency of the perpendicular bisectors of the sides of the triangle.

Example

$QC = SC = RC$

C is the circumcenter.

Spanish

Ángulo central de un círculo Un ángulo central de un círculo es un ángulo formado por dos radios que tienen el vértice en el centro del círculo.

Centroide de un triángulo El centroide de un triángulo es el punto de intersección de sus medianas.

Cuerda Una cuerda de un círculo es un segmento cuyos extremos son dos puntos del círculo.

Círculo Un círculo es el conjunto de todos los puntos de un plano situados a una distancia dada, el radio, de un punto dado, el centro. La fórmula normal de la ecuación de un círculo con centro (h, k) y radio r es $(x - h)^2 + (y - k)^2 = r^2$.

Circuncentro de un triángulo El circuncentro de un triángulo es el punto de intersección de las bisectrices perpendiculares de los lados del triángulo.

English

Circumference   The circumference of a circle is the distance around the circle. Given the radius r of a circle, you can find its circumference C by using the formula $C = 2\pi r$.

Example

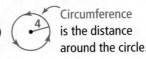

$$C = 2\pi r$$
$$= 2\pi(4)$$
$$= 8\pi$$

Circumference is the distance around the circle.

Circumference of a sphere   *See* **sphere**.

Circumscribed   A circumscribed circle of a triangle is the circle that contains the three vertices of the triangle.

Example

⊙P is the circumscribed circle of △ABC.

Collinear points   Collinear points lie on the same line.

Example

Points A, B, and C are collinear, but points A, B, and Z are noncollinear.

Combination   Any unordered selection of r objects from a set of n objects is a combination. The number of combinations of n objects taken r at a time is $_nC_r = \frac{n!}{r!(n-r)!}$ for $0 \leq r \leq n$.

Example   The number of combinations of seven items taken four at a time is $_7C_4 = \frac{7!}{4!(7-4)!} = 35$. There are 35 ways to choose four items from seven items without regard to order.

Compass   A compass is a tool for drawing arcs and circles of different sizes and can be used to copy lengths.

Complement of an event   All possible outcomes that are not in the event.
$P(\text{complement of event}) = 1 - P(\text{event})$

Example   The complement of rolling a 1 or a 2 on a standard number cube is rolling a 3, 4, 5, or 6.

Spanish

Circunferencia   La circunferencia de un círculo es la distancia alrededor del círculo. Dado el radio r de un círculo, se puede hallar la circunferencia C usando la fórmula $C = 2\pi r$.

Circunferencia de una esfera   *Ver* **sphere**.

Circunscrito   El círculo circunscrito de un triángulo es el círculo que contiene los tres vértices del triángulo.

Puntos colineales   Los puntos colineales son los que están sobre la misma recta.

Combinación   Cualquier selección no ordenada de r objetos tomados de un conjunto de n objetos es una combinación. El número de combinaciones de n objetos, cuando se toman r objetos cada vez, $_nC_r = \frac{n!}{r!(n-r)!}$ para $0 \leq r \leq n$.

Compás   El compás es un instrumento que se usa para dibujar arcos y círculos de diferentes tamaños, y que se puede usar para copiar longitudes.

Complemento de un suceso   Todos los resultados posibles que no se dan en el suceso.
$P(\text{complemento de un suceso}) = 1 - P(\text{suceso})$

English

Complementary angles   Two angles are complementary angles if the sum of their measures is 90.

Example

∠*HKI* and ∠*IKJ* are complementary angles, as are ∠*HKI* and ∠*EFG*.

Composite space figures   A composite space figure is the combination of two or more figures into one object.

Example

Composition of rigid motions   A composition of rigid motions is a transformation with two or more rigid motions in which the second rigid motion is performed on the image of the first rigid motion.

Example

If you reflect △*ABC* across line *m* to get △*A′B′C′* and then reflect △*A′B′C′* across line *n* to get △*A″B″C″*, you perform a composition of rigid motions.

Compound event   A compound event is an event that consists of two or more events linked by the word *and* or the word *or*.

Example   Rolling a 5 on a standard number cube and then rolling a 4 is a compound event.

Concave polygon   *See* **polygon**.

Concentric circles   Concentric circles lie in the same plane and have the same center.

Example

The two circles both have center *D* and are therefore concentric.

Conclusion   The conclusion is the part of an *if-then* statement (conditional) that follows *then*.

Example   In the statement, "If it rains, then I will go outside," the conclusion is "I will go outside."

Spanish

Ángulos complementarios   Dos ángulos son complementarios si la suma de sus medidas es igual a 90.

Figuras geométricas compuestas   Una figura geométrica compuesta es la combinación de dos o más figuras en un mismo objeto.

Composición de movimientos rígidos   Una composición de movimientos rígidos es una transformación de dos o más movimientos rígidos en la que el segundo movimiento rígido se realiza sobre la imagen del primer movimiento rígido.

Suceso compuesto   Un suceso compuesto es un suceso que consiste en dos o más sucesos unidos por medio de la palabra *y* o la palabra *o*.

Polígono cóncavo   *Ver* **polygon**.

Círculos concéntricos   Los círculos concéntricos están en el mismo plano y tienen el mismo centro.

Conclusión   La conclusión es lo que sigue a la palabra entonces en un enunciado (condicional), *si . . ., entonces. . . .*

English

Spanish

Concurrent Three or more lines are concurrent if they intersect at one point. The point at which they intersect is the *point of concurrency*.

Concurrente Tres o más rectas son concurrentes si se intersecan en un punto. El punto en el que se intersecan es el *punto de concurrencia*.

Example

Point *E* is the point of concurrency of the bisectors of the angles of △*ABC*. The bisectors are concurrent.

Conditional A conditional is an *if-then* statement that relates a hypothesis, the part that follows if, to a conclusion, the part that follows then.

Condicional Un enunciado condicional es del tipo *si . . ., entonces. . . .*

Example *If you act politely*, then you will earn respect.

Conditional probability A conditional probability is the probability that an event *B* will occur given that another event *A* has already occurred. The notation $P(B|A)$ is read "the probability of event *B*, given event *A*." For any two events *A* and *B* in the sample space, $P(B|A) = \frac{P(A \text{ and } B)}{P(A)}$.

Probabilidad condicional Una probabilidad condicional es la probabilidad de que ocurra un suceso *B* cuando ya haya ocurrido otro suceso *A*. La notación $P(B|A)$ se lee "la probabilidad del suceso *B*, dado el suceso *A*". Para dos sucesos cualesquiera *A* y *B* en el espacio muestral $P(B|A) = \frac{P(A \text{ and } B)}{P(A)}$.

Example $= \frac{P(\text{departs and arrives on time})}{P(\text{departs on time})}$

$= \frac{0.75}{0.83}$

≈ 0.9

Cone A cone is a three-dimensional figure that has a circular base, a *vertex* not in the plane of the circle, and a curved lateral surface, as shown in the diagram. The *altitude* of a cone is the perpendicular segment from the vertex to the plane of the base. The *height* is the length of the altitude. In a *right* cone, the altitude contains the center of the base. The slant *height* of a right cone is the distance from the vertex to the edge of the base.

Cono Un cono es una figura tridimensional que tiene una base circular, un *vértice* que no está en el plano del círculo y una superficie lateral curvada (indicada en el diagrama). La *altura* de un cono es el segmento perpendicular desde el vértice hasta el plano de la base. La *altura*, por extensión, es la longitud de la altura. Un *cono recto* es un cono cuya altura contiene el centro de la base. La *longitud de la generatriz* de un cono recto es la distancia desde el vértice hasta el borde de la base.

Example

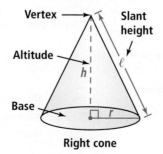

Right cone

Congruence transformation A congruence transformation maps a figure to a congruent figure. A rigid motion is sometimes called a congruence transformation.

Transformación de congruencia En una transformación de congruencia, una figura es la imagen de otra figura congruente. Los movimientos rígidos son llamados a veces transformaciones de congruencia.

English

Spanish

Congruent angles   Congruent angles are angles that have the same measure.

Ángulos congruentes   Los ángulos congruentes son ángulos que tienen la misma medida.

Example

$m\angle J = m\angle K$, so $\angle J \cong \angle K$.

Congruent arcs   Congruent arcs are arcs that have the same measure and are in the same circle or congruent circles.

Arcos congruentes   Arcos congruentes son arcos que tienen la misma medida y están en el mismo círculo o en círculos congruentes.

Example

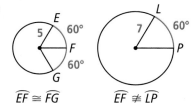

$\overset{\frown}{EF} \cong \overset{\frown}{FG}$ $\overset{\frown}{EF} \not\cong \overset{\frown}{LP}$

Congruent circles   Congruent circles are circles whose radii are congruent.

Círculos congruentes   Los círculos congruentes son círculos cuyos radios son congruentes.

Example

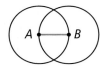

$\odot A$ and $\odot B$ have the same radius, so $\odot A \cong \odot B$.

Congruent figures   Two figures are congruent if there is a rigid motion that maps one figure to the other.

Figuras congruentes   Dos figuras son congruentes si hay un movimiento rígido en el que una figura es imagen de la otra.

Example

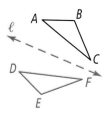

Since the reflection across line ℓ maps $\triangle ABC$ to $\triangle DEF$, $\triangle ABC$ and $\triangle DEF$ are congruent figures.

Congruent polygons   Congruent polygons are polygons that have corresponding sides congruent and corresponding angles congruent.

Polígonos congruentes   Los polígonos congruentes son polígonos cuyos lados correspondientes son congruentes y cuyos ángulos correspondientes son congruentes.

Example

$\triangle DEF \cong \triangle GHI$

English

Spanish

Congruent segments Congruent segments are segments that have the same length.

Segmentos congruentes Los segmentos congruentes son segmentos que tienen la misma longitud.

Example

$\overline{AB} \cong \overline{CD}$

Conjecture A conjecture is an unproven statement or rule that is based on inductive reasoning.

Conjetura Una conjetura es una afirmación o regla no demostrada, que está fundamentada en un razonamiento inductivo.

Example As you walk down the street, you see many people holding unopened umbrellas. You make the conjecture that the forecast must call for rain.

Consecutive angles Consecutive angles of a polygon share a common side.

Ángulos consecutivos Los ángulos consecutivos de un polígono tienen un lado común.

Example

In ▱JKLM, ∠J and ∠M are consecutive angles, as are ∠J and ∠K. ∠J and ∠L are *not* consecutive.

Construction A construction is a geometric figure made with only a straightedge and compass.

Construcción Una construcción es una figura geométrica trazada solamente con una regla sin graduación y un compás.

Example

The diagram shows the construction (in progress) of a line perpendicular to a line ℓ through a point P on ℓ.

Contrapositive The contrapositive is obtained by negating and reversing the hypothesis and the conclusion of a conditional. The contrapositive of the conditional "if *p*, then *q*" is the conditional "if not *q*, then not *p*." A conditional and its contrapositive always have the same truth value.

Contrapositivo El contrapositivo se obtiene al negar e intercambiar la hipótesis y la conclusión de un condicional. El contrapositivo del condicional "si *p*, entonces *q*" es el condicional "si no *q*, entonces no *p*". Un condicional y su contrapositivo siempre tienen el mismo valor verdadero.

Example **Conditional:** If a figure is a triangle, then it is a polygon.
Contrapositive: If a figure is not a polygon, then it is not a triangle.

Converse The converse reverses the hypothesis and conclusion of a conditional.

Expresión recíproca La expresión recíproca intercambia la hipótesis y la conclusión de un condicional.

Example The converse of "If I was born in Houston, then I am a Texan" would be "If I am a Texan, then I am born in Houston."

Convex polygon *See* **polygon**.

Polígono convexo *Ver* **polygon**.

English

Spanish

Coordinate(s) of a point The coordinate of a point is its distance and direction from the origin of a number line. The coordinates of a point on a coordinate plane are in the form (x, y), where x is the x-coordinate and y is the y-coordinate.

Coordenada(s) de un punto La coordenada de un punto es su distancia y dirección desde el origen en una recta numérica. Las coordenadas de un punto en un plano de coordenadas se expresan como (x, y), donde x es la coordenada x, e y es la coordenada y.

Example

The coordinate of P is −3.

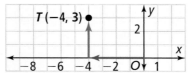

The coordinates of T are (−4, 3).

Coordinate plane The coordinate plane is formed by two number lines, called the axes, intersecting at right angles. The x-axis is the horizontal axis, and the y-axis is the vertical axis. The two axes meet at the origin, O(0, 0). The axes divide the plane into four *quadrants*.

Plano de coordenadas El plano de coordenadas se forma con dos rectas numéricas, llamadas *ejes*, que se cortan en ángulos rectos. El eje x es el eje horizontal y el eje y es el eje vertical. Los dos ejes se unen en el *origen*, O(0, 0). Los ejes dividen el plano de coordenadas en cuatro *cuadrantes*.

Example

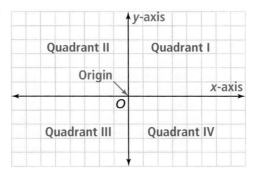

Coordinate proof *See* **proof.**

Prueba de coordenadas *Ver* **proof.**

Corollary A corollary is a theorem that can be proved easily using another theorem.

Corolario Un corolario es un teorema que se puede probar fácilmente usando otro teorema.

Example **Theorem:** If two sides of a triangle are congruent, then the angles opposite those sides are congruent.
Corollary: If a triangle is equilateral, then it is equiangular.

Corresponding angles Corresponding angles lie on the same side of the transversal t and in corresponding positions relative to ℓ and m.

Ángulos correspondientes Los ángulos correspondientes están en el mismo lado de la transversal t y en las correspondientes posiciones relativas a ℓ y m.

Example

∠1 and ∠2 are corresponding angles, as are ∠3 and ∠4, ∠5 and ∠6, and ∠7 and ∠8.

English

Spanish

Cosine ratio   *See* **trigonometric ratios.**

Razón coseno   *Ver* **trigonometric ratios.**

Counterexample   A counterexample is an example that shows a statement or conjecture is false.

Contraejemplo   Un contraejemplo es un ejemplo que demuestra que una afirmación o conjetura es falsa.

Example   **Statement:** All apples are red.
Counterexample: A Granny Smith Apple is green.

Cross section   A cross section is the intersection of a solid and a plane.

Sección de corte   Una sección de corte es la intersección de un plano y un cuerpo geométrico.

Example

 The cross section is a circle.

Cube   A cube is a polyhedron with six faces, each of which is a square.

Cubo   Un cubo es un poliedro de seis caras, cada una de las caras es un cuadrado.

Example

Cylinder   A cylinder is a three-dimensional figure with two congruent circular bases that lie in parallel planes. An *altitude* of a cylinder is a perpendicular segment that joins the planes of the bases. Its length is the *height* of the cylinder. In a *right cylinder*, the segment joining the centers of the bases is an altitude. In an *oblique cylinder*, the segment joining the centers of the bases is not perpendicular to the planes containing the bases.

Cilindro   Un cilindro es una figura tridimensional con dos bases congruentes circulares en planos paralelos. Una *altura* de un cilindro es un segmento perpendicular que une los planos de las bases. Su longitud es, por extensión, la *altura* del cilindro. En un *cilindro* recto, el segmento que une los centros de las bases es una altura. En un *cilindro oblicuo*, el segmento que une los centros de las bases no es perpendicular a los planos que contienen las bases.

Example

Right cylinder   **Oblique cylinder**

D

Decagon   A decagon is a polygon with ten sides.

Decágono   Un decágono es un polígono de diez lados.

Example

Deductive reasoning   Deductive reasoning is a process of reasoning using given and previously known facts to reach a logical conclusion.

Razonamiento deductivo   El razonamiento deductivo es un proceso de razonamiento en el que se usan hechos dados y previamente conocidos para llegar a una conclusión lógica.

Example   Based on the fact that the sum of any two even numbers is even, you can deduce that the product of any whole number and any even number is even.

English

Spanish

Dependent events   When the outcome of one event affects the probability of a second event, the events are dependent events.

Example   You have a bag with marbles of different colors. If you pick a marble from the bag and pick another without replacing the first, the events are dependent events.

Sucesos dependientes   Dos sucesos son dependientes si el resultado de un suceso afecta la probabilidad del otro.

Diagonal   *See* **polygon.**

Diagonal   *Ver* **polygon.**

Diameter of a circle   A diameter of a circle is a segment that contains the center of the circle and whose endpoints are on the circle. The term *diameter* can also mean the length of this segment.

Diámetro de un círculo   Un diámetro de un círculo es un segmento que contiene el centro del círculo y cuyos extremos están en el círculo. El término *diámetro* también puede referirse a la longitud de este segmento.

Example

$\overline{DM}$ is a diameter of $\odot C$.

Diameter of a sphere   The diameter of a sphere is a segment passing through the center, with endpoints on the sphere.

Diámetro de una esfera   El diámetro de una esfera es un segmento que contiene el centro de la esfera y cuyos extremos están en la esfera.

Example

Dilation   A dilation is a transformation that has *center C* and *scale factor n*, where $n > 0$, and maps a point R to R' in such a way that R' is on $\overrightarrow{CR}$ and $CR' = n \cdot CR$. The center of a dilation is its own image. If $n > 1$, the dilation is an *enlargement*, and if $0 < n < 1$, the dilation is a *reduction*.

Dilatación   Una dilatación, o *transformación de semejanza*, tiene *centro C* y *factor de escala n* para $n > 0$, y asocia un punto R a R' de tal modo que R' está en $\overrightarrow{CR}$ y $CR' = n \cdot CR$. El centro de una dilatación es su propia imagen. Si $n > 1$, la dilatación es un aumento, y si $0 < n < 1$, la dilatación es una reducción.

Example

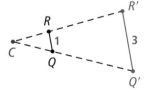

$\overline{R'Q'}$ is the image of $\overline{RQ}$ under a dilation with center C and scale factor 3.

Directrix   *See* **parabola.**

Directriz   *Ver* **parabola.**

Distance between two points on a line   The distance between two points on a line is the absolute value of the difference of the coordinates of the points.

Distancia entre dos puntos de una línea   La distancia entre dos puntos de una línea es el valor absoluto de la diferencia de las coordenadas de los puntos.

Example

$AB = |a - b|$

English	Spanish

Distance from a point to a line The distance from a point to a line is the length of the perpendicular segment from the point to the line.

Distancia desde un punto hasta una recta La distancia desde un punto hasta una recta es la longitud del segmento perpendicular que va desde el punto hasta la recta.

Example

The distance from point P to a line ℓ is PT.

E

Edge *See* **polyhedron.**

Arista *Ver* **polyhedron.**

Endpoint *See* **ray; segment.**

Extremo *Ver* **ray; segment.**

Enlargement *See* **dilation.**

Aumento *Ver* **dilation.**

Equiangular triangle An equiangular triangle is a triangle whose angles are all congruent.

Triángulo equiángulo Un triángulo equiángulo es un triángulo cuyos ángulos son todos congruentes.

Example

Each angle of the triangle is a 60° angle.

Equidistant A point is equidistant from two objects if it is the same distance from the objects.

Equidistante Un punto es equidistante de dos objetos si la distancia entre el punto y los objetos es igual.

Example

Point B is equidistant from points A and C.

Equilateral triangle An equilateral triangle is a triangle whose sides are all congruent.

Triángulo equilátero Un triángulo equilátero es un triángulo cuyos lados son todos congruentes.

Example

Each side of the triangle is 1.5 cm long.

Equivalent statements Equivalent statements are statements with the same truth value.

Enunciados equivalentes Los enunciados equivalentes son enunciados con el mismo valor verdadero.

Example The following statements are equivalent:
If a figure is a square, then it is a rectangle.
If a figure is not a rectangle, then it is not a square.

Event Any group of outcomes in a situation involving probability.

Suceso En la probabilidad, cualquier grupo de resultados.

Example When rolling a number cube, there are six possible outcomes. Rolling an even number is an event with three possible outcomes, 2, 4, and 6.

English

Expected value   The average value you can expect for a large number of trials of an experiment; the sum of each outcome's value multiplied by its probability.

Example   In a game, a player has a 25% probability of earning 10 points by spinning an even number and a 75% probability of earning 5 points by spinning an odd number.

expected value = 0.25(10) + 0.75(5) = 6.25

Experimental probability   The ratio of the number of times an event actually happens to the number of times the experiment is done.

$P(\text{event}) = \dfrac{\text{number of times an event happens}}{\text{number of times the experiment is done}}$

Example   A baseball player's batting average shows how likely it is that a player will get a hit, based on previous times at bat.

Extended proportion   *See* **proportion.**

Extended ratio   *See* **ratio.**

Exterior angle of a polygon   An exterior angle of a polygon is an angle formed by a side and an extension of an adjacent side.

Example

∠*KLM* is an exterior angle of △*JKL*.

 F

Factorial   The factorial of a positive integer n is the product of all positive integers less than or equal to n and written $n!$

Example $4! = 4 \cdot 3 \cdot 2 \cdot 1 = 24$

Flow proof   *See* **proof.**

Focus of a parabola   *See* **parabola.**

Frequency table   A table that groups a set of data values into intervals and shows the frequency for each interval.

Example

Interval	Frequency
0–9	5
10–19	8
20–29	4

Spanish

Valor esperado   El valor promedio que se puede esperar para una cantidad grande de pruebas en un experimento; la suma de los valores de los resultados multiplicados cada uno por su probabilidad.

Probabilidad experimental   La razón entre el número de veces que un suceso sucede en la realidad y el número de veces que se hace el experimento.

$P(\text{suceso}) = \dfrac{\text{número de veces que sucede un suceso}}{\text{número de veces que se hace el experimento}}$

Proporción extendida   *Ver* **proportion.**

Razón extendida   *Ver* **ratio.**

Ángulo exterior de un polígono   El ángulo exterior de un polígono es un ángulo formado por un lado y una extensión de un lado adyacente.

Factorial   El factorial de un número entero positivo n es el producto de todos los números positivos menores que o iguales a n, y se escribe $n!$

Prueba de flujo   *Ver* **proof.**

Foco de una parábola   *Ver* **parabola.**

Tabla de frecuencias   Tabla que agrupa un conjunto de datos en intervalos y muestra la frecuencia de cada intervalo.

Fundamental Counting Principle   If there are m ways to make the first selection and n ways to make the second selection, then there are $m \cdot n$ ways to make the two selections.

Principio fundamental de Conteo   Si hay m maneras de hacer la primera selección y n maneras de hacer la segunda selección, quiere decir que hay $m \cdot n$ maneras de hacer las dos selecciones.

Example   For 5 shirts and 8 pairs of shorts, the number of possible outfits is $5 \cdot 8 = 40$.

Geometric mean   The geometric mean is the number x such that $\frac{a}{x} = \frac{x}{b}$, where a, b, and x are positive numbers.

Media geométrica   La media geométrica es el número x tanto que $\frac{a}{x} = \frac{x}{b}$, donde a, b y x son números positivos.

Example   The geometric mean of 6 and 24 is 12.

$$\frac{6}{x} = \frac{x}{24}$$
$$x^2 = 144$$
$$x = 12$$

Geometric probability   Geometric probability is a probability that uses a geometric model in which points represent outcomes.

Probabilidad geométrica   La probabilidad geométrica es una probabilidad que utiliza un modelo geométrico donde se usan puntos para representar resultados.

Example

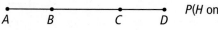

$$P(H \text{ on } \overline{BC}) = \frac{BC}{AD}$$

Glide reflection   A glide reflection is the composition of a reflection followed by a translation in a direction parallel to the line of reflection.

Reflexión deslizada   Una reflexión por deslizamiento es la composición de una reflexión seguida de una traslación en una dirección paralela a la recta de reflexión.

Example

The red G in the diagram is a glide reflection image of the black G.

Great circle   A great circle is the intersection of a sphere and a plane containing the center of the sphere. A great circle divides a sphere into two *hemispheres*.

Círculo máximo   Un círculo máximo es la intersección de una esfera y un plano que contiene el centro de la esfera. Un círculo máximo divide una esfera en dos *hemisferios*.

Example

Height   *See* **cone; cylinder; parallelogram; prism; pyramid; trapezoid; triangle.**

Altura   *Ver* **cone; cylinder; parallelogram; prism; pyramid; trapezoid; triangle.**

Hemisphere   *See* **great circle.**

Hemisferio   *Ver* **great circle.**

Hexagon   A hexagon is a polygon with six sides.

Hexágono   Un hexágono es un polígono de seis lados.

Example

English

Spanish

Hypotenuse   *See* **right triangle.**

Hipotenusa   *Ver* **right triangle.**

Hypothesis   In an *if-then* statement (conditional) the hypothesis is the part that follows *if*.

Hipótesis   En un enunciado *si . . . entonces . . .* (condicional), la hipótesis es la parte del enunciado que sigue el *si*.

Example   In the conditional "If an animal has four legs, then it is a horse," the hypothesis is "an animal has four legs."

Image   *See* **transformation.**

Imagen   *Ver* **transformation.**

Incenter of a triangle   The incenter of a triangle is the point of concurrency of the angle bisectors of the triangle.

Incentro de un triángulo   El incentro de un triángulo es el punto donde concurren las tres bisectrices de los ángulos del triángulo.

Example

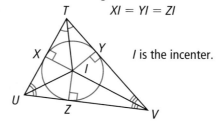

$XI = YI = ZI$

I is the incenter.

Independent events   When the outcome of one event does not affect the probability of a second event, the two events are independent.

Sucesos independientes   Cuando el resultado de un suceso no altera la probabilidad de otro, los dos sucesos son independientes.

Example   The results of two rolls of a number cube are independent. Getting a 5 on the first roll does not change the probability of getting a 5 on the second roll.

Indirect proof   *See* **indirect reasoning; proof.**

Prueba indirecta   *Ver* **indirect reasoning; proof.**

Indirect reasoning   Indirect reasoning is a type of reasoning in which all possiblities are considered and then all but one are proved false. The remaining possibility must be true.

Razonamiento indirecto   Razonamiento indirecto es un tipo de razonamiento en el que se consideran todas las posibilidades y se prueba que todas son falsas, a excepción de una. La posibilidad restante debe ser verdadera.

Example   Eduardo spent more than $60 on two books at a store. Prove that at least one book costs more than $30.
Proof: Suppose neither costs more than $30. Then he spent no more than $60 at the store. Since this contradicts the given information, at least one book costs more than $30.

Inductive reasoning   Inductive reasoning is a type of reasoning that reaches conclusions based on a pattern of specific examples or past events.

Razonamiento inductivo   El razonamiento inductivo es un tipo de razonamiento en el cual se llega a conclusiones con base en un patrón de ejemplos específicos o sucesos pasados.

Example   You see four people walk into a building. Each person emerges with a small bag containing food. You use inductive reasoning to conclude that this building contains a restaurant.

English   # Spanish

Inscribed   The inscribed circle of a triangle is the circle that intersects each side of the triangle at exactly one point.

Inscrito   El círculo inscrito de un triángulo es el círculo que interseca cada lado del triángulo en exactamente un punto.

Example

$\odot P$ is the inscribed circle of $\triangle XYZ$.

Inscribed angle   An angle is inscribed in a circle if the vertex of the angle is on the circle and the sides of the angle are chords of the circle.

Ángulo inscrito   Un ángulo está inscrito en un círculo si el vértice del ángulo está en el círculo y los lados del ángulo son cuerdas del círculo.

Example

$\angle C$ is inscribed in $\odot M$.

Intercepted arc   An intercepted arc is the part of a circle that lies between two segments that intersect the circle.

Arco interceptor   Un arco interceptor es la parte de un círculo que yace entre dos segmentos de recta que intersecan al círculo.

Example

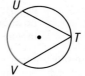

$\overset{\frown}{UV}$ is the intercepted arc of inscribed $\angle T$.

Intersection   The intersection of two or more geometric figures is the set of points the figures have in common.

Intersección   La intersección de dos o más figuras geométricas es el conjunto de puntos que las figuras tienen en común.

Example

The intersection of lines r and s is point P.

Inverse   The inverse is obtained by negating both the hypothesis and the conclusion of a conditional. The inverse of the conditional "if p, then q" is the conditional "if not p, then not q."

Inverso   El inverso es la negación de la hipótesis y de la conclusión de un condicional. El inverso del condicional "si p, entonces q" es el condicional "si no p, entonces no q".

Example   **Conditional:** If a figure is a square, then it is a parallelogram.
Inverse: If a figure is not a square, then it is not a parallelogram.

Isosceles trapezoid   An isosceles trapezoid is a trapezoid whose nonparallel opposite sides are congruent.

Trapecio isósceles   Un trapecio isosceles es un trapecio cuyos lados opuestos no paralelos son congruentes.

Example

English

Isosceles triangle An isosceles triangle is a triangle that has at least two congruent sides. If there are two congruent sides, they are called *legs*. The *vertex angle* is between them. The third side is called the *base* and the other two angles are called the *base angles*.

Example

Spanish

Triángulo isósceles Un triángulo isósceles es un triángulo que tiene por lo menos dos lados congruentes. Si tiene dos lados congruentes, éstos se llaman *catetos*. Entre ellos se encuentra el *ángulo del vértice*. El tercer lado se llama *base* y los otros dos ángulos se llaman *ángulos de base*.

K

Kite A kite is a quadrilateral with two pairs of consecutive sides congruent and no opposite sides congruent.

Example

Cometa Una cometa es un cuadrilátero con dos pares de lados congruentes consecutivos y sin lados opuestos congruentes.

L

Lateral area The lateral area of a prism or pyramid is the sum of the areas of the lateral faces. The lateral area of a cylinder or cone is the area of the curved surface.

Examples

Área lateral El área lateral de un prisma o pirámide es la suma de las áreas de sus caras laterals. El área lateral de un cilindro o de un cono es el área de la superficie curvada.

L.A. of pyramid $= \frac{1}{2}p\ell$

$= \frac{1}{2}(20)(6)$

$= 60 \text{ cm}^2$

Lateral face *See* **prism; pyramid.**

Cara lateral *Ver* **prism; pyramid.**

Law of Cosines In $\triangle ABC$, let a, b, and c represent the lengths of the sides opposite $\angle A$, $\angle B$, and $\angle C$, respectively. Then

$a^2 = b^2 + c^2 - 2bc \cos A,$

$b^2 = a^2 + c^2 - 2ac \cos B,$ and

$c^2 = a^2 + b^2 - 2ab \cos C$

Ley de cosenos En $\triangle ABC$, sean a, b y c las longitudes de los lados opuestos a $\angle A$, $\angle B$, y $\angle C$, respectivamente. Entonces

$a^2 = b^2 + c^2 - 2bc \cos A,$

$b^2 = a^2 + c^2 - 2ac \cos B,$ y

$c^2 = a^2 + b^2 - 2ab \cos C$

Example

$LM^2 = 11.41^2 + 8.72^2 - 2(11.42)(8.72) \cos 18°$

$LM^2 = 16.9754$

$LM = 4.12$

English

Spanish

Law of Detachment The Law of Detachment is a law of logic that states if a conditional statement and its hypothesis are true, then its conclusion is also true. Symbolically, if $p \to q$ and p are true, then q is true.

Regla de eliminación del condicional La ley de eliminación del condicional es una regla lógica que establece que si un enunciado condicional y su hipótesis son ambos verdaderos, entonces la conclusión también será verdadera. Desde un punto de vista simbólico, si $p \to q$ y p son verdaderos, entonces q es verdadero.

Example Suppose the following statements are true.
- If Olivia has at least $10, she can buy the book she wants.
- Olivia has $12.

Then the following is true.
- Olivia can buy the book she wants.

Law of Sines In $\triangle ABC$, let a, b, and c represent the lengths of the sides opposite $\angle A$, $\angle B$, and $\angle C$, respectively. Then $\frac{\sin A}{a} = \frac{\sin B}{b} = \frac{\sin C}{c}$.

Ley de senos En $\triangle ABC$, sean a, b y c las longitudes de los lados opuestos a $\angle A$, $\angle B$ y $\angle C$, respectivamente. Entonces $\frac{\sin A}{a} = \frac{\sin B}{b} = \frac{\sin C}{c}$.

Example

$$m\angle L = 180 - (120 + 18)$$
$$= \frac{KL}{\sin 120°} = \frac{872}{\sin 42°}$$
$$KL = \frac{872 \sin 120°}{\sin 42°}$$
$$KL = 11.26$$

Law of Syllogism The Law of Syllogism is a law of logic that states that given two true conditionals with the conclusion of the first being the hypothesis of the second, there exists a third true conditional having the hypothesis of the first and the conclusion of the second. Symbolically, if $p \to q$ and $q \to r$ are true, then $p \to r$ is true.

Ley del silogismo hipotético La ley del silogismo hipotético es una regla lógica que establece que si se tienen dos condicionales verdaderos en los que la conclusión del primero es la hipótesis del segundo, existe un tercer condicional verdadero compuesto por la hipótesis del primero y la conclusión del segundo. Desde un punto de vista simbólico, si $p \to q$ y $q \to r$ son verdaderos, entonces $p \to r$ es verdadero.

Example Suppose the following statements are true.
- If Renaldo works 20 hours this week, he earns $200.
- If Renaldo earns $200, he buys a new guitar.

Then the following is true.
- If Renaldo works 20 hours this week, he buys a new guitar.

Leg *See* **isosceles triangle; right triangle; trapezoid.**

Cateto *Ver* **isosceles triangle; right triangle; trapezoid.**

Line A line is undefined. You can think of a line as a straight path that extends in two opposite directions without end and has no thickness. A line contains infinitely many points. In spherical geometry, you can think of a line as a great circle of a sphere.

Recta Una recta es indefinida. Se puede pensar en una recta como un camino derecho que se extiende en direcciones opuestas sin fin ni grosor. Una recta tiene un número infinito de puntos. En la geometría esférica, se puede pensar en una recta como un gran círculo de una esfera.

Example

Linear pair A linear pair is a pair of adjacent angles whose noncommon sides are opposite rays.

Par lineal Un par lineal es un par de ángulos adjuntos cuyos lados no comunes son semirrectas opuestas.

Example

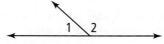

$\angle 1$ and $\angle 2$ are a linear pair.

English

Line of reflection   See **reflection**.

Line of symmetry   See **reflectional symmetry**.

 M

Major arc   A major arc of a circle is an arc that is larger than a semicircle.

Example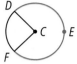

$\overarc{DEF}$ is a major arc of $\odot C$.

Map   See **transformation**.

Measure of an angle   Consider $\overrightarrow{OD}$ and a point C on one side of $\overrightarrow{OD}$. Every ray of the form $\overrightarrow{OC}$ can be paired one to one with a real number from 0 to 180. The measure of $\angle COD$ is the absolute value of the difference of the real numbers paired with $\overrightarrow{OC}$ and $\overrightarrow{OD}$.

Example

$$m\angle COD = 105$$

Measure of an arc   The measure of a minor arc is the measure of its central angle. The measure of a major arc is 360° minus the measure of its related minor arc.

Example

$m\overarc{TY} = 70$
$m\overarc{TXY} = 290$

Median of a triangle   A median of a triangle is a segment that has as its endpoints at a vertex of the triangle and the midpoint of the opposite side.

Example Median

Midpoint of a segment   A midpoint of a segment is the point that divides the segment into two congruent segments.

Example   Midpoint of $\overline{AB}$

Spanish

Eje de reflexión   *Ver* **reflection**.

Eje de simetría   *Ver* **reflectional symmetry**.

Arco mayor   Un arco mayor de un círculo es cualquier arco más grande que un semicírculo.

Trazar   *Ver* **transformation**.

Medida de un ángulo   Toma en cuenta $\overrightarrow{OD}$ y un punto C a un lado de $\overrightarrow{OD}$. Cada semirrecta de la forma $\overrightarrow{OC}$ puede ser emparejada exactamente con un número real de 0 a 180. La medida de $\angle COD$ es el valor absoluto de la diferencia de los números reales emparejados con $\overrightarrow{OC}$ y $\overrightarrow{OD}$

Medida de un arco   La medida de un arco menor es la medida de su ángulo central. La medida de un arco mayor es 360° menos la medida en grados de su arco menor correspondiente.

Mediana de un triángulo   Una mediana de un triángulo es un segmento que tiene en sus extremos el vértice del triángulo y el punto medio del lado opuesto.

Punto medio de un segmento   El punto medio de un segmento es el punto que divide el segmento en dos segmentos congruentes.

English

Spanish

Midsegment of a trapezoid   The midsegment of a trapezoid is the segment that joins the midpoints of the nonparallel opposite sides of a trapezoid.

Segmento medio de un trapecio   El segmento medio de trapecio es el segmento que une los puntos medios de los lados no paralelos de un trapecio.

Example

Midsegment of a triangle   A midsegment of a triangle is a segment that joins the midpoints of two sides of the triangle.

Segmento medio de un triángulo   Un segmento medio de un triángulo es un segmento que une los puntos medios de dos lados del triángulo.

Example

Minor arc   A minor arc is an arc that is smaller than a semicircle.

Arco menor   Un arco menor de un círculo es un arco más corto que un semicírculo.

Example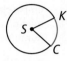

$\overset{\frown}{KC}$ is a minor arc of $\odot S$.

Mutually exclusive events   When two events cannot happen at the same time, the events are mutually exclusive. If A and B are mutually exclusive events, then $P(A \text{ or } B) = P(A) + P(B)$.

Sucesos mutuamente excluyentes   Cuando dos sucesos no pueden ocurrir al mismo tiempo, son mutuamente excluyentes. Si A y B son sucesos mutuamente excluyentes, entonces $P(A \text{ o } B) = P(A) + P(B)$.

Example   Rolling an even number E and rolling a multiple of five M on a standard number cube are mutually exclusive events.

$$P(E \text{ or } M) = P(E) + P(M)$$
$$= \frac{3}{6} + \frac{1}{6}$$
$$= \frac{4}{6}$$
$$= \frac{2}{3}$$

N

Negation   The negation of a statement has the opposite meaning of the original statement.

Negación   La negación de un enunciado tiene el sentido opuesto del enunciado original.

Example   **Statement:** The angle is obtuse.
Negation: The angle is not obtuse.

***n*-gon**   An n-gon is a polygon with n sides.

***n*-ágono**   Un n-ágono es un polígono de n lados.

Example   A polygon with 25 sides is a 25-gon.

Nonagon   A nonagon is a polygon with nine sides.

Nonágono   Un nonágono es un polígono de nueve lados.

Example

English

Oblique cylinder or prism   *See* **cylinder; prism**.

Cilindro oblicuo o prisma   *Ver* **cylinder; prism**.

Obtuse angle   An obtuse angle is an angle whose measure is between 90 and 180.

Ángulo obtuso   Un ángulo obtuso es un ángulo que mide entre 90 y 180.

Example

Obtuse triangle   An obtuse triangle has one obtuse angle.

Triángulo obtusángulo   Un triángulo obtusángulo tiene un ángulo obtuso.

Example

Octagon   An octagon is a polygon with eight sides.

Octágono   Un octágono es un polígono de ocho lados.

Example

Opposite angles   Opposite angles of a quadrilateral are two angles that do not share a side.

Ángulos opuestos   Los ángulos opuestos de un cuadrilátero son dos ángulos que no comparten lados.

Example

∠A and ∠C are opposite angles, as are ∠B and ∠D.

Opposite rays   Opposite rays are collinear rays with the same endpoint. They form a line.

Semirrectas opuestas   Las semirrectas opuestos son semirrectas colineales con el mismo extremo. Forman una recta.

Example

$\overrightarrow{UT}$ and $\overrightarrow{UN}$ are opposite rays.

Opposite sides   Opposite sides of a quadrilateral are two sides that do not share a vertex.

Lados opuestos   Los lados opuestos de un cuadrilátero son dos lados que no tienen un vértice en común.

Example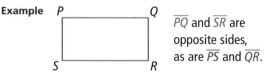

$\overline{PQ}$ and $\overline{SR}$ are opposite sides, as are $\overline{PS}$ and $\overline{QR}$.

Orientation   Two figures have opposite orientation if a reflection is needed to map one onto the other. If a reflection is not needed to map one figure onto the other, the figures have the same orientation.

Orientación   Dos figuras tienen orientación opuesta si una reflexión es necesaria para trazar una sobre la otra. Si una reflexión no es necesaria para trazar una figura sobre la otra, las figuras tienen la misma orientación.

Example   R Я   The two R's have opposite orientation.

VISUAL GLOSSARY

English	Spanish

Origin   *See* **coordinate plane**.

Origen   *Ver* **coordinate plane**.

Orthocenter of a triangle   The orthocenter of a triangle is the point of concurrency of the lines containing the altitudes of the triangle.

Ortocentro de un triángulo   El ortocentro de un triángulo es el punto donde se intersecan las alturas de un triángulo.

Example

D is the orthocenter.

Outcome   An outcome is the result of a single trial in a probability experiment.

Resultado   Un resultado es que se obtiene al hacer una sola prueba en un experimento de probabilidad.

Example   The outcomes of rolling a number cube are
1, 2, 3, 4, 5, and 6

Overlapping events   Overlapping events are events that have at least one common outcome. If *A* and *B* are overlapping events, then $P(A \text{ or } B) = P(A) + P(B) - P(A \text{ and } B)$.

Sucesos traslapados   Sucesos traslapados son sucesos que tienen por lo menos un resultado en común. Si *A* y *B* son sucesos traslapados, entonces $P(A \text{ o } B) = P(A) + P(B) - P(A \text{ y } B)$.

Example   Rolling a multiple of 3 and rolling an odd number on a number cube are overlapping events.

$$P(\text{multiple of 3 or odd}) = P(\text{multiple of 3}) + P(\text{odd}) - P(\text{multiple of 3 and odd})$$
$$= \frac{1}{3} + \frac{1}{2} - \frac{1}{6}$$
$$= \frac{2}{3}$$

P

Parabola   A parabola is the set of all points *P* in a plane that are the same distance from a fixed point *F*, the focus, as they are from a line *d*, the directrix.

Parábola   La parábola es el conjunto de todos los puntos *P* situados en un plano a la misma distancia de un punto fijo *F*, o foco, y de la recta *d*, o directriz.

Example

Paragraph proof   *See* **proof**.

Prueba de párrafo   *Ver* **proof**.

English

Parallel lines Two lines are parallel if they lie in the same plane and do not intersect. The symbol ∥ means "is parallel to."

Example $\ell \parallel m$

Parallelogram A parallelogram is a quadrilateral with two pairs of parallel sides. You can choose any side to be the *base*. An *altitude* is any segment perpendicular to the line containing the base drawn from the side opposite the base. The *height* is the length of an altitude.

Example

Pentagon A pentagon is a polygon with five sides.

Example

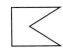

Perimeter of a polygon The perimeter of a polygon is the sum of the lengths of its sides.

Example

$$P = 4 + 4 + 5 + 3$$
$$= 16 \text{ in.}$$

Permutation A permutation is an arrangement of some or all of a set of objects in a specific order. You can use the notation $_nP_r$ to express the number of permutations, where n equals the number of objects available and r equals the number of selections to make.

Example How many ways can you arrange 5 objects 3 at a time?

$$_5P_3 = \frac{5!}{(5-3)!} = \frac{5!}{2!} = \frac{5 \cdot 4 \cdot 3 \cdot 2 \cdot 1}{2 \cdot 1} = 60$$

There are 60 ways to arrange 5 objects 3 at a time.

Perpendicular bisector The perpendicular bisector of a segment is a line, segment, or ray that is perpendicular to the segment and divides the segment into two congruent segments.

Example

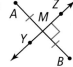

$\overleftrightarrow{YZ}$ is the perpendicular bisector of $\overline{AB}$. It is perpendicular to $\overline{AB}$ and intersects $\overline{AB}$ at midpoint M.

Spanish

Rectas paralelas Dos rectas son paralelas si están en el mismo plano y no se cortan. El símbolo ∥ significa "es paralelo a".

The red symbols indicate parallel lines.

Paralelogramo Un paralelogramo es un cuadrilátero con dos pares de lados paralelos. Se puede escoger cualquier lado como la *base*. Una *altura* es un segmento perpendicular a la recta que contiene la base, trazada desde el lado opuesto a la base. La *altura*, por extensión, es la longitud de una altura.

Pentágono Un pentágono es un polígono de cinco lados.

Perímetro de un polígono El perímetro de un polígono es la suma de las longitudes de sus lados

Permutación Una permutación es una disposición de algunos o de todos los objetos de un conjunto en un orden determinado. El número de permutaciones se puede expresar con la notación $_nP_r$, donde n es igual al número total de objetos y r es igual al número de selecciones que han de hacerse.

Mediatriz La mediatriz de un segmento es una recta, segmento o semirrecta que es perpendicular al segmento y que divide al segmento en dos segmentos congruentes.

English	Spanish

Perpendicular lines   Perpendicular lines are lines that intersect and form right angles. The symbol ⊥ means "is perpendicular to."

Rectas perpendiculares   Las rectas perpendiculares son rectas que se cortan y forman ángulos rectos. El símbolo ⊥ significa "es perpendicular a".

Example

$m \perp n$

Pi   Pi (π) is the ratio of the circumference of any circle to its diameter. The number π is irrational and is approximately 3.14159.

Pi   Pi (π) es la razón de la circunferencia de cualquier írculo a su diámetro. El número π es irracional y se aproxima a $\pi \approx 3.14159$.

Example

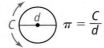

$\pi = \dfrac{C}{d}$

Plane   A plane is undefined. You can think of a plane as a flat surface that extends without end and has no thickness. A plane contains infinitely many lines.

Plano   Un plano es indefinido. Se puede pensar en un plano como una superficie plana sin fin, ni grosor. Un plano tiene un número infinito de rectas.

Example

Plane *ABC* or
plane *Z*

Point   A point is undefined. You can think of a point as a location. A point has no size.

Punto   Un punto es indefinido. Puedes imaginarte a un punto como un lugar. Un punto no tiene dimensión.

Example   • *P*

Point of concurrency   *See* **concurrent lines**.

Punto de concurrencia   *Ver* **concurrent lines**.

Point of tangency   *See* **tangent to a circle**.

Punto de tangencia   *Ver* **tangent to a circle**.

Point-slope form   The point-slope form for a nonvertical line with slope *m* and through point (x_1, y_1) is $y - y_1 = m(x - x_1)$.

Forma punto-pendiente   La forma punto-pendiente para una recta no vertical con pendiente *m* y que pasa por el punto (x_1, y_1) es $y - y_1 = m(x - x_1)$.

Example $y + 1 = 3(x - 4)$
In this equation, the slope is 3 and
(x_1, y_1) is $(4, -1)$

Point symmetry   Point symmetry is the type of symmetry for which there is a rotation of 180° that maps a figure onto itself.

Simetría central   La simetría central es un tipo de simetría en la que una figura se ha rotado 180° sobre sí misma.

Example

180°

English

Polygon A polygon is a closed plane figure formed by three or more segments. Each segment intersects exactly two other segments, but only at their endpoints, and no two segments with a common endpoint are collinear. The *vertices* of the polygon are the endpoints of the sides. A *diagonal* is a segment that connects two nonconsecutive vertices. A polygon is *convex* if no diagonal contains points outside the polygon. A polygon is *concave* if a diagonal contains points outside the polygon.

Example

Polyhedron A polyhedron is a three-dimensional figure whose surfaces, or *faces*, are polygons. The vertices of the polygons are the *vertices* of the polyhedron. The intersections of the faces are the *edges* of the polyhedron.

Example

Postulate A postulate is an accepted statement of fact.

Example **Postulate:** Through any two points there is exactly one line.

Preimage *See* **transformation**.

Prime notation *See* **transformation**.

Prism A prism is a polyhedron with two congruent and parallel faces, which are called the *bases*. The other faces, which are parallelograms, are called the *lateral faces*. An *altitude* of a prism is a perpendicular segment that joins the planes of the bases. Its length is the *height* of the prism. A *right prism* is one whose lateral faces are rectangular regions and a lateral edge is an altitude. In an *oblique prism*, some or all of the lateral faces are nonrectangular.

Example

Spanish

Polígono Un polígono es una figura plana compuesta por tres o más segmentos. Cada segmento interseca los otros dos segmentos exactamente, pero únicamente en sus puntos extremos y ningúno de los segmentos con extremos comunes son colineales. Los *vértices* del polígono son los extremos de los lados. Una *diagonal* es un segmento que conecta dos vértices no consecutivos. Un polígono es *convexo* si ninguna diagonal tiene puntos fuera del polígono. Un polígono es *cóncavo* si una diagonal tiene puntos fuera del polígono.

Poliedro Un poliedro es una figura tridimensional cuyas superficies, o *caras*, son polígonos. Los vértices de los polígonos son los *vértices* del poliedro. Las intersecciones de las caras son las *aristas* del poliedro.

Postulado Un postulado es un enunciado que se acepta como un hecho.

Preimagen *Ver* **transformation**.

Notación prima *Ver* **transformation**.

Prisma Un prisma es un poliedro con dos caras congruentes paralelas llamadas *bases*. Las otras caras son paralelogramos llamados *caras laterales*. La *altura* de un prisma es un segmento perpendicular que une los planos de las bases. Su longitud es también la *altura* del prisma. En un *prisma rectangular*, las caras laterales son rectangulares y una de las aristas laterales es la altura. En un *prisma oblicuo*, algunas o todas las caras laterales no son rectangulares.

English

Spanish

Probability   Probability is the likelihood that an event will occur (written formally as *P*(event)).

Probabilidad   Probabilidad es la posibilidad de que un suceso ocurra, escrita formalmente *P*(suceso).

Example   You have 4 red marbles and 3 white marbles. The probability that you select one red marble, and then, without replacing it, randomly select another red marble is $P(\text{red}) = \frac{4}{7} \cdot \frac{3}{6} = \frac{2}{7}$.

Probability distribution   A probability distribution for an experiment is a function that assigns a probability to each outcome of a sample space for the experiment.

Distribución de probabilidades   La distribución de probabilidades de un experimento es una función que asigna una probabilidad a cada resultado de un espacio muestral del experimento.

Example

Roll	Fr.	Prob.
1	5	0.125
2	9	0.225
3	7	0.175
4	8	0.2
5	8	0.2
6	3	0.075

The table and graph both show the experimental probability distribution for the outcomes of 40 rolls of a standard number cube.

Proof   A proof is a convincing argument that uses deductive reasoning. A proof can be written in many forms. In a two-column proof, the statements and reasons are aligned in columns. In a paragraph proof, the statements and reasons are connected in sentences. In a flow proof, arrows show the logical connections between the statements. In a coordinate proof, a figure is drawn on a coordinate plane and the formulas for slope, midpoint, and distance are used to prove properties of the figure. An indirect proof involves the use of indirect reasoning.

Prueba   Una prueba es un argumento convincente en el cual se usa el razonamiento deductivo. Una prueba se puede escribir de varias maneras. En una *prueba de dos columnas*, los enunciados y las razones se alinean en columnas. En una *prueba de párrafo*, los enunciados y razones están unidos en oraciones. En una *prueba de flujo*, hay flechas que indican las conexiones lógicas entre enunciados. En una *prueba de coordenadas*, se dibuja una figura en un plano de coordenadas y se usan las fórmulas de la pendiente, punto medio y distancia para probar las propiedades de la figura. Una *prueba indirecta* incluye el uso de razonamiento indirecto.

Example

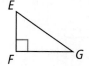

Given: $\triangle EFG$, with right angle $\angle F$
Prove: $\angle E$ and $\angle G$ are complementary.

Paragraph Proof: Because $\angle F$ is a right angle, $m\angle F = 90$. By the Triangle Angle-Sum Theorem, $m\angle E + m\angle F + m\angle G = 180$. By substitution, $m\angle E + 90 + m\angle G = 180$. Subtracting 90 from each side yields $m\angle E + m\angle G = 90$. $\angle E$ and $\angle G$ are complementary by definition.

English

Proportion   A proportion is a statement that two ratios are equal. An *extended proportion* is a statement that three or more ratios are equal.

Example $\frac{x}{5} = \frac{3}{4}$ is a proportion.

$\frac{9}{27} = \frac{3}{9} = \frac{1}{3}$ is an extended proportion.

Pyramid   A pyramid is a polyhedron in which one face, the *base*, is a polygon and the other faces, the *lateral faces*, are triangles with a common vertex, called the *vertex* of the pyramid. An *altitude* of a pyramid is the perpendicular segment from the vertex to the plane of the base. Its length is the *height* of the pyramid. The *slant height* of a regular pyramid is the length of an altitude of a lateral face.

Example

Pyramid

Pythagorean triple   A Pythagorean triple is a set of three nonzero whole numbers a, b, and c, that satisfy the equation $a^2 + b^2 = c^2$.

Example   The numbers 5, 12, and 13 form a Pythagorean triple because $5^2 + 12^2 = 13^2 = 169$.

Quadrant   *See* **coordinate plane.**

Quadrilateral   A quadrilateral is a polygon with four sides.

Example

Radian   A radian is equal to the measure of a central angle that intercepts an arc with length equal to the radius of the circle.

Example

Spanish

Proporción   Una proporción es un enunciado en el cual dos razones son iguales. Una *proporción extendida* es un enunciado que dice que tres razones o más son iguales.

Pirámide   Una pirámide es un poliedro en donde una cara, la *base*, es un polígono y las otras caras, las *caras laterales*, son triángulos con un vértice común, llamado el *vértice* de la pirámide. Una *altura* de una pirámide es el segmento perpendicular que va del vértice hasta el plano de la base. Su longitud es, por extensión, la *altura* de la pirámide. La *apotema* de una pirámide regular es la longitud de la altura de la cara lateral.

Tripleta de Pitágoras   Una tripleta de Pitágoras es un conjunto de tres números enteros positivos a, b, and c que satisfacen la ecuación $a^2 + b^2 = c^2$.

Cuadrante   *Ver* **coordinate plane.**

Cuadrilátero   Un cuadrilátero es un polígono de cuatro lados.

Radián   Un radián es igual a la medida de un ángulo central que interseca a un ángulo de la misma longitud que el radio del círculo.

English

Radius of a circle   A radius of a circle is any segment with one endpoint on the circle and the other endpoint at the center of the circle. *Radius* can also mean the length of this segment.

Example 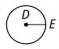 $\overline{DE}$ is a radius of $\odot D$.

Radius of a sphere   The radius of a sphere is a segment that has one endpoint at the center and the other endpoint on the sphere.

Example

Ratio   A ratio is a comparison of two quantities by division. An *extended ratio* is a comparison of three or more quantities by division.

Example   5 to 7, 5 : 7, and $\frac{5}{7}$ are ratios.

3 : 5 : 6 is an extended ratio.

Ray   A ray is the part of a line that consists of one *endpoint* and all the points of the line on one side of the endpoint.

Example

Rectangle   A rectangle is a parallelogram with four right angles.

Example

Reduction   *See* **dilation**.

Reflection   A reflection across line *r*, called the *line of reflection*, is a transformation such that if a point *A* is on line *r*, then the image of *A* is itself, and if a point *B* is not on line *r*, then its image *B′* is the point such that *r* is the perpendicular bisector of $\overline{BB'}$. A reflection is a rigid motion.

Example

Spanish

Radio de un círculo   Un radio de un círculo es cualquier segmento con extremo en el círculo y el otro extremo en el centro del círculo. *Radio* también se refiere a la longitude de este segmento.

Radio de una esfera   El radio de una esfera es un segmento con un extremo en el centro y otro en la esfera.

Razón   Una razón es una comparación de dos cantidades usando la división. Una *razón extendida* es una comparación de tres o más cantidades usando la división.

Semirrecta   Una semirrecta es la parte de una recta que tiene un *extremo* de donde parten todos los puntos de la recta.

Rectángulo   Un rectángulo es un paralelogramo con cuatro ángulos rectos.

Reducción   *Ver* **dilation**.

Reflexión   Una reflexión a través de una línea *r*, llamada el *eje de reflexión*, es una transformación en la que si un punto *A* es parte de la línea *r*, la imagen de *A* es sí misma, y si un punto *B* no está en la línea *r*, su imagen *B′* es el punto en el cual la línea *r* es la bisectriz perpendicular de $\overline{BB'}$. Una reflexión es un movimiento rígido.

English

Reflectional symmetry   Reflectional symmetry is the type of symmetry for which there is a reflection that maps a figure onto itself. The reflection line is the *line of symmetry*. The line of symmetry divides a figure with reflectional symmetry into two congruent halves.

Example

A reflection across the given line maps the figure onto itself.

Regular polygon   A regular polygon is a polygon that is both equilateral and equiangular. Its *center* is the point that is equidistant from its vertices.

Example

ABCDEF is a regular hexagon. Point *X* is its center.

Relative frequency   The relative frequency of an event is the ratio of the number of times the event occurs to the total number of trials.

Example

Archery Results					
Scoring Region	Yellow	Red	Blue	Black	White
Arrow Strikes	52	25	10	8	5

$$\text{Relative frequency of striking red} = \frac{\text{frequency of striking red}}{\text{total frequencies}}$$
$$= \frac{25}{100} = \frac{1}{4}$$

Remote interior angles   Remote interior angles are the two nonadjacent interior angles corresponding to each exterior angle of a triangle.

Example

$\angle 1$ and $\angle 2$ are remote interior angles of $\angle 3$.

Rhombus   A rhombus is a parallelogram with four congruent sides.

Example

Right angle   A right angle is an angle whose measure is 90.

Example

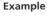

Spanish

Simetría reflexiva   Simetría reflexiva es el tipo de simetría donde hay una reflexión que ubica una figura en sí misma. El eje de reflexión es *el eje de simetría*. El eje de simetría divide una figura con simetría reflexiva en dos mitades congruentes.

Polígono regular   Un polígono regular es un polígono que es equilateral y equiangular. Su *centro* es el punto equidistante de sus vértices.

Frecuencia relativa   La frecuencia relativa de un suceso es la razón del número de veces que ocurre un evento al número de eventos en el espacio muestral.

Ángulos interiores remotos   Los ángulos interiores remotos son los dos ángulos interiores no adyacentes que corresponden a cada ángulo exterior de un triángulo.

Rombo   Un rombo es un paralelogramo de cuatro lados congruentes.

Ángulo recto   Un ángulo recto es un ángulo que mide 90.

This symbol indicates a right angle.

English

Right cone   *See* **cone**.

Right cylinder   *See* **cylinder**.

Right prism   *See* **prism**.

Right triangle   A right triangle contains one right angle. The side opposite the right angle is the *hypotenuse* and the other two sides are the *legs*.

Example

Leg   Hypotenuse   Leg

Rigid motion   A rigid motion is a transformation that preserves distance and angle measure. A rigid motion is sometimes called a *congruence transformation*.

Example   The four rigid motions are reflections, translations, rotations, and glide reflections.

Rotation   A rotation of *x* about a point *R*, called the *center of rotation*, is a transformation such that for any point *V*, its image is the point *V'*, where $RV = RV'$ and $m\angle VRV' = x$. The image of *R* is itself. The positive number of degrees *x* that a figure rotates is the *angle of rotation*. A rotation is a rigid motion.

Example

Rotational symmetry   Rotational symmetry is the type of symmetry for which there is a rotation of 360° or less that maps a figure onto itself.

Example

The figure has 120° rotational symmetry.

S

Same-side interior angles   Same-side interior angles lie on the same side of the transversal *t* and between ℓ and *m*.

Example

$\angle 1$ and $\angle 2$ are same-side interior angles, as are $\angle 3$ and $\angle 4$.

Spanish

Cono recto   *Ver* **cone**.

Cilindro recto   *Ver* **cylinder**.

Prisma rectangular   *Ver* **prism**.

Triángulo rectángulo   Un triángulo rectángulo contiene un ángulo recto. El lado opuesto del ángulo recto es la *hipotenusa* y los otros dos lados son los *catetos*.

Movimiento rígido   Un movimiento rígido es una transformación en el plano que no cambia la distancia ni la medida del ángulo. Los movimientos rígidos se conocen a veces como *transformaciones de congruencia*.

Rotación   Una rotación de x sobre un punto *R*, llamado el *centro de rotación*, es una transformación en la que para cualquier punto *V*, su imagen es el punto *V'*, donde $RV = RV'$ y $m\angle VRV' = x$. La imagen de *R* es sí misma. El número positivo de grados *x* que una figura rota es el *ángulo de rotación*. Una rotación es un movimiento rígido.

Simetría rotacional   La simetría rotacional es un tipo de simetría en la que una rotación de 360° o menos vuelve a trazar una figura sobre sí misma.

Ángulos internos del mismo lado   Los ángulos internos del mismo lado están situados en el mismo lado de la transversal *t* y dentro de ℓ y *m*.

English

Sample space   A sample space is the set of all possible outcomes of a situation or experiment.

Example   When you roll a standard number cube, the sample space is {1, 2, 3, 4, 5, 6}.

Scale   A scale is the ratio of any length in a scale drawing to the corresponding actual length. The lengths may be in different units.

Example   1 cm to 1 ft
1 cm = 1 ft
1 cm : 1 ft

Scale drawing   A scale drawing is a drawing in which all lengths are proportional to corresponding actual lengths.

Example

Scale factor   A scale factor is the ratio of corresponding linear measurements of two similar figures.

Example

$\triangle ABC \sim \triangle DEF$

$\dfrac{AB}{DE} = \dfrac{BC}{EF} = \dfrac{CA}{FD}$

Scale factor of a dilation   The scale factor of a dilation is the ratio of the distances from the center of dilation to an image point and to its preimage point.

Example

The scale factor of the dilation that maps $\triangle ABC$ to $\triangle A'B'C'$ is $\frac{1}{2}$.

Scalene triangle   A scalene triangle has no congruent sides.

Example

Spanish

Espacio muestral   Un espacio muestral es el conjunto de todos los resultados posibles de un suceso.

Escala   Una escala es la razón de cualquier longitud en un dibujo a escala en relación a la longitud verdadera correspondiente. Las longitudes pueden expresarse en distintas unidades.

Dibujo a escala   Un dibujo a escala es un dibujo en el que todas las longitudes son proporcionales a las longitudes verdaderas correspondientes.

Factor de escala   El factor de escala es la razón de las medidas lineales correspondientes de dos figuras semejantes.

Factor de escala de dilatación   El factor de escala de dilatación es la razón de las distancias desde el centro de dilatación hasta un punto de la imagen y hasta un punto de la preimagen.

Triángulo escaleno   Un triángulo escaleno no tiene lados congruentes.

English

Secant A secant is a line, ray, or segment that intersects a circle at two points.

Example

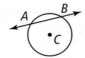

$\overleftrightarrow{AB}$ is a secant of $\odot C$.

Sector of a circle A sector of a circle is the region bounded by two radii and the intercepted arc.

Example

Sector *APB*

Segment A segment is the part of a line that consists of two points, called *endpoints*, and all points between them.

Example

Endpoints of $\overline{DE}$

Segment bisector A segment bisector is a line, segment, ray, or plane that intersects a segment at the midpoint.

Example

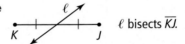

ℓ bisects $\overline{KJ}$.

Segment of a circle A segment of a circle is the part of a circle bounded by an arc and the segment joining its endpoints.

Example

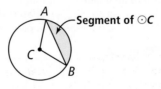

Segment of $\odot C$

Semicircle A semicircle is half a circle.

Example

Semicircle

Side *See* **angle; polygon.**

Spanish

Secante Una secante es una recta, semirrecta o segmento que corta un círculo en dos puntos.

Sector de un círculo Un sector de un círculo es la región limitada por dos radios y el arco abarcado por ellos.

Segmento Un segmento es la parte de una recta que tiene dos puntos, llamados *extremos*, entre los cuales están todos los puntos de esa recta.

Bisectriz de un segmento La bisectriz de un segmento es una recta, segmento, semirrecta o plano que corta un segmento en el punto medio.

Segmento de un círculo Un segmento de un círculo es la parte de un círculo bordeada por un arco y el segmento que une sus extremos.

Semicírculo Un semicírculo es la mitad de un círculo.

Lado *Ver* **angle; polygon.**

English

Similar figures   Similar figures are two figures that have the same shape, but not necessarily the same size. Two figures are similar if there is a similarity transformation that maps one figure to the other.

Example

Similarity transformation   A composition of one or more rigid motions and a dilation.

Similar polygons   Similar polygons are polygons having corresponding angles congruent and the lengths of corresponding sides proportional. Similarity is denoted by ∼.

Example

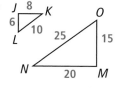

$\triangle JKL \sim \triangle MNO$

Scale factor $= \frac{2}{5}$

Sine ratio   *See* **trigonometric ratios.**

Slant height   *See* **cone; pyramid.**

Slope-intercept form   The slope-intercept form of a linear equation is $y = mx + b$, where m is the slope of the line and b is the y-intercept.

Example $y = \frac{1}{2}x - 3$

In this equation, the slope is $\frac{1}{2}$ and the y-intercept is -3.

Slope of a line   The slope of a line is the ratio of its vertical change in the coordinate plane to the corresponding horizontal change. If (x_1, y_1) and (x_2, y_2) are points on a nonvertical line, then the slope is $\frac{y_2 - y_1}{x_2 - x_1}$. The slope of a horizontal line is 0, and the slope of a vertical line is undefined.

Example

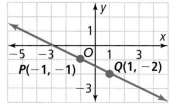

The line containing $P(-1, -1)$ and $Q(1, -2)$ has slope $\frac{-2 - (-1)}{1 - (-1)} = \frac{-1}{2} = -\frac{1}{2}$.

Spanish

Figuras semejantes   Los figuras semejantes son dos figuras que tienen la misma forma pero no necesariamente el mismo tamaño. Dos figuras son semejantes si hay una transformación de semajanza en la que una figura es la imagen de la otra.

Transformación de semejanza   Una composición de uno o más movimientos rígidos y una dilatación.

Polígonos semejantes   Los polígonos semejantes son polígonos cuyos ángulos correspondientes son congruentes y las longitudes de los lados correspondientes son proporcionales. El símbolo ∼ significa "es semejante a".

Razón seno   *Ver* **trigonometric ratios.**

Generatriz (cono) o apotema (pirámide)   *Ver* **cone; pyramid.**

Forma pendiente-intercepto   La forma pendiente-intercepto es la ecuación lineal $y = mx + b$, en la que m es la pendiente de la recta y b es el punto de intersección de esa recta con el eje y.

Pendiente de una recta   La pendiente de una recta es la razón del cambio vertical en el plano de coordenadas en relación al cambio horizontal correspondiente. Si (x_1, y_1) y (x_2, y_2) son puntos en una recta no vertical, entonces la pendiente es $\frac{y_2 - y_1}{x_2 - x_1}$. La pendiente de una recta horizontal es 0, y la pendiente de una recta vertical es indefinida.

English	Spanish

Sphere   A sphere is the set of all points in space that are a given distance *r*, the *radius*, from a given point *C*, the *center*. A *great circle* is the intersection of a sphere with a plane containing the center of the sphere. The *circumference* of a sphere is the circumference of any great circle of the sphere.

Esfera   Una esfera es el conjunto de los puntos del espacio que están a una distancia dada *r*, el *radio*, de un punto dado *C*, el *centro*. Un *círculo máximo* es la intersección de una esfera y un plano que contiene el centro de la esfera. La *circunferencia* de una esfera es la circunferencia de cualquier círculo máximo de la esfera.

Example

Square   A square is a parallelogram with four congruent sides and four right angles.

Cuadrado   Un cuadrado es un paralelogramo con cuatro lados congruentes y cuatro ángulos rectos.

Example

Straight angle   A straight angle is an angle whose measure is 180.

Ángulo llano   Un ángulo llano es un ángulo que mide 180.

Example

$$m\angle AOB = 180°$$

Straightedge   A straightedge is a tool for drawing straight lines.

Regla sin graduación   Una regla sin graduación es un instrumento para dibujar líneas rectas.

Supplementary angles   Two angles are supplementary if the sum of their measures is 180.

Ángulos suplementarios   Dos ángulos son suplementarios cuando sus medidas suman 180.

Example

$\angle MNP$ and $\angle ONP$ are supplementary,
as are $\angle MNP$ and $\angle QRS$.

Surface area   The surface area of a prism, cylinder, pyramid, or cone is the sum of the lateral area and the areas of the bases. The surface area of a sphere is four times the area of a great circle.

Área   El área de un prisma, pirámide, cilindro o cono es la suma del área lateral y las áreas de las bases. El área de una esfera es igual a cuatro veces el área de un círculo máximo.

Example

S.A. of prism = L.A. + 2*B*
             = 66 + 2(28)
             = 122 cm²

English

Symmetry A figure has symmetry if there is a rigid motion that maps the figure onto itself. *See also* **point symmetry; reflectional symmetry; rotational symmetry.**

Example

Spanish

Simetría Una figura tiene simetría si hay un movimiento rígido que traza la figura sobre sí misma. *Ver también* **point symmetry; reflectional symmetry; rotational symmetry.**

A regular pentagon has reflectional symmetry and 72° rotational symmetry.

T

Tangent ratio *See* **trigonometric ratios.**

Razón tangente *Ver* **trigonometric ratios.**

Tangent to a circle A tangent to a circle is a line in the plane of the circle that intersects the circle in exactly one point. That point is the *point of tangency.*

Tangente de un círculo Una tangente de un círculo es una recta en el plano del círculo que corta el círculo en exactamente un punto. Ese punto es el *punto de tangencia.*

Example

Point of tangency

Line ℓ is tangent to $\odot C$. Point D is the point of tangency.

Theorem A theorem is a conjecture that is proven.

Teorema Un teorema es una conjetura que se demuestra.

Example The theorem "Vertical angles are congruent" can be proven by using postulates, definitions, properties, and previously stated theorems.

Theoretical probability The theoretical probability is the ratio of the number of favorable outcomes to the number of possible outcomes if all outcomes have the same chance of happening.

$$P(\text{event}) = \frac{\text{number of favorable outcomes}}{\text{number of possible outcomes}}$$

Probabilidad teórica Si cada resultado tiene la misma probabilidad de darse, la probabilidad teórica de un suceso se calcula como la razón del número de resultados favorables al número de resultados posibles.

$$P(\text{suceso}) = \frac{\text{numero de resultados favorables}}{\text{numero de resultados posibles}}$$

Example In tossing a coin, the events of getting heads or tails are equally likely. The likelihood of getting heads is $P(\text{heads}) = \frac{1}{2}$.

VISUAL GLOSSARY

English

Spanish

Transformation A transformation is a change in the position, size, or shape of a geometric figure. The given figure is called the *preimage* and the resulting figure is called the *image*. A transformation *maps* a figure onto its image. *Prime notation* is sometimes used to identify image points. In the diagram, *X'* (read "*X* prime") is the image of *X*.

Transformación Una transformación es un cambio en la posición, tamaño o forma de una figura. La figura dada se llama la *preimagen* y la figura resultante se llama la *imagen*. Una transformación *traza* la figura sobre su propia imagen. La *notación prima* a veces se utilize para identificar los puntos de la imagen. En el diagrama de la derecha, *X'* (leído *X* prima) es la imagen de *X*.

Example

$\triangle XYZ \rightarrow \triangle X'Y'Z'$

Translation A translation is a transformation that moves points the same distance and in the same direction. A translation is a rigid motion.

Traslación Una traslación es una transformación en la que se mueven puntos la misma distancia en la misma dirección. Una traslación es un movimiento rígido.

Example

The blue triangle is the image of the black triangle under the translation $\langle -5, -2 \rangle$.

Transversal A transversal is a line that intersects two or more lines at distinct points.

Transversal Una transversal es una línea que interseca dos o más líneas en puntos precisos.

Example

t is a transversal of ℓ and *m*.

Trapezoid A trapezoid is a quadrilateral with exactly one pair of parallel sides, the *bases*. The nonparallel sides are called the *legs* of the trapezoid. Each pair of angles adjacent to a base are *base angles* of the trapezoid. An *altitude* of a trapezoid is a perpendicular segment from one base to the line containing the other base. Its length is called the *height* of the trapezoid.

Trapecio Un trapecio es un cuadrilátero con exactamente un par de lados paralelos, las *bases*. Los lados no paralelos se llaman los *catetos* del trapecio. Cada par de ángulos adyacentes a la base son los *ángulos de base* del trapecio. Una *altura* del trapecio es un segmento perpendicular que va de una base a la recta que contiene la otra base. Su longitud se llama, por extensión, la *altura* del trapecio.

Example

In trapezoid *ABCD*, $\angle ADC$ and $\angle BCD$ are one pair of base angles, and $\angle DAB$ and $\angle ABC$ are the other.

English

Triangle   A triangle is a polygon with three sides. You can choose any side to be a *base*. The *height* is the length of the altitude drawn to the line containing that base.

Example

Trigonometric ratios   The trigonometric ratios, or functions, relate the side lengths of a right triangle to its acute angles. In right $\triangle ABC$ with acute $\angle A$,

$$\text{sine } \angle A = \sin A = \frac{\text{length of leg opposite } \angle A}{\text{length of hypotenuse}}$$

$$\text{cosine } \angle A = \cos A = \frac{\text{length of leg adjacent to } \angle A}{\text{length of hypotenuse}}$$

$$\text{tangent } \angle A = \tan A = \frac{\text{length of leg opposite } \angle A}{\text{length of leg adjacent to } \angle A}$$

Example

Truth table   A truth table is a table that lists all the possible combinations of truth values for two or more statements.

Example

p	q	$p \rightarrow q$
T	T	T
T	F	F
F	T	T
F	F	T

Truth value   The truth value of a statement is "true" (T) or "false" (F) according to whether the statement is true or false, respectively.

Two-column proof   *See* **proof**.

Spanish

Triángulo   Un triángulo es un polígono con tres lados. Se puede escoger cualquier lado como *base*. La *altura*, entonces, es la longitud de la altura trazada hasta la recta que contiene la base.

Razones trigonométricas   Las razones trigonométricas, o funiones, relacionan las longitudes de lado de un triángulo rectángulo con sus ángulos agudos. En un triángulo rectángulo $\triangle ABC$ con ángulo agudo $\angle A$,

$$\text{seno } \angle A = \text{sen } A = \frac{\text{cateto opuesto a } \angle A}{\text{hipotenusa}}$$

$$\text{coseno } \angle A = \cos A = \frac{\text{cateto adyecente a } \angle A}{\text{hipotenusa}}$$

$$\text{tangente } \angle A = \tan A = \frac{\text{cateto opuesto a } \angle A}{\text{cateto adyecente a } \angle A}$$

Tabla de verdad   Una tabla de verdad es una tabla que muestra todas las combinaciones posibles de valores de verdad de dos o más enunciados.

Valor verdadero   El valor verdadero de un enunciado es "verdadero" (T) o "falso" (F) según el enunciado sea verdadero o falso, respectivamente.

Prueba de dos columnas   *Ver* **proof**.

English

Spanish

Two-way frequency table A two-way frequency table is a table that displays frequencies in two different categories.

Tabla de frecuencias de doble entrada Una tabla de frecuencias de doble entrada es una tabla de frecuencias que contiene dos categorías de datos.

Example

	Male	Female	Totals
Juniors	3	4	7
Seniors	3	2	5
Totals	6	6	12

The last column shows a total of 7 juniors and 5 seniors. The last row shows a total of 6 males and 6 females.

Uniform probability distribution A uniform probability distribution assigns the same probability to each outcome.

Distribución uniforme de probabilidad Una distribución uniforme de probabilidad le asigna la misma probabilidad a cada resultado.

Vertex *See* **angle; cone; polygon; polyhedron; pyramid.** The plural form of *vertex* is *vertices*.

Vértice *Ver* **angle; cone; polygon; polyhedron; pyramid.**

Vertex angle *See* **isosceles triangle.**

Ángulo del vértice *Ver* **isosceles triangle.**

Vertical angles Vertical angles are two angles whose sides form two pairs of opposite rays.

Ángulos opuestos por el vértice Dos ángulos son ángulos opuestos por el vértice si sus lados son semirrectas opuestas.

Example

$\angle 1$ and $\angle 2$ are vertical angles, as are $\angle 3$ and $\angle 4$.

Volume Volume is a measure of the space a figure occupies.

Volumen El volumen es una medida del espacio que ocupa una figura.

Index

A

AA ~ (Angle-Angle Similarity) Theorem, 321–322, 325

AAS (Angle-Angle-Side) Congruence Criterion, 178, 180, 187, 192, 198

algebra, 389–383, 538

Alternate Exterior Angles Theorem, 73, 75

Alternate Interior Angles Theorem, 72–73, 75

altitude, 222, 225–229, 244, 328–329, 330, 333

Angle Addition Postulate, 8, 9

Angle-Angle-Side (AAS) Congruence Criterion, 178, 180, 187, 192, 198

Angle-Angle Similarity (AA ~) Theorem, 321–322, 325

angle bisectors
concept summary of, 210, 243
construction of, 16, 17, 18, 65
defined, 16
equidistant points and, 208–212, 243
practice and problem solving, 211–212, 243
proportionality and, 340
of triangles, 216, 218, 244, 340, 341

Angle Bisector Theorem, 209, 210

angles
addition of, 8, 9
bisectors of. *See* angle bisectors
construction of, 14
defined, 5
of isosceles triangles, 159–167, 197
measuring, 4–12, 64
parallel lines and, 71–75, 79–80, 102
of parallelograms, 266, 268–269, 272, 276–277, 280, 299
of polygons, 249–255, 299
of rhombuses, 283–284, 287, 290–291, 295
of squares, 286, 287
of triangles, 86–92, 103
trigonometric inverses and, 361
vertex, 161, 167, 457, 460

angles, types of
alternate, 80, 81, 83
central, 423, 440–441, 445
complementary, 53
congruent, 9, 16, 36, 53, 64
consecutive, 268–269, 269, 299
corresponding, 73, 75, 79–80, 81, 83
of depression, 378–379, 381, 385
of elevation, 378–379, 381, 385

exterior. *See* exterior angles
inscribed, 448–454, 465
interior. *See* interior angles
opposite, 268–269, 272, 299
vertical, 51–52

Angle-Side-Angle Congruence Criterion, 175–177, 180, 187, 198

angle-sum theorems of polygons, 249–255, 298

arc length, 424–425, 428, 451, 463

arcs, 18, 423–430, 441, 445, 448, 450–452, 463

area
coordinate plane and, 392
scale factors and, 310
of sectors, 426, 428
of segment of circles, 426–427, 428
surface, 479
of triangles, 380

B

basic figure constructions. *See* constructions

biconditional statements, 38–39. *See also* conditional statements

binomial experiments, 529–530, 531, 550

binomial probability, 530, 537, 544, 550

bisectors. *See* angle bisectors; perpendicular bisectors

bridge designs, 150

building heights, 377

C

cardboard box designs, 468

Cavalieri's Principle, 475, 480, 484, 488, 491, 494, 498

center of dilation, 305, 315, 345

center of gravity, 225

center of mass, 202

central angles, 423, 440–441, 445

centroids, 223–224, 227, 244

chords, 440–447, 459, 464

circles, 420–465
arcs of, 423–430, 463
chords of, 440–447, 458, 464
circumscribed, 214–215
concept summary, 428, 436, 445, 452, 460

construction of, 13, 18
in coordinate plane system, 404–409, 4149
inscribed, 216
inscribed angles of, 448–454, 465
notations for, 405
practice and problem solving, 429–430, 437–438, 446–447, 453–454, 461–462
secant lines and segments, 455–462, 465
sectors of, 426–430, 463
similar, 317
tangent lines of, 431–438, 457, 464

circumcenters, 215, 218, 244

circumference, 424

circumscribed circles, 210–215

collinear points, 7

collinear rays, 5

combinations, probability of, 519–525, 549

compasses, 13–16, 18, 69, 205

complementary angles, 53

complement of events, 504

composite figures, 487, 493

compositions of rigid motions, 117–118, 120

conclusions
biconditional statements and, 39
conditional statements and, 35–37, 66
from deductive reasoning, 43–47, 67
defined, 35
from indirect reasoning, 59
from inductive reasoning, 27, 66

Concurrency of Altitudes, 225

Concurrency of Angle Bisectors, 216

Concurrency of Medians, 223, 399–400

Concurrency of Perpendicular Bisectors, 2013–214

concurrent lines, 214

conditional probability, 511–517, 549

conditional statements, 35–42
biconditional, 38–39
concept summary, 40, 66
defined, 35
practice and problem solving, 41–42, 66
related, 37–39
truth value, finding, 36–39
writing, 35–36

E

endpoints, 5

equations
of circles, 404–407, 418
of parabolas, 411–414, 419
of parallel lines, 97, 103
of perpendicular lines, 97–100, 103

equidistant points, 205, 209–212, 243, 410

equilateral triangles, 163–167, 197

Euler's Formula, 469–470, 472

events, probability of, 503–510, 548

expected value, 534–540, 543, 545, 550

experimental probability distribution, 528–529

exterior angles
of parallel lines, 71, 73, 75, 81, 83
of polygons, 251–252, 253, 298
of triangles, 88–889, 90

F

factorial, 520

fair decisions, 541–542

flow proofs, 80

focus, 411, 419

formulas
for arc length, 424–425, 428, 463
for area. *See* area
binomial probability, 530
for combination numbers, 522, 523
conditional probability, 511–515
of coordinate geometry, 389–393, 417
distance, 22–23, 24, 65
Euler's Formula, 469–470, 472
midpoint, 21, 22, 65, 389, 393
for permutation numbers, 521, 523
for probability. *See* probability
for sectors, 426, 428
for segments of circles, 426–427, 428
slope, 94, 97, 103, 391, 393
for volume. *See* volume

45°-45°-90° Triangle Theorem, 352, 355

Fundamental Counting Principle, 519–520

G

geometric means, 329–332, 333, 345

glide reflections, 132–135

golden ratio, 4

graphs. *See* coordinate plane systems

great circles, 493

H

hemispheres, 493

Hinge Theorem, 238, 240, 245

hydraulic lift designs, 248

Hypotenuse-Leg (HL) Theorem, 185–187, 192, 198

hypotheses
of biconditional statements, 39
of conditional statements, 35–36, 37, 39, 66
for deductive reasoning, 43–45, 47
of related conditional statements, 37

I

incenter, 216–217, 218, 244

independent events, 505–507, 508, 512–513, 515, 548

indirect proofs, 58–63, 67
concept summary, 61, 67
contradictions and, 59
contrapositives and, 60
defined, 59
indirect reasoning and, 58
practice and problem solving, 62–63, 67

indirect reasoning, 58–59. *See also* indirect proofs

inductive reasoning, 27–34, 66
concept summary, 31, 66
conjectures, 28–30
mathematical modeling of, 34
patterns and, 27–31
practice and problem solving, 32–33, 66

inequalities in triangles, 230–236, 237–242, 245

inscribed angles, 448–454, 465

Inscribed Angles Theorem, 449–450

inscribed circles, 216

intercepted arcs, 423, 448, 450–452

interior angles
of parallel lines, 72–73, 80–81, 83
of polygons, 249–250, 253, 298
of triangles, 86–88, 90

inverse of conditional statements, 37, 38, 40, 66

isosceles trapezoids, 259–262, 263

isosceles triangles, 159–167, 197

Isosceles Triangle Theorem, 160

K

kites, 257–258, 263–265, 300, 391

L

Law of Cosines, 371–376, 385

Law of Detachment, 44, 46, 47, 67

Law of Sines, 365–371, 385

Law of Syllogism, 45–47, 67

Linear Pairs Theorem, 54

lines. *See also* angle bisectors; parallel lines; perpendicular bisectors; perpendicular lines; segments
collinear points on, 7
construction of, 13, 18, 65
coordinate points on, 6, 10
defined, 4
distance on, 6
of reflection, 108–112
secant, 455–462, 465
of symmetry, 138–139, 141
tangent, of circles, 431–439, 464

M

major arcs, 423

means, geometric, 329–332, 333, 345

median, 222–224, 227–229, 244

midpoints, 21, 24, 65, 389, 393

midsegments
of trapezoids, 261–262, 263, 299, 397–398
of triangles, 338, 339, 341

minor arcs, 423

mutually exclusive events, 503–504, 508, 548

N

negation, 37, 67

non-mutually exclusive events, 504–505

notations
for angles, 5
for circles, 406
for compositions of rigid motions, 117
for dilations, 306, 308, 311
for lines, 4
for planes, 5
for points, 5
for rays, 5
for segments, 6

number lines, 4, 5, 6

O

oblique cylinders, 475

oblique prisms, 471

opposite angles, 268–265, 272, 2959

opposite rays, 5

Acknowledgments

Photography

Cover: Dmitriy Rybin/Shutterstock; Maxger/Shutterstock; FooTToo/Shutterstock

Topic 1
003: Pale Male/Getty Image; **004a:** Sergii Moscaliuk/Fotolia; **004b:** Evgeny Karandaev/Shutterstock; **004c:** Elena Ermakova/Fotolia; **004d:** Nd3000/Fotolia; **034:** Pale Male/Getty Image; **058C:** Arek_Malang/Shutterstock; **058L:** Michaeljung/Shutterstock; **058R:** Antonio Guillem/Shutterstock; **063:** Bupu/Shutterstock

Topic 2
069: Raw/Fotolia; **070a:** Sirtravelalot/Shutterstock; **070b:** Monkey Business Images/Shutterstock; **070c:** Peter Rooney/Shutterstock; **070d:** Eric Fahrner/Shutterstock; **070e:** Marius Godoi/Shutterstock; **070f:** Praewpailin Phonsri/123RF; **080:** Sherry Smith/Alamy Stock Photo; **092:** Juice Dash/Shutterstock; **101:** Raw/Fotolia

Topic 3
105: Dennis Van De Water/Shutterstock; **106a:** World History Archive/Alamy Stock Photo; **106b:** Andrey_Popov/Shutterstock; **106c:** Login/Fotolia; **140:** Ae in Wonder Land/Shutterstock; **141T:** Steve Mann/Fotolia; **141B:** Shahril Khmd/Shutterstock; **142:** Bmszealand/Shutterstock; **143:** Kichigin19/Fotolia; **144:** Dennis Van De Water/Shutterstock

Topic 4
148a: Michelle Lemon/Fotolia; **148b:** Michelle Lemon/Fotolia; **148c:** Eric Audras/Onoky-Photononstop/Alamy Stock Photo; **148d:** Frankljunior/123RF; **148e:** Mr Twister/Shutterstock; **148f:** Lakeviewimages/Fotolia; **167T:** Kosmos111/Shutterstock; **167B:** Trekandphoto/Fotolia; **189:** Chuck Eckert/Alamy Stock Photo

Topic 5
201: Luftbild Bertram/Agefotostock; **202a:** Neil Webb/Ikon Images/Alamy Stock Photo; **202b:** Jacob Lund/Fotolia; **202c:** Maksym Protsenko/Fotolia; **202d:** Aleksandr Simonov/Shutterstock; **221:** Luftbild Bertram/Age Fotostock

Topic 6
247: Africa Studio/Fotolia; **248a:** Zastolskiy Victor/Shutterstock; **248b:** Dushlik/Fotolia; **248c:** Julen Garces Carro/EyeEm/Alamy Stock Photo; **248d:** Taina Sohlman/Fotolia; **256:** Africa Studio/Fotolia; **274:** Rukawajung/Fotolia

Topic 7
303: Maxisport/Fotolia; **304a:** Pressmaster/Fotolia; **304b:** Juan Carlos Ulate/Reuters/Alamy Stock Photo; **304c:** Chris Hill/National Geographic Creative/Alamy Stock Photo; **304d:** Petrovich12/Fotolia; **336:** Maxisport/Fotolia; **343:** Oleksii Nykonchuk/Fotolia

Topic 8
347: Science photo/Fotolia; **348a:** Kadmy/Fotolia; **348b:** Robert/Fotolia; **348c:** Okamigo/Fotolia; **348d:** Makko3/Fotolia; **348e:** Dariodv/Fotolia; **377:** Science photo/Fotolia

Topic 9
387a: Luis Molinero/Shutterstock; **387b:** Prostock-studio/Shutterstock; **387c:** Prostock-studio/Shutterstock; **388a:** Hayate/Fotolia; **388b:** Aleksandr Lesik/Fotolia; **388c:** Andy Dean/Fotolia; **388d:** Jdoms/Fotolia; **388e:** Aleksandr Simonov/Shutterstock; **395:** Karen Doody/Stocktrek Images,Inc./Alamy Stock Photo; **396a:** Luis Molinero/Shutterstock; **396b:** Prostock-studio/Shutterstock; **396c:** Prostock-studio/Shutterstock; **409:** Rgb Ventures/SuperStock/Ed Darack/Alamy Stock Photo; **413:** Africa Rising/Shutterstock; **416:** Stocker1970/Shutterstock

Acknowledgments

Topic 10
421: Paul Fleet/Shutterstock; **422a:** 3Dsculptor/Shutterstock; **422b:** Tryfonov/Fotolia; **422c:** Olekcii Mach/Alamy Stock Photo; **422d:** Algol/Shutterstock; **438:** Songquan Deng/Shutterstock; **439:** Paul Fleet/Shutterstock; **454:** Vasilii Gubskii/Shutterstock; **462:** Friedrich Saurer/Alamy Stock Photo

Topic 11
467a: Andersphoto/Shutterstock; **467b:** Fotomaton/Alamy Stock Photo; **468a:** Heiner Heine/ImageBroker/Alamy Stock Photo; **468b:** AD Hunter/Shutterstock; **468c:** Aleksandr Simonov/Shutterstock; **468d:** Katyr/Fotolia; **474a:** Perutskyi Petro/Shutterstock; **474b:** Imfotograf/Fotolia; **474c:** Yellow Cat/Shutterstock; **474d:** Monkey Business/Fotolia; **478:** Cynoclub/Fotolia; **479:** Joerg Hackemann/123RF; **483a:** Andersphoto/Shutterstock; **483b:** Fotomaton/Alamy Stock Photo; **496:** Sorapong Chaipanya/123RF

Topic 12
501: Jacques Beauchamp/Glow Images; **502a:** Harvepino/Shutterstock; **502b:** Tainar/Shutterstock; **502c:** Marina Zezelina/Shutterstock; **502d:** Vasin Lee/Shutterstock; **502e:** Zeljko Radojko/Fotolia; **518:** Jacques Beauchamp/Glow Images; **533:** Grum_l/Shutterstock; **547:** Blackregis/123RF